P9-BHR-941

THE KORSUN POCKET

The Encirclement and Breakout of a German Army in the East, 1944

By
Niklas Zetterling
and
Anders Frankson

Philadelphia & Newbury

Published in the United States of America in 2008 by
CASEMATE
1016 Warrior Road, Drexel Hill, PA 19026

and in the United Kingdom by
CASEMATE
17 Cheap Street, Newbury, Berkshire, RG14 5DD

ISBN 978-1-932033-88-5

Cataloging-in-publication data is available from the Library of Congress and from the British Library.

Printed and bound in the United States of America.

For a complete list of Casemate titles, please contact

United States of America
Casemate Publishers
Telephone (610) 853-9131, Fax (610) 853-9146
E-mail casemate@casematepublishing.com
Website www.casematepublishing.com

United Kingdom
Casemate-UK
Telephone (01635) 231091, Fax (01635) 41619
E-mail casemate-uk@casematepublishing.co.uk
Website www.casematepublishing.co.uk

Contents

Preface		vii
Prologue		1
Chapter 1	Background: The War in the East	5
Chapter 2	The Battles on the Dnepr	17
Chapter 3	Planning, Preparation, and Readiness	25
Chapter 4	The Condition of the Armies	43
Chapter 5	Konev Attacks	55
Chapter 6	The Soviet Breakthrough	73
Chapter 7	Vatutin's Attack	97
Chapter 8	The Korsun Pocket	103
Chapter 9	The Red Army Squeezes the Pocket	121
Chapter 10	Von Vormann's Counterattack	139
Chapter 11	Hube Assembles a Rescue Force	151
Chapter 12	Breith's III Panzer Corps Attacks	157
Chapter 13	8th Army, 4–10 February	173
Chapter 14	Breith Tries Again	199
Chapter 15	Stalin Invervenes	215
Chapter 16	"Now or Never"	225
Chapter 17	Time is Running Out	239
Chapter 18	Breakout from the Korsun Pocket	259
Chapter 19	Aftermath	287
Notes on the Text		299
Appendix I	Orders of Battle	320
Appendix II	German Combat Units in the Battle	329
Notes on the Appendices		361
Index		370

Preface

This book deals with a battle known by two names. In Soviet literature it is usually called the battle at Korsun, or even the Korsun-Shevchenkovskii operation, while the Germans prefer to call it the battle at Tscherkassy (Cherkassy), or the "Kesselschlacht bei Tscherkassy." As the small town of Korsun for most of the time was located at the center of the pocket containing the two surrounded German corps, it seems somewhat more appropriate to call it the battle at Korsun, rather than Tscherkassy, which was situated outside the pocket and which was held by the Red Army before, during, and after the battle. Furthermore, as it was the Red Army that initiated the battle, it would seem reasonable to grant the Soviet side the favor of naming it. On the other hand, few people have a map that will show them where Korsun is located. Chances are far better that they will find Tscherkassy (or Cherkassy, depending on how it is translated) on their maps. We have opted to call it the battle at Korsun in the text and the title of this book is *The Korsun Pocket.*

Our interest in the battle at Korsun began about 20 years ago. What struck us was the unusual drama of the battle, and the fact that it was in many ways a more even battle than most Eastern Front clashes at this stage of the war. Overall the Red Army had the advantage of numerical superiority, as it had elsewhere on the Eastern Front, but by assembling a significant number of Panzer divisions, of which two were in quite good shape, the Germans managed to collect an attack force and make a determined effort to rescue the two corps that had been surrounded by the initial Soviet attack. Thus it is one of the relatively few battles in World War II where both sides were attackers as well as defenders. To this is added the foul weather, which played havoc with the plans of the generals, so that the stage was set for a dramatic battle, although its scope was not on a par with renowned confrontations like Moscow, Stalingrad, and Kursk.

Relatively little is written on the battle at Korsun. In English it is mentioned in several books, but rarely are more than a few pages devoted to it. In German there are more books written, including volumes focusing on the Korsun battle only. These include books written by men who took part in the battle, either as a high ranking commander, like Nikolaus von Vormann, or as a non-commissioned officer (NCO), like Anton Meiser. In Russian there is also some literature that describes the battle, but it does not present detailed description.

For the German side this does not pose a significant problem because the archival records of many of the units involved are available, either as microfilm at the U.S. National Archives in Washington, D.C. or in the form of the original papers at the Bundesarchiv in Freiburg, Germany. These documents have formed the basis of our description of the German forces and their actions. Other German sources have constituted a complement.

Information on the Soviet side is much more scarce. The most important source has been the Soviet General Staff Study, which was written in 1944, but it is a source with many problems. When comparing it to the German archival documents it is clear that most of the Soviet General Staff Study's statements on the Germans are wrong. Many explanations found in the study are untenable. From what we have seen of Soviet archival documents on the battle it seems that the Study was partly written as propaganda, although it was not intended for public use. Despite these limitations, we decided to use it, but with great caution. Fortunately we also obtained access to some Soviet archival records, but these were not as extensive as those for the German side. As we have preferred to say too little, rather than to risk making erroneous statements, we have not been able to give such extensive coverage of the Soviet side as we have done for the German side. This is not due to any bias on our part, but rather reflects the availability of reliable sources. Indeed, we could have described the German activities in much more detail, but we had to prioritise the material in order to produce a reasonably balanced book. For the Soviet side, on the other hand, we have included as much as possible of what we found relevant and reasonably reliable. Despite these limitations it has been our intention to present as much new information as possible, with references to enable the deeply interested reader to look for further information about the battle.

The maps deserve some comments. We have used a variety of sources to produce them and the level of detail available in the sources differed considerably. Thus the information found in the maps is varied. In some cases we have opted to include information on the location of specific units, even though we do not have information on the location of all units involved. Finally it must be said that the frontlines were not always as clearly defined as they appear on the maps. In many situations the units were stretched over wide areas, with very little infantry to maintain a coherent defensive front. In such situations both sides often resorted to maintaining control over the villages and keeping an eye on the terrain in between. In such situations the frontlines indicated on the maps can at best be regarded as approximate.

We hope to have written a book that can be read by those who wish to discover something they have not read about before, as well as by those who have a deep interest in World War II and already possess an extensive knowledge about the conflict. Whether we have succeeded or not is up to the readers to judge. Our judgment is that the book has benefited considerably by the assistance of various other people: Karl-Heinz Frieser, Kamen Nevenkin, Mirko Bayerl, and especially Egor Sjtjekotichin, who helped us with Soviet archival documents.

Both armies allowed infantry to ride on armored vehicles, in this case a German StuG III assault gun. (SIPA PRESS)

Prologue

In the afternoon on 8 February 1944, Colonel Hans Viebig, commander of the German 258th Infantry Regiment, picked up the phone and tried to contact some of his superior commanders. He had just received important information and it was necessary to immediately convey it. Within a short time Viebig had Johannes Sapauschke, the chief of staff of XXXXII Corps, at the other end of the connection. Sapauschke was told that a Soviet jeep, carrying a large white flag and accompanied by trumpet blasts, had approached the defense lines of the 258th Infantry. Obviously it was a parlayer, and Sapauschke was not surprised.

Together with the XI Corps, the XXXXII Corps had been surrounded for almost two weeks by Soviet troops. They had cut off the salient held by the two German corps and created a pocket near the Dnepr River, about 130 kilometers southeast of Kiev. By now, ammunition was running low for the surrounded Germans, who could not hold out much longer. Many soldiers who were ill or wounded had been assembled near the little town of Korsun, where doctors and nurses did their best to care for them, but shortages of medicine and other equipment made their struggles difficult. A few thousand wounded had been evacuated by air, but still there were more than 50,000 men inside the pocket created by the Soviet 1st and 2nd Ukrainian Fronts, commanded by generals Nikolai Vatutin and Ivan Konev.

The fate of the surrounded German forces hung in the balance, and had so far only been sustained by an insecure airlift operation, whose effectiveness was highly dependent on a small airfield near Korsun. Memories of the disaster that befell the German 6th Army at Stalingrad, almost exactly a year earlier, were very vivid to many of the Germans in the pocket. To Sapauschke, in the present situation, there seemed to be few realistic alternatives to receiving the parlayer. Sapauschke told Viebig that he would send an interpreter and then the small Soviet group would be brought to the staff of XXXXII Corps, of course with all due precautions to avoid revealing the location of the staff.

Blindfolded, the Russian group, headed by General M.I. Saveliev, was brought to XXXXII Corps staff, where they were taken into a small house. Sapauschke noted that the Soviet interpreter wore an unusual fur cap, leading him to believe that the man originated from the Caucasus area. At the beginning of the war the Red Army had been dominated by men from Russia, but vast casualties had increased the share of men from other parts of the Soviet Union. The Germans had also been forced to recruit in new areas, to remedy the shortages of manpower caused by the years of hard fighting that had passed.

General Saveliev opened the discussion by complaining that he had been fired upon when approaching the German positions, despite carrying a distinctive white flag. Sapauschke was convinced this was only a trick to get a better starting position for the negotiations, thus he said that the error must have been caused by the unfavorable direction of the wind, causing the flag to be difficult to see.

Saveliev asked to be introduced to the commanders of the two surrounded German corps, generals Wilhelm Stemmermann and Theobald Lieb. When this was turned down, Saveliev wanted to know who Sapauschke was. The latter replied that he was chief of staff of the German unit Saveliev had approached. Saveliev remained undaunted and handed over two letters, one each for Stemmermann and Lieb.

It was clear that Sapauschke had to get into contact with the two corps commanders, and the small Soviet delegation was brought outside the small farmer's hut. Sapauschke soon made contact with Lieb and gave him a brief description of what had taken place, whereupon Lieb asked Sapauschke to open the letters and read them. Their content was clear enough and did not contain any major surprise. The Soviets asked that a German officer with the necessary authority come into their lines before 10.00 next day to sign terms of surrender. Thus the German force would be spared the fate of their comrades at Stalingrad. All German officers would be allowed to retain their sidearms and every German soldier who according to this agreement went into captivity would be allowed to go to any country they wished when the war was over. The letters were signed by three of the most well-known Soviet officers, Zhukov, Konev and Vatutin.

Sapauschke proposed that they should pretend to accept the proposal. German panzer divisions attacking from outside the pocket were getting closer to the two surrounded corps. Possibly time could be won by provisionally accepting the terms but demanding some alterations. Lieb turned this down, since he believed that it was both a dangerous gambit and unlikely to succeed. There was to be no surrender, but the Russian officer would not be told so bluntly.

For a second time the Soviet delegation entered the small hut. Without much sign of reaction they listened to Sapauschke tell them that Lieb and Stemmermann had been informed of the content of the letters and would reply at a moment they found appropriate. Saveliev was hardly surprised. The Germans rarely surrendered. At Stalingrad they had refused to capitulate for months, until finally succumbing to starvation, disease, and Soviet attacks that had begun to shatter their cauldron. Neither he nor the high ranking officers who had signed the letters could have had any illusions about the Germans' willingness to surrender. As he probably had an exaggerated picture of the strength of the two surrounded German corps, he realized that more hard fighting was to be expected over the following days or perhaps weeks.

The subject was exhausted, but Sapauschke wanted to combine hospitality with his desire to convey the impression that the surrounded Germans were relatively well off. He asked the Soviet general if he would like to have some French Cognac. Without hesitation Saveliev accepted. Sapauschke did not have any wine or cognac glasses, but he had some tooth brushing glasses, which he filled to the edge. Sapauschke raised and proposed a toast to General Saveliev. The Soviet officer certainly did not decline. They emptied their glasses and Saveliev asked if he could have a second filling.

For a moment Sapauschke considered trying to give the Russian general so much to drink that he would unintentionally disclose some valuable information. However, since it would be impossible to validate his words, the German dropped the idea. When the glasses were empty the two officers shook hands and the Soviet delegation departed the same way it had arrived.

The battle at Korsun would continue.

CHAPTER 1

Background: The War in the East

When Adolf Hitler launched Operation Barbarossa, the assault on the Soviet Union, on 22 June 1941, he expected swift success. Initially, his hopes appeared to be justified. The German armies rapidly drove deep into Soviet territory and captured hundreds of thousands of Red Army soldiers as they advanced. However, in August, Soviet resistance increased, while German logistical difficulties mounted with the increasing distances. Nevertheless, the German high command remained optimistic. Late in August, German army groups Center and South carried out a double envelopment of the Soviet armies in the Kiev area, which resulted in the capture of 665,000 Soviet soldiers. It was a major success and was followed by yet another huge encirclement operation.

At the beginning of October, Army Group Center launched Operation Typhoon, the assault on Moscow. Immediately, the German armored spearheads broke through the Soviet defenses west of Vyazma and Bryansk. The German pincers closed behind the Soviet defenses, which resulted in perhaps the greatest losses ever inflicted upon an enemy. The Germans reported the capture of 673,000 prisoners, but time was running out. About a week into October, fall rains turned the ground into a morass, allowing the Red Army time to move reinforcements to the shattered front west of Moscow. The Germans made yet another attempt to capture the Soviet capital, but it petered out early in December. Instead, Stalin launched a counteroffensive that drove the Germans away from the gates of Moscow.

With the failure to knock the Soviet Union out of the war in 1941, Hitler doomed his country to a prolonged war, in which the weight of

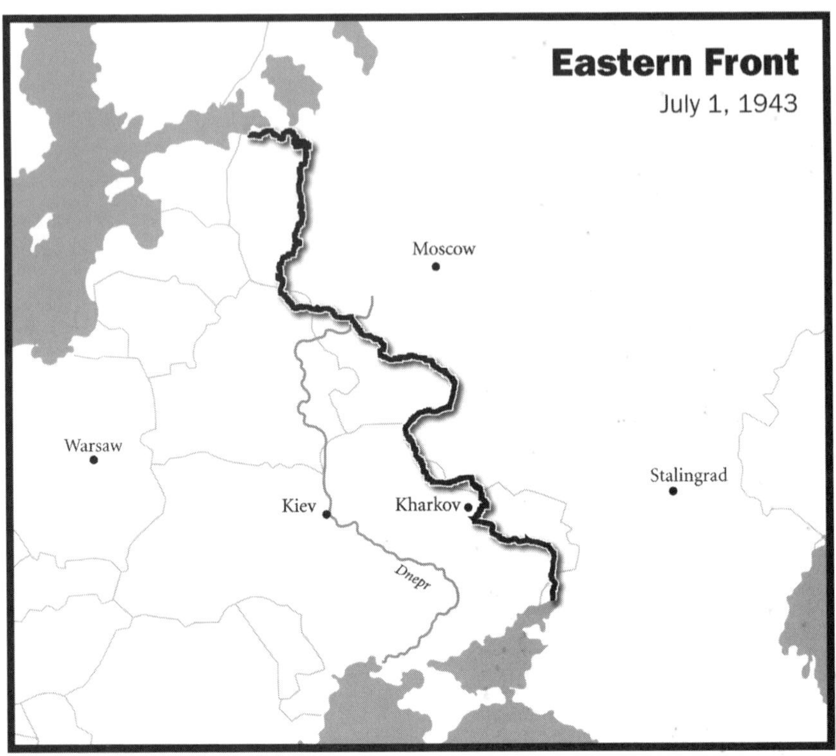

industrial and demographical resources would ultimately decide the outcome. The war in the East proved to be horrendously costly and characterized by unparalleled brutality, in particular against the civilian population and prisoners of war. From the outset Hitler had decided that the war would be a war of extermination, a challenge the Soviets took up in kind, and the result was appalling.

With hindsight, it seems clear that if Hitler had any chance of defeating the Soviet Union, he had forfeited that chance by December 1941. At the time, though, as the German armies halted the Soviet winter offensive, Hitler was poised to launch a major offensive in the summer of 1942. However, this time his resources did not suffice to attack along the entire front, as had been the case in 1941. Rather, his efforts were directed towards the oil fields in the Caucasus and towards Stalingrad. Neither of these aims was fully achieved, and in November 1942 the Red Army launched a counteroffensive that cut off the German 6th Army at Stalingrad. This success was subsequently regarded as a turning point in the war, but in fact it is probable that the balance had already shifted in Soviet favor.

The Tide Turns Against Germany

The German efforts to relieve 6th Army failed, and at the beginning of February 1943 the starved remnants of the surrounded 6th Army surrendered. About 100,000 German soldiers went into Soviet captivity. But Stalin was not content with crushing 6th Army. Other offensives were launched, which threatened to crumble the entire German front in the eastern Ukraine. At the same time German forces suffered reverses on other fronts, too. In North Africa, the battle at El Alamein in October 1942 marked the beginning of the end of the Axis forces on the southern shores of the Mediterranean. The Anglo-American invasion of Algeria and Morocco on 8 November 1942 marked the entry of American ground forces into the war against Germany.

The Allied progress continued during the first half of 1943. The Axis forces in North Africa were compressed into a bridgehead in Tunisia, where they finally surrendered in May. On the Atlantic the threat from German submarines was mastered and the Allied build-up of forces in Britain continued remorselessly. On the Eastern Front the Soviet offensives continued. Both the Don and Donets rivers were crossed and the Germans were forced to retreat from the Caucasus. Although a German counteroffensive led by Field Marshal von Manstein gave Hitler one success to boast of before the spring thaw put an end to operations, it was clear that the German situation was much worse than it had been a year ago.

Despite their recent reverses, for the summer of 1943 the Germans prepared an operation to regain the initiative on the Eastern Front, but it was much more limited in scope compared to their previous summer offensives. It was given the code name "Citadel (Zitadelle)." After many postponements, the Germans launched Operation Citadel on 5 July 1943, aiming to cut off the Soviet-held salient around Kursk. The northern prong met with little success, and after a week it stalled. The southern attack force was far more successful, and was only halted by the Red Army at great cost and after substantial reinforcements had been committed. Nevertheless Operation Citadel, which turned out to be the last major German offensive on the Eastern Front, was clearly a failure.[1]

Moreover, the Red Army, capitalizing on good intelligence, had not

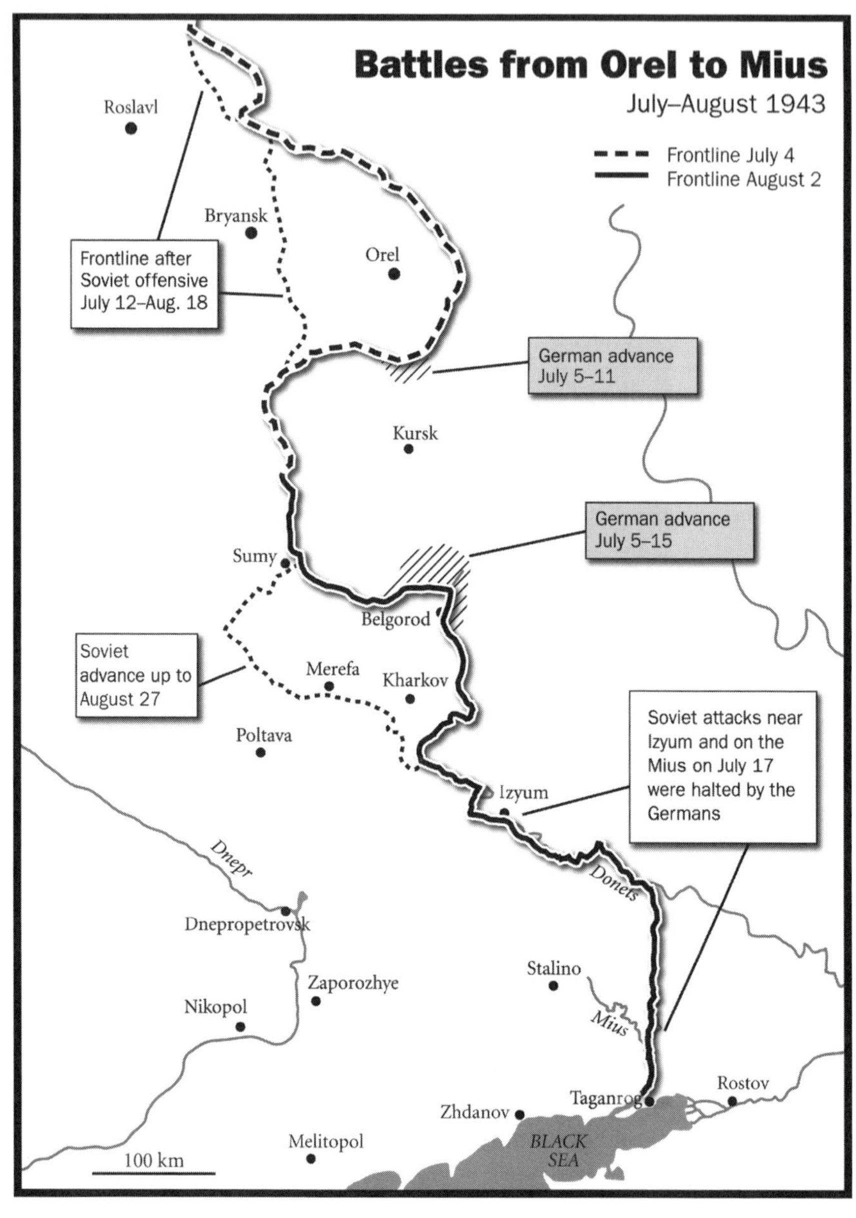

Battles from Orel to Mius
July–August 1943
Frontline July 4
Frontline August 2
Roslavl
Bryansk
Orel
Frontline after
Soviet offensive
July 12–Aug. 18
German advance
July 5–11
Kursk
German advance
July 5–15
Sumy
Belgorod
Soviet
advance up to
August 27
Merefa
Kharkov
Poltava
Soviet attacks near
Izyum and on the
Mius on July 17
were halted by the
Germans
Izyum
Dnepr
Donets
Dnepropetrovsk
Stalino
Zaporozhye
Nikopol
Mius
Rostov
Taganrog
Zhdanov
Melitopol
BLACK
SEA
100 km

only placed strong defenses where the Germans attacked, it had also built up offensive groupings which were to be committed once the German assault had been contained. The first of these Soviet counteroffensives was directed against the salient around Orel, which was held by the Germans. In fact, the northern prong of Operation Citadel was located in the Orel salient. Three Soviet fronts, West, Bryansk, and Central, were given the task of crushing the German forces in the Orel salient and on 12 July they struck. The Central Front did not achieve much success, as it had been heavily engaged during the German attack. The other two Soviet fronts consisted of fresh forces, however. The West Front in particular made good initial progress, but a prompt German reaction soon followed. The German countermeasures were insufficient to retain the Orel salient, but they did enable the Germans to conduct a fighting withdrawal and exact a heavy toll on the attacking Red Army forces, which made slow progress. Although the Soviet offensive in the Orel salient produced less decisive results than anticipated, the fighting in the Kursk–Orel area showed that the war had definitely turned in a direction that was as favorable to the Red Army as it was disadvantageous to the Germans.[2]

At the beginning of summer 1943 it was not apparent to all observers that the Germans were fighting a losing battle, although with hindsight it is clear that the war had turned against them. When Operation Citadel stopped, and the Soviet Orel offensive launched, it became clear that the Red Army had grasped the initiative and would not relinquish it. At the same time, British and American forces invaded Sicily, and a surrender in Italy soon followed. Furthermore, the intensity of the Allied bombings of German cities mounted, with the firestorm of Hamburg as the most telling example. On all fronts the Germans were forced onto the defensive and nowhere was this more apparent than on the Eastern Front.

The Orel fighting required more time and produced less decisive results than the Soviet high command had anticipated, but there were other offensives planned too. On 17 July, the South Front launched an assault on the (reconstituted) German 6th Army, which defended the Mius River. The Germans were compelled to send the II SS-Panzer Corps to the area, as well as other reinforcements. This enabled them to throw back the Soviet assault, but it weakened their defense in the Belgorod area, which was the target for the next Soviet blow.

According to the original Soviet plans, the German assault forces would be counterattacked once Operation Citadel had been halted. However, due to the substantial losses suffered when defending against the German attack, these plans had to be altered. The Germans were allowed to return to their jump-off positions, while the Soviet fronts prepared the next blow.

When the Red Army struck on 3 August, using the Voronezh and Steppe fronts, it made relatively good progress. The Germans were prompted to bring the Grossdeutschland, Das Reich, and Totenkopf divisions to the Kharkov–Belgorod area. They managed to seal off the most threatening Soviet penetrations, but could not prevent the Red Army from recapturing Kharkov, which was accomplished on 23 August. However, again the cost for the Red Army had been considerable.[3]

These operations set the pattern for the rest of 1943. The Red Army struck a blow at a chosen sector of the front, which forced the Germans to shift mechanized formations to the threatened sector. Simultaneously the Soviet high command built up forces to attack another part of the front, an attack which was unleashed once German units were engaged by the previous offensive. In this way blow after blow was struck by the Red Army against the front in the east, while the Germans shifted units back and forth. The Germans were always one step behind, and even though they eventually succeeded in containing every Soviet attack, they were gradually pushed back along most of the front.

There were two major disadvantages to the Soviet operational methods employed during the second half of 1943. The Germans never suffered a serious defeat, while the casualties incurred by the Red Army were very high. Between 1 July and 30 September 1943 the Red Army suffered appallingly, enduring almost three million casualties.[4] This can be compared to German casualties which amounted to more than 530,000 in the same period.[5] In addition, almost 180,000 Germans were evacuated due to disease or left the Eastern Front for other reasons.[6]

Replacements were wholly insufficient to cover the German losses, as less than 280,000 men arrived either as replacements or returning convalescents.[7] Furthermore, the low German replacement rate was dwarfed by the influx of replacements to the Red Army, which must have received more than two million men as replacements, returning convalescents, and reinforcements. Had the Red Army not enjoyed this massive advantage it seems highly unlikely that it could have continued its offensives.[8]

The Front in the Ukraine
Autumn 1943
The Front
August 24
September 30
December 23
Dnepr
Mozyr
Central Front
(Rokossovski)
Kursk
Voronezh
Voronezh Front
(Vatutin)
Kiev
Belgorod
Zhitomir
Steppe Front
(Konev)
Kharkov
Cherkassy
Poltava
Southwest Front
(Malinovski)
UKRAINE
Vorosilovgrad
Kirovograd
South Front
(Tolbuchin)
Stalino
Krivoi Rog
Nikopol
Rostov
Dnepr
Odessa
BLACK
SEA
Krasnodar

Evgeni Bessonov at the Bryansk Front

The enormous casualties suffered by the Red Army during its offensive operations are not only evident in the statistics. The danger was very real to the men who fought in the foxholes too. However, for them many days could pass without experiencing anything particularly harmful, until they suddenly found themselves caught up in extremely costly actions. Evgeni Bessonov spent more than a year in military service, mostly in training, until he was sent to the Bryansk Front in July 1943 to serve as a platoon commander in 4th Tank Army. Transport shortages forced him and the other soldiers he travelled with to hitchhike and walk part of the distance between Moscow and the front.[9]

At the beginning of August, Bessonov arrived at the headquarters of the Bryansk Front, from where he was passed on to the 4th Tank Army, which needed replacements. At first Bessonov spent two weeks without seeing any action, but in the middle of August the company he belonged to was sent forward to attack. Bessonov was given command of the 2nd Platoon and had very little time to get acquainted with the men subordinate to him before the fighting began.[10]

After moving up in the evening, Bessonov and his unit was ready to attack in the morning. Bessonov's company formed a line in order to advance toward a hill, together with two other companies from the battalion. They did not know whether the hill was defended by the Germans or not, but the truth soon dawned upon them. Enemy machine guns opened fire on the advancing Soviet infantry and then the Germans launched a mortar barrage. Bessonov, as he had been trained, shouted: "Forward, run!"

Except for himself, nobody followed Bessonov's order. He looked around and saw that his men had taken cover in a ravine and begun to dig in. Bessonov decided to follow their example, only to realize that he lacked equipment for the job. Fortunately he could borrow an entrenching tool from a soldier who had been quick to dig a hole for himself.[11]

The day passed and another attack was attempted during the night, but it failed too. On the following day, a further attempt was to be made and this time Bessonov warned some of the soldiers that if they did not advance in the attack, they would be severely punished for cowardice. He even told one of his subordinates, who had claimed a stomach ache as a reason for not following the attack, that he would be shot if it happened again. Such threats were, however, to little avail, as the attacks during the second day also failed. Even tank support from three T-34s was ineffective.[12]

On the third day the Soviet attack was suspended, as the positions held by Bessonov and his men were subjected to repeated German air strikes and artillery barrages. The Soviet soldiers hunkered down in their foxholes while shell after shell, bomb after bomb, exploded around them and sent splinters whizzing around the area. Bessonov later recalled that in a hell such as that to which he was subjected, time passes painfully slowly. Toward the end of the day the German fire ceased and Bessonov's unit could count its losses.[13]

Bessonov's baptism of fire was not remarkable for the men who served on the Eastern Front. The vast number of casualties necessitated a huge influx of green replacements, especially for the Red Army. Millions of men must have experienced their first combat action during the second half of 1943, and come to realize how terrifying war could be. Bessonov was one of those fortunate enough to survive the war and retell his experiences.

The War on the Eastern Front, August–November 1943

During the last three months of 1943 the costly battles continued, as fighting along the Dnepr River ensued. Soviet casualties diminished slightly, but were nevertheless very high. German losses also declined somewhat, but still exceeded the Reich's capability to replace them.[14]

In essence the war in the east during the second half of 1943 was a war of attrition. The Red Army did not cause German defenses to collapse in an operational sense; rather it succeeded in exerting sufficient pressure to push the Germans back gradually. The latter succeeded in extracting a disproportionally high toll on the attackers and, as argued above, it was only thanks to the equally exceptionally large advantage in reinforcements and replacements that the Red Army could maintain the pressure. An important factor explaining the poor casualty exchange ratio was the absence of major encirclements of German units. If German units could be surrounded, the Red Army would stand a much better chance of achieving a favorable casualty exchange ratio. However, encirclements had been difficult to achieve for the Red Army, since the Soviet forces thus far had not been able to advance quickly enough to prevent the Germans from withdrawing in relatively good order.

Although the cost in manpower was extremely high, the Red Army had made important gains. A considerable part of Ukraine had been liberated, with its valuable economic, agricultural and industrial assets. But to what extent these could be exploited was yet unclear, as the Germans had made extensive efforts to destroy industrial plants and infrastructure, remove or kill livestock, and deport part of the population, particularly those able-bodied men who could be used as labor or for military service.[15]

Of the Soviet victories thus far, Stalingrad stood out as the most complete. Not only did the Germans suffer considerable losses, their losses were also distributed among all arms. This was a major difference compared to the fighting in the second half of 1943, when German losses were mainly confined to the infantry. This made it easier for the Germans to replace casualties. Furthermore, as long as German forces were not cut off, wounded men typically made up 70–80% of the casualties.[16] Of these, almost half could be expected to return to duty within a period of time that was not inordinately long, but sometimes several years could pass before a wounded soldier returned to frontline service. Anton Meiser had served in the 79th Infantry Division in 1940, when he had been seriously wounded. After more than five months in various hospitals, he was declared capable of garrison duty. Almost three years passed while he served mainly in Metz and Nancy in eastern France. During this period he performed various office tasks, but the deteriorating situation on the Eastern Front mandated changes.[17]

The 389th Infantry Division had been destroyed at Stalingrad, but it was decided that it should be reconstituted and the remnants assembled in western France. Far too few men remained from the original division. Most of the manpower of the new formation would not be veterans of the old one, and Meiser was one of the men detailed to the new 389th Division. He was to serve in the 389th's artillery regiment, and late in August 1943 he arrived at the unit's base in western France.[18]

An autumn in France would perhaps have been a pleasant sojourn, but Meiser's lot was different. After a month with his unit, Meiser and his new comrades were loaded on trains, as was the equipment and horses. They could only speculate on what the future would bring them, but when they had reached well into the Soviet Union, the train stopped as there had been a partisan attack on the station they were to pass. The partisans had already disappeared, but the dead bodies of the railway staff remained as a sombre remainder of what could happen to anyone serving on the Eastern Front.[19]

The three years that passed between Meiser's being wounded in 1940 and his return to frontline duty was probably a longer period than most wounded German soldiers experienced. His example does, however, show something that probably was typical: the longer the period of convalescence, the less chance of returning to the original unit.

With the Germans driven out of the eastern Ukraine, and Soviet armies reaching the eastern bank of the Dnepr, it was evident that the Germans were losing their grip in the East. Also, in September Allied forces had invaded mainland Italy. Mussolini had already been arrested in the wake of the Allied invasion of Sicily, and the Allied landings at Salerno caused Italy to change sides in the war. Other German allies were to follow suit and try to get out of the war, or change sides, but the diminishing successes did not shake Hitler's resolve to continue fighting. Most of Italy was promptly occupied by German forces, and as poor weather in the English Channel area could be expected to prevent an Allied seaborne operation, Hitler decided to send some Panzer divisions from western Europe to the Ukraine, where the Soviet offensives continued.

CHAPTER 2

Battles on the Dnepr

At the end of September, four Soviet fronts reached the eastern bank of the mighty Dnepr, one of the largest rivers in Europe. Field Marshal Erich von Manstein, who, as commander of Army Group South was responsible for the defense of the Ukraine, realized that the river would have made a formidable defensive line had the Germans possessed enough resources to defend it. As it was, there were not enough German troops on hand to provide a solid defense along the entire length of the river. Furthermore, the German retreat to the Dnepr line was difficult, as only five crossing sites were available, At these, congestions occurred.

Lieutenant Fritz Hahl was a 23-year-old officer who served as company commander in the Westland Motorized Infantry Regiment of the 5th SS-Panzer Grenadier Division Wiking. He had participated in the battles along the Mius and remained with the division when it retreated after the costly battles in eastern Ukraine. The retreat over the Dnepr meant that fighting became less severe, but the situation was far from safe. As he recalled:

> *On September 27 we crossed the Dnepr on a bridge near Cherkassy and reached the western bank. Due to incorrect situation estimates the higher headquarters had failed to provide enough bridges within the 8th Army area. At the few crossing points long queues appeared, several kilometers long, with vehicles from the combat units, tanks, artillery and the baggage. It borders on the miraculous that this traffic jam was not bombed by the Red Air Force. We had been left without any air cover, as not a single German fighter could be seen in the sky and no AA units had been*

deployed to protect the river crossing.

As the Germans were retreating towards the river, the Soviet forces pushed hard to create bridgeheads across it. The Germans pursued a scorched-earth policy when withdrawing so the Soviet forces experienced difficulties finding boats, ferries, or any floating craft. But everyone in the Red Army knew how important it was to gain a foothold on the western bank of the Dnepr. The initial crossings were all dependent on the limited resources available. However, soon engineers erected new bridges and began to operate ferries. German airpower and artillery harassed the bridgeheads, but were unable to halt the flow of Soviet troops.

The Liberation of Kiev

By 1 October 1943, the Red Army had established several bridgeheads over the Dnepr, although an improvised attempt to use airborne forces had ended in failure. During the first week of October, the Soviet commanders brought up more troops and supplies before resuming the offensive. Their strike marked the beginning of several months of hard battles on the western bank of the Dnepr. In October, the 2nd Ukrainian Front, commanded by General Konev, cleared the western bank of the river between Dnepropetrovsk and Cherkassy. His troops gained a solid grip on the western bank, establishing a large bridgehead with a depth of about 100 kilometers.

In November the 1st Ukrainian Front, commanded by General Vatutin, attracted the most attention. His troops held two rather small bridgeheads, one at Bukrin, south of Kiev, and one at Lyutezh, north of Kiev.

The 3rd Guards Tank Army, commanded by General Rybalko, had withdrawn from the Bukrin bridgehead, taking great care to deceive the Germans about its true whereabouts. In fact, the Red Army made every effort to convince the Germans that the 3rd Guards Tank Army was still in the Bukrin bridgehead. German situation maps dated 3 November still indicated that the Guards tankers were in place at Bukrin. As General Zhukov admits in his memoirs, the weather had favored the Soviet regroupings: "To our good fortune the weather was unfit for flying, so during this movement enemy air reconnaissance was almost completely inactive."[20]

The tanks had to cross the Dnepr River twice to reach their new staging area, but they were not alone as they moved into the Lyutezh bridgehead. As usual, the Soviet artillery moved up in huge numbers, reaching a density of 400 guns and mortars per kilometer of frontline. Most of the infantry in the bridgehead belonged to General Moskalenko's 38th Army, and as he concluded after the war, the concentration of artillery here was so far the most massive in the war.[21]

To Vatutin, who had moved his headquarters into the Lyutezh bridgehead, it was very important that the Germans still thought his main attack would come from Bukrin. He had already tried twice from there, but failed. Vatutin needed a success very soon, because Stalin wanted Kiev to be liberated before 7 November, the anniversary of the Revolution of 1917. In addition, his fellow front commanders, Ivan Konev, Rodion Malinovskii, and Fedor Tolbukhin, had seen various successes to boast of during October, while his front was still fighting in its bridgeheads. Vatutin knew he had to try to outwit von Manstein, the opposing commander on the German side. Consequently, on 1 November he launched strong attacks from the Bukrin bridgehead in an attempt to distract German attention while the final preparations were underway for the main assault out of Lyutezh.

Vatutin began his attack from the Lyutezh bridgehead on 3 November, and, unlike his previous attempts, this one quickly met with success. Rybalko's 3rd Guards Tank Army was committed to create a breakthrough. By the morning of 5 November Rybalko's tankers had reached Svyatoshino (west of Kiev) and were blocking the main road running west from the city. Rybalko established his command post in a small house outside Svyatoshino and ordered his subordinate commanders to attend a briefing. Colonel Yakubovskii, commander of 91st Independent Tank Brigade, was the first to arrive. Rybalko seemed more agitated and excited than normal.

He asked Yakubovskii: "Do you know whose house this is?"

Yakubovskii did not note anything special about the house. It seemed quite normal to him. He answered that he did not know. Rybalko said: "Before the war I lived here with my family."[22]

The Soviet forces continued towards Kiev, which they entered on 6 November, just in time for the ceremonies in Moscow on the following day. Stalin was able to announce that the third largest city in the Soviet Union had been liberated from the enemy.

However, Vatutin's offensive did not end with the liberation of Kiev. His armies continued west, pushing the Germans more than 60 kilometers from Kiev. As a result, the Germans were largely dislodged from the west bank of Dnepr, but they managed to hang on to a 100 kilometer stretch of the river near Kanev, south of Kiev.[23] This German bulge was soon to be dented. Vatutin and Konev planned further offensives that would force von Manstein to react.

The fighting around Kiev had been costly for the 1st Ukrainian Front, not only for the infantry and tankers but also for the Communist Party members among the front troops. As Konstantin V. Krainyukov, political officer at the 1st Ukrainian Front wrote in his memoirs:

> *The heavy, prolonged offensive and offensive fighting around Kiev had hit the party organisation of communist and komsomol very hard. To replace losses we had to find reserves during the operations. Thus we mobilized, which was very unusual, party members in the rear areas to bring forward to the most important sectors at the front.*[24]

Despite the losses sustained, Vatutin continued the preparations for his offensive, which were completed in the second half of December 1943.

Vatutin Presses his Advantage

The commander of Army Group South, Field Marshal von Manstein, intended to celebrate Christmas with the 20th Panzer Grenadier Division. However, the visit was disturbed by ominous reports suggesting that a Soviet offensive could have begun. When von Manstein returned to his headquarters, he realized that Vatutin was not making some sort of diversion; rather it was a major offensive. Vatutin attacked with substantial numerical superiority and the Germans could not withstand the onslaught.[25]

Vatutin opened up the offensive with a sequence of attacks on various sectors, as he wanted to make full use of his artillery and air power on each breakthrough sector. Konstantin V. Krainyukov from the staff of the 1st Ukrainian Front was visiting 18th Army's headquarters when the offensive started. Colonel-General Lesselidse looked tensely at his wristwatch and said in a low voice: "Now, God of War, you have the first word."

The artillery opened up their barrage and the Katyushas fired. Lesselidse continued with a loud and cheerful voice: "This music one can enjoy, two hundred barrels for each breakthrough kilometer."[26]

The Red Army had improved its ability to concentrate artillery. At Stalingrad, for example, the number of guns and mortars had been less than 80 for each kilometer of front at breakthrough sectors. At the Dnepr, more than double that number of guns was available.

When the breakthroughs had been achieved, the tanks were sent into the breach, but the attack did not run smoothly. Colonel Yakubovskii, commander of 91st Independent Tank Brigade in 3rd Guards Tank Army, recalled:

> *The second day of the operation started with adverse conditions. On the morning of 25 December the weather become worse. Once more heavy rain fell. The roads turned into mud. This made it much harder to bring the second echelon forward, as well as resupplying with ammunition and fuel.*

Despite poor weather, the Soviet offensive gained ground. Vatutin managed his troops as they pushed the Germans back another 100 kilometers. However, he had to attend other affairs, too.

Late on 6 January a U.S. military delegation arrived at Kiev for a visit, headed by Major General D. H. Connolly, commanding general of the Persian Gulf command. The delegation had left Moscow on 3 January and made stops at Orel and Kursk. It also visited Zhitomir and its surroundings, before returning to Moscow on 16 January. The purpose of the journey was to study Soviet supply facilities, thus very little data on operations was gathered. Amongst other things, the report of the mission discussed the level of destruction that the war had caused to Soviet society. For example, in January 1944, Orel had a population of 55,000 compared to 110,000 before the war. Even more telling, when the Red Army liberated Orel in August 1943, the city only had a population of 25,000. The main railroad yards and buildings had been completely destroyed by the Germans during their retreat, but by January 1944 about 60% had been rebuilt. Similar data on Kursk, which had been liberated in February 1943, was available. Although the city had been in Soviet hands for almost a year, air raids during the summer battles around the city had damaged important parts of it, such as the railroad system. In January 1944 the capacity of the railroads at Kursk was about 60% below the prewar level. The city itself was not as damaged as Orel but the prewar population had been reduced from 120,000 to 60,000.

Kiev had also been severely damaged. As the U.S. military delegation arrived, the trolley lines were just starting to operate again. Its members travelled by motor cars to Zhitomir and arrived there just ten days after the Red Army had retaken the city. It was estimated that 30–40% of city was destroyed, but the electric power plant and a beer factory were still operating. On the buildings in the city it was posted that all men between 17 and 35 had to register at the city commandant. The purpose was to round up new recruits for the Red Army. Newly liberated areas were an important source for replacements. For example, during February–March 1944 the 1st Front and the 1st Belorussian Front gathered 76,000 recruits from areas they were located in.[27]

On 14 January, just before the U.S. delegation embarked on its journey back to Moscow, Vatutin ordered his armies to assume a defensive position. The offensive had cost him over 100,000 casualties, but the Germans had not yet been beaten. Field Marshal von Manstein ordered a counterstroke which was given the ironic name "Operation Watutin." It was to be conducted by two Panzer corps from General Hans-Valentin Hube's 1st Panzer Army. Hube intended to cut off the Soviet tank forces by conducting a two-pronged attack.

Konev Attacks Kirovograd, 5 January

In the meantime, General Konev had prepared a major Russian offensive further to the southeast. His aim was to attack towards Kirovograd. On paper, Otto Wöhler, commander of the German 8th Army, which was intended to take the brunt of Konev's attack, had an impressive order of battle. He possessed 16 frontline divisions, five of which were Panzer divisions. Although the divisions were in poor condition, because many of them had been fighting almost continuously since July 1943, they were not taken by surprise. On 3 January, von Manstein and Wöhler had discussed the threat of a forthcoming Soviet attack and how it could be thwarted, and it was noted in the war diary of 8th Army on 4 January that a Soviet offensive was imminent.

To what extent the Soviet commanders were aware of the German situation is unclear, but they did not underestimate the task confronting them. Early in the morning of 5 January, Marshall G. K. Zhukov arrived at the staff of 5th Guards Army. General Zhadov reported on the situation in his army. After the report Zhukov commented:[28]

> *Kirovograd may prove to be a hard nut to crack. Success in the assault is largely dependent on a swift advance by Major General Rodimtsev's units (32nd Guards Rifle Corps) to cut off the roads utilized by the enemy in the east and by 33rd Guards Rifle Corps in the northwest. Keep a vigilant eye on the unfolding of events on the flanks of the army. The fate of the entire Kirovograd operation may well hinge on the area where 5th Guards Army is going to attack.*

Zhukov's concerns were not unfounded. The German difficulties notwithstanding, there was nothing suggesting that the Red Army would score an easy victory. Previous experience also motivated the Red Army commanders to avoid making overly optimistic assumptions.

When Konev's artillery opened fire on the morning of 5 January, it signalled the beginning of yet another costly battle. After a barrage lasting half an hour, rifle troops supported by tanks and assault guns began to advance. General Rotmistrov, who as commander of 5th Guards Tank Army was expected to exploit a breach in the German defense lines, followed the progress of the attack:

> *The chilly morning of 5 January came. Dense mist covered the ground. From my observation post the trench lines and the white painted tanks were hardly visible. The fog both made us delighted and concerned. It delighted us because it would prevent the enemy from aiming accurate fire at longer distance. It caused concern that our air force would not be able to conduct its missions and thereby deprive us of air support.*[29]

During the first day, Rotmistrov's troops were successful, although not overwhelmingly so. On 6 January Marshal Zhukov visited Rotmistrov and began the conversation with a very ordinary question:

"How are you getting on?"

"It goes well."

Zhukov listened attentively to Rotmistrov's description of the events while he checked the positions of the units as they were marked on the map. Rotmistrov reported that the enemy had offered stubborn resistance to 7th Guards Army from the very beginning of the offensive, forcing Rotmistrov to reinforce the rifle units with two of his tank brigades. Somewhat later he had been forced to commit both his tank corps. Zhukov raised his head and said:

"Do you know that Konev is transferring 8th Mechanized Corps to Zhadov's army?"

Rotmistrov said he knew, as he had been informed by the chief of staff and continued: "I just can't understand why the second echelon is taken from me, which should be used exploit the success and enable me to repel enemy counterattacks when encircling Kirovograd."

Zhukov smiled cunningly: "You will have to prove that your army can fulfil its mission even without the 8th Mechanized Corps. By the way, the powerful offensive by Zhadov's army will support your attacks, as the enemy will have to divert forces from the southern and southwestern sector to the northwest."

Rotmistrov thought that Zhukov seemed friendly toward him. His stern face seemed to soften and show a bright smile:

'The commander or soldier who does not endeavour to achieve victory first is bad. I like healthy ambition."[30]

The battle raged on over the following days, with attacks followed by counterattacks. However, it was clear that the Germans fought for their survival. Soon Soviet forces reached the outskirts of Kirovograd. The Germans began to demolish important parts of the city before finally leaving it on 8 January. Konev was not satisfied with the liberation of Kirovograd. He maintained the pressure on the Germans and gradually his troops pushed forward. However, Konev did not advance quickly. When the battle finally petered out on 19 January, his front had not forced the Germans back more than about 40 kilometers.

The results of the battle at Kirovograd were perhaps meager, but combined with the gains made by Vatutin's 1st Ukrainian Front, they offered the Red Army a chance to encircle a major German force, something which had not been accomplished since von Paulus' 6th Army was surrounded at Stalingrad. In fact, already while the battle at Kirovograd was raging, Soviet planning for an encirclement operation was initiated. However, it was unclear if the Soviet offensive would be launched before von Manstein was ready to execute the counterstroke he was planning under the code name "Watutin."

CHAPTER 3

Planning, Preparations, and Readiness

Vatutin's offensives in the Kiev area, together with Konev's attacks near Kirovograd, left a German salient centered around the small town of Korsun, about 120 kilometers southeast of Kiev. It was a tempting target for the Red Army commanders. Two German corps could be encircled by a two pronged attack, launched at the respective sides of the salient. Vatutin's 1st Ukrainian Front could attack from the northwest and Konev's 2nd Ukrainian Front from the southeast. The Stavka issued a directive to the two fronts on 12 January, instructing them to prepare an operation to cut off the German forces around Korsun, which still held to a stretch of the Dnepr between Kanev and Cherkassy.

1st Panzer Army Holds Its Position, 6 January

Quite understandably, the Germans were also aware that the protruding section of the front was very exposed. Already in the afternoon of 6 January, the commander of 1st Panzer Army, General Hans-Valentin Hube, discussed the matter with Field Marshal von Manstein, commander of Army Group South. Hube proposed that his right wing, the XXXXII Corps, should be pulled back to the Rossava River. This would place the corps in a less exposed position and would enable the army to release troops for a counterattack further to the west. In his reply, von Manstein said that the 1st Panzer Army should not count on any approval for withdrawal. Nevertheless, Hube ordered both the VII and XXXXII Corps to make plans for withdrawals. Later the same day, Hube again discussed the matter with von Manstein. The field marshal

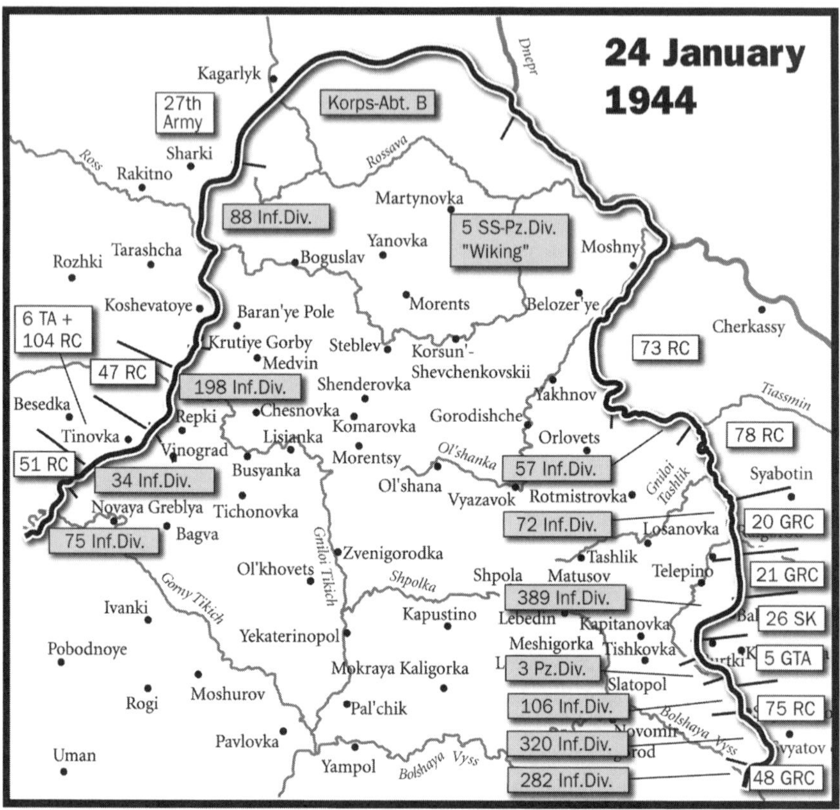

told Hube that he had previously received orders from above that the positions were to be held under all circumstances.[31]

Von Manstein did, however, discuss the issue with the army high command (OKH) and in the meantime Hube spurred the two corps to proceed with their preparations for a withdrawal. Before lunchtime, 1st Panzer Army was notified that OKH had not authorized the withdrawal, but was discussing the matter. Hube seems to have been quite optimistic, but at 14.00hrs on 7 January, the OKH replied in clear terms that any withdrawal was forbidden. This placed 1st Panzer Army in an awkward position. Soviet attacks had opened a gap between VII Corps and III Panzer Corps, and their promised reinforcements had been sent to other armies. This left Hube with no choice but to thin out his frontline to free the forces needed to counterattack the Soviet penetration.[32]

This was an obviously risky approach, yet it could conceivably work for the moment. If, however, the Red Army commanders discovered that the front had been weakened, they might well take advantage of it. Unfortunately for Hube, he had only uncertain alternatives to choose from since the best of his options had been forbidden by OKH. The war diary does not make clear whether the order emanated from Hitler, but if it did, it would most likely have passed through the OKH anyway. It seems to have been Hitler's custom to give few orders in his own name. Since he followed events on the Eastern Front closely, however, it would have been easy for him to ensure that the right wing of 1st Panzer Army was withdrawn, had he wished so.

As the option to withdraw was denied him, it remained for Hube to hope that the forthcoming Operation Watutin would upset the Soviet plans. However, it was unclear if the operation would be launched in time to prevent or weaken the expected Soviet attacks. This was a crucial question, as the threat to the right flank loomed larger. In fact, already on 8 January, a Soviet attack created serious problems for the Germans at the junction between VII and XXXXII Corps.[33] On 10 January, both aerial reconnaissance and ground observation detected Soviet reinforcements moving toward this sector, including tanks and motorized units. The Germans believed these observations suggested a shift in the direction of the main Soviet effort, presumably toward Uman.[34] The following six days passed without any remarkable Soviet efforts against the two right flank corps of 1st Panzer Army.[35]

The first signs of a Soviet buildup appeared on 17 January, when two new rifle divisions and a tank unit equipped with U.S. tanks were identified in front of the VII Corps. The Germans did not judge these forces as sufficient to mount a serious threat, but nevertheless the VII Corps was forced to assume a defensive posture.[36]

A particular problem for the VII Corps was an isolated group of Soviet units around Rubanyi Most and Bagva.[37] The Germans tried to destroy these forces, but a Soviet attack on 18 January made it difficult to detach the forces necessary. Soviet forces pushed back the 82nd Infantry Division and took Tinovka. Further observations of Soviet reinforcements moving to the Tinovka–Vessely Kut area added to German anxieties.[38] The following day, Soviet attacks in the Tinovka–Bashtechki area put strong pressure on the German VII Corps. Even more serious was the situation on the corps' north flank, where the Red Army attacked them between Krutiye Gorby and Antonovka. The

German defenses gave way and the Soviet forces almost reached Krasnogorodka. The 1st Panzer Army interpreted the attack as a clear attempt to break through the German defenses. Poor weather prevented the Luftwaffe from attacking Soviet assembly areas or providing useful reconnaissance. Nevertheless, elements of 82nd Division began to assemble for the mission to eliminate the cut-off Soviet units around Rubanyi Most and Bagva. The attack was planned for 21 January.[39]

On 20 and 21 January no significant Soviet attacks hit the German VII and XXXXII Corps, while the Germans proceeded with their preparations for further attacks by III and XXXXVI Panzer Corps. Simultaneously Soviet reinforcements continued to arrive opposite the VII Corps. Temperatures rose slightly and a thaw set in. The 82nd Division continued to pull out of the line, to be sent southwest, but left behind a Kampfgruppe to attack an encircled Soviet force near Tikhonovka.[40]

On 22 January the Germans continued to observe Soviet reinforcements moving in against the VII Corps. Three or four antiaircraft batteries were observed and this led the Germans to assume that the Red Army was preparing an offensive that was more ambitious than the attacks with limited objectives that had been conducted during the last week. In particular, German observers suspected that the newly-arrived Soviet forces might be part of a two pronged attack—with the other prong advancing from the Kirovograd area—that aimed to cut off the salient around Korsun. Since the option to withdraw from the Korsun salient had been rejected by decisions made at OKH or higher, the 1st Panzer Army could only hope that its imminent attacks would diminish the Soviet ability to create a grouping strong enough for an attack aimed at cutting off the Korsun salient.[41]

For the XXXXII Corps the preceding days had been calm, but on 23 January a major Soviet attack hit the 88th Infantry Division, along the main road from Tarashcha to Zvenigorodka. Hard fighting ensued around Koshevatoye, which fell to Soviet forces after a bitter struggle. They pushed on to Luka and the Germans were forced to detach one battalion from Korps-Abteilung B to shore up the defenses. In addition, four Soviet attacks were directed against Krutiye Gorby, some six kilometers to the south, but the German defenders managed to hold on to their positions.[42]

A major reason for the inability of the XXXXII Corps to repel the Soviet attacks was its weakness; on 22 January it only had two divisions, neither of which could be described as regular. The 88th Division had only five infantry battalions, while the Korps-Abteilung B had six.[43] This was very little to hold a front sector of more than 100 kilometers. Except for its two divisions, the XXXXII Corps had little combat power to offer: a security regiment with two battalions, an infantry battalion, and a light field howitzer battalion. The security battalions were actually intended for rear area security and anti-partisan operations, but the extended front forced Lieb, the commander of XXXXII Corps, to use them in the front line, at the 88th Division sector. Perhaps the situation could have been somewhat better if plentiful artillery had been available, but the XXXXII Corps was weak in this respect too. The 88th Division and Korps-Abteilung B had only eight and 11 artillery batteries, respectively; woefully inadequate to effectively cover such extended frontlines.[44]

The German VII Corps further south was stronger and had a shorter front to hold. Nevertheless, it too had its troubles. The Soviet attack that seemed imminent was at least somewhat countered by the Luftwaffe, which directed Stuka attacks against the Soviet preparations in the Tinovka area. However, the cut off Soviet units at Tikhonovka presented another problem. On 23 January a Kampfgruppe from 82nd Infantry Division managed to squeeze them into a smaller area, thus bringing the situation under control. However, it was unclear if these Soviet forces could be eliminated before the major Soviet attack that now seemed imminent. It was imperative that the area be secured before the morning of 25 January, since that was when the 82nd Division was supposed to be sent to the III Panzer Corps, which was preparing to launch Operation Watutin in conjunction with the XXXXVI Panzer Corps.[45]

The Soviet Build-up, 24–26 February

There were no significant Soviet attacks against the VII and XXXXII Corps on 24 January. However, the Germans observed further build-up by the Red Army in the Tinovka–Bashtechki area and also around Koshevatoye. Since prisoner interrogations had revealed that the Soviet 5th Guards Tank Corps and 5th Mechanized Corps were assembled in the Tinovka area, the Germans concluded that the Soviet main effort would be against the 34th Infantry Division, and hurried reinforcements to the threatened sector. They estimated that the Soviet preparations were almost finished and that a major attack could be expected very soon.[46]

The signs of build-up were corroborated by a Soviet deserter, a lieutenant from the antitank battalion of the 359th Rifle Division, who revealed that he had seen about 70 tanks in Tinovka. He also disclosed that the initial aim was Vinograd and that the projected attack date was 25 or 26 January. The German picture of the enemy intentions became more and more clear.[47]

In the meantime, the Kampfgruppe from 82nd Infantry Division continued its attacks on the cut-off Soviet units, which were pushed into Tikhonovka. The Kampfgruppe itself was not particularly strong, but it was supported by seven artillery batteries, and the Luftwaffe made strong efforts to provide close air support. Still, the Germans lacked sufficient strength entirely to eliminate the Red Army force, which was supplied by Soviet air power.[48]

On 24 January the German XXXXVI Panzer Corps began the attack against the Soviet 1st Tank Army. Hube could only hope that this would put such pressure on the 1st Ukrainian Front that the latter's plans would either be shelved or reduced in scope.[49]

The XXXXVI Panzer Corps continued its attacks and was joined by the III Panzer Corps on 25 January. However, the 1st Panzer Army noted that it was very concerned about the threat to VII and XXXXII Corps and urged the two Panzer corps to attack with the utmost speed and determination, to finish the offensive operation, and, as soon as possible to begin shifting units to the right flank of the army. Two Soviet tank corps were committed against the attacking German forces, a move which threatened the success of the operation.[50]

In retrospect, it is clear that 1st Panzer Army correctly identified the main Soviet attack sectors and also that they were correct in assuming that the southern thrust, from the Tinovka area, would be the main effort. Furthermore, the Germans quite accurately predicted the date the Soviet offensive was to be launched and identified that its main objective was to cut off the German forces in the Korsun area.

Unfortunately for the Germans, the general situation on the Eastern Front resembled a dyke with many holes, but with few plugs available to arrest the flow of water. Unlike water, which continues to put pressure on a wall even if it is moved back, military forces may require time before they can reapply pressure. If the XXXXII Corps had been withdrawn to the more defensible area around the Rossava River, it would have taken some time for the Red Army to bring up forces and supplies. Since Hube was required to hold his position, however, he was left with only two alternatives: he could either use his Panzer divisions to attack the 1st Ukrainian Front, or he could keep them as a reserve ready to counterattack a Soviet offensive operation. In reality, the latter was hardly a choice at all. Any army commander who had a number of Panzer divisions standing in reserve was likely to be ordered to send them somewhere else, since there was always a need for Panzer divisions on many sectors of the Eastern Front.

The Situation for 8th Army, 22–23 January

On the sector of front covered by 8th Army, 1st Panzer Army's eastern neighbor, the XI Corps held a position somewhat similar to XXXXII Corps. The XI Corps was considerably stronger, but also had a longer front to defend. The northern part of the front did not lend itself to large-scale operations, since the area was swampy and large tracts of forest created difficulties. Also, the Tyassmin River could be used to advantage by the defender. The sector held by the XI Corps south of the Tyassmin River was more open though, and here the German 389th Infantry Division, a unit that had been destroyed at Stalingrad one year earlier, formed its defense. The division had been reformed in Brittany and sent to the Ukraine in the fall. In fact, the XI Corps also had been encircled at Stalingrad and its commander, General der Infanterie Karl Strecker, had been among the men who went into Soviet captivity.

On 22 January the XI Corps was engaged in minor actions in the Smela–Beresnyaki region, but these were not major concerns for the corps. In front of the sector held by 389th Infantry Division, intensive Soviet motor traffic, including tanks, was detected in the morning, especially in the Balandino–Krasnosilka area. Later the same day, the 389th Division was attacked south of Balandino, but the attacks were repulsed. Further Soviet movement in the area was observed, and artillery fire was called on to disrupt enemy movements. The commander of XI Corps, General Stemmermann, thought that the Soviet attacks against the corps were intended to feel for weak points, as a preliminary to a major offensive. Aerial reconnaissance indicated that the Red Army was creating a force concentration around Krasnosilka, which confirmed the view put forward by the commander of XI Corps. It was more difficult to establish the direction of a Soviet attack from this staging area, but as a precaution, the 8th Army decided to pull the 11th and 14th Panzer Divisions out of the front, to create a reserve.[51]

Soviet traffic in the Balandino–Krasnosilka area continued during the evening, and artillery from the XI Corps engaged Soviet concentrations east of Burtki and Verbovka. The impression of a force build-up was reinforced on 23 January by Soviet employment of antiaircraft units and fighter cover in the Balandino–Bondyevo area. Despite this, the Germans planned air attacks against this area, to disrupt and damage the Soviet build-up. Also, it was discovered that the Red Army had moved reinforcements into the area south of the Balandino–Krasnosilka region.[52]

Signs of an imminent attack multiplied during the afternoon of 23 January. Red Army assault units tried to destroy barbed wire and other field works, and Soviet artillery units began registering targets. The Germans responded by calling for artillery fire and air strikes on the Soviet concentrations. At 19.30hrs on 23 January, the 8th Army noted that the assumed Soviet main concentration in the Balandino–Krasnosilka area had been confirmed. Recent observations further suggested that the enemy grouping extended further south, between Krasnosilka and Penkino.[53]

Preliminary Soviet Attacks, 24 January

For the Germans, the situation grew even more precarious on 24 January. In the morning, strong Soviet attacks hit the 389th Infantry Division. It was stretched thin, with a combat strength of 1,500 men spread over a sector of 21 kilometers. To remedy the situation, a small armored group from the SS-Wiking Division counterattacked near Burtki, but the results were mixed. Still, the Germans were not entirely clear about where the Soviet main effort would be directed. The attacks on 389th Division were so far made without tank support and seemed like an effort to improve positions and gain knowledge of German dispositions as a prelude to the main assault.[54]

Anton Meiser served as an NCO in the artillery regiment of the 389th Division. His battery was deployed further north, near Olyanino, when shortly after 10.00hrs General Kruse, the division's commander, arrived. Meiser climbed aboard Kruse's vehicle and the driver set out for an observation post for the artillery. When they reached the position, which Meiser had visited previously, he could not avoid being awed by the change. Recent combat had completely changed the landscape, and the snow was "burned" and showered with earth. Meiser had little time to contemplate the landscape however, as he quickly had to make everything ready to repel a forthcoming Soviet attack.[55]

He did not have to wait long before Katyusha rocket launchers (known as "Stalin organs"), mortars, and howitzers opened a murderous fire. Meiser called for fire from his tubes in response. Only a few rounds were expended, but they were sufficient to see that the fire was correctly aimed. Suddenly the Soviet weapons went silent and Soviet infantry stormed forward. First it appeared to Meiser that the German infantry froze in fear, but very soon the characteristic sound of rapid-firing MG42 machine guns was heard. Cries of pain were mixed with "Urrah" yells. Meiser wasted no time and directed his artillery to fire a barrage at the attacking Soviet troops. Under the impact of the exploding shells the assault came to a halt. The Soviet troops withdrew, but the terrain offered no cover, and the retreat became costly.[56]

Major-General Kruse was satisfied that the Soviet attack had been repelled, but he could not understand why such a significant attack had not been detected earlier. Meiser replied that he had seen signs of the coming attack, and sent the information to his battalion commander, who had rejected the threat. Kruse and Meiser had hardly begun discussing the issue when Soviet heavy weapons again opened fire. In their optics, both men could discern Soviet infantry advancing. At this moment a runner arrived with the bad news that the artillery batteries on the right had depleted their ammunition. Thus the attacking Soviet infantry was permitted to overrun the defenses of a German battalion, and motorized troops were following behind.[57]

At first Kruse tried to order tanks to the threatened area, but they were halted as Soviet antitank guns engaged them. Instead he turned to Meiser and ordered him to call down artillery fire. Meiser immediately turned to his business and used a hurriedly improvised solution to direct the guns of the battery to various targets. Behind him, Kruse seemed to be somewhat startled, but allowed Meiser to do everything in his own way. When Kruse saw that it worked smoothly and had produced the desired results, he said "My son, that is not how it is written in any field manual, but it is good! Excellent, continue!"[58]

The artillery fire put the Soviet antitank guns out of action and the German tanks that had been stalled continued to try to recapture the

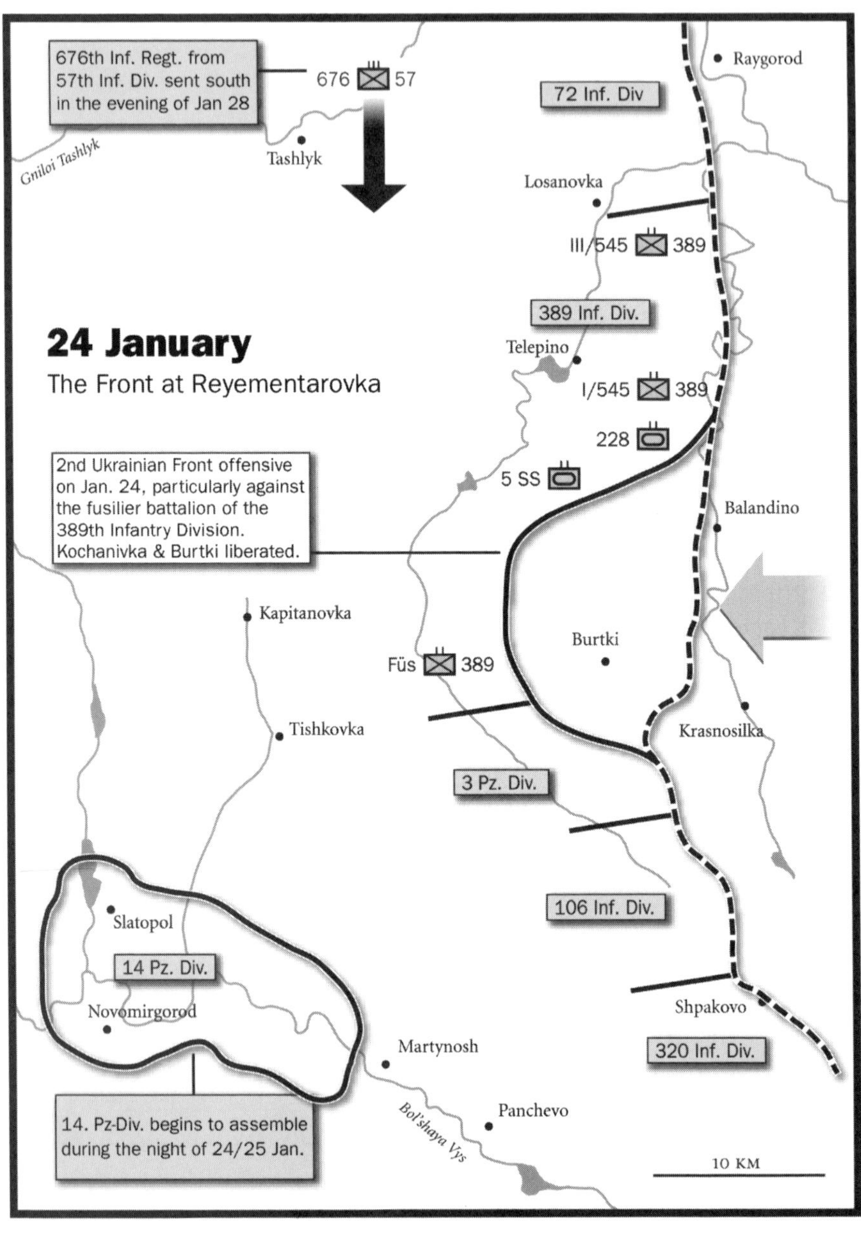
676th Inf. Regt. from 57th Inf. Div. sent south in the evening of Jan 28
676 57
Raygorod
72 Inf. Div
Gniloi Tashlyk
Tashlyk
Losanovka
III/545 389
389 Inf. Div.
24 January
The Front at Reyementarovka
Telepino
I/545 389
228
5 SS
2nd Ukrainian Front offensive on Jan. 24, particularly against the fusilier battalion of the 389th Infantry Division. Kochanivka & Burtki liberated.
Balandino
Kapitanovka
Burtki
Füs 389
Tishkovka
Krasnosilka
3 Pz. Div.
106 Inf. Div.
Slatopol
14 Pz. Div.
Novomirgorod
Shpakovo
Martynosh
320 Inf. Div.
14. Pz-Div. begins to assemble during the night of 24/25 Jan.
Panchevo
Bol'shaya Vys
10 KM

contested hill. However, the battery Meiser directed was also running short of ammunition. Fortunately for the hard-pressed German infantry, a Stuka attack was on the way, as reported on the radio receiver in Kruse's vehicle. Hardly had Kruse received the message before intense Soviet fire, from every conceivable weapon, rained down on the German positions. Meiser called for a barrage, but it was weak and soon ended when the ammunition was expended. The Russian infantry continued forward, only to be attacked by the Stukas in the nick of time.[59]

Kruse and Meiser rejoiced when they saw the aircraft, which effectively created havoc among the advancing Soviet units. After their initial effort the Stukas turned and came back for a second attack. This time, however, they made a serious mistake in attacking their own defending troops. Kruse ordered Meiser to fire a star shell to indicate that the position was held by German troops, but Meiser had none remaining. The aircraft made their attack and departed. Soviet infantry wasted no time and resumed their advance when they saw the German aircraft attacking their own infantry.[60]

The depleted German infantry, disrupted by the attack from its own air force, could not resist the Soviet assault. Soon some soldiers began running back. Kruse gave orders to break up and he set off toward his vehicle, to try to direct the tanks to counterattack where the infantry gave way. The Red Army soldiers followed the retreating Germans, but to Meiser it appeared that they did not follow very quickly; he thought that perhaps they were just as exhausted as the Germans.[61]

The battalion commander of the recoiling German infantry ordered his soldiers to hold and take new positions, but to no avail. None obeyed his orders. Meiser shouted: "Herr Major, something has to be done. If Ivan reaches the hilltop, he will see our howitzers as if they were a gift served on a plate." The major reacted and told Meiser to help him. The major, as well as a sergeant, pulled their pistols and pointed them at the fleeing soldiers, shouting, "Get into position or I will shoot you!" Meiser believed that the major or the sergeant, both very nice men, would never have shot their own soldiers, but fortunately they did not have to. The fleeing soldiers halted, got down and began firing at the approaching Soviet infantry. Some sort of defense was restored and the Soviet onslaught was temporarily checked. While these dramatic events took place Kruse had tried to get armor support to the endangered area. The time won when the major got his men to halt the Soviet advance was sufficient to allow the armor to counterattack and stabilize that sector of the front. By the evening, the Germans had mastered the difficult situation and the fighting slowed down. But though Kruse had managed to scramble a defense together, further south it was ominously quiet.[62]

Even these attacks, believed to be mere preliminaries, caused the XI Corps to use up its last reserves. The 228th Assault Gun Battalion had been committed between Radvanivka and Kokhanivka. To get some new reserves, the 57th Infantry Division was ordered to send one regiment south, to Pastorskoye, where it would be at the disposal of XI Corps. However, the reinforcements would not be available until the afternoon of 25 January.[63]

The gravity of the situation was clear to Army Group South, too. In the evening the chiefs of staffs of both the army group and 8th Army discussed the matter. They were unanimous in concluding that the action on 24 January had only been a prelude to the major assault which was to begin on 25 January or at the very latest on 26 January, and that the attack would be launched between Balandino and Penkino. There was little that the Germans could do. Air attacks had been directed against the Soviet assembly areas, but these could at best delay the Soviet preparations, not stop them. The relief of 11th and 14th Panzer Division was already underway. The 14th Panzer Division was expected to be available at Novy Mirgorod on the morning of 25 January and the 11th Panzer Division would follow slightly later. One GHQ artillery battalion, the I./Art.Rgt. 108, was ordered to leave the Grossdeutschland Division and move to Kapitanovka, to support the 389th Division, but it was unclear if it could reach the threatened area in time.[64]

Evidently the 8th Army, like its neighbor to the left, was aware of Soviet intentions and preparations. It correctly assessed where the Red Army would make its main effort and its leaders were able to follow the build-up. Indeed, the Germans even tried to interdict the build-up, but the means available to 8th Army were insufficient to the task. Wöhler tried to scramble two Panzer divisions to form a reserve, but both divisions were depleted and it was unlikely that both of them would reach the threatened area in time.

The Red Army Plans the Korsun Encirclement

For the Red Army, the planning process was somewhat simpler. Their overall superiority of forces on the Eastern Front permitted Stalin and his generals to dictate the broader events. Local German counterattacks could be a problem, but unless the Stavka played its cards completely wrong, the Germans could not be expected to create major problems for the Red Army. They could certainly be expected to offer stubborn resistance and cause the Red Army to pay a high price for any gains, but overall, the Soviets were in charge of events at this time, as they had been for the last five months.

The problems surrounding the Korsun–Shevchenkovskii operation were mainly caused by the fact that it was an operation of much greater scope than anything else currently taking place on the Eastern Front, even as other important operations were being conducted at the same time. As a result, the Red Army was juggling conflicting demands and ambitions; but that can hardly be considered an exceptional military situation. Rather, it is a quite common problem for military forces facing a competent or powerful opponent. Another problem was the depleted condition of many of the Soviet formations. However, the Germans also suffered from worn-out units.

The Stavka ordered the 1st and 2nd Ukrainian Fronts to encircle and annihilate the German forces in the Korsun–Shevchenkovskii area. The selected meeting point for the two prongs was Zvenigorodka. Since this meant that the 2nd Ukrainian Front would have 70 kilometers to cover and the 1st Ukrainian Front only 40 kilometers, the 2nd Ukrainian Front was scheduled to start moving one day earlier, on 25 January.[65]

On 15 January, General Konev held a conference at his headquarters in Boltushki. His subordinate commanders and their political commissars were present, as well as several officers from Konev's own staff. Konev opened the conference by describing the order received by the front and his preliminary opinion on how it should be carried out. According to Konev it was best to launch the main attack from the area north of Kirovograd, as the Germans were believed to have weaker defenses there. This meant that a significant part of the front's forces would have to be shifted north, among them Rotmistrov's 5th Guards Tank Army. The main weight of the initial attack would be provided by the 53rd Army and 4th Guards Army.[66]

Since both fronts had been conducting operations in diverging directions since Christmas 1943, they were compelled to do some regrouping of forces. The 1st Ukrainian Front formed a new army, the 6th Tank

Army, on 21 January. The 6th Tank Army had no real staff or GHQ units. Rather it was the 5th Guards Tank Corps commander who, in addition to his previous duties, had been given control over the 5th Mechanized Corps too. Soviet sources do not agree upon the number of tanks available to the two corps when the Soviet offensive began. The 6th Tank Army had 190 tanks and assault guns.[67] Interestingly, the 5th Mechanized Corps possessed a considerable number of lend-lease Sherman tanks.[68]

Although the 6th Tank Army was not fully up to strength in tanks, the 5th Mechanized Corps had its full complement of personnel, small arms weapons, and artillery. The 5th Guards Tank Corps suffered from shortages of soldiers in the motorized rifle units and in the artillery. The corps received replacements just before the offensive, but the new soldiers lacked experience and were poorly trained. Many of the soldiers came from recently liberated areas. Their desire to defeat the hated enemy was strong, but they lacked sufficient training.[69]

In addition to the 6th Tank Army, the 27th and 40th Armies were also to attack. The Koshevatoe and Tinovka areas were selected as their respective main efforts,[70] precisely where the Germans had expected. The 6th Tank Army was deployed behind 40th Army's shock groups, ready to exploit any penetrations.[71]

Unlike Vatutin's front, the 2nd Ukrainian Front did not create any new formations for the forthcoming operation. The 4th Guards and 53rd Armies were allotted the task of penetrating the German defenses, which the 5th Guards Tank Army should exploit. However, it was deemed necessary to use some of the tanks from the tank army in the initial attacks. Hence elements of two of the tank corps were subordinated to 53rd Army, which was very weak in armor, as it only possessed 21 tanks.[72]

While the 53rd Army was weak in tanks, it was strong in artillery. Aside from its divisional units, the army controlled five artillery brigades, one mortar brigade, one artillery regiment, and one mortar regiment. The army possessed 611 guns (larger than 45mm) and 467 mortars (larger than 82mm). Also it had more than 300 rocket launchers. The 4th Guards Army was slightly weaker in artillery, but nevertheless, the two armies mustered considerable firepower, most of which was concentrated against the German 389th Infantry Division.[73]

The 5th Guards Tank Army was supposed to exploit the breach created by 53rd Army and advance towards Shpola and Zvenigorodka.

The fighting around Kirovograd had been costly to the army and currently it consisted of three tank corps: the 18th, 20th, and 29th. The number of tanks in the army is a little unclear. On 21 January, the Tank Army possessed 156 operational tanks and assault guns, plus 91 in need of repair. Considerable efforts were made to repair vehicles and it seems that about half of them were repaired in time for the starting date of the operation.[74]

Konev had actually wanted to have his most experienced armies—Zhadov's 5th Guards Army and Shumilov's 7th Guards Army—committed in the encirclement operation, but it proved impossible to disengage them from their positions around Kirovograd and send them to the western wing of the front within the time allotted for the preparations.[75]

An important part of the Soviet planning was the deception operation staged by the 2nd Ukrainian Front. The use of dummy tanks, false artillery positions and depots, and simulated radio traffic was intended to create the illusion that a considerable force was concentrated west of Kirovograd. To this was added motor vehicle noise, field works, track marks from tanks, and other measures intended to reinforce the impression. At the same time the true build-up was hidden. These activities were conducted between 19 and 24 January,[76] in the hope of causing the Germans to place their forces, particularly their reserves, too far south.

Unsurprisingly, Soviet sources maintain that the deception was successful. This seems at most to be only partially true. For example, the Soviet General Staff Study claims that "the Germans kept all of their Panzer divisions along the Kirovograd axis."[77] However, both the 11th and 14th Panzer Divisions were pulled out and sent to the Novo Mirgorod area, which was on the real Soviet attack axis.[78]

Also, the 8th Army war diary shows clearly that the army was more concerned with the real threat than the simulated one. On 22 January, it discussed the "enemy main effort build-up and attack preparations" in the Krassnosilka area and regarded them as confirmed. The Soviet fake preparations were observed, but they were only mentioned in one sentence: "Scope of the ongoing enemy regrouping on the southern wing not yet identified."[79]

At 08.20hrs on 23 January, the LII Corps (on the southern wing of the army) reported that it had directed artillery fire on enemy concentrations.[80] This may have been caused by the Soviet deception. Also, busy traffic was reported in front of the LII Corps. However, when summing up the day on the evening of 23 January, it was clear that 8th

Army expected the Soviet main effort in the Krasnosilka–Balandino area.[81]

On the morning of 24 January, the XXXXVII Panzer Corps reported busy traffic on the roads leading north on the Soviet side of the front line, in the Penkino–Vladimirovka area northwest of Kirovograd. This observation may have been caused by Soviet deceptive measures, but the overall impression remained focused on the area east of Kapitanovka.[82]

Air Power on the Eastern Front

It was not only the Soviet deception plan that produced far less results than hoped for. At the beginning of the war in the East, the Luftwaffe quickly had gained command of the skies. However, as the number of aircraft available to the German air force on the Eastern Front was fairly small, the Luftwaffe did not have as great an effect as it had had during the campaign in the West in 1940. The smaller number of aircraft committed during Operation Barbarossa, combined with the larger theater of operations, made it difficult for the Luftwaffe to make more than local efforts. Initially this was offset by the weakness of the Red Air Force, but over time Soviet air power grew stronger. Still, even by the time of Operation Citadel, the Germans could establish local air superiority. However, the mounting Allied bombing offensive against Germany forced the Luftwaffe to commit more and more of its fighter units to the defense of the homeland, leaving the Luftflotten on the Eastern Front with few fighter aircraft. Simultaneously the strength of the Red Air Force grew.

At the beginning of 1944 the focus of air power for both sides on the Eastern Front was support of the ground units in various ways. Tactics as well as aircraft were largely adapted to this task. For the forthcoming offensive Rotmistrov intended to make effective use of air power during the breakthrough phase. A short artillery preparation was planned, and groups of four to eight aircraft were to attack enemy firing positions when they had been identified. Rotmistrov's intentions were good, but there was one major uncertainty: the weather. Fog could easily cover important parts of the battlefield and render air support impossible. Low clouds could have the same effect. The planning would have to take into account the likelihood that air power would fail to appear.[83]

Ground Logistics

In determining their strategy for the offensive, the Soviets also had to take into account the importance of logistics. More stubborn resistance on the part of the Germans than was anticipated would raise ammunition expenditure, and the attendant slowing of the advance would increase fuel consumption. It might also prove necessary to redirect reinforcements to respond to key areas of resistance. The roads were usually few and poor in Russia and the Ukraine, so important operations often required considerable efforts to improve the road network. The Korsun operation was no exception and the Soviet engineers worked to improve the roads so that they were sufficient to carry the substantial traffic that was inevitable. In particular in the area covered by the 2nd Ukrainian Front, the troop concentration was considerable, placing a strain upon the road network. Engineers from the front had only a few days to improve the existing roads and to build new ones. For example, a 35-kilometer lateral road for the 5th Guards Tank Army had to be built in four days.[84]

There were several problems involved in building and improving roads. First of all, such work could jeopardize the secrecy of the operation. Roads are generally quite visible and any work might give the enemy clear indications of their opponent's intent. Another difficulty was caused by the fact that the area had recently been a battleground. Existing roads might be mined and demolitions caused extra work. To locate mines the Red Army sappers were assisted by dogs.[85]

An alternative to roads, and one with considerably greater capacity, was, of course, railroads. They were even more susceptible to damage than roads and they too required work before they could be of use in the build-up of Soviet forces. Sleepers were scarce and the Soviet engineers resorted to using logs from buildings to remedy the shortage. Clamps had to be manufactured and were often delivered by Po-2 aircraft.[86]

There were numerous details to attend to and little time available. The planning and preparations of the two Soviet fronts had an impromptu character, but it was probably unavoidable. To spend more time on preparations would also have meant that the Germans could recover and present a more solid defense. It was probably better to try to mount the offensive as soon as possible.

Meanwhile, Hube had proceeded with the preparations for Operation Watutin, and on 24 January the XXXXVI Panzer Corps struck, followed by III Panzer Corps the next day. The two corps made fairly good but not spectacular progress. It remained to see if the German attack might affect the forthcoming Soviet offensive.

Rocket artillery, like this six-barreled German 15cm piece, was used extensively by both armies during offensive operations. (SIPA PRESS)

CHAPTER 4

The Condition of the Armies

Soviet and German Casualties up to 1944

It was the third winter in the war between Germany and the Soviet Union. For both sides, the previous years had brought considerable changes to the units involved. The war in the East was an immensely costly war. The Red Army suffered tremendous casualties in 1941 alone. Most likely the losses are not fully recorded.[87] During this year the men lost were predominantly taken as prisoners of war or killed, thus making them irretrievable. During 1942 and 1943, Soviet casualties remained very high, but wounded made up a larger portion. A significant number of the soldiers who were recorded as casualties could eventually be expected to return to duty; nevertheless, at least 12 million Soviet soldiers must have been irrevocably lost before 1944.[88]

While German casualties were not as staggering as Soviet losses, they were severe enough. Up to 31 December 1943, more than a million men were recorded as killed in action or missing.[89] But to this figure must be added the 25,000–30,000 men who died of disease or accidents.[90] Also, almost two and a half million were recorded as wounded in action and were evacuated.[91] No more than about half of the wounded could be expected to return to front line duty on the Eastern Front. Furthermore, an estimated 80,000 of the wounded men died in hospitals from complications with their injuries or other illnes. Another 100,000 had to be discharged due to injuries from accidents or disease.[92] Thus, German forces in the East must have permanently lost, at minimum, around two and a half million men from service. Considering that this was almost exactly the size of the original force that launched the invasion on 22 June 1944, it was a serious drain.

As always, casualties were most serious in the infantry. The old saying "the artillery is for the killing, the infantry is for the dying" certainly had some merit. According to Soviet figures, infantry represented 86% of the casualties in 1943–45.[93] Similar percentages are given by German sources. The turnover, to use a euphemism for bloodshed, was many times higher in the infantry than among average soldiers. As a result, many divisions mustered far fewer riflemen than their overall strength returns suggest. Furthermore, the greater strains on men in foxholes caused them to suffer more from various diseases. The German strength returns usually show the number of soldiers within the units, including those who were sick but not evacuated. Consequently, a division could be weaker than it seemed from the strength returns.

Organization and Supplies

Most divisions that took part in the Korsun battle adhered to the prescribed tables of organization and equipment, as most had been engaged in prolonged action and were consequently depleted. One example of this is Korps-Abteilung B, which held the northern part of the German Korsun salient. A Korps-Abteilung was a kind of fusion between three depleted divisions.[94] In the case of Korps-Abteilung B, the staff of 112th Infantry Division was used to form the Korps-Abteilung. To this was added elements from the 112th, 255th, and 332nd Infantry Divisions.[95] The formation of a Korps-Abteilung reflected the fact that the infantry suffered most of the casualties. When the Korps-Abteilung was formed, surplus rear services and artillery personnel and other specialists were freed and put at the disposal of OKH. The new Korps-Abteilung had a more balanced composition of manpower than that possessed by any of the three depleted divisions from which it had been formed.

Manpower was not the only shortage that troubled the armies. The Soviet Union was not a country abundant in food and other items, even before the war. In Germany the situation was much better pre-1939, but as the war progressed more and more shortages became apparent. Lack of transport could cause local food shortages, even if there was an overall surplus. Finally, almost any large organization will encounter problems in distributing items precisely where they are needed, especially a military organization engaged in a war with powerful enemies, where the situation changes rapidly and drastically in a short time.

Shortages also affected important weapon systems, like the Panther tank. The 11th Panzer Division reported that about one third of its Panthers remained in workshops for a prolonged period due to lack of spare parts. The spare part situation was somewhat better for the PzKw IV tanks and the StuG III assault guns, but they suffered from shortages of high explosive ammunition instead, which hardly was much better.[96]

Deliveries of new tanks to replace losses could vary considerably. In early February 1944, the 13th Panzer Division complained that it had not received a single new tank during the last three months. It had so many tank crews without a vehicle that it could immediately accept 30 new PzKw IVs and put them into action at once, should it receive them. Also, lack of spare parts caused many of its tanks on hand to remain at workshops.[97]

Probably the most serious German shortage, except manpower, was in motor vehicles. In particular, towing vehicles were often reported to be in very short supply, causing numerous problems both when units were to regroup and when damaged vehicles were to be salvaged. Even the German Panzer divisions, expected to be the pinnacle of mobile warfare, suffered from serious problems due to lack of motor vehicles. The result was not only a loss of mobility, but of flexibility too. As long as all parts of a Panzer division were fully motorized and provided with sufficient fuel, they could simply be ordered to move and attack or defend wherever needed or desired. When insufficient vehicles were available, vehicles had to be moved forward to the units in greatest need of them and time had to be spent on establishing where vehicles were to be found.[98]

The Red Army experienced similar troubles. Indeed, had it not been for the substantial influx of U.S. lend-lease vehicles, the Soviet forces would have experienced considerably greater difficulties than the Germans. However, at this stage of the war the Red Army, thanks to its superior resources, enjoyed the benefit of the initiative. Thus the Red Army commanders had more choice with regard to the place and time of their actions than did the German army.

The Privations of Daily Life on the Eastern Front

The daily life of the soldiers was also affected by shortages. The 3rd Panzer Division experienced a grave shortage of soap and especially shaving soap. It had received no new deliveries of soap since October 1943, which of course caused hygiene to suffer so that the men were increasingly more troubled by lice. To this was added the difficult climate, alternating between frost, mud, and rain, which made hygiene more important than ever. At the same time, the division was engaged in uninterrupted fighting. Gradually the soldiers became more and more exhausted. Mail only reached the soldiers irregularly, which appears to have made the hardships more difficult to bear. The 14th Panzer Division reported that mail from the soldiers' families had not arrived for a long time, which had a negative effect on the men, especially as they were very worried about how their families fared in a Germany that was subject to increasingly severe bombing from Allied air power.[99]

Soldiers' Motivation

The men who lived in the foxholes had by far the worst situation, and as the struggle on the Eastern Front had already continued for more than 30 months, one can legitimately ask what kept them fighting. Obviously, individual reasons varied, and what motivated one soldier to overcome the horrors and hardships of war may not have affected another, whose situation could have been quite different. Those who served in the rear services seldom had to face enemy fire, and suffered far fewer casualties than the infantry. They had better opportunities to wash, rest, get mail, find shelter from the elements, and to cook warm meals. On the other hand, the fact that these men were less likely to become casualties meant that they tended to serve for longer periods. Extended service brought along its own negative effects.

It has been suggested that soldiers are motivated to fight, and to continue fighting, by such factors as primary group cohesion, sense of duty, leadership, discipline, ideology, propaganda, and heroism. To assess the appropriate importance of each of these factors has been much more difficult. For example, before and during the war, ideology and propaganda were considered to play a prominent role in motivation and combat performance. Soon after the war, this theory fell out of favor, but about 25 years ago researchers again began to advance the idea that the effects of ideology and propaganda were a central part of the motivation of the German soldiers on the Eastern Front. This theory plays down the role of the primary group, which has often been regarded as the most plausible explanation for combat motivation.[100]

The argument against the importance of primary groups centered around the perception that the fighting on the Eastern Front was much more dangerous than on other fronts, which has been claimed to make the cohesion of primary groups an insufficient explanation. Rather, it is concluded that ideology and propaganda were chiefly responsible for the German tenacity in this area. However, in reality, casualties per division and month were actually lower in the East than, for example, in Normandy in 1944, and this holds true for German as well as British and U.S. divisions. Even the Soviet divisions did not, on average, suffer a loss rate that was higher than experienced in Normandy.[101] Of course, the overall number of casualties in the East was much higher than on other fronts, but this was the result of far more divisions being engaged over a much longer period of time.

If casualty rates have a strong negative impact on the morale of soldiers, which clearly seems plausible, it must be the number of losses suffered by individual units in a given time span that is of interest, not the overall casualties in an entire theater. In this respect the war in the East was not extreme. It is not only the fighting in Normandy that was more costly (per division and month); for example, the operations during the war between Finland and the Soviet Union in 1939–40, 1941, and 1944 showed higher casualty rates than the operations on the Eastern Front from July to December 1943, which was one of the bloodiest of all periods on that front. Furthermore, during the Yom Kippur War of October 1973, casualty rates were comparable to those on World War II's Eastern Front. There is nothing to suggest that the war on the Eastern Front was unique in its casualty rates, unit for unit.

It is inarguable that the soldiers on the Eastern Front endured severe hardships and extreme horrors, but there is no reason to assume that the soldiers' reasons to overcome these sufferings was any different from those factors identified in other theaters of war. There have been studies on Finnish, Israeli, and American soldiers in war, as well as German soldiers fighting in Western Europe, 1944–45.[102] These suggest that social factors within the combat units were chiefly responsible for cohesion and motivation, although the role of other factors, such as those discussed above, cannot be discounted completely. Nevertheless, the bonds between the men in the squads and platoons seem to have contributed the most to the men's resilience in battle, and endurance in the face of hardship.

In most military organizations, good leadership is regarded as important in keeping the men focused. However, the effect of leadership on morale is difficult to assess. A series of questionnaires distributed to American soldiers and officers who served in World War II showed that the officers attributed much more importance to good leadership than did the soldiers.[103] Partly this may have reflected the different roles, but there is another possible explanation. It may well be that the soldiers did not consciously bother much about leadership as long as it was reasonably good. When it was poor it might on the other hand have been much more obvious to them. The experience of Anton Meiser seems to be in line with this assumption. He did generally find that most officers he served under were brave, self-sacrificing, and competent, but the few exceptions seem to dominate his recollection of the Korsun battle.[104]

Leadership and Heroism

The word "hero" seems to have been used widely during the war. In many German documents it is said that a person "fand den Heldentot" ("found the hero's death"). Similarly, Soviet accounts speak liberally about heroism among soldiers. However, it seems that the soldiers themselves did not spend much time thinking about heroism. Instead, they simply tried to survive, and what time they could spare was devoted to thoughts of relatives, loved ones, friends, and other persons who mattered to them. Of course there were exceptions, like Olaf Ehlers, who served in the artillery regiment of the 13th Panzer Division. In his diary, which reveals theological tendencies, he mused over various topics, including heroism, which he wrote about on 27 January, when his division enjoyed a lull in the fighting:[105]

> *Heroism as means and self-esteem*
>
> *All I read makes me wonder about human life and existential issues. Time and again I recall the experience shared by professor Schöttle at Odessa and his stern questions that follow me.*
>
> *Today I cannot refrain from thinking on the notion of heroism. What does the "idea of heroism" actually mean? Is heroism a necessary means when politicians strive to fulfil their inevitable missions; is it thus a means justified by the aim? Can it serve as an example for the educator to advance the power men would not discover unless there is a model? Is it not the educator's task to release all power within a people to enable them*

> *to succeed in the struggle with other peoples?*
>
> *But when the ideal becomes a means to an end, then its value can not be found in itself alone and it would be a contradiction to the concept of the idealistic as a value in itself. Does the aim justify persuasion? Where can the demarcation between encouragement and persusasion be found, except in the judgement of the aim?*
>
> *Is heroism nothing but a life feeling? Wouldn't it be a terrible delusion, uncharitable destruction, a callous glorification of devastation, to fall forever into meaninglessness?*
>
> *No, we need theology, which deprives humankind of their ideas their autonomy and brings them back to their character as tools in the service of the Lord in the history of mankind. In him we can find the demarcations.*
>
> *Hence, heroism must be allied to humbleness when acting, with the pride in oneself in the service of God and with the distance the heroic personality has to maintain to itself. If not, heroism would just be an instinctive and uncritical denial of the claims of justification of others, it would be a naïve contradiction to the self-sacrificing of others.*

This is perhaps an example of thinking that was not typical, but can be seen as one example of a wide range of thoughts about how soldiers behaved on the battlefield and why.

Atrocities in War

The war in the East was particularly rife with atrocities, and this factor is also likely to have affected an unknown number of soldiers. Of course, some soldiers were fortunate enough not to be witness to atrocities; others saw but did not participate; still others took an active part. The reactions of those who saw, or who chose or were forced to participate in atrocities, varied from disgust, to an acceptance of the inevitability of such actions, even to a willingness and desire to commit them. In many cases the atrocities were ordered and planned by the top leadership, or happened as the result of policy decisions, in which cases it became a matter of duty. In other cases they were caused by more "spontaneous" action. In January 1944, Anton Meiser became witness to an event whose cause was unknown to him, as he came riding toward a village. He saw how soldiers in German uniforms assembled all men over the age of 14. Other soldiers collected the livestock. When the men and cattle had been brought outside the village, the women and children remained near their houses and begged for mercy. It was to little avail, as torches set the straw roofs ablaze.[106]

The village burned down, while the women saw their men being herded away and threatened with rifle butts. The women and the children were left in the bitter cold, with almost no possessions remaining as their houses burnt down. Some of them attempted to save objects from the burning houses, despite the danger of serious injury.[107]

Such scenes were common.

Soldiers' Pay

As the ordinary soldier on the Eastern Front was enlisted, and thus expected to do his duty to his country, he did not receive any extravagant pay. Basic pay in the German army was the equivalent of about one-eighth of what an industrial worker earned, but frontline service resulted in an extra payment per day, bring the earning up to a level of about one-third of an industrial worker's. Officers were considerably better off: a captain earned about ten times as much as an enlisted soldier in frontline service, and a general about 20–30 times a much. To some extent the low pay for a soldier was alleviated by the fact that he did not have to pay for food, lodging, clothes, etc, which he would probably have done at home.

Not that there was much else for a soldier to spend money on at the front. The canteen usually offered some merchandise, and there was always the black market, but for frontline soldiers who required a pass to get to the rear areas, access to the black market was difficult. It seems more likely that the rear services, or soldiers from units not engaged in combat, could spend their money on the products offered by the black market.

For many soldiers there was an alternative to spending the money locally, and instead they sent their money home, knowing that it would be of better use there than near the frontline. It was sometimes mentioned in letters that money had been, or soon would be, sent home to the families. At a time when the margins of life were slight, even the small amounts a soldier could send home were valuable.

The big difference in pay between an officer and a private may be interpreted as an indication of inequalities, and to a certain extent it is probably true. On the other hand, it is clear that to be an officer was a profession in peacetime too, and it would not have seemed reasonable to lower wages in war.. Furthermore, in the German army it seems that the casualty rates among officers were higher than among enlisted men, so the higher rate of pay served to recompense them for the increased danger. It is uncertain whether the officers in the Red Army suffered an equally high rate of casualties.

Conclusion

The balance of strength between the two armies opposing each other on the Eastern Front had changed considerably since the Germans invaded in June 1941. At first there had been approximate parity, but the Red Army enjoyed a massive influx of reinforcements during 1941, which the Germans did not even come close to matching. However, during the summer and early fall the Germans inflicted such immense losses on the Soviet forces that approximate numerical parity remained, despite massive Soviet reinforcements. With the advent of the fall mud and the ensuing winter, the Soviet loss rates shrank considerably and the influx of reinforcements gradually gave the Red Army an increasing numerical superiority.[108]

When the Germans launched Operation Citadel on 5 July 1943, their army in the East still was about as strong as it had been in June 1941; but from then on it almost invariably shrank, as casualty numbers were greater than reinforcements and replacements. At the beginning of 1944 the German Ostheer had shrunk to 2,528,000 men. The Red Army too found it difficult to maintain its strength, but thanks to its much greater replacements it still maintained a manpower strength of 6.1 million men. Thus the Soviet forces enjoyed a numerical superiority of 2.4:1.[109] The Soviet superiority in armor was even greater. Overall, the Red Army had a 3:1 superiority, but as many German tanks were in workshops, the Soviet advantage was at least 4:1 if only operational vehicles are counted.[110]

One possible explanation for the lower serviceability of the German tanks may be the shortages of spare parts already described. Another factor to consider is that the turnover of tanks was more rapid in the Soviet armored forces, resulting in fewer vehicles with high mileage. Also, it seems that the percentage of irrevocably destroyed vehicles was higher among the Soviet tanks put out of action, compared to the German tanks hit by Soviet fire.

With the comfort of their overall numerical superiority, the Red Army commanders could also assemble a numerically superior force in the Korsun area. The initial forces committed comprised 451 tanks and 62 assault guns operational. This was almost four times the number of available German tanks and assault guns. To compare artillery is more difficult, as the two armies did not count the pieces in the same way. Furthermore, heavy mortars were much more prevalent in the Soviet army than in the German. It can, however, be concluded that the Soviet forces assembled for the Korsun operation comprised 2,677 guns and 2,222 mortars. The former figure includes antitank guns and can be compared to the German force with slightly less than 500 pieces of artillery and 178 antitank guns. It would thus give the two Soviet fronts a numerical superiority of about 4:1 in the Korsun area, if guns and howitzers are compared. The Germans also had a number of infantry howitzers, 75mm and 150mm short-range weapons that naturally belonged to the infantry regiments. It is somewhat difficult to establish the true number of mortars and infantry howitzers in the German units, as these weapons were not included in all reports. However, the three Panzer divisions in XXXXVII Panzer Corps had, on average, 12 mortars and 13 infantry howitzers on 22 January. Simultaneously, three infantry division of the corps had, on average, 15 mortars and 12 infantry howitzers. If these strengths are representative for the German forces in the Korsun area as a whole, it can be concluded that the Germans had about 400 mortars and infantry howitzers. Thus the two Soviet fronts probably had a 5:1 advantage in this category of weapons.[111]

Overall, then, the Red Army had a numerical advantage of about 4:1 in the major heavy weapons categories. It is more difficult to assess the Soviet superiority in manpower. There are many reasons for this. First of all, the German records that have survived give detailed manpower strength for some divisions, while many other divisions lack figures of any kind. It is hardly possible to establish the overall German strength. In Soviet sources there are strength figures to be found for the overall forces committed at the beginning of the operation. However, they differ considerably. For example, one source gives a strength of 254,965 men,[112] while another give a much higher figure of 336,700 men.[113] Probably these differences are caused by using different strength categories—for example whether non-combat troops are included or

TABLE 1: GERMAN HEAVY EQUIPMENT ON JANUARY 25 IN THE KORSUN AREA			
	Tanks and Ass.Guns	Artillery Tubes	AT guns
Korps-Abteilung B	0	41	11
88th Division	0	22	14
XXXXII GHQ units	0	0	0
198th Division	0	36 (est.)	14
34th Division	0	33 (est.)	14
VII Corps GHQ units	23	10 (est.)	0
SS-Wiking	20 (est.)	52	12 (incl. 7 SP)
SS-Wallonien	10	0	9
57th Division	0	50	8
72nd Division	0	33	14
389th Division	0	26	12
XI Corps GHQ units	9 (est.)	16	0
3rd Panzer Division	20 (est.)	22	10 (incl. 5 SP)
106th Division	0	31	7
320th Division	0	24	17
282nd Division	0	36	10
14th Panzer Division	15	24	15
11th Panzer Division	25 (est.)	26	11 (incl. 5 SP)
XXXXVII Panzer Corps GHQ units	20 (est.)	11 (est)	0
Total	142	493	178

not—and whether or not all supporting echelons are included.

The latter factor is particularly important when comparing Soviet and German forces. The German divisions were, on paper, larger than their Soviet counterparts, but on the other hand, the Soviets had considerably more support from army and front resources. It is important to ensure that comparisons are made in such a manner that all the relevant factors are taken into account.

The number of divisions probably gives a fairly accurate picture of the relative troop strengths.[114] For the Korsun operation the force ratio was about 40 Soviet divisions against 15 German, giving a force ratio of 2.7:1. This at least hints at the Soviet manpower superiority.[115]

With such superior forces at its disposal in the area of the planned operation, it is no surprise that the two Soviet fronts could assemble overwhelming forces at the intended breakthrough areas. Even the Soviet General Staff Study admitted a numerical superiority of about 7:1 in infantry and 13:1 in tanks where the 2nd Ukrainian Front intended to make its attack. The fact that the Soviets generally had more men and materiél at their disposal allowed them to concentrate forces where they were needed.[116]

CHAPTER 5

Konev Attacks

The Soviet Attack on 389th Division, 25 January

Early on 25 January, Soviet artillery intensified its fire against the German 389th Division. No less than seven infantry divisions,[117] with strong armor support, were ready to attack the sector defended by the German 389th Division, which only had 1,500 infantry to cover a front of 21 kilometers.[118] Further forces were immediately made available as reserves, including two rifle divisions and most of Rotmistrov's 5th Guards Tank Army.

No less than 270 Soviet tanks were committed against the German 389th Infantry Division and its nearest neighbor to the south, the 3rd Panzer Division.[119]

Soon the infantry from 53rd Army and 4th Guards Army attacked, supported by tanks from 5th Guards Tank Army. The 389th Division was already weak. It had too little infantry to man a continuous front line, so instead it held a series of resistance points. The Soviet forces soon created holes in the German defenses. In particular, the situation in the Ositniazhka area quickly became serious, prompting the German XI Corps to try to comb out reinforcements from other units. The small armored battle group from SS-Wiking was directed towards Ositniazhka, as was the 676th Regiment from 57th Infantry Division, which was already on the march.

It soon became clear that these forces were insufficient and the decision was made to pull out the entire 57th Division and send it south.[120]

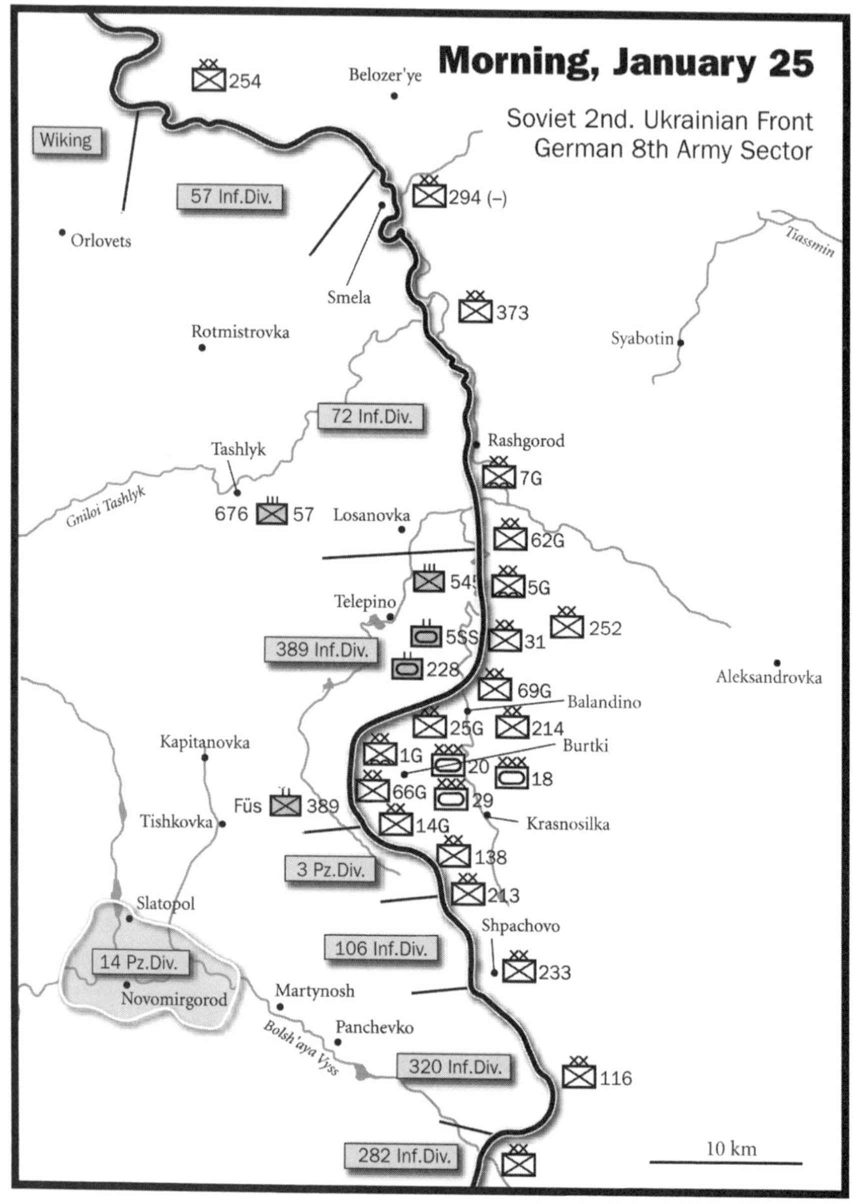
Morning, January 25
Soviet 2nd. Ukrainian Front
German 8th Army Sector
254
Belozer'ye
Wiking
57 Inf.Div.
294 (–)
Orlovets
Tiassmin
Smela
373
Rotmistrovka
Syabotin
72 Inf.Div.
Rashgorod
Tashlyk
7G
Gniloi Tashlyk
676
57
Losanovka
62G
545
5G
Telepino
252
5SS
31
389 Inf.Div.
228
Aleksandrovka
69G
Balandino
25G
214
Kapitanovka
Burtki
1G
20
18
66G
29
Füs
389
Tishkovka
14G
Krasnosilka
138
3 Pz.Div.
213
Slatopol
Shpachovo
106 Inf.Div.
14 Pz.Div.
233
Novomirgorod
Martynosh
Panchevko
Bolsh'aya Vyss
320 Inf.Div.
116
282 Inf.Div.
10 km

The Soviet Attack on 3rd Army

The Soviet attacks on the northern flank of XXXXVII Panzer Corps made less progress. Four infantry divisions—14th Guards, the 138th, 213th, and 233rd—were hurled, with armor support, against the German 3rd Panzer and 106th Infantry Divisions. The latter division, which was not subjected to particularly strong attacks, managed to hold its positions, but the fighting was harder for its northern neighbor, the 3rd Panzer Division. The strongest Soviet attacks were launched from the village of Burtki. South of the village the reconnaissance battalion of the 3rd Panzer Division tried to make a stand, but was soon pushed back. At 10.00hrs it was ordered to defend positions along the heights northeast of Reyementarovka, while the division's tanks moved forward to counterattack.[121]

The counterattack stabilized the situation temporarily, but in the afternoon the Soviet 53rd Army, commanded by Galanin, made a determined effort near Reyementarovka. After strong artillery preparation, the Soviet infantry rushed forwards. The German defenses were breached, forcing XXXXVII Panzer Corps to order the evacuation of the defenses northeast of Reyementarovka. The Soviet attack penetrated the woods southeast of Reyementarovka and severed the junction between the 3rd Panzer Division and its southern neighbor. Not until 20.00hrs did the Germans get the situation under control, when the penetration was contained and the connection between the two divisions restored.[122]

14th Panzer Division Counterattacks

Thus, the 3rd Panzer Division and 106th Infantry Division managed, barely, to maintain a defensive line, but north of XXXXVII Panzer Corps, events were developing quite differently. Soviet pressure on the southern flank of 389th Division was very strong. The German division almost fell apart, severing the connection between XI Corps and XXXXVII Panzer Corps; but reinforcements were on their way. The 14th Panzer Division had been marching during the night to be available for a counterattack and shortly after 09.00hrs the division's commander was notified that his unit would probably attack by noon. General Wöhler, the commander of 8th Army, wanted the 14th Panzer Division to conduct reconnaissance in the area where Soviet forces were breaking through. Martin Unrein, commander of 14th Panzer Division, replied that he had already ordered this and the reconnaissance was proceeding.[123]

Due to unexpectedly stubborn German resistance, the Red Army had not been as successful before noon as expected. However, the main force of 5th Tank Army was committed during the afternoon and it soon became apparent that the German 389th Infantry Division was already overtaxed.[124]

At 13.00hrs the 14th Panzer Division set out to counterattack the Soviet forces that had opened a gap between XI Corps and XXXXVII Panzer Corps. The division was divided into two groups, one operating in the Kapitanovka area and the other in the Rossochovatka area. The former was Kampfgruppe von Brese, consisting of a Panzer grenadier regiment, an armored reconnaissance battalion, an artillery battalion, and a small flak unit.[125] The other part was the armored battle group, but it was quite weak. The 14th Panzer Division only had seven PzKw IVs, four StuG IIIs, and four flamethrower tanks in running order. Together with the mechanized infantry battalion and the self-propelled artillery battalion, these were placed under the command of Colonel Langkeit.[126]

Langkeit's battle group rolled out from eastern Slatopol, along the road towards Kamenovatka, intending to turn north after a few kilometers. The fog was very dense and it was difficult to find the enemy. Neither side could use air support. Before 16.00hrs the Germans heard fire from the area north of Rossochovatka and they promptly turned north. Suddenly a column of trucks appeared in front of the German tanks, which immediately opened fire and destroyed two of the trucks before the rest disappeared, without having fired.[127]

Visibility deteriorated even further, making engagements very unpredictable. It was difficult to hear anything, due to the noise from the tank engines, and without any warning, Soviet and German tanks stumbled into each other. At a distance of only 50 meters Feldwebel Ziegler fired a shot from his tank, which hit a T-34 and set it on fire. Otherwise the engagement was inconclusive and each side seemed to be content with settling down for the evening. The tanks of the 14th Panzer Division assembled in Rossochovatka and waited for supplies, which arrived at 20.30hrs.[128]

Perhaps the tankers hoped to enjoy a calm night at Rossochovatka, but they were disappointed. At 21.30hrs a Soviet battalion-sized attack captured the northern part of the village. The German reaction followed soon. An hour later the German tanks, together with the attached Panzer grenadiers from I./Pz.Gren.Rgt. 103, recaptured the northern part of Rossochovatka.[129]

Kampfgruppe von Brese initially had somewhat more success. It reached the hills west of Ositniazhka. However, this was a dangerous position as it placed von Brese directly in the path of the Soviet advance, without having secure contact with friendly forces on either flank.[130]

Soviet Spearheads Reach Yekaterinovka, 25 January

While the 14th Panzer Division made an effort that was not particularly spectacular, Soviet progress continued along the Burtki–Kapitanovka axis. General Rotmistrov had chosen to advance with two tank corps abreast, the 20th to the north and the 29th to the south, while initially keeping the 18th Tank Corps behind the other two. General Lazarev, who commanded 20th Tank Corps, directed one tank brigade to envelop Ositniazhka. Just before 12.00hrs, the Soviet forces reached hill 222.0, four kilometers southeast of Ositniazhka.[131]

The Germans tried to scramble reinforcements to the area, but only modest forces were available. At the same time as the Red Army occupied hill 222.0, one German infantry battalion reached Ositniazhka. The Panzer group of SS-Wiking was also directed towards Ositniazhka, but it was unclear if it would arrive in time to stave off the crisis, or even if it was strong enough to do so since it possessed less than 30 tanks.[132]

In the meantime the Soviet forces pushed on. The 20th Tank Corps advanced through Pisarivka to Kapitanovka. Simultaneously the 29th Tank Corps made progress further to the south, where it managed to reach Tishkovka. Of all Soviet units, these two corps made the greatest advance during 25 January, but the penetration was by no means deep. During the day, the two tank corps had advanced 10 kilometers.[133] In itself, this would probably have been manageable for the opposing German forces, but the Soviet pressure on 3rd Panzer Division prevented it from interfering with the spearheads of 5th Guards Tank Army. However, compared to its northern neighbor, the 3rd Panzer Division was not in a particularly difficult situation. The 389th Infantry Division had borne the brunt of the Soviet offensive, and was almost falling apart under pressure from 4th Guards Army. Indeed, the 389th had been in a perilous situation already on 24 January, when the Red Army conducted its probing attacks, but as soon as the main offensive opened up, the situation became insurmountable.

The greatest danger lay in the southern sector of the 389th Division, where the Füsilier battalion initially defended, but was soon overwhelmed. By the evening of 25 January the division had lost control over the fighting on its southern sector. In the center it had been pushed back to Olyanino and Radvanovka, but was still able to maintain a continuous frontline between the northern outskirts of Ositniazhka and Yekaterinovka. North of Yekaterinovka, the 4th Guards Army had created a breach and separated one infantry battalion from the main body of the 389th Division. It was decided temporarily to subordinate the battalion to the 72nd Infantry Division. Exploiting the breach, the 4th Guards Army spearheads captured Telepino and reached the eastern outskirts of Yekaterinovka, causing the 72nd Infantry Division's south flank to be separated from other German units.[134]

Soviet Assessment of the Battle

Although the attacks by 4th Guards Army caused great difficulties for the German 389th and 72nd Divisions, Konev had expected its great preponderance of force to produce more significant results. On the evening of 26 January he issued an order in which he emphasized that the units of 4th Guards Army had operated particularly poorly on 24 and 25 January. Instead of conducting a daring and decisive maneuver they were held down in front of weakly defended villages. They had not used indirect fire from artillery and mortars against the enemy strongpoints.[135]

In an order issued the same day by the 4th Guards Army to its subordinate units, Konev's complaints were repeated in detail, as were the measures necessary to improve matters. Most important were command and control, the use of artillery, night operations, and outflanking maneuvers. The strong artillery support—with up to 121 tubes per kilometer of front in the attack sector—had not been used sufficiently and it had been poorly organized. The artillery was not close enough to the infantry, and lack of good communications hampered the coordination of the two arms. On many occasions the artillery was committed with poor timing, especially during the decisive moments, such as in support of attacks or during enemy counterattacks with tanks and infantry. Division commanders had not used their antitank assets with sufficient resolve when fending off enemy tank attacks. Rather they wasted ammunition.

Furthermore, command and control was poorly organized, particularly the communications between divisional staffs and the regiments. For example, the 7th Guards Airborne Division had no signals communication with its regiments during the night before 25 January and during 25 January itself. Due to communication breakdowns the commanders of 31st and 69th Guards Rifle Divisions could not command their troops and influence the events. Neither main nor secondary communications were used. Despite personal instruction by the army commander, orderlies remained unused. Finally, staff and observation posts, especially those of the 7th Guards Airborne Division and 20th Guards Corps, remained too far back from the combat units. Some commanders had not been present with their combat units during the fighting, instead remaining in shelters or villages.[136]

Wöhler Shores Up his Defenses

When summing up the events that had taken place on 25 January, both sides had reason to be disappointed with the results achieved. While the 2nd Ukrainian Front had made notable progress, it still could not claim to have made a clear breakthrough, despite committing the 5th Guards Tank Army, its main mobile force. Obviously the German 389th Division had been hard hit and was fighting desperately to hold a front. However, the penetration achieved by Rotmistrov's tanks was relatively narrow and shallow. If the Germans had mobile reserves in the vicinity they might close the gap at Kapitanovka and Tishkovka. The second day of the offensive could prove to be decisive.

If Konev was worried, he nevertheless had a far lighter burden on his shoulders than Wöhler. Due to Soviet pressure, the 3rd Panzer Division had been fully engaged and unable to send any units north. The 14th Panzer Division had duly moved forward, but its depleted strength prevented it from halting the Soviet attack. As was to be expected from the grave situation, the XI Corps had committed all its reserves, but more were needed. Risks had to be accepted. There had been relatively little Soviet activity in the sectors held by the German 72nd and 57th Infantry Divisions. Also, the SS-Wiking Division had hardly been troubled by the enemy. It was possible that some of these units could be disengaged and sent south. Already at 08.45hrs, Wöhler had decided that the entire 57th Infantry Division, which had previously sent its 676th Infantry Regiment to support the 389th Division, should be pulled out of the front line and sent south. Fifteen minutes later orders were sent to effect this decision.[137]

It was a difficult decision, since the divisions of the XI Corps were already thinly stretched, but considering the gravity of the situation on the corps' right flank, it was probably unavoidable to shift forces south. The SS-Wiking was ordered to take over the sector held by the 57th Infantry Division, but it would take some time before it was in a position to relieve the 57th. At best it could be available on 27 January.[138]

In the present situation this was all that could be done by the XI Corps, unless its positions along the Dnepr River were abandoned, an option that had already been ruled out. The 8th Army had one card yet to play, however: the 11th Panzer Division was ready to go into action early on 26 January, and further reinforcements were on the way.[139]

While Wöhler struggled to get more forces to the endangered sector, Konev had committed most of his resources. He could do little more than exhort his men to accomplish the desired breakthrough on 26 January.

The weather had been an important factor during the day, with temperatures hovering around 0° C, but the condition of the roads was still good. Dense fog covered much of the battlefield and made air support largely ineffective, despite attempts by both sides to put planes in the air. The fog also made it difficult to command the combat units. Forecasts indicated that more troublesome ground conditions could be expected in the future. Indeed, on the morning of 26 January a thaw began, with rain clouds above the battlefield. For the moment the roads were icy in places, but there were stretches that quickly became weakened by the thaw.[140]

The German Defense Continues, 25–26 January

The fighting continued on the night of 25 January, although at a somewhat lower intensity. The German 3rd Panzer Division had to create a new main defense line to be able to resist the renewed Soviet attacks that were expected. The German soldiers worked in the darkness and managed to create a coherent defense line on the sector held by Colonel Lang's division. The situation was less clear to the north of 3rd Panzer, where Soviet units probed westwards, but made no substantial gains. The 4th Guards Army kept pressure on the north flank of the German 389th Infantry Division, causing the connection between the 389th and the 72nd Division to be fragile. In the evening, the German 72nd Infantry Division had been forced to withdraw its southern flank, to establish contact with 389th Division, a process that continued on the morning of 26 January.[141]

Rotmistrov's aim for 26 January was clear: to achieve a complete penetration of the German defenses to enable his units to advance towards Zvenigorodka. He ordered his corps to continue to the west. It was obvious that delays would enable the Germans to position reinforcements in the path of his units. Time was of paramount importance, and yesterday's gains were not particularly impressive. The offensive must continue.[142]

It was perhaps not fully clear to the Soviet commanders, but the German defenses in front of 5th Guards Tank Army were indeed thin.[143] When the 20th Tank Corps attacked in the morning, with its 8th Guards Tank Brigade in the lead, it made good progress. The Brigade, commanded by Colonel Orlov and supported by two SU regiments, evicted the Germans from Kapitanovka and pushed on towards Zhuravka. Thus there were no longer any notable German forces between Rotmistrov's spearheads and Zvenigorodka.[144]

At 08.25hrs Colonel Gaedke and Major-General Speidel, the chiefs of staff of XI Corps and 8th Army, respectively, discussed the situation over a telephone line. The 14th Panzer Division had obviously not been able to close the gap at XI Corps' southern flank, and Gaedke told Speidel that numerous Soviet tanks had assembled on the hills north of Rossochovatka, and that further enemy reinforcements were arriving. Fighting was going on near the bridge at Tishkovka. Gaedke continued by emphasizing that a breakthrough towards Kapitanovka was occurring. The situation on the north flank of the 389th Division was also serious. Gaedke concluded his description of the situation by relating that the armored battle group of SS-Wiking had been sent to the Telepino–Yekaterinovka area, to help stabilize the situation there.[145]

Speidel did not doubt the gravity of the situation and asked: "What reserves do you have available; when can 57th Division go into action?"

"The 57th Division will not be relieved until tonight," Gaedke replied. "For the moment we have no reserves."

"Are there any rear positions designated or prepared?"

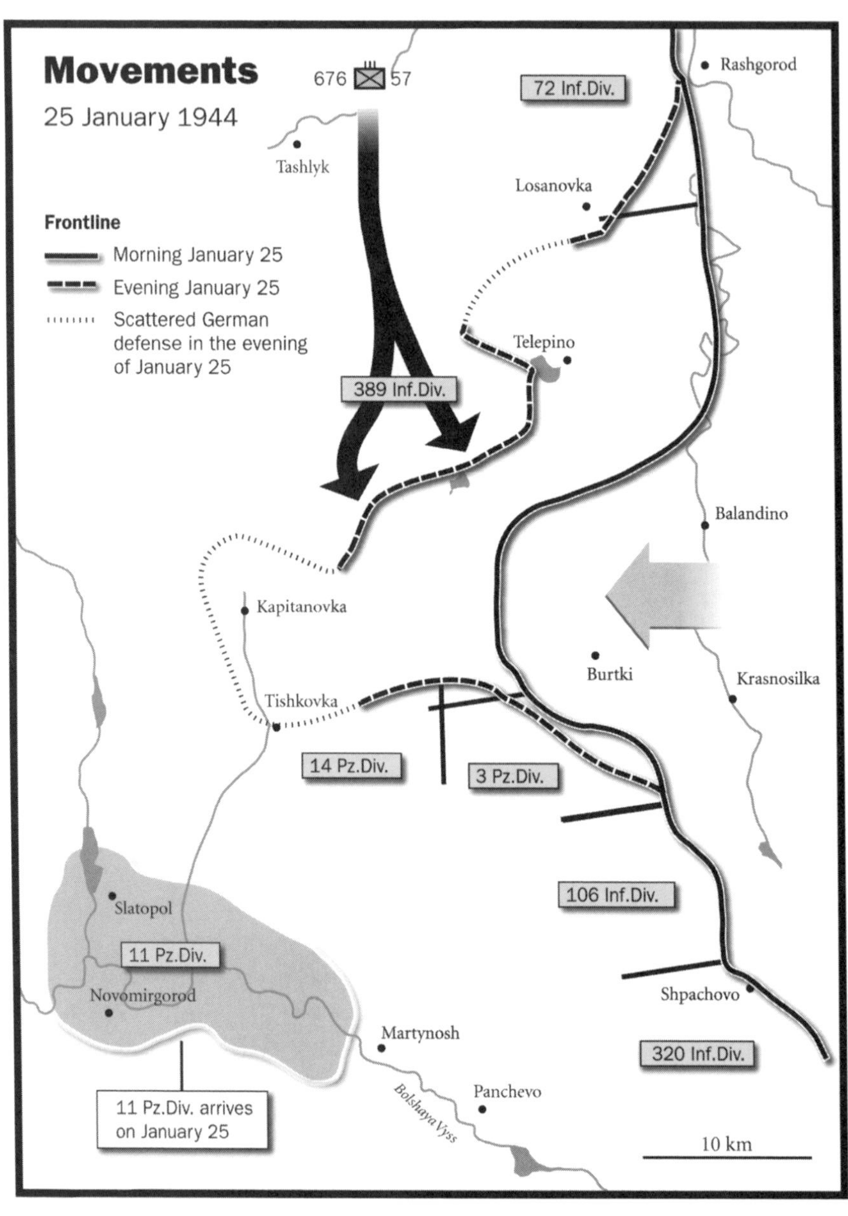
Movements
25 January 1944
676
57
Tashlyk
Frontline
Morning January 25
Evening January 25
Scattered German defense in the evening of January 25
72 Inf.Div.
Rashgorod
Losanovka
Telepino
389 Inf.Div.
Balandino
Kapitanovka
Burtki
Krasnosilka
Tishkovka
14 Pz.Div.
3 Pz.Div.
106 Inf.Div.
Slatopol
11 Pz.Div.
Novomirgorod
Shpachovo
Martynosh
320 Inf.Div.
Panchevo
Bolshaya Vyss
11 Pz.Div. arrives on January 25
10 km

"Yes, there is a line from Rotmistrovka over Stepok, the hill 1.5 kilometers east-south-east of Tashlyk, the railroad station at Serdykovka and the farms just north of Pastorskoye. It will have to connect to the Irdyn line via Beresnik and Sapadnaja. However, only the northern section, between Rotmistrovka and the Serdyukovka railroad station, is prepared."

"I will have to talk with the army commander to prepare him for future decisions," Speidel replied.

Gaedke continued to describe the situation in dark colors: "Concerning the situation west of Ositniazhka, it is doubtful if the corps can ward off the enemy unless reinforcements arrive. Also, it appears doubtful whether the 57th Division will be available in time."

"The army is not able to help in the northern sector of 389th Division," Speidel replied.

"If so, we must certainly consider the rear position I described."

"You are probably right. I can add that the army commander wants the 11th Panzer Division to attack near Kapitanovka."

Gaedke and Speidel spoke over the telephone again, an hour and a half later. Gaedke suggested that 72nd Division should be withdrawn to the "Hamster" position in one leap during the night. This would enable the 57th Division to pull out without first being relieved by the SS-Wiking. However, Gaedke argued that this could not be done without the consent of the army group.[146]

According to earlier German military tradition, such a procedure would not be necessary. Rather the local commander would have made the decision. However, since the winter of 1941–42, Hitler had usually enforced a "no retreat" policy, which obliged field commanders to ask for permission from OKH before retreating. The necessity of asking permission from higher command brought with it many disadvantages, not least of which was loss of time.

While Gaedke and Speidel discussed their options, the battle continued. At about 09.00hrs the 11th Panzer Division received orders to attack over Pisarivka. However, the division was not yet in position and required a few more hours before it could go into action. In the meantime, the Red Army continued its advance. While the 11th Panzer Division received its orders, Soviet tanks reached a point 1.5 kilometers north of Slatopol. This was serious, as there were few bridges over the

Bolshaya Vyss River. The most important were at Novo Mirgorod and at 09.45hrs the 14th Panzer Division reported that 10 T-34s were approaching the town. If the Germans were going to close the gap between the XXXXVII Panzer Corps and XI Corps, it was necessary to keep a solid position on the northern bank of the Bolshaya Vyss River. All reinforcements would have to arrive from the south, and if they then had to face an opposed river crossing, their difficulties would be considerably greater. To counter this threat the 8th Assault Gun Battalion was ordered to throw back the advancing Soviet tanks.[147]

Slatopol and Novo Mirgorod were not located on the main axis of the 5th Guards Tank Army attack. The 155th Tank Brigade passed between Tishkovka and Kapitanovka and continued towards Zhuravka. At noon it reached the outskirts of Zhuravka.[148] Thus the Soviet forces had advanced about 14 kilometers during the last 48 hours.[149]

At this moment Major-General Wenck, Chief of Staff of 1st Panzer Army, called Speidel and told him that the 1st Ukrainian Front had attacked the inner flanks of VII and XXXXII Corps. The Red Army had committed strong infantry and tank forces. Speidel immediately replied that this attack was connected to the attack on the south flank of XI Corps, which appeared to be heading in the general direction of Shpola. The aim seemed to be to effect a junction between the 1st and 2nd Ukrainian Fronts.[150]

This was news that added to Speidel's troubles, since half an hour earlier Colonel Gaedke had again called and reported that Kapitanovka was occupied by the enemy, and no reports were received from the 389th Division. Furthermore, Gaedke had told Speidel that there was no information about the situation in the Slatopol–Zhuravka area. But worse was to come.[151]

As Gaedke had asked him earlier, Speidel asked Army Group South about the proposed withdrawal of the 72nd Division. Since the question of withdrawals had been discussed before the Soviet offensive begun, and been turned down, probably by Hitler, it was understandable that Gaedke and Speidel brought the issue to Army Group South. However, later they would probably regret that they did not silently act on their own, because just before noon Theodor Busse, the Chief of Staff of Army Group South, replied that permission to withdraw 72nd Division was not granted; rather it would be better to see the results of the 11th Panzer Division's attack.[152]

Busse had not made the decision himself, but he knew that the issue was sensitive and he simply did not want anything to happen while he consulted OKH. Within a few hours he got a negative reply: the 72nd Division could not retreat. At 15.50hrs he told Speidel about the decision. Wöhler seems to have expected that the decision would be negative, because at noon he had instructed that 72nd Division should pull out elements from its forward positions and put these in the "Hamster" position, before he received orders to keep 72nd Division in the line.[153]

The Soviet Advance Continues, 26 January

Konev and his subordinate commanders did not have similar problems. Rather than delaying the movements of their units they were anxious to speed them up. The dense concentration of forces would make it possible to cover the flanks of the advancing armored spearheads, assuming that the latter advanced to provide room for the follow-up forces. This did, in fact, happen. By 15.00hrs, the village of Zhuravka had been cleared by units from 20th Tank Corps, which could then continue towards Lebedin.[154] The advance was welcome, but it remained unclear if it was enough, because a slow advance rate could also cause another difficulty. Since the armored spearheads had advanced more than 10 kilometers, the Soviet artillery was not in a position to provide fire support unless the guns also moved forward. With the large number of units cramming the roads, it would be difficult to move substantial amounts of artillery forward, at least if they were to get forward in time to provide useful support to the forward units.

As the XI Corps lacked any significant reserves, the German hopes rested on their 11th and 14th Panzer Divisions. The actions on 25 January had been somewhat hesitant, perhaps understandable considering the very low tank strength of the 14th Panzer Division. The 11th Panzer Division was somewhat stronger, with approximately 20 Panthers and a handful of Panzer IV and Panzer III tanks. Still, this was far fewer than the 200 tanks with which the 5th Guards Tank Army had begun the offensive.[155]

On 25 January, the 14th Panzer Division had been split into two groups. The armored group, commanded by Colonel Langkeit, was located at Rossochovatka in the morning of 26 January, and at 08.00hrs it received orders to attack towards Ositniazhka. Fog reduced visibility to 40–60 meters, and at 10.00hrs the German tanks stumbled into a

Soviet antitank front and a firefight ensued. Soon Soviet tanks arrived. One tank commander, Lieutenant Bauer had been wounded 11 days previously, but he remained with his company. When the Soviet tanks counterattacked, his tank received three direct hits and he was killed. It was not possible to recover the tank so the battalion commander ordered the assault guns to fire upon the stricken vehicle to destroy it. The Germans claimed to have destroyed one T-34 and three antitank guns.[156]

While this action took place, Soviet forces attacked southeast of Rossochovatka, threatening to cut off the 14th Panzer Division from 3rd Panzer Division. Colonel Langkeit's tanks had to turn around and try to reestablish contact with 3rd Panzer Division, whose armored group was also sent to restore the situation southeast of Rossochovatka. This succeeded late in the afternoon, but in the meantime Soviet forces captured Rossochovatka.[157]

In the morning of 26 January, Kampfgruppe von Brese from 14th Panzer Division held positions on the hills west of the cemetery at Ositniazhka, but was surrounded by Soviet forces. Rather than halting the Soviet advance, von Brese had to ensure that his force was not engulfed. During the day he managed to inch his battle group slightly northwards, but he could only watch as most of the 5th Guards Tank Army continued towards Tishkovka and Kapitanovka.[158]

With the 14th Panzer Division struggling to keep its positions, the 11th Panzer Division was the remaining German hope. However, the division received its orders fairly late and it also had to move along poor roads to get into position to attack. At 13.00hrs it attacked, from the Kamenovatka area, with the armored group to the right and the 111th Panzer Grenadier Regiment to the left. The armored group pushed on to Hill 205.4, west of Pisarivka, while the 111th PzG Regiment took the southern half of Tishkovka before dusk.[159]

Although the 11th Panzer Division did capture some terrain that looked valuable on the map, it did not really have much of an effect on the Soviet advance. From hill 205.4 it would have been possible to direct artillery fire onto the Soviet columns streaming west, but the approaching darkness prevented this. Also, the last two days had seen much fog, especially in the morning. If similar conditions prevailed on 27 January, the value of the hill would be limited. It seemed likely that the 11th Panzer Division would have to advance further the following day, but it was doubtful if the division had sufficient strength, despite receiving the 905th Assault Gun Battalion as reinforcements during the evening.[160]

The 11th Panzer Division's activities on the southern flank of 5th Guards Tank Army were disturbing, but not decisive. As there were follow-up forces available, the 20th Tank Corps could resume the offensive after clearing Zhuravka late in the afternoon. With two tank brigades it continued along the valley northwest of Zhuravka, and by 23.00hrs the Soviet spearheads had reached the outskirts of Lebedin. The 29th Tank Corps, operating on an axis to the south of 20th Tank Corps, made slightly less progress, but had liberated Turiya by the end of the day.[161]

For the German XI Corps the situation grew more and more dangerous with every hour. The 389th Division had been able to maintain a continuous defense line during the day, but the division was seriously weakened and completely unable to interfere with the Soviet breakthrough on its southern wing. The situation on the division's northern flank was better, since it had been possible to close the gap between the 389th and 72nd Divisions. During the evening, elements of SS-Wiking began to relieve the 57th Division, which assembled near Tashlyk, thus presenting some kind opportunity to General Stemmermann, but clearly his corps remained in a very perilous situation.[162]

In fact, the 389th Division was disintegrating. Already, on the previous day, Meiser's battery had lost contact with the battalion and had pulled back toward Pastorskoye, on the initiative of the battery commander. In the morning of 26 January some 12 howitzers from various battalions of the 389th Artillery Regiment had assembled at Pastorskoye, and Meiser's battery commander, Lieutenant Sorajewski assumed command of the motley collection of gunners and their equipment.[163]

While Sorajewski tried to reach his battalion commander by radio, the men kept everything ready for a hasty departure, as no one knew if Soviet forces were in the vicinity; perhaps the ragged force was already surrounded, a fear that seemed to be shared by many of the soldiers in the group. During the preceding days, various Soviet leaflets extolling the benefits of surrender had rained down on the German soldiers, but they seemed to have had little effect. The soldiers feared that becoming Soviet prisoners would mean being killed or sent to Siberia. The latter

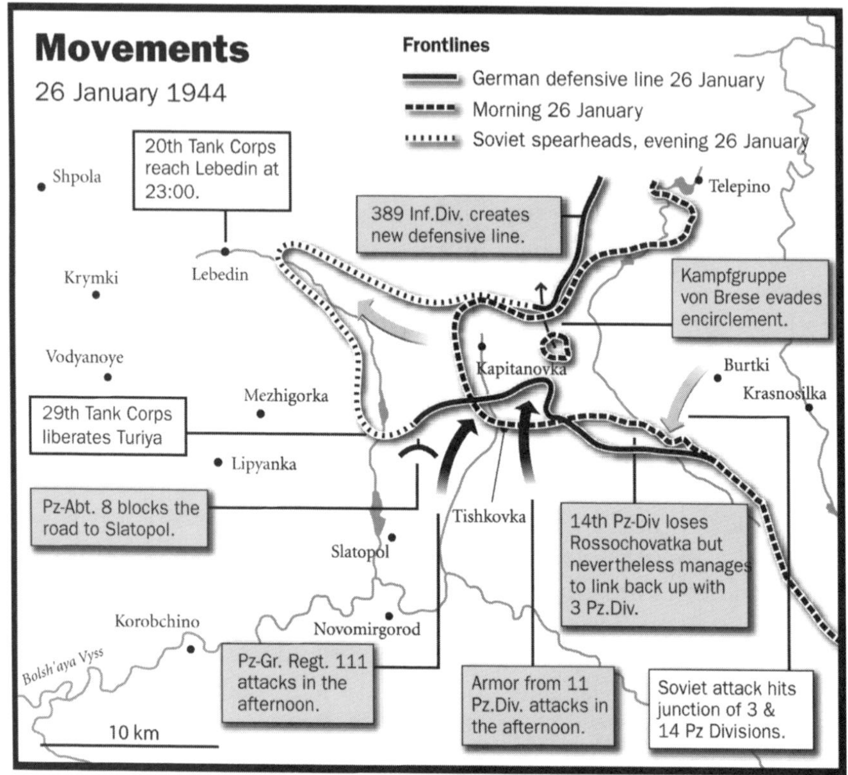

was a nightmare to the German soldiers, who were determined to avoid capture.[164]

During 26 January, the XI Corps received some reinforcements. The fact that 11th and 14th Panzer Divisions had been subordinated to the corps was perhaps not seen as reinforcements, since these extra units also meant that the corps had the added responsibility to close the Soviet penetration. However, an artillery battalion with 10.5cm guns arrived, and also the 905th Assault Gun Battalion had been transferred from the XXXXVII Panzer Corps and sent to the 11th Panzer Division.[165]

In turn, the 2nd Ukrainian Front moved forward some substantial reinforcements, the most important of which was the 5th Guards Cavalry Corps. During the day it received orders to move to the Telepino–Burtki line, a move that was initiated at 20.00hrs. The corps was also reinforced with an antitank brigade. The 18th Tank Corps had been held in reserve by Rotmistrov but was ready to advance on 27 January. It might well be needed if the German counterattacks from the south were intensified.[166]

A Soviet tanker has been captured after his tank was knocked out.
(SIPA PRESS)

CHAPTER 6

The Soviet Breakthrough

Soviet Forces Reach the German Rear

January 26 ended in a way reminiscent of the previous day. Rotmistrov's tanks had advanced farther to the west, but still they had not accomplished a clear breakthrough. The advance rate remained relatively slow: between the beginning of the offensive on 25 January and 23.00hrs on 26 January, the 5th Guards Tank Army had advanced only 20 to 25 kilometers. However, the Germans had no real defense to the west of the Soviet armored spearheads. If the 5th Guards Tank Army could contain the threat to its flanks, the road to the west was open. This opportunity was exploited by the 20th Tank Corps. After midnight, the 8th Guards and 155th Tank Brigades, with reconnaissance formations in the lead, began to advance towards Shpola. The town was weakly defended and by 10.00hrs on 27 January it had been cleared by the Soviet forces.[167]

By this stroke the Soviet spearheads had reached the German rear area, where they could expect to meet little opposition from German units. The loss of Shpola was probably not a surprise to the Germans. After all, they had suspected that this was the operational axis to be followed by the 2nd Ukrainian Front, and the weakness of the defenses made their collapse likely.

The 8th Army had no forces available that could block the Soviet thrust to the west, so Wöhler could only hope that the attacks on the shoulder of the Soviet penetration would succeed, thereby cutting off the Soviet spearheads.

11th Panzer Division Checks the Soviet Advance

The strongest German force was the 11th Panzer Division, which resumed its attack at 05.30hrs on 27 January. Fog dominated the battlefield and reduced visibility considerably. Nevertheless, the tanks of the division initially made good progress. Advancing from the hills east of Tishkovka, which had been captured on 26 January, the armor of the division managed to take the high ground east of Kapitanovka. Shortly thereafter, at 09.10hrs, the tanks made contact with Kampfgruppe von Brese, which had been cut off for nearly two days and had been forced to take up positions in a forest northeast of Kapitanovka.[168]

This meant that the 11th Panzer Division sat astride all the roads running east to west, which the Soviet spearheads depended on for supplies and reinforcements. However, given the low tank strength of the division, its grip on these vital roads could not be regarded as solid. Soviet follow-up forces would most likely try to open the route to the west as soon as possible. Later on 27 January, the 11th Panzer Division would report that it had 12 Panthers and three PzKw IVs operational, plus 15 StuG IIIs in the three assault gun battalions that were subordinated to the division.[169]

This was hardly an impressive assembly of armor, but still it was much more than the 14th Panzer Division could muster. In the evening it reported only three PzKw IVs and two StuG IIIs operational. Clearly the Germans had very little armor available and reinforcements were sorely needed. At noon a Panther battalion, the I./Pz.Rgt. 26 which had been temporarily subordinated to the Grossdeutschland Division, began to move to the 11th Panzer Division, but it was not expected to be ready to attack until the following day.[170]

When the 11th Panzer Division interrupted the Soviet east–west communications, Rotmistrov faced a delicate situation. He could either order the spearheads of 20th and 29th Tank Corps to turn back to restore the connection to the rear units, or he could order them to continue west and rely on the following forces to open the corridor. The existing circumstances clearly favored the latter alternative. Rotmistrov had not yet sent the 18th Tank Corps into action, and the 5th Guards Cavalry Corps was available in its assembly area a few kilometers east of the positions occupied by the German 11th Panzer Division. Also, the 4th Guards Army continued to push the German 389th Division back, while 53rd Army maintained pressure on the 3rd Panzer Division. These circumstances suggested that Rotmistrov should not turn 20th and 29th Tank Corps back, but that they should continue forward, while relying on the 18th Tank Corps and 5th Guards Cavalry Corps to reopen communications.[171]

Wöhler probably felt certain that the 1st and 2nd Ukrainian Fronts intended to encircle XI and XXXXII Corps. The chances of preventing this by blocking the 20th and 29th Tank Corps were indeed slim. All his combat units were at the shoulders of the Soviet penetration, and the thaw began to soften the roads, which deteriorated rapidly. In these conditions it would be time-consuming to shift units westward. His only realistic chance was to cut off the Soviet spearheads, which the 11th Panzer Division had actually managed to do. However, the 4th Guards Army attacked the German 389th Division's southern wing, focusing on Pastorskoe. If this attack was successful it would enable the 2nd Ukrainian Front to restore communications to its forward units, even if the 11th Panzer Division managed to hold on to the vital ground it had occupied early on 27 January.[172]

The situation on the 389th Division's southern wing was indeed critical, and available elements of 57th Division were sent to the Pastorskoe area. The 4th Guards Army had reached the railroad station at Serdyukovka, threatening to reopen the breach between the German 72nd and 389th Divisions, which they had managed to close with great difficulty. In the afternoon a regiment from 57th Division and elements from 4th Guards Army clashed in the forest north of Pastorskoe. The fighting was inconclusive, but at least the Soviet advance in this area had been temporarily checked.[173]

Anton Meiser on Reconnaissance

Together with many other soldiers, Anton Meiser of the 389th Division had assembled near Pastorskoye. During the night of 26 January nothing in particular happened, but the motley group of gunners and howitzers had yet no contact with other friendly units, and little knowledge about the enemy. Early in the morning of 27 January, it was decided to send three NCOs to reconnoiter, and Meiser was one of them. Each was given his own direction to scout, together with two men who would follow. Meiser was given the task of reconnoitering in a west-northwesterly direction.[174]

Little time was available to prepare and carry out the reconnaissance, and Meiser decided to conduct it from horseback. The cadet Damen volunteered to follow Meiser, to the latter's delight. The second person to follow Meiser was a soldier who was a good horseman. All of them were told that if they had not returned at dusk, they would be assumed lost.[175]

With their personal weapons, plus a machine gun, a few hand grenades, and some food in a sledge, the three men set off, to good wishes from Lieutenant Sorajewski and several of the soldiers. As silently as possible they passed through the small forest, through which it would be possible to move the howitzers if needed. Soon they reached a square opening in the forest. The thick snow made it difficult to tell what it was, but Meiser assumed they had found a sports field.[176]

The three men continued along the road leading to the west, noting that the falling snow would cover the tracks left by the small reconnaissance group. Meiser tried to keep an even pace, to enable a correct judgment of the distance covered. So far the road had continued in a westerly direction, but when it twisted it became more difficult to assess the distance traveled. At about 11.00hrs the three men reached the western edge of the forest and at a distance of about 300 meters the small village, which was their aim, appeared.[177]

So far they had not seen any signs of the enemy. The three Germans lay concealed at the edge of the forest and observed the village, but nothing transpired. Meiser decided that they would stalk toward the nearest houses. The impression of a deserted village remained when they reached the buildings. However, when Meiser entered one of the houses he found a weeping woman who told him that Soviet troops had recently taken away all the men in the village. For the moment there were no Soviet troops there. When Meiser realized he was not likely to encounter enemy troops, he told the woman to cook some eggs for him and his two companions. After a quick meal they continued westward.[178]

Signs of enemy activity remained scarce, but traces of felt boots could be seen, a type of footwear worn by soldiers in the Red Army. Nothing more was found by Meiser and his companions before they had reached as far west as they had been asked to reconnoiter. Meiser decided that they should follow the main road to Pastorskoye when they returned, a fortunate choice since no enemy troops were encountered. However, on entering a second deserted village, the men encountered a different sort of enemy. On a few houses they saw signs indicating that typhus fever had ravaged the area. As a precaution they covered their mouths with handkerchiefs, and even covered the mouths of their horses, before continuing toward Pastorskoye as quickly as possible.[179]

At about 15.30, Meiser's group returned to Pastorskoye, soon followed by the other two reconnaissance parties. Meiser could report that the route investigated by him was free of enemy troops, and that after the removal of a few trees, it could be used to move the howitzers. Meiser was ordered to go again along the route and mark it, but this time he was unlucky. When he and his men reached the village that had been deserted because of typhus, mortar shells began to explode nearby. Small arms fire immediately followed and Meiser and his two fellows galloped hastily back to Pastorskoye. Meiser's bad luck continued. After reporting that the route had been blocked by enemy forces, he was ordered to assume command of a platoon in the northern part of Pastorskoye. He had hardly got there before he collided with a car and injured his leg so that he was unable to walk, a very precarious condition for a soldier who was probably encircled. He would be dependent on others to escape the trap.[180]

The Fighting around Kapitanovka and Tishkovka

In the meantime fighting continued in other sectors, not least in the Kapitanovka region. After capturing the high ground east of Kapitanovka, Major-General von Wietersheim, the commander of 11th Panzer Division, ordered one infantry battalion, supported by assault guns, to capture Pisarivka.[181] The soldiers soon launched the attack, but it was unsuccessful. After some regrouping another attempt to capture the village was made, this time supported by rocket launchers, but it too failed. The armored battle group of the division was more successful. It managed to capture the southern half of Kapitanovka by noon on 27 January. In addition, when von Wietersheim's division established contact with the 14th Panzer Division, the Tishkovka area was brought under firm control.[182]

So far, the 11th Panzer Division had been quite successful. Indeed, given its limited strength it could probably not have hoped for more, but its neighbors to the right, the 14th and 3rd Panzer Divisions, had made far fewer gains. The 53rd Army launched spoiling attacks on the 3rd Panzer Division, but it could contain these and send its armored group to assist the 14th Panzer Division, which was trying to recapture Rossochovatka.[183] At first the 103rd Infantry Regiment from the 14th Panzer Division, supported by four tanks, had managed to capture the center of Rossochovatka, despite encountering lend-lease tanks. However, a Soviet counterattack pushed the Germans out of Rossochovatka, and two German attacks in the afternoon were unsuccessful. The inconclusive seesaw battles around Rossochovatka were costly. For example, from the morning on 26 January to the evening of 27 January, the 14th Panzer Division suffered 310 casualties. This was more than a quarter of all the casualties the division suffered during the entire month of January.[184]

Perhaps the disrupted communications affected the Soviet advance, since 20th Tank Corps did not move further westward after capturing Shpola, though it brought up its rifle brigade to defend the Shpola area. The 29th Tank Corps made more gains southeast of Shpola, where it took Vodianoe, Lipianka, and Meshigorka.[185]

It was imperative that the connection to his two forward tank corps be restored, and Rotmistrov could not wait for his northern neighbor to open a new route. Since the 18th Tank Corps and 5th Guards Cavalry Corps were available, he ordered them to reopen the corridor to the west. These efforts were not successful, but late in the afternoon Soviet forces attacking from the west, assisted by thick fog, sneaked through the 11th Panzer Division's positions and opened a very tenuous link to the Soviet forces in Ositniazhka.[186]

Confused fighting in the Kapitanovka–Tishkovka area continued during the evening. The Soviet General Staff Study on the battle states that, by the end of the day, a German grouping with 70 tanks and 30 assault guns encircled Tishkovka. This statement is wholly unfounded; the Germans had nowhere near that number of tanks and assault guns available near Tishkovka. Whether this is an example of the confusion caused by fog and darkness, or deliberate distortion is difficult to tell with certainty, but of course neither explanation excludes the other.[187]

At the end of the day neither side could be said to have complete control over the Kapitanovka–Pisarivka–Tishkovka area. Rather, each side held a series of scattered positions. The 2nd Ukrainian Front had committed substantial reinforcements during the day, of which the tank corps and the cavalry corps were of course most important, but the latter had also been reinforced by an antitank gun brigade. German reinforcements were far more modest. At 16.00hrs Major Glässgen, the commander of I./Pz.Rgt. 26 (the Panther battalion that had been on its way), arrived at the staff of XXXXVII Panzer Corps, but his battalion was not yet available. Fifteen minutes later the commander of a GHQ artillery battalion also arrived at the staff, with the same general message.[188]

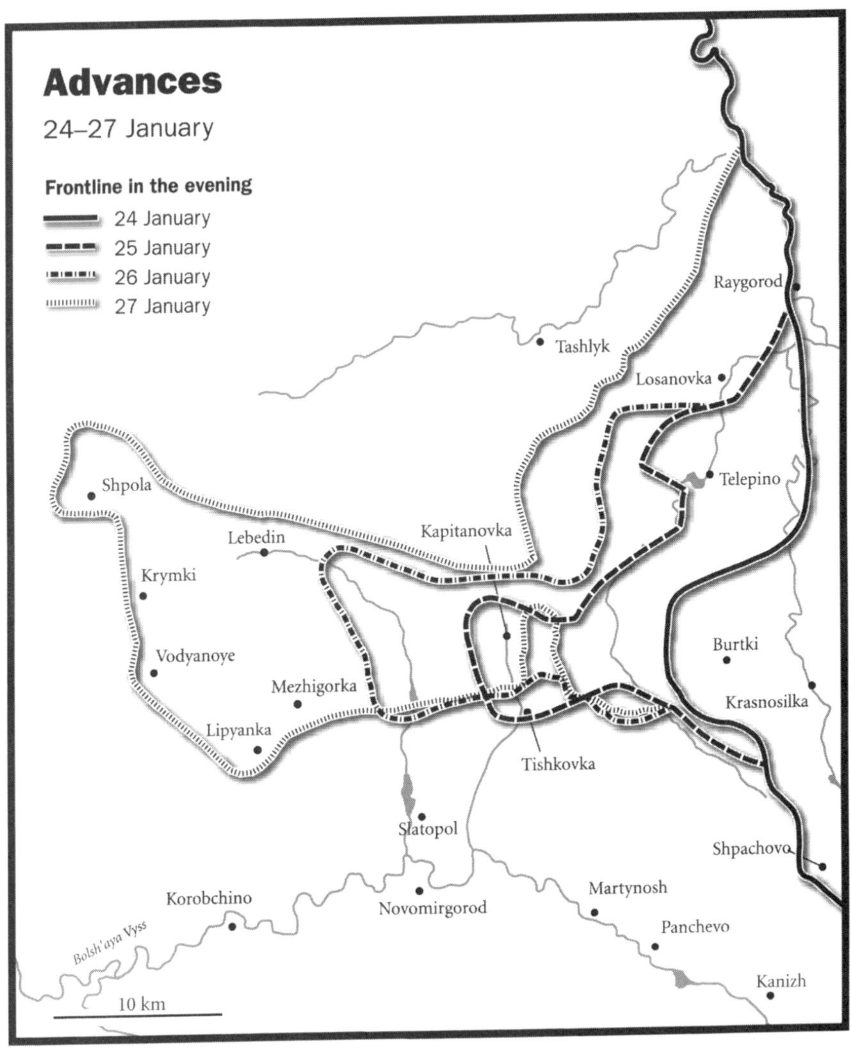

72nd Division Begins to Withdraw

Towards the evening the Germans made some changes to their command structure. Since they had been brought into action, the 11th and 14th Panzer Divisions had been under the command of the XI Corps. From the evening of 27 January, they were instead subordinated to the XXXXVII Panzer Corps. Considering the Soviet breakthrough, this probably was a more effective command structure, allowing the XI Corps to concentrate on the situation north of the Soviet penetration and the XXXXVII Panzer Corps to focus on the situation to the south.[189]

The situation north of the Soviet penetration certainly gave XI Corps enough to think about. At Serdyukovka and Krasny Kutor, the fighting rolled back and forth over the railroad line before noon. Although the 72nd Division managed to keep its line, the situation was critical. A regiment from the 57th Division was ordered to counterattack in the afternoon. While the regiment moved up, Soviet forces pushed further to the west and it soon became apparent that the 72nd Division was unable to hold the railroad line.[190]

Gaedke realized that the Soviet pressure in the Serdyukovka sector tied up German troops that were more needed elsewhere. At 17.40hrs he again brought up the issue of withdrawing 72nd Division to the Hamster positions, when he had a telephone discussion with Speidel. Again Speidel replied that he needed permission from the army group and that he would have to call back later. Speidel immediately discussed the issue with Wöhler, who promptly called Army Group South. At 19.20hrs Speidel spoke with Gaedke and told him that the permission had been given.[191]

It is, of course, uncertain whether the German situation would have been considerably improved by an earlier withdrawal to the Hamster line, but it certainly did not help matters to keep the division in the Smela salient, where it performed no useful role. Had the division retreated it would have been possible to send the 57th Division south at an earlier stage. While this would have been desirable, it must be remembered that the most important German effort was on the southern shoulder of the Soviet assault, where the 11th and 14th Panzer Divisions attacked. These divisions were too weak in tanks to have much prospect of making a decisive contribution. It has not been possible to establish their exact strength at the beginning of the Soviet offensive, but it seems that they had at most 40 to 50 operational tanks and assault guns between them. This was not much at all when compared to the 323 tanks and assault guns fielded by the 2nd Ukrainian Front for the operation on 25 January. Granted, Konev could not use all of them against these two German Panzer divisions, but the figures still give some indication of the odds.[192]

The arrival of the Panther battalion that had been on its way was, in this context, a considerable reinforcement. Actually the battalion was supposed to be part of the 26th Panzer Division, which was fighting in Italy at the time, but it never joined its parent division. It spent 1943 waiting for tanks and was finally transferred to the Eastern Front in January 1944. Initially the battalion was with the Grossdeutschland Division, but seems not to have seen any action with it. On 27 January it began to move to the XXXXVII Panzer Corps. It was almost at full strength, having reported 67 operational Panthers before leaving Grossdeutschland. On the march to the XXXXVII Panzer Corps, one Panther caught fire in its engine room and became a complete loss. Other tanks suffered mechanical breakdowns, but on the morning of 28 January the battalion could still field 61 combat-ready Panthers.[193]

This was a substantial reinforcement if we compare it with the tank strength of the XXXXVII Panzer Corps on 27 January. Nevertheless, one tank battalion and one artillery battalion could not have a major effect on a battle that involved hundreds of tanks, several thousand guns, and hundreds of thousands of men. Still, this was the only fresh German formation that could be expected to make its presence felt on 28 January. With such slender reinforcements there was no real reason for optimism among the German commanders.

Soviet Forces Join at Zvenigorodka, 28 January

It is less clear how Konev, Rotmistrov, Galanin, and Ryzhov regarded the prospects for the ongoing operation. The Soviet General Staff Study, which was written later in 1944, presents the German forces in the Kapitanovka area as quite strong. Subsequent Soviet literature conforms to this view. Yet the figures on German strength are inflated, possibly as a result of conscious manipulation after the battle, or possibly because they reflect the genuine perspective of the enemy held by the Soviet commanders. If the Soviets really believed their inflated figures, they were very likely to be concerned, but the reality was that the German situation was desperate. The Soviet operation could only be jeopardized if the commanders lost their nerve, and this did not happen.

On the morning of 28 January, the 20th Tank Corps' lead brigades set out from Shpola towards Zvenigorodka. They met only scattered resistance as they advanced through Lozovatka towards their objective. To the Germans, the city was already almost lost. At 10.00hrs Speidel had called Busse and bluntly told him that unless prompt action was taken, Zvenigorodka could not be held. There were only about a hundred Cossacks in Zvenigorodka and they could not be expected to repel the approaching Soviet tank brigades. Busse and Speidel clearly realized that it was only a matter of hours before the XI and XXXXII Corps were cut off.[194]

Just before noon, the Soviet 8th and 155th Tank Brigades closed in on Zvenigorodka from the east and southeast. No particular resistance could be observed, but it was always prudent to be cautious when advancing in populated areas with tank formations. However, the town was easily cleared and soon another force approached from the northwest. It was the lead elements from 6th Tank Army; Konev's and Vatutin's fronts had made contact at Zvenigorodka.[195]

While the 20th Tank Corps continued its advance to the west, the Germans continued their attempts to control the Kapitanovka area. As mentioned before, the I./Pz.Rgt. 26 Panther Battalion was the strongest German unit taking part in the effort. As this unit made its combat debut, it is worth following its actions on 28 January in detail, to give some impression of the difficulties that an unseasoned unit could face in battle.

I./Pz.Rgt. 26 Panther Battalion, 28 January

During the summer and fall of 1943 the I./Pz.Rgt. 26 had been forming and training in France, while waiting for its tanks. It was not until the beginning of December that it finally received its full complement of 76 Panthers plus two Bergepanther recovery vehicles. Orders to depart for the Eastern Front would be received shortly.[196]

On the evening of 5 January 1944 the battalion began loading its tanks on trains, at six small railroad stations in northern France. All in all the battalion required 12 trains to move to the Eastern Front. It took three days for the trains to arrive and to be loaded. Just before midnight on 6 January, one Panther's engine caught on fire while on board the train. Despite frantic attempts by the men, the fire could not be extinguished and the tank became a total loss before it had even begun its journey to the front.[197]

The first elements of the battalion arrived at Pomoshnaia in the Ukraine on 14 January, and the battalion commander, Major Glässgen, contacted the Grossdeutschland Division, to which his battalion was to be attached. During its two weeks with the Grossdeutschland the battalion saw no action, even though its 2nd Company took up defensive positions in the front line. At 11.17hrs on 27 January the battalion received orders to transfer to XXXXVII Panzer Corps, and by 12.30hrs it began to move with its 63 operational tanks. The distance was not particularly great, about 75 kilometers, but losses nevertheless occurred. One Panther spontaneously caught fire in its engine room, just before reaching Mal. Viski, and was completely burnt out. A Bergepanther also caught fire, but the flames were extinguished before the tank suffered extensive damage. Nevertheless, as the battalion had only two Bergepanthers, it was a serious loss to have one of them rendered unserviceable. In the coming days there would be many damaged tanks to recover. Another Panther crashed through a bridge, but was recovered. A further four tanks suffered mechanical breakdowns, but during the night the rest of the battalion arrived in the Slatopol area.[198]

While the tankers assembled for the attack on 28 January, Glässgen and his company commanders received information on both the friendly and enemy forces in the area. They learned that Kampfgruppe von Brese was located in a forest two to three kilometers northeast of Kapitanovka. Somewhat further to the southwest, on a hill east of Kapitanovka, some 11th Panzer Division Panthers under the command of Major von Sievers were in defense. The southern part of Tishkovka was occupied by German infantry, while the northern and central parts were in Soviet hands. Pisarivka was controlled by the Red Army, but the Germans held positions south of the village. Similarly, the central part of Tishkovka was in enemy hands. Furthermore, intercepted radio messages suggested that the Soviet forces that had broken through to the west were suffering from lack of ammunition and fuel. The radio traffic caused the Germans to assume that the Soviets would turn east, to enable the replenishment of their supplies.[199]

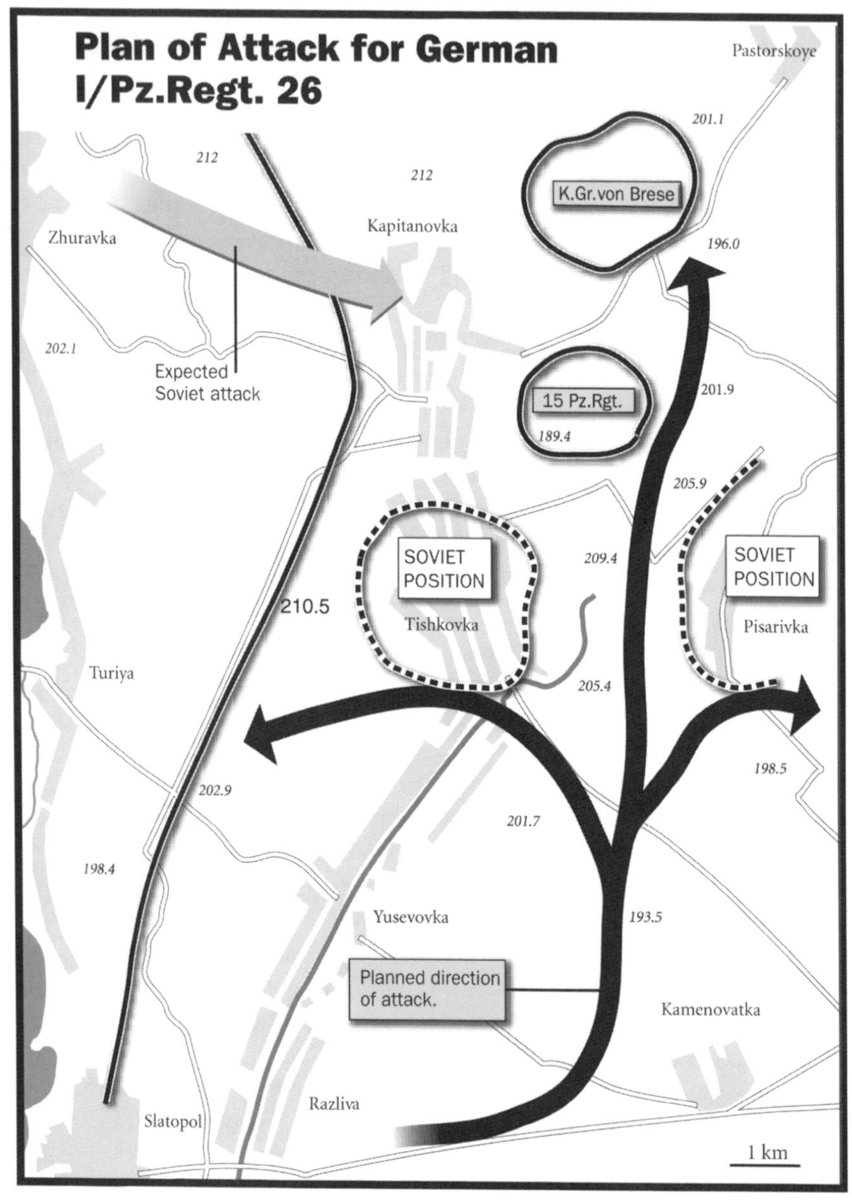

Plan of Attack for German I/Pz.Regt. 26
Pastorskoye
201.1
212
212
K.Gr.von Brese
Zhuravka
Kapitanovka
196.0
202.1
Expected Soviet attack
15 Pz.Rgt.
201.9
189.4
205.9
SOVIET POSITION
209.4
SOVIET POSITION
210.5
Tishkovka
Pisarivka
Turiya
205.4
198.5
202.9
201.7
198.4
Yusevovka
193.5
Planned direction of attack.
Kamenovatka
Razliva
Slatopol
1 km

The circumstances led Colonel Büsing, who was responsible for the enterprise, to order I./Pz.Rgt. 26 to attack to link up with Kampfgruppe von Brese and the Panthers commanded by Major von Sievers, and thereafter to occupy positions to repel the Soviet forces expected to return eastward. To accomplish this mission, it was decided that the battalion should move out from the Slatopol area along the road to Kamenovatka, then turn north approximately two kilometers west of the town. By advancing between Tishkovka and Pisarivka, the battalion hoped to reach the area occupied by von Brese and von Sievers. Major Glässgen ordered the 2nd Company to take the lead, with the 1st and 4th Companies on the left and right flank respectively, and the 3rd Company behind as reserve.[200]

While the plans matured, the soldiers continued to drive their tanks towards the assembly area. At 19.45hrs the first combat elements had reached Mal. Viski, which meant that about two thirds of the distance to Slatopol had been covered. A pause was ordered, to check the tanks and to give the crews some chance to get a little rest. At 22.30hrs the battalion resumed its march and at 01.00 on 28 January the first elements reached Slatopol. As the battalion was supposed to attack next day, the soldiers sorely needed to sleep, but only a few hours remained until dawn on 28 January. To make matters worse, time also had to be spent on other activities. The tanks had to be maintained, refueled, and loaded with rations for combat. It was vital to ensure that the tanks were in the best possible mechanical condition, because breakdowns on the battlefield could prove fatal when under enemy fire, both for the tanks and their crews. Neither did the commanders get much sleep. At 02.45hrs Glässgen summoned his company commanders, Captain Mayer (1st Company), Captain Lemmer (2nd Company), Lieutenant Wartmann (3rd Company), and Lieutenant Kirchhoff (4th Company), to give them further details on the pending attack, which was to begin within three hours.[201]

It was a tired group of soldiers who drove their tanks out of Slatopol at 06.00hrs on 28 January, but most likely they also felt a mixture of excitement and fear when they looked forward along the road to Kamenovatka. The mechanics had worked during the night and 61 Panthers, two of them command tanks, were available to the battalion in the morning—a considerable force for the Germans at this time in the war. Soon the lead elements had reached a point about two kilometers west of Kamenovatka and the tankers steered their vehicles to the north. They did not know that, further north, strong elements of the Soviet 18th Tank Corps had been given the task of reopening and securing the corridor that led to the units of 5th Guards Tank Army, which were advancing toward Zvenigorodka.[202]

Lieutenant Kirchhoff recalled that the battalion made a brief halt soon after veering off to the north, to enable it to adopt a formation suitable to the attack, after having rolled in column along the road from Slatopol. The break was too short to allow for this reformation, and instead frantic orders to drive faster were issued over the radio, although the tanks were already driving at high speed.[203]

With Major Glässgen and Captain Lemmer in the lead, the battalion proceeded towards its objective. It passed German positions south of Tishkovka and Pisarevka and proceeded into No Man's Land, or rather land that was thought to be unoccupied by the enemy. It soon became obvious that the Red Army had observers overlooking the approaching German tanks, as Soviet artillery shells began to explode around them. The Panther battalion did not sustain any losses but continued north at high speed. The artillery barrage ceased and Major Glässgen ordered a short halt so that further instructions could be given.[204]

Lieutenant ten Brink, who commanded a tank platoon, recalled that his company, in relatively closed formation, crossed a small hill about one kilometer southeast of Tishkovka and proceeded into a depression. When he saw it, he feared that his tanks would be easy to observe from Tishkovka. His fears were justified. When the tanks reached the middle of the depression, Soviet antitank guns opened fire on his platoon's flank. Without delay, ten Brink's Panthers turned ninety degrees to the left, to present their heavily armored fronts, and opened fire on the antitank guns.

In the meantime, the other two platoons in the company continued forward and soon ten Brink received orders to follow. He continued north with all his tanks except one, which had to be temporarily left behind, as it could not disengage from the enemy antitank guns without exposing its less well armored side. The Panther continued to fire on the antitank guns, and when they had all been silenced it caught up with ten Brink and the other tanks in the platoon.[205]

While ten Brink's platoon engaged the antitank guns near Tishkovka, the remaining two platoons of the 2nd Company continued towards hill 205.4, between Tishkovka and Pisarevka, which they reached at about 09.00hrs. Suddenly, ten Brink heard on the radio that enemy tanks had been discovered behind them, to the right. The company halted, while a few of its Panthers turned around and attacked the approaching enemy tanks. The Soviet tanks were shot up, but ten Brink saw that a few German tanks had been hit too. The brief firefight was soon over and ten Brink expected that orders to continue north would come at any moment, but nothing was heard from the company commander, Captain Lemmer.[206]

While the 2nd Company advanced in the lead, the 4th and 1st Companies followed closely on the flanks. Captain Mayer led his company and observed the Soviet tanks that attacked the 2nd Company in the flank. He estimated that it was about a dozen T-34s and immediately ordered his company to attack them. Within a few minutes all Soviet tanks had been shot up, according to Mayer. Soon thereafter Lieutenant Kirchhoff, who commanded the 4th Company, came close enough to see the wrecks of 10–12 T-34s and also a few Panthers.[207]

In fact, with Panthers from the 2nd Company turning around, as the 1st Company joined the fight, the Soviet tanks were caught from two directions. This certainly made them very vulnerable, but it also meant that the inexperienced German tank crews may have risked friendly fire. Fortunately for them the silhouettes of Panthers and T-34s were quite different, but in the heat of battle mistakes can easily occur. We have not found any evidence suggesting that friendly fire incidents did occur during this action, but it seems that neither the 1st nor 2nd Company was fully aware of what the other company did.

Just as the brief firefight was over, Captain Mayer received orders to turn his company to the left. Hardly had the radio silenced before Soviet antitank guns opened fire on his company. Mayer could see that well dug-in Soviet antitank guns occupied positions to the north as well as to the east. If he turned his company west, as he had just been ordered, his tanks would be exposed to side or rear hits, where the Panthers' armor not was as strong as on the front. His watch showed a few minutes after 09.00hrs, as Mayer informed the battalion commander by radio. The receipt of his message was acknowledged, but nothing more was heard on the radio.

After some hesitation, Mayer decided to comply with the order and began to turn his tank. Suddenly it shuddered when an AP round hit. Both the driver and the radio operator had been wounded, and within seconds, the tank was hit by three more rounds. One of them jammed the turret, giving Mayer no choice but to order the tank abandoned. He ran to another Panther and climbed aboard, while the Soviet fire seemed to intensify. In the meantime tanks from his company returned fire and seemed to have silenced two or three of the enemy guns, but it must be emphasized that such judgments can be very difficult to make in the heat of battle. Once Mayer had entered the new tank he shouted on the radio that the company should reverse 200 meters, to take advantage of the crest line at hill 205.4, where he also found tanks from the 2nd and 4th Companies. Still, there was no contact with the battalion commander. Mayer decided to go back to Colonel Büsing's command post to see if he could obtain some information from him.[208]

The 3rd Company, commanded by Lieutenant Wartmann, had initially struggled to catch up with the battalion, and had still not managed to do so when flashes from Soviet antitank guns could be seen at the southeast part of Tishkovka. The Panthers almost immediately replied with high explosive shells and machine gun fire. Soon the southeast part of Tishkovka was on fire, forcing the Soviet forces to withdraw to the north. Wartmann observed this and realized that the 2nd Company had an excellent opportunity to attack them in the flank. He tried to contact Glässgen and Lemmer on the radio, but his efforts were in vain. Later in the day Wartmann would learn that both Glässgen and Lemmer had been killed by this time.[209]

Lemmer's death was in fact soon known, as his tank, number 201, burst into flames when hit by an AP round. Shortly afterwards, Lieutenant ten Brink assumed command of the 2nd Company. Glässgen's fate was unclear for some time. It is possible that his tank, number 101, had already fallen out due to engine trouble, and that consequently he had climbed aboard another vehicle. His adjutant had turned back in order to check on the progress of 3rd Company, so he did not see what happened to the battalion commander.[210]

Perhaps the early death of the battalion commander, which was unknown for some time, contributed to the battalion's rather hesitant behavior after it reached hill 205.4 at about 09.00hrs. Lieutenant Kirchhoff observed that, in addition to his own 4th Company, the 1st and 2nd Companies took up defensive positions on the hill and a sort of deadlock ensued. After a while Captain Mayer, who had been at Colonel Büsing's command post, informed the battalion that both Major Glässgen and Captain Lemmer had been killed. Despite this, the attack was to continue further north. The objective remained the same as it had been a few hours earlier. Mayer, who was the senior surviving officer, was to command the battalion.[211]

Both Mayer and Kirchhoff could see that Soviet forces held strong positions north of hill 205.4, as well as along the outskirts of Pisarivka and Tishkovka. To continue forward would be very difficult, not least because fog and snow squalls made it almost impossible to discern the antitank guns. However, the German tanks remained visible to the Soviet antitank guns, which opened fire the moment Kirchhoff's Panthers began to move forward. To him it seemed that every round hit, but no German tanks appear to have been knocked out. Still, threatened by antitank guns that he could not locate with sufficient accuracy to fire upon in turn, Kirchhoff was not inclined to continue. Rather he ordered his company to reverse, to take advantage of the crest line behind. He hoped to use the range advantage of the Panther guns to knock out the antitank guns one by one.[212]

At this moment Colonel Büsing arrived and said that he himself would command the battalion, not Captain Mayer. Colonel Büsing's role in the command chain had been somewhat unclear. Actually he served with the Grossdeutschland Division, but had accompanied the I./Pz.Rgt. 26 when it departed from the division. As Major von Sievers, who commanded the Panzer regiment in 11th Panzer Division, was surrounded by Soviet forces, Büsing led the effort to open a connection. However, the only formation Büsing had was the I./Pz.Rgt. 26. Thus he was merely a link between the 11th Panzer Division commander and Glässgen, until the death of the latter. In any case, Büsing quickly concluded that the situation demanded another method of attack than had hitherto been attempted. So far, the tanks had attacked without any support from infantry, artillery, or air power. Büsing intended to arrange for artillery support before the tanks went forward again.[213]

Unfortunately artillery was not immediately available; in fact it could not be expected before 14.00hrs. Büsing and the commanders of the 3rd and 4th Companies decided to use the opportunity personally to reconnoiter the enemy positions. It became apparent that in front, on hill

209.4, the Red Army had a strong position defended by antitank guns, and also on the road between hill 209.4 and Tishkovka. Furthermore, there were also strong antitank defenses at the western outskirts of Pisarivka, just as Kirchhoff had observed previously. This time the German commanders also saw about 10 T-34s on the eastern and western slopes of hill 209.4. Suddenly a Soviet artillery barrage crashed down on the German officers. A shell splinter wounded Lieutenant Wartmann in the head and he had to be evacuated. He was replaced by Lieutenant Muth. Thus, within a few hours the battalion had lost its commander and two of its four company commanders.[214]

Anxiously the tankers waited for the artillery barrage that had been promised. There was not much they could do for the moment, except keep a vigilant eye on their surroundings. As they were without any infantry they had to ensure that Soviet antitank squads did not sneak too close to the Panthers. Perhaps they spent some time thinking about what had transpired so far on their first day of combat. They had begun the day with 61 tanks; now only about 35 remained. In fact, most of the Panthers could be repaired, but it is unclear if the tankers realized it at this moment.[215]

The tankers had to wait for the artillery barrage longer than desired. While the German tanks waited, the Soviet units improved their defenses. Finally, at about 14.50hrs the German artillery opened fire, then Stukas attacked Pisarevka. Unfortunately, the tankers had not been informed of the timing and duration of this attack, so they were unable to coordinate their attack with that of the artillery and Stukas. As a result, the delay between the air and artillery bombardment and the Panthers' advance was too long, allowing the Soviet defenders enough time to recover. Furthermore, the artillery had fired first, before the Stukas attacked Pisarevka. Thus the Soviet defenders north and west of the Panthers received even more time to recover. Finally, the artillery barrage was not particularly strong and the Stuka attack was not very effective either, because the aircraft were met by strong antiaircraft fire and forced to release their bombs at too high an altitude.[216]

When the Panthers began to roll forward at 15.35hrs, with 3rd Company in the center and the 1st and 4th Companies on the left and right, they faced defenders who were far from destroyed or disrupted. Their task was to capture hill 209.4 and wait there until German infantry arrived, whereupon the Panthers were to continue forward. Lieutenant Muth, who had commanded the 3rd Company since Wartmann became wounded, was particularly worried about flanking fire from Pisarivka, where the Soviet defenders most likely concealed antitank guns. His fears were fully justified. When the Panthers rolled forward, two tanks belonging to the 4th Company burst into flames after being hit in the side. Soon tanks from the 3rd Company received hits too, and Muth ordered his tanks to open fire on the Soviet guns. Hardly had Muth's Panthers taken up positions to fire on the Soviet guns before Colonel Büsing ordered the company commanders to come to his command post.[217]

At twilight, Muth and Kirchhoff arrived at Büsing's command post, on the southern slope of hill 205.4. Büsing greeted them by blaming them for the battalion's slow progress since the artillery barrage. He even threatened to court martial them if their units did not show more daring. Büsing's threat was not confined to the two commanders who had already arrived, but also included the other two. The battalion adjutant was sent to find Captain Mayer, as he was one of the two who had not yet arrived.[218]

Muth and Kirchhoff returned to their units, and it is unclear what they thought about Büsing's court martial threat. In the after action reports, written by the company commanders a few days later, neither gave a flattering impression of Büsing's command. Rather the reports were quite critical. Amongst other complaints, they pointed to the fact that they were not informed about the timing of the artillery barrage and the Stuka attack. This criticism seems justified, since it was indeed impossible for them to take advantage of an attack of which they had not been informed. An even more direct criticism of Büsing is the comment that time was lost by calling the company commanders back to the battalion command post. Daylight would soon be gone and every minute could be valuable. In darkness the Panthers would be robbed of the advantage they possessed with the much superior range of their guns.[219]

The attack got rolling, but the 1st Company had hardly advanced more than 800 meters when the battalion adjutant found Mayer and ordered him to go to Büsing. Thus, in the midst of the attack, the senior company commander had to go back to the command post. When Mayer reached Büsing he was accused of delaying the attack. Büsing harshly told him: "I command the battalion, you have nothing at all to give orders to." Again Büsing tried to instil urgency, but as Mayer wrote three days later, by the time he got back to his company it was already dark. He could discern vehicles lit up by star shells, and the muzzle flashes from guns and machine guns, but it seemed that most of his own tanks had lost their orientation when they tried to carry out the order to capture hill 209.4.[220]

Mayer's company had been accompanied by the 3rd and 4th Companies when they advanced, while ten Brink's company covered the left flank. As could be expected from the observations made in the afternoon, flanking fire from Soviet antitank guns was very strong. Almost immediately, the tank commanded by 2nd Lieutenant Neumeyer, who led one of the platoons in Kirchhoff's company, was hit and caught fire. Kirchhoff's tankers found that in the darkness they were unable to locate the enemy antitank guns with sufficient precision to destroy them. Even though their muzzle flashes were visible, it was impossible to assess the distance to the guns.[221]

Nevertheless, Kirchhoff drove to Muth to continue forward. They shot a light flare and discovered Soviet vehicles on the road between Tishkovka and hill 209.4. On the radio Kirchhoff gave orders to fire on these vehicles, but almost immediately Büsing commanded on the radio: "Immediately cease firing on the vehicles and continue forward towards the objective." In fact, Büsing's order seems to have been justified, because the Panthers reached hill 209.4, where one or two T-34s were shot up and the rest withdrew.[222]

The German tankers took a short break when they had reached the northern edge of the hill. At this moment Kirchhoff heard Büsing on the radio ordering that the road north of hill 209.4 should not be crossed until Büsing himself arrived. After that, nothing was heard from Büsing for a long while. Instead, Soviet antitank guns opened flanking fire on the Panthers, causing the Germans to pull back 50 to 100 meters to find less exposed positions. However, by this maneuver Soviet infantry came close to the German tanks. Kirchhoff, with his head, shoulders, and arms up through the cupola, tried to shoot Soviet riflemen with his pistol. In the darkness it was very difficult to hit them. Behind his tank he saw two other German tanks, with the crews preparing to tow one of them. Furthermore, he made out infantry and horse-drawn vehicles very close to the tanks. The engine noise of the Panthers had drowned out the sound from the Russians. Kirchhoff immediately ordered his crew to turn the turret, but it was too late. A Soviet antitank gun opened fire at point blank range and hit one of the two German tanks that had been prepared for towing. Kirchhoff frantically urged the German tanks not to become stationary, but to keep moving.[223]

Kirchhoff tried to reach Büsing on the radio several times to inform him about the situation. All the attempts were unsuccessful and Captain Mayer took command of the battalion. As there was no clear mission and the tanks lacked infantry protection, even as enemy infantry and antitank units infiltrated their position, Captain Mayer gave orders that the battalion should move east, in particular to avoid standing in an area lit up by burning vehicles. The German tanks formed a hedgehog position and soon heard from Büsing on the radio. He ordered that Mayer should fire green and white flares to indicate his position. However, Mayer did not fire flares, because he feared that they would illuminate his own tanks and make them easy targets for the Soviet gunners. Instead Kirchhoff took a flare gun and ran away from the Panthers before he fired. After some time, two German half tracks showed up, giving the Panthers some sort of infantry cover in the darkness. However shortly thereafter Büsing issued orders over the radio that the battalion should pull back to hill 205.4, which, after some hesitation, was done.[224]

As there were Soviet troops between the main body of the Panther battalion and Büsing's command post, this maneuver was not as easy to accomplish as it might appear. However, Captain Mayer instructed his tankers to form columns and steadily move south. In the dark night it was very difficult for the Soviet infantry to identify the Panthers. As they moved in columns, it seems they were mistaken for Soviet tanks. The Germans escaped south and reached Büsing's command post without a shot being fired.[225]

Several of the Panthers were very low on fuel and ammunition, and their crews had expected to find replenishment when they reached south of hill 205.4, but none was to be found. They were told that the supply column had been subjected to Soviet artillery fire and suffered losses. Also, Soviet antitank guns could fire on the area reached by the Panthers. It seemed better for most of the tanks to continue towards the supply column, and to leave a screen at hill 205.4.[226]

Thus ended a very long first day in combat for the tankers of I./Pz.Rgt. 26. They had set out with 61 Panthers in the morning of 28 January, and 24 hours later 17 runners remained, for a loss of 44 tanks. Of these, 10 had to be written off, and the remainder could be salvaged and repaired. A considerable number had simply broken down due to mechanical defects. Sixteen had been rendered inoperable due to engine damage; in many cases connecting rod bearings were found to be damaged. The mechanics would have to work hard to raise the number of operational Panthers in the battalion.[227]

This first day in action had hardly been impressive, and the performance of the battalion was discussed in higher command echelons. The 11th Panzer Division, to which the I./26 was subordinated, was very dissatisfied with the battalion's combat performance, and Wietersheim commented on the unit when he spoke with XXXXVII Panzer Corps and 8th Army. Büsing was, unsurprisingly, critical too, and on the morning of 29 January he relieved Captain Mayer from the command of 1st Company, although the threat of court martial never materialized. Thus, within 24 hours the battalion lost its commander, who was killed, one of the company commanders, also killed, one company commander wounded, and one sacked. The only one who remained was Lieutenant Kirchhoff.[228]

It is questionable whether the harsh verdict regarding the battalion's performance is justified. Perhaps it was, but it is also possible that the situation was exaggerated. For example, at 11.00hrs on 29 January it was noted in the 8th Army war diary that the battalion had only 17 Panthers left out of its initial 61, and that it had suffered 20 complete losses. However, a more detailed investigation showed that only 10 tanks were complete write-offs. Nevertheless, that was still a significant loss. In the ensuing action at Korsun, the battalion lost only a further three Panthers, which suggests that the battalion quickly learned combat lessons.[229]

It must be remembered that the unit faced several disadvantages. On 28 January the battalion went into battle without any support or cooperation from infantry, artillery, air power, or any other arm. Also, when the battalion was promised support from infantry, artillery, and air power, time was lost by waiting for these assets to be available. Another problem was intelligence, which was available but was not detailed. The strength of the enemy defenses was assessed by officers to whom Glässgen's battalion was subordinated. Indeed it appears that the battalion was rather haphazardly given a mission that was more difficult than assumed.

Büsing's conduct was not beyond question either. If he found fault with Captain Mayer's leadership after the death of Glässgen, then he ought to have gone forward rather than trying to command the battalion from behind, as he did on 28 January.

There were many examples of insufficient radio communication during the actions of 28 January, so it seems especially important that the acting commander should not stay behind. In fact, it was a well established tradition in the German army that the commander should lead from the front, not from the rear. Why Büsing refrained from this is somewhat mysterious, as he was a very experienced commander.[230] Colonel Büsing's threats did not instil his untried soldiers with the confidence needed to face the horror and chaos of combat. On the other hand, the commanders threatened by Büsing do not seem to have taken him seriously, and they certainly did not shy away from criticizing him in their after action reports.

Captain Mayer may be accused of hesitancy in his actions. For example, he went back to Büsing's command post at 09.00hrs rather than remaining forward to ensure that the attack regained momentum. Also, he appeared uncertain when the battalion should attack after the artillery barrage just before 15.00hrs. While it may very well be correct to emphasize the fact that he lacked information on when the barrage would end, German doctrine emphasized that in unclear situations it was better to act than remain passive. Mayer seems not to have acted according to this tradition in that particular situation.

Unfortunately, Büsing was killed three weeks after the end of the Korsun battle and did not leave any comments on the event. The surviving war diaries of 8th Army and XXXXVII Panzer Corps mention, in sharp words, the poor conduct of the I./Pz.Rgt. 26 on 28 January, something that does not occur for any other unit, as far as we have been able to see from the records that have survived the battle.

The Soviet Encirclement Completed

Whatever the causes of the failed attack, the Germans had lost the chance to prevent Konev from reaching his first goal. With the failure of the only fresh German unit, the XXXXVII Panzer Corps had to struggle hard to hold its positions. At the end of the action the situation was not much different from what it had been 24 hours earlier. Both sides held scattered positions in the Kapitanovka area, with neither in full control of the situation. The cost had been high to the Soviet 18th Tank Corps, too, which seems to have been the main opponent of the I./Pz.Rgt. 26, as it reported the loss of 29 T-34s and eight lend-lease tanks, which had been burned or destroyed by enemy fire. However, it could at least find some consolation from the fact that it received 22 tanks as replacements, unlike the German units, which seem not to have received a single replacement tank.[231]

Until 28 January the Germans had made relatively minor command rearrangements, but the Soviet thrust to Zvenigorodka prompted more substantial changes. When the Soviet pincers closed, the Germans combined the XI and XXXXII Corps into Gruppe Stemmermann, which was placed under the command of 8th Army. The forming of Gruppe Stemmermann was in fact little more than recognition of what had happened. As General Stemmermann was the senior officer in the surrounded German force he was given overall command of it. Also, it was regarded as a simpler command situation if the entire pocket was placed under one army HQ, rather than being split between two.[232]

It was also clear that the XXXXVII Corps was too weak to cope with the situation on its left flank. It was decided that the 320th Infantry Division should be shifted west, but also the corps needed substantial reinforcements. The 13th Panzer Division was to be immediately relieved and sent to the XXXXVII Panzer Corp's left flank. The 376th Infantry Division was to be relieved and sent to the same area, even though its shift could not be done as quickly as with the 13th Panzer Division. These units already belonged to 8th Army, but the army was also promised 24th Panzer Division as reinforcement, a unit that was with 6th Army further south.[233]

Given the distances involved, and the weather that threatened to turn the roads into mud, these units needed at least a few days before they could reach the battle area. The XXXXVII Panzer Corps would have to struggle to hold its positions until these units arrived.

After hard fighting, the 2nd Ukrainian Front had secured a corridor to Zvenigorodka. However, a double encirclement required two prongs to succeed. Konev's front had attacked from the southeast. In the meantime, Vatutin's 1st Ukrainian Front was attacking from the northwest.

CHAPTER 7

Vatutin's Attack

The Attack on Tinovka and Koshevatoe, 26 January

Unlike the 2nd Ukrainian Front, Nikolai Vatutin's 1st Ukrainian Front did not attack on 25 January. Rather it was forced to begin the operation one day later, since the assembly of the attacking formations could not be completed earlier. This was perhaps not a significant disadvantage. If the 2nd Ukrainian Front made good progress on 25 January, the Germans might not realize immediately that they were facing a two-pronged offensive.

Vatutin and his staff planned attacks on a rather wide front, but there were two areas where a major effort was focused: near Tinovka and near Koshevatoe. The southern attack force—in the vicinity of Tinovka—was the strongest, but the German defense was stronger in this sector. The Soviet 6th Tank Army concentrated on the Tinovka–Krasilovk–Besedka–Bashtechka area. Of the two corps belonging to the army, the 5th Mechanized Corps was the strongest, with 106 tanks and 46 SP guns, while the 5th Guards Tank Corps had only 54 tanks and four SP guns. The 5th Mechanized Corps was almost up to strength, while the 5th Guards Tank Corps suffered from considerable manpower shortages before the offensive. Replenishment took place during preparations and assembly, but many of the new soldiers were inexperienced and poorly trained.[234]

The 5th Mechanized Corps was supposed to penetrate just south of Tinovka, in cooperation with the 104th Rifle Corps, rush towards Shubennyi Stav, and then continue to Zvenigorodka. It was expected to capture Shubennyi Stav at the end of the first day and reach the Shpola region during the second day. A tank brigade and an SP gun regiment from the 5th Mechanized Corps was held as army reserve.[235]

After a 40-minute artillery preparation, the 1st Ukrainian Front launched its attack.[236] The infantry divisions of the 104th Rifle Corps, supported by the main body of the 5th Mechanized Corps, encountered stiff German resistance and made scant progress. After the 58th Rifle Division had failed to penetrate the German defense during the first half of the day, the commander of the 5th Guards Tank Corps ordered his brigades to "complete the penetration" of the first German defense line and to exploit success themselves. This was to little avail, however, since the attack bogged down with heavy losses. The German VII Corps claimed to have knocked out 82 tanks during 26 January. At the end of the day, the Soviet attackers had only managed to capture the first German defense line.[237]

In fact, the main 1st Ukrainian Front attack was almost completely unsuccessful. It had hit the German 34th Infantry Division, belonging to the VII Corps, but the corps was more worried about the Soviet secondary attacks. The small Soviet gains south of Tinovka were contained, but Soviet pressure on the 34th's northern neighbor, the 198th Infantry Division, caused more problems. Its left flank was pushed back to Votylevka and Repki where it barely managed to hold. Its northern flank was in even greater trouble.[238]

Captain Georg Grossjohan commanded the II Battalion of 308th Grenadier regiment (198th Division). Later he recalled the fierce battles his battalion fought:[239]

> *On the morning of 26 January heavy Soviet artillery fire rained down not only on Votylevka, but along the entire front line. The Russians must have used hundreds of batteries in support of their attack against us. Shells of every caliber fell on our positions. Waves of 132mm rockets added to the cacophony with their howling noise, before they hit the ground around us. Especially, the enemy focused on the junction to our northern neighbor, the 88th Infantry Division. Clearly, it was a major attack.*
>
> *We only had a few seconds to get our weapons and our clothes before we jumped down in the narrow ditch we had dug and covered with logs, earth, and hay. A few minutes later only pathetic fragments remained of the hut we had just left. Just before my lieutenant Armbruster jumped into the ditch he got hold a bottle of brandy, which was passed*

around after the first seconds of shock had abated. It helped to relieve the trauma caused by the impact of the heavy artillery fire that just went on and on.

At exactly 6 am, precisely after going on for 80 minutes, the enormous artillery fire ceased. There was dead silence.

The soldiers of the Red Army began their assault, tactically correct, immediately when the artillery fire ceased. We left our shelters and saw that everything in Votylevka, with few exceptions, was completely demolished. Even the few trees had been stripped to skeletons. Only a few chimneys still remained erect in the smoking lunar landscape that was filled with large craters.

The Germans regarded the situation in the sector of the 88th Infantry Division, which belonged to the XXXXII Corps, as most ominous. The division was stretched so thinly that it could not withstand the Soviet attacks in the Baranye Pole area, which was captured by a Soviet force of regimental size supported by tanks. After this success, Vatutin's forces could advance along the Koshevatoye–Medvin–Lisyanka–Zvenigorodka road, which was one of the better roads in the area. The link between the 88th and 198th Divisions, and thus also between the XXXXII and VII Corps, was broken. The Germans had to do something, but there were few units available. Despite the Soviet pressure on the VII Corps, the latter was ordered to dispatch the 239th Assault Gun Battalion to the 88th Infantry Division, but no other reinforcements were available to send to the XXXXII Corps.[240]

To General Vatutin, commander of the 1st Ukrainian Front, the main attack must have been a disappointment, but on the other hand the secondary attack in the Baranye Pole area made much better progress. He thus had the option to keep pressure on the German 34th Division, while shifting mobile forces to the northern attack sector. A mobile force was built around the 233rd Tank Brigade, which had been held in reserve. Major General M. I. Savalev was instructed to take command of a task force consisting of the tank brigade, reinforced by an SP gun regiment, a motorized rifle battalion, and an antitank battery. In all, it had 55 tanks and assault guns and four antitank guns.[241] The force was committed along the Medvin–Lisyanka road, but it did not make its presence felt before the end of the day.

The Soviet attack of 26 January was obviously the offensive that the

German 1st Panzer Army had expected. The only uncertainty was whether the Soviet intention was to liberate the encircled Soviet force around Tichonovka, or if the intention was to cut off the XXXXII Corps. It was serious enough in either case.[242] The only thing the army could do was to conclude Operation Watutin—the attacks conducted by XXXXVI Panzer Corps and III Panzer Corps further west—as rapidly as possible. But even if these attacks were terminated immediately, it would still take a few days to move the units to the threatened sector. That would probably mean they would come too late to prevent an encirclement of XXXXII Corps.

The Attacks Continue, 27–28 January

On 27 January, the staff of 1st Panzer Army and its commander, General Hans Hube, considered pulling out the 17th Panzer Division as soon as possible and sending it to the VII Corps. This was only to be done when it did not endanger Operation Watutin. Hube also repeated his demands that the northern part of XXXXII Corps should be withdrawn, to give it at least some chance of mastering the situation by freeing forces to send south.[243]

The Soviet gains on the southern wing of the XXXXII Corps had caused VII Corps' northern wing to became almost surrounded at Chesnovka, and it seemed inevitable that the Red Army would cross the Gniloi Tikich River at Lisyanka, thereby liberating the encircled Soviet forces in the Tikhonovka area. The Germans expected this to happen no later than 28 January. The danger to the VII Corps' right wing affected its ability to withstand the attacks on the sector held by the 34th Infantry Division in the center. Since the German Corps was forced to focus more on the threat to its northern flank, the Soviet pressure in the center became more dangerous. In order to cope with the situation, the corps was ordered to take its right flank behind the Gniloi Tikich River. The 40th Army pushed back the Germans from Tinovka to Vinograd, which was taken in the evening.[244]

While the Red Army had only attacked the southernmost part of XXXXII Corps on 26 January, it extended its attacks to the northern part the following day. This of course made it more difficult for the Germans to disengage units and send them south to the sector where the Red Army had broken through. Another factor to consider was the weather, which became warmer. While the previous days had seen frost, on 27 January the temperature reached 0°C. If this trend continued, a thaw could set in at any time and the roads would quickly be reduced to mud, making redeployment of forces even more difficult.[245]

On 28 January the weather was still balancing between frost and thaw and the Soviet spearheads proceeded relatively unhindered by the elements, although occasional drifts of snow caused difficulties.[246] Kravchenko's tanks continued their advance towards Zvenigorodka, where they linked up with advance elements of 5th Guards Tank Army in the afternoon. Thus the encirclement of the two German corps was accomplished.[247]

While the 1st Ukrainian Front spearheads approached Zvenigorodka, other units put pressure on the German 198th and 34th Divisions. This, together with the threat posed by the open flank of the German VII Corps, pushed the Germans far south of the Gniloi Tikich River. The Soviet forces near Tichonovka, which had been surrounded for a long time, were freed.[248]

The 1st Ukrainian Front was not content with pushing the VII Corps south and establishing contact with the 5th Guards Tank Army. It also advanced towards the Rossava River and threatened the rear of the XXXXII Corps, whose entire left flank was wide open. However, pressure on the German VII Corps slackened after the Soviet force at Tikhonovka had been relieved. Part of the 198th Division was also surrounded in the Bossovka–Dadushkovka area, but these elements broke out to the south, thereby saving the Germans from an even greater debacle than the one that loomed.[249]

Perhaps Vatutin had hoped to catch the German 198th Division, but although this did not happen, he could still be satisfied with the results of the operation so far. At this moment he seems to have worried more about the developments further west, where the operation launched by the Germans, carrying his own name, caused him to order Kravchenko to send most of the 5th Mechanized Corps west.

The Germans' Operation Watutin was also designed to create an encirclement, but a much smaller one than the pocket created by the 1st and 2nd Ukrainian Fronts. It met with success, as the Soviet 1st Tank Army was badly hit. The Germans claimed to have captured or destroyed 701 tanks and assault guns. When Operation Watutin was concluded on 30 January, it had scored a notable success, although not sufficient to disrupt the Soviet operation. When Vatutin ordered the 5th Mechanized

Corps to disengage and move west, the encirclement of the German XI and XXXXII Corps had already been accomplished.

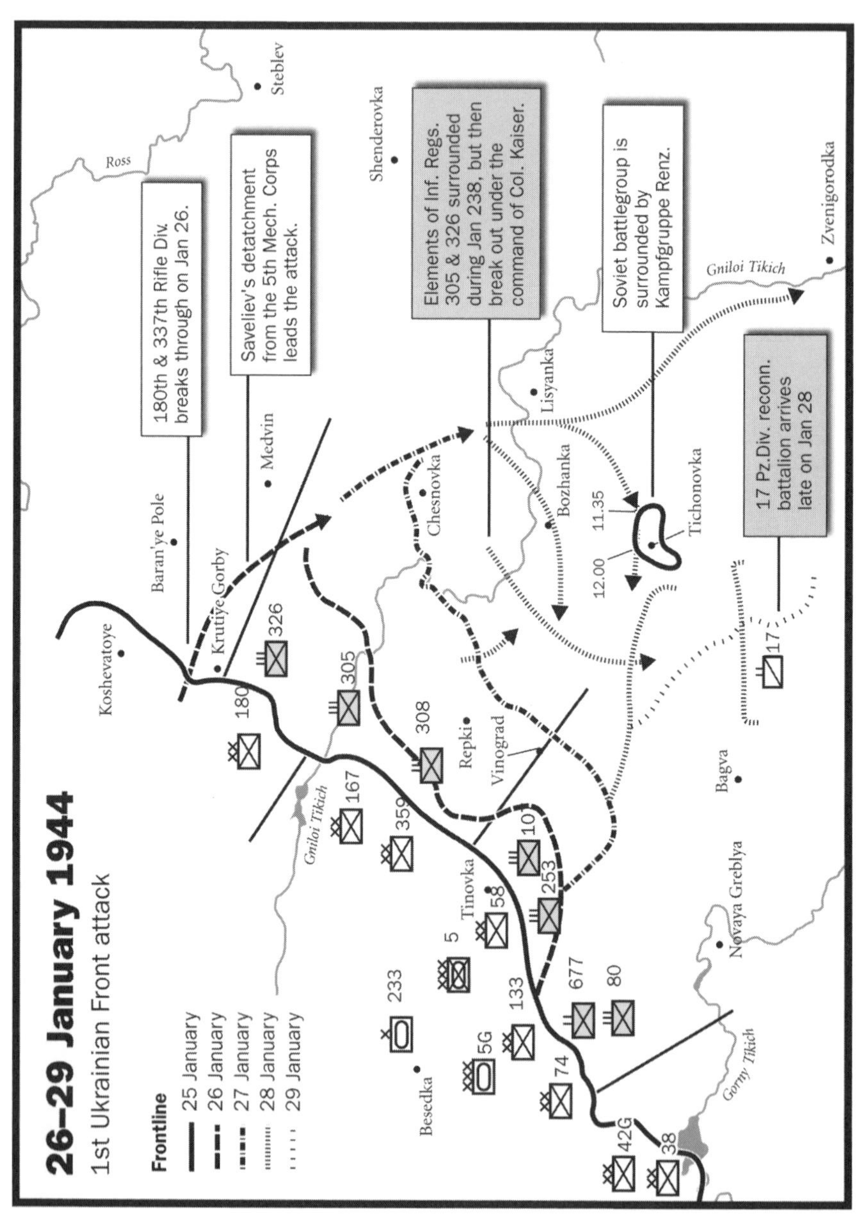

CHAPTER 8

The Korsun Pocket

When the 1st Ukrainian Front began its offensive on 26 January, the threat of encirclement was clear to the senior German commanders, including Lieb and Stemmermann. The situation deteriorated quickly, especially for Lieb's XXXXII Corps. Both his divisions—88th Infantry and Korps-Abteilung B—were spread out on a very wide front. The corps had to defend a sector more than 100 kilometers wide, which made it difficult to pull out units to create reserves, and time-consuming to move them where they were needed. When the Soviet 180th and 337th Divisions attacked the southern wing of the German 88th Division, there was little Lieb could do, at least in the short term, especially as Korps-Abteilung B also had to fend off enemy attacks.[250]

The rapidly deteriorating situation on the southern flank gave Lieb few options. He had to shift units south, despite the ensuing risks to the defenses in the north. Two artillery batteries were sent from Korps-Abteilung B to reinforce the 88th Division and, in addition, one artillery battalion from Korps-Abteilung B and an infantry battalion from the 88th Division had to be sent to the Boguslav area, where important bridges over the Rossava River were threatened by approaching Soviet forces. Finally Lieb ordered Korps-Abteilung B to send two battalions to Olkhovets, where they could constitute a reserve.[251]

During the night of 26 January Lieb decided to form "Sperrverband Foquet," which was to be a varied collection of units under the command of Colonel Foquet. His main task was to protect the southern flank of the XXXXII Corps, which was dangerously exposed.

Fortunately for him the Ross River formed a suitable defense line, and by the end of the day on 27 January weak positions had been established along the river, from Steblev to Dybnitsy. For the moment this was a very weak line and would not withstand a determined Soviet attack, but the main direction for the 1st Ukrainian Front was toward Medvin and Zvenigorodka, far to the south of Foquet's positions.[252]

On 28 January the Soviet 27th Army continued to press the northern part of the front, and also threatened the south flank of the German XXXXII Corps by attacking Nikolayevka and Sidorevka. These two villages were on the route to Steblev, an important town on the Ross River that the Germans could ill afford to lose. Divisionsgruppe 255 from Korps-Abteilung B, a regimental-sized unit, and the recently arrived 239th Assault Gun Battalion were ordered to hold the Steblev area. The 88th Division was ordered to pull back its front line during the night of 28 January and to take up new positions along the Ross River east and north of Boguslav.[253]

The Germans Defend Olshana

Lieb's eastern neighbor, Stemmermann's XI Corps, faced a slightly different situation. With its four divisions it was stronger than Lieb's Corps. Also, since it was given command over the 11th and 14th Panzer Divisions it could attack the Soviet breakthrough, unlike Lieb's corps, which could only adjust its front, trying to prevent its rear from being overrun. However, with the loss of Shpola, the XI Corps' southern flank had to be protected or else its rear would be dangerously exposed. When the Soviet pincers met at Zvenigorodka, the Soviet units turned northeast, confirming German fears. The Soviet 20th Tank Corps sent a detachment towards Olshana, an important road hub on the Olshana River. It was possible that Olshana could be occupied before the Germans reacted.[254]

The SS-Wiking Division had seen relatively little action in the days before 27 January. It had sent its few tanks and assault guns to support other units, but otherwise its units had remained in calm sectors, spread out over a large area. On 27 January news reached the division that Shpola had been occupied by Soviet units. Reconnaissance was initiated in the Shpola–Olshana area, but soon further alarming news was received. The Steblev region was also threatened. The latter danger could directly affect the SS-Wiking, as it had two units located at

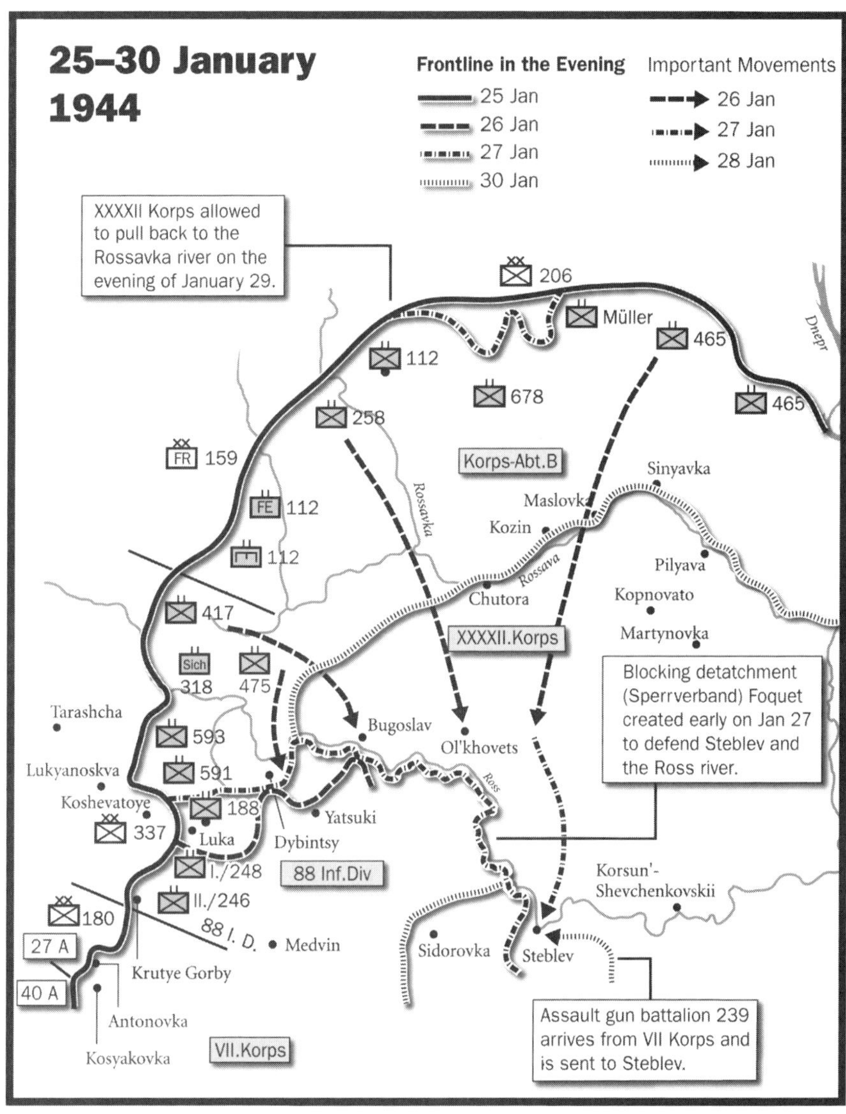

Steblev: the field replacement battalion and a school for combat engineers. In Olshana, the SS-Wiking formed alarm combat units from soldiers combed out from rear services. These did not have the same combat value as regular combat units, but at least they provided some kind of defense. Their worth was soon to be tested.[255]

Lieutenant Colonel Herbert Gille, the commander of SS-Wiking, did not consider the forces available in Olshana sufficient to defend the town. On 28 January he personally instructed Lieutenant Hein to take four assault guns to secure Olshana. In the evening, Hein's small force reached its destination and realized that the Red Army had already entered the outskirts of the town. In the darkness it was difficult to make an accurate assessment, but it was clear to Hein that the improvised defenders needed the support of his small force. On the way to Olshana the radio in his assault gun had broken down, but he assembled his tankers and ordered a counterattack, which succeeded in pushing the Russians out of the town. Later in the night, Hein sent two assault guns to the nearby village of Kirilovka, where they salvaged petrol stores that were brought to Olshana.[256]

Hein's small force was not the only reinforcement sent to Olshana. The SS-Wallonien had an assault gun company which had been included in the brigade in a somewhat unusual way. In the fall of 1943, at the training center at Debica, an assault gun company had been formed for Wallonien. Simultaneously an assault gun company had been forming for the 4th SS-Panzer Grenadier Division "Polizei." The training of the latter company had proceeded faster and in mid-November it was decided to exchange the companies, and send the one intended for SS-Polizei to SS-Wallonien instead, where it arrived at the end of November. The company did not have to take part in heavy combat immediately but was allowed some time to get acquainted with its new parent unit. As the soldiers in the Wallonien were from Belgium, there was a language barrier between them and the German soldiers of the assault gun company.[257]

The period of relative calm came to an end on 28 January, when Captain Planitzer, an officer with considerable experience who commanded the assault gun company, received orders to take two of his platoons to Olshana to help shore up the defenses of the vital communications center. His force was soon to be joined by another unusual unit, the SS-Narwa battalion, an infantry formation composed of Estonians, which would arrive at Olshana in the evening.[258]

The Encirclement Is Completed, 28 January

For the 389th Division the troublesome period continued, and Anton Meiser was among the soldiers in that division who were fully aware of their perilous situation. Early in the morning of 28 January, the surrounded group of artillery he belonged to was subjected to a Soviet attack from the east, which was repelled. The German gunners began withdrawing to the west. Meiser was given command of two howitzers and some extra infantry. His group was to set out first, and occupy a position from which it would be possible to provide covering fire for the remainder of the battalion-sized force.[259]

Due to the injury he had suffered earlier, Meiser was unable to walk and had to lead from horseback. Initially, everything went according to plan. He was able to rely on the instructions received from one of the scouting parties that had been sent out on the previous day, but after a while the small group reached a ravine. The road twisted down the ravine and the glassy ice made the descent very slippery. Meiser realized that it would be a demanding descent. He gave orders to round up the local inhabitants. With ropes attached to the wagons and howitzer carriages it was possible to make a slow descent, and the group took up their assigned covering position. Meiser sent a radio message that the remainder of the force could begin to move. He emphasized the difficulties encountered at the ravine.[260]

Without being harassed by Soviet units, the motley German force began to move westward. The journey went well, except for one of the last carriages. The driver did not take the same precautions as Meiser had done and the gun carriage began to slide, pushing the harnessed horses forward and crushing them when it reached the bottom of the ravine. After hard work the carriage was salvaged but the horses were dead. Eventually all the howitzers were saved, but the Germans were puzzled why there was so little interference from the Red Army. Perhaps the Soviet commanders knew that the small German group was heading into another encirclement, but that was yet unknown to Meiser and his fellows.[261]

In the evening, Meiser got an inkling of what might lie ahead. He spent the evening and night in a small house owned by an elderly Russian man who spoke good German. The old man told Meiser that the Red Army had created a large cauldron, and even outlined the situation on a map. He even compared the situation to that at Stalingrad and said it would be better to surrender. Meiser was flabbergasted and thought the man had had too much to drink. Even though it had been suspected for a while, Meiser did not want to believe that the threat of encirclement was true.[262]

Meiser and his fellows were not alone in their ignorance about the overall situation. It seems that the rank and file seldom knew the larger picture, especially in critical situations like the present one. Arne Hansen was a Norwegian who had volunteered for the Waffen-SS and had served in the SS-Wiking for a long time. In August 1943 he had been on leave to his home in Norway, but returned to the division on 3 September and from then on saw continuous action until the division went into the Korsun area. When the Soviet pincers closed, the antiaircraft battery he served with was stationed near Gorodishche. Little news trickled down to Hansen and his comrades, but when they observed large numbers of transport aircraft landing and taking off from the Korsun airfield they realized something serious must have happened.[263]

To Hube and his staff it was evident the encirclement they had long feared had taken place. On the evening of 28 January, Hube received the order that XXXXII Corps should leave the 1st Panzer Army and be placed under command of 8th Army, which he duly forwarded to his units. He ended his message to the departing corps with the words: "I will fight you out."

The Number of Encircled Troops

If General Hube failed to fulfil his promise, the result would be a disaster for the Germans, similar to that at Stalingrad although on a smaller scale. Hube was well aware of what had happened at Stalingrad. He had himself been among the encircled, but had been flown out before the destruction of 6th Army. At Stalingrad five corps had been surrounded, compared to two at Korsun. The number of corps does not give a clear indication of how many men were trapped, however. As with Stalingrad, the size of the encircled German force at Korsun has been subject to some debate. The Soviet sources maintain that 10 German divisions plus the Wallonien Brigade were encircled at Korsun, but this is patently wrong. Only six divisions could be claimed to be encircled.[264] Had such a force been at full strength, it would probably have amounted to close to 100,000 men, including corps and army troops.

Perhaps fortunately, the trapped divisions were not at full strength, for a variety of reasons. Each of the divisions had taken casualties in previous actions and a significant number of soldiers were on leave. Exactly how many is not clear, but information exists on the number of returning soldiers who assembled outside the pocket (see table).

SOLDIERS RETURNING FROM LEAVE	
Division	Number. of Soldiers[265]
57th Infantry	1,851
72nd	984
389th	352
88th	630
Korps-Abteilung B	1,597

These figures should be regarded as the lower limit on the number of soldiers on leave, since there may well have been more soldiers who had not yet returned from leave when the battle ended.

In addition, there were always soldiers who were hospitalized due to disease or injuries from accidents. These hospitals could be located outside a potential encirclement. Furthermore, a division, even a fresh one, could have some of its soldiers away at various courses or schools, which could be located well to the rear. Thus, even if a division was at full strength, in the sense that all positions called for in its organization tables had a person assigned, it could often have 10–20% of its soldiers absent due to leave, disease, accidents, or training.

Corporal Josef Eisner provides an example of one of the ways in which a soldier might be absent from his unit. He was an Austrian who served with the music platoon of the Westland Regiment, one of the motorized infantry regiments of 5th SS-Panzer Division Wiking. Together with six other musicians and a few other soldiers he left the division towards the end of September 1943 to take equipment to Münich for extensive repairs. Having accomplished their mission they enjoyed a fairly long leave, before going to Warsaw to pick up four Wespe SP Artillery pieces in December. On New Year's Eve, Eisner and his fellows unloaded the

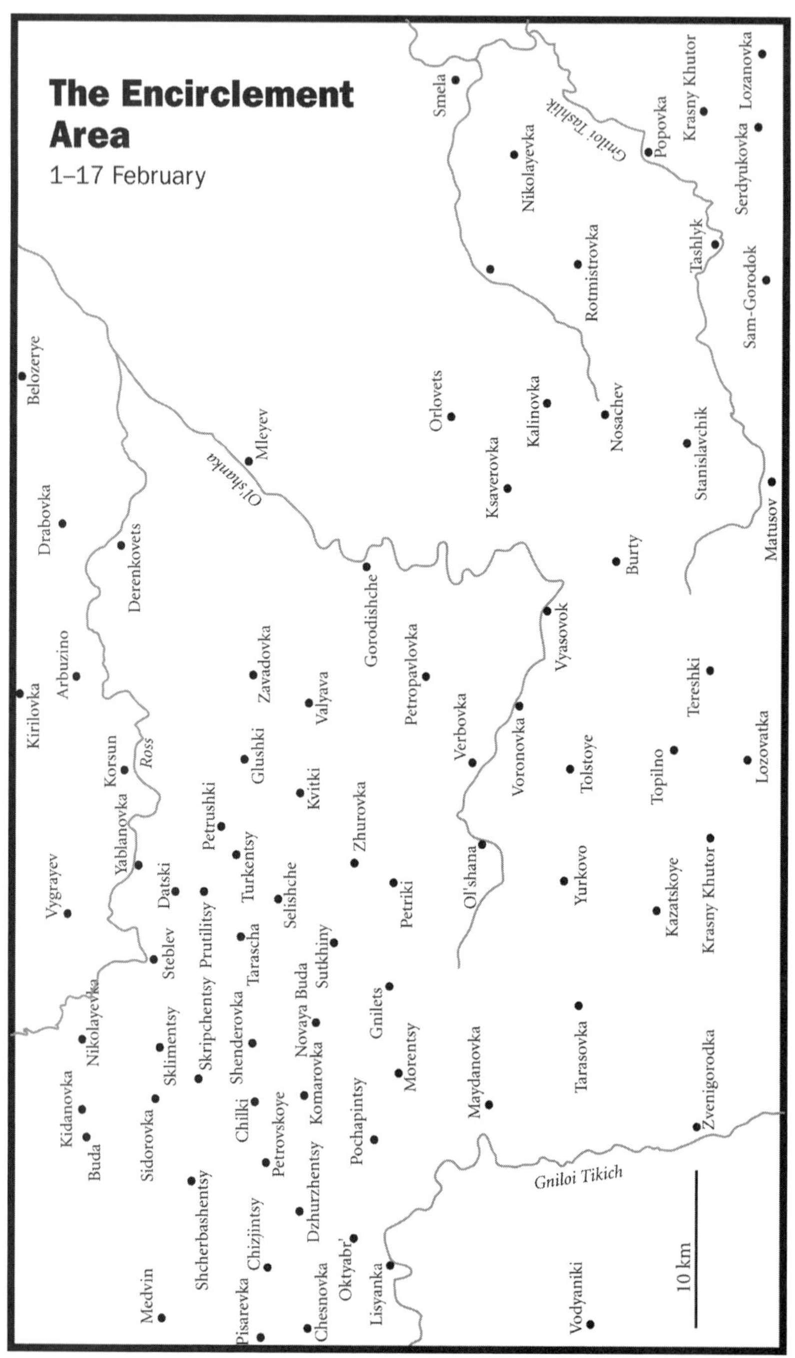
The Encirclement Area
1–17 February
Smela
Nikolayevka
Gniloi Tashlik
Popovka
Krasny Khutor
Lozanovka
Serdyukovka
Tashlyk
Sam-Gorodok
Rotmistrovka
Belozerye
Mleyev
Ol'shanka
Orlovets
Kalinovka
Nosachev
Stanislavchik
Ksaverovka
Matusov
Drabovka
Derenkovets
Burty
Gorodishche
Vyasovok
Arbuzino
Kirilovka
Zavadovka
Valyava
Petropavlovka
Tereshki
Verbovka
Voronovka
Tolstoye
Topilno
Lozovatka
Korsun
Ross
Glushki
Kvitki
Yablanovka
Petrushki
Turkentsy
Zhurovka
Vygrayev
Datski
Prutilitsy
Selishche
Petriki
Ol'shana
Yurkovo
Kazatskoye
Krasny Khutor
Steblev
Tarascha
Sutkhiny
Nikolayevka
Sklimentsy
Skripchentsy
Shenderovka
Novaya Buda
Gnilets
Morentsy
Maydanovka
Tarasovka
Zvenigorodka
Kidanovka
Buda
Sidorovka
Chilki
Komarovka
Petrovskoye
Pochapintsy
Shcherbashentsy
Chizjintsy
Dzhurzhentsy
Oktyabr'
Lisyanka
Gniloi Tikich
Medvin
Pisarevka
Chesnovka
Vodyaniki
10 km

four Wespes from a train at Berdishev, but were soon informed about the Soviet offensive not far away. It was deemed necessary to use the Wespes immediately and they had to be handed over to the 1st SS-Panzer Division. There was nothing left for Eisner and his group but to try to reach their division, which at the moment was more than 200 kilometers away. The trains made long detours to avoid advancing Red Army forces, but finally the soldiers reached their destination. A day or two later the Soviet pincers met at Zvenigorodka and Eisner and his fellow soldiers were trapped.[266]

In the case of the battle at Korsun it must also be taken into account that the encirclement was comparatively shallow. This meant that elements of the units, especially rear services, were fortunate enough to find themselves outside the encirclement. For example, no less than 1,858 soldiers belonging to the rear services of the 88th Infantry Division found themselves outside the Soviet pincers.[267] The net effect of all of this was that the surrounded German force numbered slightly less than 59,000 men.[268]

Still, this was a considerable force and the first major encirclement of German soldiers since Stalingrad in 1943. Aside from the numerical loss if this force were destroyed by the Red Army, the loss of so many of their comrades was likely to significantly lower the morale of the remaining German troops on the Eastern Front. Consequently, the German commanders seem to have felt a moral obligation to rescue the surrounded soldiers but were also undoubtedly aware of the importance of a rescue attempt on morale.

How the rescue attempt should be conducted was, however, not self-evident. Field Marshal von Manstein, commander of Army Group South, conceived a plan that, if successful, would not only save the surrounded forces, but also encircle and destroy the Soviet spearheads that had encircled the two German corps. The plan called for massing several Panzer divisions by both 1st Panzer Army and 8th Army. These were to attack in a northerly direction initially, and then turn towards the two encircled corps. In this way, the two corps would be liberated and the 5th Guards Tank Army and the 6th Tank Army, plus other Soviet units, would be surrounded instead.[269]

It was an ambitious plan, but Army Group South was far better provided with Panzer divisions than any other major German formation.

Of the 26 combat-ready German Panzer divisions at the time, no less than 20 were subordinated to Army Group South.[270] The main uncertainty was the weather.

Encirclement As a Strategy

For an army successfully to encircle its enemy had long been regarded as one of the pinnacles of military achievement. The battle between the Romans and the Carthaginians at Cannae in 216 BC is the classic example of an army encircled and annihilated. However, despite the temptations, in the two thousand years since Hannibal's victory, his success had proven difficult to repeat. The advantage of encirclement is that it provides a way to defeat the enemy army completely, rather than just pushing it back and allowing it to fight another day. However, an army attempting to encircle a force may be at risk from encirclement itself, which is possibly why field commanders refrained from the attempt. Another plausible explanation is that vigorous pursuit offers an alternative to encirclement for the commander who intends to annihilate his opponent. Napoleon often emphasized the importance of a pursuit, when the fruits of victory in battle could be harvested.

Still, the idea of the encirclement battle retained its lure. The Schlieffen Plan was heavily influenced by the concept of encirclement, but few World War I battles can truly be described as encirclements. Partly this was because of lack of mobility except by railroads. However, the railroads were much more suitable for moving reserves behind the lines than for exploiting a breakthrough, and as they were the chief means of quick movement, encirclements were difficult to achieve, especially on the Western Front.

To the Germans the idea of an encirclement battle remained highly appealing in the interwar period, since they realized that a prolonged war was unlikely to end with a German victory. Thus a quick and decisive victory on the battlefield was regarded as indispensable in future conflicts. Merely pushing the enemy forces back would provide their opponents with time to gather overwhelming resources. At the height of the Blitzkrieg the Germans conducted numerous encirclement operations, where in particular German armor divisions cut through enemy defenses and quickly pushed behind the opposing forces, to cut them off from their supplies and place them in a hopeless situation. Encirclement operations were much in evidence on the Eastern Front in 1941, but although they inflicted immense losses on the Red Army, they failed to knock out the Soviet Union entirely.

Even though the Germans failed to achieve their aim, it does not follow that the encirclement operations were either conceptually flawed or ineptly implemented. It is common to evaluate military operations relative to the aims set forth, but that seems to be a mistake. After all, the outcome of an operation is not only the result of the planning and conduct of the operation. For example, the failure to achieve the planned result can be the result of an unrealistic ambition. Conversely, an ineptly planned and conducted operation can achieve its goal, if the goal is modest enough, or the opposition is very weak in comparison to the friendly forces. Thus, even if an operation failed to achieve its aim, it may still have been the best way to pursue an objective, even if perhaps the resources available were simply insufficient. The opposite scenario, in which a poorly planned and conducted operation succeeds only due to overwhelming resources, is also conceivable.[271]

Encirclement Operations on the Eastern Front

German encirclement battles undoubtedly inflicted immense losses on the enemy, while keeping German losses comparatively low. The fact that the Germans did not defeat the Soviet Union can be attributed to an overwhelming task, rather than inherent flaws in the concept or poor execution of it. It is clear that the Red Army at least tried to use the same concept on the Germans during the Soviet winter offensive of 1941–42, but the results were mostly disappointing.

In many ways the German encirclement operations between 1939 and 1942 constitute the zenith of that kind of operation. Many factors converged to produce the outcome. One of the most important was the great differences in mobility between the relatively few mechanized units and the majority of the armies, which relied on the legs of humans and horses. As the German armored spearheads advanced at rates of up to 80 kilometers per day, it was almost impossible for the slower moving enemy units to escape encirclement, even if they had been ordered to retreat in time. However, when the Red Army tried to use the same idea against the Germans, it never managed to achieve the exceptionally high advance rates.[272] Thus the Germans usually had time to take countermeasures. Another important factor was air supply. The Germans often managed to supply those forces that had been cut off by using the Luftwaffe. In the winter of 1941–42, air power had been instrumental in supplying several German ground formations. Stalingrad is another example where air power played a part, although the Luftwaffe did not have sufficient capacity to sustain such a large force as the 6th Army. Not only surrounded German army formations were supplied from the air. Advancing spearheads could also receive airborne supply, the most recent example being that of the 1st SS-Panzer Division during its offensive action near Lipovets on 27 January, the day before the Soviet pincers met at Zvenigorodka.[273]

While the Red Army attempted many encirclement operations before the Korsun battle, only Stalingrad could be regarded as an undisputed success.

From 1944 onwards, the German Army gradually became less mobile, due to shortages of vehicles and lack of fuel. Furthermore, the "no-retreat policy" exacerbated the situation. Consequently, during the last 11 months of World War II, German units found themselves encircled more often and at that stage of the war there was little hope for any successful air supply operations, as by then the Luftwaffe was a spent force.

An encirclement is a dramatic experience for a modern army, since military doctrine usually assumed that the army's rear is fairly safe. The frontline troops are dependent on a constant supply of ammunition, fuel, food, spare parts, and a miscellany of other items. Occasionally these may be stored in advance in such a way that units retain a healthy supply if encircled, but such occasions are rare. More often, armies in war find themselves operating with many shortages, forcing them to live from hand to mouth. In the case of the German army during World War II, fuel is a good example of a commodity that could be in short supply. It is doubtful if German fuel production—imports from Romania and synthetic fuel production plants notwithstanding—was sufficient to provide enough fuel to supply the aircraft and motorized vehicles used to wage a modern war. The army suffered periodic shortages that made it impossible for the frontline units to build up significant reserves of fuel nearby. Instead, fuel had to be delivered regularly to cover consumption. Ammunition was in slightly better supply, but not much. A few days of intensive combat could deplete the stores held by a corps. If an encirclement lasted longer, food would also become scarce.

It was not only transportation of supplies to the combat units that became difficult or impossible when formations were cut off. A combat unit also had to send important traffic in the opposite direction, including any wounded men who required evacuation. Although the divisions had their own means for taking immediate care of the wounded, the seriously wounded were supposed to be transported to medical facilities in the rear where they could receive proper treatment.

Supplying the Pocket

At Korsun, the two surrounded German corps faced an additional difficulty, since some of the medical resources belonging to the divisions were outside the pocket, due to the relative shallowness of the encirclement. Consequently, it was more difficult to treat even those who were only lightly wounded.[274]

The Germans only had two realistic options to alleviate the situation in the pocket. The first was the relief attempt. However, it would take days to move up the Panzer divisions, and the encircled soldiers needed help soon. The second option would provide assistance more rapidly, but its overall capacity was limited. This option was an air lift operation, the need for which was immediately clear to the German commanders. When the Soviet tank armies met at Zvenigorodka, the Germans were already preparing the air supply operation, and before noon on 29 January, 14 aircraft took off from the air base at Uman with 30 tons of ammunition on board. They landed on the airstrip at Korsun, a facility that was to play a prominent role in the following weeks.[275]

Artillery caused most of the casualties. Heavy pieces, like this Soviet 20.3cm howitzer, had great firepower. To alleviate the problems associated with the weight, this howitzer is mounted on a tracked carriage. (SIPA PRESS)

CHAPTER 9

The Red Army Squeezes the Pocket

When the spearheads of the two Soviet fronts met on 28 January, the first phase of the operation was successfully concluded. The Soviet generals may have celebrated their success, but much hard fighting lay ahead before they could claim a final victory. The Red Army could choose either to squeeze the pocket until it collapsed or attempt to starve the German troops into submission. In either case it was necessary to prevent German relief attempts from breaking in. In order to keep the pocket isolated, an outer ring of Soviet forces was created, from Panchevo in the east to Konstantinovka in the west. About two thirds of the distance was covered by troops from the 2nd Ukrainian Front. The 5th Guards Tank Army took responsibility for the sector between Zvenigorodka to Vodianoe, and the area east of Vodianoe was allotted to 53rd Army.[276]

Initially, Pavel Rotmistrov's Tank Army only had its three tank corps, but it was reinforced with the 49th Rifle Corps, consisting of three rifle divisions and also a combat engineer brigade. The tank corps were not intended to occupy defensive front lines, and Rotmistrov was pleased to receive the rifle divisions. The length of the front line forced him to keep his armor at the front too, but the arrival of the infantry allowed him to allot shorter defensive sectors to his tank corps and even to create some reserves.[277]

Andrei Kravchenko, the commander of 6th Tank Army, was in a much more precarious position. On 28 January he received orders to detach his most powerful unit, the 5th Mechanized Corps, and send it 100 kilometers to the west. The reason was the dire situation created by the Germans' Operation Watutin in the Balabanova area. Kravchenko did retain the battle group built around the 233rd Tank Brigade from the 5th Mechanized Corps.[278]

The 5th Mechanized Corps, with attached units, became temporarily subordinated to the 40th Army. In deplorable weather, the corps marched the 100 kilometers. Rain and snow fell, and lack of vehicles in the rifle brigades forced many men to march by foot. The men had to walk fully equipped, wearing felt boots and fur coats. Despite the difficult conditions, the corps reached its destination near Staryj Zhivotin and took up defensive positions. The Germans detected the presence of the corps and refrained from attacks against it. The 5th Mechanized Corps conducted some minor attacks. However, on the third day after its arrival, the corps was ordered to return to 6th Tank Army.[279]

Since the mechanized brigades had a far stronger infantry component compared to the tank corps, the loss of the 5th Mechanized Corps was sorely felt by Kravchenko. He found some consolation in the fact that the 47th Rifle Corps, with two rifle divisions, was subordinated to his army, and further reinforcements were on the way. Within a few days the 2nd Guards Airborne Division would arrive and take up defensive positions in the Ryshanovka area. But whether Kravchenko's defenses would prove sufficient depended above all on whatever reinforcements the Germans might send to oppose his tank army. He already knew that the lead elements of the 17th Panzer Division had arrived. Further Panzer divisions might follow.[280]

General Filipp Zhmachenko's 40th Army had been given responsibility for the sector to the right of the 6th Tank Army, from Kobyliaki westwards. His divisions were extended; the four that covered the sector east of Okhmatovo had, on average, 11 kilometers to cover, although Zhmachenko was heartened by the fact that the opposing German divisions had to cover sectors that were roughly twice as large.[281]

Vatutin and Konev chose to keep a defensive line to the south, despite the fact that there were tempting targets not far away. In particular, Uman was only 55 kilometers from the positions held by 6th Tank Army, with almost no German units positioned to arrest a Soviet thrust to the city. Uman was a very important logistical center for the Germans, and also a very important air base. The air base played a prominent part in the ensuing German airlift operation. It was a tempting target for the Soviets and one wonders why the Red Army did not exploit this opportunity to take control of it. Still, it must be remembered that, with the exception of Stalingrad, encirclement operations had not been a Soviet strength. Either the Germans had broken out of encirclement or else the Soviet spearheads had been halted. In some cases the Soviet armored spearheads had been destroyed. With this experience, the Soviet generals had good reason to exercise caution.

There were also other factors that could have influenced the decisions. Both the 5th Guards and 6th Tank Armies were stretched thin already on 28 January, and Kravchenko was about to lose half his mobile force. The Soviet commanders did not have a considerable force available to pursue an attack on Uman, and they could not know for sure that the Germans had little strength available to stop an advance towards that target.

The unstable weather, a mixture of snow, rain, and thaws, must also be taken into consideration as an argument against a Soviet advance on Uman. It was possible that the forces would be delayed on the roads, just when they might be desperately needed elsewhere. All factors considered, it seems that the Soviet choice to keep a defensive line to the south was cautious but realistic, especially if they based their decisions on an inflated picture of the strength of the surrounded German force. Thus Vatutin and Konev allotted the forces they deemed sufficient to hold the outer defense ring, and tried to reduce the pocket as soon as possible.

With the 40th, 53rd, 5th Guards Tank, and 6th Tank Armies allocated to the outer ring, Vatutin could use the 27th Army to cover the cauldron, while Konev gave the same task to the 4th Guards and 52nd Armies. Neither the 27th, nor the 52nd Armies were particularly strong initially. The 4th Guards Army was undoubtedly the largest, having seven divisions on 29 January, compared to three each for the other two armies.[282]

But the mere fact that the divisions were available was not at all the same thing as having them in place. On the morning of 29 January, the bulk of 4th Guards Army had not advanced far from the initial position it held on 25 January, and the 52nd Army had not advanced at all. The area where the 5th Guards Tank Army had penetrated was still contested, which in fact meant that most of the forces Konev had designated to the inner encirclement ring would have to fight their way to create the desired inner ring around the pocket.

Vatutin's forces had made better progress. The 27th Army had reached the outskirts of Steblev and Shenderovka, which meant that almost one third of the distance that separated the 1st and 2nd Ukrainian Fronts had been covered. However, the difficulties of keeping the units sufficiently supplied with fuel, ammunition, and other necessities, as well as the fact that 27th Army for the moment only had two divisions available on this sector, excluded the possibility that the 1st Ukrainian Front could push much further to the southeast. It was imperative that Konev's armies make more progress.

As we have seen, on 27 January the German 11th Panzer Division managed to cut off the 20th and 29th Tank Corps from their comrades further to the east. Rotmistrov instructed the two tank corps to continue towards Zvenigorodka, and ordered the 18th Tank Corps and the 5th Guards Cavalry Corps to reopen the communications cut by the German 11th Panzer Division. The first attempt by the two Soviet corps, on 28 January, may hardly be described as successful. They did manage to poke some holes in the German blocking position, but it is certainly an exaggeration to claim that a corridor had been reopened.

The arrival of substantial Soviet reinforcements eventually turned the scales.[283] On 29 January the Soviet grip on the Turiya–Pisarevka area tightened, even though the German I./Pz.Rgt. 26 Panther battalion clung to hill 205.4 west of Pisarevka, and fired upon Soviet tanks and other troops that tried to advance west. The German tanks inflicted substantial losses on the Soviet units, but the Panthers also received many hits, even though only one tank was lost. Eventually the German commanders had to acknowledge that the Soviet defenses had become too strong in the Kapitanovka region. In a discussion with Wöhler, von Vormann suggested that the 14th Panzer Division should for the moment be split. Its 108th Panzer Grenadier Regiment was already cut off north of Kapitanovka, and von Vormann's intention was to subordinate the other Panzer grenadier regiment to 3rd Panzer Division, which would extend its front further to the west. The armored battle group of 14th Panzer Division would be placed under 11th Panzer Division, which in turn should shift further west, to try to cut off the Soviet spearheads by attacking west of Turiya. Wöhler agreed with von Vormann, who quickly briefed his division commanders. The Germans also pulled back the tanks of 11th Panzer Division, which had held a position between the I./Pz.Rgt. 26 and Kampfgruppe von Brese.[284]

With the corridor at Kapitanovka gradually being cleared, Konev considered how to use his forces effectively. The 18th Tank Corps, which had been fighting on the southern shoulder of the corridor, was to continue forward, to link up with the rest of 5th Guards Tank Army. The 5th Guards Cavalry corps was sent northwest, to create a solid ring around the two surrounded German corps. This maneuver constituted an important step in the process of constricting the cut-off German forces.[285]

Once the bottleneck had been secured, the Guards Cavalry was directed towards Shpola, with the intention that it should turn north as soon as that town had been reached. Between Kapitanovka and Shenderovka there was a large gap, with only scattered units on either side. This was both a problem and an opportunity. If the Germans could assemble strong forces from the two surrounded corps, they might break the encirclement. On the other hand, if the Soviets could use the opportunity, they could strike towards Korsun and perhaps split the pocket into smaller parts, a task suited to cavalry. It would take a day or two for the Guards Cavalry Corps, commanded by Major-General Selivanov, to reach Shpola, but assuming that the situation remained static, the chance of splitting the pocket was a tempting one for the Soviet commanders.[286]

German Reorganizations

The staff of XXXXVII Panzer Corps had little reason to rejoice during the afternoon of 29 January. At noon the Rossokhovatka–Reyementarovka line had been abandoned and positions further south had been occupied. Still, the Germans had some overview of the area where the Red Army was advancing west. At 14.20hrs approximately 1,500 horsemen, accompanied by T-34 tanks, were observed moving west from Pisarevka. The German observers directed artillery fire on the column, but could not do anything else. Somewhat later the Germans observed intense supply traffic heading west, in the Ositnyazhka–Pisarivka area, but with the increasing darkness there was little they could do. Clearly the 2nd Ukrainian Front had opened the route to its spearheads at Zvenigorodka. Another cause for concern was Kampfgruppe von Brese, which had been cut off for a couple of days. It received orders to try to move to Zhuravka, so that it could cooperate with the 11th Panzer Division, which had been tasked with chasing the Soviet units northwest of Novo Mirgorod.[287]

The mood was hardly better among the staff of 8th Army. Already at 00.35hrs on 29 January, the XI Corps reported that Soviet forces had broken into Tashlyk, near the junction between the 389th and 72nd Divisions. During the morning fighting continued, but before noon the Germans had lost Tashlyk and left the mopping up of the village to the Red Army. Major Norbert Bittl, a staff officer from 8th Army, was ordered to fly into Korsun, to get an up-to-date report on the situation there. The heavy clouds and intermittent rain showers that had dominated the morning had settled so that the aircraft landed safely at Korsun. Major Bittl's flight probably offered encouragement to the officers trapped inside the pocket, but his aircraft was not the only one to arrive. Before noon, 23 Ju-52s had landed at Korsun, bringing badly needed supplies and heralding the beginning of the airlift operation that was instrumental in keeping the soldiers inside the pocket supplied with ammunition and fuel.[288]

To Bittl and the commanders of the XI and XXXXII Corps it was abundantly clear that the XXXXII Corps was vastly over-extended. The Soviet breakthrough at the corps' southern sector extended the already long front line even further, as the Red Army advanced along the southern bank of the Ross River. It had only been possible to create anything resembling a defense along the Ross line in the south by stripping the northern front. Towards the end of the day on 29 January, only three battalions from Korps-Abteilung B were defending the corps' northern front, a sector almost 75 kilometers wide. Although the Soviet forces conducting the attacks on Korps-Abteilung B were weak, the situation was clearly untenable, especially as the defenses in the southern part of the pocket were anything but secure. The shifting of battalions within the XXXXII Corps was robbing Peter to pay Paul, rather than a tenable strategy.[289]

The top priority for the German commanders in the pocket was to reestablish contact with 1st Panzer Army and 8th Army. The southern part of the cauldron was clearly the most important, and forces had to be shifted south. The most powerful unit available was the SS-Wiking Division, which had seen relatively little action lately, except for its Panzers. It was located far to the north, at a sector where there was only slight Soviet activity, so it was a suitable choice to be sent south where it might even be transferred to the XXXXII Corps, since the XI Corps was in a more stable situation.[290]

Major Bittl returned from the pocket at 16.00hrs and gave a briefing, but before he returned, Wöhler and Speidel had discussed the plans with Army Group South. It was agreed that the most important area was the southern part of the pocket, a conclusion that was corroborated by Bittl's visit. Army Group South emphasized that the Boguslav area was vital because of the planned counterattack, and Steblev also had to be held under all circumstances.[291]

General Lieb was convinced that it was necessary to withdraw the thinly held northern front, but he did not receive clear consent from his superior commanders. Despite this, he initiated a withdrawal to the Rossava River line in the afternoon. He reported this to 8th Army, but the transmission was delayed and the staff did not receive the message until 23.10hrs.[292]

The withdrawal was an important maneuver, one of several vital alterations made by the German forces during the afternoon and evening. As we have seen, the 11th Panzer Division had been reinforced with the armored group from the 14th Panzer Division and several non-divisional armor and assault gun units.[293] This force shifted further west, but 8th Army was doing even more reshuffling of its deck. To cover the sector held by 11th and 14th Panzer Divisions, the 320th Division arrived in the evening. Its previous positions had been taken over by the 10th Panzer Grenadier Division. Furthermore, the 13th Panzer and 376th Infantry Divisions were on the way and could be expected to arrive within a day or two. The 24th Panzer Division was also moving towards the XXXXVII Panzer Corps, but it would have to negotiate long and muddy roads before it could influence the battle at Korsun.[294]

Changes were also implemented inside the pocket. The SS-Wiking Division was mostly transferred from XI to XXXXII Corps. Eleven tanks from the SS-Wiking Division were detached to the 72nd Division, which still remained with the XI Corps, and sent to the village of Matusov. Nevertheless, the decision contributed to a shift of forces to the southern part of the pocket.[295]

Anton Meiser's Withdrawal, 29 January

The intermingling of units became worse as the battle progressed. Sometimes it was the result of deliberate orders, sometimes due to enemy pressure, and sometimes it was caused by units being cut off, like the group of artillery that Anton Meiser accompanied.

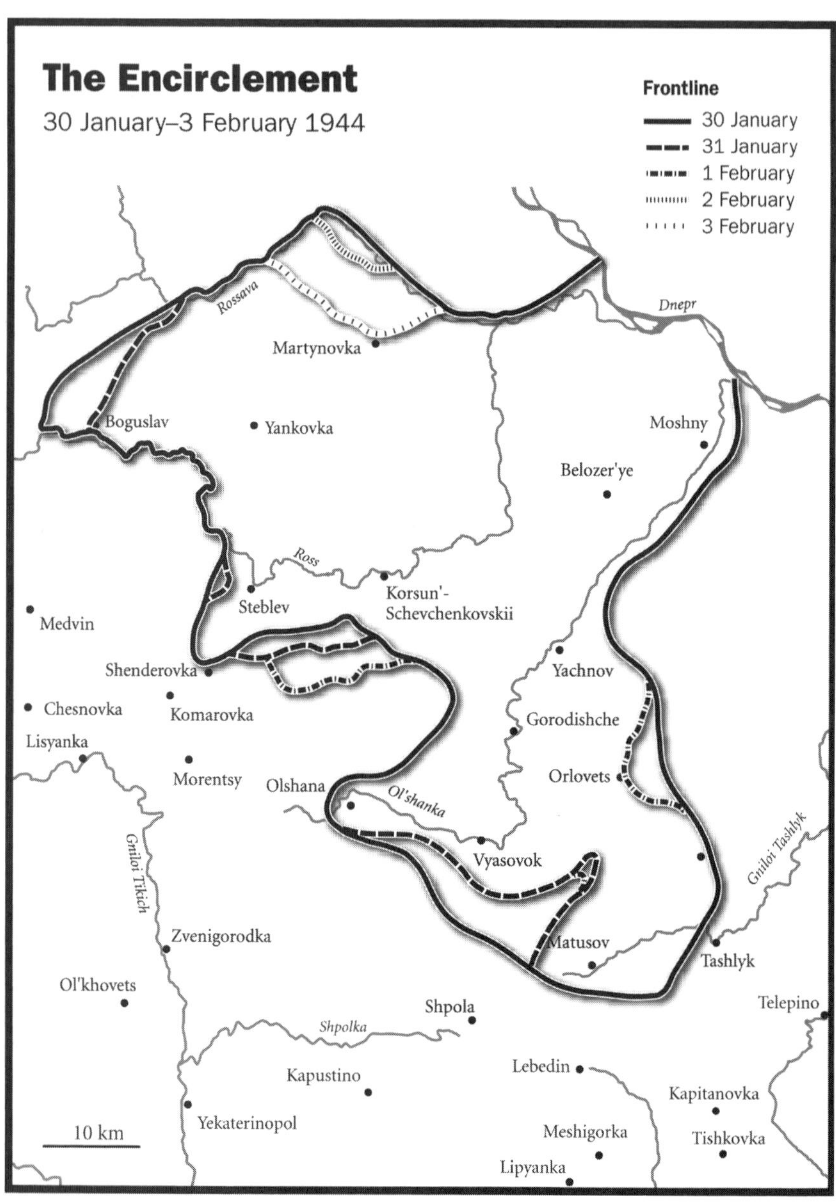

On the morning of 29 January, Meiser's artillery group continued westward, at least initially unhindered by enemy action. After a while they reached a hilly area. The road followed the southern slope of a hill, then turned right only to turn left again before reaching a bridge over a river. From there it continued on the southern slope of yet another hill. When moving onto the slope of the first hill, the Germans heard artillery shells exploding, and realized that the bridge seemed to be the target, but the shells, optimized for shrapnel and with impact fuses, had not caused any damage to the bridge and only marginally affected the road.[296]

The men could cross the river further south, but for the carriages there was no alternative to crossing the river by the bridge, and a risky solution had to be adopted. The howitzers halted in cover by the first hill, while Lieutenant Sorajewski took up a position southwest of the bridge, where he could direct the horse drawn carriages. He had observed that the Soviet gunners fired at very regular intervals. One by one the horse drawn carriages moved forward to his position, and with a clock in his hand he gave the order for one vehicle at a time to dash over the bridge. It was not an easy task for the drivers, as it was necessary to travel quickly to cross the bridge before the next Soviet round exploded, but not so quickly that the horses and carriages slid on the icy road.[297]

At first everything worked according to plan and several vehicles crossed the road and reached a point where Meiser waited for them and directed them towards a place where they were covered from enemy observers. However, when a light wagon, drawn by two horses, was about to cross the bridge, the Soviet artillery fired after a shorter interval. Shrapnel from an exploding shell tore off two feet from one of the horses. For a while it stumbled forward on the stumps that remained, but fell next to the bridge and pulled the other horse into the ditch. The wagon remained on the road, but across it, thereby blocking the entire road. The driver had the presence of mind to unharness the unscathed horse before he himself took cover.[298]

Fortunately, Lieutenant Sorajewski had been foresighted enough to place a group consisting of an NCO and six men next to Meiser. They promptly dashed toward the stricken carriage. When they had reached the bridge, they immediately took cover. After an artillery salvo had crashed down, the men sprang forward from their cover, unharnessed the dead horse, and pushed the wagon aside before taking cover again, just in time before another salvo landed. Again the men moved out from their cover when the shells had exploded and dashed to the wagon, at the same time as a rider with an extra horse galloped up. Working feverishly they managed to harness the horses to the wagon and the driver began to urge the horses to pull as hard as they could. Soon another salvo exploded, shrapnel whizzed around, but nobody was hurt. After this drama, all other carriages and wagons passed the bridge without incident. The isolated force continued west, until another river was crossed and it halted for the night. Meiser was given command of a small number of infantrymen and received the task of defending the bridge that had just been crossed. Except for a minor skirmish the night passed uneventfully.[299]

Further to the west, where the Soviet 40th Army and 6th Tank Army had clashed with the German VII Corps, both sides seemed to settle down, relatively content with the positions they held and beginning to prepare for the next round. Indeed, it seemed as if the fighting diminished on the XXXXVII Panzer Corps' sector too, with both sides busy reorganizing their units, but inside the pocket the situation remained uncertain.

Soviet Pressure Increases

Once the 2nd Ukrainian Front had secured the connection to its spearheads at Zvenigorodka, it concentrated on the surrounded German units. As it reached Shpola, the 5th Guards Cavalry Corps was directed towards Burty and Olshana, while rifle divisions tried to keep up on its right flank. Selivanov chose to commit his 63rd Cavalry Division on the left, while the 12th Guards Cavalry Division advanced on the right and the 11th Guards Cavalry Division in the center. It was important to gain ground. The corridor held by the 2nd Ukrainian Front was little more than 20 kilometers wide, far less than on the sector held by the 1st Ukrainian Front.

The German attacks on the southern side of the corridor had abated, but if they were renewed, with the aid of substantial reinforcements, such a small depth could prove dangerous. It would be prudent to try to push back the Germans towards Gorodishche.[300]

On 30 January Selivanov's cavalry advanced towards Burty and by the end of the day they could see the outskirts of the village. The distance to Olshana was greater however, and by the end of the day the forward units of 63rd Cavalry Division had only reached Zelenaya Dubrova, still about 8 kilometers from Olshana. The fighting for Olshana would have to wait until next day.[301]

Further east, Anton Meiser woke up in the morning, only to find that Soviet troops had crossed the river about two kilometers south of the bridge he was responsible for defending. His wounded leg was recovering by now, which was fortunate as he saw no alternative except to withdraw, and decided to avoid the roads. Instead, his little group plodded through the snow that covered the terrain, until they reached a village held by infantry from the same battalion as Meiser's grenadiers. In the afternoon the village was abandoned and the withdrawal continued. During the retreat, two of Meiser's comrades were killed, one by a shot to the head and one by a shot in the chest. In the darkness a snow-clad hill was chosen as position for the night, and foxholes were dug for an all around defense. The hungry soldiers, whose wet clothes provided little protection from the elements, prepared for the cold night.[302]

In the morning of 30 January Wöhler decided to visit some of his division commanders. He flew to the 320th Infantry Division as well as the 11th and 14th Panzer Divisions. He learned that 320th Division had relieved the 11th Panzer Division according to plan and that von Wietersheim's tanks were ready to advance towards Zhuravka and Meshigorka. He had some complaints, though. The I./Pz.Rgt. 26 Panther Battalion was very inexperienced, and the battalion commander had been killed. He was to be replaced by a more experienced officer from the Grossdeutschland Division, who hopefully would manage to lead the battalion more efficiently. Von Wietersheim also complained about the poor air support, claiming that the Luftwaffe reconnaissance was insufficient and had led to friendly fire incidents, as when his own troops had been bombed by German aircraft. But von Wietersheim did not only complain, he also had some praise for the Soviet cavalry, which he had found consisted of very good troops.[303]

At the 14th Panzer Division command post, Wöhler was informed that Kampfgruppe von Brese, which had been out of communication for a few days, had managed to break out in a north-westerly direction and had reached Vyasovok. Thus the battle group had actually only succeeded in breaking out from its own encirclement into the larger pocket consisting of XI and XXXXII Corps. With Kampfgruppe von Brese more or less permanently removed from the 14th Panzer Division, Unrein's division was weak in infantry as well as tanks.[304]

Wöhler departed before von Wietersheim's tanks began to advance at noon. Meeting only weak opposition, they drove through Meshi-

gorka and on towards Zhuravka, where they surprised Soviet units marching westward. In the confusion caused by the sudden appearance of German tanks, the Soviet columns suffered losses, before the German tanks turned back towards Meshigorka. The lack of infantry to protect them made it risky for the German tanks to maintain forward positions during darkness.[305]

While Wöhler consulted with some of the commanders in the XXXXVII Panzer Corps, Lieb was busy assembling a varied attack force near Steblev. It struck at 11.00hrs, advancing towards Shenderovka. Aside from the obvious advantage of getting closer to the main German forces outside the pocket, the purpose of the attack was to take some pressure off the weak German forces defending in the Olshana–Burty region. Initially the Germans made good progress, reaching the outskirts of Shenderovka within three hours. At that point Soviet reinforcements arrived, while the attacking German forces had become extended, causing the attack to ground to a halt.[306]

Information on the outcome of the fighting at Steblev reached 8th Army staff at 16.30hrs, and Wöhler concluded that the northern front of the pocket should be shortened in order to release units that could be sent to Steblev. At 18.00hrs Wöhler called Busse at Army Group South to discuss the idea, but the answer was blunt. Field Marshal von Manstein considered a withdrawal to be out of the question, as the army group was bound by orders from OKH. Two hours later, 8th Army received an order from Army Group South that the positions in the north of the pocket should be held.[307]

Almost simultaneously, Lieb sent a radio message to 8th Army that he would have to pull out a reinforced battalion from the assault group at Steblev, in order to hold the front line in the north. Perhaps this gave von Manstein and Busse second thoughts. At 22.15hrs Lieb was instructed to report as soon as possible what forces he could release by a withdrawal of the northern front.[308]

While the generals wasted time by debating, there were pressing matters to take care of. More than 1,000 wounded men remained within the pocket. It had been hoped that they might be flown out from Matusov, but the advance by the Red Army ruled out the use of Matusov as an air field. Instead, the wounded were to be transported over muddy roads to the Korsun air strip and from there evacuated from the pocket.[309]

The weather continued to be difficult to predict, but the thaw seemed to continue. The roads had frozen during the night of 29 January, but when temperatures rose during the following day they became muddy. Some of the smaller roads were no longer negotiable, except for tracked vehicles. On 31 January the troublesome weather continued. The sky was covered by clouds in the morning, but they began to clear before noon. Again the temperature was just above freezing. The roads deteriorated further.[310]

Early in the afternoon, ominous clouds gathered again and soon rain showers and snow squalls took turns making life even more miserable for the troops. The German infantry in the positions closest to the enemy suffered the most. In worn-out clothing and Zeltbahnen (waterproof fabric with which soldiers were issued) the riflemen of 14th Panzer Division got little cover from the elements. They became wet during the day and froze during the night. Covered by dirt they soon resembled moving clods of clay. It was no surprise that the number of soldiers who got ill increased sharply. The only means of lessening the hardship for the soldiers would have been to provide them with sufficiently frequent periods of rest in better quarters. However, the very low trench strength, caused by the prolonged fighting, meant that all available soldiers were needed at the front. In this way a vicious circle was created. Casualty rates forced the units to rely on fewer men, who then had to spend more time at the trenches. This in turn meant that the burden increased on the remaining soldiers, who became more prone to suffer from disease or from the accidents that were more likely to happen because of their exhausted condition. More men subsequently had to be evacuated, and the pressure on the remaining soldiers increased. The 14th Panzer Division was by no means unique among the German units fighting at Korsun, and most likely many soldiers of the two Soviet Fronts would probably find the description accurate too.[311]

Even if there was a daytime thaw, the temperature at night could still be bitterly cold. When Anton Meiser woke up in the morning on 31 January he saw that two of his comrades did not move. One of them had frozen to death during the night; the other was still alive, but so deeply chilled that he could not move his legs. Both were placed on a sledge and sent north, where it was believed that a dressing station was located. Meiser never found out if they had reached their destination.[312]

During the night Lieb and his staff had pondered how many units would be released by shortening the front in the north. The answer, received by 03.40hrs at 8th Army staff, was two battalions and three artillery batteries. Hardly an impressive force, but given the overall strength of the XXXXII Corps it was not insignificant. The information did not provoke any immediate reaction from the decision makers higher up in the command structure.[313]

Nevertheless, Lieb was not alone in realizing the need for a withdrawal from the Dnepr. At 09.00hrs Speidel and Busse held a telephone conversation in which Busse emphasized that the order to hold on to the Dnepr originated from OKH. Busse said that there should not be any talk of withdrawing the front, but of the enemy pushing the front back.

It was evident that none of the German commanders in the Ukraine would do the utmost to hold on to the Dnepr. They could only hope that Soviet pressure would be strong enough to offer an excuse for a retreat, but not so strong that it was a serious menace. With the policy practised by Hitler, retreats were only possible when units were under attack.[314]

Despite the shortage of troops, the German attack force south of Steblev did make some progress on 31 January, even though results were more modest than on the day before. Tarashcha, Turkentsy, and Petrushki were taken, but the advance was only two to three kilometers.[315]

Build-up to the German Counterattack on Shpola

The situation at Olshana had been critical for a few days, and on 31 January Soviet forces, most likely from Major-General Beloshnichenko's 63rd Cavalry Division, attacked near Verbovka, which was situated just east of Olshana. This move threatened to cut off Olshana from the rest of the pocket held by XI and XXXXII Corps. Very weak elements of the SS-Wiking Division were defending the corridor between Olshana and XI Corps' main forces, a corridor in which Verbovka was an important part. Fortunately for the defenders, Kampfgruppe von Brese arrived to bolster the lines.[316]

One can not help wondering what von Brese thought about this situation. First his Kampfgruppe had been surrounded and isolated for several days near Kapitanovka. After having extricated most of his force from there, he was now ordered to stick his nose into another dangerous location where the threat of isolation was imminent. If von Brese did have such fears, events further to the east probably strengthened his worries. Early on 31 January the Red Army attacked west of Matusov and made good progress, reaching Nosachev, about 10 kilometers north of Matusov, where the Germans still defended. By committing its last reserves, the XI Corps managed to create something resembling a defense line, but they could only hold on and hope that the Soviets did not send reinforcements. The Germans were fortunate that the 2nd Ukrainian Front was at the moment still moving the main forces of 4th Guards Army forward, but this was not known to Stemmermann.[317]

The western part of the pocket, where the German 88th Division defended, had seen relatively little action since the Germans withdrew to the Rossava River line. One reason was that the 1st Ukrainian Front had few units with offensive capabilities in the area. This sector was mostly covered by units from the 54th and 159th fortified regions, units that were mainly suited to defense. The 27th Army had, quite correctly, sent most of its more mobile units into the breakthrough, but on 31 January it was again able to attack the German-held, nose-shaped front west of Boguslav. The Germans were pushed back to the Khutora–Boguslav line before halting the Soviet attack.[318]

At the XXXXVII Panzer Corps staff, some optimism was nurtured. The 13th Panzer Division began to arrive, and at 15.00hrs Major-General Hans Mikosch, the division commander, entered Reinhard's staff room to discuss the forthcoming operations. His division was not particularly strong, since it had only 18 combat-ready tanks and less than half of them had arrived. The division was also short 4,152 officers and men. Furthermore, the muddy roads caused delays, and von Vormann suspected that only 100 riflemen from the division would be available to attack at dawn on 1 February. Nevertheless, this was the first major reinforcement von Vormann could throw into the Korsun battle in a way he chose, rather than being forced to dance to the tune played by Konev.[319]

He derived additional consolation from the successful raid carried out by 11th Panzer Division, which again had sent its tanks roving around Meshigorka. In this attack, which was just a prelude to the main assault planned for 1 February, von Wietersheim's tankers claimed to have destroyed 15 enemy tanks. The 11th Panzer Division was intended to strike from its staging area northwest of Novo Mirgorod and the 13th Panzer Division was to jump off from its bridgehead over the Bolshaya Vyss River at Petro Ostrov. They were to converge and cross the Shpolka River west of Shpola. It was hoped that Soviet pressure on Gruppe Stemmermann would thereby be reduced.[320]

Still, von Vormann remained skeptical of the chance of success, and at 16.00hrs he talked with Speidel over the telephone. Von Vormann thought that only the armored group plus a weak infantry regiment with only 100 riflemen would be available from 13th Panzer Division, and he doubted if the planned attack could take place.

"Under all circumstances must the armored group and the infantry regiment from 13th Panzer Division thrust forward tomorrow," Speidel replied.

"The mission is unclear," von Vormann responded, "whether the thrust should go over Shpola, or west of Shpola."

"The first mission is to thrust into the flank and rear of the enemy group at Shpola, but the group must be prepared to thrust west of Shpola."

"But then we must we must have more information on the enemy and friendly forces west of Shpola."

"The attacking units themselves will have to establish the enemy situation. The XI Corps is at Matusov. 8th Army can not wait another 24 hours. Tomorrow the 11th and 13th Panzer Divisions must attack."

"But the 11th Panzer Division is engaged at Turiya and Tishkovka," von Vormann protested, "and its armored group is fighting at Lebedin, where it has knocked out 15 enemy tanks."

"The thrust tomorrow will have to be carried out. We can not leave XI Corps in the lurch."

"But with a mere 100 riflemen I cannot thrust north with an unlimited objective."

"The objective is not unlimited; the objective is the south wing of XI Corps."[321]

Thus ended the discussion, but an hour and a half later Wöhler called von Vormann and again emphasized the need for attacking as early as possible the following day, with all available elements of the 11th and 13th Panzer Divisions, without concern for the flanks, in order to establish contact with the XI Corps. Von Vormann again had objections.

"I fully understand the need for the attack, but what should I do if the enemy thrust southwest from Shpola?"

"Cover the flank with a battalion," Wöhler replied.

"But I don't have a battalion to spare."

"The attack is ordered and I demand that it will begin as soon as possible tomorrow. I also ask you to relieve 3rd Panzer Division with 376th Infantry division more rapidly. It seems that the enemy is getting weaker in that sector."[322]

Wöhler's decision was a difficult one, of course. Possibly he was reassured that it was the right one when Wenck called a few minutes later. The 1st Panzer Army had reconnoitered the roads south of Zvenigorodka and found all of them to be empty of Soviet units. Also, the Red Army had dug in opposite the VII Corps. This suggested that the threat to von Vormann's western flank was weak or non-existent. Von Vormann's attack at least stood a fairly good chance of releasing some of the enemy pressure on Gruppe Stemmermann, and might perhaps even manage to establish contact with it.[323]

Stemmermann needed every respite he could get. The southeastern part of the pocket seemed to be on the verge of becoming cut off from the rest of his forces, something he could ill afford. On muddy roads it had been possible to move 750 wounded to Korsun, out of the roughly 1,000 men who had previously been assembled near Matusov. They still had to be flown out however, and one could never trust the weather to be cooperative. Everything that might prevent the Red Army from closing in on the airfield was desirable.[324]

CHAPTER 10

Von Vormann's Counterattack

At 06.00hrs on 1 February, the armor of the 11th Panzer Division which, including subordinated units, possessed 35 tanks and assault guns,[325] began attacking towards Meshigorka. Meeting weak opposition, the division made rapid progress. Wöhler flew to the staff of the XXXXVII Panzer Corps at 09.30hrs and received good news about the progress of the attack. However, he also learned that there was an urgent need for more manpower. The divisions were chronically short of riflemen, but there was little Wöhler could do about it.[326]

By 11.30hrs von Wietersheim's division had reached Skotorevo, more than 20 kilometers from the jump-off area. Continuing towards Kapustino it met with fierce resistance, but the Panzers captured the village and moved on to Iskrennoye, where they established a bridgehead over the Shpolka River in the early afternoon. So far, von Wietersheim could be very satisfied, but difficulties soon became apparent.

There was only one bridge over the Shpolka River at Iskrennoye, but it seemed quite strong. A Panther tank moved on to the bridge and successfully crossed to the northern side of the river, but when the second Panther tried, the weight of the tank proved too great and the bridge collapsed.[327]

The 13th Panzer Division had jumped off two hours later than the 11th, but it also made good progress and was able to cover the left flank of von Wietersheim's division, as the latter closed in on Kapustino. However, since neither division possessed the necessary equipment to construct a new bridge to replace the one that had collapsed, the requisite materials would have to be brought up and that would take time.[328]

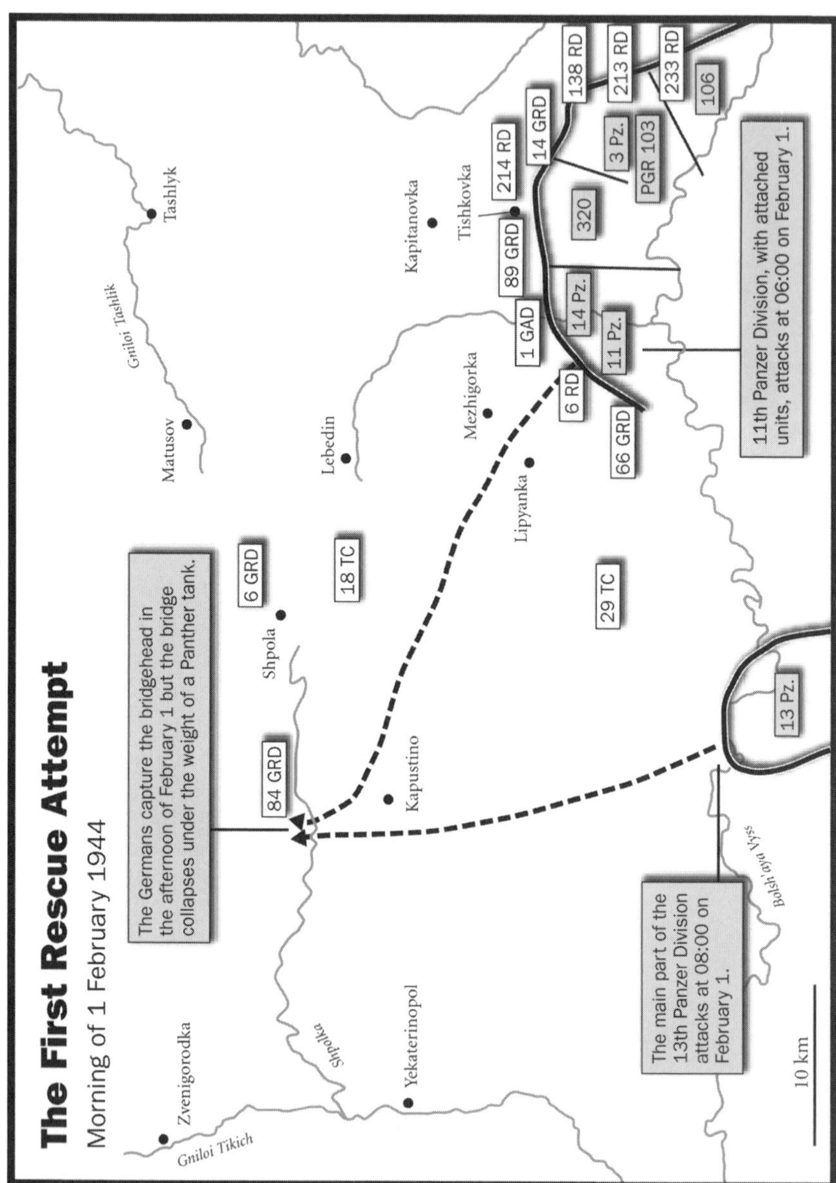

On 1 February, von Vormann, as well as Mikosch and von Wietersheim, set up their command posts at Mokraya Kaligorka, little more than 15 kilometers south of the bridgehead at Iskrennoye. Before noon the commander of the 55th Nebelwerfer Regiment arrived at the

XXXXVII Panzer Corps command post. His regiment, except one battalion which had been detached, was not far away and it was decided to subordinate it to 11th Panzer Division.[329]

Later in the afternoon the first Soviet counterattacks took place. Rotmistrov had dispatched tanks from 29th Tank Corps, which operated from Vasilkovka and probed the east flank of 11th Panzer Division, especially at Skotorevo. The German commanders were well aware of the exposed east flank. They planned to use the 3rd Panzer Division to cover the flank, as soon as it had been relieved by the 376th Infantry Division, a process that began at dusk. The intent was to resume the advance north from the bridgehead at Iskrennoye on 2 February.[330]

There was every need for the XXXXVII Panzer Corps to continue its attack, as the XXXXII Corps' attack south of Steblev made relatively little progress. Having set out at 08.00hrs, the hodgepodge German force had slowly advanced during the day, finally penetrating into Selishche and Kvitki, where street fighting was still raging at dusk.[331]

Lieb had every reason to worry about the slow progress south of Steblev, as the Red Army would certainly not stand idle. In the morning, the 27th Army resumed its attacks on the northern sector of the pocket, where it probed the German defenses at Maslovka and Kosin. However, Lieb was reassured by the progress of the Steblev group, which had managed to double the distance between the Soviet ground forces and the vital airfield at Korsun. For the moment, the Red Army could only interfere with the activity on the airfield by using long range artillery.[332]

There remained another threat to the air supply operation: the Red Air Force. On 1 February, some of the wounded were flown out of the pocket, but before noon, two Ju-52s loaded with wounded were shot down by Soviet fighters just after take-off. One officer who was brought on board a Junkers was Heinz Moritz, commander of the 1st Company of the tank battalion of SS-Wiking, who had become ill and it was decided that he should be flown out. Perhaps some of his fellow soldiers considered him fortunate to be evacuated from the pocket. However, he was aboard one of the Junkers that was shot down and he was killed when the aircraft crashed, together with the crew and the other wounded men.[333]

Of the other 11 aircraft that took off, two had to make emergency landings right after take-off and one was delayed, presumably due to Soviet fighter activity. The remaining eight seem to have made it to the air bases outside the pocket. Lieb demanded that the Luftwaffe should provide continuous fighter cover over the airfield. This was easy to demand but more difficult to achieve, since the weather remained fickle. Fog could suddenly close in on the air base and the thaw made the runways soft. Both sides had reason to complain that it was difficult to provide air support in a timely and well planned fashion.[334]

Gruppe Stemmermann had little air defense units available. The two corps had no independent Flak units, all available Flak belonging organically to the divisions. The infantry divisions usually had only a company of light AAA. The SS-Wiking had a few 88mm guns, but since the troops also had to have some air defense, it was difficult to concentrate much AAA on the air field. The Flak company of Korps-Gruppe B was sent to protect Korsun airfield, and on 1 February it was able to shoot down a Yak-7.[335]

Since he had been defending a bridge on the night of 29 January, Anton Meiser had been separated from his artillery battery. He found it again early in the morning of 1 February. The march westward continued, sometimes on roads littered with destroyed vehicles and dead horses. At noon a new threat appeared, one which they had been spared thus far during the arduous retreat. Soviet fighter aircraft began to strafe the German artillery vehicles as the latter approached a small village. Thanks to a brave initiative by Lieutenant Sorajewski, all carriages made it through the village. The small force continued toward Vyasovok and finally reached its parent corps. However, the men had only succeeded in moving from a small pocket into a larger one.[336]

Aside from Vatutin's attack on the northern face of the pocket, which was more an attempt to get an accurate picture of the German defenses, Konev's 2nd Ukrainian Front made the only effort on 1 February to dent the pocket, when the attacks in the Burty sector were repeated. These failed, however, even though the XI Corps was strained. Stemmermann reported that casualties were about 300 men per day, and the supply brought in by air was insufficient to replace them. The losses were concentrated among the combat units, where the manpower situation was strained already before the battle began.[337]

While Gruppe Stemmermann remained at risk, 8th Army continued to exert pressure on von Vormann. Just before midnight, Speidel and von Vormann spoke on the telephone and von Vormann said that he could not carry out the strike north the following day. The long flank could not be covered and the collapsed bridge at Iskrennoye was a serious obstacle, exacerbated by the delay in getting bridging equipment forward.

Speidel insisted however: "The army is well aware of the situation, but the attack must under all circumstances continue, to establish connection with Gruppe Stemmermann. The 3rd Panzer Division is moving forward. There is no alternative."

"I could certainly thrust forward to XI Corps with my tanks, but then I would have to call them back, since I don't have the infantry to cover the long corridor that would be the result, and the tanks can not be left without infantry in the terrain."

"We know that, but it would be an important accomplishment if connection could be established, and a supply convoy could be sent into the pocket. Also it would mean that the enemy rear would be interrupted. Furthermore, it would have positive effects on the morale of the encircled soldiers."[338]

Speidel continued to emphasize that the mission assigned by the 8th Army remained, and that he regarded this as the last opportunity to assist the XI Corps. Von Vormann required the 3rd Panzer Division to cover his east flank, and Speidel said that the deployment of 3rd Panzer Division was von Vormann's decision. Von Vormann replied that he would make the final decision early in the morning.[339]

Time was pressing for von Vormann, but he could do little more than stand by as a spectator on 2 February, while the engineers worked hard to rebuild the destroyed bridge at Iskrennoye. Not only did the delay mean that Gruppe Stemmermann would be more exposed, but also the Soviet 5th Guards Tank Army would have more time in which to attack the German bridgehead, which was still only weakly defended. Before noon his fears were partly realized. Rotmistrov directed an attack towards the 11th Panzer's east flank, on the southern side of the Shpolka River. Von Wietersheim's division repelled the threat, but the attack was an ominous sign of what might come.[340]

If he were to advance north from the Iskrennoye bridgehead at 14.00hrs as planned, von Wietersheim needed reinforcements. These were on their way. The 3rd Panzer Division had been relieved by the 376th Infantry Division and had been marching toward its assembly area since 05.00hrs, but the muddy roads had caused delays.[341] Perhaps even more important to von Vormann was the 24th Panzer Division, which had been located near Nikopol, about 300 kilometers from Korsun, when it received orders to reinforce the XXXXVII Panzer Corps. Struggling on bad roads that had been weakened by the thaw, it had not only lost time, but also used up an inordinate amount of fuel and caused many of its vehicles to bog down or break down. Flying in a Fieseler Storch, von Vormann went to see how the division progressed. What he learned was not encouraging. The march had been troublesome from the beginning, but became progressively worse the closer to Korsun the columns came. In the evening the division began to cover the last part of its arduous journey, from Novo Archangelsk to Yampol.

Of the 192 vehicles in one of the Panzer grenadier regiments, 40 become stranded along the road, while the repair services had a very difficult time just reaching the vehicles that needed repair. As the tanks negotiated the mud, the fuel consumption rose alarmingly, forcing them to wait for replenishment.[342]

At 12.00hrs Wöhler arrived by aircraft at von Vormann's command post, where he also met Hans Mikosch and Wend von Wietersheim. They discussed the situation and Wöhler learnt that so far only a provisional bridge with a maximum capacity of 10 tons had been constructed. Equipment for a K-Bridge would soon arrive, but such a bridge could only support 24 tons and would not carry a Panther. In fact, within the entire army area there was no J-Bridge equipment available, a type that had a capacity of 60 tons.[343]

Von Vormann's complaints about the exposed flanks were also confirmed. On 1 February the Soviet forces had quickly noted that the German attack had begun, and soon countermeasures were initiated. In particular these were directed at the flanks of the German attack force. Nevertheless, Wöhler still insisted that the attack should proceed to the encircled corps.[344]

Before he left, Wöhler reprimanded von Vormann. Wöhler was very disappointed with the previous day's discussions and told von Vormann that his reports on the situation must be clear and precise, and that there should be no debate. The army was in no position to give missions covering several days. Von Vormann should not complain about the missions he received, rather he should focus on keeping his divisions together instead of splitting them up. Currently, everything was about breaking through to Stemmermann, thus flank protection should be kept as thin as possible.[345]

Obviously Wöhler was very disappointed with von Vormann, but in fairness it must be said that the problems the XXXXVII Panzer Corps' commander saw were very real. At the same time, Wöhler seems to have felt a responsibility to help Gruppe Stemmermann by whatever means possible.

On the following day, Wöhler admitted that an attack to the north from the bridgehead was futile. By that time the K-Bridge had been built, allowing Panzerz IVs and StuG IIIs to cross the river, but since Panthers made up half von Vormann's tank strength, the bridge was insufficient. The fact that there was no available bridging equipment capable of taking the weight of a Panther was hardly von Vormann's fault, as no such equipment was available in Wöhler's entire army.[346]

Around 12.00hrs, the 3rd Panzer Division began to assemble southeast of Iskrennoye, but it had to fend off counterattacks on its right flank while on the march. In any case, bridge construction at Iskrennoye required more time than expected, partly because of Soviet fire directed at the area where the bridge was to be constructed. Von Vormann would have to wait one more day before advancing from the bridgehead.[347]

The 376th Infantry Division received two battalions with replacement personnel on 2 February. Often it was the lack of riflemen that set the limit on how wide a frontage the divisions could cover, and by this addition of new soldiers, the 376th Division could widen its front, thereby enabling 320th Division to take over the sector held by the 14th Panzer Division, which in turn became free for von Vormann to use. The 14th Panzer Division was weak, but nevertheless it was an added asset.[348]

Along the frontline of the pocket, little remarkable happened on 2 February. At Kvitki, the Germans continued to press on, but made slow progress. Similarly the Soviet attempts at cutting off Olshana persisted, but made little progress, although heavy fighting continued near the sugar factory between Olshana and Verbovka, where civilians had sought refuge in cellars and buildings. Civilians were often reluctant to leave their homes, which is understandable, but which meant that they were often wounded or killed by fire aimed at soldiers.[349]

Far in the north the Soviet 27th Army intensified its attacks, after having probed the front line on the previous day. The northernmost point of the pocket was at Sinyavka, and from there to Pilyava in the southeast, Soviet forces crossed the Rossava River and established a bridgehead more than ten kilometers wide and a few kilometers deep. This threat again caused Lieb to scramble forces from various sectors. Late in the evening he decided that there had to be a retreat from some front sectors, notably by pulling back from the Dnepr.[350]

Morale Inside the Pocket

The main idea with encirclements was to put the enemy units at a disadvantage, which would cause them to fight less effectively due to, for example, supply shortages. Ideally the surrounded soldiers would consider the situation hopeless and surrender after little or no resistance. Indeed, the morale of the enemy soldiers had been a tempting target long before the encirclement battles. In the interwar period there seems to have been a rather strong belief in the effectiveness of propaganda, both for peacetime purposes and in war. A surrounded force might be particularly susceptible to such efforts, and the Red Army tried to convince the surrounded German soldiers that they should surrender rather than continue fighting.

At Stalingrad a number of high-ranking German officers had been captured and some of them had been convinced to cooperate with their captors. The first sign of their activity at Korsun was a gas mask box found by German troops during a local counterattack. It contained a letter from General Korfes, who had commanded the 76th Infantry Division when it was destroyed at Stalingrad. The discovery was soon followed by Soviet artillery firing propaganda shells, containing a call for surrender from the "Free Germany Committee," which consisted of German officers captured at Stalingrad. So far the propaganda effort was meager, but the Germans were soon to see more attempts to convince them of the futility of resistance.[351]

In any case, the encirclement itself was a very clear threat to the Germans, and many precautions were taken as a result of the situation. Meiser was ordered to collect diaries, letters, and money and burn them, to ensure that everything was fully destroyed. He was happy to have sent his diary home just before it was too late, but still he kept a small note book, to record at least something of what was to transpire over the following days. It was actually forbidden to make such notes when inside a pocket, but Meiser disregarded the ban. Instead he concentrated his energy on collecting money and eventually rounded up more than 60,000 Reichsmarks. This impressive amount of money was useless inside the pocket and was duly burned.[352]

As no ammunition remained for the howitzers in the battalion, Meiser belonged to, its name was changed from IV./Art.Rgt. 389 to Kampfgruppe Stelzner, after Major Stelzner, the battalion commander. The lack of ammunition meant that a considerable part of the manpower of the battalion was combed out to form infantry, while the remaining soldiers had the task of caring for the howitzers and safeguarding them.[353]

Since little information trickled down to the rank and file inside the pocket, rumors and wild schemes became prevalent. The soldiers hoped, correctly, that there would be a relief attempt from the outside, but knowledge about how well it progressed was scarce. Some of Meiser's comrades suggested to Lieutenant Sorajewski that they should try to break out themselves, to approach the relief force coming from the south. Sorajewski turned them down, stating that such an attempt had little or no chance to succeed, and would amount to leaving the other surrounded soldiers in the lurch.[354]

Von Vormann's Counterattack Continues

The thaw had continued and the ground became progressively muddier, which made the original timetables too optimistic. Lieb had intended to attack Kvitki on 3 February, but first he had to report that the attack had to be delayed at least to 13.00hrs, then he had to postpone the attack to the following day. The regrouping required far more time on the muddy roads than had been initially assumed.[355]

It was naturally easier to attack if the forces were already in position, but still by no means easy. In the north the 27th Army continued to widen the bridgehead taken on 2 February, reaching Kopnatovo and Martynovka. Also the protracted struggle for the sugar factory between Olshana and Verbovka continued. Still, the Germans held on to Olshana, and a corridor to the rest of Gruppe Stemmermann, but their position remained exposed, especially as Soviet units managed to penetrate into Verbovka.[356]

The air supply operation continued, as did the Soviet efforts to shoot down the slow German transport aircraft. Corporal Grotjohann accompanied a transport aircraft that flew from Uman to Korsun on 3

February. The first flight went well. His aircraft landed at Korsun, unloaded the cargo, filled the aircraft with wounded, and took off to land safely at Uman. Soon it was loaded once more and another attempt to fly to Korsun was made. This time Soviet fighters appeared, but the pilot evaded them and landed safely on Korsun's airstrip. Grotjohann was sent to help repair another aircraft, but it was not easy to reach it in the thick mud. Grotjohann recalled that for almost every step he took, he had to pull his boots up from the sticky mud on the way to the other end of the airfield. When he had almost made it, Soviet IL-2 ground attack aircraft strafed the airfield. On the flat airstrip there was not much cover to be found from the numerous small bombs. Many of them seemed to be duds and Grotjohann remained unscathed when the IL-2s disappeared. He went back to the aircraft he had arrived with, only to find that the crew had just counted 80 hits from machine gun bullets. The left landing wheel had been shot through and no replacement wheel was available at Korsun. There was no alternative but to wait until a new wheel could be brought to the strip by air.[357]

Grotjohann and the rest of the aircrew were invited to sleep at the hospital, where they received dinner and straw sacks to sleep on. All of them slept very well, except a sergeant who spent the night hunting lice. In the morning he claimed 96 kills. Grotjohann and the rest of the aircrew had to wait another day before the spare wheel arrived. The mud made the work to fit the new wheel arduous, but the poor flying weather saved them from strafing Soviet aircraft while working to make the return flight to Uman possible. Finally everything was ready, and with relief Grotjohann and the rest of the aircrew could safely fly to their main base.[358]

On 3 February, von Vormann's troops began to attack from the bridgehead at Iskrennoye, but it was difficult to compensate for the delay caused by the collapsed bridge. With temperatures around 5°C the thaw continued, but the sky was relatively clear. Mud on the ground was little hindrance to aircraft that had taken off, and when the Germans detected Soviet troop concentrations near the bridgehead air strikes were directed on them.

Rotmistrov chose to continue the probing attacks on the east flank of the German salient at Iskrennoye. Using infantry from the 49th Rifle Corps and tanks from 29th Tank Corps, the Soviets harassed the 11th Panzer Division. The action was quite modest and von Vormann realized that it would be better to wait until 4 February for the main event, which would then coincide with the III Panzer Corps opening up its offensive. The 24th Panzer Division was assembling at Yampol, some 30 kilometers south of Zvenigorodka, and would be available to von Vormann on 4 February, giving him a stronger hand to play with. Indeed, without the 24th Panzer Division his task would probably have been impossible.[359] Von Vormann's attacks had been quite weak thus far, but meanwhile a stronger counterattack was being prepared in the sector of 1st Panzer Army, further west.

CHAPTER 11

Hube Assembles a Relief Force

Preparations for Operation Wanda

The first major combat unit sent to the staging area for the relief attempt by 1st Panzer Army was the 17th Panzer Division. The decision was taken on 28 January and the division was expected to be ready for action in the VII Corps' area early on 31 January.[360] It was to be followed by the 16th Panzer Division, the SS-Panzer Division Leibstandarte Adolf Hitler and the heavy Panzer regiment Bäke.[361] These units were to disengage during the night of 30 January and to be ready to attack on 3 February.[362]

On 29 January, 1st Panzer Army ordered that 16th Panzer Division and the units of Breith's III Panzer Corps should be the first to disengage, followed by the SS-Leibstandarte.[363] In the meantime the weather deteriorated. The thaw caused the ground to become muddy so that it was necessary to improve roads and bridges to cope with the traffic resulting from the movement of several Panzer divisions. Since many 45-ton Panthers and 57-ton Tigers were to participate, bridges had to be constructed or reinforced to carry 60-ton loads.[364]

Engineers and construction units subordinated to 1st Panzer Army were ordered to end their current work and begin to transfer to the VII Corps' area. The army engineer commander (Armee-Pioniere-Führer) was sent to VII Corps to coordinate the work. At least two roads were required that could support heavy tanks moving toward the assembly area. Rail transport was to be used for most of the tracked vehicles of the relief force, but since the railroads did not cover the full distance to the staging area, some road travel would still be necessary.[365]

In addition to its own resources, 1st Panzer Army was to be reinforced by the 1st Panzer Division, commanded by Major-General Richard Koll. The division had been engaged in action with the 4th Panzer Army, but was still a strong unit. It would not be available on 3 February, however, when the relief operation was planned to commence, since the distances involved were considerable. Also, the whole division could not immediately be relieved. Consequently, it created a strong advance detachment to be taken out of the line almost immediately and moved to the VII Corps' area. Breith must have realized that he could not count on committing the 1st Panzer Division as a complete division. Rather he would have to expect to use Koll's division in a piecemeal fashion.[366]

In the meantime, the XXXXVI and III Panzer Corps finished off the Soviet forces encircled in the Balabanovka area. The Germans claimed that Operation Watutin was a considerable success. It was reported that 701 Soviet tanks and assault guns had been destroyed or captured, together with 213 artillery pieces and 468 anti-tank guns.[367] While such claims are often exaggerated, it should be noted that German claims were usually relatively close to the mark,[368] so it is reasonable to conclude that Soviet equipment losses were indeed considerable.

The planned relief operation was given the code name "Wanda" on 30 January. Formal orders were issued to the III Panzer Corps, in which it was given the mission of attacking in the direction of Medvin–Koshevatoe, with the purpose of establishing contact with the encircled German forces and destroying the Soviet forces in the area between the VII Corps and 8th Army. The corps was to attack at dawn on 3 February, using the 16th and 17th Panzer Divisions, plus the heavy tank regiment Bäke. The SS-Leibstandarte was expected to be available one day later. The 198th Infantry Division would be temporarily subordinated to Breith's Corps, as might the 34th Infantry Division.[369]

In the war diary of 1st Panzer Army for 30 January it was noted that the operations section of the staff assembled in a separate room for a short celebration of the 12th anniversary of Hitler's assumption of power in Germany, through which "the Reich regained its freedom. The highest mission for every soldier was to defend this freedom with all his powers in the proud feeling of connection with the struggling German nation."[370] It should be noted that this passage in the war diary is a very rare example of anything with political connotations in the documents.

While the planning and preparations proceeded, the front was relatively serene on the VII Corps' sector after 28 January. The Red Army conducted nothing greater than local battalion-sized attacks, and the Germans were content with holding their positions.[371] At this time the front line ran along the Pobodna–Shubennyi Stav axis.

The condition of the roads had deteriorated considerably due to the warm weather, making it difficult for the III Panzer Corps to complete its assembly in the prescribed time. Early on 2 February, 1st Panzer Army suggested that the attack be postponed one day, a proposition that III Panzer Corps found very welcome. After lunch, Field Marshal von Manstein arrived at the 1st Panzer Army staff and he concurred with the proposal. The III Panzer Corps suggested that it should employ its forces not mainly according to tactical and operational factors, but rather in response to the prevailing conditions of the muddy terrain. It was necessary to select attack directions where it was possible to advance without getting completely stuck in mud. The corps was given full freedom to choose attack routes.[372]

On 3 February the thaw continued. No combat actions took place across the 1st Panzer Army front, except for sporadic exchanges of artillery fire and some patrol activity. While the III Panzer Corps struggled to get its units in position for the attacks that were to be launched within less than 24 hours, the weather and Soviet pressure on the two encircled corps caused a change to the plan. Originally it was intended that the III Panzer Corps should attack northward, cross the Gniloi Tikich River, proceed to Medvin and then turn east, toward the surrounded corps. Due to the muddy ground, which would make the attack proceed more slowly than originally anticipated, and the fact that the pocket had been compressed, it was decided that the III Panzer Corps should turn right almost immediately after crossing the Gniloi Tikich River.[373]

In mud and slush, the soldiers of the III Panzer Corps struggled to get their equipment in position. The force that managed to assemble for the attack was fairly strong. Although the 17th Panzer Division had only 15 Panzer IVs operational, these were complemented by eight Panthers and eight Tigers from the heavy Panzer regiment Bäke. All of these were available on the morning of 4 February in time for the attack. The 16th Panzer Division had 40 Panthers, 26 Panzer IVs, and 18 StuG IIIs operational. Also the s.Pz.Abt. 506 with eight combat-ready Tigers

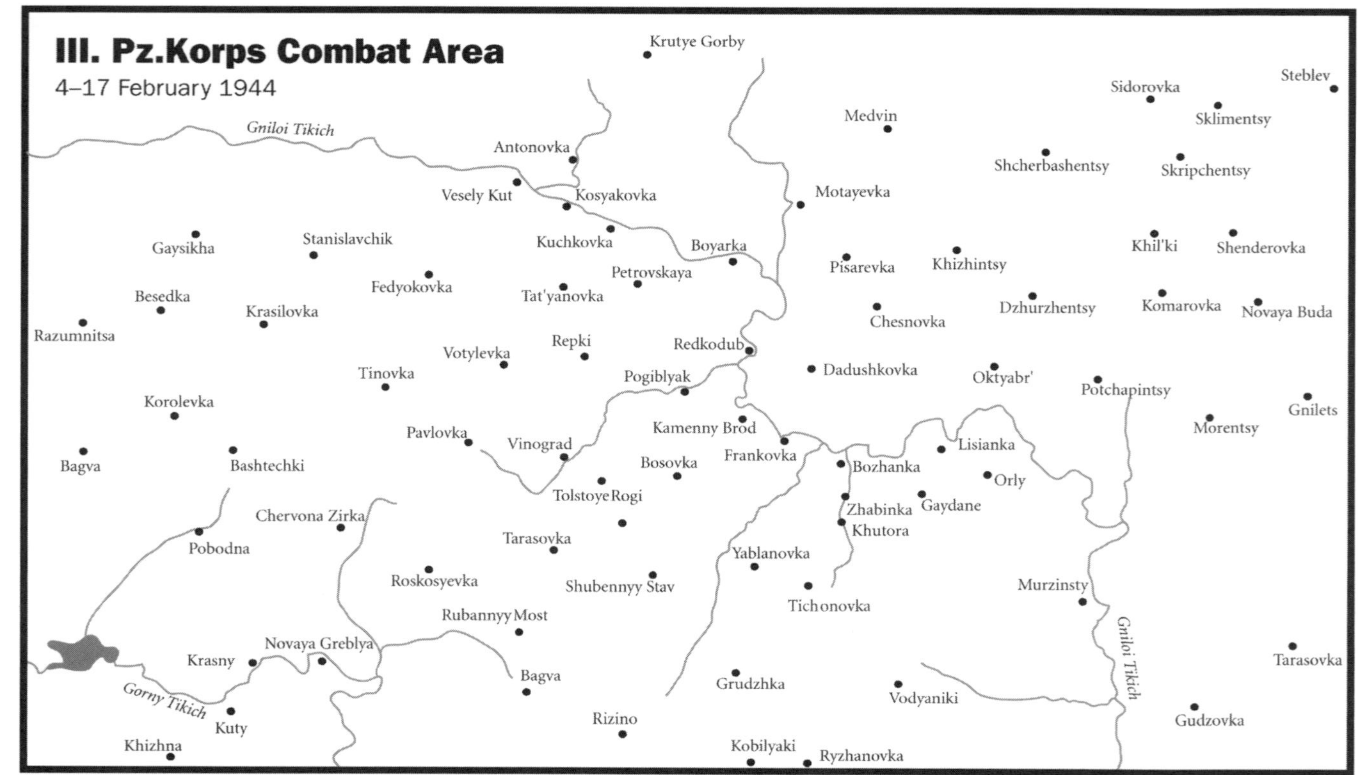
III. Pz.Korps Combat Area
4–17 February 1944
Krutye Gorby
Gniloi Tikich
Antonovka
Vesely Kut
Kosyakovka
Medvin
Sidorovka
Steblev
Sklimentsy
Shcherbashentsy
Skripchentsy
Motayevka
Gaysikha
Stanislavchik
Kuchkovka
Boyarka
Pisarevka
Khizhintsy
Khil'ki
Shenderovka
Fedyokovka
Petrovskaya
Tat'yanovka
Besedka
Krasilovka
Chesnovka
Dzhurzhentsy
Komarovka
Novaya Buda
Razumnitsa
Repki
Redkodub
Votylevka
Tinovka
Pogiblyak
Dadushkovka
Oktyabr'
Potchapintsy
Korolevka
Gnilets
Kamenny Brod
Morentsy
Pavlovka
Vinograd
Frankovka
Lisianka
Bagva
Bashtechki
Bosovka
Bozhanka
Orly
Tolstoye Rogi
Zhabinka
Gaydane
Chervona Zirka
Khutora
Tarasovka
Pobodna
Yablanovka
Roskosyevka
Shubennyy Stav
Murzinsty
Tichonovka
Rubannyy Most
Novaya Greblya
Krasny
Gniloi Tikich
Tarasovka
Bagva
Grudzhka
Vodyaniki
Gorny Tikich
Kuty
Rizino
Gudzovka
Khizhna
Kobilyaki
Ryzhanovka

was attached to the 16th Panzer Division and the StuG.Abt. 249 was attached to the 17th Panzer Division. The assault gun battalion was quite weak, though, as on 1 February it only had three StuG IIIs operational. Thus the corps had 126 tanks and assault guns available at the beginning of Operation Wanda.[374]

For the Germans in 1944 this was a pretty impressive attack force, especially considering that more than half the tanks were Panthers and Tigers. Furthermore, the corps knew that the 1st SS-Panzer Division and the 1st Panzer Division would soon arrive and be able to provide flank cover. Thus the initial attack force could concentrate on pushing forward.

As we have seen, the second prong of the German relief attack, the XXXXVII Panzer Corps, had not been in a position to assemble such a strong force. In fact, von Vormann made little specific preparations, but instead he was forced to try to create an attack force from the midst of a defensive battle. This attack force had already been committed on 1 February and had largely got stuck. Von Vormann's hopes rested with the 24th Panzer Division, since it was the only new force he could commit. However, the 24th Panzer could not be regarded as a fresh division up to strength. It was short of 4,168 officers and men and had only 17 Panzer IVs and 14 StuG IIIs operational, plus a few command tanks.[375]

As a result, the German rescue attempt depended on Breith's corps, which not only possessed a much stronger armored punch, but had recently concluded a successful encirclement, which may well have boosted morale. In addition, the formations had been given a few days free from combat. Admittedly the soldiers had had to struggle in the mud to reach the assembly areas, but most likely that was preferable to the horrors of combat. In comparison, von Vormann had only one advantage—a shorter distance to the pocket. This mattered little if his forces proved insufficient to break through the Soviet defenses.

Ju-87 Stuka divebombers are taking off from a German airfield while Me-109 fighters are parked in the foreground. Both types were in use from the beginning to the end of the war. (SCANPIX)

CHAPTER 12

Breith's III Panzer Corps Attacks

Hermann Breith was a very experienced Panzer commander. In October 1941 he had taken command of the 3rd Panzer Division and led it during the battles outside Moscow in the harsh winter of 1941–42. He continued to command the division during the Kharkov battle in May 1942, where a quarter of a million Soviet soldiers were captured. In the summer offensive that followed, Breith led the 3rd Panzer Division when it advanced into the Caucasus until he left the division on 1 October 1942. Three months later, he was given command of the III Panzer Corps, a position he held, with the exception of a few short periods, until the end of the war. During his combat career he had seen many difficult actions, especially the retreat from the Caucasus and the extrication through the Rostov bottleneck in January–February 1943. All these actions had been very important, but the task given him in February 1944 was the most important and difficult thus far, as was signified by the forces given to him. At the beginning of the offensive, his units had 105 tanks and 21 assault guns.[376] Sixty-four of the tanks were Tigers or Panthers.

The number of tanks available at the outset of the offensive was impressive for the German army at this stage of the war. Breith also knew that both the 1st and 1st SS-Panzer Divisions were on the way to reinforce his corps. He could count on them adding more than 150 operational tanks and assault guns to his initial force, of which more than half were Tigers or Panthers.[377] In fact, more than half of all Tigers and Panthers on the Eastern Front were either with Breith's corps, or on the way to it. These figures compared very favorably to the forces available to von Vormann, whose XXXXVII Panzer Corps only had 58 tanks and assault guns in running order on 4 February, with little prospect of being reinforced.[378] If Breith could not fight his way to the surrounded Germans, nobody would succeed.

According to the plan, the 16th Panzer Division, commanded by Major-General Hans-Ulrich Back, would attack from the line at Chervona Sirka– Poboika, via Tinovka, and establish a bridgehead across the Gniloi Tikich River in the Kosyakovka–Veselyy Kut region. From there it was to advance south of Medvin toward Morentsy. The 17th Panzer Division, commanded by Major-General Karl-Friedrich von der Meden, would jump off from the area north of Roskoshevka over Pavlovka and Votylevka, and take a bridgehead over the Gniloi Tikich River between Semenovka and Boyarka. From there it would proceed to Morentsy via the Lisyanka area.[379]

Soviet Opposition to Breith's Forces

The main Soviet formation blocking the projected German attack was the 104 Rifle Corps, with the 58th and 133rd Rifle Divisions. However, there were reserves available. The 6th Tank Army was deployed between Vinograd and Zvenigorodka, with many of its combat units behind the line. This meant that the army was deployed east of the direction along which the Germans were going to attack.[380]

We have seen that the 5th Mechanized Corps was withdrawn from 6th Tank Army after Zvenigorodka had been liberated. On the evening of 3 February it returned and took up positions between Zhabinka and Yablonovka. The 5th Mechanized Corps was not only a valuable asset that could prove useful if the Germans struck, it was also a boost to the morale of the men in 6th Tank Army to get back the unit that had been absent for almost a week.[381]

It is unclear why the Soviet 6th Tank Army was deployed east of the German attack axis. Possibly it just remained there as a result of its advance towards Zvenigorodka. Whether Soviet intelligence identified the German attack direction or not is unclear. The deployment of 6th Tank Army could be interpreted either way. It may have been placed along the Vinograd–Zvenigorodka axis to block a German advance along the most direct route to the two encircled corps. But it may also have been placed there to be in position to launch a flanking attack against a German attack along the Roskoshevka–Boyarka axis. The latter interpretation has its problems though; in particular the fact that the muddy roads would make it time consuming to move the 6th Tank Army west if it were to strike the Germans in the flank.

To the Germans, it appeared that the attack on 4 February had come as a surprise to the Red Army.[382] This fact suggested that at least the direction of the attack was not the one anticipated by the 1st Ukrainian Front. Another possibility is that the Soviet commanders hoped that their holding attacks would prevent the Germans from forming an attack force, but such hopes were not fulfilled. The Soviet General Staff Study claims that already on 31 January the 1st Ukrainian Front had reached the conclusion that the Germans intended to attack in a northeasterly direction from the Russalovka–Rubannyi Most–Pavlovka sector.[383] Such statements should be taken with a grain of salt, but if true, it is not surprising that the 6th Tank Army was in fact deployed east of the German attack axis.

The German Push Toward the Gniloi Tikich River, 4–5 February

The morning of 4 February was sunny, except for a few clouds. The temperature was well above freezing and the thaw continued. The thaw did not augur well for the Germans, but the attack could no longer be postponed, especially as nothing suggested that colder weather could be expected within a day or two. The only alternative was to launch the attack according to the plans already made.

At 6.00hrs the 17th Panzer Division, including the heavy Panther and Tiger tanks of Panzer Regiment Bäke, jumped off. The Soviet defense consisted mainly of infantry and antitank guns protected by minefields. Despite Soviet flanking fire, the Germans broke through the first and second Soviet defense lines. Panzer Regiment Bäke was concentrated on the left. It managed to cross the railroad and by 10.00hrs it had penetrated into Pavlovka. Progress was slower on the right wing, where infantry attacked through a partly forested area and fighting continued there well into the afternoon. After taking Pavlovka, Bäke continued the advance in a north-northeast direction and joined forces with Pz.Rgt. 39, which had advanced west of Vinograd. Together the two tank formations broke into Votylevka at 12.45hrs.[384]

Half an hour later than 17th Panzer Division, at 06.30hrs, the 16th Panzer Division began its attack. Strong Soviet resistance was initially

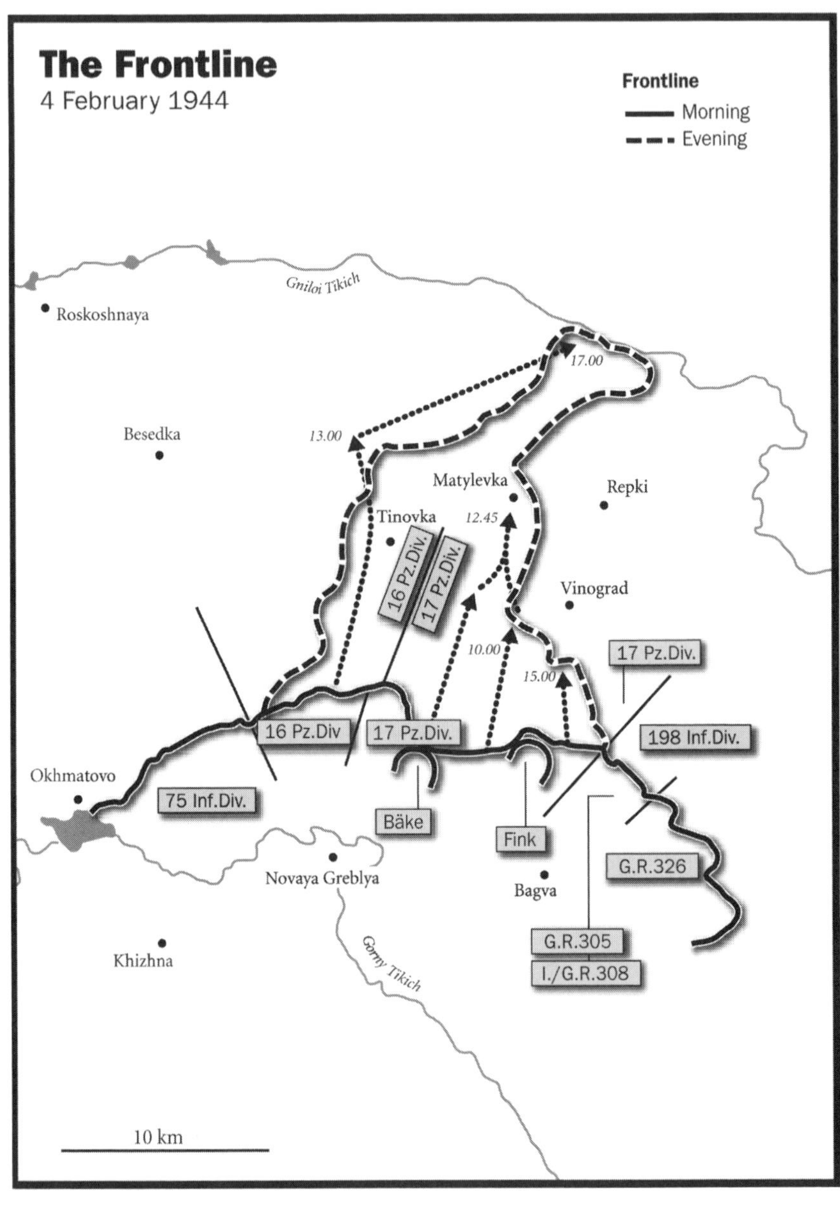
The Frontline
4 February 1944
Frontline
Morning
Evening
Gniloi Tikich
Roskoshnaya
17.00
Besedka
13.00
Matylevka
Repki
Tinovka
12.45
16 Pz.Div.
17 Pz.Div.
Vinograd
10.00
17 Pz.Div.
15.00
16 Pz Div
17 Pz.Div.
198 Inf.Div.
Okhmatovo
75 Inf.Div.
Bäke
Fink
G.R.326
Novaya Greblya
Bagva
G.R.305
I./G.R.308
Khizhna
Gorny Tikich
10 km

encountered, especially when the division crossed the railroad embankment a few kilometers south of Tinovka. Despite enemy opposition and ground softened by thaw, the tanks battled on, captured Tinovka and reached hill 229.8 (two kilometers east-southeast of Stanislavchik) by 13.00hrs.[385]

The two Panzer divisions had made good progress so far, but the 198th Infantry Division had less success with its flanking attack. It did not manage to take advantage of the breakthrough made by 17th Panzer Division. Strong Soviet frontal opposition was supported by flanking fire from Shubenyy Stav and hill 243.4. The fighting raged for hours until noon, when the Soviet defenders began to evacuate their positions. They retreated to the Vinograd–Bosovka–Yablonovka area and the Germans took the low hills between Vinograd and Shubenyy Stav (240.6 and 236.9). The 198th Division prepared to attack the new Soviet positions, but this could not be done before the artillery had replenished its ammunition.[386]

While the 17th Panzer Division had been very successful before noon, it made far less progress in the afternoon. The infantry found it difficult to follow the tanks and the latter had to halt at Votylevka. Not until 15.00hrs could the infantry begin to clear Pavlovka, and allow Reconnaissance Battalion 17 to begin to open the road to the tanks in Votylevka. The 107th Infantry Regiment, subordinated from 34th Infantry Division, approached the southern outskirts of Vinograd, with the mission of covering the right flank of 17th Panzer Division.[387]

The 16th Panzer Division made better progress during the afternoon. After a short break, the tanks that had reached hill 229.8 turned towards Fedyukovka, which was soon taken. This opened the way to Kosyakovka on the Gniloi Tikich River, and at dusk the tanks broke into the southern parts of Kosyakovka. Unlike the 17th Panzer Division, Back's division had managed to push its infantry forward much faster. At the end of the day, it had reached almost as far as the tanks. Possibly this was due to the fact that the 16th Panzer Division was much better supplied with armored half-tracks for the grenadiers.[388]

Vatutin reacted to the German attack by moving elements from the 6th Tank Army west. They were unsuccessfully employed in the defense of Pavlovka but also, and with greater success, against the German 198th Infantry Division. In addition, the 2nd Tank Army, which had been in the 1st Ukrainian Front reserve, was moving to counterattack the III

Panzer Corps. The 2nd Tank Army did not arrive in time to take part in the fighting on 4 February, but it assembled in the Goisika–Razumnitsa area during the night of 4 February.[389]

The Germans also had reinforcements moving up. Kampfgruppe Huppert was the first element of 1st Panzer Division expected to arrive, and it was decided that this formation would join 198th Infantry Division and try to take the high ground between Shubenyy Stav and Bosovka. The intent was to open a supply route over Frankovka/Bushanka to use for the later stages of Operation Wanda. Further to the west, the lead elements of the 1st SS-Panzer Division had reached the Novaya Greblya–Krasny area early in the afternoon, but it could not be assumed that they would be ready for action before 10.00hrs on 5 February.[390]

The 1st Panzer Army was disappointed that the 17th Panzer Division had not reached the Gniloi Tikich River, and requested that a night attack be made by the division. It was also proposed that the division could be supplied by air. Orders were issued to 17th Panzer Division at 22.00hrs. However, General von der Meden, 17th Panzer's commander, disagreed, since the area in front of the division was covered by mine fields and an attack through those during darkness would lead to heavy casualties. Furthermore, due to the catastrophic condition of the roads, the division was already low on supplies. Von der Meden recommended that the division move out at first light and try to reach a bridgehead over the Gniloi Tikich River at noon on 5 February. The III Panzer Corps concurred.[391]

While these discussions took place, the 16th Panzer Division cleared Kosyakovka, but found that the bridges over the Gniloi Tikich River had been blown up. The bridge column was stuck in mud south of Tinovka and could not be expected to arrive in Kosyakovka before dawn. The 16th Panzer Division was ordered to retain its hold on Kosyakovka but attack to the east with most of its strength. It was hoped that it could find a river crossing at Boyarka. Still, the efforts to create a crossing at Kosyakovka continued.[392]

The condition of the roads became a matter of paramount importance. During the night of 4 February, only incomplete replenishment of ammunition and fuel could be made for Heavy Panzer Regiment Bäke.[393] Any major effort by the regiment was inconceivable. Also, the regiment had to pull back its elements in Votylevka during the night, since they were running out of supplies, allowing Soviet forces to reoccupy parts of Votylevka. Reconnaissance Battalion 17 counterattacked from the west and managed to limit the Soviet gains.[394]

The partial loss of Votylevka upset Breith, and he ordered the commander of 17th Panzer Division to explain why Bäke had pulled out of Votylevka without orders to do so. Von der Meden replied that the muddy roads had made the supply of the advanced elements impossible and that there was no alternative. Ernst Merck, chief of staff of the III Panzer Corps, told von der Meden to make every use of the local population, carts, and animals to haul supplies forward. The 1st SS-Panzer Division was also told to make "ruthless" use of civilians to improve the roads.[395]

How difficult the mud was to deal with can best be illustrated by the fact that even the lead elements of 1st SS-Panzer Division, still not in contact with the enemy, could not be resupplied. Only the tracked vehicles had made any reasonable progress, but most of the division was stuck with its wheeled vehicles in the deep mud. Similarly, the 17th Panzer Division reported that only tracked vehicles could negotiate the roads. There was not much Hube could do for the moment, but at least the 1st Panzer Army offered a construction battalion to improve the roads in the III Panzer Corps' sector. Had not fog made air supply impossible the Luftwaffe might have furnished Breith's troops with fuel and ammunition, but for the moment that solution had to be disregarded. Hube could do little more than exhort the III Panzer Corps to do its utmost to get the attack rolling again.[396]

The Panthers, with their wide tracks, had quite low ground pressure, despite their weight. Of all German vehicles they were among the best suited to negotiate the mud. Still, on the road just west of Krivets, where most of the Leibstandarte tried to move forward, the mud was so deep that even Panthers got stuck. When its 700hp engine could not move the 45-ton tank forward, the men had to work extremely hard. The 1st SS-Panzer Division seems only to have been able to send one battle group, Kampfgruppe Heimann, into action on 5 February. This consisted of 12 assault guns with infantry from SS-Panzer Grenadier Regiment 1 riding on them. At noon it moved out from Novaya Greblya to the Tinovka area, where hard fighting was raging.[397]

Vatutin intended to add to the German difficulties. During the night 40th Army, 6th Tank Army, and the recently arrived 2nd Tank Army had assembled to counterattack. The 40th Army attacked in a southeasterly direction from the line Goisika–Olshanka–Konela, with the aim of taking Kuty, Antonovka, and Krachkovka. Kravchenko's 6th Tank Army had the mission of attacking from the Ryzhanovka–Popovka area, to reach Krachkovka, Popuzhintsy, Pashchevoe, and Sokolocha. The plan was far too ambitious and the attack failed to make substantial progress.[398]

Since supplies could not be brought forward to the spearheads of 16th Panzer Division, the projected advance toward Boyarka had to be postponed and the positions held on 5 February. Instead the Red Army initiated counterattacks. Units from 6th Tank Army in the east and 40th Army in the west attacked the flanks of the 16th Panzer Division, whose positions protruded far into the Soviet lines. The Soviet attacks met with some success and the German spearhead in the Kosyakovka region was cut off. Further strong Soviet attacks were directed against Tinovka.[399]

Supply difficulties also beset Heavy Panzer Regiment Bäke and the 17th Panzer Division. The division already had its reconnaissance and antitank battalions fighting in the outskirts of Votylevka. When the engineer battalion arrived in Pavlovka, the division sent Kampfgruppe Fink (I./Pz.Gren.Rgt. 40 and II./Pz.Gren.Rgt. 63), supported by a few of Bäke's Tigers, to Votylevka. After hard fighting most of Votylevka was recaptured by the Germans, but Soviet forces still held the eastern parts.[400]

Before noon the 198th Infantry Division sent one battalion, strongly supported by artillery and rocket artillery, to attack toward Vinograd. It managed to penetrate the town and clear the southern parts. The rest of the division faced strong Soviet resistance and made little progress.[401]

At about 16.00hrs Panzer Regiment Bäke had been sufficiently replenished with fuel and ammunition to send elements to reestablish connection with the 16th Panzer Division's spearhead. A major tank battle ensued. According to German estimates, about 40 Soviet tanks participated, of which 31 were claimed to have been knocked out. Such claims should not be taken at face value, but the figures do suggest that hard fighting took place. Just after midnight Bäke's tanks accomplished the link up, but the road conditions remained as difficult as ever.[402]

Revised Plans, 6–7 February

It was clear to the Germans that, while the opening of the offensive had been a success, by the second day the attack was bogging down. At about 18.00hrs on 5 February, Colonel Ernst Merck, Chief of Staff of the III Panzer Corps, discussed the matter with Major-General Walther Wenck, Chief of Staff of 1st Panzer Army. Merck argued that the corps could count on succeeding in attacking toward Bushanka; that is, in an eastern direction rather than the more northerly direction pursued thus far. The disadvantage with this solution was that it would cause the formation of yet another narrow protruding section of the front, which would require more precious troops to cover it. Nevertheless, Merck favored this option and wanted to use the Kampfgruppe Huppert and 17th Panzer Division to attack Repki. This would enable the corps to get a wider and more secure basis from which to continue its attacks, whether it continued according to the original plan or shifted its attack direction almost 90 degrees. Wenck said he would take up the matter as soon as possible with Hube, and within less than an hour Wenck reported that Hube had agreed.[403]

Hube was also in contact with von Manstein. When the original plan was conceived, the ground conditions were much better, and this kind of thaw in early February was not something the German forces had experienced during their previous winters in the Soviet Union. Hube was quite confident that his Panzers could roll over any Soviet defense consisting of infantry and antitank guns.[404] Given the battles his forces had fought during the second half of January and the first day of Operation Wanda, this confidence was possibly justified.

However, the immense supply difficulties and the fact that the roads were almost impassable to wheeled vehicles (which made up the majority of the armored units on both the German and Soviet side), meant that the punch of the Panzers was to little avail. Von Manstein considered that it might be worthwhile to try to attack in another direction, since the slow progress on 5 February had made it possible for the Red Army to shift its tank and mechanized corps to block the III Panzer Corps in its present direction. Hube replied that 1st Panzer Army had already considered this, but the loss of time that would be associated with a regrouping would be unacceptable. With the present condition of the roads, a regrouping that would normally take a few hours required days.[405]

Von Manstein's assumption that Soviet reinforcements were moving up was correct. As we have seen, Vatutin had already sent Bogdanov's 2nd Tank Army to attack the western side of the wedge that the III Panzer

Corps had driven into the 1st Ukrainian Front. Further units arrived on 6 February. The 202nd and 340th Rifle Divisions moved up on the western side of the protruding spearheads of the III Panzer Corps, while the 32nd Antitank Brigade occupied defensive positions north of the Gniloi Tikich River. Vatutin led the reinforcement race, even though the two rifle divisions were not immediately ready to go into action. The 2nd Tank Army was ready for combat, however, and had been tasked with counterattacking in the Tinovka area on the morning of 6 February, but the attack failed to make any progress.[406]

Another aspect to consider for Hube and von Manstein was the meager progress the XXXXVII Panzer Corps had made. Its low strength meant that there was little prospect of improving von Vormann's chances for success. Consequently the original idea, to encircle the Soviet 5th Guards and 6th Tank Armies in the vicinity of Zvenigorodka

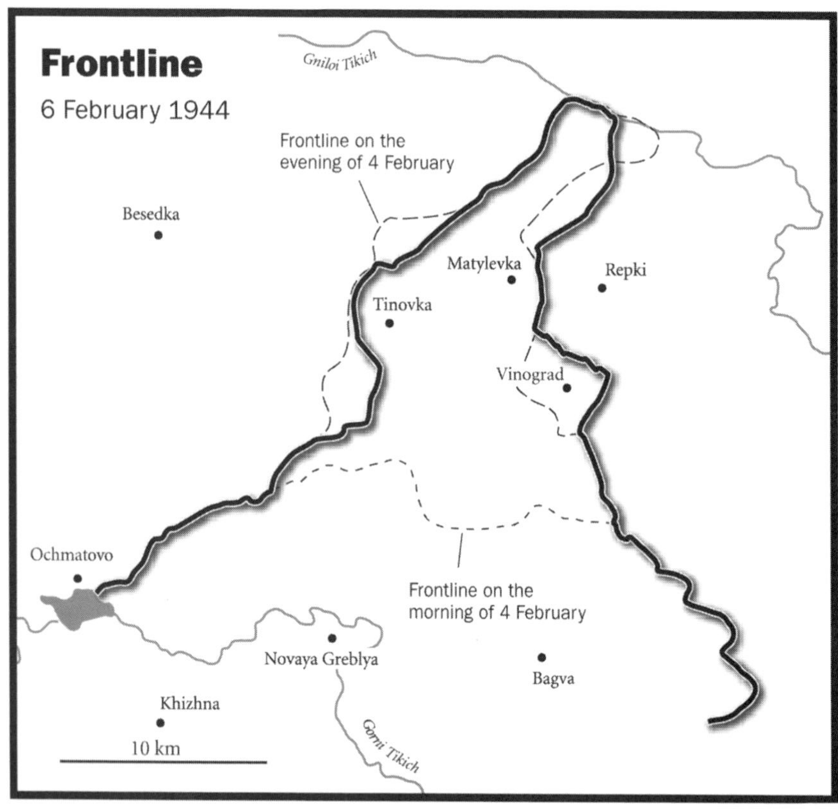

at the same time as the two encircled German corps were rescued, had little prospect of succeeding. Accordingly, it might be better to use the III Panzer Corps to attack along the shortest path to make contact with Gruppe Stemmermann. Given the difficulties of supplying the spearheads of the III and XXXXVII Panzer Corps, it might have been better to use an attack route that was as short as possible.

While the debate raged in the higher echelons of German command, the struggle continued at the front. For most of 6 February, heavy Panzer Regiment Bäke was engaged with covering the tenuous link to the 16th Panzer Division's spearhead at Kosyakovka. It did what it could to bring supplies forward to Kosyakovka, where the Germans had been very low on supplies for a while. The mud was very deep. 17th Panzer Division reported that the roads were barely passable even for tracked vehicles. Even halftracks got stuck.[407]

The mud not only hampered progress toward the battlefield, it also made evacuation of the wounded difficult. Near the front neither side had the capacity to take good care of the seriously wounded, who were supposed to be evacuated to the rear where they could receive better care. The field ambulances fought an unequal battle with the mud to reach the medical facilities. The wounded endured long and agonizing journeys, and the duration of each journey meant that fewer wounded men could be evacuated per day. Some of the wounded waiting to be evacuated died before they could be moved to the ambulances.[408]

On 6 February Kampfgruppe Huppert, the first elements of the 1st Panzer Division, joined the German attack. Reinforced with some engineers and assault guns, plus a battalion of infantry from 198th Infantry Division, the Kampfgruppe attacked from Pavlovka at 09.45hrs and broke through the Soviet positions west of Vinograd. Soon the church in Vinograd was reached and during the afternoon the town was cleared. A Soviet counterattack followed, but it was repelled.[409]

The 34th Infantry Division and elements from the Leibstandarte assumed responsibility for the defense around Tinovka, which was hotly contested. A Soviet attack forced its way into the northeastern parts of Tinovka, but units from the 16th Panzer Division restored the situation. The latter division was also able to send one of its Panzer grenadier regiments toward Tatianovka and the northern half of the village was taken, despite determined Soviet resistance.[410]

Further elements of the 1st Panzer Division were arriving. Initially these were used to secure the southeastern part of the flank of 1st Panzer Army. The sub-units had been unable to maintain an even advance rate in the mud and so arrived piecemeal. For example, many of the tanks of the Panther battalion had arrived, but not much else. Thus the battalion as a whole was not combat ready, although its 51 Panthers were technically fit for action.[411]

The chiefs of staff of German formations and higher command echelons took a very active part in the decision-making, both during prior planning and the conduct of operations. On 6 February, Lieutenant-General Hans Speidel, Chief of Staff of 8th Army, visited the staff of 1st Panzer Army to discuss the ongoing battle. Both Wenck and Speidel agreed that the two armies should make their main efforts near the junction between the two armies, in the general direction of Morentsy. Also it was agreed that the two surrounded corps would break out toward Morentsy. Time was pressing, as it was estimated that from 9 February supplies would almost be depleted within the pocket.[412]

The conclusions from the discussion were immediately sent to Army Group South, and very soon a new order was received at 1st Panzer Army and 8th Army. Essentially, it contained what Wenck and Speidel had suggested. The III Panzer Corps was to destroy the Soviet armored formations in front of the Gniloi Tikich River and then proceed northwards along the Bushanka–Lisyanka–Morentsy road to link up with Gruppe Stemmermann. The 8th Army should attack with at least two Panzer divisions over the Iskrenoe–Yerki–Olshana line to prevent enemy forces in the Zvenigorodka–Kasazkoe area from interfering with the III Panzer Corps' operations. Gruppe Stemmermann should be made ready to break out toward the west and southwest.[413]

These orders showed that the original grand design had been reassessed. The more limited, but still vital, task of rescuing Gruppe Stemmermann remained. Given the quagmire on the ground, the poor flying weather, and the low strength of the XXXXVII Panzer Corps, there was probably no alternative.

For much of 7 February, Soviet attacks forced the III Panzer Corps to assume a defensive position. The 34th Infantry Division managed to hold on to its positions from Tinovka southward. Soviet pressure on the 16th Panzer Division spearhead at Kosyakovka was very strong and forced the Germans back. On the other hand, the 16th Panzer Division captured all of Tatianovka, which had been partly taken the previous day. The Leibstandarte managed to move elements forward, to create a screening line between Tinovka and Kosyakovka, which ensured that the 16th Panzer Division would be supplied for the following day.[414]

On the night of 6 February, Soviet forces penetrated into Votylevka, forcing the 17th Panzer Division, together with heavy Panzer Regiment Bäke, to spend the morning of 7 February clearing the village. At the beginning of the afternoon, Bäke attacked toward Repki but his Panzers soon collided with a Soviet tank unit and neither side made any progress.[415]

On the eastern flank of the salient, the III Panzer Corps had driven into the Soviet lines. 198th Infantry Division and Kampfgruppe Huppert tried to clear Vinograd and capture the high ground east of the village. There was some disagreement between the 198th Infantry Division and the III Panzer Corps on how to use the Kampfgruppe Huppert. The corps wanted Huppert to bypass Vinograd from the south and continue toward the high ground east of the village. However, at 09.20hrs the 198th Infantry Division suggested that the Kampfgruppe should attack through Vinograd and from there proceed east. Too much time would be lost by regrouping Huppert's forces. Wenck reluctantly assented, but clearly pointed out that this was not a proper way to use mechanized units. However, due to Soviet pressure, neither the 198th Division, nor Kampfgruppe Huppert began any attack before noon. At 13.55hrs the III Panzer Corps again ordered that the attack to the east had to be made. The attack finally got rolling at 16.45hrs, with two infantry battalions, one infantry company, and a tank company, but an hour later the 198th Division reported that the tanks were stuck only 500 meters east of Vinograd, and the infantry was engaged by stubbornly defending Soviet forces. German progress on this sector remained unimpressive.[416]

During 7 February the mud continued to be the dominant factor in the battles. On the German side, the roads were so bad that in many places only tracked vehicles could negotiate them. The countryside was a morass. The tanks of the 1st Panzer Division's Panther battalion remained in the Tshernaia Kamenka–Ivanki area, since no supplies could be brought to them. Soldiers sometimes had to throw off their boots and continue barefoot. However, in the evening temperatures fell slightly and during the night there was a light frost. If this continued, the ground would improve.[417]

The Red Army also experienced considerable problems due to the mud. Second Lieutenant Murashkin was a veteran from 1941, but late in 1942 he had been sent to an armor school at Rybinsk, where he stayed for more than a year. In December 1943 he was sent to Chelyabinsk, which was a center for tank production. Murashkin was not allowed to see anything of the tank production factories. The reason he had been sent to Chelyabinsk was to follow a replacement unit to the front. On 25 January, together with green tank crews and 32 T-34s, he entrained for a journey toward Kiev. Eventually, the trains unloaded at Belaya Tserkov on 4 February, where an officer from 21st Guards Tank Brigade waited and informed the men that the tanks and their crews, including Murashkin, constituted the 2nd Battalion in the 21st Guards Tank Brigade. The unit was ordered to proceed by road to Tolstoye Rogi, a journey of approximately 80 kilometers.

The T-34 had a good reputation for its ability to negotiate difficult ground conditions, but the relatively short journey was a real challenge. Of the 32 tanks, no less than 19 got stuck in the mud or suffered mechanical breakdowns. Early on 8 February, 13 T-34s arrived at the front and were immediately sent into battle. Murashkin and the other tankers received virtually no information on the situation, the enemy, or neighboring units. The only advice they received was that American tanks were used in some of the Soviet units, hence it would be better to be cautious when firing. With such poor guidance it is perhaps no surprise that Murashkin was taken prisoner on the same day as he arrived at the front.[418]

The Effects of Supply Difficulties

Kampfgruppe Huppert was more successful during the morning of 9 February than the previous day. By 08.45hrs it had taken Tolstoye Rogi, which also enabled the 308th Infantry Regiment of 198th Division to take the ground between Vinograd and Shubenyy Stav. This was as far as they got, however, as Soviet counterattacks forced them on the defensive.[419]

For the 17th Panzer Division and heavy Panzer Regiment Bäke, the day began with a Soviet attack toward Votylevka, just before 07.00hrs. It was repelled, and three hours later the Germans attacked. At 11.30hrs, the Germans entered Repki, but it took more than two hours to secure the village. The attack was intended to advance toward Kharchenkov, on the Gniloi Tikich River, but this had to be cancelled due to lack of fuel.[420]

Similarly, the 16th Panzer Division had to call off its attack on Petrovskaya due to lack of fuel. Fuel shortages were common for the Germans on this day, almost entirely due to the impassable roads. In the evening, Wenck asked both the 16th and 17th Panzer Divisions if the lack of notable results during the day was due to enemy resistance or insufficient supplies. He also wanted the divisions to consider whether the slow progress had given the Red Army time to reinforce to such an extent that there was no purpose in continuing the current attacks. Finally Wenck asked the two divisions to consider whether it would be better to regroup and attack from the Rizino area toward Lisyanka, even though he estimated that such a regrouping would require two days given the poor condition of the roads.[421]

Both 16th and 17th Panzer Divisions were of the opinion that the lack of progress during the last days was caused by the supply problems and the catastrophic condition of the roads. They considered that the new proposal from the corps was the most suitable solution.[422]

The main forces to be committed in the new direction were the 16th and 17th Panzer Divisions plus the heavy Panzer Regiment Bäke, which had also been the main attack force on 4 February. In addition, the main body of the 1st Panzer Division would be in position for the new attack, while the Leibstandarte would cover the northern flank.[423]

As the German commanders saw it, there were four advantages with the new direction of attack. First, the northern flank would be shorter and could partly be based on rivers and streams and would thus require fewer forces. Second, the supply routes would be shorter. Third, the three attack divisions would converge on the Gniloi Tikich River, where Soviet resistance was expected to be strong. Fourth, the protection of the south flank would be simplified, since the three Panzer divisions would attack through the 198th Infantry Division, which would thus be freed for flank protection.[424]

Still, the main problem remained. The divisions and the corps' staff unanimously regarded the difficult road conditions, and the resulting supply problems, as the main bottleneck thus far and not the strength of the opposition. However, the decision was made to see what results were achieved on 9 February before fully committing to the new proposal.[425]

The hopes for any significant progress on 9 February were soon dashed. During the night of 8 February, the Red Army launched several attacks against Kampfgruppe 79 (formed around Pz.Gren.Rgt. 79 of 16. Pz.Div.) in Tatianovka. The Germans managed to hold the village, despite running low on ammunition and being rendered immobile due to lack of fuel. Just after 08.00hrs the 17th Panzer Division reported that it could not attack before noon due to supply difficulties, and soon the 16th Panzer Division reported that it also had to postpone its attack. Effectively, this decided the issue, and at 12.35hrs both divisions were ordered to reassemble in the Rubannyi Most area as soon as possible.[426]

The final phase of the relief operation was about to begin. However, while Breith had endeavored to cross the Gniloi Tikich River, dramatic events had taken place within the pocket and on the sector held by von Vormann's corps.

CHAPTER 13

8th Army, 4–10 February

Hitler Interrupts the Planning, 4 February

At 20.00hrs on 3 February, Nikolaus von Vormann received orders to shift 11th Panzer Division further west, to make it possible to combine 11th and 24th Panzer Divisions for a concerted attack on 5 February. Thus its two strongest divisions would be combined, which probably was the best solution for XXXXVII Panzer Corps, given the intention to push forward to the pocket.[427]

However, far away decisions were made that ruined the idea of combining 11th and 24th Panzer Divisions. Hitler had suddenly decided to send the 24th Panzer Division south, to Army Group A. After its long and difficult struggle along the muddy roads, it had reached its assembly area 30 kilometers south of Zvenigorodka, only to turn around 180 degrees and move to southern Ukraine. The news reached 8th Army at 02.50hrs on 4 February, when an order from Army Group South arrived. Aside from the decision by Hitler, the new order contained instructions that von Vormann's corps should be used to tie up Soviet armor, to prevent it from being shifted to block Breith's attack.[428]

At least there was some logic in the new order from Army Group South. With the loss of a major component for the planned attack, it was quite reasonable to reduce the level of ambition. Wöhler and Speidel, however, did not want to accept the situation. At 09.00hrs Speidel spoke with Busse and declared that neither he nor Wöhler could understand the decision to send 24th Panzer Division back south, considering the combat situation as well as the weather and the condition of the roads. Busse did not need any persuasion since he was of the same opinion. In fact, Army Group South had already objected to the order, but to no avail. Minutes later, Wöhler had to inform von Vormann about Hitler's decision.[429]

Von Manstein and Busse still worked to change the decision. The 6th Army was to receive 24th Panzer Division, according to Hitler's order, but after a brief discussion the army declared that it did not need the Panzer division, what it needed was more infantry. Von Manstein and Busse conceived the idea that the 2nd Parachute Division, currently employed by the 8th Army near Kirovograd, should be sent to 6th Army. At 10.50hrs Busse called Speidel to ask how 8th Army regarded the proposal. Speidel almost immediately spoke with Wöhler, who needed very little time to make up his mind. Within minutes Speidel could again speak with Busse and say that 8th Army had no objections. The risks involved in pulling out 2nd Parachute Division had to be accepted in order to keep 24th Panzer Division in von Vormann's corps.[430]

Von Manstein and Busse immediately sent the proposal to OKH and nervously waited for a reply. The proposal seemed quite reasonable, especially as 6th Army had declared that it did not need the 24th Panzer Division. However, at about 13.00hrs they were informed that the proposal had been declined. The 24th Panzer Division should be sent to 6th Army. Obviously von Manstein and Busse were very disappointed, but there was little they could do, except convey the bad news to 8th Army.[431]

Hitler's role in German military operations has been a subject of intense discussion since the end of World War II. It has been argued that his influence, directly as well as indirectly, was a serious disadvantage, leading to many unnecessary disasters for the German forces. Unsurprisingly the German field commanders, in their postwar writings, have been proponents of this idea. On the other hand there have been those who have argued that the German generals exaggerated the role of Hitler, in order to avoid taking responsibility for their own military disasters in the field. In the case of the Korsun battle, the records clearly support the view that the field commanders were hampered by disadvantageous decisions made by Hitler. The back and forth movement of the 24th Panzer Division is a good example. After having reached its assembly area on 4 February, it needed almost a week to travel back to Nikopol, where the battle was almost over when it arrived. It spent most of its time moving back and forth on muddy roads, between two battles, without making any particularly useful effort in either. The records clearly show that the field commanders realized that too much valuable time would be lost by shifting 24th Panzer Division back and forth, but they were overruled.

Inside the Pocket, 4 February

Whatever von Manstein, Wöhler, von Vormann, and the other officers may have thought about it, they had to adjust to the new situation created by the diversion of 24th Panzer Division. For the moment there was probably not much else to do beyond carrying on with the order already given to von Vormann, that XXXXVII Panzer Corps should prevent Soviet tank units, in particular Rotmistrov's 5th Guards Tank Army, from shifting west where they could block Breith's III Panzer Corps.

Wöhler had been trying to do his utmost to assist the two encircled corps, but with the departure of 24th Panzer Division his ability to help them was seriously reduced. Perhaps this contributed to his decision to fly into the pocket, together with Major Bittl who had already made the journey a few times. Wöhler informed the commanders that he would land at Korsun at about 16.30hrs and asked Stemmermann and Lieb to meet him there.[432]

Inside the pocket, the XXXXII Corps continued attacking toward Kvitki, but progress was slow. One prong reached the southeast part of Kvitki, but most of the fighting occurred inside Kvitki, where fierce house to house fighting took place. Even though this was not the main attack in the effort to reestablish contact, it was yet another indication that each stage of the attack was taking longer than had been anticipated, which of course was very serious in the difficult situation. At 11.20hrs the previous day it had been estimated that XI Corps only had supplies for another two days.

The XXXXII Corps was somewhat better off, with supplies for three or four days. Gruppe Stemmermann was completely dependent on the supplies provided by air, but bad weather could easily render flights impossible. However, the Luftwaffe was able to fly in or drop 160 tons of supplies on 3 February, while 2,800 wounded men had been flown out between 27 January and 3 February. The supply situation nevertheless remained precarious. At 10.50hrs on 4 February, Stemmermann reported that the daily ammunition consumption was 180 tons, despite strict rationing.[433]

With supplies running lower and lower, time was also running out for the Germans. But it was not only the problem of supplies that prompted the Germans to act as quickly as possible. The Soviet commanders were not sitting idle and waiting for the Germans to act. Reinforcements had been moved to the Korsun area. The Kirovograd battle had been costly for the 2nd Ukrainian Front, but during the two weeks that had passed since, it had been possible to replenish the units. Konev had sent some of these to take part in the Korsun battle. On 4 February, tanks as well as infantry and artillery arrived from 5th and 7th Guards Armies. Tank and antitank assets were particularly important, both for compressing the pocket and for blocking the German relief attempts. Among the units that arrived on 4 February were 27th Tank Brigade from the 7th Guards Army and the 34th Antitank Gun Brigade from 5th Guards Army.[434]

In the afternoon, Wöhler and Bittl climbed aboard the aircraft that would take them to Korsun. Clouds obscured the sky, but posed no hindrance to take off. The pilot set course toward the Korsun airfield and initially the journey was uneventful. As they approached Korsun, however, the situation changed. The flashes and noise from exploding Soviet antiaircraft shells forced the aircraft to turn back. Wöhler was disappointed, but it was decided that Major Bittl would try again later in the evening.[435]

German Defense of the Iskrennoye Bridgehead, 4 February

With the order to send back 24th Panzer Division, von Vormann had few options left. His tank strength was low. The 11th Panzer Division was strongest with 21 Panthers (including the attached I./26 battalion) and eight assault guns (including attached assault gun units). The 3rd Panzer Division had 12 Panzer IVs, while the 14th Panzer Division had five Panzer IVs and four StuG IIIs. The 13th Panzer Division only had four Panzer IVs and one Panzer III. There were also four command tanks and artillery observation tanks within the units. Thus the entire corps, with its four nominal Panzer divisions, had only 59 tanks and assault guns available, about one third of a single, full strength Panzer division.[436]

The units possessed many more tanks and assault guns, but they had either bogged down in the mud or were at workshops waiting for repairs, and there was little prospect of quickly raising the number of operational tanks. Indeed, the Germans would probably have to be content with keeping the number of operational tanks at the current level.

The infantry situation was not much better for the Panzer divisions. Even though a division might have fairly high manpower strength, this did not necessarily translate to high infantry strength. The overall manpower ranged from 8,942 men (for the 14th Panzer Division, whose Kampfgruppe von Breese was inside the pocket and unable to report) to 12,464 (for the 11th Panzer Division).[437] However, the infantry combat strength was only 724 for the 3rd Panzer Division. The other three Panzer divisions, 11th, 13th, and 14th, had 1,100, 1,420, and 551 infantry respectively.[438]

With these meager resources von Vormann not only had to cover a sector almost 40 kilometers wide, from Listopadov, north of Novomirgorod, to the Iskrennoye bridgehead, but also to attack toward the pocket. Even though the original scope of the attack had been reduced, it was still not an easy task. Probably Wöhler thought along similar lines, because the reprimands he had subjected von Vormann to during the preceding days seem to have ceased, at least for a while.

The weather remained troublesome. Olaf Ehlers noted in his diary on 4 February: "After the rain yesterday, it is sunny and so warm today that we can lay down on the rapidly drying straw and sleep in the open. In the night it was a bit cold. The snow has become thin and in many places naked ground was exposed. In the field works we have found cockchafers and we have also seen the first violets blossom."[439] The first signs of spring were joyful to behold, but they were definitely a hindrance to operations, and were indeed likely to prove transitory.

Despite the weakness of his divisions and the filthy weather, von Vormann decided to attack Vodianoe and Lipyanka, using both 3rd and 11th Panzer Divisions. While von Wietersheim's Division attacked Vodianoe from the northwest, Lang sent part of his division toward Vodianoe from the southwest. By surprising the enemy, the spearheads of the 11th Panzer Division captured Vodianoe. Simultaneously, the remainder of the 3rd Panzer Division approached Lipyanka. However, assisted by minefields, the defending Soviet forces were able to hold their positions along the stream flowing through Lipyanka.[440]

The 13th Panzer Division retained the bridgehead at Iskrennoye, but in the afternoon Soviet concentrations were observed to the east and northwest of Iskrennoye, and they seemed to be preparing for an attack on the bridgehead. The Germans called for Stukas to attack the concentrations. According to German estimates the air attacks were quite effective, but it must, as always, be remembered that such estimates are difficult to make. In any case it was important for the XXXXVII Panzer Corps to hang on to the bridgehead. The advance to the north was still planned to go ahead, according to an order from 8th Army at 17.45hrs, and the bridge over the river was to be reinforced to carry 60 tons as soon as possible.[441]

Initial Plans for the Breakout, 4 February

In the evening, Major Bittl again attempted to fly to Korsun. This time he was luckier, perhaps aided by the radio beacon at Korsun, and at about 19.00hrs he landed safely on the air strip. He soon met General Lieb and Colonel Gaedke, and handed over instructions to them. These included two alternatives for a breakout. The first, which was be initiated on the code word "Frühlingsglaube," called for a concentration southwest of Gorodishche and a breakout toward the bridgehead at Iskrennoye.

The second alternative, to be initiated when the code word "Betriebsausflug" was received, involved concentrating the XI Corps in the Kvitki–Glushki–Derenkovets area. From this staging area together, with XXXXII Corps, it should thrust toward Morentsy, eventually to join up with III Panzer Corps. In either case, permission had to be obtained from Hitler.[442]

Preparations for the two alternatives could be initiated immediately, in the hopes that Hitler could be persuaded to accept one of them. The shortage of supplies demanded that an urgent decision be made. Major Bittl had been fortunate to reach Korsun by air. Some 19 Ju-52s, loaded with ammunition, had been forced to turn back to avoid Soviet fighters. Another attempt to fly supplies in would be made during the night, but when Bittl departed it was too early to tell if the attempt would be successful.[443]

That evening XXXXVII Panzer Corps received orders to support the efforts by III Panzer Corps and Gruppe Stemmermann. By employing mobile tactics, von Vormann was to attract Soviet units. Von

Vormann was to be especially active on his west wing, but he was not to neglect opportunities to strike from Iskrennoe towards Vyasovok. The bridge at Iskrennoe should be reinforced to be able to take 60-ton vehicles.[444]

During the night of 4 February, the air supply operation continued. The VIII Air Corps reported that 81 tons were flown into the pocket and 259 wounded were brought out by the returning aircraft. This was barely enough to sustain Gruppe Stemmermann. During the night the 8th Army quartermaster had flown to Korsun. He confirmed that the ammunition available would only be sufficient for three days, at most. Some consolation could be found from the fact that nearly 3,000 wounded had been flown out so far, but there were approximately 300 soldiers who became wounded each day. There was every reason to continue with the air supply operation, but the weather was threatening to shut it down. The air strip at Korsun was not hardened, and the mud made it very soft. It might soon prove impossible to land and take off. Parachutes for supply drops were not immediately available, but had to be acquired somehow.[445]

The gravity of the situation was clear to von Manstein and his chief of staff, Busse. At 09.05hrs Busse informed Wöhler that perhaps Army Group South would, on its own responsibility, give orders to Gruppe Stemmermann to break out. To let the two corps remain in the pocket to succumb to the Soviets was out of the question. However, first an attempt was made to get permission from OKH. Such a decision was usually difficult to get and involved waiting for hours, perhaps days. When 1st Panzer Army reported that the III Panzer Corps was stuck in mud, and was not receiving even the most essential supplies, the need for a quick decision seemed even more urgent.[446]

Von Vormann Attacks Lipyanka, 5 February

On the XXXXVII Panzer Corps' sector there were no major battles while both sides suffered from the mud, but still they persisted with local attacks. Rotmistrov's 5th Guards Tank Army conducted several minor attacks on the German bridgehead at Iskrennoe, but all were repelled. It seems that they were not intended to do more than harass the Germans there. Von Vormann, on the other hand, concentrated his efforts at the Lipyanka area, where elements of 3rd and 14th Panzer Divisions had been tasked with capturing the town.[447]

The eastern prong of the attack was led by the commander of Panzer Regiment 36. He commanded a Kampfgruppe consisting of one tank battalion, one armored infantry battalion, and one battalion with SP howitzers, a fairly common composition for a German Kampfgruppe. The mission was received at 06.00hrs and included clearing Lipyanka and capturing the high ground north of the village. The Panzer grenadiers were delayed due to the mud, but eventually the attack began, and at about 10.00hrs the first Soviet positions were reached. Initially visibility had been very poor, but at this moment it cleared, with the sun appearing behind the advancing German tanks. Suddenly a mine exploded beneath an assault gun, putting it out of action, although nobody in the vehicle was injured.[448]

The Panzer grenadiers had lagged behind the tanks and assault guns, and some of the crews had to jump out from their vehicles to fight with pistols and hand grenades. The first Soviet infantry positions were cleared in close combat. Soon Soviet antitank guns opened fire from hill 205.2, but as the Germans had the sun behind them, the Soviet gunners were blinded. The commander of III./Pz.Rgt 36, Major Bernau, decided to take advantage of the situation and ordered his tankers to roll over the enemy position, which they did without suffering any losses.[449]

By noon the Germans had reached the outskirts of Lipyanka. The Panzer grenadiers received orders to proceed into the village to clear it, while the tankers provided covering fire. However, the attack did not get rolling and Major Bernau decided to proceed with his tanks and assault guns. They entered the village through a fruit garden, and fierce fighting soon erupted. A mortar shell landed on 2nd Lieutenant Rheinbaben's tank, and he was seriously wounded by the explosion. Soon thereafter Major Bernau was wounded, and Lieutenant Müller assumed command of the battalion. Despite these losses the Germans cleared the southern half of the village and took defensive positions for the night. Supplies arrived in timely fashion in the evening, as did two previously damaged Panzer IV tanks that had been repaired.[450]

The western prong of the attack on Lipyanka consisted of elements from 3rd Panzer Division. Encountering weak resistance, the Germans advanced into Lipyanka from the west, but they were too late to prevent the Soviet defenders from blowing up the bridge over the small river in the northern part of the village. The 3rd Panzer Division was therefore unable to assist the Kampfgruppe from 14th Panzer Division to take the northeastern part of Lipyanka. Still, most of the village was in German hands and the booty taken included nine 12.2cm guns, 10 antitank guns, and two T-34s.[451]

At 17.15hrs Speidel and Wenck spoke over the telephone about the situation. Wenck emphasized the supply difficulties caused by the mud. The III Panzer Corps was helplessly stuck, while simultaneously fighting strong enemy tank formations. Speidel also focused on supplies, pointing to the fact that the air supply operation so far had barely been sufficient to keep Gruppe Stemmermann struggling, and with the deep mud on the airfield at Korsun, it seemed that the situation would only deteriorate.[452]

Kampfgruppe Haack

Neither 1st Panzer Army nor 8th Army had any reason to hope for reinforcements. 1st Panzer Army still struggled to get 1st Panzer Division and 1st SS-Panzer Division into the frontline, but after these two division had arrived, nothing more was scheduled. 8th Army had nothing to expect, but perhaps it mattered little, since more units would aggravate the already difficult logistical situation. On the other hand, if the weather changed and the ground froze again, any reinforcements could prove valuable. In 1944, though, the Germans were hard pressed on many other sectors of the Eastern Front, and it was difficult to find reinforcements. In contrast, because of their overall superiority of numbers, it was comparatively easier for the Red Army commanders to redeploy units. Konev continued to move units from other sectors of his front, to insert them into the battle at Korsun. On 5 February the 41st Guards Rifle Division was detailed to move toward the pocket.[453]

Without such resources at their disposal, the Germans were forced to resort to more desperate methods to scramble units. Many soldiers from the encircled units had been on leave when the Soviet pincers closed. Some of these had returned from leave and had arrived outside the pocket, only to learn that their parent units had been surrounded. These soldiers became the nucleus of a new Kampfgruppe, which was to be led by Major-General Werner Haack.[454]

Haack could use his artillery division staff,[455] which received a number of different units, in addition to the returning soldiers from 57th Division, 72nd Division, 88th Division, 389th Division, and Korps-Abteilung B, which was used as infantry. He was also instructed to include three artillery battalions, three Nebelwerfer battalions, and one engineer battalion in his Kampfgruppe. Five assault guns that belonged to 228th Sturmgeschütz Battalion were also allotted to Haack. The latter unit was actually part of Gruppe Stemmermann, but some of its damaged assault guns had been in workshops outside the pocket and five of them had by this time been repaired.[456]

A unit of the kind Haack had to lead lacked cohesion, as it had no prior training as a unit. This was particularly apparent among the infantry unit, which was composed of soldiers who had little knowledge about each other. One of the most important factors behind the soldiers' ability to withstand the strain of combat seems to have been the connection they had developed to each other within a group of limited size. When they were thrown together in this manner, there was little or no time to develop such bonds. In fact, to send such improvised units into combat was counter to German ideas on what was important to develop effective combat units; but the situation was becoming desperate.[457]

Haack's mission at least partly reflected the disadvantages from which his formation suffered. He was ordered to secure crossings over the Shpolka River southeast of Zvenigorodka, and to cover the gap between 1st Panzer Army and 8th Army. His Kampfgruppe was to be prepared to receive XI and XXXXII Corps if they broke out. Since only weak Soviet units were present in the area south of Zvenigorodka, the mission did not seem unduly difficult and would not involve hard fighting, at least in the short term.[458]

Major Bittl continued to fly to the pocket and back. In the afternoon he reported to the 8th Army staff on Gruppe Stemmermann's situation. No dramatic frontline changes had occurred. The salient at Burty had been evacuated, but the thick mud made all movements very slow. It was just as difficult for the German soldiers to withdraw as it was for the Soviet soldiers to pursue them. Stemmermann reported that the great strain on the soldiers had pushed them to crisis point. The soldiers' exhaustion, coupled with the great losses among the officers, made actions slow both to initiate and to carry out. With fighting going on in daytime and regrouping taking place in darkness, there were few opportunities for the officers and men to sleep.[459]

The Evacuation of Olshana

The soldiers fighting at Olshana were in desperate need of sleep, but they could not hope that the coming night would offer them any rest.

The defenders, of whom the Estonian soldiers of the "Narwa" battalion made up a major part, faced an untenable situation and there was no alternative but to pull out. At 23.00hrs orders were issued for the evacuation of Olshana. Tanks were sent to receive the garrison when it had broken out. The tanks were indeed observed by the garrison late in the evening and the troops began to leave Olshana. Unfortunately a bridge broke under a heavily laden truck. The bridge was along the only road available to the Germans, and the withdrawal ground to a halt. An attempt was made to haul the most important items from the truck to the other side of the now collapsed bridge, but the work had hardly begun before Soviet machine gun fire raked the column. The trucks were visible against the lighter night sky, while the Soviet troops were concealed in the darkness. Soon some of the trucks caught fire, thereby further illuminating the German vehicles.

The only alternative remaining for the German soldiers was to run as fast as possible from the trucks and throw themselves into the ditches along the road. In the darkness it was not apparent, but as soon as they got into them, the Germans became painfully aware that the ditches were clogged with melting snow, mud, and water. Crawling through the slush the German soldiers reached their goal and the temporary safety of other units belonging to XI Corps. They managed to bring many of the wounded along, but the infantry's howitzers, the mortars, and other heavy equipment had to be left behind.[460]

The Soviet Attempt to Split the Pocket, 5–6 February

On the morning of 6 February the two German corps had been encircled for more than a week, but still they held a fairly large area. As long as the encircled forces could be supplied by air, the Soviet commanders had reason to fear that the operation would be prolonged. Perhaps they recalled the Stalingrad operation one year earlier, when the German 6th Army had held out for almost two and a half months before finally succumbing. Such a protracted operation was better avoided since it was likely to result in more casualties.

In addition, the Korsun pocket was tying up important elements of the Red Army that could better be employed elsewhere. The most important of these were Rotmistrov's and Kravchenko's tank armies, which were committed to defending parts of the outer encirclement ring. The tank armies had not been designed for such a task, but there were no other options available to Vatutin and Konev. If the pocket could be compressed, or even broken up, it was likely that the battle could reach a rapid conclusion. Even if the battle did not end more quickly, a compressed pocket would require fewer troops to cover, which would free up some of the forces currently holding the inner ring to relieve the tank armies at the outer ring. These were strong arguments favoring a continued and even intensified offensive against Gruppe Stemmermann. Finally, Konev and Vatutin had to consider the German relief attempts, especially those conducted by III Panzer Corps. If the pocket could be pushed north, the distance to cover would be greater for the German forces south of the encirclement ring.

Accordingly, during the night of 5 February, Konev issued orders to 4th Guards Army and 5th Guards Cavalry Corps to take Gorodishche, 20 kilometers southeast of Korsun. Selivanov, the commander of the 5th Guards Cavalry Corps, decided to attack toward Valiava, located on the road between Gorodishche and Korsun. If Valiava could be taken, a German withdrawal from Gorodishche would become much more difficult, especially with heavy equipment. There was the possibility not only of capturing Gorodishche, but also of inflicting considerable losses on the German XI Corps.[461]

Selivanov's Cossacks and elements of four rifle divisions from Smirnov's 4th Guards Army hit the junction between XI and XXXXII Corps when they attacked after dawn. Intense fighting ensued, as Lieb ordered that the road between Gorodishche and Korsun had to be held at all costs. He asked for the return of the Panzers from SS-Wiking, so that they could be used together with 72nd Division to halt the Soviet attack. To Stemmermann, it was obvious that the Soviet commanders intended to split the pocket into two parts. On 6 February the German soldiers prevented this from happening by offering stubborn resistance. The progress was much slower than the Soviet commanders had hoped.[462]

The question was how long this resistance could be maintained. The hard fighting caused ammunition expenditure to rise, and on 6 February very little could be flown into the pocket. Of the 19 Junkers aircraft that had taken off, only one landed at Korsun. Twenty Heinkels flew toward the pocket, loaded with canisters to be dropped, but none of them managed to drop their loads inside the pocket. The chief of staff of Luftflotte 4, Major-General Karl-Heinrich Schulz, issued a statement to the effect that the utmost had been done to keep the two surrounded corps supplied, but the atrocious weather made it well nigh impossible to fly in supplies. Indeed, Lieutenant-General Seidemann, commander of VIII Fliegerkorps, said when he met Speidel in the afternoon that a regular supply could not be expected, despite the best efforts of the air crews.[463]

The rift between the field commanders and the decision makers in Berlin became even wider. The OKH had not given permission to break out, as Busse informed Speidel over the telephone in the morning. In any case, the III Panzer Corps was still about 30 kilometers away from the pocket, too far for a successful breakout. Either that distance must be reduced or any attempted breakout would be a disaster. Still, Army Group South sent a written demand for permission to break out to OKH. Although Busse and Speidel still thought it was somewhat too early to order a breakout, their previous experience suggested that the OKH would take time in reaching a decision; it was better to have the permission first and then issue the orders at the appropriate moment.[464]

Meanwhile, the mud was causing supply difficulties for the Red Army. At 08.20hrs Colonel Reinhard, chief of staff of XXXXVII Panzer Corps, informed 8th Army that the enemy remained silent along most of the corps' front. At the sectors defended by 106th and 376th Divisions, there was no enemy activity worth noticing. The 320th Division was subjected to some local attacks, but these were relatively easy to repel. The 11th and 13th Panzer Divisions faced an almost silent opponent. To the Germans, it seemed very clear that lack of ammunition prevented the Soviet forces from doing much more. Only at Lipyanka did significant fighting take place, a continuation of the attack initiated by the German 3rd and 14th Panzer Divisions on 5 February. But even at Lipyanka the fighting was not intensive. The Soviet troops had already blown up most of the bridges, making it difficult for the Germans to attack the northern part of the village.[465]

Despite the fact that it would take several days for reinforcements to reach the battle area, Wöhler decided to try to make some additional forces available. By thinning out the line near Kirovograd, the 2nd Parachute Division could be pulled out and sent to the Korsun area. It was a risk to take the 2nd Parachute Division from LII Corps, but Wöhler had to accept the risk. He ordered the corps commander to relieve the division and to make it available for new missions.[466]

Anton Meiser: Village Fighting

In the poor weather the villages assumed a greater importance. The houses could provide shelter for the soldiers and offer them some chance to dry their clothes, which provided little protection against the chilliness when they were wet. Fighting often raged in or near the villages, something Anton Meiser, who had been relegated to an infantry role as his battery was out of ammunition, became involved in. Early on 6 February a runner brought an order from Major Stelzner, who was Meiser's battalion commander, ordering the unit to take a small village. Meiser had no confidence in Stelzner, who he regarded as a poor commander who spent most of his time sitting in a warm house a few kilometers from the front.[467]

Lieutenant Sorajewski, who still commanded Meiser's battery, was an officer for whom Meiser had the greatest respect, as he combined competence, courage, and good leadership skills. Sorajewski devised a scheme for taking the village, which actually only consisted of a few houses on each side of a road. Sorajewski's plan was a good example of how to combine fire and movement, and initially it worked very well. Covering fire was provided by a pre-positioned machine gun, as well as from the houses when they had been captured. One by one, the houses were attacked with hand grenades thrown though the windows. However, after taking four houses, Lieutenant Sorajewski was hit in the chest, just as he was about to take the fifth house. Meiser saw it happen and ordered the machine gunners to cease firing. He dashed to Sorajewski, only to find that his life could not be saved. Sorajewski's last words were "Tell my mother and give her my watch. And now please take the remaining buildings." A few minutes later all the buildings had been captured, but the loss of Lieutenant Sorajewski, who had been such a respected and beloved commander, made the success seem hollow. There was no time to mourn, however, as it became clear that Soviet soldiers were hiding in the cellars in some of the houses, alongside the civilians. These soldiers shot two of the Germans.[468]

German calls for surrender were met with silence. Meiser decided that one of the buildings with a cellar should be set on fire, which soon persuaded five men to come out with their hands held high. All were dressed in civilian clothes but had still been firing, a breach of the Geneva Convention. However, in the war on the Eastern Front, breaches of the Geneva Convention were far too frequent. It would not have been unusual if the Soviet "soldiers" had been summarily shot, but Meiser sent them to a nearby house where they could be guarded.[469]

The inhabitants of one cellar refused to surrender. Meiser heard that there were women and children present, before a shot was fired from the cellar. It was aimed at a corporal who approached the entrance. He replied immediately with a hand grenade, and screams followed the explosion. A woman with a wounded child came out, followed by two soldiers. Inside the cellar Meiser's men found the corpses of two soldiers and a woman.[470]

As the action was over, Meiser began to scribble a report. He decided to write a separate report about the death of Lieutenant Sorajewski, but first he tried to finish the report on the action. He concluded that the casualties, except for Sorajewski, amounted to two killed and one wounded. Just as he finished his report, rifle shots cracked. Both the machine gunners, who had raised their heads from cover out of curiosity, were hit in the head. Meiser had to add two more killed to the tally, a price he thought was far too high for the capturing of a village that was likely to prove untenable, as the Red Army controlled the high ground dominating it. Meiser's confidence in Stelzner diminished further when in the afternoon, after having buried the dead, he received orders to abandon most of the captured village. Furthermore, the order from Stelzner included a detailed plan on how the defense should be established and where the company command post should be placed. Meiser found the solution exceptionally unsuitable, as did the infantrymen with him. They wrote a message to Stelzner protesting the order, and sent it with the runner.[471]

Soon a second lieutenant arrived with the message that he was replacing Meiser as commander of the company Meiser had led since the death of Sorajewski. Meiser shrugged and let the officer take the responsibility of carrying out Stelzner's orders, even though he pointed out the risks inherent in the position the battalion commander had ordered. However, the latter remained in effect, and Meiser could only wait and see what would happen.[472]

Soviet Attempts to Split the Pocket, 7–10 February

On the morning of 7 February the quartermaster at the staff of 8th Army studied the supply situation for Gruppe Stemmermann carefully. He concluded that, at the most, the two corps' supplies would last until

9 February, but no longer. The critical factor was ammunition; the situation was better with food. General Lieb visited his old unit, the Korpsgruppe B, on 7 February to see how the soldiers fared. Afterward he noted in his diary that there was plenty of sausages, bread, sugar, and cigarettes, at least sufficient for another 10 days. The availability of food was a consolation, but it would not scare away the Red Army.[473]

It was very difficult to travel by car in the deep mud, and even the small Storch aircraft found it very risky to land on anything but hardened surfaces. Thus it was difficult for the commanders to meet each other. The railroad tracks were not affected by mud and Wöhler decided to take the train to meet von Vormann's staff. Wöhler wanted to take two of his Panzer divisions out of the line, move them to the extreme left wing of the corps, and attack in a northerly direction. As usual, von Vormann saw many difficulties with the plan, but promised to do everything possible to get the Panzers to the designated area[474]

Selivanov had hoped that his Cossacks would take Valiava on 6 February, but the stubborn German defense prevented them from reaching their aim as quickly as their commander wished. Early on 7 February Valiava finally fell, after hard house-to-house fighting. The Germans soon staged a counterattack to retake the village, but the results were mixed when darkness fell. Fighting continued to rage in the village during the night, and continued for some days. With the Red Army in Valiava, the threat of splitting the XI and XXXXII Corps was very clear to the German commanders. One option was to evacuate the positions around and southeast of Gorodishche, and concentrate the units of XI Corps in the area currently held by XXXXII Corps. Since it seemed far more likely that III Panzer Corps could get closer to the pocket than the much weaker XXXXVII Panzer Corps, it was realistic to assume that a breakout could be staged from the Shenderovka area. However, giving up the positions along the Olshanka River would also disclose German intentions to their opponents. Neither von Manstein nor Wöhler wanted to hand that knowledge to Konev and Vatutin.[475]

At this stage of the battle many Soviet units also experienced supply shortages. The mud was not the only cause. Since III Panzer Corps had reached the Gniloi Tikich River, important Soviet formations, such as the 6th Tank Army, found their supply lines much longer than they were previously. On 6 February the 2nd Air Army began to prepare for supplying the ground troops, and on 8 February the 2nd and 6th Tank armies, plus the 40th Army, began to receive supplies from Po-2 aircraft. The air supply operation continued for the remainder of the battle. Even though the quantities delivered were not as great as those the Germans received by air, the contribution was nevertheless valuable.[476]

At 09.30hrs on 8 February, Speidel went to Mal. Viski, where he met the chiefs of staff of XXXXVII Panzer Corps, 10th Panzer Grenadier Division, 14th Panzer Division, 106th Infantry Division, and 320th Infantry Division. Speidel outlined the forthcoming operations, which required some regrouping. The main effort was to be on the extreme left of XXXXVII Panzer Corps, where the 11th Panzer Division was to be committed. The divisions represented at Mal. Viski would take over longer defensive sectors to release von Wietersheim's division. Considerable reshuffling would take place, which inevitably would mean further struggle with the mud.[477]

An example of the difficulties caused by the mud is provided by the war diary of the Panzer battalion of 14th Panzer Division. The battalion had to rely on a flame thrower tank belonging to the regiment staff for its courier services. To get spare parts, a Panzer IV chassis was used to move them forward to the few tanks remaining for the battalion. Indeed, the Panzer IV chassis, which was actually supposed to be used to train drivers, remained the primary means for the battalion to receive its supplies for the remainder of the thaw. Since the Germans first encountered the Russian mud, in the fall of 1941, it had been clear to them that only vehicles using tracks could be relied upon to negotiate it. To build them was another matter. Aside from tanks and halftracks, the Germans built a few transport vehicles, like the Maultier and the Raupenschlepper Ost that used tracks, but such vehicles were expensive to build and maintain, and they consumed more fuel than conventional trucks. Consequently, there was never enough of them. Still, the Germans were at least somewhat better off than the Red Army, which had no domestic production of such vehicles at all.[478]

February 8 brought two surprises for XXXXII Corps. One was the Soviet call for surrender (described in the prologue); the other was a Soviet attack across the Ross River, upstream from Steblev. Crossing near Nikolayevka, a few Soviet companies entered a forest east of the river before hurriedly scrambled German troops managed temporarily to seal off the bridgehead. Further east, at Valiava, a stalemate ensued, but the situation at Gorodishche remained difficult. Lieb noted in his diary that "vehicles, artillery, heavy weapons from 72nd, 389th, and Wiking, as well as hundreds of wounded, were stuck at Gorodishche. To pull back the present lines would result in unbearable losses of men, weapons and equipment. The lines would have to be held for another 24 hours."[479]

Anton Meiser Withdraws

The company Meiser served with, composed of artillerymen from his own battery and some infantry from an infantry company, had not seen much action during the preceding day. However, Meiser and an infantry NCO had observed how Soviet troops moved up on the flanks of the Germans. Both were certain that the position was utterly untenable and tried to persuade the company commander to disregard Stelzner's order. Second Lieutenant Rudel, who commanded the company, had however been sent to the front before completing his training and had virtually no combat experience. As a result he did not force the issue, but stuck to the orders he had received from Stelzner.[480]

On 8 February, Soviet forces launched an attack that threatened to envelop the German position. As Stelzner and the infantry NCO had predicted, the German force was far too weak to halt the Soviet attack, especially as the position held was too extended. The Germans recoiled, but the infantry NCO managed to turn a threatening rout into a more controlled retreat, although losses had been considerable. When he and his men found an infantry lieutenant with about 30 men, they quickly attached themselves to the officer. They had had enough of being put into hopeless positions by a remote artillery major.[481]

Meiser continued walking to reach Stelzner's command post, where he found the major and reported. Meiser did not spare any critique of Stelzner's orders, and before he had finished, Stelzner became red in the face from anger and shouted, while he took hold of his pistol: "Herr Fahnenjunker, you are mad. Go immediately back to your company!"

"Herr Major, you should know that you can not deal with me like that," Meiser replied. "Herr Major, you seem not to have understood my report; the company does not exist anymore. Check with the other units. And now, Herr Major, I report myself ill! I have had great pains from my old wound."

Stelzner seemed to be on the verge of losing his composure, but Meiser moved into a nearby house while still keeping an eye on the major. As expected, Meiser found the battalion doctor there, who said that Meiser had done very well, and then he was interrupted by the telephone. It was Stelzner, who said that Meiser should be examined with a very critical eye, to get medical proof that he was trying to shirk away from service. The doctor calmly replied that Meiser was no lazybones and that his wound certainly justified him in staying in the rear. Furthermore, Meiser was so chilled that he would have to be spared from service for a week.

Stelzner angrily hung up without saying anything further. Meiser was put on the sick-list, but did not remain long at the cottage hospital. Without letting Stelzner know, Meiser declared himself fit. The doctor said that Meiser was crazy, but let him go after providing him with some painkillers. Meiser joined a hastily cobbled-together infantry troop. Like many other similar formations it was not a success in battle and Meiser soon found himself searching for his parent division again.[482]

Air Supplies to the Pocket

There were also some favorable developments for Gruppe Stemmermann. Most important was the fact that the air supply was quite successful on 8 February. During the day, the initial reports showed that 20 tons of ammunition and 14 cubic meters of fuel were landed at Korsun, in addition to 127 canisters with various contents that were dropped in the pocket. Furthermore, during the night of 8 February, another 100 tons of ammunition and 32 cubic meters of fuel were landed, and 566 wounded were brought out with the aircraft. In fact, it later transpired that these initial reports gave a conservative estimate, because it was reported that between the morning of 8 February and the morning of 9 February, 150 tons of ammunition and 60 cubic meters of fuel were flown in to Gruppe Stemmermann. This was the largest amount so far to be flown in during any 24-hour period.[483]

The arrival of the much needed supplies, in particular ammunition, gave Gruppe Stemmermann some respite. It was indeed in the nick of time, as the quartermaster of 8th Army had predicted that the ammunition on hand would be exhausted on 9 February. Still, when Speidel and Busse discussed the situation on the morning of 9 February, they concluded unanimously that Gruppe Stemmermann would have to break out no later than 11 February.[484]

Even though a significant number of wounded men had been flown out, many remained. Late in the evening of 8 February it was reported that approximately 1,400 wounded were in Korsun. Some of these were among those evacuated by air during the following night, but still about 1,000 must have remained.

Casualties had not been slight during the two weeks that had elapsed since the two Soviet fronts began their offensive. The 389th Infantry Division had been weak already before the beginning of the battle, and by now it was so depleted that its combat elements were distributed to other formations and the division staff was used to control traffic within the pocket. To the soldiers in the pocket there was probably nothing remarkable in this. Almost from the very beginning, units had been shuffled back and forth. Even though sectors had been allotted to divisions, elements of various divisions were intermingled to a considerable extent.[485]

Anton Meiser Joins the Wallonians

It was not only the movements ordered by the senior commanders that caused units to be intermingled. In many cases soldiers were cut off from their units and wandered around in the pocket, some searching for their unit, some trying to hide from the fighting. Together with four other soldiers, Anton Meiser had reached Gorodishche, where they searched for their division after finding some food and rest. Two of the soldiers had little inclination to be "sacrificed," as they called it. Meiser attempted to convince them that if everyone thought like that, nobody would get out of the pocket. It was to no avail and Meiser tried to argue that one day or another, deserters would get into difficulties, but failed to make any impression on the two soldiers. Meiser left them, but the other two soldiers followed him and continued to search for their division. After a while they met a sergeant, who told them he had seen vehicles with the 389th Division insignia north of Gorodishche. Meiser was skeptical about this, but did not rule out the prospect that the sergeant was correct. After all, they had been pushed northward.[486]

By now the ground had frozen and it was much easier to walk, compared to the days before when the deep mud had made every step a challenge. After a long walk Meiser and his two comrades reached the Wallonien Brigade. To turn back was out of the question; neither Meiser nor the other two soldiers wanted to walk back and forth unnecessarily, so instead they decided to report themselves at one of the Wallonien companies, where they were also given food. Meiser and his comrades were included in the Wallonien ranks without much formality. Meiser could not avoid reflecting on his appearance and that of the other two soldiers. None of them had shaved for several days, and their clothes were more akin to rags than uniforms. The well dressed Wallonians seemed amazed when they saw the three ragged veterans from the 389th Division. Still, the newcomers were given ammunitions for their small arms, two hand grenades each, and rations. The commanding officer said that he would send them to 389th Division as soon as he received information about its location. In the meantime, Meiser and the two soldiers stayed with the Wallonien Brigade, where they were treated very well.[487]

Stemmerman Withdraws from the East of the Pocket

As the advance in the Valieva area had progressed far less rapidly than Konev had hoped, he ordered Selivanov to use the 63rd Cavalry Division to cover the sector from Valiava to Klichkovo, and to use the rest of his forces to attack towards Zavadovka. Simultaneously, 52nd Army was to attack towards Zavadovka, from the northeast, thereby cutting off the German salient around Gorodishche.[488]

Stemmermann also had plans for the forthcoming days, which he outlined in a radio message to 8th Army at 04.45hrs on 9 February. Until the night of 9 February the present line was to be held, even though elements had been pulled out from the Gorodischche area. Under cover of darkness the southeastern front should be withdrawn to the line of Glushki–Derenkovets. On 10 February the 72nd Division and elements of SS-Wiking should be shifted to the Shenderovka area, in order to be ready to attack on 11 February, with the aim of advancing along the road from Shenderovka to Morentsy. Thus, Gruppe Stemmermann would attack toward III Panzer Corps.[489]

Stemmermann's plans could not be carried out exactly to the letter. Soviet pressure and difficult roads conspired to upset the schedule. However, by the end of 9 February the situation was approximately as planned. Konev's troops entered Gorodishche, which had been abandoned by the Germans. For the moment, German food reserves were sufficient for five days, but as a precaution Lieb ordered the bread rations to be cut back to 500 grams per day within his corps. The number of wounded remained high. On 8 February Gruppe Stemmermann had suffered 350 casualties, and approximately 1,100 wounded were in Korsun.[490]

As so often in war, where true information is scarce, rumors spread inside the Korsun pocket. Some of them at least had a trace of substance while other were wildly off the mark. For example, there was speculation about rifts between the German commanders. Such perceptions may have held a grain of truth, but the stories were exaggerated with each person who retold them. Another rumor was that the German generals had negotiated with the Soviet commanders. Exactly how this rumor originated is unclear, but a possible explanation is that some soldiers of Korps-Gruppe B may have observed that a high ranking Soviet officer came to the chief of staff. Assumptions of the outcome of that meeting may have spread quickly. Another strange rumor was that General Stemmermann had been arrested and General Gille had assumed command. The basis for such a rumor is even more difficult to guess at.[491]

Perhaps it was not only among the rank and file that rumors were prevalent. It is possible that decision makers much higher in the chain of command also heard strange tales. In the midst of all the other business he had to attend to, Stemmermann was asked to send a more detailed report on the Soviet call for surrender and the circumstances surrounding it. He was also informed that it was Hitler who wanted to know. A report was duly sent, but Hitler's interest in the issue remains puzzling. It is unclear if some strange rumor had reached his ear, or if it was just a manifestation of his distrustfulness.[492]

Von Vormann did not have to bother about strange questions from the Führer, but was able to concentrate on shifting his units westward. The 106th Division was on its way to relieve the 14th Panzer Division, which, together with the 3rd Panzer Division, was to relieve the 11th Panzer Division. The latter, together with the armor elements of the 13th Panzer Division, was to attack from Verbovets toward Zvenigorodka. As usual, delays occurred, but late in the evening of 9 February von Vormann reported that he would have the entire 11th Panzer Division ready to attack on the morning of 11 February, but not all elements of 13th Panzer Division. At the same time, Kampfgruppe Haack was assembling around Yampol, and would be available to cover the flank of the attacking units from 11th and 13th Panzer Divisions.[493]

At 01.45hrs on 10 February another strange question from Hitler reached the 8th Army staff. The Führer had heard that foreign news agencies reported that Leon Degrelle had been taken prisoner by the Red Army. Thus Hitler wanted to know where Degrelle was. In fact he remained as adjutant to Lippert, the commander of SS-Sturmbrigade Wallonien. Whether the information that had reached Hitler's ears was just one of the many rumors that pops up in war, or some ploy of the Soviet authorities, remains unknown.[494]

Of greater concern was the supply situation, but again the German air force had managed to fly considerable quantities into the pocket. From the morning of 9 February to the morning of 10 February, 190 tons of ammunition and 68 cubic meters of fuel had been landed or dropped in the pocket, while 442 wounded had been brought out. The immediate supply crisis was averted, but Stemmermann, as well as the other commanders, was fully aware that a few days of unsuitable weather could again bring the two corps dangerously close to collapsing from lack of ammunition and fuel.[495]

Stemmermann's withdrawals from the eastern part of the pocket continued, but Soviet pressure meant that it was a fighting withdrawal. Vatutin's 1st Ukrainian Front had relatively weak forces, the 27th Army with two divisions and two fortified regions, on the western side of the pocket. These could be regarded as sufficient to keep the Germans contained, but lacked the punch to do more than dent the positions held by the German XXXXII Corps. Konev had far stronger forces, two armies with nine divisions, plus the 5th Guards Cavalry Corps. The fighting in and around Valieva had been raging for a few days, but on the morning of 10 February the 5th Guards Cavalry Corps finally had the village under control. But it was too late to cut off the Germans who were retreating from the Gorodishche area.[496]

Von Vormann's Attack Toward Morentsy

Nevertheless, Stemmermann and Lieb had their share of complications to ponder. For some reason, elements of the SS-Westland Regiment gave up their position, forcing the Germans to extend the retreat further than planned. Perhaps worse was the fact that units from 72nd Division had to be committed to seal off the Soviet penetration. It had been planned to use the 72nd Division for the attack from Shenderovka toward Morentsy. If the division was frittered away, the intended attack force

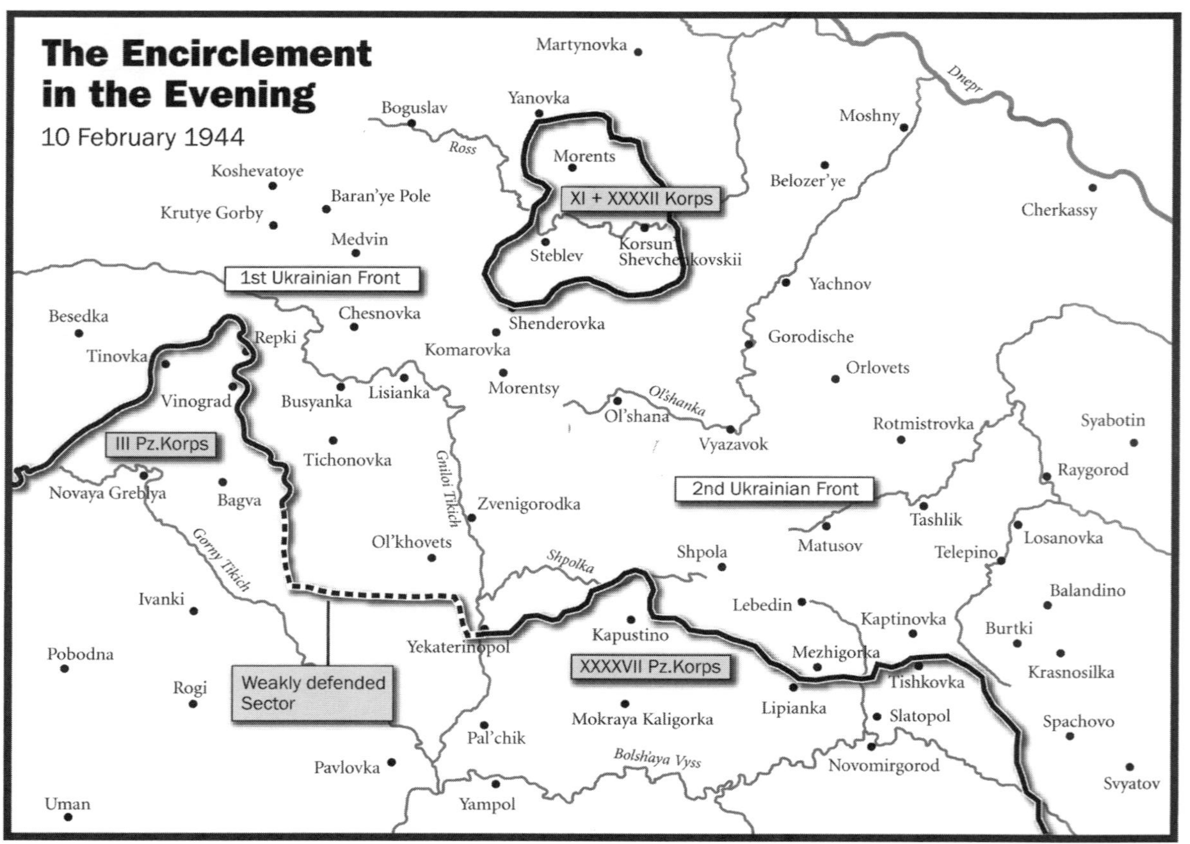
The Encirclement in the Evening
10 February 1944
Martynovka
Boguslav
Yanovka
Ross
Dnepr
Moshny
Morents
XI + XXXXII Korps
Koshevatoye
Baran'ye Pole
Krutye Gorby
Belozer'ye
Cherkassy
Medvin
Steblev
Korsun Shevchenkovskii
1st Ukrainian Front
Yachnov
Besedka
Chesnovka
Shenderovka
Repki
Gorodische
Komarovka
Tinovka
Orlovets
Morentsy
Lisianka
Busyanka
Vinograd
Ol'shanka
Ol'shana
Rotmistrovka
Syabotin
Vyazavok
III Pz.Korps
Tichonovka
Raygorod
2nd Ukrainian Front
Novaya Greblya
Bagva
Zvenigorodka
Gniloi Tikich
Tashlik
Losanovka
Matusov
Ol'khovets
Gorny Tikich
Shpolka
Shpola
Telepino
Balandino
Lebedin
Ivanki
Kaptinovka
Burtki
Kapustino
Yekaterinopol
Pobodna
Mezhigorka
Krasnosilka
XXXXVII Pz.Korps
Tishkovka
Rogi
Weakly defended Sector
Lipianka
Mokraya Kaligorka
Slatopol
Spachovo
Pal'chik
Bolshaya Vyss
Novomirgorod
Pavlovka
Svyatov
Uman
Yampol

might prove to be too weak. Another danger brought by the withdrawals was the diminishing distance between Soviet ground forces and the airfield at Korsun. On 10 February Soviet artillery began to fire on the radio beacon the Germans had at their airfield. Despite this, the VIII Air Corps was determined to continue flying in darkness to maintain the flow of supplies to Gruppe Stemmermann.[497]

Wöhler traveled by trolley to von Vormann's command post to discuss the attack planned for the following day, 11 February. Wöhler became convinced that the commanders and soldiers of XXXXVII Panzer Corps had done their utmost to assemble for the attack. Unfortunately the vehicles had been subjected to considerable wear, due to the very difficult roads. The strain on the vehicles multiplied many times in the mud.[498]

All tanks that the corps could make available were subordinated to the 11th Panzer Division, which was given the lead role in the attack. It might seem to be remarkable to commit all available tanks from a Panzer corps, but the reality was not particularly impressive. By far the strongest component was the I./Pz.Rgt. 26 Panther Battalion, which reported 17 operational tanks on 10 February. Most likely it possessed at least half the tanks available to von Vormann.[499]

According to the plan, von Wietersheim's division, with the subordinated elements from 13th Panzer Division and supported by Kampfgruppe Haack, should take a bridgehead over the Shpolka River at Yerki and then continue north to support III Panzer Corps' attack towards Morentsy. It was decided to hold the bridgehead at Iskrennoe at least for 11 February, but to evacuate it later. The troops made available should then reinforce the 11th Panzer Division. The reason for not immediately evacuating the Iskrennoe bridgehead was to keep the opposing Soviet generals uncertain about where the Germans would make their main effort.[500]

A major concern was of course the weather. More rain fell on 10 February and the ground softened even more. Nevertheless, there was no thought of postponing the attack. There were still 54,000 Germans within the pocket, and with the Red Army getting closer to the vital airfield there was no margin for postponement. The final German attempt to save the two surrounded corps would begin at dawn on 11 February.[501]

Konev pondered about what the Germans were up to. Unlike Vatutin, who had to consider the threat from III Panzer Corps, which was much stronger than XXXXVII Panzer Corps, Konev could focus more on what to do about the two surrounded enemy corps. It was evident that the Germans had been pulling back from the eastern parts of the pocket. It was equally evident that the major threat of a German relief attack came from Breith's Panzer Corps. Thus, it seemed most likely that the Germans would attempt to attack along a line that ran between Medvin and Zvenigorodka. At 04.30hrs on 11 February Konev ordered Selivanov to prepare his cavalry divisions to shift further to the west, to be able to block a German attack from the Steblev region toward the southwest. However, there was no order to actually carry out such a maneuver. Konev still hesitated. As yet the German intentions were not fully clear.[502]

Selivanov's cavalry was not the only part of 2nd Ukrainian Front that was moved west. Rotmistrov's 5th Guards Tank Army had 160 tanks, which made it many times stronger than the opposing forces of XXXXVII Panzer Corps. One of its tank corps, the 18th, was moved to a position a few kilometers east of Zvenigorodka. The 20th Tank Corps had been employed on the extreme west wing of 5th Guards Tank Army since it reached Zvenigorodka. Thus Rotmistrov's army held positions that would enable it to mount effective resistance to von Vormann's projected attack.[503]

CHAPTER 14

Breith Tries Again

The days that had passed between 4–10 February had taken their toll on the III Panzer Corps. Its tank losses due to enemy action were small, but many more tanks had been rendered inoperable due to technical problems and the very poor condition of the roads. However, it was hoped that these would soon be brought back into running order. For example, on 10 February heavy Panzer Regiment Bäke had 10 Tigers and 16 Panthers operational, but it was hoped that a total of 40 tanks would be available to the regiment on 11 February.

The situation was worse for the 17th Panzer Division, which only had one Panzer III and four Panzer IVs operational on 10 February. On the other hand, the 16th Panzer Division reported 16 Panthers, 16 Panzer IVs, and 10 StuG IIIs on the same day. Again it was supposed that more tanks would soon be operable again. The 16th Panzer Division was reinforced by a company with 10 PzKw IV tanks from SS-Leibstandarte. The 506th heavy Panzer Battalion had only two operational Tigers on 10 February, and the 249th Assault Gun Battalion was little better off, with four StuG IIIs.[504]

This meant that the units that had begun Operation Wanda now consisted of 79 tanks and assault guns, a reduction of 39% since the beginning of the operation. To supplement these units, more formations from the 1st Panzer Division had arrived, including 18 Panzer IVs and 48 Panther tanks. Thus, on the evening of 10 February the III Panzer Corps had, together with the tanks from SS-Leibstandarte, 155 tanks and assault guns available in the units that were to attack at dawn the following day. More than half were heavy Panthers and Tigers.[505]

Hube had previously claimed that his Panzers could roll over any Soviet defense consisting of infantry and antitank guns. For the attack on 11 February he had collected an impressive attacking force by German 1944 standards, and one that was much stronger than anything von Vormann could hope for. It remained to see if Hube's confidence in his Panzer units was justified. After all, the ground remained very soft and muddy, and the opposing Soviet 6th Tank Army had been given several days to prepare its defensive positions.[506]

Breith had chosen to place the 16th Panzer Division, with heavy Panzer Regiment Bäke and the II./Art.Rgt. 67 Artillery Battalion, in the center, just west of Shubennyi Stav. The division was complete, except for one infantry battalion, which remained with the SS-Leibstandarte covering the western and northern flank of III Panzer Corps. The weak 17th Panzer Division was placed on the left flank. Elements from the 1st Panzer Division were still stuck in the mud further south, but the division was to attack alongside the 16th Panzer Division, with its elements available at dawn on 11 February.[507]

The plan was quite straightforward. The tanks, in particular heavy Tank Regiment Bäke and Kampfgruppe Frank, the latter consisting of the Panther battalion and SPW battalion of 1st Panzer Division, were to crush the enemy defenses between Ryshanovka and Shubennyi Stav. Two Nebelwerfer regiments were to support the 16th and 17th Panzer Divisions. After breaking through the Soviet defenses the tanks were to make a dash toward the Gniloi Tikich River to capture crossings between Kamenyy Brod and Lisyanka, thereby enabling III Panzer Corps to continue toward Gruppe Stemmermann.[508]

Hans-Valentin Hube spent most of 10 February—a Thursday characterized by fog, snow squalls, and thaw—visiting III Panzer Corps. The Leibstandarte, which had the task of holding the western part of the III Panzer Corps, had very little infantry. On the previous day it had only been able to muster 180 men in the trenches, a small number for a division that had to cover a front of approximately 15 kilometers. The II./Pz.Gren.Rgt. 79, a motorized infantry battalion from 16th Panzer Division, had to remain with the Leibstandarte, or else the division could not be expected to hold its positions.[509]

The mud caused Hube great concern. It had taken a heavy toll on the vehicles. For example, one of the artillery battalions of 1st Panzer Division had lost 11 of its 15 prime movers for the guns and was stuck in the mud further south. The staff of III Panzer Corps only had three vehicles in order and was unable even to organize itself according to the normal procedures. If the mud continued to be such a factor, the other arms might find it well nigh impossible to follow the tanks when the offensive began.[510]

Despite the mud, the battles that had raged since 4 February had been quite intense. The III Panzer Corps claimed to have knocked out 300 tanks since Operation Wanda began. These claims were said to be confirmed and were regarded as reliable. Hube was shown a tank graveyard near Pavlovka, where countless U.S. lend-lease tanks and Soviet T-34s could be seen. Furthermore, the 1st Ukrainian Front archival records show that Vatutin's troops had lost 337 tanks and assault guns irretrievably during the first 10 days of February.[511] As most of its armor was employed against III Panzer Corps during these days, and little action took place elsewhere, it seems that the German claims were not too far off the mark. Whatever the true number of destroyed Soviet tanks, it was certainly considerable, and ample testimony to the fierceness of the fighting. In exchange, German tank losses due to enemy fire were slight.[512]

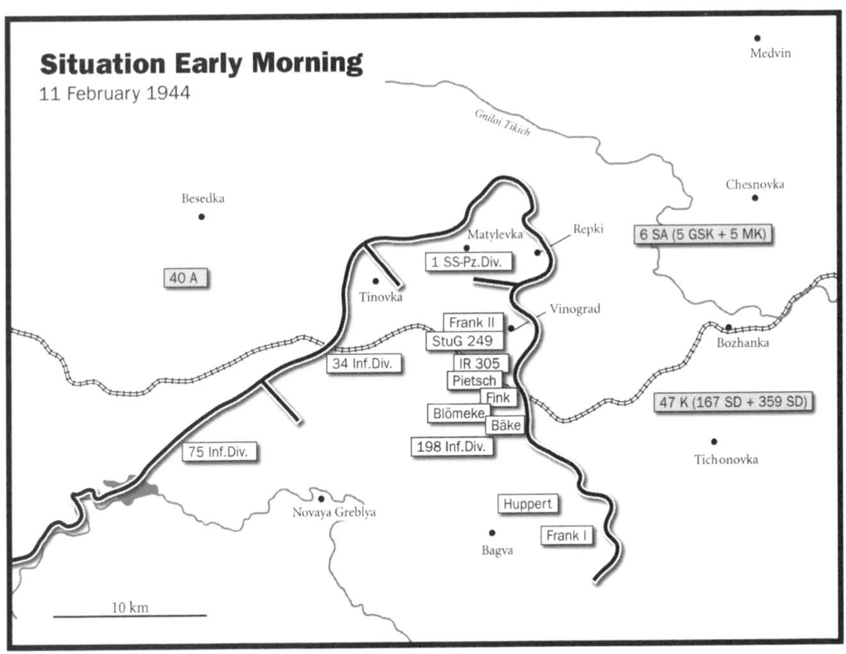

Table 2: III PANZER CORPS ON THE MORNING OF FEBRUARY 11, 1944	
1. SS-PANZER-DIVISION:	
Reinforced with	II./Pz.Gren.Rgt. 79 (from 16. Pz.Div.)
Detached	Company from II./SS-Pz.Rgt. 1
17. PANZER-DIVISION	
Reinforced with	Stug.Abt. 249, s.Pz.Abt. 506, II./Art.Rgt. 62
Kampfgruppen formed	Fink with: I./Pz.Gren.Rgt. 40, II./Pz.Gren.Rgt. 63
	Pietsch with: II./Pz.Rgt. 39, s.Pz.Abt. 506
	Frank II with: Pz.Pi.Btl. 27, elements Pz.Aufkl.Abt. 17
16. PANZER DIVISION	
Reinforced with	II./Pz.Rgt. 23, s.Pz.Abt. 503, II./Art.Rgt. 67, one company from II./SS-Pz.Rgt. 1
Kampfgruppen formed	Bäke with: I./Pz.Rgt. 2, II./Pz.Rgt 23, s.Pz.Abt. 503, II./Pz.Gren.Rgt. 64, 3./Pz.Pi.Btl. 16
	Blömeke with: Pz.Gren.Rgt. 64 (except II. Btl.), 2./Pz.Art.Rgt. 16, II./Pz.Rgt. 2, 1 Company from II./SS-Pz.Rgt. 1
1. PANZER-DIVISION (still not fully arrived)	
Reinforced with	Pi.Btl. 127 (mot)
Kampfgruppen formed	Frank I with: Pz.Rgt. 1 (except II.), II./Pz.Gren.Rgt. 113, one battalion from Inf.Rgt. 326 (198. I.D.)
	Huppert with: II./Pz.Rgt. 1, II./Pz.Gren.Rgt. 1, Pz.Aufkl.Abt. 1
198. INFANTERIE-DIVISION	
Reinforced with	One company Pz.Zerst.Btl. 471.
Sources: Anlagen zum KTB PzAOK 1 Ia, 09.00, 11.2.44, T313, R70, F7306656; KTB III. Pz.Korps Ia, T314, R208, F000044-51; Lagekarte III. Pz.Korps, 10.2.44, T314, R212, F000416; KTB Pz.Gren.Rgt. 64, BA-MA RH 37/6257; KTB Pz.Rgt. Bäke, BA-MA RH 39/677; III. Pz.Korps Ia Nr 248/44, 10.2.44, T312, R208, F000815.	

It is likely that Hube was thoroughly confident in the combat skills of his Panzer units, but whether it was sufficient to save Gruppe Stemmermann was another matter. However, there was no alternative to trying, no matter what it might cost.

Bridgehead at Bushanka

Franz Bäke had placed the 503rd Tiger Battalion in the center, the II./Pz.Rgt. 23 Panther Battalion on the left and the I./Pz.Rgt. 2 Panther Battalion (from the 16th Panzer Division) on the right, when his battle group moved up toward the front. Frost during the night did make it somewhat easier to move, but it was unlikely that the ground would remain frozen during the day. Bäke gave the forward signal at 07.00hrs, and at least 10 Tigers and 32 Panthers began to advance against the Soviet defenses facing the German tanks. Behind them followed the infantry of Kampfgruppe Blömeke from 16th Panzer Division, but Captain Blömeke chose to go with the tanks in the lead.[513]

Blömeke's decision to go with the tanks in the lead proved to be a wise choice, as the tanks made very rapid progress. Within two hours hill 239.1 had been reached, which was about eight kilometers from the jump-off positions. Bäke's tanks kept the attack going, and if anything even increased the pace. Under a clear sky the Tigers reached Bushanka at 10.00hrs, only to find that all bridges capable of taking tanks and other vehicles had been blown up. A small bridge, which allowed soldiers to pass, was undamaged, but that was all. However, the II./Pz.Rgt. 23 Panther Battalion was more fortunate. While the Tigers reached Bushanka the Panthers rushed into Frankovka, stormed over the bridge over the Gniloi Tikich River, which had demolition charges attached, and secured it before the Red Army had time to destroy it. The crew of the tank that first crossed was rewarded by an extra eight days' leave.[514]

The Gniloi Tikich River was a major obstacle and with a river crossing secured, the chances of reaching Gruppe Stemmermann had improved considerably. At III Panzer Corps staff the news about the success at Frankovka caused elation, and the following radio message was sent to General Stemmermann: "We are coming. Bridgehead and bridge at Frankovka 11.00."[515]

South of Kampfgruppe Bäke, the 1st Panzer Division attacked with Kampfgruppe Frank. At 06.30hrs, supported by one artillery battalion from 1st Panzer Division and the artillery of 198th Infantry Division,

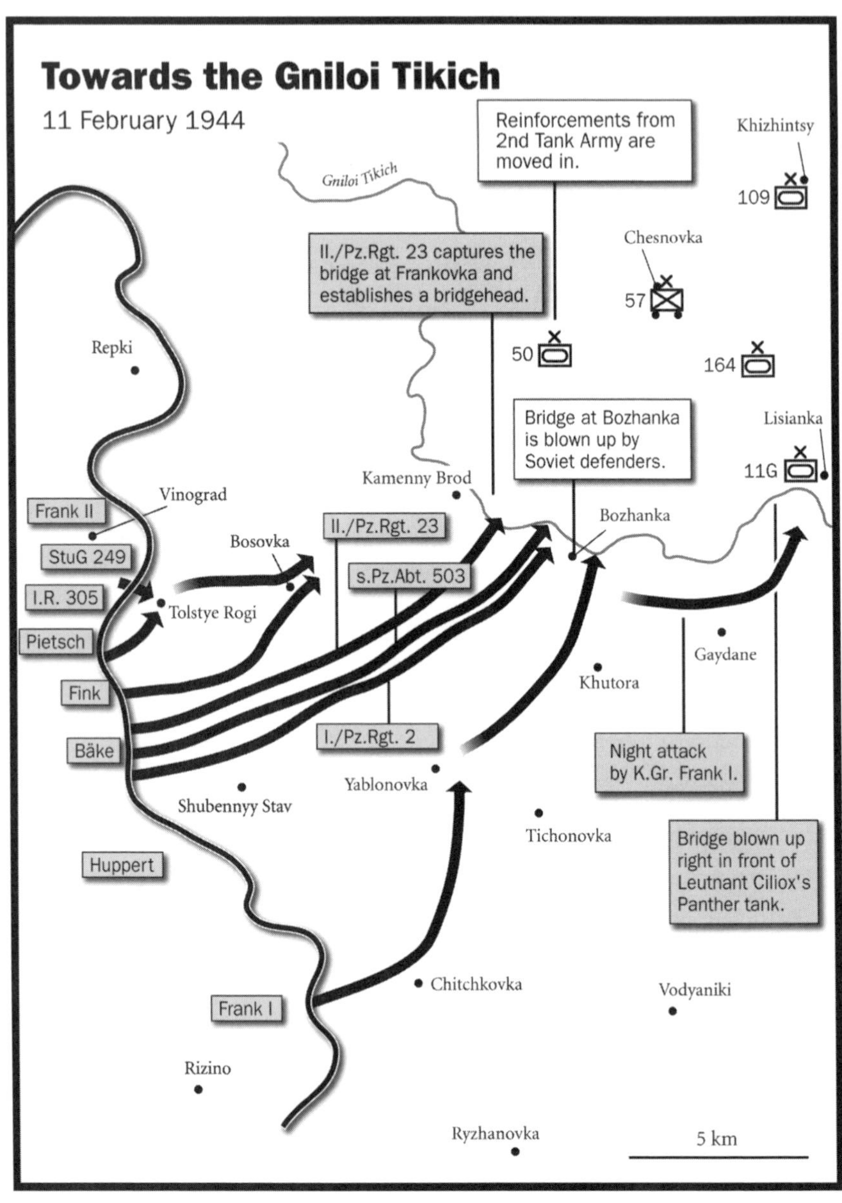

Frank sent his tanks forward. In the lead was a Panther company, commanded by Lieutenant Seemann. There were no Panzer grenadiers riding on his tanks, but the companies following behind did have Panzer grenadiers with them. As the divisions' SPW-units had not yet arrived, there was no other possibility of bring the grenadiers along in the mud. Success was swiftly achieved. After two hours Chizkhovka was taken, and the tanks veered to the left and squeezed a Soviet rifle battalion between the 1st and 16th Panzer Divisions. The Soviet battalion was quickly defeated.[516]

Frank's tanks continued north, troubled by minefields but still making good progress in bright, warm weather that was more akin to spring than the beginning of February. When the Panthers reached the outskirts of Yablonovka, several T-34s appeared, but they were quickly shot up or forced to withdraw by the gunfire from the Panthers. Without losing much time, the German tanks continued toward Zhabinka, which they bypassed, and continued to the Gniloi Tikich River. The river was reached at noon, at Bushanka. The tanks could not cross, but the Panzer grenadiers established a bridgehead.[517]

Within six hours, Kampfgruppe Frank had advanced 15 kilometers, through mud, minefields, and prepared enemy defenses. Contact was established with the 16th Panzer Division, which had also reached Bushanka, and preparations for the continuation of the offensive were made. Bridges over the Gniloi Tikich River were of paramount importance, and as yet only one that could carry tanks had been taken undamaged. It was decided to send the entire Panzer Regiment Bäke over the bridge at Frankovka.[518]

Somewhat later than Kampfgruppe Bäke and Kampfgruppe Frank, at 07.15hrs, von der Medens' 17th Panzer Division began to attack. As it was weak in tanks, it had been assigned to protect the northern flank of Breith's relief attack. Kampfgruppe Fink advanced just north of the II./Pz.Rgt. 23 Panther Battalion of Bäke's group. It made good progress, but could not quite match the pace of the Panthers, especially when it encountered strong resistance near Stepok. The 305th Infantry Regiment (from 198th Division) and the few operational tanks from Kampfgruppe Pietsch had orders to take the hamlet of Tolstyye Rogi, which was accomplished just before noon. The tanks replenished ammunition and fuel, before setting off toward Bosovka. Also, Kampfgruppe Fink, which had broken the resistance at Stepok, reached Bosovka in the afternoon. Together with the tanks of Kampfgruppe Pietsch, the southern half of the village was taken, but fighting still continued in the northern parts at dusk.[519]

Before Bäke could shift all his tanks to Frankovka, a sudden threat appeared. Many of his tanks had bunched up on the south bank of the Gniloi Tikich River, close to the destroyed bridge at Bushanka. Suddenly a number of Soviet assault guns emerged on the other side of the river, which was not particularly wide. The German tankers estimated that it was 17 assault guns and promptly opened fire on them. According to German claims, all 17 assault guns were knocked out.[520]

Bäke was able to begin to shift the rest of his Kampfgruppe toward the bridgehead at Frankovka, held by II./Pz.Rgt. 23. However, supply difficulties again began to plague his units. Soviet forces in the Bosovka area harassed the supply route for his Kampfgruppe. Neither did the air supply he asked for materialize, forcing him to send some of his tanks back, to ensure that at least some supplies arrived at his forward units.

Another problem was that the bridge captured at Frankovka seemed not to be strong enough to carry Tigers. It was unthinkable that any risks should be taken with the only major bridge over the Gniloi Tikich River that had been captured undamaged. A closer inspection of the river and its banks suggested that it might be possible to find a ford. When track marks were found where Soviet tanks had previously forded the river, it was decided to make an attempt. Under Soviet artillery fire, the first Tiger made it through the Gniloi Tikich River and was soon followed by the rest. Together with the Panthers already across the river, defenses were solidified on the northern side.[521]

In the meantime, Kampfgruppe Frank had consolidated its positions in Bushanka. Frank and Bäke met in Bushanka and discussed the situation. It was decided that Kampfgruppe Bäke should continue through the bridgehead at Frankovka, while Kampfgruppe Frank attacked along the southern bank of the Gniloi Tikich River, toward Lisyanka. An infantry company was to hold the small bridgehead, supported by the guns from a Panther company during the night, as it was expected that 16th Panzer Division would have occupied the northern bank by the morning of 12 February. The other elements of Kampfgruppe Frank would continue east, hoping to capture a bridge at Lisyanka by a surprise attack at night.[522]

A supply center was established at Bushanka, and the Germans found a dressing station that the Soviet forces had hastily abandoned. It was well provided with medicines and other equipment. The prisoners taken thus far were sent into a damaged church, where they were guarded by 10 German soldiers.

Fuel and ammunition were urgently required. Already by 15.40hrs,

Frank radioed that he urgently needed more fuel, but the combination of the thaw and the remaining pockets of resistance behind the Panzers, conspired to make resupply difficult. Perhaps the supply situation was one of the reasons behind Frank's decision to attack Lisyanka in the night, rather than immediately.[523]

In darkness, Frank deployed his Panthers for the attack toward Lisyanka, which was a rather drawn-out town, divided by the Gniloi Tikich River. There was a road running from Bushanka to Lisyanka, which served well as a navigation aid in the darkness. Without being hindered by Soviet opposition, the German tanks reached within a few hundred meters of the southeastern outskirts of Lisyanka. Lieutenant-Colonel Frank rolled forward in his Panther, which carried the designation "R01," and gave the order to attack:[524] "Kampfgruppe takes Lisyanka on the move; 1st company to the left of the main road, 2nd company to the right. 3rd company follows, Panzer grenadiers remain on the tanks as long as possible, wedge on right wing, to protect the flank."

The Panthers quickly lined up for the attack and rapidly closed the distance to the village. When they were about 30 meters from the first buildings, they encountered Soviet resistance in the form of tanks and antitank guns. However, the Germans had the advantage of surprise, and the Panthers from 1st Company quickly rolled over the Soviet defenses. Only one or two Soviet guns had time to open fire. Somewhat later, 2nd Company met similar defenses, which were equally quickly defeated. German losses were negligible, but when continuing into Lisyanka, after letting the Panzer grenadiers jump off, the Panthers ran into a minefield. First Sergeant Bohlken's tank was put out of action, quickly followed by Sergeant Schäfer's. Also Frank's adjutant, Captain von Lüttichau, had his tanks put out of action by mine damage. The tempo was lost and a bitter house-to-house fight ensued.[525]

Frank was well aware that with the current ground conditions it would take too much time to build a new bridge, if none in Lisyanka were taken intact. Over the radio he ordered "Ciliox—quickly toward the bridge." Lieutenant Ciliox continued forward, but the Soviet defenders, who had by now recovered from their initial surprise, fired from tanks, antitank guns, field guns, antitank rifles, and other weapons. Nevertheless, Ciliox battled on, but the resistance slowed his tanks. Finally he saw the bridge and immediately moved toward it. His

Panther was just about to move onto the bridge when it blew up. He would have to find another way to cross the river.[526]

The German attack on 11 February, which continued overnight, must have come as a shock. Soviet sources maintain that the attack was expected, but that statement seems hard to reconcile with the very rapid advance made by the German Panzers. Within five hours, Breith's tanks had covered approximately one third of the distance to the pocket, and secured a crossing over the most significant obstacle. Such a development could hardly have been expected. Perhaps the attack itself was no surprise but at the very least the intensity and speed of the attack seem not to have been anticipated in time to complete countermeasures.[527]

During the day, Bogdanov's 2nd Tank Army was relieved by rifle units and transferred to the Chesnovka–Pisarevka area. Vatutin also sent the 206th Rifle Division, which was part of the 27th Army, to the Pisarevka area. He also ordered attacks on the positions held by the 34th and 1st SS-Panzer divisions, but neither was strong enough to cause more than local difficulties for the Germans. The 1st Ukrainian Front did not manage to offer a serious threat to the rear of the attack force that Breith had sent to the Gniloi Tikich River.[528]

The German Attack Toward Yerki and Nova Buda, 11–12 February

Konev, too, had some forces to spare. He sent the 5th Guards Airborne Division and 62nd Rifle Division to the Morentsy–Maydanovka area, which was about 10 kilometers east of Lisyanka. Previously he had ordered Selivanov to prepare his cavalry corps to move west. Selivanov's troops had already spent most of the night moving over muddy roads, and the soldiers and horses were exhausted. Selivanov sent reconnaissance troops to the Selishche–Shenderovka–Novo Buda area, while the remainder of his corps got some rest around Kvitki–Valiava area, before setting out toward Novo Buda in the evening.[529]

There was every reason for Konev to be concerned about the situation in the Novo Buda sector. By shortening the frontline of the pocket, Stemmermann and Lieb had strived to assemble an attack force that could attack from the area south of Steblev toward Shenderovka and Novo Buda. This consisted of units from different divisions. The Germania regiment from SS-Wiking seems to have been the first to arrive, and was quickly sent to attack Shenderovka, which was captured during the day. Otherwise the main attack force was mainly formed of elements from the 72nd Division, which had disengaged from the eastern part of the pocket on 10 February. Major Kaestner, who commanded the 105th Infantry Regiment in 72nd Division, reconnoitered the area between Tarashcha and Shenderovka, and found that his regiment would have to attack down a slope which was very exposed to enemy observers and fire. Except for a few small depressions there was no cover to be found. Furthermore, despite recent deliveries from the Luftwaffe, artillery ammunition remained scarce. The attacking forces could not count on continuous artillery support; the most they could expect was a short barrage just before the attack was about to begin.

Kaestner concluded that there was little prospect of success if the regiment attacked in daylight. Instead he suggested that a surprise night attack should be staged, and his proposal was approved. Major Siegel, who commanded the neighboring 266th Infantry Regiment, would also attack with his regiment in darkness and to that end he assembled his troops during the day. To his surprise, Siegel found a paved road, which made advancing considerably easier, but his delight did not last long, as the good road was soon followed by the ordinary dirt roads that had been turned into channels of mud by the weather. Nevertheless, Siegel's regiment was ready to attack when the sun set.[530]

As we have seen, during the preceding days, von Vormann had been shifting forces toward the area south of Zvenigorodka. The most important role was given to 11th Panzer Division, and at 20.00hrs on 10 February, von Wietersheim issued orders for the attack on 11 February. He was particularly concerned at the lack of bridges that could carry Panthers, so he separated the Panthers from the other tanks and assault guns that could cross rivers on less sturdy bridges. Accordingly, several Kampfgruppen were formed. The most powerful was Kampfgruppe von Sievers, led by Major von Sievers, who was commander of the Panzer regiment of the division. The Kampfgruppe consisted of the Panthers from 11th Panzer Division and the I./Pz.Rgt. 26, one or two infantry battalions, one artillery battalion, and some engineers. Some elements of the 11th Panzer Division were still in the Iskrennoye area, as they had not been relieved in time, but Kampfgruppe Haack and elements of the 13th Panzer Division were to join the attack.[531]

Von Wietersheim assembled his Kampfgruppe commanders at midnight and issued the final orders. Kampfgruppe von Sievers would

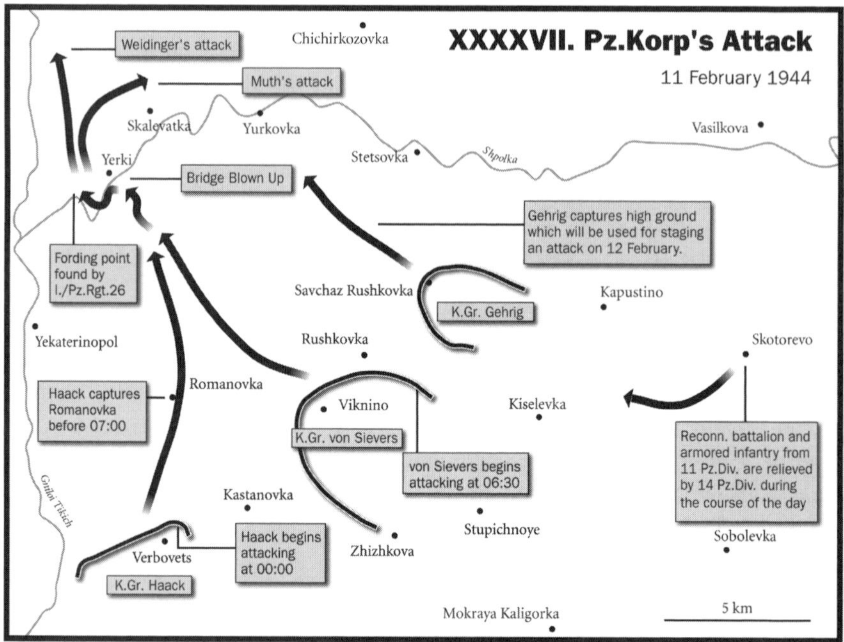

attack from the Viknino area toward Yerki, where a bridgehead was to be secured. The 110th and 111th Infantry Regiments would follow Kampfgruppe von Sievers and secure the flanks and captured areas, allowing von Sievers to continue forward. Kampfgruppe Gehrig from the 13th Panzer Division, reinforced with the few operational PzKw IV tanks possessed by 11th Panzer Division, as well as the assault guns from Pz.Abt. 8, was to attack from the area around the state farms at Rushkovka, and follow on the right wing of Kampfgruppe von Sievers. The divisional engineer battalion would follow behind Kampfgruppe von Sievers and ensure that bridges with a capacity of at least 60 tons were created or maintained. The various units would jump off between 04.30hrs and 05.30hrs.[532]

Kampfgruppe Haack, which had assembled near Brodetskoye, was not as mobile as von Wietersheim's units. Accordingly, it had to begin its attack at midnight, when von Wietersheim issued orders to his Kampfgruppe commanders. At first it was an uneventful march in darkness and mud. Without meeting much resistance, Romanovka was occupied just before 07.00hrs. By then, von Wietersheim had already launched his units.[533]

Most of the punch von Sievers possessed came from the 18 operational Panthers of I./Pz.Rgt. 26, which, with grenadiers riding them, passed through Vilknino at 06.30hrs and continued toward Yerki. The roads were, as usual, very soft and wet, and the tanks mostly moved off the roads. However, in the boggy ground the tanks ploughed forward in second or third gear (the Panthers had seven forward gears). Hardly any resistance was met until they approached a crossroads two to three kilometers southeast of Yerki. Soviet infantry opposed the German tanks, but as the defenders only had antitank rifles, the Panthers brushed aside the opposition and continued toward Yerki. At this moment the lead elements of Kampfgruppe Haack appeared to the left.[534]

There was no time to lose, and under low-hanging clouds that precluded air support, the attack immediately continued toward Yerki. When the outskirts of the town were reached, the Panzer grenadiers jumped off the tanks and escorted the tanks on foot as they entered the settlement. Von Sievers directed his troops toward the northeastern part of Yerki, where there was a bridge over the Shpolka River. With the tanks advancing as quickly as they dared, the southern end of the bridge was approached, only for the German forces to see it destroyed by an explosion. The Germans turned left and followed the Shpolka River downstream. They soon found another bridge that had already been destroyed, but the tankers had more luck further south, where an intact bridge was discovered. It was not strong enough to take Panthers, but it might prove possible to ford the Shpolka River close to the bridge. Lieutenant Wartmann inspected the river and its banks, and decided it was worth trying. Luck accompanied the Germans, and all the Panthers were able to cross at the ford. The first step of XXXXVII Panzer Corps' mission had been accomplished—to create a bridgehead over the Shpolka River.[535]

Farther east, Kampfgruppe Gehrig set out from its staging area at the Rushovka farms. Without drama it reached the high ground about three kilometers southeast of Yurkovka at noon. Its purpose was twofold. The maneuver served both to protect the right flank of the 11th Panzer Division and also to capture a staging area for further attacks to the north. More forces were expected to become available on 12 February, when the relief of 11th and 13th Panzer Divisions had been completed.[536]

After securing Yerki, Kampfgruppe von Sievers and Kampfgruppe Haack continued. The I./Pz.Rgt. 26 had 15 Panthers operational (three had suffered mechanical breakdowns), on which infantry from Kampfgruppe Haack climbed. The tanks were divided into two groups, one commanded by Lieutenant Weidinger, which advanced along the road to Zvenigorodka, and one commanded by Lieutenant Muth, which advanced further east, toward Skalevatka. Soon Soviet mortar shells exploded around the Panthers, forcing the infantry to jump off the tanks and take cover. Almost immediately Soviet antitank guns joined the action. The Panthers fired back and defeated the guns, without a tank being knocked out. Weidinger's group pushed further north and captured hill 161.2, just east of Stebnoye. In the meantime Muth was approaching his objective, the road and railroad crossing north of Skalevatka. A concealed antitank gun suddenly opened fire on Muth's tanks after they had passed, but it was silenced by fire from Weidinger's group before it could knock out any tanks, which were then able to reach their objective. Together with infantry from Kampfgruppe Haack, the crossroads was secured.[537]

Low clouds had blocked air support, but when Muth's tanks had reached Skalevatka, a low flying Soviet reconnaissance aircraft appeared. Muth ordered his gunner to fire on the small aircraft. Using machine guns and firing high explosive shells, the aircraft was shot down. Otherwise, antitank guns were the main opponent for the Panthers on 11 February. Soviet tanks had not appeared, despite the fact that the area was defended by 20th and 29th Tank Corps. Rotmistrov's engineers had been more active during the day, placing over 5,000 mines in the area north of Yerki.[538]

The effects of the mines had thus far been negligible, but that might change during the following day. Even though the German forces had been able to advance despite the poor ground condition, von Vormann and his staff was concerned about the fuel supply, as it had become apparent that consumption was about five times higher than normal. The ground was also one of the most important factors behind von Vormann's proposal that the main direction of the attack should be west, rather than east of Tarasovka. It was imperative to avoid low lying river crossings as much as possible, something which spoke in favor of the area west of Tarasovka. Von Vormann's suggestion was approved, but before Tarasovka could be approached it would be necessary to see what results were achieved on 12 February.[539]

As usual, fuel was a prerequisite for success and von Vormann wanted the Luftwaffe to fly fuel to his spearheads. Wöhler, of course, agreed, and later in the evening it was confirmed that the Luftwaffe had prepared to fly 35 cubic meters of fuel to von Vormann. Reinforcements were also required, but the only major unit that could be counted on was the 2nd Parachute Division, which would require days before it could be inserted into the front line.[540]

As we have seen, Gruppe Stemmermann had been preparing to attack in a south-westerly direction. The 105th Infantry Regiment would lead 72nd Division's attack on Novo Buda. Major Kaestner chose to place the submachine-gunners and machine-gunners in the lead, to generate as much firepower as possible at the front of his attacking regiment. As the attack first and foremost relied on surprise, there would be no artillery preparation, which perhaps was one of the factors that led Kaestner to place the automatic weapons in the lead.[541]

During the day, Kaestner's troops had been hiding further back, but after sunset they moved forward to the positions from where the attack would be launched. Including the attached elements, Kaestner's force numbered 689 officers and men. There was no moonlight, but with the snow on the ground it was not completely dark; it was light enough for the soldiers to find their positions without allowing the Soviet defenders to discover what was going on. Silently the Germans crouched while they waited, until at 20.30hrs the attack began. In snow smocks they stealthily stalked forward, toward the Soviet defenses that had been revealed by previous observations. The Germans held their fire as long as possible. No signs of discovery were observed until they got very close to the Soviet positions, but then the Soviet troops seem to have noticed that something was going on. Immediately the Germans opened fire and assaulted the Soviet defenses, which were captured after a brief close-quarters combat action.[542]

There was no time to spare if the initial success was to be exploited. The lead elements continued forward while other troops protected the flanks. By midnight the northeastern outskirts of Novo Buda had been reached, when noise from moving vehicles was heard from the area around Sukhiny. The German spearhead halted and discovered a column of about 30 vehicles, plus a rocket launcher. Kaestner had ordered that 20mm antiaircraft guns should be brought along right behind the lead infantry. It had been arduous to move them through the snowdrifts, but at this moment they proved useful. When the guns opened fire at about 200 meters, the trucks were soon riddled with shells from the rapid-firing 20mms. Some of the trucks were evidently loaded with fuel, as they burned violently, illuminating the remainder of the column. The rocket launcher opened fire on the Germans, but as the Soviet troops were firing into the dark, they could not aim accurately, and after firing a few rounds the rocket launcher was silenced. After destroying the column, Kaestner's troops quickly reorganized and continued toward Novo Buda, which was taken without fighting at about 02.30hrs.[543]

Kaestner's regiment had been the spearhead, but was not alone in the attack. The other two regiments of 72nd Division, plus elements of SS-Wiking and SS-Wallonien had also taken part, and at dawn the Germans held Nova Buda, Komarovka, and the northern part of Khilki. Less than 20 kilometers now separated Gruppe Stemmermann from the spearheads of III Panzer Corps.[544]

CHAPTER 15

Stalin Intervenes

The Germans' successes on 11 February and the following night seem to have caused consternation among the top Soviet leadership. Zhukov had been coordinating the two Soviet fronts, but on the morning of 12 February he suffered from fever and fell asleep. He could not recall how long he had slept when his adjutant, Leonid Fedorovich Minyuk, woke him and said that Josef Stalin was on the telephone. The Soviet supreme commander had learned about Breith's breakthrough, and also the recent attack by Gruppe Stemmermann, which had swept through Khilki and Novo Buda. When Zhukov was asked if he knew anything about it, he had to admit that he was uninformed. Stalin told him to check it and report later.[545]

Zhukov immediately called Vatutin, who told him how the situation had developed during the night. After a brief discussion, Zhukov called Stalin and told him everything he knew. According to Zhukov, Konev had just talked with Stalin and proposed that his 2nd Ukrainian Front take command of all Soviet forces around the pocket, thus including Trofimenko's 27th Army, which had hitherto been part of Vatutin's 1st Ukrainian Front. According to Konev's proposal, Vatutin would control the forces constituting the outer ring, defending against Breith's and von Vormann's latest attacks. Zhukov replied that the defeat of the surrounded German forces was only a matter of three or four days, and that a change of command structure would only cause delay.[546]

Stalin paid little attention to Zhukov's objection and replied, before hanging up: "Let Vatutin personally supervise the operations of the 13th and 60th Armies in the area of Rovno–Lutsk–Dubno, while you assume responsibility for preventing a breakthrough by the enemy striking force from the Lisyanka area." A few hours later this was confirmed in the form of a written directive, which also included the order to transfer the 27th Army, with the 180th, 202nd, and 337th Rifle Divisions, plus the 54th and 159th Fortified Regions, to Konev's 2nd Ukrainian Front. To what extent Stalin's order affected the operations is of course difficult to tell, but compared to force ratios, weather, logistics, and other factors it probably had relatively little effect. The order did mean that Vatutin's front would not be honored with the expected victory over the encircled Germans.[547]

General Konev gives a slightly different description of events in his memoirs. According to Konev it was Stalin who proposed to transfer 27th Army to 2nd Ukrainian Front, but Konev claims to have advised against the idea. He valued Trofimenko as a commander, but Konev believed it would be difficult for him to lead and assist an army on the other side of the cauldron. However, Stalin remained firm and 27th Army was transferred.[548]

Following the directive to place 27th Army under the command of 2nd Ukrainian Front, Konev decided to establish a forward command post where 4th Guards Army had located its staff. He was told that the ground was too soft for a Po-2 aircraft to land, but as it would take too much time to travel by car in the mud, Konev ordered that a temporary landing strip should be created. Finally, two Po-2s left the 2nd Ukrainian Staff headquarters, one of them with Konev as a passenger and the other with his adjutant. The latter aircraft was attacked by German fighter aircraft and did not reach its destination, but Konev arrived at his forward command post to lead his units.[549]

The German Spearhead Continues, 11–12 February

It was of course very important that the Germans should capitalize on their possession of the bridgehead at Frankovka as quickly as possible. Late in the evening, Bäke was ordered to conduct a night attack from the bridgehead toward the Luka–Lisyanka road. However, due to resupply difficulties the attack could not be launched until after dawn. Using 10 Panthers from the II./Pz.Rgt. 23 and elements of the reconnaissance battalion of 16th Panzer Division, the attack was to unfold south of Dadushkovka and Chesnovka. However, south of Dadushkovka, fire from Soviet antitank guns in ambush positions, assisted by poor visibility due to fog, knocked out several Panthers. Four of them seem to have been permanently lost, and the attack was halted.[550]

The dearth of supplies continued to be a restraining factor for Kampfgruppe Bäke, which remained fairly inactive during 12 February. Kampfgruppe Blömeke also saw little action. An attempt was made to advance toward Kamenyy Brod, but after some initial success the German troops returned to the positions held during the morning. Neither did the 17th Panzer Division see much action. It moved its elements forward, to be in a better position to cover the flank of the 16th Panzer Division, as the latter would continue to drive northeast as soon as possible.[551]

The other three divisions of III Panzer Corps were involved in more difficult fighting during 12 February. At Vinograd, the Soviet 3rd Guards Airborne Division launched several battalion-sized attacks, which penetrated into Vinograd and continued to the center of the village. As the German defenders only consisted of 35 riflemen, four machine guns and an antiaircraft platoon from the 198th Division, they could not withstand the attack. The Germans were forced to withdraw to the southern part of Vinograd. To restore the situation, the 326th Infantry Regiment, the Füsilier battalion, and one artillery battalion from the 198th Division were directed toward Vinograd. Also Breith sent two batteries from the 202nd Assault Gun Battalion, which had just been transferred from VII Corps, to reinforce the 198th Division at Vinograd. Finally, a Kampfgruppe from SS-Leibstandarte was ordered to counterattack along the road from Votylevka toward Vinograd. The latter only consisted of one Panther and 12 riflemen. By twilight it was still to early to tell what effect Breith's countermeasures would have.[552]

The Soviet 58th Division put pressure on the SS-Leibstandarte, especially at Repki, which was attacked early in the morning. The reconnaissance battalion of the 1st SS was soon forced out of Repki. Otherwise, Leibstandarte was beset with supply problems, just like virtually every other unit. Due to the poor condition of the roads, its field kitchens had still not arrived. The soldiers had been given cans of meat, to heat by themselves, but the unbalanced diet gave the division doctor cause for concern about the health of the men. Ammunition also remained scarce. Lieutenant-Colonel Stoltz looked for a means to alleviate the transportation difficulties. As so often in this war, the local population and its assets were used. About 150 horse-drawn vehicles were commandeered and sent to the front, each loaded with 200 liters of fuel.

A stretch of narrow-gauge railroad had been found, leading to a brickyard, and it was decided that it too could be used. Work was begun on connecting it to the front so that rail hoppers could be drawn by horses on the tracks. For the moment these measures had not yet proved useful, but at least they presented some hope for improvement.[553]

The 1st Panzer Division, on the other side of the protruding salient that the III Panzer Corps had driven into the Soviet lines, also spent much of 12 February worrying about supplies. Kampfgruppe Frank at Lisyanka was very low on fuel and ammunition. As we have seen, one Panther company and some infantry, under the command of Lieutenant Wall, had been left at Bushanka. It was decided to move them to Lisyanka, which would provide Frank with some fresh forces that were also better furnished with ammunition and fuel. When the Panther company began to move it met very little resistance.

The distance between Bushanka and Lisyanka was only six kilometers. In good conditions it would take less than a quarter of an hour for Wall's Panthers, but when he set out in the morning he could not count on perfect conditions and he probably expected the journey to take more time. It seemed likely that there would be little opposition from the Red Army, and Lieutenant Wall's force proceeded unmolested until Lisyanka was within sight. However within 300 meters of Lisyanka, a shot from a Soviet antitank gun hit his tank, killing or wounding the infantry who rode on top of the Panther. Sergeant Strippel, who commanded the tank following behind Wall, saw what happened and radioed to the other tanks to halt before reaching the field of fire of the Soviet guns.

Covered by fire from Lieutenant Wall's Panther, Strippel ordered his driver to run the tank over the open field at full speed to Lisyanka. It was a daring maneuver, but Strippel was a very experienced tanker, who had clocked up an impressive score of knocked out enemy tanks. Strippel's Panther made it to Lisyanka without being hit, and he took cover. It was difficult to locate the Soviet antitank guns, so Strippel found it prudent to climb out from the tank while it remained in cover, and proceed on foot to locate the guns. Having successfully done that, he went back to his Panther and rolled forward to open fire on the antitank guns, which were silenced. Subsequently the remainder of Wall's company proceeded safely to Lisyanka.[554]

Otherwise, Lieutenant-Colonel Frank had little for which to be thankful. During 12 February, 40 aircraft flew supplies to the III Panzer

Corps. All of it had to be dropped in canisters, and Frank did not get much, as only two of the aircraft dropped their loads in the area held by his Kampfgruppe. In frustration he saw that many other canisters fell in a forest south of Lisyanka, which was held by Soviet troops. Also, the link between his Kampfgruppe and other parts of Koll's Division was very weak, as the roads running west and southwest from Lisyanka were harassed by Soviet forces. Already during the night of 11 February, a column of German vehicles loaded with supplies became painfully aware of the threat. When it reached the area between Yablonovka and Tikhonovka, it was shot up by Soviet antitank guns and assault guns. This boded ill for the urgent need to get supplies to Frank. Furthermore, unless a corridor could be held open, through which Stemmermann's beleaguered soldiers could move, there was no point in the German armored spearheads reaching the pocket.[555]

Breith's Panzer corps had not fired its last shot. During the night a supply column reached Kampfgruppe Bäke, bringing precious ammunition and fuel to the Panthers and Tigers, thereby making it possible to resume offensive actions. Breith gave clear orders to his units for 13 February to continue the offensive. The 16th Panzer Division, with Bäke's regiment, was to break through the Soviet defenses near Dadushkovka and reach Khizhintsy, to link up with Gruppe Stemmermann, no matter what it took to do so. Kamfpgruppe Frank should ford the Gniloi Tikich River at Lisyanka, and if necessary give up the southern part of the town. Breith's orders carried the suggestion that the attempt would succeed here or fail completely, because he was aware that Gruppe Stemmermann could not hold out for more than a few days.[556]

One reason for the sense of extreme urgency was the situation at Korsun airfield, which was very close to the front line. Gruppe Stemmermann had about 2,000 wounded who had not been evacuated by air, most of whom were located near the Korsun airfield. Since the air evacuation operation was now at an end, they were to be moved to Steblev. From now on, the only remaining hope of getting out of the pocket was to move to the southwest. Lieb visited Khilki, which had just been taken. It was an important step toward linking up with the III Panzer Corps, but Lieb could not avoid noting how exhausted the soldiers were. Seeing that it was uncertain if they had the strength to accomplish a breakout, Lieb sent a message on the radio, saying that it was "urgently necessary that Breith as soon as possible reached

Petrovskoye." The latter village was located three kilometers west of Khilki, and if the III Panzer Corps got that close, a breakout stood a good chance of succeeding. Lieb asked his orderly to burn his papers and to distribute clothes and other items to his staff. Perhaps they would have more use for them during a breakout.[557]

The possibility of a breakout depended on whether III Panzer Corps could advance further, but still von Vormann's corps had to continue attacking. If he did not, Konev would be able to release units from 2nd Ukrainian Front and place them between Gruppe Stemmermann and Breith's Panzer corps. According to the plans previously prepared, the bridgehead at Iskrennoe was evacuated before sunrise. The remaining elements of the 13th Panzer Division were finally relieved by the 14th Panzer Division and were sent west, to join von Wietersheim's attack.[558]

Before noon, the 11th Panzer Division mopped up Skalevatka, which had been captured the day before. From Skalevatka, Kampfgruppe von Sievers would attack toward Zvenigorodka, although the aim was to take hill 204.8, which was located about 4 kilometers north-northwest of Skalevatka, halfway to Zvenigorodka. Panthers from the 15th Panzer Regiment and I./Pz.Rgt. 26, with infantry riding on the tanks, would conduct the attack, which was scheduled to begin at 12.15hrs. Just before beginning the attack it was decided to proceed without infantry riding on the tanks, a decision that proved fortunate since Soviet mortars shelled the Panthers as soon as they rolled north. The infantry would most likely have suffered serious losses if they had sat on the tanks while shells exploded around them.[559]

The tanks proceeded unmolested to bypass hill 204.8 to the west, but soon Soviet antitank guns joined the mortars. The Germans found themselves in a crossfire, and Lieutenant Wartmann, who commanded the I./Pz.Rgt. 26 with its 10 operational Panthers, directed Sergeant Fangerow, with some of the Panthers, to engage the enemy to the east, while Lieutenant Weidinger with some of the other tanks attacked the Soviet forces to the west. Wartmann placed himself at the tip of the attack, to bypass hill 204.8 and attack it from the north.[560]

As was customary in the German Panzer troops, Wartmann commanded with his head up through the cupola on the roof of the Panther turret. This gave him better visibility compared to that from the vision aids within the tank, but of course also meant that he took a greater risk. While proceeding toward the hill, which he carefully studied through his binoculars to see if it was free of enemy troops, Soviet shells suddenly exploded near the German tanks. A splinter hit Wartmann in the wrist, making him unable to command the battalion.[561]

Lt. Weidinger assumed command and continued the attack, which succeeded in capturing hill 204.8 at about 14.30hrs. The Panthers had reached the objective, but had also suffered some losses. One tank was rendered unsalvageable, although the crew bailed out unharmed. Another tank was hit, but did not suffer extensive damage. Its crew was less fortunate, although there were no fatalities. Furthermore, the fuel tanks of the Panthers were almost empty at the end of the day. No fuel reached the forward tanks, and even a few tanks that drove back to Yerki for fuel found nothing. Weidinger's tanks had to sit out the night almost immobile while waiting for fuel to arrive on the following day.[562]

On the morning of 12 February, Wöhler had set out to visit 11th Panzer Division and Kampfgruppe Haack, but only reached a point two kilometers north of Yampol, when he had to turn back because the roads were impassable. Thus he did not even get within 25 kilometers of von Wietersheim's spearheads.[563]

Further north, the 13th Panzer Division attempted to gain a crossing over the Shpolka River at Yurkovka. On 11 February, the elements of the division that were subordinated to the 11th Panzer Division had occupied the high ground south of Yurkovka. At 13.00hrs that group, supported by the 911th Assault Gun Battalion, resumed the attack toward Yurkovka, and one and a half hours later penetrated into the village. A Soviet counterattack pushed the Germans back, but they still retained a small bridgehead when darkness fell. Hope remained that, when more troops from the 13th Panzer Division reached the area, the bridgehead could be expanded.[564]

Inside the Pocket

Anton Meiser had been sent to take part in the defense of Korsun, and was given command of 20 men and subordinated to a lieutenant-colonel from the infantry. He took part in the vital defense of a hill behind which the airfield was located. Many wounded men were treated in Korsun, and during a lull in the fighting Meiser went to see some of them. The wounded men, often suffering severely from pain, were crammed on the floor of a house. Many of them seemed to be apathetic, others were in despair. The medical staff had much to do, but their resources were very limited.

Walking further in, Meiser found the cadet Damen, who had been shot through his hand and now also suffered from a high fever. Next to him lay another man from his old battery, a corporal who had been shot through the neck. Fortunately the bullet had passed straight through, without wobbling or hitting the trachea, arteries, or any other vital parts. Both Meiser's comrades had "flight tickets," a certificate written by a doctor that allowed them to be evacuated by air. After a while Meiser became aware that many of the soldiers held firmly to their "flight ticket." He asked why and received the answer that there were people who walked around and tried to steal the certificates from the seriously wounded. Neither the wounded nor the thieves knew that by this time the evacuation by air had ceased.[565]

During the day the Red Air Force was more active in the skies above the ground troops than the Luftwaffe. Soviet fighters strafed the roads between Korsun, Steblev, and Shenderovka, causing Stemmermann to ask on the radio, at 13.25hrs, where the Luftwaffe was. The Soviet fighters continued attacking ground targets in the pocket, without being hindered by German fighters. At 14.45hrs Stemmermann again radioed to ask why nothing was being done to stop the Red Air Force. Less than an hour later the Luftwaffe representative at 8th Army staff replied that only a few fighters had been able to take off from the airfield, to escort transport aircraft and also to patrol at Steblev. He also reported that two groups of Stukas, with 40 and 15 aircraft respectively, had attacked northwest of Yurkevka, in support of XXXXVII Panzer Corps.[566]

The Luftwaffe continued to concentrate on supply deliveries, which were vital to the armored spearheads in III and XXXXVII Panzer Corps, since ground conditions precluded supplies being moved by road. Heinz Lampe was a radio operator on board a Ju-52, which, on 12 February flew toward Lisyanka to drop fuel for Kampfgruppe Frank. After a short briefing, Lampe and the rest of the crew climbed on board the aircraft. Another Junkers, piloted by staff sergeant Kern, took the lead when they set off on the mission. By flying low the pilots of the slow transport aircraft hoped that they would escape detection by Soviet fighters. With 10 barrels of gasoline on board, any fighting would be dangerous indeed. Lampe could easily distinguish the signs of recent fighting on the ground: he saw burnt out houses, tanks, and other vehicles. There were no beacons or any other navigation aids, so the air crews had to rely on their experience to find the places where they should drop the fuel barrels.[567]

The air crews kept a watchful eye out for enemy fighters, but also scanned the ground. No fighters, enemy or friendly were detected, but soon troops on the ground could be discerned. Lampe saw German tanks engaging Soviet forces. Fortunately the Junkers were not detected by the Soviet troops on the ground. Clearly the front line had been reached, which was confirmed when a white flare was fired from a German tank. However, the Luftwaffe crews realized that they had only reached the flank of the III Panzer Corps. Only a few minutes remained before they reached Lisyanka.[568]

The Junkers aircraft continued at an altitude of only 150 meters and Lampe clearly saw corpses of Russian soldiers, killed horses, and burning vehicles littering the ground below. Soon three or four German tanks appeared. They fired a white flare and this time the two transport aircraft were on target. Feverishly Lampe began to untie the fuel barrels, but almost immediately the aircraft shuddered. It had been hit by machine-gun fire. The mechanic, Sergeant Ehrlich, hurried to help Lampe. They pulled two barrels to the opening and waited for the horn that would sound when they had reached the exact spot where the barrels should be released. Lampe cursed the machine-gun fire, which still raked the aircraft, when finally the horn gave the signal for them to push out the barrels. Lampe saw the parachutes work properly and the barrels landed safely close to the tanks.[569]

Several fuel barrels remained, however, and the aircraft flew another turn to release more of them. Just when they were to push the barrels out of the aircraft, the rear gunner was hit in the back, but he could still walk and made it to the forward part of the aircraft. Lampe and Ehrlich sweated while they struggled with the heavy barrels, and Lampe thought it was real donkey work to drag the barrels to the door. On the second turn they managed to get three barrels out, but the "bolshevik fire" became more and more intense. Still there were two barrels remaining, far forward in the machine. Lampe ran forward to the pilot, Staff Sergeant Golbik, and shouted in his ear: "One more turn, at the lowest level." The last two barrels lacked parachutes, requiring the aircraft to fly as low as possible. Fortunately it seemed to be more difficult for the Soviet gunners to aim when the Junkers flew extremely low, and Lampe and Ehrlich successfully shoved the remaining barrels out of the aircraft.[570]

Lampe grabbed a first-aid kit and rushed to the wounded gunner. While bullets still hit the machine, he began to bandage the gunner, who was not seriously wounded. As a precaution Lampe radioed to the base that an ambulance should be available when they landed. After taking care of the gunner, Lampe inspected the aircraft, to see what damage the machine-gun fire had caused. The only serious damage he could find was a loss of fuel. One of the fuel tanks of the aircraft left a small stream of fuel in the air. The other Junkers also showed similar damage. However, as they had gotten out of reach of the Soviet fire, and the distance to the base was not excessive, there was no undue cause for alarm. Both of the Ju-52s landed safely and an ambulance took care of the wounded gunner. There were many holes in the aircraft, but the following day Lampe and his comrades were in the air again, to drop more supplies to the troops on the ground.[571]

The air supply operation in support of the III Panzer Corps involved dropping almost seven tons of ammunition for Tigers and Panthers, plus 37 cubic meters of fuel. As the complete rounds for Tigers and Panther weighed about between 10 and 20 kilograms, and the fuel capacity of the tanks were slightly less than one cubic meter, this was a welcome contribution.[572]

At 18.35hrs Wenck and Speidel spoke over the telephone about the situation. Wenck explained that due to the destroyed bridges at Lisyanka it had not been possible to make much progress during the day. Tomorrow an attempt would be made to advance toward Dzhurzhentsy. Speidel emphasized that had the 24th Panzer Division, which inexplicably had been withdrawn, been available, it could have been used to expand the bridgehead at Yerki. The lack of the division was sorely felt. At least, Speidel continued, the limited attacks that had been made had attracted enemy reinforcements. Thus some kind of success had been achieved.[573]

Due to the German attack at Khilki and Novo Buda, Konev decided to commit Selivanov's cavalry corps, which suffered from serious shortages of fuel. Many vehicles were stranded along the muddy roads and could not take part in the ensuing action. Only gradually did the corps get into position to counterattack the German forces that had captured Novo Buda, Khilki, and Shenderovka. Otherwise no major changes seem to have taken place among the Soviet forces on 12 February. Perhaps the top commanders were busy reorganizing, due to Stalin's order as to how the command responsibilities should be divided.[574]

CHAPTER 16

"Now or Never"

As we recall, Breith had given a "now or never" order for 13 February. Bäke's Panzer regiment played the most important part in the attack, and in the morning it rolled forward, with its Tiger battalion to the left and its Panther battalion to the right. Forces from the 16th Panzer Division advanced on Bäke's left flank. The initial aim was the crossroads east of Chesnovka, but first Dadushkovka had to be captured, where the 2nd Tank Army had prepared defenses in and south of the village.[575]

Almost immediately the Germans caught a glimpse of two T-34s before they disappeared in a small depression. Sensing that his opponent might be up to something, Bäke called for air support. At Uman a Stuka-Staffel had already taken off, and through the wireless set in his command tank Bäke was able to direct it toward the suspected Soviet position. He ordered the 503rd Tiger Battalion to continue forward as soon as the dive bombers had attacked, while the Panthers to the right conducted a flank move.[576]

Walter Scherf commanded the Tigers and ordered that white flares should be fired as soon as the Stukas became visible. The tankers ensured that AP as well as high-explosive ammunition was easily accessible, as both tanks and antitank guns could be expected. Scherf had ordered that his tanks should move forward as soon as the first Stukas had released their bombs, but this did not work out as planned. When the Stukas attacked, the Soviet tanks moved forward, perhaps because they were located in a position that was suitable for ambushing advancing German tanks, but that did not provide cover from the air. Instead,

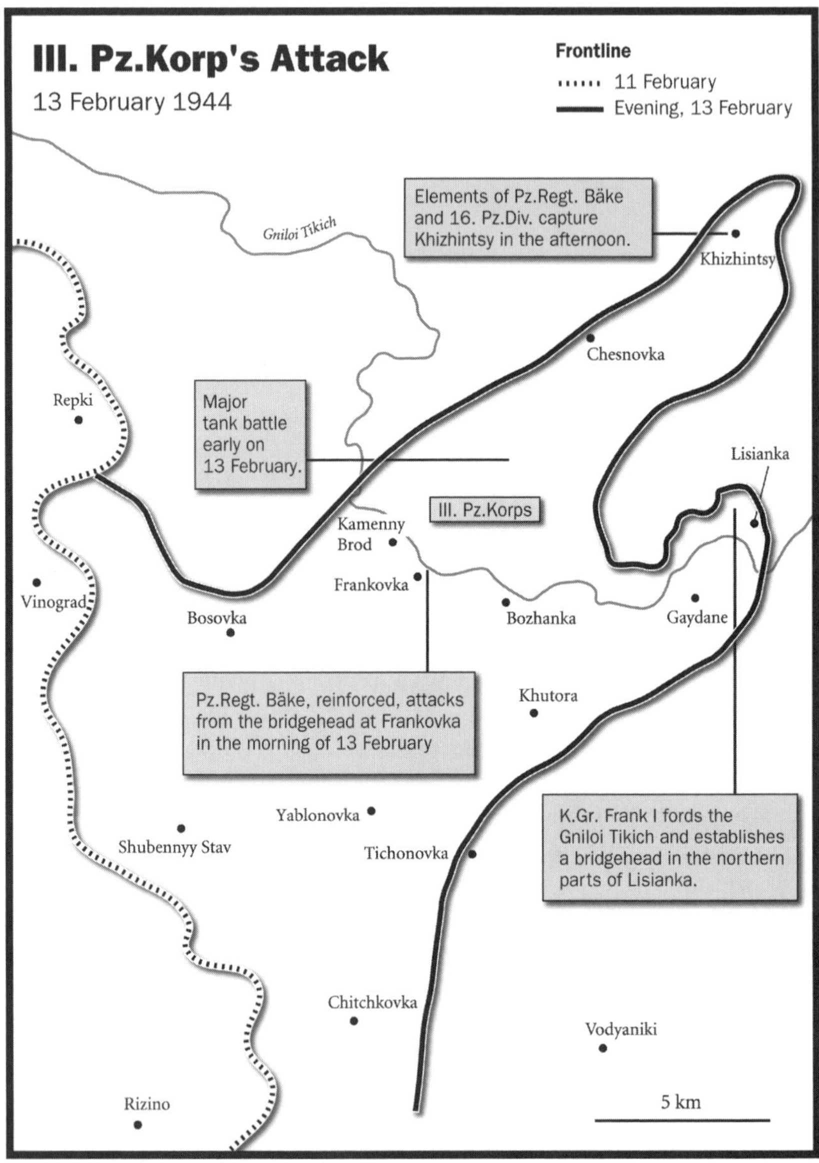

the T-34s rolled straight toward the guns of the Tigers. At a distance of about 1,800 meters the Tigers opened fire and destroyed all the T-34s, save a few who turned back in time.[577]

Scherf ordered his Tigers forward when the Soviet tanks withdrew and soon became engaged in a life and death battle with Soviet tanks and antitank guns. Fortunately the flanking move by the Panthers now paid off, as they effectively engaged the Soviet tanks. However, the Soviet forces had further cards to play, when they threatened to outflank Scherf's Tigers on the left; but again Scherf was lucky, as a Panther company from 16th Panzer Division arrived in time to stave off the threat. Meanwhile the Stukas continued attacking and proved especially effective at silencing the Soviet antitank guns. Finally the Germans got the upper hand, and when the battle was over they estimated they had knocked out about 70 tanks and 40 antitank guns. Five Tigers and four Panthers had been put out of action.[578]

When the strong Soviet position had been defeated, German troops from 16th Panzer Division occupied Dadushkovka at about 10.00hrs. There was no time to rest, as it was necessary to take advantage of this hard-fought success. In the mud the tanks and SPWs pushed on and took Chesnovka at 11.20hrs. One and a half hours later, Bäke's regiment took up positions at hill 239.8, which was located about five kilometers north of Lisyanka, on the main road from Lisyanka to Baranye Pole. It was the very road Kravchenko's tanks had used when they'd first headed for Zvenigorodka to encircle XI and XXXXII Corps.[579]

The Tigers kept blocking the road, while four Panthers, together with 12 SPWs from the reconnaissance battalion of 16th Panzer Division, continued toward Khizhintsy, which was taken in the afternoon. Thus the 16th Panzer Division and heavy Panzer Regiment Bäke had covered another 12 kilometers. Only 10 kilometers remained before they reached Gruppe Stemmermann. This was an impressive achievement, and von Manstein sent a radio message to III Panzer Corps and the 1st, 16th, and 17th Panzer Divisions, with the following content:[580] "Bravo—despite mud and Russians, already much accomplished. Now it is about the last step. Teeth together and forward. Now or never. This step will succeed too." [581]

The Germans Hold Lisyanka

Further south, at Lisyanka, Kampfgruppe Frank searched for a way to cross the Gniloi Tikich River. The thaw had caused the water to rise and the current was swift. The banks were steep and the condition of the river bed was unknown. That morning Soviet attacks had claimed the Kampfgruppe's attention, but at noon Sergeant Strippel found a place where it might be possible to ford the river. Together with soldiers who volunteered for the task, he crossed the river further west of the bridge that had been blown up just in front of Lieutenant Ciliox's Panther a day and a half earlier. Six more Panthers were collected, all with crews who volunteered, and, supported by Stukas, they managed to cross the river safely.[582]

With Strippel's Panther in the lead, the Germans expanded the bridgehead. It was important to get infantry across too, and under cover from the guns of the Panthers that had already crossed, soldiers from the 6th Company of 113th Panzer Grenadier Regiment began crossing. In what amounted to a mixture of swimming and fording, the soldiers challenged the ice-cold water and swift current, but all made it to the other side. Once over they faced hard fighting, but by midnight the Germans had taken control of the western half of Lisyanka. Engineers began to repair the bridge, but it was too early to tell if it would be strong enough to carry Panthers. The muddy ground made it difficult to move forward essential repair equipment.[583]

Despite the uncertainty of the bridge at Lisyanka, the events of 13 February amounted to a major success for III Panzer Corps, which kindled hopes for the imminent rescue of Gruppe Stemmermann. The major concern was, as ever, the resupply of the spearheads. In the evening Frank had 22 Panthers fully operational and six that were not. In addition, most of Panzer Grenadier Regiment 113 and elements of Engineer Battalion 37 (both units belonging to First Panzer Division) were available to Frank at Lisyanka.[584]

Maintaining Supply Lines

This was all that 1st Panzer Division could make available for the advance toward Gruppe Stemmermann, since the rest of the division was either busy hauling supplies, covering the eastern flank, or had simply not yet arrived. In the Rizino area the divisional antiaircraft battalion was employed, but it was immobile. It had been stripped of its half-tracks, which were employed in moving supplies forward. The supply route was under constant threat from roving Soviet forces, and to escort supply convoys from Tichonovka to Lisyanka, Koll had to use some of his PzKw IV tanks and Wespe and Hummel SP artillery pieces, in addition to one engineer company and elements of the SPW battalion. To cover the flank from Koblyaki to Tikhonovka, Koll disposed the reconnaissance battalion, the PzKw IV battalion, one antitank company, one infantry company, and three artillery batteries. The rest of his division was stuck in mud further south.[585]

Evidently Koll could only use a fraction of his division to push forward. Especially noteworthy is the relegation of the PzKw IV tanks to the role of securing supply lines to the Panthers, which led the attack. When the Germans had decided that each Panzer division should have one battalion of Panther tanks and one with PzKw IVs, several factors influenced the decision. One of the most important was that a complete shift to Panthers could not be done without seriously interrupting tank production, just at a time when it was critical that the rate of production should be increased. Thus the PzKw IV, which was old but not obsolete, was retained in the Panzer divisions. In fact production of the Panzers continued until the end of the war, which was sensible, considering that by February 1944 only seven Panther battalions had yet reached the front. Of these all but one were engaged in the battle to save Gruppe Stemmermann.

The idea to place Panthers at the tip of the attack, and use the older PzKw IVs to cover the flanks could usually not be carried through in practice, as most Panzer divisions had to rely on the PzKw IV and StuG III. At Korsun there was an usually high number of Panthers and Tigers available, and indeed almost all terrain gained by III Panzer Corps was taken with them in the lead. The lighter PzKw IV and StuG III were mainly used for flank protection. It had probably never been envisaged that the lighter vehicles should be employed as far back as Koll used them at this stage of the operation, but reality is a much stronger factor in determining dispositions than doctrine, and it is difficult to see what Koll could have done differently under the circumstances.

The whole of III Panzer Corps had a long flank and extended supply routes to worry about. North of the 1st Panzer Division, the attack force consisted of only Panzer Regiment Bäke, the 506th Tiger Battalion, and the Panther Battalion, the SPW battalion, and the reconnaissance battalion of the 16th Panzer Division. The rest of 16th Panzer Division, as well as the entire 17th Panzer Division and all of the Leibstandarte, fought to protect the flank and keep the supply route to the lead units open. The last component of III Panzer Corps was the 198th Division, which was fighting at the base of the salient that III Panzer Corps had driven into Vatutin's front, and which had succeeded in recapturing Vinograd and reestablishing the connection with SS-Leibstandarte.[586]

The extended flanks called for reinforcements, and during 13 February Hube instructed the XXXXVI Panzer Corps to make a plan showing how quickly the 4th Mountain Division could be relieved and sent to III Panzer Corps. Initially the 4th Mountain Division could be relieved by the 6th Panzer Division, but Hube demanded that the latter division would later have to be made available as a reserve.[587]

One reason for Hube's concern may have been the presence of Zhmachenko's 40th Army, which attacked the 34th Infantry Division near Tinovka. After a thorough preparation by mortars and rocket launchers, infantry supported by tanks assaulted. The attack carried into Tinovka and street fighting ensued, while the advancing Soviet forces isolated German defenders on Hill 235 west of the village. Eventually the 34th Division halted the Soviet attack, but clearly reserves at hand would be preferable. If Zhmachenko succeeded in breaking through, the consequences could be disastrous for the Germans. Not only would the relief attempt be impossible, the entire III Panzer Corps could be cut off.[588]

For the moment German intelligence did not suggest that Zhmachenko had strong armored forces on hand, and the ground conditions were as much a hindrance to Soviet mobile operations as they were to the Germans; but circumstances could change. It was more prudent to begin moving the 4th Mountain Division soon. As a further consideration, the gap between 1st Panzer Army and 8th Army was still almost undefended. More troops would be needed to prevent the Red Army from exploiting it.[589]

Maintaining the Bridgeheads

During 13 February, von Vormann's XXXXVII Panzer Corps made very little progress. Almost all of the tanks in 11th Panzer Division were out of fuel, as not even tracked vehicles designed to pull other heavy equipment could get forward. The I./26 Panther Battalion had three tanks still running. One of them was commanded by second lieutenant Fisch, who moved forward toward suspected Soviet tanks. Within a short time his tank was struck repeatedly and he was hit by splinters in the back and head. Fisch was killed almost instantly, but his crew drove the tank back to safety. Little else happened in the 11th Panzer Division's sector. The tank crews tried to alleviate the supply problems by distributing the scarce ammunition between the tanks, to ensure that each had at least some rounds of both high-explosive and armor-piercing. For the moment, supply was the limiting factor on the readiness of the tanks. The I./26 Battalion actually had 20 Panthers in running order, but the majority of them were inoperable due to lack of fuel or ammunition.[590]

Somewhat more success was achieved by the 13th Panzer Division at Yurkovka, but still the gains were only modest. The bridgehead was slightly enlarged, but that was about it. From an armchair general's point of view, it could be argued that it would have been better to send 13th Panzer Division to reinforce the bridgehead already taken by 11th Panzer Division. However, that would mean two divisions on a road network that already was overstrained in the present weather conditions. Colonel Reinhard, the Chief of Staff of XXXXVII Panzer Corps, had to borrow a Storch aircraft to get forward and visit the 11th Panzer Division's command post. It cannot have been an encouraging trip, since it must have been obvious to Reinhard that only tanks could still move, and then only at great strain to their engines and transmissions, and by consuming scarce fuel. Furthermore, many German soldiers had been afflicted by "Volhynian fever," a kind of typhoid disease. It seemed that von Wietersheim and his chief of staff had also been infected.[591]

More drama took place inside the pocket, as fighting raged on its perimeter. During the night, fighting had continued at Komarovka, Shenderovka, and Novo Buda and the struggle for these vital localities continued into the morning of 13 February. The Germans penetrated into the furthest parts of Komarovka at about 08.00hrs, but soon faced a Soviet response. At 09.10hrs heavy Soviet artillery fire rained down on the German positions around Novo Buda. Stemmermann asked for air power to attack the positions of the Soviet artillery units, because lack of ammunition prevented his artillery from effectively countering that of the enemy. In the meantime, the German soldiers could only hunker down in their foxholes and wait for the major attack that seemed certain to follow soon.[592]

The German fears were fully justified. During the night, Selivanov's cavalry had moved to get into position to attack on 13 February. He had his 11th and 12th Guards Cavalry Divisions available to assault Novo Buda and Shenderovka, while 63rd Cavalry Division, supported by 19 tanks, attacked Komarovka. It was vital to prevent the Germans inside the pocket from moving further to the southwest, where the German III

Panzer Corps constituted the gravest threat among the enemy forces outside the pocket.[593]

After an artillery preparation lasting more than an hour, the Soviet forces, supported by tanks, attacked and penetrated Novo Buda, where the Wallonien Brigade had just relieved the 266th Infantry Regiment. The commander of the latter unit, Major Siegel, was still in Novo Buda when Soviet tanks rolled into the streets between the houses. He watched helplessly as a Soviet tank slowed down and stopped very close to him. His orderly had just left with the only available Panzerfaust to fight another tank and Siegel could only wait in silence. Fortunately for Siegel, Lieutenant Peters was not far away and he stalked the imprudent tank and hit it with another Panzerfaust.[594]

The 266th Infantry Regiment had not gotten far from Novo Buda and swiftly conducted a counterattack, which recaptured the village. The Wallonians once again assumed responsibility for the village, but the Soviet soldiers remained just outside. Major Lippert, who commanded the Wallonian Brigade, was about to direct his soldiers to their positions when he was hit in the chest just as he stepped out from a house. The wound was severe and Lippert passed away quickly. His adjutant, Leon Degrelle, assumed command over the Brigade while Soviet artillery began to shell the village. Lippert's body was placed in a coffin, which was later fastened to an SP gun in an attempt to bring the corpse out of the pocket and bury it.[595]

The fighting at Novo Buda was only a prelude to a greater battle. Stemmermann's pleas for air support increased, as Soviet artillery continued to shell Novo Buda. The Luftwaffe liaison officer at the 8th Army staff replied that he had already asked the I. Fliegerkorps to support the ground units fighting in the Shenderovka–Steblev area. In the meantime the 2nd Ukrainian Front continued its attacks on Komarovka and Shenderovka. A force of about a dozen Soviet tanks attacked from Morentsy, along the road to Novo Buda and Komarovka, but was repulsed. Within the villages, bitter house-to-house fighting ensued, but neither side made much progress. However, Konev's chief aim was to prevent the Germans from moving further toward the south or west. At least temporarily, this objective was achieved.[596]

The complaints from Gruppe Stemmermann about lack of air support continued, and late in the afternoon a message was received that air power had been directed to support the armored spearheads attacking toward the pocket. All available aircraft had been used in those areas, leaving nothing to support Gruppe Stemmermann. Perhaps this was a reasonable decision. After all, priorities had to be made, and the fate of the Gruppe was probably more dependent on the progress made by III and XXXXVII Panzer Corps than on air cover directly above the pocket. The rapid progress made by III Panzer Corps on 13 February was at least partly aided by the air support it received.[597]

At the same time, papers produced by "Nationalkomitee Freies Deutschland" continued to rain down into the pocket. They seem seldom to have had the intended effect, and on this day they had a completely different effect. One of the papers was brought to General Lieb, who found that they contained statements about the size of the German force inside the cauldron. To his relief, Lieb concluded that the enemy estimates of the size of the surrounded force were grossly exaggerated, which might lead the Red Army to be more cautious in its dealings with them.[598]

The Loss of Korsun Airfield, 13 February

For two weeks the air field at Korsun had provided a lifeline for Gruppe Stemmermann, but on 13 February it was finally captured by Konev's forces. Although supplies could still be dropped from the aircraft, wounded soldiers could no longer be evacuated by air. However, very few wounded had been evacuated by air in the preceding days, since the landing strip had become so soft that aircraft were hardly able to land and take off. The loss of the airfield had been anticipated, since the Germans had been shifting forces from the northeastern part of the pocket to the southwest. All trust was placed on the hope that the III Panzer Corps could reach Gruppe Stemmermann.[599]

It seemed unlikely that the German forces inside the pocket could hold out for long. Gruppe Stemmermann had lived from hand to mouth for days, and on 13 February it received very few supplies as the radio beacon did not work. In the atrocious weather the beacon was indispensable for aircrews, as it was almost impossible to navigate to the pocket without it. Despite the poor weather, 50 He-111s dropped 39 cubic meters of fuel and 25 canisters with ammunition, but how much of it that was retrieved by Gruppe Stemmermann is unclear.[600]

Somewhat better conditions prevailed over the III Panzer Corps, and it received 61 cubic meters of fuel and 34 tons of ammunition for its

Tigers and Panthers. Obviously, however, the aircraft could not drop their load exactly where the tanks were located. First of all, it was imprudent to drop the loads precisely on the troops, and secondly it was not always easy to locate the tanks, which tended to stay under cover. Finally, it was always difficult to place the load exactly where intended. Lieutenant Lappe, Bäke's adjutant, recalled how the fuel reached the tanks:[601]

> *Finally, on 13 February, we reached the small town of Khizhintsy. We had been told that the outer ring of the pocket would be found there. Unfortunately erroneous! The advance thus far had caused almost all the tanks to fall out. The last tanks ploughed forward in the mud, which reached up to the mudguards, meter by meter. Fuel consumption was enormous, Panthers could consume a full fuel load on 3.5–4 km. Low flying Ju-52s dropped petrol barrels, which often landed in the mud 200–300 meters from the tanks. Steel wires had to be connected to the barrels, which could thereby be winched to the tanks with some fuel remaining.*[602]

The German Link-up at Lisyanka, 14–15 February

Although fuel and ammunition were scarce, at least some reached the front units. In the armored spearheads, shortages of food also became critical. Unlike Gruppe Stemmermann, which could live to some extent on stores from an area that had been held for a while, the soldiers of the III Panzer Corps advanced through an area that had been held by the enemy for a couple of weeks. No stores could be counted upon except those captured by chance. As the limited capacity of the supply aircraft was devoted to fuel and ammunition, the officers and men had to continue without receiving any more food. When their rations had been consumed, they had to go on fighting despite empty stomachs.[603]

The soldiers who reached Khizhintsy were not only forced to contend with hunger, they also had to cope with the discouraging discovery that the terrain east of the town was wholly unsuited for tanks, something that became clear to the higher commanders in the evening. This was a bitter disappointment. What had appeared as a short distance separating the pocket from the relief force suddenly became much further. One possibility was that Gruppe Stemmermann might traverse the area east of Khizhintsy, as infantry would find it easier to cross the difficult terrain. Wenck asked Speidel about this in the evening, but 8th

Army had already suggested that the encircled corps should concentrate all available forces to reach III Panzer Corps.[604]

To Zhukov it must have become apparent by now that the major threat was not von Vormann's corps, but Breith's corps. Consequently Rotmistrov was ordered to shift forces from the sector southeast of Zvenigorodka to the area between Dzhurzhentsy and Komarovka. There was some risk involved in weakening the defenses against the German XXXXVII Panzer Corps, but this had to be weighed against the risks in the area between III Panzer Corps and Gruppe Stemmermann. Evidently the latter problem was deemed more threatening, and hindsight certainly does not contradict that judgment.[605]

Bad roads, of course, plagued the Soviets as well as the Germans. Aside from the time and fuel used up in the movement, vehicles were strained and rendered unusable. It seems that the 18th Tank Corps, which previously had been in reserve, was the first unit to arrive in the new area. With 30 operational tanks it reached Dzhurzhentsy in order to take up defensive positions for the following day. From the 20th Tank Corps, two tank brigades were directed to Lisyanka and one tank brigade was sent to 4th Guards Army, while the rifle brigade remained southeast of Lisyanka. Finally, the 29th Tank Corps was sent to the Komarovka area.[606]

To move the units and their supplies through the mud called for hard work from the soldiers, but the tank units also used oxen and horses to drag supply items forward. The local population was also drafted to help. Despite these measures, only one third of a basic load of fuel was available to Rotmistrov's troops at the new deployment area. Certainly this was a serious impediment, but their opponents were not better off. The following day would show whether the Soviet countermeasures were sufficient or not.[607]

On 14 February Breith decided to fly in a Fieseler Storch to Lisyanka. A pilot could usually find a suitable place to land such a small aircraft close to the unit to be visited. On this occasion the pilot landed at Lisyanka, where Breith met both Koll and Frank near the bridge. The commander of III Panzer Corps could see for himself that hard fighting raged north of the Gniloi Tikich River, where Frank's troops tried to advance toward Oktyabr, a small village northeast of Lisyanka. Attack was followed by counterattack and the margins between success and failure were slight. The border between life and death was slight too, which was well illustrated by a German tank commander who, as was common, fought with his head up from the cupola. For some reason he decided to get into the tank and had just got his head down through the cupola when an armor piercing round hit the hatch which he had not yet closed.[608]

Oktyabr was separated from Lisyanka by a stream that flowed to the Gniloi Tikich River. The stream was not wide, but would still be difficult for the tanks to cross. However, when darkness fell the platoon commanded by Sergeant Strippel captured a 40-ton bridge over the stream. The bridge was undamaged and Strippel's tank and crew shot up two T-34s that had been tasked with protecting it. Thus Strippel was credited with the destruction of 60 enemy tanks so far in the war.[609]

The opening of the route to the northeast was an important achievement. Hitherto the 16th Panzer Division, with the attached Panzer Regiment Bäke, had attacked along the main axis, while 1st Panzer Division had a flanking role. However, on 14 February it was decided that the main effort would be made from the Lisyanka area due to both the difficult terrain east of Khizhintsy and the stiff Soviet resistance.[610]

To cover the gap between 1st and 16th Panzer Divisions, Kampfgruppe Pietsch from the 17th Panzer Division had been ordered to advance north of the Gniloi Tikich River late on 13 February, and to descend on Lisyanka from the northwest. Just before midnight the Kampfgruppe began to move from Frankovka, with one PzKw IV, three StuG IIIs from Stug.Abt. 249, and a few SPWs with infantry. However, soon one StuG and all the SPWs had broken down. The infantry—one officer, two NCOs, and 27 men—had to sit on the PzKw IV and the remaining two StuGs. After spending 10 hours moving to Chesnovka, a journey of less than 10 kilometers, the first goal was finally reached. Three Tigers from s.Pz.Abt. 506 joined Kampfgruppe Pietsch before the move toward Lisyanka was resumed, by following the main road toward Lisyanka.

Halfway between Chesnovka and Lisyanka the small German force met small arms fire from Soviet infantry. A commander of one of the Tigers was wounded in the head before the Soviet troops withdrew. When only two to three kilometers separated Kampfgruppe Pietsch from Lisyanka, more infantry opposed the German advance, but again were brushed aside. In the skirmish the turret on the PzKw IV jammed and rendered the tank unable to take part in further fighting. Also, a shot from a Soviet assault gun penetrated one of the Tigers, but its crew bailed out unharmed. After the brief action, Kamfpgruppe Pietsch struggled through the mud, and at twilight its armored vehicles were discovered by soldiers from Kampfgruppe Frank. Pietsch's troops had by then reached a hill just north-northwest of Lisyanka. However, Pietsch and Frank did not link up until the following day.[611]

Even though Kampfgruppe Pietsch was not particularly strong, it was a welcome addition to the low combat strength of Kampfgruppe Frank. As we have seen, many tanks were inoperable, and the infantry was very week too. Casualties had not been particularly high, but there were many cases of frostbite, trench foot, and disease caused by the poor conditions. The infantry were the main sufferers, and their combat strength declined considerably. Kampfgruppe Bäke suffered from exactly the same problems, and soon various combat teams would be scrambled from units fighting further west.

To pull elements out of units at the flanks put those sectors in jeopardy, though as we have seen, on 13 February, Hube had instructed XXXXVI Panzer Corps to prepare pulling out one division. The issue was again discussed by Hube and von Manstein on 14 February. Von Manstein proposed that 6th Panzer Division should be sent to III Panzer Corps. Normally this would have been a logical choice, but Hube considered 4th Mountain Division to be a better candidate. The 6th Panzer Division was not very strong in tanks. It had 15 operational PzKw IVs, and on the muddy roads several would no doubt break down, but it possessed valuable infantry. However, Hube did not believe that 6th Panzer Division, delayed by its trucks that had only limited cross-country capability, could transfer east quickly enough along roads that were quagmires of mud. The fact that considerable parts of 1st Panzer Division still struggled on the roads was sufficient testimony to this belief. Instead, he preferred to pull out the 4th Mountain Division and send it to III Panzer Corps. Von Manstein asked Hube to examine this question more closely.[612]

After checking with the chief of staff of XXXXVI Panzer Corps (to which both divisions were subordinated) and the transport officer in 1st Panzer Army, Hube called von Manstein again and it was decided that 4th Mountain Division should be sent to III Panzer Division, largely by utilizing railroads. It was uncertain if it would arrive in time to assist in the rescue of Gruppe Stemmermann.[613]

Terrain, weather and the poor roads in eastern Europe often made it difficult for conventional trucks to move. Halftracks had better mobility in difficult conditions, but were expensive to produce and sustain.
(SIPA PRESS)

CHAPTER 17

Time Is Running Out

Breith's III Panzer Corps made little progress on 14 February, thus further increasing the need for air supplies to reach Gruppe Stemmermann in the pocket. To help the aircraft find the drop zones for their cargo, three bonfires were lit in the shape of a triangle. The Luftwaffe had asked that headlights from vehicles should illuminate the area where loads were to be dropped, but the muddy roads proved so difficult that all attempts to get vehicles properly positioned failed. The fires were probably of some help to the aircrews, as 44 aircraft out of 74 dispatched dropped their loads, consisting of 20 tons of ammunition and 18 cubic meters of fuel. These supplies were very welcome, but if one considers that a single division could easily expend more than twice as much ammunition during a day's fighting, it begins clear how precarious the situation was. Six divisions were located inside the pocket, although they were far from full strength. During the night, the weather deteriorated even further, making it impossible for more aircraft to reach the pocket.[614]

Mud also prevented XXXXVII Panzer Corps from having much of an impact on the positions of 2nd Ukrainian Front. Von Vormann observed that the fuel consumption of his tanks was five times higher than normal, due to the sticky mud. A Panther consumed one basic fuel load per 18 kilometers under the current terrain conditions. Other vehicles could hardly move at all, and there was simply not enough fuel available to get any significant attack moving. The XXXXVII Panzer Corps was plainly not in a position to exploit the fact that the Soviet defenses had been weakened by moving most of Rotmistrov's armor to

the region between III Panzer Corps and Gruppe Stemmermann.[615]

Already in the morning, the soldiers of Gruppe Stemmermann suspected that they would need all the ammunition they could get. Noise from approaching Soviet tanks could be heard south and east of Novo Buda. Probably these belonged to 29th Tank Corps, which had been sent to reinforce the 5th Guards Cavalry Corps and the 202nd, 254th, and 62nd Rifle Divisions that were already fighting in the Komarovka–Novo Buda area.[616]

The Soviet tanks were soon thrown into the fighting for the important villages at the southwestern perimeter of the pocket, while the

Germans tried to continue further to the southwest. Neither side made much progress during the day, but casualties continued to mount. Lieb reported that there were around 2,000 wounded in the pocket. These had to be brought along as the pocket tried to wander southwestward, as its eastern and northern perimeters were gradually pulled back. Originally it had been hoped that this would free troops that could be used to attack toward III Panzer Corps, but in the end the added troops only compensated for losses suffered in the units already committed to the attack. The lack of ammunition seriously hampered the Germans. It been intended to attack from Khilki at noon, but this attack had to be postponed due to lack of ammunition. Thus, at the end of the day the positions were much the same as at the beginning of the day, a result that probably pleased Konev much more than his counterparts on the German side.[617]

Army Group South was extremely concerned about the situation of Gruppe Stemmermann, and at 18.05hrs Wöhler called von Manstein to briefly describe the situation. Von Manstein replied: [618] "Since the first day Gruppe Stemmermann has not got forward at all."

Wöhler said: "In the afternoon I ordered that Gruppe Stemmermann should pull together all forces to bolster the offensive strength and that all forces north of the Ross River should be withdrawn to the southern side. Lack of fuel and ammunition, due to the poor weather which prevented air supply, hampered the movements."

"To move south of the Ross River is the last movement Gruppe Stemmermann can make," Manstein said. "After that it must unconditionally break through."

"I have already ordered Stemmermann several times to break out. Perhaps Lieb is more active," Wöhler responded.

"Well, then one perhaps has to place all forces under Lieb. It must be clear to Gruppe Stemmermann that it has to break through to Dzhurzhentsy by its own forces. How many men are there in the cauldron?"

"54,000."

"Can not the 11th Panzer Division be reinforced?," von Manstein asked.

"Unfortunately not, and currently it is almost impossible to keep 11th Panzer Division supplied."

"I would like to ask you to consider whether the 3rd Panzer Division can be released."

"Unfortunately it is impossible for the moment," Wöhler replied.

Thus ended the conversation, and it seems that Wöhler was correct when he regarded it as impossible to release the 3rd Panzer Division. Even if it could be done, it would require days given the condition of the roads. By then the fate of Gruppe Stemmermann would already be sealed. It is somewhat ironic that Wöhler, who had been pushing a reluctant von Vormann to advance, was now being pushed by his superior, who perhaps found Wöhler lacking some energy. However, the mud was a very real hindrance, and it seems that the closer a commander was to the troops in their struggle with the mud, the more realistic he became.

Other reinforcements had been considered and discussed previously, first and foremost the 2nd Parachute Division. Later in the evening Busse called Speidel and suggested that this division should be used to relieve 3rd Panzer Division. As it seemed that the Soviet 20th Tank Corps had been pulled out and sent northwest, it would be desirable to get the 3rd Panzer Division free for other missions. Speidel replied that it would take about 10 days for the 2nd Parachute Division to arrive. For the moment, the only thing that could be done was to send two battalions with replacement personnel to Kampfgruppe Haack.[619]

The lack of progress on 14 February was a bitter disappointment to all the German soldiers remaining inside the pocket. By this time, the knowledge of the loss of the Korsun airfield must have become fairly well known, and the conclusion was obvious. If the rescue did not succeed quickly, everything would be lost. General Stemmermann was well aware of the seriousness of the situation, and concluded that if the tanks of III Panzer Corps did not reach the pocket on 15 February a crisis would occur. It was not a far fetched opinion. The XI and XXXXII Corps were compressed into a small oblong area, where the few roads, weakened by the mud, were crammed with vehicles. Many of them carried wounded, who had to endure several hours in traffic jams, but it was imperative to move them to Shenderovka, as Steblev was evacuated by the Germans later in the day.[620]

Neither did the fighting seem to go well for the Germans in the pocket. The 72nd Division continued to advance from the Khilki area, but made no net progress as Soviet forces launched counterattacks. A Soviet attack at Nova Buda threatened to expel a battalion from SS-Wiking's Germania Regiment, which had just relieved the Wallonians. As the Soviet infantry was accompanied by tanks they stood a good chance of pushing the Germans out of the village. However, the remaining PzKw IV tanks of SS-Wiking were near by and averted the threat.[621]

Again neither side made much progress, but as time was working against the Germans, Konev could remain fairly satisfied with the situation around the pocket. He was probably not too worried about the situation on the outer ring either, although von Vormann's troops launched a renewed attack in the morning. This time it was Kampfgruppe Haack, supported by tanks from 11th Panzer Division, which captured some terrain southwest of Zvenigorodka, not far from hill 204.8 which had been reached by the tanks of 11th Panzer Division on 12 February. German gains were modest, however, and a snowstorm also hampered the actions. In any case, German tank strength in the area was very low. On paper it may have looked impressive, as two tank regiments, Panzer Regiment 4 from 13th Panzer Division and Panzer Regiment 15 from 11th Panzer Division operated in the area, supported by one Panther battalion (I./Pz.Rgt. 26) and two assault gun battalions (Pz.Abt. 8 and StuG.Abt. 911). However, these units only counted six tanks and three assault guns operational. Had such a force been at full strength it would have had over 500 tanks and assault guns.[622]

With such low tank strength on the German side, it seems clear that few risks attended Konev's decision to shift Rotmistrov's 5th Guards Tank Army. Furthermore, no immediate improvement in the German tank strength could be expected. Lack of spare parts made repairs of the many damaged tanks in workshops impossible, and the delivery of new tanks from factories was impossible under the conditions. But it was not only the machines that were at the end of their tether; the soldiers were exhausted too. The men were utterly overstrained and many had become completely apathetic. Indeed, von Vormann seems to have been at the end of his strength and contemplated moving his command post backward, something to which Wöhler strongly objected. Given the low strength of XXXXVII Panzer Corps and its immense supply difficulties, it is doubtful that von Vormann could have much impact on the rescue of Gruppe Stemmermann, no matter where he was located.[623]

As we have seen, III Panzer Corps made relatively little progress on 14 February. The temperature had fallen and frost had set in, which might have offered better roads for the wheeled vehicles. However, heavy snowfalls began in the afternoon of 14 February, so the roads remained as difficult as ever for the vehicles that made up the majority of the German divisions. It was still up to the few operational tanks of

1st Panzer Division, Bäke's Regiment, and Kampfgruppe Pietsch to effect a link-up with Gruppe Stemmermann, provided of course that fuel and ammunition could be brought forward.[624]

Early in the morning of 15 February, Breith and Back, who had flown in a Fieseler Storch, arrived at Bäke's command post. The two generals conveyed the message that Bäke's regiment would have to shift south to attack along the Lisyanka axis, a decision that could hardly have been a surprise to Bäke, as he had himself concluded that the terrain east of Chesnovka was unsuitable for his tanks. Given the very small number of vehicles available to Bäke, six Tigers and eight Panthers, he could not send many tanks south. It was decided that the Panthers would remain in the Chesnovka–Khizhintsy area, but evacuate the latter village to fight against the Soviet tanks south of Medvin, while the Tigers moved south, toward Lisyanka.[625]

Before noon the Tigers, commanded by Scherf, set out on their journey to Lisyanka. Almost immediately a Tiger received a hit in the rear which penetrated into the engine room. In poor visibility the remaining Tigers took up the fight and claimed to have knocked out four T-34s within a short time. The fighting continued, as the Soviet tankers tried to use the undulating terrain to find cover. It was to little avail, however, as the Tigers still found opportunities to fire on the Soviet tanks, and claimed to have knocked out another seven T-34s. The Germans also suffered losses. One Tiger had its drive sprocket shot away, and another received track damage from a hit by an artillery shell. Both these vehicles were rendered immobile by the hits. Also, Scherf's tank was hit: a Soviet shell tore away the spare track fastened to the side of the turret, but due to the angle of the shot no other damage was sustained. Finally, one Tiger had been penetrated, whereby two men were killed and one wounded.[626]

Meanwhile the Panther battalion of Panzer Regiment Bäke had also been hotly engaged when a Soviet force, estimated to consist of about a dozen tanks by the Germans, attacked from the north. The attack was repelled and the Germans claimed to have knocked out eight tanks, but suffered losses too, as three Panthers were put out of action, one of them by a shot that ricocheted on the lower part of the gun mantlet and hit between the turret and the chassis, jamming the turret.[627]

In addition to the tanks put out of action, there were soldiers who had been wounded. They had to be evacuated, but this was not easy to accomplish. With Soviet tanks operating in the area it was risky to send them in SPWs without escort by tanks. For the moment the wounded had to wait, hungry and frozen, like the other soldiers who continued fighting. Since it left Frankovka, Bäke's regiment had received no rations except the emergency rations kept in the tanks. They had gone without any real sleep for weeks, but it was realized that their comrades in the pocket were in an even worse condition.[628]

During the night, engineers of Kampfgruppe Frank had improved the bridge at Lisyanka. Thus it would be easier for Frank's forces to continue toward the pocket, but only if the supply of fuel and ammunition could be ensured. A heavily protected supply convoy, led by Major Feig, managed to reach Lisyanka in the afternoon of 15 February. While Feig labored to get supplies forward, the fighting continued in Lisyanka. At the end of the day Frank's soldiers had managed to get control over the entire village, and could spend the night preparing to attack toward Oktyabr the following day.[629]

Of course some hopes could be nurtured about the intention to attack from Lisyanka, over Oktyabr and toward Komarovka, but it was clear to the German commanders that the available forces were very weak. Kampfgruppe Pietsch did not bring much strength to the Lisyanka area. In the morning of 15 February it only counted one PzKw IV and one StuG III, plus some infantry from 17th Reconnaissance Battalion. The Kampfgruppe supported Kampfgruppe Frank in the fighting for the northern parts of Lisyanka, but clearly more forces were needed. As the situation in the sector held by the SS-Leibstandarte was not as difficult as it had been a few days ago, it was decided to detach elements of that division to reinforce the thrust toward the pocket. However, all the division could scavenge from its depleted ranks were four armoured fighting vehicles: one StuG III, one PzKw IV, one Panther, and one Tiger. A few Panzer grenadiers rode on top of the tanks. The difficult terrain and roads made travelling arduous. Late in the afternoon the battle group had only reached Shubennyi Stav. It would not be able to influence the situation at Lisyanka until the following day. In fact, the entire journey, of some 21 kilometers, required 36 hours.[630]

With such scant reinforcements to throw into the thrust toward the pocket, it was clear that time was running out for the Germans. At the same time, a breakout would be very hazardous. It would mean that many wounded men would have to be left behind, and probably much heavy equipment would be lost too, even if everything went as well as the Germans could hope. If the breakout failed, however, it could turn into a bloodbath. The fighting during the preceding days suggested that Soviet forces around the pocket had been reinforced, which would make a breakout very difficult. Nonetheless, there was no longer any viable alternative.

Plans for the Breakout, 15 February

Early on 15 February, Stemmermann and Lieb met to discuss the breakout. Several measures had already been taken to enable the attempt. Secret papers had been burnt and many vehicles that could not be expected to accompany a breakout because of the terrain or the lack of fuel had been destroyed. Considerable amounts of other heavy equipment had been destroyed too.

The most difficult decision probably concerned the wounded. There were about 2,100 wounded men in Shenderovka, of whom 1,450 were in such condition that they could only either lie down or sit. Lieb and Stemmermann agreed that these men would have to be left behind. To bring them along would jeopardize the breakout without helping the wounded, since the transports to take them would most likely not be able to traverse the difficult terrain, especially in the prevailing bad weather. So it was decided that those who could not walk would be left at the provisional hospital, together with medical staff. A doctor from each division would stay behind. Hopefully the Soviet forces would treat them reasonably well.[631]

For the breakout it was envisaged that Lieb's corps, with the Korps-Abteilung B, the 72nd Division, and the SS-Wiking division would constitute the vanguard, while Stemmermann's corps, with 57th and 88th Divisions, would make up the rearguard. From the Komarovka–Khilki area the vanguard would break through the enemy defenses and take the shortest route toward Oktyabr, where III Panzer Corps was expected to be waiting. At 23.00hrs on 16 February the breakout would begin, hopefully benefiting from darkness and surprise.[632]

In principle the plan seemed simple, but of course the reality was more difficult. In the afternoon Lieb spent some time in the house he used as a command post. From there he could see the entire pocket, except when snow squalls reduced visibility. About 50,000 men were crammed inside the small area. To move them without disclosing their intentions to the enemy was not easily accomplished. But it must have been evident to the Soviet commanders that the Germans could hardly effect a link-up between the pocket and their outside forces except along the shortest route.[633]

The soldiers of the Red Army who had been taken prisoner by the Germans and who were cooperating with them, known as the Hillfswillig (abbreviated to HiWi), were of particular concern. Hundreds of thousands of HiWis were serving in German units on the Eastern Front. Unsurprisingly, they were regarded as traitors if they were captured by Soviet forces and the HiWis had even more reason than the German soldiers to fear Soviet captivity. Ten HiWi had served with Anton Meiser's battery, but at the beginning of February they all disappeared. They had been doing good service with the Germans, but when they understood that the two German corps were encircled, they seem to have deserted. Meiser realized that they most likely would have been shot if captured, and he assumed that they had tried to find partisan groups to join.[634]

As is well known, the war in the East witnessed numerous atrocities against soldiers and civilians. This is perhaps reflected in the final paragraph of Stemmermann's order for the breakout: "Violations of international law may under no circumstances occur, or else enemy acts of cruelty against the wounded are to be expected." [635]

Ammunition, in particular for small arms, was of course an important prerequisite for the breakout. A night attempt that relied on surprise would not have much call for artillery, but if this attempt did not go according to plan, artillery might well prove necessary. Furthermore, more fighting was to be expected before the breakout, and Gruppe Stemmermann was already critically low on ammunition. More supplies by air were urgently needed.[636]

Outside the pocket, many measures were taken to receive the soldiers of Gruppe Stemmermann. If all of the estimated 50,000 men made it to the III Panzer Corps it would be a considerable task to accommodate them. The local population was evacuated from villages near the front line, to provide housing for the soldiers who had broken out. Dressing stations had to be prepared to deal with the anticipated significant number of wounded. Near the front they would only receive first aid. As quickly as possible the wounded would be brought to the rear area, where trains were ready to take them to hospitals. Further preparations were made to evacuate the wounded by air.[637]

Soviet Forces on the Eve of the Breakout

Whether these German measures were to prove useful was of course at least partly up to the Soviet forces. Konev had three armies—the 4th Guards, 27th, and 52nd—surrounding the two encircled German corps. The 5th Guards Cavalry Corps had been fighting together with these armies for more than two weeks, and elements of 5th Guards Tank Army had recently been added. The units were worn from prolonged combat, however, in particular the corps of Rotmistrov's tank army. Lazarev's 20th Tank Corps only mustered six operational tanks on the evening of 15 February. Kirichenko's 29th Tank Corps was marginally better off, counting 15 operational tanks.[638]

Still, Konev had more forces to play with than Stemmermann and Lieb. The three armies around the pocket numbered 11 divisions and were supported by Selivanov's Cavalry Corps and Kirichenko's Tank Corps. Even though comparisons based on the number of divisions should always be done with caution, it seems clear that the forces constituting the ring around the pocket were stronger than the surrounded force. Furthermore, it seems that the most powerful Soviet units, in particular armor, were placed between Gruppe Stemmermann and the III Panzer Corps. The odds did not favor the planned German breakout, as Konev and Zhukov must have known.[639]

Build-up to the Breakout

Twenty-four more hours remained before the breakout began. Under better weather conditions much could happen in that time span, but with the poor ground condition, low supply levels, and exhaustion that afflicted the soldiers, no dramatic changes could be expected. On the other hand, the distance between Gruppe Stemmermann and III Panzer Corps was such that even small changes could be significant. Especially important were the villages Khilki, Komarovka, and Novo Buda, which were on the southwestern perimeter of the pocket. It would be valuable for either side to hold them and hard fighting was to be expected, which would cause ammunition stocks to shrink to dangerously low levels.

Fortunately for the Germans, the Luftwaffe made a considerable effort to provide more supplies. During 15 hours, from 15.00hrs on 15 February to 06.00hrs on 16 February, Ju-52 and He-111 aircraft flew repeatedly to drop supplies to Gruppe Stemmermann. Indeed some of the air crews made seven sorties in this brief period. The efforts paid off, and 140 tons of ammunition, 57 cubic meters of fuel, and other valuable items were dropped. General Lieb noted in his diary on 16 February that his corps was considerably better supplied with ammunition after the efforts by the Luftwaffe on the preceding night.[640]

Perhaps the Germans received the ammunition in the nick of time. On the evening of 15 February the 105th Infantry Regiment had assembled for a night attack on Khilki. The soldiers were physically exhausted, but the importance of the attack was clear to anyone who wanted to get out of the cauldron, and the troops arrived at the staging area in time. Since the attack on Nova Buda four days ago, the regiment had gained experience in night fighting and it succeeded in capturing the objective this night too, helped by the fact that the village was not particularly strongly defended by Soviet forces. A Soviet counterattack, supported by armor, was launched in the morning, but was repulsed. However, at 16.00hrs a more determined Soviet attack was launched, again with armor support. It managed to penetrate into the southwest part of Khilki, but that was as far as the Soviet success extended. Major Kaestner, the commander of the 105th Regiment, committed his reserve, including assault guns, and counterattacked. In the evening the village was in German hands.[641]

Further south, at Komarovka, the roles were reversed. At dawn on 16 February the Germans held the village, but at noon the German XI Corps reported that Soviet infantry and tanks had penetrated into the village. Heavy fighting continued to rage from house to house, and by the afternoon the western half of Komarovka was in Soviet hands while the eastern part was controlled by the Germans. At Nova Buda too, intense fighting raged during the day, but the soldiers from SS-Wallonien and the SS-Wiking Division managed to keep their grip on the village.[642]

Thus the positions along the vital southwestern edge of the pocket changed slightly but not to such an extent that they affected the German breakout plans. However, Stemmermann felt certain that the III Panzer Corps would have to defeat the Soviet forces defending to the northeast of Lisyanka. At most, he expected his own troops to be counted upon to break the inner ring around the pocket, not the outer ring. His skepticism may have reinforced the doubts, held by some of the higher German commanders, that Stemmermann was capable of leading his force in such an exceptionally difficult situation. At 10.00hrs von

Manstein again said to Speidel that he doubted that Stemmermann had the necessary energy and drive to conduct the breakout. Speidel replied that Wöhler had already ordered that Lieb should lead the breakout.[643]

As we have seen, Wöhler nurtured doubts about other commanders too. In the morning he flew to Verbovets and from there continued by a Kübelwagen to Yerki, where the command posts of Kampfgruppe Haack and 11th Panzer Division were located. Also, present were von Vormann and the commanders of the 13th and 14th Panzer Divisions, Major-Generals Mikosch and Unrein. The assembled officers testified that they lacked critical supplies, not only fuel and ammunition but also bread, boots, socks, and other items. The troops were simply worn out and suffered terribly from lice, since a further consequence of the poor supply situation was that it made it difficult for the soldiers to maintain their personal hygiene. Furthermore, the number of tanks and towing machines that had broken down, due to mud and lack of maintenance, was higher than ever before. Together with infections, all these factors combined to render combat power at a level lower than experienced before.[644]

As we have seen, disease also affected the commanders. Von Wietersheim, who suffered from "Volhynian fever," received injections in order to stay in command of 11th Panzer Division. His chief of staff, Major Drews, suffered from the same disease and was confined to bed. Martin Unrein was afflicted by some kind of stomach disease, but stayed in command of 14th Panzer Division, even though he was clearly weakened by the illness. Von Vormann was not necessarily ill, but cold and nervous strain seemed to have exhausted him, or at least this was Wöhler's impression. Despite all these difficulties, Wöhler demanded that XXXXVII Panzer Corps should continue to attack. In particular hill 208.9, east of Zvenigorodka, was to be taken. Spoiling attacks should also be made, in order to prevent 2nd Ukrainian Front from shifting troops to other areas.[645]

Olaf Ehlers: An Incident Near Yurkovka, 16 February

In the end, the XXXXVII Panzer Corps saw little action on 16 February. Most of the front line was calm, but some fighting took place over a few small hills northwest of Yurkovka. The Germans committed scattered units in this action. Olaf Ehlers was among the soldiers from 13th Panzer Division who participated, and he described his experiences in his diary. Early in the morning his Kampfgruppe formed, consisting of about 60 men. Ehlers, as observer for the artillery, brought with him a radio operator and radio equipment. However the few available vehicles did not allow Ehlers, his radio operator, and the equipment to be transported. Both the crates for the radios could be loaded in an SPW, but there was only room for either Ehlers or the radio operator. Ehlers thought it was best to let the operator go with the radios, while he followed on foot.[646]

Armed with a pistol, Ehlers struggled through the snow that covered the muddy ground beneath, following the tracks of the Kampfgruppe. The vehicles had already disappeared when he heard the unmistakable sounds of combat. It seemed to be a very brief action, as it soon became silent, and when Ehlers had squelched forward he found a few corpses of Soviet soldiers who had recently been killed. The German vehicles had continued forward and were invisible to Ehlers, because they had passed a crest line.[647]

Ehlers had not had anything to eat in the morning, but next to one of the fallen soldiers he found a bag with some bread and cheese, which he brought along. Before he continued forward, he took a Russian machine pistol, as he had lost his own a few days earlier. After only a few steps he found the bodies of two other Soviet soldiers, but there was something strange about them, as they lay in the snow without any trace of blood. With the newly acquired machine pistol he hit one of them on the boot, and suddenly the Soviet soldier moved up with his arms raised, and then the other "corpse" got up too. It was clear to Ehlers that these young boys had no intention of killing him, which they could easily have done when he walked toward them, had it been their intention. Rather they had thrown away their weapons and pretended to be dead.[648]

Unexpectedly Ehlers found himself in the possession of two prisoners of war, and decided to bring them along, as he was needed further forward. It was unthinkable to leave them, as they could get back to their unit and inform their commanders about the German forces they had encountered. Ehlers realized that he could have shot them, but he would not do that, even though he had seen Soviet soldiers kill Germans who had surrendered.[649]

Accompanied by his two prisoners, Ehlers continued forward. After walking for about half an hour they met a German tank which was loaded with killed and wounded soldiers, and had no space for the two prisoners. Ehlers continued the arduous march forward accompanied by the Soviet soldiers.[650]

After plodding through the snow for two and a half hours, Ehlers found his Kampfgruppe, which was busy improving foxholes that had been captured from the Soviet forces who had been defending earlier, but who had disappeared before Ehlers arrived. The Germans soldiers looked with amazement on the two Soviet soldiers Ehlers brought with him as he walked toward the command post. This was located in a small hut whose roof had been shot away. Ehlers let a grenadier guard the prisoners as he reported to the lieutenant who commanded the Kampfgruppe. The officer told Ehlers that they would have to prepare an all around defense, and his observation position would have to be part of the perimeter defense, since few riflemen were available.[651]

Ehlers concurred and said he could use his prisoners to dig. The lieutenant agreed and asked Ehlers to hurry, as an enemy counterattack could be expected at any moment. When Ehlers asked that the prisoners should be taken to the rear as soon as a suitable vehicle arrived, the officer replied that it would probably be difficult, as the only armored vehicle available was on its way with ammunition and rations, and would take wounded German soldiers to a dressing station after it had unloaded the supplies.[652]

Ehlers, the radio operator, and the two prisoners began working and had created a useful dugout when, in the afternoon, a blizzard set in. In the hope of using the whirling snow as concealment, Soviet forces launched an attack against the German Kampfgruppe, but Ehlers had contact with his battery and called artillery fire on the approaching enemy, whose attack halted under the fire from the German howitzers and machine guns.[653]

The Soviet attack on the position had been successfully repulsed, but it soon became apparent that the German position was almost cut off, as Soviet forces could fire upon the area behind the small hill held by the Germans. The tank that was supposed to bring food and ammunition had to wait until darkness before it could reach the exposed position. When it arrived it became clear to the soldiers that the amount of food was scarce and Ehlers' two prisoners only got some bread. Ehlers' hopes that the two prisoners would be taken to the rear with the tank were dashed, as not even all of the wounded German soldiers could be evacuated by the tank.[654]

About an hour after the tank had left with the wounded, Ehlers received a runner who conveyed an order from the lieutenant that the prisoners should be shot. Ehlers sent the runner back without any reply. He had no intention of killing the prisoners, and rather used his radio set to get into contact with Captain Iwohn, his commander, and described the situation. Iwohn replied that he would personally intervene to ensure that the tank came back once more, or else he would try to find another vehicle that could get the prisoners.[655]

After arming himself with the words of his commander, Ehlers went to the lieutenant at his command post. Ehlers told the lieutenant that the two Soviet soldiers were his personal prisoners and that he himself had the responsibility to ensure that they were treated according to international law.

"Now hear this," the lieutenant bragged to two other NCOs next to him. "According to the international law, it is not allowed to put prisoners to dig fieldworks." The lieutenant turned to Ehlers and said: "Herr Oberfänrich, I have given you the clear order to shoot the prisoners."

"Herr Oberleutenant," Ehlers replied sharply, "You have no right to order me, I am detailed to cooperate with you, but I am not your subordinate."

"Hear this," the lieutenant said to the other NCOs in the room, before turning to Ehlers again. "You are Oberfähnrich and still not an officer and you refuse to follow an order from an officer? I will report you for punishment."

However, Ehlers did not back off:

"Here I do my service as observation officer and I hold the Iron Cross just as you do. And as for the artillery fire I do not decide, due to the shortage of ammunition, but my commander at the battery decides."

"We are surrounded," the lieutenant replied, "and as commander of the strongpoint I can order anyone within it, including you, to be part of the garrison. Thus I again give you the formal order to shoot the prisoners."

Ehlers walked back to his foxhole and once more contacted Captain Iwohn on the radio. After hearing Ehlers' description of what had transpired, Iwohn said that he could not prevent Ehlers from becoming part of the garrison, but nevertheless he strictly ordered Ehlers and the radio operator that they should not, under any circumstances, shoot the prisoners. During the radio conversation Ehlers noted that the two Soviet soldiers became white in the face; perhaps they understood some

German. To Ehlers' relief it turned out that the regimental commander, Colonel Daude, had forbidden the shooting of the prisoners, and armed with this information he returned to the hut, where the lieutenant had demanded a report on the execution.[656]

When Ehlers told him about Colonel Daude's message, the lieutenant changed tactics: "Good, I understand your problem, but consider this. Here in the hut there is no room for the prisoners. Even when the wounded have been evacuated the available space has to be used for my soldiers to get some rest. For the moment they can only squat in their foxholes, and to send the prisoners back to the Russians is out of the question. Also, during the night we have too few men to spare to guard the prisoners. And what if we come under attack? As we are only 42 men, every soldier will be needed to fight, none can be spared to guard prisoners."

"Perhaps we can tie up the prisoners to prevent them from escaping."

"Well, if they are tied they will have to lie on the ground. If they do they will have frozen to death in the morning. However, I cancel my order that you should shoot them. Rather I order you to hand the prisoners over to me."

Ehlers went to his foxhole, where he found that the radio operator was talking to Captain Iwohn, who said that the prisoners would have to be handed over to the commandant of the strongpoint, but the regiment commander was working to arrange a transport. With weak knees Ehlers walked back to the command post, bringing the prisoners along. They stepped into the hut and Ehlers, with some exaggeration, reported that Colonel Daude had personally worked to make a transport available. The lieutenant dryly replied that so he had apprehended. He ordered one of the NCOs to take charge of the prisoners and take them outside, and soon two pistol shots cracked. With heavy heart, Ehlers walked back to his foxhole and he had hardly arrived when Soviet mortar shells landed and exploded. Ehlers ordered his radio operator to call for barrages on both sides of the position.[652]

The fate of prisoners captured on the Eastern Front was far too often deplorable. In this particular situation, it seems that the initial intent was to treat the Soviet soldiers as international law demanded, but still they were killed in the end. Perhaps such circumstances influenced Stemmermann's order for the breakout, where he emphasized that there should be no violations of international law. During a breakout it would be difficult to make proper arrangements for prisoners. On the other hand, there was actually little risk of just letting them go, after removing their weapons. There would be little valuable information they could possibly reveal when they again found a Soviet unit to report to. Before the breakout it was of course wholly different, as secrecy had to be maintained, but as long as the breakout had not begun it would be relatively easy to guard prisoners.

The German Attack Toward Oktaybr, 16 February

As we recall, Stemmermann deemed it necessary that 1st Panzer Division should defeat the Soviet units defending northeast of Lisyanka. Breith of course realized the importance of gaining ground northeast of Lisyanka and flew to the village early in the morning, with the intention of staying there until the soldiers of Gruppe Stemmermann had reached safety. At the same time as Kampfgruppe Frank began to attack toward Oktyabr, Breith's Fieseler Storch landed.[658]

As Breith could see for himself, the attack did not get off to an auspicious start. Kamfgruppe Pietsch, which was to support Frank, consisted of one PzKw IV, one StuG III, and 19 officers and men from the 17th Reconnaissance Battalion. However, the StuG III fell out due to a broken drive shaft before even getting in position, halving the armor strength of the Kampfgruppe. Furthermore, a Soviet attack by T-34 tanks had to be repelled by a Panther company, but during the action two Panthers crashed into small ravines that were covered by snow and thus invisible to the tank drivers. Both tanks were eventually recovered, but only after much work.[659]

Another Soviet attack followed soon. The Germans estimated that the attack force was made up of 30 T-34s. Sergeant Strippel, with three Panthers, was sent to counterattack. Fortunately for him he received reinforcements; first two more tanks were detailed to him, then another two followed. With his seven Panthers Strippel repulsed the Soviet attack, and it was claimed that no less than 27 T-34s had been knocked out in the action as opposed to only one Panther. Whatever the true loss to the Soviet attack force, this success paved the way for a German attack on Oktyabr, which was launched after noon.[660]

While Kampfgruppe Frank attacked toward Oktyabr, another Germans force approached from the north. It was heavy Panzer

Regiment Bäke, which was attacking toward hill 239.0, situated about two kilometers east-northeast of Oktyabr. Bäke's regiment had seen its strength decline considerably. At the moment it amounted to two platoons of Panther tanks and two platoons of Tigers, rather than a battalion of each type. He deployed his Panthers to the right and the Tigers to the left, as his force attacked toward hill 239.0.[661]

When the tanks had reached a point approximately two kilometers north of hill 239.0, the small force halted, as Stukas from Geschwader Immelmann launched attacks on a forest east of Oktyabr. Also, a stretch of forest east-southeast of Dzhurzhentsy was attacked by the aircraft. Both these areas were good positions for Soviet antitank guns to hide in. After about 15 minutes the Luftwaffe had made its contribution, and Bäke's tanks rolled forward. Walter Scherf, in command of the Tigers, almost immediately heard gunfire. It turned out that a number of T-34s had been observed and were taken under fire by the Panthers, who eliminated the threat from the Soviet tanks and thereafter engaged enemy antitank guns near Oktyabr.[662]

Scherf's Tigers proceeded uneventfully until they reached close to the area where the Stukas had attacked. Fires could be observed, and Scherf concluded that the Stukas had done their job. However, it soon became apparent that the Soviet soldiers were tenacious. At the edge of the forest east of Oktyabr a few antitank guns had survived the Stuka attack, and the Red Army soldiers strived to man their weapons as the Tigers approached. Unfortunately for them, the crews of Scherf's Tigers had already seen them and had the advantage of power traverse for their guns. The Germans opened fire first and knocked out the antitank guns before they could respond, but the troubles for the Tigers were not over. A firefight with T-34 tanks broke out, and one Tiger was hit in the engine compartment and caught fire. The crew bailed out in time and saw how the ammunition exploded. After further actions with Soviet tanks the other Tigers reached their goal and established a defense at hill 239.0.[663]

In the meantime, Kampfgruppe Frank had battled on toward Oktyabr, after receiving an air resupply, especially of fuel. Rather than attacking straight on from Lisyanka, Frank chose to send his few available tanks and scarce infantry in a "left hook," to take Oktyabr from the north. Despite the fact that three Panthers bogged down in marshes that had been concealed by recently fallen snow, Frank's troops pushed on to take Oktyabr. They managed to create a weak screen west of

Dzhurzhentsy, but to clear the forest east of Oktyabr proved beyond their strength.[664]

Toward the end of the day Kampfgruppe Frank counted barely a dozen operational Panther tanks. The infantry companies of II./ Pz.Gren.Rgt. 113 had a combat strength of only about a dozen men each. Within or near Lisyanka there were also many tanks that had suffered minor damage or had bogged down. As it was clear that the position held by Kampfgruppe Frank was dangerously exposed, and the condition of the terrain made rapid recovery of damaged tanks unlikely, many of the immobile tanks were prepared for demolition.[665]

It was not only Bäke's and Frank's battle groups that were depleted; the strength of the entire III Panzer Corps was exhausted. More troops were needed in the Lisyanka area, and the only possible source seemed to be the 1st SS-Panzer Division. However, as we have seen, although the first elements of this division had begun the arduous journey early on 15 February, they did not arrive until late in the afternoon on the 16th. Although further small forces from 1st SS-Panzer Division were on the way, they could not be expected to arrive soon, given the poor condition of the roads.[666]

Not only were the German forces around Lisyanka weak in numbers. The soldiers were exhausted from the strain of combat, lack of sleep, and shortage of food. Hot meals had not been served to the spearheads for half a week, but on this day Walther Sherf received a surprise. Bäke asked Scherf to come to the regimental command post to report about the recent action. Scherf's Tiger was located only about 400–500 meters from Bäke's command post, and Scherf's driver took it to a point about 80 meters away, whereupon Scherf walked the remaining distance. Once he had arrived at the command post only a few minutes were spent discussing military matters. Suddenly a plate with fried potatoes was placed in front of Scherf and Bäke said, "Enjoy your meal." The potatoes and the lard they were fried in had been found in an earth cellar.[667]

CHAPTER 18

Breakout from the Korsun Pocket

By dusk on 16 February, the III Panzer Corps had fought its way slightly closer to the pocket, but still about seven kilometers separated its spearhead, heavy Panzer Regiment Bäke, from the surrounded Gruppe Stemmermann. Part of the reason for the remaining distance was the Soviet attack on Komarovka, which had succeeded in capturing the western half of the village. The part of Komarovka held by the 2nd Ukrainian Front was the only significant built-up area on the shortest route between Gruppe Stemmermann and the leading elements of the III Panzer Corps.

After the dash forward by the III Panzer Corps on 13 February, German hopes for a rescue had been high, but optimism faded as it became clear that fatigue, casualties, mechanical breakdowns, supply difficulties, and longer front lines had gradually sapped the corps' attack strength. On the morning of 16 February it was clear that the chances for a breakthrough to Gruppe Stemmermann were slim indeed. At Shenderovka, Stemmermann discussed the situation with his fellow corps commander Lieb and the division commanders.[668]

"Gentlemen, you all know our situation," Stemmermann said before giving a brief description of the situation, after which he continued: "We have no other chance; it is now or never. We will have to proceed as follows: The entire cauldron will move toward Lisyanka. General Lieb will be responsible for the breakthrough. We will employ three columns, with army units to the right, Waffen-SS to the left and the 72nd Division in the center. The 57th and 88th Divisions will make up the rear guard. I will stay with those who leave the cauldron last. Xhour for the operation will be 23.00, today February 16. Any questions?"

"What shall we do with the vehicles?" asked General Lieb.

"We can't take them along. All vehicles will have to be destroyed. Only tanks and other tracked vehicles can accompany the operation," replied Stemmermann.

"And the wounded?"

"All the wounded that can be transported will be loaded on carts and sledges, the others will have to remain at Shenderovka with voluntary medical staff."

At this moment the commander of the SS-Wiking Division, Lieutenant-General Gille, broke into the discussion and asked: "Who will provide the main force that will break through the Soviet defense perimeter?"

"That is a task for you, Gille," Stemmermann replied.

"I would have suggested it, Herr General," was Gille's immediate response, which also marked the end of the discussion.

Finally the die had been cast. The commanders went to their units, passing through Shenderovka where signs of German military units could be seen everywhere. Small buildings with their straw roofs were chock-full of wounded. In between, various staffs and signals units competed for space. Soldiers who enjoyed a short rest tried to find some warmth and shelter in the buildings, at least to get a chance to dry their wet clothes. However, during the last days their clothes rarely, if ever, got really dry.[669]

Frantic activity took place in Shenderovka. Staff members were burning various papers which could not be taken along, nor allowed to fall into enemy hands. Still, some papers did survive, such as the order for the breakout issued by Divisions-Gruppe 112, one of the component parts of Korps-Abteilung B. The order reflected the precarious situation. As it was part of the first echelon, the Divisions-Gruppe 112 was to attack at 23.00hrs on 16 February. It would have to be in position at least an hour earlier, partly because other elements of Gruppe Stemmermann would also have to move forward.[670]

Surprise was of paramount importance to the breakout attempt. Remarkably, the soldiers of Divisions-Gruppe 112 were to attack with rifles unloaded. The order for the attack continued: "Any unnecessary shooting is a crime and jeopardizes the entire breakthrough. Each soldier who sees an enemy in front of him and does not immediately attack and kill him, is himself to be killed silently. This has to be made clear to everyone. More serious matters are at stake than the life of a single person." [671]

Undoubtedly this was a rather severe order, but it has to be remembered that the situation was very grave. A large force was surrounded, and after three weeks consisted largely of exhausted men, who tended to be either desperate or apathetic. Exactly how many men still remained with Gruppe Stemmermann is unclear. The staff of XI Corps estimated that about 45,000 men were inside the pocket and still in condition to fight. Also it was estimated that there were about 2,100 wounded inside the cauldron. However, by this time accurate monitoring of manpower strength was not possible, and it is likely that the strength of Gruppe Stemmermann was slightly greater. Whatever the true number, the final chance for all of them rested on surprise, and in addition to the instructions mentioned above, other measures were taken to keep the Soviets unawares. For example, it was forbidden to set fires, smoke, speak, or cause any unnecessary noise near the frontline. Vehicles had to be destroyed using means other than explosives or fire. Radio traffic was kept normal until the very last moment.[672]

Doing their best to observe these precautions, the Germans made themselves ready for the breakout. Nevertheless some firing was heard by Anton Meiser as he waited for the order to begin the breakout, but perhaps total silence in a combat area might have appeared even more suspicious to the Soviet forces nearby. Meiser was not with the foremost units who were to conduct the initial breakthrough of the Soviet defense perimeter. The units that had received this task probably had greater reason to observe silence.[673]

One of the units in the first echelon was Major Kaestner's 105th Infantry Regiment. For the breakout his regiment had been reinforced by men from various dissolved or broken up units. However, he regarded these elements as having little combat value, and he relied on his own troops to provide the assault power. As his regiment had conducted several successful night attacks during the preceding week, Kaestner relied on the experiences gained and intended to use similar methods during the breakout.[674]

The 105th Infantry Regiment, as part of 72nd Division, was placed in the center of the first echelon, with Korps-Abteilung B to the north and SS-Wiking to the south. The central position of 72nd Division would hopefully ensure that its flanks would be protected. However, in the darkness, orientation could easily be lost. The aim was Lisyanka, but the small town was no shining beacon. Rather, the troops would have to find their way over ground covered by snow. Maps were scarce; Kaestner was fortunate to have a map in the scale 1:10000, which had been taken from a captured Soviet officer, but with all the difficulties inherent in a night operation there was always the possibility of confusion and units becoming mixed. Furthermore, if hard fighting began, it would be very difficult for the officers to lead their men except those who were nearby.[675]

The Breakout: 72nd Division

The last hours before the breakout were characterized by nervous waiting. It was impossible to tell what resistance the Red Army would mount in the area between the cauldron and Lisyanka. All the Germans knew was that they would certainly encounter two defense lines. Perhaps the Soviet commanders had placed further units in the path the Germans intended to use. Nobody could know for sure, but perhaps it mattered little at this moment. There was only one recourse left, and at 23.00hrs, as scheduled, the breakout attempt began.

Major Kaestner's regiment was among the first to jump off. As stealthily as possible his soldiers, heavily laden with ammunition, began to move forward from their staging area near Khilki. The sky was dark with clouds obscuring the light from the moon and the stars, conditions that would make it more difficult for Soviet forces to realize what was happening. Kaestner's lead men made no sounds that might betray them, and at close range attacked the first Soviet defense line with edged weapons and small arms. Surprise assisted the Germans and they managed to defeat the first Soviet defense line quickly. A second Soviet defense position was also defeated swiftly and the mass of the regiment followed closely behind the lead elements.[676]

Only on two occasions did Kaestner's regiment get embroiled in somewhat more intense combat. In both cases his soldiers stumbled into Soviet artillery batteries, which were captured in close combat. By making use of terrain features, the 105th Regiment continued in a southwesterly direction and at about 03.30hrs they reached the road from Dzhurzhentsy to Pochapintsy. Small reconnaissance teams were sent toward Dzhurzhentsy, where it was found that five T-34s guarded the entrance to the village. About two kilometers south of Dzhurzhentsy, silhouettes of a few tanks and vehicles were also discerned. After reporting by radio to the division, Kaestner's men sneaked past the enemy vehicles, making use of the undulating terrain. Nothing indicated that the Soviet troops had any inkling of what was happening, as the Germans crossed the road and continued west. Suddenly a new Soviet position was encountered. This time it was clearly oriented in a westward direction. The outer Soviet defense ring had been reached. The Soviet soldiers were found asleep in their foxholes, and the Germans attacked them with knives and the butts of their weapons.[677]

The action was brief, as the Germans again capitalized on surprise and quickly overcame the defenders. However, the latter shot off a few rounds, which attracted the attention of a Soviet tank. It lit a searchlight, but while it did not discover Kaestner's men, elements of the 72nd Division who followed behind the 105th Regiment were discovered and became embroiled in fighting. Kaestner's men continued forward, and southeast of Khizhintsy they again encountered tanks. Scouts were sent out and as they crept closer they saw, to their immense delight, the familiar "Balken" cross that marked all German tanks. They had made it to the spearheads of III Panzer Corps.[678]

Kaestner's regiment had conducted an almost textbook breakout. It had probably worked better than anyone in the regiment had dared to hope, largely thanks to stealth and surprise. However, not all units were as fortunate as Kaestner's. Soon after the beginning of the breakout, command and control broke down throughout the mass of the column. To what extent that really mattered is unclear, as the commanders did not have a particularly clear picture of enemy dispositions, intentions, and capabilities. It was probably unavoidable that the breakout developed into a number of individual actions and fates, channelled along the same general direction.

Major Siegel's 266th Regiment followed behind Kaestner's 105th. Initially everything went well, but as soon as the first hill was reached, Soviet mortars and machine guns targeted Siegel's regiment. In the darkness, accuracy was poor and only a few of the German soldiers were hit. Siegel heard a wounded soldier shout: "Take me along! Take me along!" Perhaps it was Sergeant Reisch. Siegel told him to wait until a field ambulance could come and pick him up.[679]

Siegel's men continued forward and met no resistance until they made out the road between Dzhurzhentsy and Pochapintsy. As Soviet tanks were positioned along the road, Siegel concluded that his men had no chance to break through the enemy curtain, since they lacked anti-tank weapons. Siegel sent Lieutenant Ohlendorf to reconnoiter, and he soon returned with information that Soviet tanks were coming from Dzhurzhentsy to reinforce the screen along the road. There was no alternative except to veer off south. Siegel checked his compass and gave the necessary instructions, when Colonel Hummel, from the 124th Regiment, came by. Like Siegel he saw no alternative but to try to bypass the Soviet screen to the south.[680]

Soon after turning south Siegel's men were again fired upon by Soviet units, this time from the forest between Potchapintsy and Oktyabr. Siegel shouted loudly: "Here is Major Siegel. 266th Regiment to me!" Men from various parts of the 72nd Division appeared. As there was no time to waste, Siegel gave instructions to the men as they emerged and the movement south continued along the edge of the forest. However, Captain Knostmann assembled a small Kampfgruppe and attacked the Soviet machine gunners in the forest, pushed them back, and then continued through the trees. He and his men managed to reach the 105th Regiment, as the latter had just linked up with the III Panzer Corps, even though casualties were suffered. Among the losses was Lieutenant Ohlendorf, who was wounded and subsequently captured.[681]

Neither Siegel nor anyone else was aware of the success achieved by Captain Knostmann and his men. Instead they continued south and reached the southeast corner of the forest. As the daylight began to illuminate the area, two sledges appeared at some distance. It seemed to be the morning soup that was to be delivered to some Soviet units nearby. Siegel and his men stayed silent and the two drivers did not seem to have noticed the nearby Germans. Soon Siegel sent a small Kampfgruppe to capture the sledges, but after crouching forward, without yet reaching the sledges, they discovered a Soviet artillery battery. It was swiftly stormed and the guns were rendered inoperable before the Germans continued south.[682]

Siegel's men soon reached within a stone's throw of the Gniloi Tikich River, where Siegel established a bridgehead. He did not himself go to the river bank, as he wanted to ensure that his grenadiers held a perimeter around it. Furthermore, he observed five Soviet tanks and feared the worst, but the tanks remained inactive. Siegel collected men from his own regiment, as well as from 124th Regiment and SS-units that had reached the area. He made clear that they would have to defend the bridgehead to allow the soldiers following behind an opportunity to cross the river and reach safety.[683]

Most of the men were "old foxes," veterans who understood what they needed to do and quickly took action. Lieutenant Grosse from the 124th Regiment assumed command of the eastern flank and Siegel took responsibility for the western side. Siegel gave an SS-officer the task of building an emergency crossing over the Gniloi Tikich River. Siegel walked back and forth between his own flank and the east flank, checking that everything was in order, while more and more soldiers from the pocket reached the bridgehead. Through the branches of the trees near the river, Siegel could see German soldiers on the other side. Thus everything seemed to be working as well as could be hoped.[684]

Except for offering harassing fire, Soviet forces made little effort to disturb the crossing of the Gniloi Tikich River. After about an hour, some armored vehicles from SS-Wiking appeared, shortly followed by a Soviet tank, which charged into the bridgehead and fired on some of the German baggage vehicles. It soon drove into a deep gully and was immobilized. At about 08.30hrs Siegel gave orders to his men to cross the river, since the flow of men from the pocket increased without any signs of enemy attacks.[685]

As Siegel came within sight of the river, which was about 20–30 meters wide, he saw no bridge or any other means of crossing. Attempts to push panje wagons into the river to create a makeshift bridge were futile because the current was too strong. The men tried to cut down trees to form a bridge, but in vain. There was no resort but to swim in the ice cold water. At about 09.15hrs, Siegel had crossed the river and most of his men made it too, although a number of them succumbed to the cold water and swift current and drowned.[686]

The soldiers who reached the southern bank of the Gniloi Tikich River had brought little else than their soaking wet clothes. Many small arms weapons, as well as all heavy equipment, were lost. A determined Soviet attack would have wrought havoc among Siegel's wet and freezing men. They walked some two or three kilometers and reached Lisyanka, suffering few losses along the way, despite being subjected to Soviet fire. Probably the deep snow dampened the effects of the exploding shells. Siegel recalled that one soldier who was wounded, not far from Lisyanka, was helped by a Russian woman, who had served as a

HiWi at a field kitchen and taken part in the breakout. She received a decoration for courage.[687]

At Lisyanka, Siegel became aware that he had already been reported as killed. He was able to prove otherwise, but his case was far from unique. It was many days before the Germans had an accurate picture of how many soldiers had escaped, and in what condition.[688]

Most of the 72nd Division, which assembled about 4,000 men for the breakout, made it to Lisyanka. Probably around 90% of its personnel got out of the pocket, despite the fact that the majority of them had to diverge from the planned route. The loss of equipment was almost total, much of it east of the road between Dzhurzhentsy and Pochapintsy, where the terrain was very difficult.[689]

Some of the German soldiers had made only narrow escapes. One example is Sergeant Peter Reisch, who served with the 4th Company of the 266th Infantry Regiment. He was only about one kilometer east of Shenderovka when he was severely wounded in the leg by shrapnel from Soviet mortar fire. He was unable to walk and quickly concluded that he could only be saved by begging or threats. After Captain Ochten and Major Siegel had spoken to him, a medical orderly came and cut off his trouser leg. Reisch received a bandage and was told to attend himself, while the medical orderly went to find somebody who could help to carry him. The orderly never returned.[690]

Helpless, Reisch lay in the snow, watching the flow of vehicles, panje wagons, and soldiers heading southwest. None made any effort to help him until a signals unit had to halt due to traffic jams ahead. After some discussion Reisch was loaded onto one of the wagons. He was cold and in severe pain, but at least he got closer to the III Panzer Corps. In darkness the transport proceeded slowly but steadily until dawn, when a traffic jam blocked further movement. Reisch was moved to a covered wagon, which was more comfortable, but he could not orient himself as he could not see anything of the surroundings. He was not alone in the wagon; two other wounded soldiers were there too.[691]

The wagon remained immobile for a long time and Reisch began to wonder what had happened. A traffic jam would not have caused a complete standstill for such a long period of time. He and the other two wounded soldiers began to shout, but received no reply. Reisch crawled forward and cut a hole in the fabric to see what had happened. To his consternation he discovered that there was no horse harnessed to the wagon.[692]

Reisch's wagon, which was situated in a depression, was bypassed by an artillery unit from the Waffen-SS. Its guns got stuck, and to Reisch's relief, some of the horses were used to harness his wagon. However, after a while the men who attached the horses began to try to persuade Reisch to give himself up as a prisoner to the Red Army. Reisch did not listen to them. He was desperate to get out of the pocket or die, even if it would take a shot from his own pistol. Faced with such determination, the SS-soldiers lifted Reisch from the wagon and placed him in the snow.[693]

That was all the help he got however, as he soon found himself deserted. Other German soldiers had fled the field due to Soviet fire. With his wounded leg he could not walk, so he decided to crawl toward a forest. En route he encountered another wounded German soldier, trying to do exactly the same thing. For a while they joined in their efforts to crawl forward, but after a while the other soldier lagged behind and soon Reisch did not see him anymore. At last Reisch reached the forest, where a muddle of vehicles was trying to avoid Soviet tanks.[694]

Luckily Reisch found a horse-drawn staff vehicle, which he could accompany by sitting on one of the horses. To get out of the forest was difficult because there were Soviet tanks nearby, but when these moved away, Reisch asked the officer of the unit he had encountered to let more wounded follow in the wagon. Together with some other wounded soldiers Reisch was placed in the wagon. As the horses toiled, the wagon bumped over the rough ground, causing the wounded to cry with pain. When the wagon reached the road running south from Dzhurzhentsy, rounds from Soviet mortars exploded and the wagon crashed into a ditch. The driver unharnessed the horses and rode away, leaving the wounded men in the wagon to their fate.[695]

Reisch was helped by some SS-soldiers, who took him on board their panje wagon along with other wounded soldiers, but he did not get far. The road was blocked by wrecks, and again the driver lost his nerve and rode away on the horse. In a little while, two doctors walked past and Reisch asked them to harness the wagon. In their haste to continue on their way they refused, but Reisch pulled his pistol, pointed it at them and said: "If we don't get away from here, neither will you." The threat had the desired effect and the doctors shouted to some passing soldiers, who cleared the road and harnessed the wagon once more.[696]

Reisch and the other wounded soldiers on the wagon continued on their journey. Not far from hill 239.0 Reisch saw a general, possibly

Major-General Kruse, who was directing soldiers near the forest south of hill 239.0. Reisch's wagon continued south, but soon got stuck in a marsh. Reisch was transferred to another wagon, but could only get a place to sit, not lie down. As the wagon shuddered over the bumpy terrain, the movement caused horrible pains to his wounded leg. When Lisyanka came within sight he even asked that he should be placed on the ground to crawl the final distance, but nobody listened to him. He had to remain in the wagon but he reached Lisyanka alive, to his immense relief.[697]

The Breakout: Korps-Abteilung B

On the northern wing of Gruppe Stemmermann, Korps-Abteilung B made itself ready for its breakout on the evening on 16 February. Its strength was reported as 6,257 German officers and men, plus 1,155 HiWi, making it one of the strongest formations to take part in the breakout. Its first wave was lead by Colonel Viebig and consisted of Divisions-Gruppe 112, made up of Regimentsgruppe 110, Regimentsgruppe 258, Field Replacement Battalion 112, Engineer Battalion 112, and Antitank Battalion 112. The artillery of the Korps-Abteilung B was led by Colonel Böhm and made ready to fire against the Petrovskoye–Dzhurzhentsy area, before beginning to move west. One light field howitzer battery was to accompany each infantry wave, to provide direct fire. It was deemed impossible to save the heavy howitzers, which were to be destroyed after firing their last rounds.[698]

Despite congestion, the units reached their designated positions in time, and at 23.00hrs the Regiments-Gruppe 258 silently began to advance, followed ten minutes later by Regiments-Gruppe 110. Like Kaestner's regiment, the Regiments-Gruppe 258 achieved surprise and attacked with edged weapons when it reached the first Soviet defenses. Almost complete success was achieved and the assault continued southwest, where another Soviet defense position was overrun south of Petrovskoye. The lead battalions of Korps-Abteilung B continued south of Dzhurzhentsy, crossed the road, and reached Oktyabr at about 05.00hrs.[699]

The elements of Korps-Abteilung B that followed behind Viebig's men were not as successful. Only a few kilometers southwest of Khilki it was found that the howitzers could not be moved across the difficult ground, so they had to be destroyed. When the men continued forward they reached the screen of Soviet tanks along the Dzhurzhentsy–Pochapintsy road, which forced them to veer off south. They became intermingled with elements of the 72nd Division and SS-Wiking, and continued toward the Gniloi Tikich River, which they then had to cross.[700]

In some cases soldiers became separated from their parent units even before the breakout began. Nikolaus Romes served in Korps-Abteilung B, but found himself in Novo Buda, together with men from the SS-Wallonien Brigade. These elements still held positions in Novo Buda on the morning on 17 February when Soviet forces attacked. At about 10.00hrs the German defense gave way and the position had to be abandoned. Romes withdrew through the valley where Shenderovka was situated. A pitiful picture appeared before him. Long columns of panje wagons with wounded German soldiers had assembled in the hope that they could be moved out of the pocket. However, their dreams of rescue were literally crushed, as Soviet tanks crashed over the wagons. For Romes there was no alternative but to flee westward, and the German soldiers around him all seemed only to focus on one thing: to save their skin.[701]

All German soldiers still able to walk moved west, hoping to reach Oktyabr. Romes was engulfed in the crowd. Corpses of men and horses littered the snow-covered ground. Horses came galloping by with dead or half-dead men hanging in their stirrups, while fire from Soviet weapons riddled the closely bunched German soldiers. At about 11.00hrs General Stemmermann passed by in a halftrack, but the vehicle was hit by an antitank round while only a few meters from Romes. He did not see anyone come out alive from the halftrack, but at this stage of the breakout no one cared about the dead; everyone ran for his life.[702]

Romes, too, found his path to rescue blocked between Dzhurzhintsy and Potchapintsy. Together with the Wallonians, he veered off south, toward the Gniloi Tikich River. He halted in the forest south of hill 239.0, where Leon Degrelle had assembled numerous soldiers from shattered formations. By now daylight had passed, and not until early morning on 18 February did the assembled soldiers begin to move toward the bank of the Gniloi Tikich. Romes still had his horse, and when he reached the river he tried to cross it while mounted. The horse drowned in the crossing, possibly after heart failure, but Romes was able to swim the last few meters himself and continue walking to

Lisyanka, still draped in his soaking wet clothes that only accentuated the cold.[703]

Romes might have hoped that the walking would be over when he reached Lisyanka, but the village was now a very exposed position. Almost immediately he and thousands of other soldiers had to continue walking, eventually reaching Uman where Romes found some survivors of his squadron. The remnants of Korps-Abteilung B were soon used to reconstitute other formations, and in a short time Romes was transferred to the 88th Division.[704]

The Breakout: SS-Wiking Division

The strongest formation of Gruppe Stemmermann was SS-Wiking, which was reported to have assembled about 11,500 men for the breakout. It also possessed more heavy weapons than the other formations. For example, it still had seven tanks and three assault guns, and its artillery consisted of nine Wespes and three Hummels, in addition to 25 light field howitzers, six heavy field howitzers, and four 10cm guns.[705]

The preparations were hampered by traffic congestion, but at 23.30hrs the SS-Wiking Division began its breakout, about half an hour later than Korps-Abteilung B and 72nd Division. Initially no opposition was met. A hilly area about two kilometers south of Petrovskoye was reached, where a few Soviet machine gun positions were overrun. When Soviet antitank guns opened fire on SS-Wiking's flank, the Wespe SP howitzers quickly silenced the guns and the advance continued. However, the Soviet defense in the woods north of Potchapintsy proved too strong and the Germans were forced to bypass the forest on the northern side.[706]

Fritz Hahl had received a special mission for his company. He was the only officer commanding a company in his battalion, since the high casualty rates among the officers meant that all the other companies were commanded by NCOs. Perhaps this fact contributed to him receiving the mission to attack and hold a piece of high ground southwest of Shenderovka until all other units had passed. To Hahl it seemed like a "Himmelfahrtskommando," a suicide mission. Nevertheless, when the breakout began he duly carried out his task. The high ground was captured with ease, and except for one Soviet solider captured, no enemy was seen. Hahl could not see any threatening Soviet forces, and after a while he began to question the judiciousness of clinging to the position.

He saw how the men of his division moved westward and the tactical value of his position seemed marginal at best, but he had his orders. Fortunately the battalion commander arrived. Hahl reported the situation and asked how long the position was to be held. Spontaneously the battalion commander said, "Youngster, I leave that to your intelligence," whereupon he continued west. Hahl recalled the words of General Hausser, which he had heard at the SS-Junkerschule Bad Tölz: "The Prussian discipline is the discipline of independent decision making, not subservient obligingness." Without much hesitation Hahl ordered: "Company, march toward Lisyanka, Parole Freiheit."[707]

The soldiers of SS-Wiking continued west, where they were met by fire from Dzhurzhentsy. One battalion from the Westland Regiment attacked, reaching the church in the town. So far the breakout had proceeded quite well for SS-Wiking, but it too found the terrain impossible for vehicles and heavy equipment, which had to be destroyed. Furthermore, the Soviet tank screen along the road south of Dzhurzhintsy caused the SS troops to veer off south, like so many other German units had done.[708]

The longer the march through snow and darkness continued, the more the units became intermingled. Officers could only command the men nearby, but as everyone seemed bent on reaching Lisyanka it probably mattered little. The men of SS-Wiking skirted the forest south of hill 239.0 and proceeded toward the Gniloi Tikich River. A marsh caused the last vehicles to bog down. The troops continued toward the river, where Fritz Hahl found some of the soldiers of his company, at about the same time as the rising sun began to illuminate the landscape.[709]

With the advent of the morning the Germans could no longer count on surprise and darkness. Soviet countermeasures became more obvious, although they could not be described as vigorous. Hahl recalled that artillery fire was directed toward the fleeing German soldiers, and some T-34s also went into action. The latter was a particularly serious threat, as the Germans hardly possessed any antitank weapons. German casualties rose, and Hahl was hit in the back by splinters from a shell fired from a T-34. He was fortunate that the wound was slight, as he too saw how wagons with wounded were rolled over by the T-34 tanks. Without being particularly hampered by the wound, Hahl continued toward a small forest, where he found remnants of his company. Suddenly a small Soviet infantry force appeared only 30 meters from

Hahl's company. Without much hesitation Hahl's men stormed forward and got the upper hand in a brief but bitter close combat.[710]

Only a small distance remained before Hahl reached the Gniloi Tikich River, where he, like so many other German soldiers found that there was no bridge or any other means of crossing. The cold and swift water appeared ominous; however, fire from a T-34 on a crest about 500 meters away shattered any doubts about the need to cross as quickly as possible, even as it made searching for a suitable crossing place more difficult. With his company dispersed and out of control, Hahl quickly decided to swim, despite the fact that the temperature in the air was almost -10°C. He jumped into the water and swam as quickly as he could. His uniform became soaked and heavy, threatening to pull him down under the current. Despite wet clothes, cold water, and the rushing current Hahl made it to the bank on the other side, where he briefly recovered in the brushwood.[711]

Together with an officer from the Germania Regiment, who had crossed the Gniloi Tikich just after him, Hahl began to walk toward Lisyanka. On the southern side of the river the threat from Soviet units was much weaker, and the two walked until they saw a German tank next to a cottage. As they approached, Hahl and the officer noticed that the commander in the turret of the tank looked curiously at them. Somewhat hesitantly they asked him: "Have we got out?" Cheerfully the tank commander said "Yes." Hahl and the other officer fell into each other's arms. It was just as well. Apart from three rounds left in his machine pistol and one hand grenade, Hahl was unarmed.[712]

Two days later Hahl wrote a short letter to his parents:

> *Dear parents! For weeks I have not been able to write to you, as all communications to the rest of the world were severed. Two days ago we broke out of the cauldron. We had to endure many hardships and many times the situation was not rosy. However, everything is well now. I was wounded a fifth time during the breakout, but made it anyway. I will send you more later.*[713]

Another wounded soldier of the SS-Wiking Division was Otto Brieger. He served in the 11th Battery of the artillery regiment and had previously injured his foot, which of course boded ill for his chances of getting out of the pocket. He recalled:

In the morning it all began. As we could not bring our gun along, it was destroyed. I was offered to accompany a tank during the breakout. I climbed up but had no positive feelings about it. After travelling for a few hundred meters a half-track passed by and I swiftly moved to it. However, we did not come far before the vehicle got stuck in a muddy valley. The vehicle tried to get up, but slid down again. We had no choice but to abandon it and continue on our own. After about a kilometer we came across SS-Major Dorr, who had assembled a small battle group. We accompanied the group, but as I was hampered by my wounded foot I was soon alone. When I reached a crest I did no longer see the other men. I reached a covering forest. All the time, groups of men came walking in bunches, but due to my slowness I soon found myself alone again. Or Not! There was a Russian position ahead and it had to be overcome. In this attack I joined a group led by SS-Captain Degrelle. I threw my last hand grenade and fired all the remaining ammunition.

Soon I was alone again and had reached the end of the forest. Suddenly there was machine gun fire from the right. I could see the bullets striking the ground to the left of me. No doubt the fire was aimed at me, but I was so tired I just looked at the impacts as if I were a remote observer. Anyhow, I had the fortune to get away unharmed. Thereafter I ran a fairly long distance until I saw a straw stack covering a tank. Briefly I was filled with fear, but then I realised it was a German tank. I had got through.[714]

Breakout: The 57th and 88th Divisions

The units who made up the rear guard had a more difficult task, since the element of surprise was lost by the time they began to move west. Daylight also increased the dangers from Soviet artillery and armor. Furthermore, while it could be hoped that the Soviet soldiers would be confused during the initial phase of the breakout, as it progressed it was likely that the German soldiers themselves would become muddled.

General Stemmermann had decided that the 57th and 88th Divisions would provide most of the rear guard. The 88th Division was on the northern corner of the pocket, giving Count von Rittberg's division the longest distance to the spearheads of the III Panzer Corps. This division would have to set off later than those of the first echelon.

However, it was envisaged that soldiers who were not needed to man the rear defenses could join other units which began the breakout earlier. It is unclear how successful this plan was, as traffic jams caused delays among the units closer to the western edge of the pocket.[715]

The breakout began at 23.00hrs, but already on the evening of 16 February some elements of 88th Division had begun to pull back from the northeastern perimeter of the cauldron. At 17.00hrs the Division-Gruppen 323 and 332 pulled back and moved into Shenderovka. During the night the 88th Division held its positions, but at 05.15hrs on 17 February it received orders from Stemmermann to begin its breakout.[716]

As dawn provided some visibility, the 88th began to move, while Soviet units fired into the division's northern flank. In front of the division there was practically no resistance, probably because it followed other German units. At the road between Dzhurzhentsy and Pochapintsy the lead elements of 88th Division encountered the same Soviet tank screen as had obstructed so many German units earlier. The troops of 88th Division also found the forest south of hill 239.0 held by Soviet troops. However, hastily collected troops from the 88th attacked the Soviet defenses in the forest, broke through, and reached Lisyanka. Not all soldiers of 88th Division were aware of the events in the forest. Instead they continued south and reached the Gniloi Tikich River. The troops set about constructing a crossing, but the work was made difficult by the fire from Soviet tanks and antitank guns. A brief panic broke out, but calm was soon restored and footbridges were built, which even allowed the wounded to cross the river.[717]

Thus the lead elements of the 88th Division were successful, but more problems were encountered by the rearward parts. At the western edge of Shenderovka, traffic jams hampered the breakout. There was only one bridge available at the exit of the village, and it was not strong enough for heavy vehicles. These should already have been destroyed but, contrary to orders, several vehicles had been driven toward the bridge. When they could not cross, the bridge was blocked and the heavy equipment had to be left at Shenderovka.[718]

The soldiers managed to get past the blocked bridge, so that despite its rear position at the beginning of the breakout, the 88th Division managed to save a significant share of its men, probably more than had been expected.[719]

At 13.00hrs on 16 February General Trowitz of the 57th Division personally gave the orders to his regiment commanders. The original orders for the breakout had to be altered somewhat, as Soviet forces had penetrated into Komarovka, on the southern edge of the pocket. As a result, the units of the 57th Division would have to take a slightly northerly route compared to the original plan. At 17.00hrs the infantry regiments defending the eastern part of the pocket were to disengage from the enemy and move toward Shenderovka. The 676th Regiment should thereafter take up positions to screen off the Soviet forces in the Komarovka area.[720]

In the evening of 16 February the division's units began to carry out their orders as planned, but many hours passed without the 57th Division receiving any orders from the XI Corps. Orders to begin the final breakout were requested on many occasions, but not received until the order was relayed by 88th Division. As late as 06.15hrs on 17 February Trowitz's Division finally began its breakout attempt. Despite the late start, enemy opposition was initially no impediment to the troops, but the traffic jam at the western exit of Shenderovka was a major hindrance. Only one of 57th Division's artillery batteries made it over the bridge, whereupon it took up its designated position.[721]

The disengagement from Soviet units in the east posed almost no difficulties for the Germans, but Soviet tanks attacked into the southern part of Shenderovka, from where they could threaten the troops of the 57th Division in the flank. The Soviet commander had brought infantry, mortars, antitank guns, tanks, and artillery to the heights on the sides of the German breakout path. The Soviets had recovered from their initial surprise, and the three main routes could not be made out, so Trowitz's Division followed on the heels of the SS-Wiking Division.[722]

Heavy Soviet fire from the Khilki area prevented many vehicles and horse-drawn wagons from getting far from Shenderovka. Soviet tanks attacked from both sides, causing casualties, confusion, and disorder. The German escape to the west was made even more difficult by the many ravines and marshy areas that ran across the route in that direction. Many vehicles were lost, and Trowitz was of the opinion that, even without Soviet fire, the terrain alone would have proved impossible for the vehicles.[723]

Despite the difficulties, the German soldiers continued southwest. Indeed, they had little choice. Following behind the SS-Wiking Division,

the troops of 57th Division also encountered opposition at the forest south of hill 239.0. Some elements of the division persisted in moving through the forest, which brought them to Lisyanka almost unmolested. Other elements of the 57th continued south and were forced to cross the Gniloi Tikich River east of Lisyanka. This turned out to be the more dangerous route, as Soviet units directed fire against the Germans who bunched up near the river bank. No bridge was found, and many soldiers drowned in the cold, swift running water. Trowitz estimated that most of the casualties suffered during the breakout were incurred at the Gniloi Tikich River crossing. By the morning of 18 February some provisional bridges had been created, which even allowed about 20 panje wagons with wounded to cross the river. About 600 wounded were brought out of the pocket this way.[724]

Despite its difficult task the 57th Division managed to save most of its men, but like the other divisions its heavy equipment and vehicles were lost. To the Germans it seemed that Soviet resistance had been weaker than expected. The major hindrance appears to have been the tank screen south of Dzhurzhentsy and the infantry in the forest south of hill 239.0. Otherwise only flanking fire harassed the German columns, but this did cause significant casualties. In retrospect, the route through the Soviet defenses along the Dzhurzhentsy–Potapintchy road and in the forest south of hill 239.0 was the best one to take. Those German soldiers who made it to the Gniloi Tikich River, on the other hand, faced the dual threat from the river itself and from the Soviet units that were able to fire at German soldiers grouped on the river's banks.

The Breakout: Anton Meiser

Although the five divisions played the main roles during the breakout, there were many soldiers who did not belong to any of them. For example, the 389th Division had practically been dissolved. Its soldiers had largely been distributed among other units, and the division commander, Major-General Kruse, had little more than his staff to command. He nevertheless managed to assemble about 2,500– 3,000 assorted men near the forest south of hill 239.0, from where he led them along the railroad north of the Gniloi Tikich River, to reach Lisyanka. Many wounded on panje wagons were thus brought to the temporary safety at Lisyanka.[725]

As somewhere around 50,000 men were inside the pocket at the time of the breakout, the fates of individual soldiers could differ considerably. Anton Meiser found himself in Novo Buda when the breakout began, at 23.00hrs on 16 February. He belonged to a unit that was to cover the flank until the morning, when it was to leave its positions and join the breakout. During the nervous night hardly anyone could sleep. Anxiously, the soldiers waited until their part in the breakout was to begin. Finally, at dawn a rider came with the order for Meiser's group: "Breakout has begun according to plan. Spearheads advance successfully. Enemy must however be pushed back further. All are to advance according to plan."[726]

The men cheered briefly before beginning to move westward. Meiser froze in the icy air, as his thin coat provided little shelter. From the hill he could make out the columns of vehicles heading west, using the last of their fuel, and the horse-drawn wagons carrying the wounded. The deep snow made it hard work to get forward, and many vehicles came to a halt because of the ground, the snow, and the traffic jams. Suddenly tank engines were heard. Due to the snowfall, visibility was poor, but occasionally the wind cleared the air and Meiser could see Soviet tanks approaching both from south and east. The nine men of his little group only had six rifles, three machine pistols, two pistols, and a few hand grenades, hardly proper weapons to defeat tanks. There was no alternative but to flee southwest.[727]

In front of Meiser there was a flat, snow-covered area. He and many others fled over the field, only to discover that it was a small lake, covered by a thin sheet of ice under a blanket of snow. Unable to carry the weight of the large number of soldiers, the ice sheet broke and Meiser, like many around him, sank into the water up to his chest. Some drowned there, but the other soldiers were determined to survive. Meiser continued forward until he finally found solid ground under his feet. He had lost his machine pistol in the water, but he continued southwest as fast as he could, now freezing in his wet clothes.[728]

All semblance of order had disappeared. Those who were hit were left behind and lost, all who still had strong enough legs continued westward as fast as they could, hastened by the fire from Soviet units on both sides of the corridor. Sometimes Meiser stumbled over a corpse, occasionally an arm from someone who was still dying could be seen above the snow. The frightful sounds from the wounded completed the terrible scene. A lieutenant from the SS-Wallonien Brigade shook his head and said: "What has become of the German army?" He, Meiser, and a sergeant assembled to discuss bringing the rout into some kind of order. They had hardly begun when strange sounds were heard from what was believed to be a corpse. When they looked closer they found a major who had suffered a complete nervous breakdown. The three men asked him to get up, to assume command, and halt the rout, but even kicking him had no effect. Most likely he soon froze to death.[729]

Together with the other two men Meiser continued southwest, but the three were soon met by soldiers hastening eastward. They said that there were Soviet tanks behind the next hill. Only with difficulty could the soldiers be convinced that they were fleeing in the wrong direction. In fact the Soviet tanks had previously been knocked out. The now enlarged group strove further toward Lisyanka, and after a while encountered a number of abandoned German vehicles, two of them loaded with food and clothes. Meiser used the opportunity to get better clothing and something to eat. Some cans were also taken by the other soldiers.[730]

After the short break at the vehicles, the escape was resumed. Meiser had not got far when he was hit by a bullet at one of the pockets of his trousers. The pain caused him to bend over and he grabbed his pistol. He had seen enough people bleed to death in the snow, and he would rather shoot himself than suffer that fate. Before he had the time to pull the trigger, he became aware that he had neither seen nor felt any blood. He looked closely at his trousers but saw no trace of blood. He pulled away his trousers and saw that he had a bruise but nothing more. There was a hole in the trouser, at the pocket. Inside the pocket he found a bullet, whose impact had been absorbed by a magazine. Meiser put his pistol back in its holster.[731]

A sergeant next to him was less fortunate, as he was hit in the foot. Meiser bandaged the wound, but it soon proved impossible for the man to walk, even when Meiser supported him. The sergeant, a father of two children, feared for his life. He realized that those who were wounded had virtually no chance to continue by themselves. Captivity or death were the only realistic alternatives. Meiser assured the man he would find him some help. The sergeant scarcely believed him, but Meiser went away and soon encountered a Russian riding on a German horse, probably a Cossack or HiWi who had joined the Germans. By threatening the Russian with his pistol, Meiser stole the horse from him and brought it to the wounded sergeant and helped him to mount.[732]

Soon Meiser was only about four kilometers north of the Gniloi Tikich River, with hill 239.0 to the right and Potschapintsy to the left. Except for a brief combat action, he and the small group he temporarily belonged to reached the Gniloi Tikich relatively swiftly. At the river bank more soldiers were waiting, conferring about what to do. Meiser recalled that it had been said that there would be three columns during the breakout, and that they had belonged to the left column. Thus he found it better to walk along the river, to the west. Not all were convinced, but Meiser set off west together with a few other soldiers.[733]

Passing dead soldiers and horses, Meiser struggled west with the handful of men, generally facing no obstructions other than the marshy ground. Suddenly, bullets whizzed around, forcing Meiser and the other men to take cover. They soon found that the Soviet units firing at them were quite distant and could not achieve much accuracy. The German soldiers dashed from cover to cover without being hit, and soon reached a forested area along the river, where they were protected. Cautiously they continued west until fater a short while Meiser heard a shout: "Parole!" All the men in Meiser's little group immediately replied "Freiheit!" the code word to be used to identify the soldiers who broke out. They had finally reached the III Panzer Corps—the breakout was over for them and they were still alive.[734]

The Breakout: Sergeant Fiebelkorn

As we have seen, once the breakout was begun at 23.00 on 16 February there was little overall command and control. Still most of the men were saved, and it seems that the main reason for loss of equipment was the difficult terrain. There were numerous ravines, difficult slopes, marshes, and other relatively small obstacles. These caused the loss of a large number of vehicles, wagons, and other heavy equipment. Subsequently the Gniloi Tikich River was a major obstacle that caused further losses of equipment. The latter hindrance could possibly have been overcome by better command and control. It seems that a fairly significant number of troops and equipment managed to move west along the northern side of the river and it is probable that losses could have been reduced if more units had followed that route. However, it must be emphasized that there is little evidence suggesting that the higher German commanders had enough of a clear picture of the terrain and the enemy dispositions that they could have given the proper directions. Rather, each one, regardless of rank, seems to have had knowledge only of what transpired in the immediate vicinity. The force behind the breakout was the will of the individual soldiers to avoid imprisonment and to get a chance to see their families again.

An almost extreme example of willpower is the fate of Sergeant Fiebelkorn. He served in the 1st Company of SS-Panzer Battalion 5 of the Wiking Division. On 14 February his tank was hit in the engine compartment and caught fire. The crew bailed out in time, but Fiebelkorn broke one of his feet when he jumped from the tank. He remained with the tank battalion until the breakout began, when he was provided a seat on a prime mover. Unfortunately the vehicle was hit by fire from Soviet antitank guns when it had reached about seven kilometers from Novo Buda. Fiebelkorn survived and was loaded on a panje wagon, and his unit reached the edge of the forest southeast of Dzhurzhentsy.[735]

Suddenly a number of T-34 tanks appeared on a hill, and a brief tank battle ensued as the German tanks returned fire. The Soviet tanks pulled back and the Germans continued. However, during the action Fiebelkorn had been brought into cover in a piece of forest, where he remained on a wagon, with four horses harnessed and a driver. He was told to make it to Lisyanka by himself, as the remaining distance was deemed short. As the fighting petered out, the driver urged the horses on and moved out from the forest. After they had traveled about a kilometer, Soviet fire raked the area and the driver panicked and fled, leaving Fiebelkorn alone.[736]

After a while, Fiebelkorn's cries for help were heard by an officer in the Waffen-SS, who helped him get down from the wagon. Seconds later the wagon was hit and the SS officer killed. Fiebelkorn stayed in cover for a few hours and waited for sunset. Under cover of darkness he began to crawl forward, and after a little while he encountered two other wounded soldiers doing the same thing. Of course it was a painstakingly slow way of moving, and despite spending the entire night crawling, the soldiers did not reach Lisyanka. As the sun rose, Fiebelkorn realized that they had come unpleasantly close to an enemy position. They dug themselves into the snow and waited for the sun to set again.[737]

At dusk the three men resumed their incredibly arduous attempt to reach Lisyanka. However, one of the men froze to death soon after they began to crawl that evening. Within minutes the other soldier succumbed to the cold too, and Fiebelkorn found himself alone. Despite the appalling conditions he struggled on, thinking of his family to find the strength to continue, until he finally reached one of the outposts of III Panzer Corps.[738]

When he reached the outpost Fiebelkorn was completely exhausted and lost consciousness. He did not reawaken until he was on an aircraft. Then he found that in addition to the wound received before the breakout, both hands, both feet, and one knee was frost-bitten. Still, he lived and would get a chance to see his family again, including his wife who was carrying their second child.[739]

The Success of the Breakout

Soldiers arrived in various conditions over a period of some days after the breakout began, so it was difficult for III Panzer Corps to establish how many managed to escape. Lieutenant-General Mattenklott, the commander of XXXXII Corps who had been on leave when the Soviet pincers closed at Zvenigorodka three weeks earlier, was given the task of collecting and counting the survivors of Gruppe Stemmermann before sending them by rail or air toward facilities in the rear. It took almost two weeks for Mattenklott and his staff to count the survivors. Their final count showed that 27,703 German soldiers and 1,063 HiWis had broken out unscathed. In addition 7,496 wounded and injured had managed to reach III Panzer Corps. These were soldiers who had either been wounded during the breakout or who had been wounded beforehand but nevertheless been brought out. Hence, 36,262 had managed to escape the pocket. Also, 4,161 wounded and sick had been evacuated prior to the breakout aboard aircraft. Thus a total of 40,423 men had survived the encirclement without becoming prisoners.[740]

Since an estimated 59,000 men were trapped inside the encirclement on 28 January, about 19,000 men seem to have been killed or taken prisoner. About 11,000 were wounded, giving an overall casualty figure of about 30,000. This was of course a serious loss, but at least it was far from the disaster at Stalingrad, which appears to have loomed as a specter for many of the Germans who took part in the Korsun battle, whether on the ground or within the higher commands.[741]

The German soldiers' fear of a new Stalingrad is also evident in Soviet archival records. For example, a German soldier who was taken prisoner and interrogated by 4th Guards Army said that the encirclement was regarded as a "second Stalingrad" by the German soldiers.

They did not want to surrender due to fear of Siberia.[742]

Equipment losses were of course extensive. According to estimates by Mattenklott's staff, there were 141 10.5cm howitzers, 33 15cm howitzers, eight 10cm guns, three 17cm guns, 41 7.62cm field guns, 51 7.5cm antitank guns and 13 other towed antitank guns inside the pocket when it was formed. There were also 12 Wespes, four Hummels and seven SP antitank guns inside the pocket. Thus 313 guns and howitzers had been encircled and virtually none came out.[743]

Soviet sources give grossly exaggerated figures on the German losses. First of all they inflate the strength of Gruppe Stemmermann; secondly they play down the number of soldiers who got out. Soviet sources claim that 75,000 Germans were surrounded, with 270 tanks and assault guns and 1,100 guns. Of these it is said that 52,000 soldiers were killed and 11,000 taken prisoner, while all equipment was lost. The only one of these figures that seems reasonable is the number of prisoners. All other are grossly inflated. It should be noted that these Soviet figures were released as soon as the battle ended, in an official bulletin. It seems wholly unreasonable that the full picture of the German losses could have been clear by then. It can only have been a figure deemed suitable for propaganda purposes, but was not changed in subsequent Soviet historiography.[744]

In his memoirs, Konev claims that the surrounded German force comprised the 57th, 72nd, 82nd, 88th, 167th, 168th, and 332nd infantry divisions, plus the SS-Panzer Division Wiking and the 213th Security Division. Also, he clams that the SS-Brigade Wallonien, an independent cavalry regiment, and a regiment each from the 389th and 198th Divisions, as well as a regiment from 14th Panzer Division and a number of supporting units were in the pocket. Compared to the German units that actually were in the pocket, Konev's claims contain a number of errors, and some of the divisions given by Konev no longer existed.[745]

The dubious Red Army information on the German divisions is perhaps not surprising. After the Allies landed in Normandy, an exchange of intelligence took place between the Western Allies and the Soviet Union. The Western Allies were clearly disappointed with the information provided by their comrades at arms in the East. It revealed that the Red Army had poor knowledge about which German divisions were actually present on the Eastern Front.

A lesser controversy is that regarding the possession of hill 239.0

northeast of Lisyanka. The III Panzer Corps reported that the position had been taken, but many officers who broke out of the pocket maintained that the hill was occupied by Soviet forces. The fire from these forces contributed considerably to the fact that many Germans veered off toward the Gniloi Tikich River. One important factor behind the diverging opinions is that hill 239.0 is, in fact, not much of a hill. Rather it is just a point on a gently rolling area. It was difficult to identify the point, which may be the reason for the different opinions expressed in the reports.[746]

According to Konev's memoirs, he ordered the commander of 27th Army to defend hill 239.0 with an antitank regiment, to prevent German tanks from breaking into the pocket. The order was issued on 14 February. Thus it seems possible that the defense of hill 239.0 was mainly designed to prevent attacks from the west, not east.[747]

The Soviet resistance in the area around hill 239.0 area was not typical of the German impression of the Soviet opposition. German reports often explicitly or implicitly express surprise at the weakness of the Soviets' resistance to the breakout. One reason may have been that Konev concentrated his efforts on the southeast and northwest flanks of the pocket, and for example, only on 17 February, when the German breakout was already in full swing, did 5th Guards Cavalry Corps shift to the proper area.[748]

The true reason for the weak Soviet resistance may perhaps be found with more extensive research in Soviet archives. Soviet secondary sources maintain that virtually no German soldiers broke out of the encirclement, but this is patently wrong and seems mainly to be a cover-up for the failure to completely destroy Gruppe Stemmermann.

One possible explanation for the lack of opposition the Germans faced is that snow storms reduced visibility. The 4th Guards Army noted that the intense thaw in the first half of February ended on 14 February, when temperatures fell and snow began to fall. On 16 February, as the wind increased the snowfall gradually turned into a storm, which became especially intense during the evening of 18 February. The roads, which had been very bad previously, deteriorated even further as drifting snow closed them in many places. Soviet movements to block the German breakout were seriously hampered.[749]

Although the two Soviet fronts failed to deliver the coup de grace to Gruppe Stemmermann, the fact that the two German corps had suffered a major defeat should not be disregarded. Virtually all equipment had been lost, and almost one third of their men were dead or prisoners. Furthermore, many of those who broke out were in very poor condition. Already before the breakout the soldiers were exhausted by continuous fighting, regrouping, creating field works, and other activities that left little time for rest. The harsh weather imposed further strains, as did the knowledge of being cut off from friendly units for weeks, with the accompanying dread of capture and the uncertainty of what would happen if wounded. Finally, the breakout with its horrors and drama drained the last ounce of strength from many soldiers. Walther Wenck judged that the soldiers had indeed performed remarkably, but only a few men, by their nature hardened, would be able to stand up to such trials again.[750]

The significant number of wounded men placed considerable strain on the medical facilities that were waiting for them. Professor Stoll served with a facility that received the wounded and gave them first aid and conducted emergency surgery. He recalled that it was located in a large factory building:[751]

> *We received about a thousand men each day. Often a surgical treatment was impossible, rather we could only bandage and delouse. Sometimes we could not even do that. I worked as a surgeon. We did surgery on three operating-tables in the factory hall, where we did surgery and bandaging. At each table a doctor and a medical orderly worked, often also a third man who assisted. There were also two men who brought the wounded to and from the operating table.*
>
> *Crêpe paper rollers served as first aid bandages, which had excellent absorption capacity. The floor was soon covered by removed bandages and more and more piled up. The stench was terrible. We had covered the upper part of our boots with bandages drenched with lysol, to prevent lice from getting into the clothes, since the bandages of the wounded were full of lice. It must have itched enormously; at least there were many wounded who scratched under their bandages by using small sticks. The number of wounded we received was so great that we could not cope. Abscesses were opened, sometimes rifle bullets were removed, when the entry hole was clean and the bullet was located near the skin. Despite all the difficulties we stood eight hours at the operating-tables, spent another eight hours on visiting the wounded and caring for them and prepared the treated soldiers for evacuation. The remaining eight hours could be used for rest*

> *and sleep. We drank coffee immensely and smoked a lot. Alcohol was avoided.*
>
> *We could not treat the head wounds. We strived to send these cases away by air. Cases with abdominal wounds were – I have to say: placed in a corner – and given morphine to die. This was the reality, as we could not perform surgery on men who had been hit in the stomach. Such an operation would have lasted two to three hours and soldiers who could quickly be helped would be lying unattended. We simply did not have the time.*

With so many wounded and exhausted men among the survivors of Gruppe Stemmermann it would take months of rest, training, and rebuilding before the surviving troops were again ready for action. These troops would be sorely missed on the Eastern Front, but before other operations could be initiated, the soldiers of Gruppe Stemmermann would have to be brought to the rear. 1st Panzer Army had prepared to receive and quickly move the exhausted soldiers, but the weather still contributed to logistical difficulties.[752]

Those soldiers who could still walk usually had to make their own way from the exposed salient held by the III Panzer Corps spearheads. Transport was mainly reserved for the wounded, and time was scarce. The III Panzer Corps was dangerously extended, and on 19 February it began to pull back from the Lisyanka salient. By then it was assumed that no more soldiers from Gruppe Stemmermann would be rescued.[753]

CHAPTER 19

Aftermath

German Losses

Both sides tried to portray the Korsun battle as a victory once it had ended. Obviously propaganda purposes played a prominent role in the spreading of such images. In any case, the Red Army had some reason to label the hard-fought battle a victory. The Germans had finally been driven away from the Dnepr in the Ukraine, and two enemy corps had been defeated; but the success was less than claimed. Soviet propagandists asserted that no German soldiers escaped from the cauldron. All in all it was claimed that Gruppe Stemmermann lost 52,000 men killed and 11,000 taken prisoner, a gross exaggeration, at least of the number of killed. Furthermore, it was claimed that the German relief forces—the III and XXXXVII Panzer Corps—lost 20,000 officers and men killed and more than 600 tanks, another gross exaggeration. The Soviet sources did not say anything about the losses incurred by their own forces, since to mention the losses suffered by the Red Army in individual battles was virtually a forbidden topic prior to 1990. According to Krivosheev, the Soviet casualties in the Korsun-Shevchenkovskii operation (24 January–17 February) amounted to 80,188, of which 24,286 were killed or missing.[754]

Reports from the two Soviet fronts support the level of losses given by Krivosheev. Vatutin's 1st Ukrainian Front reported 16,545 killed, 46,410 wounded, and 14,997 missing between 20 January and 20 February. The Konev's 2nd Ukrainian Front incurred 10,669 killed, 34,613 wounded, and 1,886 missing during the same period. Equipment losses included 1,711 guns and 512 mortars for the 1st Ukrainian Front and 221 guns and 154 mortars for the 2nd.[755]

Given the scope of the fighting on the Eastern Front, the Soviet casualties suffered in the Korsun battle were slight, and compared to the results achieved they were low by Red Army standards. However, tank losses could not be described as slight by any standards.

In Moscow a 20-shot salute was fired by 224 guns on 18 February, but the consequences of Stalin's decision to assign the 2nd Ukrainian Front responsibility for the annihilation of the pocket became evident on this occasion too. In Stalin's congratulation, the 1st Ukrainian Front was not mentioned at all. The council at Vatutin's front listened to the broadcast of the salute and the congratulation. None of the members could conceal their disappointment. Krainjukov at the staff of the 1st Ukrainian Front later said that the members of the council thought someone had not informed Stalin correctly and objectively about the efforts of the front. When the indignance had settled somewhat, Vatutin said: "The most important thing to do is to defeat the enemy. Later, historians can try to find out who has done what." [756]

As we have seen, the casualties suffered by Gruppe Stemmermann amounted to approximately 19,000 killed or missing and approximately 11,000 wounded. The forces outside the pocket of course also suffered losses, but compared to the two encircled corps they suffered far less. During its relief attempt, the 1st Panzer Army endured about 3,300 casualties, of which more than 70% were wounded. The elements of the Panzer army that did not take part in the relief attempt suffered less than 900 casualties during the first 20 days of February, ample testimony to the fact that relatively little action took place outside the areas where the III and VII Panzer Corps fought.[757]

It is perhaps somewhat surprising that the divisions fighting at the base of the salient created by the III Panzer Corps—the 34th and 198th Divisions plus the 1st SS-Panzer Division—suffered more casualties than the three Panzer divisions thrusting toward Gruppe Stemmermann. In fact, the 1st, 16th, and 17th Panzer Divisions suffered approximately half the casualties incurred by 34th Division, 198th Division, and 1st SS-Panzer Division, despite the former three being mainly on the offensive and the latter three on the defensive. There are a few likely explanations. First of all, we must question the notion that it is more costly to attack than to defend. Usually the attacker has some important

Table 3: 1ST PANZER ARMY CASUALTIES 1-20 FEBRUARY 1944			
	Killed	Wounded	Missing
1. Pz.Div.	35	212	3
1. SS-Pz.Div.	82	219	17
16. Pz.Div.	90	380	50
17. Pz.Div.	77	225	25
34. Inf.Div.	170	707	105
75. Inf.Div.	23	64	6
198. Inf.Div.	105	509	147
Werfer-Brig. 1	17	32	0
Other 1. Pz.Armee Units	205	637	39
TOTAL	804	2,985	392
Source: PzAOK 1, IIa, Verlustübersicht vom 1. bis einschl. 20. February 1944, NARA T313, R74, F7312637.			

advantages, such as superior firepower, surprise, numerical advantage, local air superiority, more ammunition available, or rested troops. These factors often overshadow the advantage of defensive posture.[758]

In the case of the III Panzer Corps' attack toward Gruppe Stemmermann, it must also be emphasized that tanks bore the brunt of the fighting, while infantry probably carried the main weight at the base of the salient. Thus it could be expected that the units at the base of the salient suffered greater losses in men, though fewer losses in armor. Indeed, the German armored spearheads suffered much greater tank losses, but how the losses arise is perhaps not self-evident.

Table 4: 1st PANZER TANK ARMY LOSSES IN THE KORSUN BATTLE, FEBRUARY 1944						
	Enemy Fire	Mines	Spontaneous Ignition	Mechanical Failure	Collapsed Bridge	Stuck in Terrain
1. Pz.Div.	16	3	2	25	0	5
16. Pz.Div.	6	3	4	18	1	0
17. Pz.Div.	6	0	0	10	0	0
II./Pz.Rgt. 23	6	2	2	15	0	0
s.Pz.Abt. 503	1	2	1	3	0	0
s.Pz.Abt. 506	0	0	0	7	0	0
TOTAL	35	10	9	78	1	5

Source: PzAOK 1, Stabsoffizier für Panzer-Bek., 3.3.1944, Fernschreiben PzAOK 1 Ia 423/44, Betr. Panzerausfälle, T313, R70, F7307174-6.

Comment: The table does not include all units of 1st Panzer Army. For more details see the text.

All in all, the tank units in Table 4 lost 138 tanks, but only 35 of these had been hit by enemy fire. Furthermore, not all of those tanks hit by enemy fire had suffered fatal damage, but lack of recovery means and poor weather prevented the Germans from salvaging them before they withdrew. Instead they had to be blown up. The recovery difficulties were also responsible for the losses due to mechanical failures given in the table. There were further tanks that suffered mechanical breakdowns, but were recovered.

The nine cases of spontaneous ignition included eight Panthers and one Tiger, which developed fires in their engine compartments, none of which could be extinguished in time to save the tanks from becoming complete write-offs. Thus self destruction constituted a significant share of the Panther tanks irrevocably lost. The main cause of loss, however, was the difficulty of recovering damaged tanks. At the onset of Operation Wanda the units of the III Panzer Corps only had about half their prescribed number of recovery vehicles operational, and breakdowns may very well have occurred in the deep mud that characterized much of the operation. The mud and snow caused further recovery difficulties, and the retreat from the exposed salient around Lisyanka was too quick to allow a significantly greater number of tanks to be recovered.[759]

In addition to the losses suffered by the units listed in Table 4, the 1st SS-Pz.Div. seems to have lost eight tanks and 10 assault guns, thus bringing the tank losses incurred by 1st Panzer Army to 156. But there were also many tanks in need of repairs. For example, of the 187 Panthers in the 1st Panzer Army on 29 February, no less than 171 were in workshops. It would take some time to bring them back to operational readiness, and if the units became embroiled in heavy combat it would be veritably impossible to bring all the tanks back to running order before new tanks needed repair.[760]

The men also needed time away from the frontline. On 24 February the III Panzer Corps reported that uninterrupted heavy fighting in mud and snow had exhausted the men to such an extent that they were at the end of their tether. Poor food had contributed to the grave situation, since the field kitchens had not been able to move forward to the frontline troops, who had to resort to cold emergency rations. The soldiers had not had any real sleep for weeks, which of course sapped them of their strength. Warm shelter had been lacking, and their clothes were worn out, especially their footgear. In the Leibstandarte and the 16th Panzer Divisions, there were units where up to 70% of the men suffered from various foot infections. Also many men suffered from trench foot or frostbite. For example, in a subunit of 1st Panzer Division there were 20 cases of frostbite in a single day, quite considerable considering that the unit had only 70 men. Finally, the poor weather conditions and supply difficulties conspired to cause hygiene to deteriorate. Almost all the men had lice, and the 16th Panzer Division reported that about 50–60% of its men suffered from scabies.[761]

Between 1 and 20 February the divisions of 1st Panzer Army received 8,505 replacements, more than twice as many replacements as casualties incurred. However, it must be remembered that casualties only refer to those soldiers who are killed, wounded, or missing due to enemy action. Soldiers absent due to exhaustion, frostbite, disease, injury, and other non-combat causes are not included. Hence, it may well be possible that the divisions of 1st Panzer Army had a much lower combat value after the relief of Gruppe Stemmermann compared to their condition at the beginning of February, especially as it seems that the divisions of III Panzer Corps received comparably less replacements.[762]

It is more difficult to pinpoint the casualties suffered by VII Corps during its defensive battles of 26–31 January. Some indication is given by the fact that the 34th and 198th Divisions lost 692 killed, 1,907 wounded and 316 missing during the entire month of January. Since the two divisions were involved in action for much of the month, it seems realistic to estimate that the defensive battles during the Soviet offensive caused losses amounting to about 1,000 men, of whom the majority were wounded. Tank losses must have been very low for the Germans during that phase, as no tanks and only a handful of assault guns participated. Thus it could be estimated that the forces of 1st Panzer Army that participated in the Korsun battle outside the pocket suffered casualties of about 4,000–4,500 men, of whom about two thirds were wounded, and about 160 tanks and assault guns that were irretrievably lost.[763]

The situation for the XXXXVII Panzer Corps was fairly similar to that which the III Panzer Corps experienced. Casualties seem to have been slight. For example, the 13th Panzer Division lost 559 men killed, wounded, and missing in February, while the 376th Division reported 399 casualties. This seems to be well in line with the losses reported for the entire 8th Army, which were very low in February.[764]

Except for the units inside the pocket, the losses for 8th Army in February were considerably smaller as compared to January, and especially when set against those of the Kirovograd battle. It is difficult to establish the losses for the Korsun operation, largely because it is not self-evident which units of the XXXXVII Panzer Corps participated. No doubt the 3rd, 11th, 13th, and 14th Panzer Divisions participated, but it is less clear which of the infantry divisions on the right flank to include. Neither is it entirely clear which units Krivosheev has included in his data on Soviet casualties, as shown above. However, as little combat activity took place on the right flank of the XXXXVII Panzer Corps, the effect on an estimate of the overall casualties is slight. If it is assumed

Table 5: 1st PZ ARMY & 8th ARMY CASUALTIES ACCORDING TO WEHRMACHT VERLUSTWESEN						
	1-10 January	11-20 January	21-31 January	1-10 February	11-20 February	21-29 February
1st Panzer Army	720	3,907	4,501	3,596	3,243	26,281
8th Army	4,093	7,883	5,481	2,032	1,467	696
Total	4,793	11,790	9,982	5,628	4,710	26,977

Source: Wehrmacht Verlustwesen ten day reports, T78, R414, F6383320-6383333.

Comment: The ten day reports sometimes suffered from lagging behind. In this case we have compared the losses suffered by 1st Panzer Army with the data in the sources given for Table 1. Overall casualties for the period 1 January–20ruary Feb differ by a mere 3%, but it seems that there is a spill over from 21-31 January into 1-10 February, caused by delayed reporting. The very high casualties for 1st Panzer Army dating to 21-29 February are most likely caused by the preliminary reports for the losses sustained by Gruppe Stemmermann.

that the elements that participated in the Korsun battle incurred half the casualties sustained by 8th Army during the period 20 January–20 February, about 4,500 casualties would have to be accounted for.

Even though the casualties sustained were not particularly high, the units were badly worn from prolonged fighting in very poor weather conditions. The 11th Panzer Division, which had been almost continuously engaged since the beginning of the battle at Kursk in July 1943, was so exhausted that it was decided to send it to southern France for rest and refit. The 13th Panzer Division was very low on combat-ready tanks, but otherwise in fairly good shape. The 376th, on the other hand, complained about lack of many personal items for the soldiers, such as tents, water bottles, mess tins, boots, socks, uniforms, and means for taking care of hygiene. Furthermore, some of its replacements had been conscripted from Slovenia and Croatia, and these soldiers seem to have been more prone to leave the front line without permission. Even cases of self-mutilation had occurred in order to avoid combat.[765]

Still, the several months of fighting before the Korsun Battle was the main reason for the strains experienced by the units of XXXXVII Panzer Corps.

Unfortunately it is much more difficult to establish tank losses for XXXXVII Panzer Corps, compared to III Panzer Corps. One thing is clear: the number of operational tanks was generally much lower for XXXXVII Panzer Corps. In fact for much of the operation the number of operational tanks was so low that major tank losses due to enemy action were simply impossible. Reports for a few units are available. For example, the I./Pz.Rgt. 26 Panther battalion lost 10 Panthers on 28 January, but thereafter only five more during the Korsun battle. Similarly, its personnel casualties were low during February, only 10 officers and men.[766]

The 3rd Panzer Division suffered more extensive losses, reporting that it had lost 26 tanks during the Korsun battle. To a significant degree, this was due to the lack of towing vehicles, which meant that equipment with only slight damage or that had simply bogged down in mud had to be abandoned.[767]

It has been more difficult to establish the tank losses for other units of the XXXXVII Panzer Corps involved in the Korsun battle, but they seem to have been slight, as is indicated by their strength on 1 March, as shown in Table 6. Of the Panzer divisions, it seems that von Wietersheim's 11th Panzer Division contributed most of the tank strength, and it mainly possessed Panthers. On 20 January, it had eight operational Panthers and 39 in workshops, thus its number of Panthers on hand actually increased by at least 17 by 1 March, possibly more as some of the four command tanks may well have been Panthers. However, as the I./Pz.Rgt. 31 Battalion had been ordered to hand over its Panthers to the 11th Panzer Division, it must be considered that the I./Pz.Rgt. 31 had 39 Panthers on 20 January.[768]

To what extent the I./Pz.Rgt. 31 really handed over its tanks is unclear. Although orders instructed it to hand over all its Panthers, and probably the battalion retained no Panthers when it departed from the Eastern Front, not all the tanks were necessarily given to the 11th Panzer Division (for example, tanks requiring extensive repairs may

Table 6: TANK STRENGTH IN XXXXVII PANZER CORPS ON 1 MARCH 1944						
	Panther	Pz IV	Pz III	Flamm-Panzer	StuG	Command Tanks
11th Pz.Div. (operational)	10		4			3
11th Pz.Div. (short repair)	43	7	2			1
11th Pz.Div. (long repair)	11					
13th Pz.Div. (operational)		5	1			2
13th Pz.Div. (short repair)		5	2			1
13th Pz.Div. (long repair)		2	1			1
14th Pz.Div. (operational)		6		2	4	6
14th Pz.Div. (short repair)		1		2	2	2
14th Pz.Div. (long repair)		3	1		1	
I./Pz.Rgt. 26 (operational)	6					
I./Pz.Rgt. 26 (short repair)	22					1
I./Pz.Rgt. 26 (long repair)	29					
StuG.Abt. 203 (operational)					4	
StuG.Abt. 203 (short repair)					2	
StuG.Abt. 203 (long repair)					5	
StuG.Abt. 905 (operational)					11	
StuG.Abt. 905 (short repair)					3	
StuG.Abt. 905 (long repair)					5	
StuG.Abt. 911 (operational)					8	
StuG.Abt. 911 (short repair)		2			7	
StuG.Abt. 911 (long repair)					3	

Source: XXXXVII. Pz.Korps Ia, "Panzer-und Sturmgeschütz-Lage Stand 1.3.44", T314, R1132, F000724.

Comment: Vehicles in short repair were repairable within 14 days, long repairs would take longer than two weeks.

have been sent back to Germany). However, it is most likely that the majority of them were handed over to 11th Panzer Division. Thus it would seem reasonable to assume that the 11th Panzer Division lost about 20 Panthers between 20 January and 1 March, and perhaps 15 of them were lost during the Korsun battle. As the division hardly had any operational tanks except its Panthers, it seems likely that no more than about 20 tanks were lost irretrievably in the Korsun battle.[769]

The war diary of III./Pz.Rgt. 36, the only tank battalion in the 14th Panzer Division, shows one tank lost on 26 January and an assault gun the following day. A further tank was lost on 1 February. Of these three vehicles the assault gun was burnt out and destroyed, while the two tanks had been damaged by enemy fire and could not be recovered due to enemy action. On 16 February the battalion lost two tanks in a more peculiar way. They were trying to tow away an SPW, but they all bogged down in mud and all attempts to recover the vehicles failed, partly due to the fact that the area was under Soviet fire.[770]

For the remaining tank units of XXXXVII Panzer Corps we have found no useful information in the German archival records. However, as the units discussed above contained the bulk of the armor employed in the fighting, it seems that an estimate of about 80 tanks and assault guns lost for the entire XXXXVII Panzer Corps is not far off the true figure. Thus the German forces outside the pocket probably lost about 240 tanks and assault guns. The SS-Wiking Division probably had around 25 tanks and assault guns, the SS-Wallonien Brigade had about 10 assault guns, and the two army assault gun battalions within the pocket—the 228th and 239th—probably had about 15 assault guns. Hence, about 50 tanks were lost to Gruppe Stemmermann. All in all it seems that the Korsun battle cost the Germans close to 300 tanks and assault guns.[771]

Soviet Losses

Soviet claims asserted that the Germans lost all tanks within the pocket, which seems quite correct, but erroneously stated that they possessed at least 270 tanks. Furthermore, Soviet sources claim that the German forces outside the pocket—mainly III and XXXXVII Panzer Corps—lost more than 600 tanks. In total, the Germans should have lost approximately 900 tanks, or about three times the true number.[772]

Unfortunately, Soviet sources are much more silent on their own tank losses. According to German claims, the Soviet tank losses were considerable. For example, the III Panzer Corps claimed to have destroyed or captured 606 tanks and assault guns during 4–18 February. How well these claims stand up to scrutiny is somewhat difficult to tell, but at least some observation can be concluded from the available figures.[773]

To begin with, the Soviet forces engaged in the liberation of the western Ukraine between 24 January 1943 and 17 April 1944 lost on average 40 tanks and assault guns per day. If this figure is also representative for the period when the Korsun battle was fought, about 920 tanks would have been lost irretrievably in the days between 25 January and 17 February. Of course, that would include losses in other sectors too, but it seems that most of the fighting involving Soviet tank forces during that period took place at Korsun. Nevertheless, such a figure is of course only a very crude estimate. Fortunately somewhat more useful figures are available, as presented in Table 7.[774]

Table 7: 1st UKRAINIAN FRONT ARMOR LOSSES

	Tanks	Assault Guns	Total
1-10 January 1944	314	65	379
11-20 January 1944	294	88	382
21-31 January 1944	513	146	659
1-10 February 1944	243	95	338
11-20 February 1944	193	38	231

Source: Tsamo RF, Fond 236, opis 2673, delo 311, list 12, 39, 64, 85

Comment: Losses refer to complete write-offs.

During the period 1–20 February the 1st Ukrainian Front was not engaged in any heavy fighting except the Korsun battle. This seems to have been especially true for its tank units. Consequently almost all the losses of 1–20 February, 569 tanks and assault guns, as given in Table 5, must have been incurred at the Korsun battle, in particular in the actions against III Panzer Corps.[775]

It seems that the claims made by III Panzer Corps were not too far off the mark. Admittedly, not all the tank losses sustained by the 1st Ukrainian Front were caused by the III Panzer Corps, but on the other hand the III Panzer Corps also fought against units of 5th Guards Tank Army, which belonged to 2nd Ukrainian Front. Nevertheless, it seems that III Panzer Corps claims were exaggerated, but not by much, and certainly were far less inflated than the Soviet claims.[776]

To assess the tank losses sustained by 1st Ukrainian Front during the initial phase, from 26 January to 31 January, is somewhat tricky. While Vatutin's troops on his eastern flank attacked, the Germans conducted offensive operations against his center. The latter fighting seems to have resulted in far heavier tank losses than the actions by 6th Tank Army and 27th and 40th Armies, but given the archival data in Table 5 it seems that about 600 tanks lost irretrievably is a reasonable estimate for 1st Ukrainian Front.

The tank losses sustained by the 2nd Ukrainian Front are more difficult to establish. There is little doubt that they were smaller than for 1st Ukrainian Front, as the latter had to ward off the attack from III Panzer Corps. The threat from the XXXXVII Panzer Corps was much less menacing, as is evidenced by the fact that parts of the 5th Guards Tank Army were shifted toward the area where III Panzer Corps attacked. It is clear that Konev's front lost as complete write-offs 324 tanks and assault guns in the period of 20 January–20 February. Of these, the vast majority must have been lost during the Korsun battle. If we assume that 250 were lost in the Korsun battle, the overall Soviet tank and assault gun losses in the Korsun operation would be approximately 850.[777]

As is evident, it has been impossible for us to establish German as well as Soviet losses without resorting to estimates. However, it seems clear that the Soviet casualties were about twice as high as those incurred by the Germans. Soviet tank losses seem to have been close to three times as high. Furthermore, it must be remembered that German data on tank losses may include vehicles lost due to action between 20 and 29 February. Corresponding losses for the Soviet side have not been included in the estimates, as we have no data at all for that period.

Despite the fact that our figures are partly based on estimates, it is clear that Soviet casualties were about twice as high, and tank losses about three times as high, as the Germans incurred. Given their preponderance of strength and favorable strategic situation, that does not appear to be a particularly impressive achievement, but it still seems to be a considerable improvement compared to the performance of the Red Army during the summer and fall of 1943. Furthermore, the German casualties in the Korsun battle included an unusually high proportion of killed and missing, which made the German losses more difficult to replace. Of the wounded soldiers, a significant share could return to service eventually, but hardly any of the men taken prisoner returned.

The remnants of the XI and XXXXII Corps would be absent from the German order of battle for some months. Hence, the immediate consequences of the battle were more favorable to the Red Army than is suggested by the raw casualty data. The same phenomenon could to some extent be seen in the armor branch. As we have seen, the German Panzer units had very few operational tanks by the end of the battle, but a considerably greater number of tanks in workshops awaiting repairs. For a few weeks the men in the German tank repair units would have to work hard, but without spare parts it would have been impossible to improve the supply of available tanks.

After the Battle

The 1st and 2nd Ukrainian Fronts resumed offensive operations in March, culminating in another encirclement, this time encompassing the entire 1st Panzer Army. Eventually the Germans broke out, but again considerable amounts of equipment had to be abandoned. Hans-Valentin Hube, who had led the 1st Panzer Army since 29 October 1943, was promoted to colonel-general and awarded the Knights Cross with oak leaves, swords and brilliants on 20 April, as a recognition of how he led his army in two difficult operations. Ironically, he was killed in an aircraft crash near Obersalzberg the following day.

For much of the time, Vatutin had been Hube's opponent, and he too suffered a violent fate. On 29 February he was travelling by car to the 60th and 13th Armies on the north wing of his front. Ukrainian partisans, opposing restored Soviet rule, had arranged an ambush and Vatutin was seriously wounded in the firefight that ensued. The efforts of the doctors were eventually in vain, as Nikolai Fedorovich Vatutin succumbed to his wounds on 15 April, less than a week before Hube's aircraft crash.

Most of the other high-ranking commanders involved in the Korsun battle survived the war, for example Konev, Zhukov, Rotmistrov, Kravchenko, Galanin, as well as Wöhler, von Vormann, Breith and von Manstein. Even a commander like Franz Bäke, who led from the front to a very great extent, had the luck to survive the war.

Many other soldiers who survived the Korsun battle did not live to see the end of the war. The Soviet armies continued fighting many hard battles until the fall of Berlin. Probably close to an additional nine million Red Army soldiers were killed, wounded, or taken prisoner before the end of the war, ample testimony to the fact that the remainder of the war was not an easy march to the west. The battle at Korsun was just one battle in what must have seemed an almost endless series of battles. For many Westerners it is easy to forget the magnitude of the battles fought in Eastern Europe, but with combined Soviet and German casualties numbering between five and ten million each year, even the horrible battles on the Western Front during World War I pale in comparison.[778]

Most of the German divisions fighting outside the pocket remained on the Eastern Front, but the survivors of the surrounded divisions were sent to various training facilities, to reform or become part of other formations. The 57th Division was sent to Debica in Poland to reform. It spent about three months there, before being sent to the German 4th Army in Byelorussia, only to be surrounded again when the great Soviet summer offensive was unleashed. After that disaster, the 57th Division was disbanded. The 72nd Division was sent to Hrubieszov in Poland to reform, but in April it was sent to the Kowel area and was subsequently engaged in costly battles until the end of the war. The 88th Division reformed at Deba in Poland, before being involved in battles near Baranov in the summer of 1944. It remained near Baranov until the Soviet winter offensive along the Vistula, when the 88th Division was destroyed.

The 389th Division spent two months in Hungary, before in May transferring to Latvia. A few months later it found itself bottled up at

Courland. In February 1945 it was shipped to West Prussia, where it was once again cut off and largely captured by the Red Army. The Korps-Abteilung B was dissolved after the Korsun battle and most of its survivors were used to reconstitute the 57th and 88th Divisions, and thus shared their fates. In contrast, the Waffen-SS units, Wiking and Wallonien, were maintained until the end of the war. Wallonien was even expanded to a division, the 28th SS-Division, which fought in Pomerania and Brandenburg in 1945, while the SS-Wiking Division ended the war in Austria.

Even though the Germans tried to keep soldiers of a formation together, they did not always succeed, and as the war progressed it became more and more difficult. The fate of Anton Meiser illustrates this. Like many of his comrades he fell victim to the Volhynian fever, which in his case coincided with appendicitis, and he was moved to a hospital at Prague. As he spent eight weeks at hospital he did not follow the reconstituted 389th Division when it moved to the northern sector of the Eastern Front. Rather he was sent to a training unit near Stettin in Germany, and eventually he was transferred to an artillery unit on the Western Front, where he was taken prisoner by the Americans at the end of the war.

Meiser spent some 15 months as a prisoner of war before he was released in September 1946. This was a much shorter period of imprisonment than that endured by most German soldiers who were taken prisoner by the Red Army. Many were not allowed to return until 10 years after the end of the war, and of course there were many who did not return at all. Prisoners of war have often been treated badly, and the war on the Eastern Front was no exception. The mortality rates of the German soldiers taken prisoner at Korsun, however, seems to have been notably lower than among those captured at Stalingrad.

In the context of World War II, the battle at Korsun was a minor one, but with an unusually high degree of drama. The Soviet commanders took advantage of their considerable numerical superiority on the Eastern Front and decided to attack an exposed German position, which Hitler stubbornly decided to hold, despite many objections. The initial phase of the Soviet operation proceeded fairly well. As usual with military plans, the Soviet attack did not work out exactly as intended, but the initial aim was achieved. But the elimination of the cauldron did not proceed as planned, nor could the expected German relief attempts be repelled in the desired way. Nevertheless, the Soviet position, relative to the Germans, was stronger after the battle than before, so Korsun may be viewed as a Soviet victory, even though it was bought at a considerably higher price than it ought to have been.

Notes on the Text

1 For more information on the battle at Kursk, see N. Zetterling and A. Frankson, *Kursk 1943, A Statistical Analysis* (Frank Cass, London 2000).

2 Soviet casualties in the Orel fighting (12 July–18 August) amounted to 429,890, and 2,586 tanks and assault guns were written off. See G. F.Krivosheev, *Grif Sekretnosti Sniat* (Voenizdat, Moscow 1993), pp. 189 and 370. The two German armies that fought in the Orel salient, 9th Army and 2nd Panzer Army, suffered 89,688 casualties between 11 July and 20 August. See Zetterling and Frankson, *Kursk 1943*, p. 200. It has not been possible to establish German tank losses, but all tank and assault gun formations in the Orel salient lost 371 tanks and assault guns irrevocably during July 1943 (see Pz.Offz. b. Chef Genst.d.H. Bb. Nr. 562/43 g.Kdos, 14.8.1943, BA-MA RH 10/48). Since this also included losses during the German offensive operation, and considering the generally less intensive fighting in August, it seems reasonable to assume that German losses did not exceed 400.

3 The Red Army suffered 255,566 casualties during the Belgorod-Kharkov operation according to Krivosheev, *Grif Sekretnosti Sniat*, p. 190. This can be compared to the fact that the defending German armies (4th Panzer Army and Army Detachment Kempf) reported 51,724 casualties 1–31 August. See Zetterling and Frankson, *Kursk 1943*, p. 200.

4 The exact figures are 2,864,661 casualties. Of these, 1,829,666 were wounded and 231,139 were hospitalized due to disease. See Krivosheev, *Grif Sekretnosti Sniat*, pp. 146f.

5 German combat losses were 533,025 (see BA-MA RH 2/1343), of which 72% were wounded. The rest were killed in action or missing. The percentage is derived from the ten-day reports of the Heeresarzt for the period, found in NARA T78, R414, F6383353-6383369. Since these reports sometimes suffer from delayed reporting, we have opted to use the BA-MA RH 2/1343 file to establish overall losses for the period.

6 The more precise figure of 176,871 is given by BA-MA RH 2/1343.

7 BA-MA RH 2/1343. Another document – NARA T78, R414, F6383154 – shows marginally higher figures. According to this document 114,000 convalescents and 188,000 replacements were sent to the Eastern Front during July, August and September 1943. Given the small disagreement (only 8%) between the two documents, it is quite possible that one document gives the number of replacements dispatched, or ordered, while the other gives the number that had actually arrived. Thus the difference between the two figures is actually the soldiers in transit. If this assumption is true, it would be expected that the error (in percent) would get smaller the longer the time period studied. This is indeed the case. Both documents give replacements and convalescents also for the period 1 July 1943–31 May 1944. The RH 2/1343 shows 1,205,030 replacements and convalescents, while NARA T78, R414, F6383154 shows 542,000 convalescents and 685,000 replacements, which gives a difference of less than 2%.

8 On 1 July 1943 the manpower ratio was 6,856,800 soldiers on the Soviet side vs 3,138,000 Germans, or 2.2:1. Had neither side received any new manpower, the force ratio would have been reduced to 4 million vs 2.4 million, or 1.67:1. As it was, in October the Red Army numbered 6.6 million men pitted against 2.68 million Germans, or a ratio of 2.5:1.

9 Evgeni Bessonov, *Tank Rider* (London: Greenhill, 2003) p. 33.

10 Ibid, pp. 35–36.

11 Bessonov, *Tank Rider*, pp. 36–37.

12 Ibid, pp. 37–38.

13 Bessonov, *Tank Rider,* pp. 38–40.

14 See casualty chart in BA-MA RH 2/1343.

15 Examples of documents on this can be found in Anlagenband zum KTB AOK 8 Qu., Jan–März 1944, T312, R63, F7580590 and F7580602.

16 Up to 31 May 1944, the German casualties on the Eastern Front amounted to 751,237 killed in action, 2,824,807 wounded in action and 541,043 missing in action (Der Heeresarzt om OKH GenSt d H/GenQu Az 1335 c/d (IIb), Personelle blutige Verluste des Feldheeres, Berichtigte Meldun für die Zeit vom 1.6.1944 bis 10.1.1945, T78, R414, F6383234). This means that wounded constituted 69% of the casualties. However, since this figure includes some cases where German forces were surrounded, the wounded must have constituted a slightly greater share than in those situations where German units were not surrounded.

Between 1 July 1943 and 1 June 1944 1,900,490 losses were suffered (OKH/Gen.St.d.H./Org.Abt. Nr. I/18941/44 g.Kdos, v. 7.9.44 (National Archives, Microfilm Publication T78, Roll 414, Frame 6383114). The figure does not include forces in Finland. Of these about 1.3 million were wounded. Simultaneously 542,000 convalescents returned to the eastern front (NARA T78, R414, F6383154).

17 Anton Meiser, *Die Hölle von Tscherkassy* (Schnellbach, Verlag S. Bublies 2000), pp. 12–37.

18 Idem.

19 Meiser, *Die Hölle von Tscherkassy*, pp. 12–37.

20 G. F. Zhukov, *Vospominanija i razmysjlenija*, vol III (Novosti, Moscow 1986), p. 83.
21 K. S. Moskalenko, *Na Yugo-Zapadnom Napravlenii 1943–1945, Kniga 2.* (Nauka, Moscow 1973), p. 162.
22 Richard Armstrong, *Red Army Tank Commanders, The Armored Guards.* (Schiffer Military /Aviation History, Atglen 1994), p. 201.
23 The Germans also held along the west bank of the Dnepr between Nikopol and the river estuary.
24 K.V. Krainyukov, *Ot Dnepra do Visly* (Voenizdat, Moscow 1971), page 92.
25 Vatutin had 831, 000 front troops, almost 11,400 guns and mortars, 297 rocket artillery launchers and over 1,100 tanks and assault guns combat ready at his disposal (see A.N.Grylev; *Dnepr. Karpaty, Krim* [Nauka, Moscow 1970], pp. 40-41). The German 4th Panzer Army, which faced Vatutin's front, had a ration strength of 360,000 (Anlage 7 zum KTB Meldungen (Beute, Verpflegungsstärken) v. 1.7.1943–31.12.1943). As German army ration strengths included large numbers of men from categories not included in the Soviet returns, the true force ratio was even more favorable to Vatutin than these figures suggest.
26 Krainyukov, *Ot Dnepra do Visly*, p. 101.
27 The report was written by Lieutenant-Colonel Robert E.McCabe. See Public Record Office, War Office 193/651. Trip to Kiev Front 3–16 January 1944.
28 A. S. Zjadov, *Tjetyre Goda Vojny* (Moscow: Voenizdat 1978), p. 157.
29 P.A. Rotmistrov. *Stalnaja Gvardija.* (Voenizdat, Moscow 1984.) p. 254.
30 Rotmistrov, *Stalnaja Gvardija,* p. 256.
31 PzAOK 1 Ia KTB Nr. 13, 6 January 1944, T313, R69, F7305767f.
32 PzAOK 1 Ia KTB Nr. 13, 7 January 1944, T313, R69, F7305769f.
33 PzAOK 1 Ia KTB Nr. 13, 8 January 1944, T313, R69, F7305773f.
34 PzAOK 1 Ia KTB Nr. 13, 10 January 1944, T313, R69, F7305779.
35 PzAOK 1 Ia KTB Nr. 13, 11-16 January 1944, T313, R69, F7305783-99.
36 PzAOK 1 Ia KTB Nr. 13, 17 January 1944, T313, R69, F7305800.
37 These units – according to German intelligence consisting of elements from the 32nd, 136th, and 167th Rifle Divisions – were not particularly strong, but nevertheless far more than a nuisance (See PzAOK 1 Ia KTB Nr. 13, 17 January 1944, T313, R69, F7305801). It seems that the German intelligence was at least partially accurate, since the Soviet General Staff Study says that elements of the 136th and 167th Rifle Divisions, plus the 6th Motorized Rifle Brigade were encircled in the area (*The Korsun'-Shevchenkovskii Operation* [The Cherkassy Pocket] [January-February 1944] The Soviet General Staff Study. Translated and edited by David M. Glantz and Harold S. Orenstien. p. 12).
38 PzAOK 1 Ia KTB Nr. 13, 18 January 1944, T313, R69, F7305803f.
39 PzAOK 1 Ia KTB Nr. 13, 19 January 1944, T313, R69, F7305806f.
40 PzAOK 1 Ia KTB Nr. 13, 20-21 January 1944, T313, R69, F7305809-15; Tagesmeldung VII. A.K. Ia, 20.1.44 and 21.1.44 in Anlagen zum KTB PzAOK 1 Ia, T313, R69, F7306320 & F7306341.
41 PzAOK 1 Ia KTB Nr. 13, 22 January 1944, T313, R69, F7305816f.
42 PzAOK 1 Ia KTB Nr. 13, 23 January 1944, T313, R69, F7305818.
43 Kriegsliederung PzAOK 1, 22 January 1944, T313, R69, F7306352. Actually both divisions had seven infantry battalions (including Füsilier battalions) but two had been detached from the 88th Division to the 68th Division and one had been detached from Korps-Abteilung B to VII Corps.
44 Kriegsliederung PzAOK 1, 22 January 1944, T313, R69, F7306352.
45 PzAOK 1 Ia KTB Nr. 13, 23 January 1944, T313, R69, F7305818f; VII. A.K. Ia Tagesmeldung 23.1.44, in Anlagen zum KTB PzAOK 1 Ia, T313, R69, F7306377.
46 PzAOK 1 Ia KTB Nr. 13, 24 January 1944, T313, R69, F7305820.
47 VII. A.K. Ia Nr. 159/44 g.Kdos,Fernschreiben an PzAOK 1 Ia, 24.1.44, 13.00 Uhr, in Anlagen zum KTB PzAOK 1 Ia, T313, R69, F7306385.
48 PzAOK 1 Ia KTB Nr. 13, 24 January 1944, T313, R69, F7305820f.
49 PzAOK 1 Ia KTB Nr. 13, 24 January 1944, T313, R69, F7305821.
50 PzAOK 1 Ia KTB Nr. 13, 25 January 1944, T313, R69, F7305823-5.
51 AOK 8 Ia KTB Nr. 3, 22 January 1944, T312, R64, F7581722-5.
52 AOK 8 Ia KTB Nr. 3, 23 January 1944, T312, R64, F7581726-38.
53 Ibid.
54 AOK 8 Ia KTB Nr. 3, 24 January 1944, T312, R64, F7581739f.
55 Meiser, *Die Hölle von Tscherkassy*, p. 181.
56 Meiser, *Die Hölle von Tscherkassy*, pp. 181–2.
57 Meiser, *Die Hölle von Tscherkassy*, p.182.
58 Meiser, *Die Hölle von Tscherkassy*, pp. 182–3.
59 Meiser, *Die Hölle von Tscherkassy*, pp. 183–4.
60 Meiser, *Die Hölle von Tscherkassy*, pp. 183–4.
61 Meiser, *Die Hölle von Tscherkassy*, pp. 184–5.
62 Meiser, *Die Hölle von Tscherkassy*, pp. 184–5.
63 AOK 8 Ia KTB Nr. 3, 24 January 1944, T312, R64, F7581740-2.
64 AOK 8 Ia KTB Nr. 3, 24 January 1944, T312, R64, F7581740-4.
65 *The Korsun'-Shevchenkovskii Operation,* p. 7. Note that the source gives slightly longer distances than we have given. It seems to be a rather common practice by Soviet sources to inflate distances, to produce more impressive advance rates.
66 *Studies on Soviet Combat Performance*, pp. 20–22.

67 In fact, the Soviet General Staff Study (p. 10) from 1944 says the army had 91 tanks and 16 self-propelled guns, while an article in the Soviet General Staff's military history journal in 1969 says the army had 168 tanks and 22 self-propelled guns ("Dokumenti i materiali: Korsun-Shevchenkovskaya operatsiya v tsifrakh," *Voenno-Istoricheskii Zhurnal* no 7 [1969], pp. 45–52). The latter figure seems more likely. The most likely explanation for this discrepancy is that the General Staff Study actually used a figure that referred to the situation a few days before the offensive began, but during those days, tanks returning from workshops raised the strength of the army to the figure given by the article.

68 Soviet General Staff Study, p. 104.

69 G.T.Zavizion & P.A.Kornjusjin, *I na Tikhom okeane*. (Voenizdat, Moscow 1967), p. 16.

70 *The Korsun'-Shevchenkovskii Operation*, p. 10.

71 Ibid, map 4, p. 19.

72 *The Korsun'-Shevchenkovskii Operation*, pp. 8, 18 and 172; *Studies on Soviet Combat Performance*, pp. 28–30.

73 *The Korsun'-Shevchenkovskii Operation*, p. 172.

74 *The Korsun'-Shevchenkovskii Operation*, pp. 126, 127, 172.

75 I.S.Konev, *Zapiski Komandujusjego Frontom*. (Voenizdat, Moscow 1982.) p. 98.

76 *The Korsun'-Shevchenkovskii Operation*, pp. 13–15.

77 *The Korsun'-Shevchenkovskii Operation*, p. 15.

78 AOK 8 Ia KTB Nr. 3, 22-25 January 1944, T312, R64, F7581722-7581744.

79 AOK 8 Ia KTB Nr. 3, 22 January 1944, T312, R64, F7581725.

80 AOK 8 Ia KTB Nr. 3, 23 January 1944, T312, R64, F7581726.

81 AOK 8 Ia KTB Nr. 3, 23 January 1944, T312, R64, F7581736.

82 AOK 8 Ia KTB Nr. 3, 24.1.44, T312, R64, F7581739-44.

83 *The Korsun'-Shevchenkovskii Operation*, p. 127.

84 *The Korsun'-Shevchenkovskii Operation*, p. 147.

85 *The Korsun'-Shevchenkovskii Operation*, pp. 147–8 & 159.

86 *The Korsun'-Shevchenkovskii Operation*, pp. 147–8 & 159.

87 This is discussed further in N. Zetterling & A. Frankson, "Analyzing World War II East Front Battles," *Journal of Slavic Military Studies, vol 11, no 1* (March 1998), pp. 176–203.

88 We have used Krivosheev's figures (see G.F. Krivosheev, *Grif Sekretnosti Sniat* [Voenizdat, Moscow 1993] p. 146) which should be seen as a minimum. Krivosheev states that 8,708,318 soldiers were killed, died of wounds or went missing 22 June 1941–31 December 1943. Also 10,992,283 were wounded or evacauated due to disease or frostbite. Here it has been assumed that one third of them did not return to duty (note that unlike the German figures, Krivosheev's figures of dead include those who died of wounds in hospital). This yields a total of 12,374,412. However, most likely Krivosheev's figure for 1941 is at least one million too low. He records 2,335,482 missing, while the Germans took more than three million prisoners.

89 1,075,773 were reported as killed in action or missing according to Der Heeresarzt b. Oberkommando des Heeres Nr. I/080/44 g.Kdos, Personelle Blutige Verluste vom 22. juni 1941 bis 31. Dezember 1943, T78, R414, F6383333.

90 This is an estimate. Up to 20 February 1944, the German army lost 795,698 killed in action and 32,724 who died of accidents or disease (Der heeresarzt im OKH GenStdH/GenQu Az 1335 (IIb) Nr I./01867/44 g.Kdos 6.3.1944, BA-MA RW 6/v. 555). This gives a ratio of 24:1, which has been used to calculate the number killed on the Eastern Front up to 31 December 1943 (655,164, source as in the note above). This is of course an estimate, but since more than 80% of all deaths in action were incurred on the Eastern Front, this can hardly be considered a daring estimate.

91 2,438,198 were reported as killed in action or missing according to Der Heeresarzt b. Oberkommando des Heeres Nr. I/080/44 g.Kdos, Personelle Blutige Verluste vom 22. juni 1941 bis 31. Dezember 1943, T78, R414, F6383333.

92 Der heeresarzt im OKH GenStdH/GenQu Az 1335 (IIb) Nr I./01867/44 g.Kdos 6.3.1944, BA-MA RW 6/v. 555. This document gives losses for the entire army from the beginning of the war up to 20 February 1944. Here it has been assumed that 80% of the losses were incurred on the Eastern Front 22 June 1941–31 December 1943.

93 See J. Erickson & D. Dilks (eds.), *Barbarossa–The Axis and the Allies* (Edinburgh University Press, Edinburgh 1994), p. 261.

94 How the Korps-Abteilungen were to be organized is described in the document Oberkommando des heeres GenStdH/Org.Abt. Nr. I/430/43 g.Kdos, "Zusammenlegung von Inf.div., 24 September 1943." A copy of this document can be found in Anlagenband Nr. 1 zum KTB Nr. 9 XXXXVII. Pz.Korps Ia, T314, R1132, F000615ff.

95 G. Tessin, *Verbände und Truppen der deutschen Wehrmacht und Waffen-SS* (Mittler & Sohn, Frankfurt am Main and Biblio Verlag, Osnabrück 1966–1975), entry for units beginning with letter "B."

96 11. Pz.Div. Monatliche Zustandmeldung, Stand 1.2.44, in Anlagenband Nr. 1 zum KTB Nr. 9 XXXXVII. Pz.Korps Ia, T314, R1132, F000656.

97 13. Pz.Div. Monatliche Zustandmeldung, Stand 1.2.44, in Anlagenband Nr. 1 zum KTB Nr. 9 XXXXVII. Pz.Korps Ia, T314, R1132, F000668.

98 See reports on the condition of the divisions of the XXXXVII. Pz.Korps, in Anlagen zum KTB XXXXVII. Pz.Korps Ia, T314, R1132, F000629-674.

99 3. Pz.Div. Monatliche Zustandmeldung, Stand 1.2.44, in Anlagenband Nr. 1 zum KTB Nr. 9 XXXXVII. Pz.Korps Ia, T314, R1132, F000649ff; 14. Pz.Div. Monatliche Zustandmeldung, Stand 1.2.44, in Anlagenband Nr. 1 zum KTB Nr. 9 XXXXVII. Pz.Korps Ia, T314, R1132, F000668.

100 Omer Bartov presented this argument in a 1983 PhD thesis and in subsequent books, for example: *The Eastern Front 1941–1945: German Troops and the Barbarisation of Warfare* and *Hitler's Army* (Houndmills, Palgrave 1986); *Hitler's Army* (Oxford, Oxford University Press, 1992).

101 This is discussed further in N. Zetterling, *German Ground Forces in Normandy* (Fedorowicz, Winnipeg, 2000), pp. 434–6 and the footnotes on pp. 437f

102 Knut Pipping, *Kompaniet som samhälle* (Åbo Akademi, Åbo 1947); Ben Shalit, *Konfliktens och stridens psykologi* (Liber, Stockholm 1983); S.A. Stouffer, *The American Soldier, vol 1 & 2* (Princeton University Press, 1977); E.A. Shils & M. Janowitz, "Cohesion and Disintegration in the Wehrmacht in World War II," *Public Opinion Quarterly*, Summer 1948. For further discussion of the issue, see for example, Bruce Newsome, "The Myth of Intrinsic Combat Motivation," *Journal of Strategic Studies*, vol 26, no 4 (December 2003). For examples of how soldiers react in adverse military situations, see M. Connelly & W. Miller, "The BEF and the Issue of Surrender on the Western Front in 1940," *War in* History *2004*, 11 (4).

103 More on this can be found in Stouffer, *The American Soldier, vol 1 & 2.*

104 Meiser, *Die Hölle von Tscherkassy*, pp. 229–40.

105 Olaf Ehlers' Diary, BA-MA MSg 2/3200.

106 Meiser, *Die Hölle von Tscherkassy*, p. 164.

107 Meiser, *Die Hölle von Tscherkassy*, p. 164.

108 A. Frankson, "Summer 1941," *Journal of Slavic Military Studies*, vol 13, no 3 (September 2000); N. M. Rekkedal & N. Zetterling, *Grundbok i operatioonskonst* (Försvarshögskolan, Stockholm 2004), pp. 281-4.

109 "Entwicklung der Iststärke des Ostheeres," NARA T78, R414, F6383128; *Geschichte des Grossen Vaterländichen Krieges der Sowjetunion*, vol 4, page 25, Deutscher Militärverlag, Berlin 1965. The book is a translation of *Istoria Velikoi Otechestvennoy Voiny Sovetskogo Soyoza* (Moscow 1964). The figure does include STAVKA reserves, but not personnel in the air force and the navy.

110 The Red Army had 7,753 tanks and assault guns in the frontline units and 2,232 in operational reserves. In comparison, the German forces in the East merely numbered 3,356 tanks and assault guns. Of these only 1,285 were operational, the remainder were in workshops. Of course there were Soviet tanks in workshops too. It seems that there were 5,357 operational tanks in the Soviet frontline forces, plus an unknown number in the operational reserves. Thus the Red Army enjoyed a 3:1 advantage in tanks and assault guns, if all vehicles are included, and more than 4:1 if only operational vehicles are included. Panzer-Lage Ost (Nach Gen.Qu.), BA-MA RH 10/61 and StuG-Lage Ost (Nach Gen.Qu.), BA-MA RH 10/62. Included in the figures are 118 obsolete tanks (Pz II, Pz 38, Pz III L42, Pz IV L24) 135 command tanks, 349 Panthers and 232 Tigers. The Soviet tank strength comes from *Geschichte des Grossen Vaterländichen Krieges der Sowjetunion* (East German translation of *Istoriya Velikoy Otechestvennoy Voyny Sovetskogo Sojuz*), vol 4 (Deutscher Militärverlag, Berlin 1965), p.26

111 Soviet strength from N. Tereshchenko, "Korsun-Shevchenkovskaia operatiia v tsifrakh," *Voenno-istoricheskii zhurnal* (July 1969), German strength from Appendix 2, table 1 and "Gefechtsstärken und einsatzber. Waffen," 22.1.44, in Anlagen zum KTB XXXXVII Pz.Korps Ia, T314, R1132, F000577-82.

112 Tereshchenko, "Korsun-Shevchenkovskaia operatiia v tsifrakh."

113 Krivosheev, *Grif Sekretnosti Sniat*, p. 227.

114 A useful concept is the "divisional slice," which means that the front, army, and corps assets are distributed equally on the divisions. It is of course an abstraction, but it shows how strong the average division was, when the support from higher echelons is included. When 1943 shifted to 1944 the German Ostheer had a divisional slice of almost exactly 15,000 men per division. Note that the German strength is Iststärke, thus it actually include soldiers on leave, hospitalized (except those who were evacuated from their units) or on separate training. The real divisional slice probably was less than 14,000. (168 divisions on 26 December 1943 [KTB OKW 1943, pp. 1397ff] and 2,528,000 men on the Eastern Front ["Entwicklung der Iststärke des Ostheeres," NARA T78, R414, F6383128])

For the Red Army the divisional slice was about 12,500 men per division (calculation based on the number of soldiers, taken from *Geschichte des Grossen Vaterländichen Krieges der Sowjetunion*, vol 4 [Deutscher Militärverlag, Berlin 1965], p. 25. The book is a translation of *Istoria Velikoi Otechestvennoy Voiny Sovetskogo Soyoza* (Moscow 1964). The figures do include STAVKA reserves, but not personnel in the air force and the navy. Soviet Tank, Mechanized, and Cavalry corps have been equated with divisions. Thus, counting divisions may actually provide a quite reasonable picture of the manpower ratio.

115 It should be emphasized that the number of divisions employed is partly a matter of definition, as neither side only employed complete corps or armies. Rather the boundaries of the operation did not fully coincide with the boundaries of the corps and army sectors.

116 *The Korsun'-Shevchenkovskii Operation*, p. 9, gave these ratios. However, as it usually inflates the German strength, it is possible that the real Soviet advantage was greater.

117 The Soviet divisions were, from north to south: 31st Rifle Division, 375th Rifle Division, 69th Guards Rifle Division, 25th Guards Rifle Division, 1st Guards Airborne Division, 66th Guards Rifle Division, and 14th Guards Rifle Division. See *The Korsun'-Shevchenkovskii Operation*, maps on pp. 184–5.

118 AOK 8 Ia KTB Nr. 3, 24 January 1944, T312, R64, F7581743.

119 The Rifle Divisions were the 252nd and 214th. See *The Korsun'-Shevchenkovskii Operation*, pp. 9 & 185.
120 AOK 8 Ia KTB Nr. 3, 25 January 1944, T312, R64, F7581745-7. See also *The Korsun'-Shevchenkovskii Operation*, p. 127.
121 KTB XXXXVII. Pz.Korps Ia, 25 January 1944, T314, R1132, F000425; AOK 8 Ia KTB Nr. 3, 25 January 1944, T312, R64, F7581745-7. See also *The Korsun'-Shevchenkovskii Operation*, pp. 18 & 185.
122 KTB XXXXVII. Pz.Korps Ia, 25 January 1944, T314, R1132, F000425-6.
123 AOK 8 Ia KTB Nr. 3, 25 January 1944, T312, R64, F7581747.
124 *The Korsun'-Shevchenkovskii Operation*, p. 127 and map on p. 185. Strangely the Soviet General Staff Study maintains that "the tank corps had advanced from 18–20 kilometers during the 5–6 hours of combat" (p. 127). This cannot be true. When the two tanks corps were committed, Soviet forces were already fighting along the Reyementarovka–Ositjyashka line, which is only 6–8 kilometers from the Kapitanovka–Tishkovka line.
125 The exact composition was Pz.Gren.Rgt. 108, Pz.Aufkl.Abt. 14, II./Pz.Art.Rgt. 4 and a Flak-Kampftrupp.
126 Langkeit's group consisted of Pz.Rgt. 36, I./Pz.Gren.Rgt. 103 and I./Pz.Art.Rgt. 4. KTB AOK 8 Ia, 25 January, T312, R64, F7581727-9; R. Grams, *Die 14. Pz.Div. 1940–1945* (Podzun, Bad Nauheim 1957), pp. 164-6.
127 KTB III./Pz.Rgt. 36, 25 January, BA-MA RH 39/380.
128 KTB III./Pz.Rgt. 36, 25 January, BA-MA RH 39/380.
129 KTB III./Pz.Rgt. 36, 25 January, BA-MA RH 39/380.
130 Tagesmeldung XI. Armee-Korps Ia vom 25.1.1944, found in Anlagen zum KTB AOK 8 Ia, T312, R66, F7584343.
131 AOK 8 Ia KTB Nr. 3, 25 January 1944, T312, R64, F7581747;*The Korsun'-Shevchenkovskii Operation*, pp. 127f & 185.
132 AOK 8 Ia KTB Nr. 3, 25 January 1944, T312, R64, F7581747; Proschek papers, MSg 2/5648. The infantry battalion arriving in Ozitniazhka at 11.15hrs was the II./Gren.Rgt. 676.
133 Strangely there are Soviet statements that the two tank corps advanced 18–20 kilometers during 5–6 hours of fighting on 25 January (*The Korsun'-Shevchenkovskii Operation*, p. 127). This is clearly at odds with the locations reached, as stated by the Soviet accounts, and which are corroborated by the German war diaries.
134 XI. A.K. Ia Morgenmeldung, 25.1.44, in Anlagen zum KTB AOK 8 Ia, T312, R66, F7584360; XI. A.K. Ia Tagesmeldung, 25.1.44, in Anlagen zum KTB AOK 8 Ia, T312, R66, F7584343. The battalion that became separated from 389th Division was the III./Gren.Rgt. 545.
135 Tsamo RF, fond 4.gd.A.(320), Opis 4522, delo 114.
136 Tsamo RF, fond 4.gd.A.(320), Opis 4522, delo 114.
137 AOK 8 Ia KTB Nr. 3, 25 January 1944, T312, R64, F7581746.
138 AOK 8 Ia KTB Nr. 3, 25 January 1944, T312, R64, F7581746f & F7581727-30; XI. A.K. Ia Tagesmeldung, 25.1.44, in Anlagen zum KTB AOK 8 Ia, T312, R66, F7584343.
139 AOK 8 Ia KTB Nr. 3, 25 January 1944, T312, R64, F7581746f & F7581727-30.
140 AOK 8 Ia Tagesmeldung 25.1.44, T312, r66, f7584340-2; XI. A.K. Ia Tagesmeldung, 26.1.44, in Anlagen zum KTB AOK 8 Ia, T312, R66, F7584323.
141 AOK 8 Ia KTB Nr. 3, 25 January 1944, T312, R64, F7581729-30. AOK 8 Ia, "Morgenmeldungen der Korps 26.1.44", T312, R66, F7584338.
142 *The Korsun'-Shevchenkovskii Operation*, p. 128.
143 Some Soviet sources mention a German "second defensive belt." This suggests a much stronger defense than was actually the case. There was actually no coherent German defense between Slatopol and Ositniazhka.
144 *The Korsun'-Shevchenkovskii Operation*, p. 128; AOK 8 Ia KTB Nr. 3, 26 January 1944, T312, R64, F7581731-35 & F7581748-51.
145 AOK 8 Ia KTB Nr. 3, 26 January 1944, T312, R64, F7581731-32.
146 AOK 8 Ia KTB Nr. 3, 26 January 1944, T312, R64, F7581734.
147 AOK 8 Ia KTB Nr. 3, 26 January 1944, T312, R64, F7581733-35 &F7581749; KTB XXXXVII. Pz.Korps Ia 26 January 1944, T314, R1132, F000427.
148 *The Korsun'-Shevchenkovskii Operation*, p. 128.
149 Note that Soviet sources often give higher advance rates. We prefer to check the advance rates ourselves, using the locations given in the sources and measuring the distances on the map. Thus we ensure that we get reliable and consistent figures, useful for anyone who wants to compare advance rates.
150 AOK 8 Ia KTB Nr. 3, 26 January 1944, T312, R64, F7581734.
151 AOK 8 Ia KTB Nr. 3, 26 January 1944, T312, R64, F7581734.
152 AOK 8 Ia KTB Nr. 3, 26 January 1944, T312, R64, F7581735.
153 AOK 8 Ia KTB Nr. 3, 26 January 1944, T312, R64, F7581735 & F7581748.
154 *The Korsun'-Shevchenkovskii Operation*, p. 128.
155 See Appendix 2 for a discussion of the 11th Panzer Division's tank strength. Soviet Tank strength from *The Korsun'-Shevchenkovskii Operation*, pp. 126, 127, 172..
156 KTB III./Pz.Rgt. 36, 26 January, BA-MA RH 39/380; Verlustliste III./Pz.Rgt. 36 BA-MA RH 39/380.
157 KTB III./Pz.Rgt. 36, 26 January, BA-MA RH 39/380.
158 XI. A.K. Ia Tagesmeldung, in Anlagen zum KTB AOK 8 Ia, T312, R66, F7584323.

159 Ia-Tagesmeldung 11. Pz.Div. vom 26.1.1944, in Anlagen zum KTB AOK 8 Ia, T312, R66, F7584325; Tagesmeldung AOK 8 Ia, T312, R66, F7584320.
160 AOK 8 Ia KTB Nr. 3, 26 January 1944, T312, R64, F7581733-35 &F7581749.
161 *The Korsun'-Shevchenkovskii Operation*, pp. 127f.
162 XI. A.K. Ia Tagesmeldung, in Anlagen zum KTB AOK 8 Ia, T312, R66, F7584323-4.
163 Meiser, *Die Hölle von Tscherkassy*, pp. 186–190.
164 Meiser, *Die Hölle von Tscherkassy*, pp. 186–190.
165 The artillery battalion was the I./Art.Rgt. 108, which had been supporting the Grossdeutschland Division. See XI. A.K. Ia Tagesmeldung, in Anlagen zum KTB AOK 8 Ia, T312, R66, F7584323-4; Kriegsgliederung AOK 8, Stand 28.1.44, T312, R64, F7582625; AOK 8 Ia/Art Nr. 212/44 geh. 24.1.44, T312, R64, F7582982. Note that there is a typing error in the first document; it is said that the unit was I./A.N. 108, rather than I./A.R. 108 as it should be.
166 *The Korsun'-Shevchenkovskii Operation*, pp. 53–5.
167 *The Korsun'-Shevchenkovskii Operation*, pp. 128–9; AOK 8 Ia KTB Nr. 3, 27 January 1944, T312, R64, F7581752-3. Note that the Soviet General Staff Study claims that the German defense of Shpola counted up to a regiment of infantry and a training battalion. We have not found any evidence at all of German combat units in Shpola. It seems only to have been occupied by various rear services.
168 KTB XXXXVII. Pz.Korps Ia, 27 January 1944, T314, R1132, F000428; AOK 8 Ia KTB Nr. 3, 27 January 1944, T312, R64, F7581752-3.
169 Fernschreiben 11. Pz.Div. Ia an AOK 8, 16.25 Uhr, 27.1.44, in Anlagen zum KTB AOK 8 Ia, T312, R66, F7584303. The three assault gun battalions were Pz.Abt. 8 (one StuG III), StuG.Abt. 905 (ten StuG III) and StuG.Abt. 911 (four StuG III). The Soviet General Staff Study grossly exaggerates the German tank strength, stating that the SS-Wiking attacked from the north with 50 tanks and the 14th Panzer Division with 70 tanks (see *The Korsun'-Shevchenkovskii Operation*, p. 56). Neither division had that number before the operation began and had not recieved any reinforcements since then. Even if we assume that the Soviet Study actually means all German tank units operating on the 5th Guards Tank Army's southern flank when speaking about the 14th Panzer Division, it is impossible to reach anywhere near 70 tanks. Also, the SS-Wiking Division was not even employed in this area, its tanks being further to the north; see Proschek collection, BA-MA MSg 2/5648.
170 Fernschreiben 14. Pz.Div. Ia an AOK 8, 23.40 Uhr, 27.1.44, in Anlagen zum KTB AOK 8 Ia, T312, R66, F7584304; AOK 8 Ia KTB Nr. 3, 27 January 1944, T312, R64, F7581754.
171 *The Korsun'-Shevchenkovskii Operation*, pp. 18–20, 56–58, 128–130.
172 AOK 8 Ia KTB Nr. 3, 27 January 1944, T312, R64, F7581752-8.
173 Ibid.
174 Meiser, *Die Hölle von Tscherkassy*, pp. 191–2.
175 Ibid.
176 Meiser, *Die Hölle von Tscherkassy*, p. 192.
177 Meiser, *Die Hölle von Tscherkassy*, pp. 192–3.
178 Ibid.
179 Meiser, *Die Hölle von Tscherkassy*, pp. 193–4
180 Meiser, *Die Hölle von Tscherkassy*, pp. 194–5.
181 The battalion was the II./Pz.Gren.Rgt. 110 and the assault guns belongred to StuG.Abt. 905. See Fernschreiben 11. Pz.Div. Ia an AOK 8, 16.25 Uhr, 27.1.44, in Anlagen zum KTB AOK 8 Ia, T312, R66, F7584303.
182 Fernschreiben 11. Pz.Div. Ia an AOK 8, 16.25 Uhr, 27.1.44, in Anlagen zum KTB AOK 8 Ia, T312, R66, F7584303.
183 KTB XXXXVII. Pz.Korps Ia, 27.1.44, T314, R1132, F000428; AOK 8 Ia KTB Nr. 3, 27 January 1944, T312, R64, F7581754.
184 AOK 8 Ia KTB Nr. 3, 27 January 1944, 20.40, T312, R64, F7581752-8; Fernschreiben 14. Pz.Div. Ia an AOK 8, 23.40 Uhr, 27.1.44, in Anlagen zum KTB AOK 8 Ia, T312, R66, F7584304; KTB XXXXVII. Pz.Korps Ia, 27.1.44, T314, R1132, F000428; 14. Pz.Div., monthly report to the Inspector-General of Panzer Troops, 1.2.44, BA-MA RH 10/152.
185 *The Korsun'-Shevchenkovskii Operation*, pp. 18–20, 56–58, 128–130.
186 Fernschreiben 11. Pz.Div. Ia an AOK 8, 16.25 Uhr, 27.1.44, in Anlagen zum KTB AOK 8 Ia, T312, R66, F7584303; AOK 8 Ia KTB Nr. 3, 27 January 1944, T312, R64, F7581755-6; *The Korsun'-Shevchenkovskii Operation*, pp. 18--20, 56–58, 128–130.
187 *The Korsun'-Shevchenkovskii Operation*, p. 58. The Only German units operating in the area were the 11th and 14th Panzer Divisions, plus three assault gun battalions. These only had 18 tanks and 17 assault guns. Also, not all of them were involved in the encirclement of Tishkovka.
188 *The Korsun'-Shevchenkovskii Operation,* pp. 18–20, 54–58, 128–130; KTB XXXXVII. Pz.Korps Ia, 27.1.44, T314, R1132, F000428-30; Proschek papers, BA-MA MSg 2/5654. The artillery battalion was the III./Art.Rgt. 140.
189 KTB XXXXVII. Pz.Korps Ia, 27.1.44, T314, R1132, F000428-30.
190 AOK 8 Ia KTB Nr. 3, 27 January 1944, T312, R64, F7581754-5.
191 AOK 8 Ia KTB Nr. 3, 27 January 1944, T312, R64, F7581755-8.
192 See Appendix 2 for data on the German divisions; Soviet strength from "Dokumenti i materiali: Korsun-Shevchenkovskaya operatsiya v tsifrakh," *Voenno-Istoricheskii Zhurnal*, no 7, (1969), pp. 45–52.
193 For more on the I./Pz.Rgt. 26, see Appendix 2.
194 *The Korsun'-Shevchenkovskii Operation*, pp. 20–21, 130; AOK 8 Ia KTB Nr. 3, 28 January 1944, T312, R64, F7581761.
195 *The Korsun'-Shevchenkovskii Operation*, pp. 20–21, 130, 188.

196 For tank deliveries, see Lieferung der Pz.-Fahrz., Bd. Ab Mai 1943, BA-MA RH 10/349.
197 KTB I./Pz.Rgt. 26, BA-MA RH 39/599.
198 KTB Nr. 3, I./Pz.Rgt. 26 and Anlage 3 &25 zum KTB Nr. 3, I./Pz.Rgt. 26, BA-MA RH 39/599.
199 KTB Nr. 3, I./Pz.Rgt. 26 and Anlagen 4, 5, 6a, 6b and 7 zum KTB Nr. 3, I./Pz.Rgt. 26, BA-MA RH 39/599.
200 Ibid.
201 KTB Nr. 3, I./Pz.Rgt. 26 and Anlagen 4, 5, 6a, 6b and 7 zum KTB Nr. 3, I./Pz.Rgt. 26, BA-MA RH 39/599.
202 KTB Nr. 3, I./Pz.Rgt. 26 and Anlagen 4, 5, 6a, 6b and 7 zum KTB Nr. 3, I./Pz.Rgt. 26, BA-MA RH 39/599; Tsamo RF, Fond 332, opic 4948, delo 154, list 28,29,30.
203 Ibid.
204 KTB Nr. 3, I./Pz.Rgt. 26 and Anlagen 4, 5, 6a, 6b and 7 zum KTB Nr. 3, I./Pz.Rgt. 26, BA-MA RH 39/599; Tsamo RF, Fond 332, opic 4948, delo 154, list 28,29,30.
205 Anlage 5 zum KTB Nr. 3, I./Pz.Rgt. 26, BA-MA RH 39/599.
206 Ibid.
207 Anlage 5 zum KTB Nr. 3, I./Pz.Rgt. 26, BA-MA RH 39/599.
208 Anlage 4 zum KTB Nr. 3, I./Pz.Rgt. 26, BA-MA RH 39/599.
209 Anlage 6a zum KTB Nr. 3, I./Pz.Rgt. 26, BA-MA RH 39/599.
210 KTB Nr. 3 & Anlage 25 zum KTB Nr. I./Pz.Rgt. 26, BA-MA RH 39/599. It is known that tank I01, the battalion commander's tank, suffered from engine damage and had to be towed away to the workshop. Exactly when this took place is unknown.
211 Anlage 7 zum KTB Nr. 3, I./Pz.Rgt. 26, BA-MA RH 39/599.
212 Anlage 7 zum KTB Nr. 3, I./Pz.Rgt. 26, BA-MA RH 39/599.
213 Anlage 7 zum KTB Nr. 3, I./Pz.Rgt. 26, BA-MA RH 39/599.
214 Anlage 6a & 7 zum KTB Nr. 3, I./Pz.Rgt. 26, BA-MA RH 39/599.
215 KTB Nr. 3, I./Pz.Rgt. 26, BA-MA RH 39/599. All in all, the battalion lost 10 tanks destroyed on 28 January. Some of these losses occurred after 15.00hrs, see Anlage 7 & 25 zum KTB Nr. 3, I./Pz.Rgt. 26, BA-MA RH 39/599.
216 Anlage 4, 6b & 7 zum KTB Nr. 3, I./Pz.Rgt. 26, BA-MA RH 39/599.
217 Anlage 6b zum KTB Nr. 3, I./Pz.Rgt. 26, BA-MA RH 39/599.
218 KTB Nr. 3, I./Pz.Rgt. 26, BA-MA RH 39/599 and Anlage 4-7 zum KTB Nr. 3, I./Pz.Rgt. 26, BA-MA RH 39/599.
219 Anlage 4-7 zum KTB Nr. 3, I./Pz.Rgt. 26, BA-MA RH 39/599.
220 Anlage 4 zum KTB I./Pz,Rgt. 26, BA-MA RH 39/599.
221 Anlage 7 zum KTB I./Pz.Rgt. 26, BA-MA RH 39/599.
222 Anlage 7 zum KTB I./Pz.Rgt. 26, BA-MA RH 39/599.
223 Anlage 7 zum KTB I./Pz.Rgt. 26, BA-MA RH 39/599.
224 Anlage 7 zum KTB I./Pz.Rgt. 26, BA-MA RH 39/599.
225 Anlage 7 zum KTB I./Pz.Rgt. 26, BA-MA RH 39/599.
226 Anlage 7 & 8 zum KTB I./Pz.Rgt. 26, BA-MA RH 39/599.
227 KTB I./Pz.Rgt. 26, BA-MA RH 39/599; Anlage 25 zum KTB I./Pz.Rgt. 26, BA-MA RH 39/599.
228 AOK 8 Ia KTB Nr. 3, 28 January 1944, T312, R64, F7581761-3. Also see the comments on the battalion in AOK 8 Ia KTB Nr. 3, on 30 January, 09.30, T312, R64, F7581777; KTB I./Pz.Rgt. 26, BA-MA RH 39/599; Anlage 4 zum KTB I./Pz.Rgt. 26, BA-MA RH 39/599.
229 AOK 8 Ia KTB Nr. 3, 29 January 1944, T312, R64, F7581770; Anlage 25 zum KTB I./Pz.Rgt. 26, BA-MA RH 39/599.
230 One example of the German penchant for leading from the front, especially in the armored troops, is OKW, "Richtlinien für Führung und Einsatz der Panzer-Division," vom 3. Dezember 1940, T78, R201, F6144287. Also useful is Wolfgang Schneider, *Panzertaktik* (Fedorowicz, Winnipeg 2000).
231 *The Korsun'-Shevchenkovskii Operation*, pp. 20–21, 58, 130; AOK 8 Ia KTB Nr. 3, 28 January, T312, R64, F7581759-66; Tsamo RF, Fond 332, opic 4948, delo 154, list 28,29,30..
232 AOK 8 Ia KTB Nr. 3, 28 January 1944, T312, R64, F7581760-6.
233 KTB XXXXVII. Pz.Korps Ia, 28.1.44, T314, R1132, F000432.
234 *The Korsun'-Shevchenkovskii Operation*, pp. 108f.
235 *The Korsun'-Shevchenkovskii Operation*, pp. 109f.
236 *The Korsun'-Shevchenkovskii Operation*, p. 110. The war diary of the 1st Panzer Army mentions an artillery preparation of half an hour (PzAOK 1 Ia KTB Nr. 13, 26 January 1944, T313, R69, F7305827).
237 *The Korsun'-Shevchenkovskii Operation*, pp. 110f. PzAOK 1 Ia KTB Nr. 13, 26 January 1944, T313, R69, F7305827-31.
238 PzAOK 1 Ia KTB Nr. 13, 26 January 1944, T313, R69, F7305829.
239 G. Grossjohann, *Five Years, Four Fronts, The War Years of Georg Grossjohann.* (Aegis Consulting Group, Bedford 1999), pp. 70–71.
240 PzAOK 1 Ia KTB Nr. 13, 26 January 1944, T313, R69, F7305828.
241 *The Korsun'-Shevchenkovskii Operation*, p. 111.
242 PzAOK 1 Ia KTB Nr. 13, 26 January 1944, T313, R69, F7305827.
243 PzAOK 1 Ia KTB Nr. 13, 27 January 1944, T313, R69, F7305832.
244 PzAOK 1 Ia KTB Nr. 13, 27 January 1944, T313, R69, F7305832f.
245 PzAOK 1 Ia KTB Nr. 13, 27 January 1944, T313, R69, F7305832.
246 PzAOK 1 Ia KTB Nr. 13, 28 January 1944, T313, R69, F7305836.
247 *The Korsun'-Shevchenkovskii Operation*, pp. 113 & 130.

248 PzAOK 1 Ia KTB Nr. 13, 28 January 1944, T313, R69, F7305839; Soviet General Staff Study, pp. 22–3.

249 Tagesmeldung VII. A.K. Ia, 28.1.44 and Tagesmeldung XXXXII. A.K. Ia, 28.1.44, both in Anlagen zum KTB PzAOK 1 Ia, T313, R69, F7306464 and F7306470.

250 XXXXII. A.K. Tagesmeldung 26.1.44, in Anlagen zum KTB PzAOK 1 Ia, T313, R69, F7306434; Situation map in RH 24-11/98K.

251 XXXXII. A.K. Tagesmeldung 26.1.44, in Anlagen zum KTB PzAOK 1 Ia, T313, R69, F7306434; Situation map in RH 24-11/98K.

252 Fernschreiben XXXXII. A.K. Ia an PzAOK 1, 10.25 Uhr 27.1.44, in Anlagen zum KTB PzAOK 1 Ia, T313, R69, F7306438; Tagesmeldung XXXXII. A.K., 27.1.44, in Anlagen zum KTB PzAOK 1 Ia, T313, R69, F7306442.

Sperrverband Foquet initially received two battalions and an artillery battery from Korps-Abteilung B: Rgt.Gr. 258, Rgt.Gr. 475 and 6./Art.Rgt. 86 (Tagesmeldung XXXXII. A.K., 27.1.44, in Anlagen zum KTB PzAOK 1 Ia, T313, R69, F7306442 and Morgenmeldung XXXXII. A.K., 28.1.44, in Anlagen zum KTB PzAOK 1 Ia, T313, R69, F7306449).

253 Tagesmeldung XXXXII. A.K., 28.1.44, in Anlagen zum KTB PzAOK 1 Ia, T313, R69, F7306470.

254 *The Korsun'-Shevchenkovskii Operation*, p. 133. The detachement from the 20th Tank Corps was reinforced by the the 1st Guards Motorcycle Regiment plus elements from the 5th Guards Cavalry Corps.

255 Proschek papers, BA-MA MSg 2/5648.

256 Proschek papers, BA-MA MSg 2/5648.

257 Gunther Jahnke & Bernd Lerch, *Der Kessel von Tscherkassy 1944* (Donauwörth, Merkle Druck, 1996).

258 Jahnke and Lerch, *Der Kessel von Tscherkassy*, pp. 52–4.

259 Meiser, *Die Hölle von Tscherkassy*, pp. 196-9.

260 Ibid.

261 Ibid.

262 Meiser, *Die Hölle von Tscherkassy*, p. 200.

263 F. Halle, *Fra Finland till Kaukasus – Nordmenn på Østfronten 1941–1945* (Dreyers Forlag, Oslo 1972,) pp. 47–57.

264 For example, *The Korsun'-Shevchenkovskii Operation* maintains that the German force consisted of 75,000 soldiers and officers, 1,700 machine guns, 1,100 guns (including 108 self-propelled), 540 mortars, and 270 tanks and assault guns(p. 41). However, the German documents show that the pocket consisted of around 55,000 men, 313 guns (including 23 self-propelled) and less than 70 tanks and assault guns. Such exaggerations are common in Soviet sources. Whether they reflect inaccurate wartime estimates or conscious post-battle distortions is unclear. However, these two possibilities do not exclude each other. It is worth recalling that the Soviet sources invariably inflate German strength, they do not underestimate it.

265 Gruppe Mattenklott 18 Februar 1944, Nicht im Kampfraum XI. und XXXXII. A.K. befindlichen Teile, T313, R72, F7310468-70.

266 Jahnke & Lerch, *Der Kessel von Tscherkassy*, pp. 28–9.

267 Gruppe Mattenklott 18 February 1944, Nicht im Kampfraum XI. und XXXXII. A.K. befindlichen Teile, T313, R72, F7310468-70.

268 The documents are not entirely in agreement. An entry in the 8th Army war diary on 11 February states that Gruppe Stemmermann consisted of 56,00 men of all ranks. However, another entry, on 14 February, gives the figure as 54,000 men. At first glance it could be assumed that the difference is caused by wounded soldiers flown out of the pocket. This is however unlikely, as the air evacuation had ceased during the period 11–14 February. It seems also quite unlikely that losses in killed and missing would be more than a few hundred men. Either the figure 56,000 refers to a date much earlier than 11 February, or else the figure 54,000 is the result of a more careful investigation. Another report (AOK 8/O.Qu Nr. 277/44 geh. 11.2.44, T312, R63, F7581371) confirms the latter figure and also shows that 3,904 wounded and sick had been evacuated by air since 29 January. Thus the total would have been 58,000 when the pincers closed. However to this must be added soldiers killed or taken prisoner since the pocket was formed. We estimate that number to approximately 1,000. Hence we arrive at the figure 59,000.

269 PzAOK 1 Ia KTB Nr. 13, 30 January 1944, T313, R69, F7305845-8. See also Edgar Röhricht, *Probleme der Kesselschlacht* (Condor Verlag, Karlsruhe 1958), pp. 147–9.

270 The following Panzer divisions were with Army Group South: 1, 3, 6, 7, 8, 9, 11, 13, 14, 16, 17, 19, 23, 24, 25, Grossdeutschland, Leibstandarte, Das Reich, Totenkopf, Wiking. The 4th, 5th, 12th, and 20th were with Army Group Center and the 26th Panzer Division was in Italy, as was the Hermann Göring Division. The rest of the German Panzer divisions were forming or refitting.

271 A good example is the Soviet victory in the Winter War 1939–40. It seems perfectly clear that the Red Army prevailed only thanks to overwhelming military resources, but the use of these resources was far from efficient.

272 For more on advance rates, see N. Zetterling & A. Frankson, "Analyzing World War II Eastern Front Battles," *Journal of Slavic Military Studies*, vol 11, No 1 (March 1998), pp. 192–8.

273 KTB PzAOK 1 Qu, 27 Jan 1944, T313, R74, F7312709.

274 Gruppe Mattenklott 18. February 1944, "Nicht im Kampfraum XI. und XXXXII. A.K. befindlichen Teile," T313, R72, F7310468-70.

275 KTB PzAOK 1 Qu, 28-29 Jan 1944, T313, R74, F7312710.

276 *The Korsun'-Shevchenkovskii Operation*, p. 21.
277 *The Korsun'-Shevchenkovskii Operation*, pp. 21 & 133. The three divisions were the 84th Rifle Division, 94th Guards Rifle Division, and 6th Guards Airborne Division.
278 *The Korsun'-Shevchenkovskii Operation*, p. 112f,
279 G.T.Zavizion & P.A.Kornjusjin, *I na Tichom okean.* (Voenizdat, Moscow), p. 22.
280 *The Korsun'-Shevchenkovskii Operation*, pp. 116 & 189.
281 *The Korsun'-Shevchenkovskii Operation*, p. 116.
282 *The Korsun'-Shevchenkovskii Operation*, p. 189.
283 *The Korsun'-Shevchenkovskii Operation* claims that the Germans transferred large tank forces to the Kapitanovka area on 29 January, units that included a considerable number of Tigers, Panthers, and Ferdinands, and that the correlation of forces turned out to be in favor of the Germans (p. 132). This is hard to accept. First, the German 8th Army did not send any Ferdinands or Tigers into the Korsun battle. Second, it seems unlikely that the Germans had an advantage in numbers. On 27 January the 14th and 11th Panzer Divisions reported five and 30 tanks and assault guns respectively. These figures include the non-divisional assault gun units attached to the divisions, but not the I./Pz.Rgt. 26 Panther Battalion, which had 17 operational Panthers on 29 January. The available reports for 1 February and 4 February suggest that if anything the number of tanks in the German units decreased after 27 January. In the absense of accurate Soviet strength figures it is difficult to settle the issue conclusively, but it seems unlikely that the Red Army, with the comittment of the relatively fresh 18th Tank Corps, would have had less than around 50 tanks and assault guns. (See Fernschreiben 14. Pz.Div. 27.1.44, 23.40 Uhr, in Anlagen zum KTB AOK 8 Ia, T312, R66, F7584304; Fernschreiben 11. Pz.Div. 27.1.44, 16.25 Uhr, in Anlagen zum KTB AOK 8 Ia, T312, R66, F7584303; KTB AOK 8 Ia, 29 Jan, 11.00, T312, R64, F7581770; XXXXVII. Pz.Korps Ia Tagesmeldung 1.2.44, T314, R1132, F000594; AOK 8 Ia Nr. 845/44, geh., 4.2.44, T312, R64, F7582968).
284 KTB XXXXVII. Pz.Korps Ia, 29 Jan, T314, R1132, F000432ff; Anlage 7 zum KTB I./Pz.Rgt. 26, BA-MA RH 39/599.
285 *The Korsun'-Shevchenkovskii Operation*, pp. 56–62 & 131–133.
286 *The Korsun'-Shevchenkovskii Operation*, pp. 21–22.
287 KTB XXXXVII. Pz.Korps Ia, 29 Jan 1944, T314, R1132, F000432-4; AOK 8 Ia KTB Nr. 3, 27 January 1944, T312, R64, F7581767-75.
288 AOK 8 Ia KTB Nr. 3, 27 January 1944, T312, R64, F7581767-75; AOK 8 Ia Nr. 712/44, Tagesmeldung 29.1.44, T312, R66, F7584252ff.
289 AOK 8 Ia KTB Nr. 3, 27 January 1944, T312, R64, F7581767-75; AOK 8 Ia Nr. 712/44, Tagesmeldung 29.1.44, T312, R66, F7584252ff; XXXXII. A.K. Funkspruch an AOK 8, 29.1.44, 18.05.Uhr, in Anlagen zum KTB AOK 8 Ia, T312, R66, F7584240.
290 AOK 8 Ia KTB Nr. 3, 27 January 1944, T312, R64, F7581767-75; AOK 8 Ia Nr. 712/44, Tagesmeldung 29.1.44, T312, R66, F7584252ff.
291 AOK 8 Ia KTB Nr. 3, 27 January 1944, T312, R64, F7581767-75; AOK 8 Ia Nr. 712/44, Tagesmeldung 29.1.44, T312, R66, F7584252ff.
292 XXXXII. A.K. Funkspruch an AOK 8, 29.1.44, 18.05 Uhr, in Anlagen zum KTB AOK 8, T312, R66, F7584240.
293 These were the I./Pz.Rgt. 26 Panther battalion, the Pz.Abt. 8 (with StuG III assault guns), the StuG.Abt. 905 and the StuG.Abt. 911.
294 AOK 8 Ia Nr. 712/44, Tagesmeldung 29.1.44, T312, R66, F7584252ff; KTB XXXXVII. Pz.Korps Ia, 28.1.44, T314, R1132, F000432.
295 AOK 8 Ia Nr. 712/44, Tagesmeldung 29.1.44, T312, R66, F7584252ff; AOK 8 Ia KTB Nr. 3, 30.1.44, 00.40 Uhr, T312, R64, F7581776; Funkspruch von XI. A.K. an AOK 8, 29.1.44, 23.30 Uhr, in Anlagen zum KTB AOK 8 Ia, T312, R66, F7584231.
296 Meiser, *Die Hölle von Tscherkassy*, pp. 200–1.
297 Ibid.
298 Mesier, *Die Hölle von Tscherkassy*, pp. 201–2.
299 Meiser, *Die Hölle von Tscherkassy*, pp. 201–5.
300 *The Korsun'-Shevchenkovskii Operation*, pp. 60–61 & 190.
301 *The Korsun'-Shevchenkovskii Operation*, p. 61.
302 Meiser, *Die Hölle von Tscherkassy*, pp. 205–6.
303 AOK 8 Ia KTB Nr. 3, 30 January 1944, T312, R64, F75817777-8.
304 AOK 8 Ia KTB Nr. 3, 30 January 1944, T312, R64, F75817777-8.
305 KTB XXXXVII. Pz.Korps Ia, 30.1.44, T314, R1132, F000434-5.
306 AOK 8 Ia KTB Nr. 3, 30 January 1944, T312, R64, F75817778; Funkspruch von XXXXII. A.K. an AOK 8, 30.1.44, 14.45 Uhr, in Anlagen zum KTB AOK 8 Ia, T312, R66, F7584212; Funkspruch von XXXXII. A.K. an AOK 8, 30.1.44, 19.20 Uhr, in Anlagen zum KTB AOK 8 Ia, T312, R66, F7584210; AOK 8 Ia, Tagesmeldung vom 30.1.44, T312, R66, F7584203-4.
307 AOK 8 Ia KTB Nr. 3, 30 January 1944, T312, R64, F75817779-82.
308 Funkspruch von XXXXII. A.K. an AOK 8, 30.1.44, 19.20 Uhr, received by AOK 8 at 20.20, found in Anlagen zum KTB AOK 8 Ia, T312, R66, F7584210; AOK 8 Ia KTB Nr. 3, 30 January 1944, T312, R64, F75817783.
309 AOK 8 Ia KTB Nr. 3, 30 January 1944, T312, R64, F75817783.
310 AOK 8 Ia, Tagesmeldung vom 30.1.44, T312, R66, F7584203-5; AOK 8 Ia, Tagesmeldung vom 31.1.44, T312, R66, F7584170-2.
311 AOK 8 Ia, Tagesmeldung vom 31.1.44, T312, R66, F7584170-2. R. Grams, *Die 14. Panzer-Division 1940–1945* (Podzun Verlag, Bad Nauheim 1957), p. 173.
312 Meiser, *Die Hölle von Tscherkassy*, pp. 206–7.
313 Funkspruch von XXXXII. A.K. an AOK 8, 31.1.44, 02.42 Uhr, in Anlagen zum KTB AOK 8 Ia, T312, R66, F7584187.
314 AOK 8 Ia KTB Nr. 3, 31 January 1944, T312, R64, F75817786.
315 Funkspruch von XXXXII. A.K. an AOK 8, 31.1.44, 18.22 Uhr, in Anlagen zum KTB AOK 8

Ia, T312, R66, F7584173.

316 Funkspruch von XI. A.K. an AOK 8, 31.1.44, 15.40 Uhr, in Anlagen zum KTB AOK 8 Ia, T312, R66, F7584177.

317 Funkspruch von XI. A.K. an AOK 8, 31.1.44, 09.15 Uhr, in Anlagen zum KTB AOK 8 Ia, T312, R66, F7584181; Funkspruch von XI. A.K. an AOK 8, 31.1.44, 12.45 Uhr, in Anlagen zum KTB AOK 8 Ia, T312, R66, F7584180; Funkspruch von XI. A.K. an AOK 8, 31.1.44, 15.40 Uhr, in Anlagen zum KTB AOK 8 Ia, T312, R66, F7584177; Funkspruch von XI. A.K. an AOK 8, 31.1.44, 18.30 Uhr, in Anlagen zum KTB AOK 8 Ia, T312, R66, F7584174; *The Korsun'-Shevchenkovskii Operation*, pp. 62–3.

318 Funkspruch von XXXXII. A.K. an AOK 8, 31.1.44, 18.22 Uhr, in Anlagen zum KTB AOK 8 Ia, T312, R66, F7584173; *The Korsun'-Shevchenkovskii Operation*, pp. 62–3.

319 AOK 8 Ia KTB Nr. 3, 31 January 1944, T312, R64, F7581790; KTB XXXXVII. Pz.Korps Ia, 31.1.44, T314, R1132, F000437; Monatszustandmeldung 13. Pz.Div., Stand 1.2.44, in Anlagen zum KTB XXXXVII. Pz.Korps Ia, T312, R1132, F000637. On 1 February only six Pz IV and one Pz III were available to the 13. Pz.Div., see XXXXVII. Pz.Korps Ia Tagesmeldung 1.2.44, T314, R1132, F000594.

320 KTB XXXXVII. Pz.Korps Ia, 31.1.44, T314, R1132, F000435; AOK 8 Ia Nr. 763/44, 31.1.44, T312, R66, F7584172.

321 AOK 8 Ia KTB Nr. 3, 31 January 1944, T312, R64, F7581791.

322 AOK 8 Ia KTB Nr. 3, 31 January 1944, T312, R64, F7581792.

323 AOK 8 Ia KTB Nr. 3, 31 January 1944, T312, R64, F7581792.

324 Funkspruch von XI. A.K. an AOK 8, 31.1.44, 13.55 Uhr, in Anlagen zum KTB AOK 8 Ia, T312, R66, F7584178.

325 The division had five Panthers operational, plus the following number of tanks operational from subordinated units: I./Pz.Rgt. 26 had 17 Panther; Pz.Abt. 8 had seven StuG, StuG.Abt. 911 had six StuG, see XXXXVII. Pz.Korps Is Tagesmeldung, 1.2.44, T314, R1132, F000594 and StuG.Abt. Monatszustandmeldung, Stand 1.2.44, in Anlagen zum KTB XXXXVII. Pz.Korps Ia, T312, R1132, F000663. Note that the units had many more Panzers in workshops.

326 KTB XXXXVII. Pz.Korps Ia, 31.1.44, T314, R1132, F000437-8; AOK 8 Ia KTB Nr. 3, 1 February 1944, T312, R64, F7581799.

327 KTB XXXXVII. Pz.Korps Ia, 31.1.44, T314, R1132, F000437-8; AOK 8 Ia KTB Nr. 3, 2 February 1944, T312, R64, F7581808.

328 KTB XXXXVII. Pz.Korps Ia, 31.1.44, T314, R1132, F000437-8.

329 XXXXVII. Pz.Korps Is Tagesmeldung, 1.2.44, T314, R1132, F000594; KTB XXXXVII. Pz.Korps Ia, 31.1.44, T314, R1132, F000437-8.

330 XXXXVII. Pz.Korps Is Tagesmeldung, 1.2.44, T314, R1132, F000594; KTB XXXXVII. Pz.Korps Ia, 31.1.44, T314, R1132, F000437-8;The Korsun'-Shevchenkovskii Operation, p. 122.

331 Funkspruch von XXXXII. A.K. an AOK 8, 1.2.44, 10.50 Uhr, in Anlagen zum KTB AOK 8 Ia, T312, R66, F7585239; Funkspruch von XXXXII. A.K. an AOK 8, 1.2.44, 12.45 Uhr, in Anlagen zum KTB AOK 8 Ia, T312, R66, F7585236; Funkspruch von XXXXII. A.K. an AOK 8, 1.2.44, 19.00 Uhr, in Anlagen zum KTB AOK 8 Ia, T312, R66, F7585228.

332 Funkspruch von XXXXII. A.K. an AOK 8, 1.2.44, 10.50 Uhr, in Anlagen zum KTB AOK 8 Ia, T312, R66, F7585239.

333 Funkspruch von XXXXII. A.K. an AOK 8, 1.2.44, 12.45 Uhr, in Anlagen zum KTB AOK 8 Ia, T312, R66, F7585236; Jahnke/Lerch, pp. 35–6.

334 Funkspruch von XXXXII. A.K. an AOK 8, 1.2.44, 12.45 Uhr, in Anlagen zum KTB AOK 8 Ia, T312, R66, F7585236.

335 Funkspruch von XXXXII. A.K. an AOK 8, 2.2.44, 06.30 Uhr, in Anlagen zum KTB AOK 8 Ia, T312, R66, F7585220.

336 Meiser, *Die Hölle von Tscherkassy*, pp. 202–13.

337 Funkspruch von XI. A.K. an AOK 8, 1.2.44, 15.30 Uhr, in Anlagen zum KTB AOK 8 Ia, T312, R66, F7585234; Funkspruch von XI. A.K. an AOK 8, 1.2.44, 17.40 Uhr, in Anlagen zum KTB AOK 8 Ia, T312, R66, F7585232; Funkspruch von XI. A.K. an AOK 8, 1.2.44, 18.00 Uhr, in Anlagen zum KTB AOK 8 Ia, T312, R66, F7585233; Funkspruch von XI. A.K. an AOK 8, 1.2.44, 18.00 Uhr, in Anlagen zum KTB AOK 8 Ia, T312, R66, F7585226; Funkspruch von XI. A.K. an AOK 8, 1.2.44, 17.40 Uhr, in Anlagen zum KTB AOK 8 Ia, T312, R66, F7585232.

338 AOK 8 Ia KTB Nr. 3, 1 February 1944, T312, R64, F7581804-5.

339 AOK 8 Ia KTB Nr. 3, 1 February 1944, T312, R64, F7581804-5.

340 KTB XXXXVII. Pz.Korps Ia, 2 february 1944, T314, R1132, F000440-441.

341 KTB XXXXVII. Pz.Korps Ia, 2 february 1944, T314, R1132, F000440-441.

342 N. von Vormann, *Tscherkassy* (Scharnhorst Buchkameradschaft, Heidelberg 1954), p. 76; Proschek papers, BA-MA MSg 2/5648.

343 AOK 8 Ia KTB Nr. 3, 2 February 1944, T312, R64, F7581807-8.

344 AOK 8 Ia KTB Nr. 3, 2 February 1944, T312, R64, F7581807-8.

345 AOK 8 Ia KTB Nr. 3, 2 February 1944, T312, R64, F7581807-8.

346 AOK 8 Ia KTB Nr. 3, 3 February 1944, T312, R64, F7581815.

347 KTB XXXXVII. Pz.Korps Ia, 2.2.44, T314, R1132, F000440-1.

348 KTB XXXXVII. Pz.Korps Ia, 2.2.44, T314, R1132, F000440-1.

349 Funkspruch von XXXXII. A.K. an AOK 8, 2.2.44, 11.11 Uhr, in Anlagen zum KTB AOK 8 Ia, T312, R66, F7585200; Funkspruch von XXXXII. A.K. an AOK 8, 2.2.44, 15.15 Uhr, in

Anlagen zum KTB AOK 8 Ia, T312, R66, F7585205; Funkspruch von XI. A.K. an AOK 8, 2.2.44, 15.00 Uhr, in Anlagen zum KTB AOK 8 Ia, T312, R66, F7585204. Jahnke/Lerch, p. 54

350 AOK 8 Ia Tagesmeldung 2.2.44, T312, R66, F7585193-5; Funkspruch von XXXXII. A.K. an AOK 8, 2.2.44, 23.40 Uhr, in Anlagen zum KTB AOK 8 Ia, T312, R66, F7585191.

351 AOK 8 Ic/AO–Ic Morgenmeldung 3.2.44, in Anlagen zum KTB AOK 8 Ia, T312, R66, F7585186.

352 Meiser, *Die Hölle von Tscherkassy*, p. 213.

353 Meiser, *Die Hölle von Tscherkassy*, p. 214.

354 Meiser, *Die Hölle von Tscherkassy*, pp. 216–7.

355 Funkspruch von XXXXII. A.K. an AOK 8, 3.2.44, 10.10 Uhr, in Anlagen zum KTB AOK 8 Ia, T312, R66, F7585177; Funkspruch von XXXXII. A.K. an AOK 8, 3.2.44, 13.45 Uhr, in Anlagen zum KTB AOK 8 Ia, T312, R66, F7585172.

356 Funkspruch von XXXXII. A.K. an AOK 8, 3.2.44, 10.10 Uhr, in Anlagen zum KTB AOK 8 Ia, T312, R66, F7585177.

357 Gefr. Heinr. Grotjohann, 5./TG 3, 10.4.1944, "Drei Tage im Kessel," BA-MA RL 10/641, Bl. 13.

358 Gefr. Heinr. Grotjohann, 5./TG 3, 10.4.1944, "Drei Tage im Kessel," BA-MA RL 10/641, Bl. 14.

359 AOK 8 Ia Nr. 826/44, Tagesmeldung 3.2.44, T312, R66, F7585159; KTB XXXXVII. Pz.Korps Ia, 3.2.44, T314, 1132, F000441-3; *The Korsun'-Shevchenkovskii Operation*, pp. 133–136 & 194.

360 KTB PzAOK 1 Ia, 28 January 1944, T313, R69, F7305837.

361 See Appendix 2 for a description of s.Pz.Rgt. Bäke.

362 KTB PzAOK 1 Ia, 28 January 1944, T313, R69, F7305838.

363 KTB PzAOK 1 Ia, 29 January 1944, T313, R69, F7305842f.

364 KTB PzAOK 1 Ia, 29 January 1944, T313, R69, F7305843.

365 KTB PzAOK 1 Ia, 29 January 1944, T313, R69, F7305843.

366 KTB PzAOK 1 Ia, 29 January 1944, T313, R69, F7305843f.

367 KTB PzAOK 1 Ia, 30 January 1944, T313, R69, F7305846f.

368 Zetterling & Frankson, *Kursk 1943*, pp. 125–7.

369 KTB PzAOK 1 Ia, 30 January 1944, T313, R69, F7305846f.

370 KTB PzAOK 1 Ia, 30 January 1944, T313, R69, F7305847f.

371 KTB PzAOK 1 Ia, 29-30 January 1944, T313, R69, F7305841-8.

372 KTB PzAOK 1 Ia, 2 February 1944, T313, R69, F7305852f.

373 KTB PzAOK 1 Ia, 3 February 1944, T313, R69, F7305854f.

374 The tank strength is taken from Appendix 2, where the references are also found. How the units were subordinated is derived from III. Pz.Korps Ia Nr. 193/44, 2.2.44, "Korpsbefehl für den Angriff," T314, R208, F000411.

375 24. Pz.Div. Zustandmeldung an Gen.Insp.d.Pz.Tr., Stand 1.2.44, BA-MA RH 10/160.

376 See Appendix 2.

377 Ibid.

378 Anlagen zum KTB AOK 8 Ia, Fernschreiben 4.2.44, 12.20 Uhr an Heeresgruppe Süd, T312, R64, F7582968.

379 III. Pz.Korps Ia Nr. 193/44 geh. 2.2.44, "Korpsbefehl für den Angriff," T314, R208, F000411 and III. Pz.Korps Ia Nr. 205/44 geh. 3.2.44, "Korpsbefehl für den 4.2.44," T314, R208, F000436.

380 *The Korsun'-Shevchenkovskii Operation*, pp. 116, 194.

381 Zavizion & Kornjusjin, *I na Tichom okeane*, p. 23.

382 PzAOK 1 Ia KTB Nr. 13, 5 February 1944, T313, R69, F7305859.

383 *The Korsun'-Shevchenkovskii Operation*, p. 24. It should be noted that the study presents this as a sign of excellence on behalf of the Soviet command. With hindsight, it turned out to be true. The Germans did eventually attack along this direction, but not until one week later. By then the Soviet forces had been moved back and forth to such an extent that the original dispositions were no longer recognizable.

384 Anlagen zum KTB III. Pz.Korps Ia, Tagesmeldungen der Div. am 4.2.44, T314, R208, F000465 and Kriegstagebuch III. Pz.Korps Ia, 4.2.44, T314, R206, F001238-40.

385 Anlagen zum KTB III. Pz.Korps Ia, Tagesmeldungen der Div. am 4.2.44, T314, R208, F000467 and Kriegstagebuch III. Pz.Korps Ia, 4.2.44, T314, R206, F001238-40.

386 Anlagen zum KTB III. Pz.Korps Ia, Tagesmeldungen der Div. am 4.2.44, T314, R208, F000465 and Kriegstagebuch III. Pz.Korps Ia, 4.2.44, T314, R206, F001238-44.

387 Anlagen zum KTB III. Pz.Korps Ia, Tagesmeldungen der Div. am 4.2.44, T314, R208, F000465 and Kriegstagebuch III. Pz.Korps Ia, 4.2.44, T314, R206, F001238-44.

388 Anlagen zum KTB III. Pz.Korps Ia, Tagesmeldungen der Div. am 4.2.44, T314, R208, F000467 and Kriegstagebuch III. Pz.Korps Ia, 4.2.44, T314, R206, F001244-48. Zustandmeldungen der 16. & 17. Panzer-Divisionen an Gen.Insp. der Panzertruppe, Stand 1.2.44, BA-MA RH 10/153 & RH 10/154.

389 *The Korsun'-Shevchenkovskii Operation*, p. 28.

390 KTB III. Pz.Korps Ia, 4.2.44, T313, R206, F001246; Anlagen zum KTB III.Pz.Korps Ia, Morgenmeldungen der Div. am 5.2.44, T314, R208, F000479.

391 KTB III. Pz.Korps Ia, 4.2.44, T314, R206, F001246-48.

392 KTB III. Pz.Korps Ia, 4.2.44, T314, R206, F001248-50.

393 Michael Schadewitz, Einsätze des "schweren Panzerregiments Bäke" vom 24. Januar bis 17. February 1944, p. 8, BA-MA MSg 2/4396.

394 KTB III. Pz.Korps Ia, 5.2.44, T314, R206, F001254.

395 KTB III. Pz.Korps Ia, 5.2.44, T314, R206, F001256 and F001262.

396 KTB III. Pz.Korps Ia, 5.2.44, T314, R206, F001252 & F001256; PzAOK 1 Ia KTB Nr. 13, 5 February 1944, T313, R69, F7305859; Anlagen zum KTB III.Pz.Korps Ia, Morgenmeldungen der Div. am 5.2.44, T314, R208, F000479.

397 Anlagen zum KTB III. Pz.Korps Ia, Tagesmeldungen der Div. am 4.2.44, T314, R208, F000503. Number of assault guns taken from KTB III. Pz.Korps Ia, 5.2.44, T314, R206, F1266.

398 Soviet General Staff Study, p. 28.

399 Anlagen zum KTB III. Pz.Korps Ia, Tagesmeldungen der 16. Pz.Div. am 5.2.44, T314, R208, F000506 and Soviet General Staff Study, p. 28.

400 KTB III. Pz.Korps Ia, 5.2.44, T314, R206, F1252ff.

401 KTB III. Pz.Korps Ia, 5.2.44, T314, R206, F1258-60.

402 KTB III. Pz.Korps Ia, 5.2.44, T314, R206, F1258-60 and 6.2.44, T314, R206, F1272; Michael Schadewitz, Einsätze des "schweren Panzerregiments Bäke" vom 24. Januar bis 17. Februar 1944, p. 9, BA-MA MSg 2/4396; Tagesmelddung III. Pz.Korps 5.2.44, T313, R71, F7308406.

403 KTB III. Pz.Korps Ia, 5.2.44, T314, R206, F1266ff.

404 PzAOK 1 Ia KTB Nr. 13, 6 February 1944, T313, R69, F7305861-3.

405 Ibid.

406 *The Korsun'-Shevchenkovskii Operation*, pp. 28–29.

407 PzAOK 1 Ia KTB Nr. 13, 6 February 1944, T313, R69, F7305862; KTB III. Pz.Korps Ia, 5.2.44, T314, R206, F1272ff; 17. Pz.Div. Tagesmeldung an III. Pz.Korps am 6.2.44, T314, R208, F543; III. Pz.Korps Ia, "Morgenmedlungen der Div. am 7.2.44," T314, R208, F569.

408 U. von Alvensleben, *Lauter Abschiede* (Ullstein, Frankfurt am Main, 1971), p. 379.

409 KTB III. Pz.Korps Ia, 5.2.44, T314, R206, F1274. The infantry battalion was the II./Gren.Rgt. 305. Probably the assault guns belonged to 249. StuG.Abt., which was on the eastern half of III. Pz.Korps on 5 February (see III. Pz.Korps Ia Nr. 216/44, "Gliederung des III. Pz.Korps am 5.2.1944," NARA T314, R208, F000518).

410 KTB III. Pz.Korps Ia, 6.2.44, T314, R206, F1274-6. The attack towards Tatianovka was made by Pz.Gren.Rgt. 79.

411 See, III.Pz.Korps Ia Nr 219/44 geh., 5.2.44, 23.00 Uhr, T314, R208, F514 and 1. Pz.Div. Tagesmeldung an III. Pz.Korps am 6.2.44,, T314, R208, F541.

412 PzAOK 1 Ia KTB Nr. 13, 6 February 1944, T313, R69, F7305863; KTB AOK 8 Ia, 6 February 1944, 19.15-21.30, T312, R64, F7581841f.

413 KTB AOK 8 Ia, 6 February 1944, 19.15-21.30, T312, R64, F7581841f; KTB PzAOK 1 Ia, 7.2.44, T313, R69, F7305864f. The order from von Manstein (HGr Süd Ia Nr 652/44 gKdos, 6.2.44, 19.55 Uhr) can be found in the Anlagen zum KTB PzAOK 1 Ia, T313, R70, F7306559-63.

414 KTB PzAOK 1 Ia, 7.2.44, T313, R69, F7305864-7; KTB III. Pz.Korps Ia, 7.2.44, T314, R206, F1278-82 and T314, R207, F0004-10.

415 KTB III. Pz.Korps Ia, 7.2.44, T314, R206, F1278-82. According to Michael Schadewitz, Einsätze des "schweren Panzerregiments Bäke" vom 24. Januar bis 17. Februar 1944, p. 9, BA-MA MSg 2/4396, p. 9, Repki was taken on 7 February. However according to the KTB III. Pz.Korps Ia, Repki was in German hands at 14.00hrs on 8 February. Since the latter source is more detailed and also a primary source, it has been relied upon here.

416 KTB III. Pz.Korps Ia, 7.2.44, T314, R206, F1278-82 and T314, R207, F0004-10. The units were I. and II. Btl. from Gren.Rgt. 305, one company from II./Pz.Gren.Rgt. 1 plus a tank company, most likely froom II./Pz.Rgt. 1. See 198. Inf.Div. Tagesmeldung an III. Pz.Korps am 7.2.44, T314, R208, F602.

417 Tagesmeldung 1. Pz.Div. an III. Pz.Korps am 7.2.44, T314, R208, F601. KTB III. Pz.Korps Ia, 7.2.44, T314, R206, F1278-82 and T314, R207, F0004-10; KTB PzAOK 1 Ia, 7.2.44, T313, R69, F7305864-7. Weather from KTB PzAOK 1 Ia, 8.2.44, T313, R69, F7305868 and KTB III. Pz.Korps Ia, 8.2.44, T314, R207, F00011.

418 III. Pz.Korps Ic, 10.2.44, Gefangenenvernehmung, T314, R212, F000598.

419 KTB III. Pz.Korps Ia, 8.2.44, T314, R207, F00012-20.

420 KTB III. Pz.Korps Ia, 8.2.44, T314, R207, F00012-14.

421 KTB III. Pz.Korps Ia, 8.2.44, T314, R207, F00018-20.

422 KTB III. Pz.Korps Ia, 8.2.44, T314, R207, F00020-22.

423 KTB III. Pz.Korps Ia, 8.2.44, T314, R207, F00022.

424 KTB III. Pz.Korps Ia, 8.2.44, T314, R207, F00022-24.

425 Ibid. It should be noted that the opinion that supply and not the Red Army was the main obstacle is not hindsight, but an opinion recorded at the time of the battle.

426 KTB III. Pz.Korps Ia, 9.2.44, T314, R207, F00028-30; III. Pz.Korps Ia, Morgenmeldungen der Div. am 9.2.44, T314, R208, F687.

427 KTB XXXXVII. Pz.Korps Ia, 3.2.44, T314, R1132, F000443; AOK 8 Ia KTB Nr. 3, 3 February 1944, T312, R64, F7581819.

428 AOK 8 Ia KTB Nr. 3, 4 February 1944, T312, R64, F7581821.

429 AOK 8 Ia KTB Nr. 3, 4 February 1944, T312, R64, F7581822.

430 AOK 8 Ia KTB Nr. 3, 4 February 1944, T312, R64, F7581823.

431 AOK 8 Ia KTB Nr. 3, 4 February 1944, T312, R64, F7581824.

432 AOK 8 Ia KTB Nr. 3, 4 February 1944, T312, R64, F7581824.

433 AOK 8 Ia KTB Nr. 3, 3 February 1944, T312, R64, F7581815-9; AOK 8 Ia KTB Nr. 3, 4 February 1944, T312, R64, F7581823; Funkspruch von XXXXII. A.K. an AOK 8, 4.2.44, 10.20 Uhr, in Anlagen zum KTB AOK 8.

Ia, T312, R66, F7585141; Funkspruch von XXXXII. A.K. an AOK 8, 4.2.44, 13.16 Uhr, in Anlagen zum KTB AOK 8 Ia, T312, R66, F7585139.

434 *The Korsun'-Shevchenkovskii Operation*, pp. 31–35.

435 AOK 8 Ia KTB Nr. 3, 4 February 1944, T312, R64, F7581825-6.

436 AOK 8 Ia, Fernschreiben an HGr Süd, 4.2.44, 12.20 Uhr, T312, R64, F7582968.

437 See Monatszustandmeldungen in Anlagen zum KTB XXXXVII. Pz.Korps Ia, T314, R1132, F000649-000674.

438 AOK 8 Ia, Fernschreiben an HGr Süd, 4.2.44, 12.20 Uhr, T312, R64, F7582968.

439 Olaf Ehlers' personal diary, 4 February 1944, BA-MA MSg 2/3200.

440 XXXXVII. Pz.Korps Ia Tagesmeldung 4.2.44, in Anlagen zum KTB AOK 8 Ia, T312, R66, F7585129f.

441 AOK 8 Ia KTB Nr. 3, 4 February 1944, T312, R64, F7581825.

442 AOK 8 Ia KTB Nr. 3, 4 February 1944, T312, R64, F7581825-6. For some days the Germans had had a radio beacon at Korsun, to aid landing in darkness and poor weather; see Ofw. Günter Schmidt, O. U., den 29.6.1944, "Bericht über meine Einsätze in den Kessel von Tscherkassy," BA-MA RL 10/641, Bl. 28.

443 AOK 8 Ia KTB Nr. 3, 4 February 1944, T312, R64, F7581827.

444 AOK 8 Ia KTB Nr. 3, 4 February 1944, T312, R64, F7581825.

445 AOK 8 Ia KTB Nr. 3, 5 February 1944, T312, R64, F7581829-32.

446 AOK 8 Ia KTB Nr. 3, 5 February 1944, T312, R64, F7581828-33.

447 KTB XXXXVII. Pz.Korps Ia, 5.2.44, T314, R1132, F000447.

448 KTB III./Pz.Rgt. 36, BA-MA RH 39/380. The units in the Kampfgruppe were III./Pz.Rgt. 36, I./Pz.Gren.Rgt. 103 and I./Pz.Art.Rgt. 4.

449 KTB III./Pz.Rgt. 36, BA-MA RH 39/380.

450 KTB III./Pz.Rgt. 36, BA-MA RH 39/380.

451 Tagesmeldung XXXXVII. Pz.Korps Ia, 5.2.44, in Anlagen zum KTB AOK 8 Ia, T312, R66, F7585094.

452 AOK 8 Ia KTB Nr. 3, 5 February 1944, T312, R64, F7581831.

453 *The Korsun'-Shevchenkovskii Operation*, p. 35.

454 AOK 8 Ia KTB Nr. 3, 5 February 1944, 21.00, 6 February 1944, 09.10 & 17.00, T312, R64, F7581833, F7581836 & F7581839; AOK 8 Ia Nr. 918/44 geh. 6.2.44, T312, R64, F7582954.

455 Haack was commander of "Artillerie-Division zur besondere Verwendung 310." Originally it had been a regiment staff, used to coordinate artillery from different units, but it seems to have been uprated in fall 1943. However, it remained a staff only, with no actual firing units.

456 AOK 8 Ia Nr. 918/44 geh. 6.2.44, T312, R64, F7582954. For more on Kampfgruppe Haack, see Appendix 2

457 This thesis was originally put forward by E. A. Shils & M. Janowitz, "Cohesion and Disintegration in the Wehrmacht in World War II," *Public Opinion Quarterly, Summer 1948*, but has been subject to critisism by, for example, Omer Bartov. However, Bartov's methodology is fundamentally flawed in several aspects. It should be noted that studies on Israeli soldiers (Ben Shalit, *Konfliktens och stridens psykologi* [Liber, Stockholm 1983], as well as U.S. soldiers [Stouffer, *The American Soldier, vol 1 & 2*], have resulted in simliar conclusions to those put forward by Shils and Janowitz.

458 AOK 8 Ia KTB Nr. 3, 6 February 1944, T312, R64, F7581836.

459 AOK 8 Ia KTB Nr. 3, 5 February 1944, T312, R64, F7581830; XI. AK Funkspruch an AOK 8, 5.2.44, 11.40 Uhr, T312, R66, F7585108; XXXXII. AK Funkspruch an AOK 8, 5.2.44, 11.45 Uhr, T312, R66, F7585107; XI. AK Funkspruch an AOK 8, 5.2.44, 11.40 Uhr, T312, R66, F7585108.

460 Jahnke & Lerch, *Der Kessel von Tscherkassy*, pp. 54f.

461 *The Korsun'-Shevchenkovskii Operation*, pp. 65–67.

462 Funkspruch von XXXXII. A.K. an AOK 8, 6.2.44, 19.27 Uhr, T312, R66, F7585068; XI. A.K. Tagesmeldung 6.2.44, in Anlagen zum KTB AOK 8 Ia, T312, R66, F7585057;*The Korsun'-Shevchenkovskii Operation*, p. 67.

463 AOK 8 Ia KTB Nr. 3, 7 February 1944 08.00, 6 February 09.45, T312, R64, F7581842, F7581836, F7581837.

464 AOK 8 Ia KTB Nr. 3, 6 February 1944, 09.10, T312, R64, F7581836.

465 KTB III./Pz.Rgt. 36, BA-MA RH 39/380; AOK 8 Ia KTB Nr. 3, 6 February 1944, 08.20, T312, R64, F7581835.

466 AOK 8 Ia KTB Nr. 3, 6 February 1944, 19.05, T312, R64, F7581840.

467 Meiser, *Die Hölle von Tscherkassy*, p. 221.

468 Meiser, *Die Hölle von Tscherkassy*, pp. 222–4.

469 Ibid.

470 Ibid.

471 Meiser, *Die Hölle von Tscherkassy*, pp. 222–8.

472 Meiser, *Die Hölle von Tscherkassy*, pp. 227–9.

473 AOK 8 Ia KTB Nr. 3, 7 February 11.25, T312, R64, F7581844; Lieb diary, 7 February, NARA MS # T-12.

474 AOK 8 Ia KTB Nr. 3, 6 February1944, 19.05, T312, R64, F7581844.

475 AOK 8 Ia KTB Nr. 3, 7 February1944, 07.00, 15.55 & 19,30, T312, R64, F7581842, F7581845 & F7581846.

476 *The Korsun'-Shevchenkovskii Operation*, p. 93.

477 AOK 8 Ia KTB Nr. 3, 8 February 1944, 09.30, T312, R64, F7581847.

478 KTB III./Pz.Rgt. 36, 8 February 1944, BA-MA RH 39/380.

479 AOK 8 Ia KTB Nr. 3, 8 February 1944, 13.20, T312, R64, F7581848; Lieb diary, 8 February 1944, NARA MS # T-12.

480 Meiser, *Die Hölle von Tscherkassy*, p. 229.

481 Meiser, *Die Hölle von Tscherkassy*, pp. 229–230.

482 Meiser, *Die Hölle von Tscherkassy*, pp. 231–244

483 AOK 8 Ia KTB Nr. 3, 8 February1944, 19.20 and 9 February 07.50, T312, R64, F7581850-1; "Erfahrungsbericht über die Luftversorgung des XI. und XXXXII. A.K. und der Panzerspitzen III. und XXXXVII. Pz.K.", 21.2.44, T313, R74, F7312885.

484 AOK 8 Ia KTB Nr. 3, 9 February1944, 09.05, T312, R64, F7581852.

485 AOK 8 Ia KTB Nr. 3, 8 February1944, 21.40, T312, R64, F7581850; Jahnke & Lerch, *Der Kessel von Tscherkassy*, p. 23.

486 Meiser, *Die Hölle von Tscherkassy*, p. 244.

487 Meiser, *Die Hölle von Tscherkassy*, pp. 244–5.

488 *The Korsun'-Shevchenkovskii Operation*, pp. 67–8.

489 AOK 8 Ia KTB Nr. 3, 8 February1944, 04.45, T312, R64, F7581851.

490 *The Korsun'-Shevchenkovskii Operation*, p. 68; Tagesmeldungen XI. and XXXXII. A.K. 9.2.44, in Anlagen zum KTB AOK 8 Ia, T312, R66, F7584964-5; AOK 8 Ia KTB Nr. 3, 9 February 1944, 10.35, 11.15, 12.10, 13.40, 14.35, 14.40, 15.50, 18.00, 21.20, T312, R64, F7581852-5.

491 Gen.Kdo. XXXXII. A.K. Ia, "Meldung zu PzAOK 1 Ia Nr 370/44 geh. vom 19.2.44," 24.2.44, in Anlagen zum KTB PzAOK 1 Ia, T313, R72, F7310519.

492 AOK 8 Ia KTB Nr. 3, 9 February 1944, 11.35, 16.35, T312, R64, F7581853-4.

493 Tagesmeldung XXXXVII. Pz.Korps Ia, 9.2.44, T312, R66, F7584968; AOK 8 Ia KTB Nr. 3, 8 February 1944, 10.15 & 21.45, T312, R64, F7581852-5.

494 AOK 8 Ia KTB Nr. 3, 9 February 1944, 01.45, T312, R64, F7581856.

495 AOK 8 Ia KTB Nr. 3, 10 February 1944, 20.00, T312, R64, F7581862.

496 *The Korsun'-Shevchenkovskii Operation*, p. 68; XI. A.K. Ia, Tagesmeldung 10.2.44, in Anlagen zum KTB AOK 8 Ia, T312, R66, F7584930.

497 XI. A.K. Ia, Tagesmeldung 10.2.44, in Anlagen zum KTB AOK 8 Ia, T312, R66, F7584930; AOK 8 Ia KTB Nr. 3, 10 February 1944, 11.07, 12.05, 16.25, 18.45, 19.15, 19.40, 20.00, T312, R64, F7581858-61.

498 AOK 8 Ia KTB Nr. 3, 10 February 1944, 09.15, T312, R64, F7581857.

499 KTB I./Pz.Rgt. 26, 10.2.44, BA-MA RH 39/599. The tank strength for the other units participating has not been possible to establish. However, given the low tank strength on 4 February and the ardous movement over muddy roads that must have caused further breakdowns, it seems unlikely that they had more than about 15 tanks and assault guns.

500 AOK 8 Ia KTB Nr. 3, 10 February 1944, 09.15, T312, R64, F7581857-8.

501 AOK 8 O.Qu. Nr. 277/44 geh., 11.2.44, T312, R63, F7581371; AOK 8 Ia KTB Nr. 3, 10 February 1944, 19.15, T312, R64, F7581860.

502 *The Korsun'-Shevchenkovskii Operation*, pp. 68–9.

503 *The Korsun'-Shevchenkovskii Operation*, p. 138.

504 Anlagen zum KTB PzAOK 1 Ia, "Besprechungspunkte (Besuch bei III. Pz.Korps am 10.2.1944)," T313, R70, F7306641-3. Number of operational tanks for s.Pz.Rgt. Bäke, s.Pz.Abt. 506, StuG.Abt. 249 and 16. Pz.Div. on 10 February given by PzAOK 1 Ia Tagesmeldung 10.2.44, T313, R70, F7306649. Number of operational tanks for 17. Pz.Div. on 10 February given by Anlagen zum KTB III. Pz.Korps Ia, Tagesmeldung der 17. Pz.Div. am 10.2.44, T314, R70, F7306649. The contribution from SS-Leibstandarte is given by the KTB Pz.Grent.Rgt. 64, 10.2.44, BA-MA RH 37/6257.

505 This is also supported by an unusual map. In the Anlagen of the PzAOK 1 Ia, dated 3 March 1944, there is a map showing the location of the tanks and other armored vehicles lost by III. Pz.Korps during the operation. In the area where 16. and 17. Pz.Div., plus the s.Pz.Rgt. Bäke, s.Pz.Abt. 506 and StuG.Abt. 249 operated during the first phase of the relief operation, there are 10 AFVs indicated as lost due to enemy action. Note that this includes APCs too. Thus, at most 10 tanks may have been lost by these units. In the National Archives, the map is found at T313, R70, F7307179. However the map employs color coding to distinguish between losses due to enemy action and other losses and as the microfilm copy is in black and white, important information is missing on the microfilm copy. The original map, today at the Bundesarchiv-Militärarchiv in Freiburg, is in color and a color copy has kindly been provided to us by Dr. Karl-Heinz Frieser at the Militärgeschichtliches Forschungsamt. For the tank strength of the German units see Appendix 2. It should be noted that the Soviet General Staff Study claims that the Germans attacked with 200 tanks (*The Korsun'-Shevchenkovskii Operation*, p. 30) but this is, as usual, an exaggeration.

506 PzAOK 1 Ia KTB Nr. 13, 6 February 1944, T313, R69, F7305861-3.

507 III. Pz.Korps Lagekarte, 10.2.44, T314, R212, F000416; III. Pz.Korps Ia Nr. 248/44 geh., T314, R208, F000815; KTB III. Pz.Korps Ia, 10.2.44, T314, R203, F000042-50. Stoves, p. 497-9; III. Pz.Korps Ia Tagesmeldung an PzAOK 1, 10.2.44, T314, R208, F000787.

508 III. Pz.Korps Ia Nr. 237/44 geh. 9.2.44, T314, R208, F000730-1.

509 Anlagen zum KTB PzAOK 1 Ia, "Besprechungspunkte, Besuch bei der III. Panzerkorps am 10.2.1944," T313, R70, F7306641.

510 Anlagen zum KTB PzAOK 1 Ia, "Besprechungspunkte, Besuch bei der III. Panzerkorps am 10.2.1944," T313, R70, F7306641.

511 Tsamo RF, Fond 236, opic 2673, delo 311, list 85.

512 Anlagen zum KTB PzAOK 1 Ia, "Besprechungspunkte, Besuch bei der III. Panzerkorps am 10.2.1944," T313, R70, F7306641.

513 KTB Pz.Rgt. Bäke, BA-MA RH 39/677, note that the dates have shifted by mistake in the war diary, it is indicated that the attack began on 10 February, but in fact it began on 11 February, which is corroborated by numerous other documents; KTB Pz.Gren.Rgt. 64, 11.2.44, BA-MA RH 37/6257; Rubbel, p. 132. Captain Blömeke had taken over as commander of Panzer Grenadier Regiment 64 on 6 February when Colonel Hesse became ill.

514 KTB Pz.Rgt. Bäke, BA-MA RH 39/677; KTB Pz.Gren.Rgt. 64, 11.2.44, BA-MA RH 37/6257; Alfred Rubbel (ed.), *The Combat History of schwere Panzer-Abteilung 503* (Bassum, privately published 1990), p. 132; Proschek papers, BA-MA MSg 2/5649.

515 III. Pz.Korps, Funkspruch Nr. 117, an XI. A.K., 11.2.44, T314, R208, F000844.

516 Rolf Stoves, *1 Panzer Division 1935–1945* (Bad Nauheim, Podzun Verlag 1961), pp. 499–500.

517 Stoves, *1 Panzer Division*, pp. 500–2.

518 KTB Pz.Rgt. Bäke, BA-MA RH 39/677; Stoves, *1 Panzer* Division, pp. 500–1.

519 Tagesmeldung 17. Pz.Div. an III. Pz.Korps, 11.2.44, T314, R208, F000852.

520 KTB Pz.Rgt. Bäke, BA-MA RH 39/677.

521 Proschek papers, BA-MA MSg 2/5649.

522 Stoves, *1 Panzer* Division, pp. 502–3.

523 Stoves, *1 Panzer Division*, pp. 502–3; Anlage 760 zum KTB III. Pz.Korps Ia, 15.40, 11.2.44, T314, R208, F0008484; Tagesmeldung 1. Pz.Div. 11.2.44, in Anlagen zum KTB III. Pz.Korps Ia, T314, R208, F000856.

524 Stoves, *1 Panzer Division*, p. 503.

525 Stoves, *1 Panzer Division*, p. 504.

526 Stoves, *1 Panzer Division*,pp. 504–5.

527 For example, the Soviet General Staff Study (pp. 29–30) claims the attack was expected. However, as it gives quite erroneous information on the German attack force (grossly exaggerating the tank strength and mixing up the divisions of III Panzer Corps), it can not be excluded that the claim is a rationalization after the battle.

528 *The Korsun'-Shevchenkovskii Operation*, pp. 29–32; R. Lehmann and R. Tiemann, *The Leibstandarte, vol IV/1* (Winnipeg, Fedorowicz 1993), pp. 29–30; LSSAH Tagesmeldung 11.2.44 an III. Pz.Korps Ia, T314, R208, F000854; KTB PzAOK 1 Ia, 11.2.44, T313, R69, F7305880.

529 *The Korsun'-Shevchenkovskii Operation*, pp. 29–32.

530 Bericht über die Kämpfe des Grenadier-regiments 266 der 72. Infanterie-Division im Kessel von Tscherkassy und des großen Kessels von Korsun in der Zeit vom 22.11.1943 bis 17.2.1944, BA-MA RH 37/6609; Bericht Major Siegel, BA-MA MSg 2/3570; Jahnke & Lerch, *Der Kessel von Tscherkassy*, p. 42.

531 The following units were part of Kampfgruppe von Sievers: Pz.Rgt. 15 (except Pz IV tanks), I./Pz.Rgt. 26, II./Pz.Rgt. 110, I./Pz.Art.Rgt. 119 and Elements of Pz.Pi.Btl. 209. If the I./Pz.Gren.Rgt. 110 had been relieved in time it would also have participated in von Sievers' Kampfgruppe. Among the units of the 11th Panzer Division that had not yet been relieved were the SPW-battalion (I./Pz.Gren.Rgt. 110) and the recon battalion, which still were near Skotorevo, more than 10 kilometers further east. 11. Panzer-Division Ia Nr. 236/44, "Befehl für den Angriff am 11.2.1944", in Anlagen zum KTB Nr. 3 der I./Pz.Rgt. 26, BA-MA RH 39/599; KTB XXXXVII. Pz.Korps Ia, 11.2.44, T314, R1132, F000458.

532 KTB Nr. 3 der I./Pz.Rgt. 26, 11.2.44, BA-MA RH 39/599; 11. Panzer-Division Ia Nr. 236/44, "Befehl für den Angriff am 11.2.1944", in Anlagen zum KTB Nr. 3 der I./Pz.Rgt. 26, BA-MA RH 39/599.

533 KTB XXXXVII. Pz.Korps Ia, 11.2.44, T314, R1132, F000458.

534 KTB Nr. 3 der I./Pz.Rgt. 26, 11.2.44, BA-MA RH 39/599; KTB XXXXVII. Pz.Korps Ia, 11.2.44, T314, R1132, F000458.

535 KTB Nr. 3 der I./Pz.Rgt. 26, 11.2.44, BA-MA RH 39/599; KTB XXXXVII. Pz.Korps Ia, 11.2.44, T314, R1132, F000458; KTB AOK 8 Ia, 09.30, 11.2.44, T312, R64, F7581864.

536 KTB XXXXVII. Pz.Korps Ia, 11.2.44, T314, R1132, F000458-9; KTB AOK 8 Ia, 11.00 & 19.05, 11.2.44, T312, R64, F7581864 & F7581867.

537 KTB Nr. 3 der I./Pz.Rgt. 26, 11.2.44, BA-MA RH 39/599.

538 KTB Nr. 3 der I./Pz.Rgt. 26, 11.2.44, BA-MA RH 39/599; Soviet General Staff Study, pp. 139 & 154.

539 KTB XXXXVII. Pz.Korps Ia, 11.2.44, T314, R1132, F000459.

540 KTB AOK 8 Ia, 18.15, 11.2.44, T312, R64, F7581864 &F7581867.

541 Bericht Major Kaestner, BA-MA MSg 2/3570.

542 Bericht Major Kaestner, BA-MA MSg 2/3570; Proschek papers, BA-MA MSg 2/5649.

543 Bericht Major Kaestner, BA-MA MSg 2/3570.

544 Bericht Major Kaestner, BA-MA MSg 2/3570; Bericht über die Kämpfe des Grenadier-regiments 266 der 72. Infanterie-Division im Kessel von Tscherkassy und des großen Kessels von Korsun in der Zeit vom 22.11.1943 bis 17.2.1944, BA-MA RH 37/6609; Jahnke & Lerch, *Der Kessel von Tscherkassy*, pp. 41–42; Lieb Diary, NARA MS # T-12.

545 G. K. Zhukov, *The Memoirs of Marshal Zhukov* (New Delhi: Natraj, 1985), p. 507.

546 Zhukov, *The Memoirs of Marshal Zhukov*, p. 507.

547 Zhukov, *The Memoirs of Marshal Zhukov*, pp. 507–8.

548 I. S. Konev, *Zapiski Komandujusjego Fronto.* (Voenizdat, Moskva 1982), s. 118.

549 Konev, *Zapiski Komandujusjego Frontom*, ss. 118–121.

550 KTB PzAOK 1 Ia, 12.2.44, T313, R69, F7305882-3; KTB s.Pz.Rgt. Bäke, BA-MA RH 39/677; Proschek papers, BA-MA MSg 2/5649. This is also supported by the map in the Anlagen of the PzAOK 1 Ia, dated 3 March 1944, showing the location of the tanks and other armored vehicles lost by III. Pz.Korps during the operation. Near Dadushkovka there are four AFVs marked as lost due to enemy action. Note that the map does not differentiate between tanks and APCs. Thus, at most four tanks may have been lost by II./Pz.Rgt. 23 at Dadushkovka. In the National Archives, the map is found at T313, R70, F7307179. However, the map employs color coding since the microfilm copy is in black and white, important information is missing on the copy. The original map, today at the Bundesarchiv-Militärarchiv in Freiburg, is in color and a color copy has kindly been provided to us by Dr.

Karl-Heinz Frieser at the Militärgeschichtliches Forschungsamt.

551 KTB Pz.Gren.Rgt. 64, 12.2.44, BA-MA RH 37/6257; Anlagen zum KTB III. Pz.Korps Ia, Tagesmeldungen der Div. am 12.2.44, 17. Pz.Div., T314, R208, F000965; 16. Pz.Div. Ia Tagesmeldung an III. Pz.Korps Ia, 12.2.44, Anlagen zum KTB III. Pz.Korps, T314, R208, F000972. Note that some sources describe a major tank battle on 12 February, with s.Pz.Rgt. Bäke playing a major role. However, according to the war diary of III. Pz.Korps, that battle took place on 13 February, something which is also backed up by the reports submitted to III. Pz.Korps during the battle, as well as the war diary of Pz.Gren.Rgt. 64.

552 Anlagen zum KTB III. Pz.Korps Ia, Tagesmeldungen der Div. am 12.2.44, 198. Inf.Div., T314, R208, F000966; KTB III. Pz.Korps Ia, 12.2.44, T314, R208, F000060-62; Lehmann & Tiemann, *The Leibstandarte, vol IV/1*, p. 31.

553 KTB III. Pz.Korps Ia, 12.2.44, T314, R208, F000060; Lehmann & Tiemann, *The Leibstandarte, vol IV/1*, pp. 31–2.

554 Stoves, *1 Panzer Division*, pp. 505–7; Proschek papers, BA-MA MSg 2/5649.

555 Anlagen zum KTB PzAOK 1 Ia, 12.2.40, 22.00 Uhr, T313, R70, F7306704; 1. Pz.Div. Ia Tagesmeldung an III. Pz.Korps Ia, 12.2.44, T314, R208, F000967.

556 Anlagen zum KTB III. Panzer Korps Ia, 13.2.44, 0745 Uhr, T314, R208, F001017; III. Pamzer Korps Ia Nr. 267/44, "Korpsbefehl für den 13.2.44," T314, R208, F000977.

557 XI. A.K. Funkspruch an AOK 8, 12.2.44, 12.12 Uhr, T312, R66, F7584883; KTB AOK 8 Ia, 12.2.44, T312, R64, F7581870-5; Lieb Diary, 12.2.44, MS # T-12.

558 KTB XXXXVII. Pz.Korps Ia, 12.2.44, T314, R1132, F000460-3.

559 KTB XXXXVII. Pz.Korps Ia, 12.2.44, T314, R1132, F000460-3; KTB I./Pz.Rgt. 26, 12.2.44, BA-MA RH 39/599.

560 KTB I./Pz.Rgt. 26, 12.2.44, BA-MA RH 39/599.

561 KTB I./Pz.Rgt. 26, 12.2.44, BA-MA RH 39/599.

562 KTB XXXXVII. Pz.Korps Ia, 12.2.44, T314, R1132, F000460-3; KTB I./Pz.Rgt. 26, 12.2.44, BA-MA RH 39/599.

563 KTB AOK 8 Ia, 12.2.44, 06.30, T312, R64, F7581868.

564 KTB XXXXVII. Pz.Korps Ia, 12.2.44, T314, R1132, F000460-3.

565 Meiser, *Die Hölle von Tscherkassy*, pp. 257-8.

566 KTB AOK 8 Ia, 12.2.44, T312, R64, F7581872.

567 Bericht Ofw. Heinz Lampe, 5./TG 3, BA-MA RL 10/641, Bl. 18-21.

568 Bericht Ofw. Heinz Lampe, 5./TG 3, BA-MA RL 10/641, Bl. 18-21.

569 Bericht Ofw. Heinz Lampe, 5./TG 3, BA-MA RL 10/641, Bl. 18-21.

570 Bericht Ofw. Heinz Lampe, 5./TG 3, BA-MA RL 10/641, Bl. 18-21.

571 Bericht Ofw. Heinz Lampe, 5./TG 3, BA-MA RL 10/641, Bl. 18-21.

572 PzAOK 1/O.Qu./Qu.1 Nr. 530/44 geh, 12.2.44, T313, R74, F7312907.

573 KTB AOK 8 Ia, 12.2.44, 18.35, T312, R64, F7581875.

574 *The Korsun'-Shevchenkovskii Operation*, p. 70.

575 Proschek papers, BA-MA MSg 2/5649; KTB s.Pz.Rgt. Bäke, BA-MA RH 39/677; KTB Pz.Gren.Rgt. 64, BA-MA RH 37/6257; Michael Schadewitz, Einsätze des "schweren Panzerregiments Bäke" vom 24. Januar bis 17. Februar 1944, p. 10, BA-MA MSg 2/4396; Rubbel, *The Combat History of schwere Panzer-Abteilung 503*, p. 127; 16. Pz.Div. Tagesmeldung an III. Pz.Korps Ia, 13.2.44, T314, R208, F001063; *The Korsun'-Shevchenkovskii Operation*, pp. 29–30. Note that some of the sources state that the described action took place on 12 February. However, the war diaries, radio messages, and other documents from III Panzer Corps and 1st Panzer Army make it clear that the battle took place on 13 February. Note also that Scherf (in Proschek papers) speaks of "Totalausfälle," but probably he means vehicles put out of action, as other reports show that it can not be Totalausfälle, which means vehicles written off.

576 Ibid.

577 Proschek papers, BA-MA MSg 2/5649; KTB s.Pz.Rgt. Bäke, BA-MA RH 39/677; KTB Pz.Gren.Rgt. 64, BA-MA RH 37/6257; Michael Schadewitz, Einsätze des "schweren Panzerregiments Bäke" vom 24. Januar bis 17. Februar 1944, p. 10, BA-MA MSg 2/4396; Rubbel, *The Combat History of schwere Panzer-Abteilung 503*, p. 127; 16. Pz.Div. Tagesmeldung an III. Pz.Korps Ia, 13.2.44, T314, R208, F001063;*The Korsun'-Shevchenkovskii Operation*, pp. 29–30. Note that some of the sources state that the described action took place on 12 February. However, the war diaries, radio messages, and other documents from the III Panzer Corps and the 1st Panzer Army make it clear that the battle took place on 13 February. Note also that Scherf (in Proschek papers) speaks of "Totalausfälle," but probably he means vehicles put out of action, as other reports show that it can not be Totalausfälle, which means vehicles written off.

578 Ibid.

579 KTB Pz.Gren.Rgt. 64, BA-MA RH 376257; 16. Pz.Div. Tagesmeldung an III. Pz.Korps Ia, 13.2.44, T314, R208, F001063.

580 KTB Pz.Rgt. Bäke, BA-MA RH 39/677; KTB III. Panzer Korps Ia, T314. R208, R000070; 16. Pz.Div. Tagesmeldung an III. Pz.Korps Ia, 13.2.44, T314, R208, F001063.

581 Funkspruch von Manstein an III. Pz.Korps, 1., 16. und 17. Pz.Div., in Anlagen zum KTB III. Pz. Korps Ia, T314, R208, F001081.

582 Proschek papers, BA-MA MSg 2/5649; 1. Pz.Div. Tagesmeldung an III. Pz.Korps, 13.2.44, T314, R208, F001065.

583 Proschek papers, BA-MA MSg 2/5649; 1. Pz.Div. Tagesmeldung an III. Pz.Korps, 13.2.44, T314, R208, F001065.
584 1. Pz.Div. Tagesmeldung an III. Pz.Korps, 13.2.44, T314, R208, F001065; PzAOK 1 Ia, 13.2.44, 15.30 Uhr, "Gliederung der 1. Pz.Div.," T313, R70, F7306727.
585 1. Pz.Div. Tagesmeldung an III. Pz.Korps, 13.2.44, T314, R208, F001065; PzAOK 1 Ia, 13.2.44, 15.30 Uhr, "Gliederung der 1. Pz.Div.," T313, R70, F7306727.
586 III. Pz.Korps Ia, Tagesmeldungen der Div., 13.2.44, T314, R208, F001061-5.
587 KTB PzAOK 1 Ia, 14.2.44, T313, R69, F7305889-90.
588 VII. A.K. Tagesmeldung 13.2.44, in Anlagen zum KTB PzAOK 1 Ia, T313, R70, F7306734; KTB PzAOK 1 Ia, 13.2.44, T313, R69, F7305891.
589 The Germans of course monitored the Soviet troop movements as closely as they could. See the reports of III. Pz.Korps Ic 10-15. Febr., T314, R212, F890-900.
590 KTB XXXXVII. Pz.Korps Ia, 13.2.44, T314, R1132, F000463-5; KTB I./Pz,Rgt. 26, 13.2.44, BA-MA RH 39/599; Anlage 25 zum KTB I./Pz,Rgt. 26, 13.2.44, BA-MA RH 39/599; KTB AOK 8 Ia, 13.2.44, 11.05 Uhr, T312, R64, F7581878.
591 KTB XXXXVII. Pz.Korps Ia, 13.2.44, T314, R1132, F000463-5; KTB AOK 8 Ia,13.2.44, 11.05, 16.20, 17.50, 20.00, T312, R64, F7581876-81.
592 KTB AOK 8 Ia, 13.2.44, 07.00, 08.20, 10.06, 10.25, 10.40, T312, R64, F7581876-81; Bericht Major Kaestner, BA-MA MSg 2/3570; BA-MA RH 37/6609.
593 *The Korsun'-Shevchenkovskii Operation*, p. 70.
594 KTB AOK 8 Ia, 13.2.44, 11.30 Uhr, T312, R64, R7581878; Bericht Major Siegel, BA-MA RH 37/6609.
595 Bericht Major Siegel, BA-MA RH 37/6609; Jahnke & Lerch, pp. 51–2.
596 KTB AOK 8 Ia, 13.2.44, 11.30, 11.45, 12.10, 14.00 Uhr, T312, R64, R7581878-9; Jahnke & Lerch, *Der Kessel von Tscherkassy*, pp. 43–4.
597 KTB AOK 8 Ia, 13.2.44, 16.15 Uhr, T312, R64, R7581879.
598 Lieb Diary, NARA MS # T-12.
599 Jahnke & Lerch, *Der Kessel von Tscherkassy*, p. 34; KTB PzAOK 1 Ia, 11.2.44, T313, R69. F7305880.
600 KTB PzAOK 1 Ia, 13.2.44, T313, R69. F7305888; KT-B AOK 8 Ia, 13.2.44, 15.10 Uhr, T312, R64, F7581879.
601 KTB PzAOK 1 Ia, 13.2.44, T313, R69. F7305888.
602 Michael Schadewitz, Einsätze des "schweren Panzerregiments Bäke" vom 24. Januar bis 17. Februar 1944, p. 10, BA-MA MSg 2/4396.
603 Michael Schadewitz, Einsätze des "schweren Panzerregiments Bäke" vom 24. Januar bis 17. Februar 1944, p. 11, BA-MA MSg 2/4396.
604 KTB s.Pz.Rgt. Bäke, p. 76, BA-MA RH 39/677; KTB AOK 8 Ia, 13.2.44, 19.22 Uhr, T312, R64, F7581880.
605 *The Korsun'-Shevchenkovskii Operation*, pp. 139–40.
606 *The Korsun'-Shevchenkovskii Operation*, pp. 138–40.
607 *The Korsun'-Shevchenkovskii Operation*, pp. 140–1.
608 Stoves, *1 Panzer Division*, pp. 510-512; Proschek papers, BA-MA MSg 2/5649.
609 Stoves, *1 Panzer Division*, pp. 510-512; Proschek papers, BA-MA MSg 2/5649.
610 KTB III. Pz.Korps Ia, 14.2.44, T314, R207, F000074-82; Tagesmeldung 16. Pz.Div., 14.2.44, T314, R208, F001179; Stoves, *1 Panzer Division*, pp. 510-512; Proschek papers, BA-MA MSg 2/5649.
611 II./Pz.Rgt. 39, 23.2.44, "Gefechtsbericht für die Zeit vom 13. - 19.2.44 (Lissjanka)," in Anlagen zum KTB III. Pz.Korps Ia, T314, R209, F000475; Anlagen zum KTB III. Pz.Korps Ia, Funkspruch 14.2.44, 16.45 Uhr, T314, R208, F 001169; KTB III. Pz.Korps Ia, 14.2.44, T314, R207, F000074-82.
612 XXXXVI. Pz.Korps, Tagesmeldung an PzAOK 1, 13.2.44, T313, R70, F7306733; KTB PzAOK 1 Ia, 14.2.44, T313, R69, F7305889-90.
613 KTB PzAOK 1 Ia, 14.2.44, T313, R69, F7305890.
614 KTB AOK 8 Ia, 14.2.44, 14.20, 20.50 & 22.00 Uhr, 15.2.44, 07.00 Uhr, T312, R64, F7581884-8; Gerhard Donat, *Der Munitionsverbrauch im Zweiten Weltkrieg im operativen und taktischen Rahmen* (Biblio Verlag, Osnabrück 1992), pp. 67–73.
615 KTB XXXXVII. Pz.Korps Ia,14.2.44, T314, R1132, F000465-7; KTB AOK 8 Ia, 14.2.44, 19.15 Uhr, T312, R64, F7581886-7.
616 KTB AOK 8 Ia, 14.2.44, 08.35 Uhr, T312, R64, F7581883; *The Korsun'-Shevchenkovskii Operation*, pp. 70–71.
617 KTB AOK 8 Ia, 14.2.44, 10.05, 11.25, 14.55, 15.50, 18.00 Uhr, T312, R64, F7581883-5.
618 KTB AOK 8 Ia, 14.2.44, 18.05 Uhr, T312, R64, F7581885-6.
619 KTB AOK 8 Ia, 14.2.44, 18.55 Uhr, T312, R64, F7581886.
620 Funkspruch XXXXII. A.K. an AOK 8, 14.2.44, 18.55 Uhr, in Anlagen zum KTB AOK 8 Ia, T312, R66, F7584800; KTB AOK 8 Ia 15.2.44, 06.30, T312, R64, F7581889; Jahnke & Lerch, *Der Kessel von Tscherkassy*, p. 57.
621 KTB AOK 8 Ia 15.2.44, 11.40 & 12.00 Uhr, T312, R64, F7581892; Jahnke & Lerch, *Der Kessel von Tscherkassy*, pp. 57f.
622 KTB XXXXVII. Pz.Korps Ia, 15.2.44, T314, R1132, F000467-9; KTB I./Pz.Rgt. 26,15.2.44, BA-MA RH 39/599; Fernschreiben XXXXVII. Pz.Korps and AOK 8, 15.2.44, 17.30 Uhr, in Anlagen zum KTB AOK 8 Ia, T312, R66, F1584761.
623 Fernschreiben XXXXVII. Pz.Korps and AOK 8, 15.2.44, 17.30 Uhr, in Anlagen zum KTB AOK 8 Ia, T312, R66, F158476; Fernschreiben XXXXVII. Pz.Korps and AOK 8, 13.2.44, 20.45 Uhr, in Anlagen zum KTB AOK 8 Ia, T312, R66, F1584827; KTB AOK 8 Ia, 15.2.44, 10.35 Uhr, T312, R64, F7581891; Lieferungen der Pz. Fahrzeuge, BA-MA RH 10/359.

624 KTB Pz.Gren.Rgt. 64, 14.2.44, BA-MA RH 37/6257; Stoves, *1 Panzer Division*, pp. 512f.
625 Proschek papers, BA-MA MSg 2/5649; Anlagen zum KTB PzAOK 1 Ia, Panzerlage III. Pz.Korps 15.2, 11.10 Uhr, T313, R70, F7306803.
626 Proschek papers, BA-MA MSg 2/5649; KTB III. Pz.Korps Ia, 15.2.44, T314, R208, F000082.
627 Proschek papers, BA-MA MSg 2/5649.
628 Proschek papers, BA-MA MSg 2/5649.
629 Stoves, *1 Panzer Division*, pp. 512–4.
630 II./Pz.Rgt. 39, 23.2.44, "Gefechtsbericht für die Zeit vom 13. – 19.2.44 (Lissjanka)," in Anlagen zum KTB III. Pz.Korps Ia, T314, R209, F000475; KTB III. Pz.Korps Ia, 15.2.44, T314, R208, F000082-8; Jahnke & Lerch, p. 74.
631 Lieb Diary & p. 44 in MS # T-12; Gen.Kdo. XI. A.K. Ia Br.B.Nr. 19/44, 23.2.1944, p. 6, in Anlagen zum KTB PzAOK 1 Ia, "Gefechtsberichte Gruppe Stemmermann," T313, R72, F7310500.
632 Gruppe Stemmermann, Ia Nr. 236/44 geh. 15.2.44, "Befehl für den Durchbruch," in Anlagen zum KTB PzAOK 1 Ia, "Gefechtsberichte Gruppe Stemmermann," T313, R72, F7310503.
633 Lieb Diary in MS # T-12.
634 Meiser, *Die Hölle von Tscherkassy*, p. 214.
635 Gruppe Stemmermann, Ia Nr. 236/44 geh. 15.2.44, "Befehl für den Durchbruch," in Anlagen zum KTB PzAOK 1 Ia, "Gefechtsberichte Gruppe Stemmermann," T313, R72, F7310503.
636 KTB AOK 8 Ia, 15.2.44, 17.20 Uhr, T312, R64, F7581893.
637 KTB PzAOK 1 Ia, 16.2.44, T313, R69, F7305897.
638 *The Korsun'-Shevchenkovskii Operation*, p. 141.
639 *The Korsun'-Shevchenkovskii Operation*, p. 206.
640 KTB AOK 8 Ia, 16.2.44, 10.30 Uhr, T312, R64, F7581900; Anlagen zum KTB Nr. 6, AOK 8 O.Qu, Bl. 299, T312, R63, F7581303; Lieb Diary, MS # T-12.
641 KTB AOK 8 Ia, 16.2.44, 10.38 Uhr, T312, R64, F7581900; Bericht Major Kaestner, BA-MA MSg 2/3570.
642 KTB AOK 8 Ia, 16.2.44, 12.00 & 13.20 Uhr, T312, R64, F7581901; 5. SS-Pz.Div. Ia, Gefechtsbericht, 24.2.44, Anlage 10 zu Pz.AOK 1 Ia Nr. 158/44 g.Kdos. v. 28.2.44, T313, R72, F7310541.
643 KTB AOK 8 Ia, 16.2.44, 09.00 & 10.10 Uhr, T312, R64, F7581898-9.
644 KTB AOK 8 Ia, 16.2.44, 10.00 Uhr, T312, R64, F7581898-9.
645 KTB AOK 8 Ia, 16.2.44, 10.00 Uhr, T312, R64, F7581898-9.
646 KTB XXXXVII Pz.Korps Ia, 16.2.44, T314, R1132, F469-471; Olaf Ehlers' Diary, BA-MA MSg 2/3200.
647 Olaf Ehlers' Diary, BA-MA MSg 2/3200.
648 Olaf Ehlers' Diary, BA-MA MSg 2/3200.
649 Olaf Ehlers' Diary, BA-MA MSg 2/3200.
650 Olaf Ehlers' Diary, BA-MA MSg 2/3200.
651 Olaf Ehlers' Diary, BA-MA MSg 2/3200.
652 Olaf Ehlers' Diary, BA-MA MSg 2/3200.
653 Olaf Ehlers' Diary, BA-MA MSg 2/3200.
654 Olaf Ehlers' Diary, BA-MA MSg 2/3200.
655 Olaf Ehlers' Diary, BA-MA MSg 2/3200.
656 Olaf Ehlers' Diary, BA-MA MSg 2/3200.
657 Olaf Ehlers' Diary, BA-MA MSg 2/3200.
658 KTB III. Pz.Korps Ia, 16.2.44, T314, R208, F000088.
659 II./Pz.Rgt. 39, 23.2.44, "Gefechtsbericht für die Zeit vom 13.-19.2.44 (Lissjanka)," in Anlagen zum KTB III. Pz.Korps Ia, T314, R209, F000476; Proschek papers, BA-MA MSg 2/5650.
660 Proschek papers, BA-MA MSg 2/5650; Stoves, *1 Panzer Division*, p. 518.
661 Proschek papers, BA-MA MSg 2/5650.
662 Proschek papers, BA-MA MSg 2/5650; Stoves, *1 Panzer Division*, p. 522.
663 Proschek papers, BA-MA MSg 2/5650.
664 Stoves, *1 Panzer Division*, p. 517-9; Funkspruch Gen. Breith an III. Pz.Korps Ia, 16.2.44, 13.50 Uhr, T314, R209, F000158.
665 Stoves, *1 Panzer Division*, p. 522.
666 Lehmann & Tiemann, *Liebstandarte IV/1*, p. 35.
667 Proschek papers, BA-MA MSg 2/5650.
668 Proschek papers, BA-MA MSg 2/5650.
669 Jahnke & Lerch, *Der Kessel von Tscherkassy 1944*, p. 84.
670 Jahnke & Lerch, *Der Kessel von Tscherkassy 1944*, pp. 84–5.
671 Jahnke & Lerch, *Der Kessel von Tscherkassy 1944*, p. 85.
672 Gen.Kdo. XI. A.K., Ia Br.B.Nr. 19/44, in Gruppe Mattenklott papers, PzAOK 1, T313, R70, F7310494-7310502; Jahnke & Lerch, *Der Kessel von Tscherkassy 1944*, p. 85.
673 Meiser, p. 267.
674 Bericht Major Kaestner, BA-MA MSg 2/3570, p. 21-24; Anlage 3 zum Gen.Kdo. XI. A.K. Ia Nr. 19/44 g.Kdos, "72. Inf.-Div. Gefechtsbericht," 23. 2.44, in Anlagen zum KTB PzAOK 1, T313, R72, F7310527-30.
675 Bericht Major Kaestner, BA-MA MSg 2/3570, pp. 21–24.
676 Bericht Major Kaestner, BA-MA MSg 2/3570, p. 23-26; Anlage 3 zum Gen.Kdo. XI. A.K. Ia Nr. 19/44 g.Kdos, "72. Inf.-Div. Gefechtsbericht," 23. 2.44, in Anlagen zum KTB PzAOK 1, T313, R72, F7310527-30.
677 Bericht Major Kaestner, BA-MA MSg 2/3570, p. 23-26; Anlage 3 zum Gen.Kdo. XI. A.K. Ia Nr. 19/44 g.Kdos, "72. Inf.-Div. Gefechtsbericht," 23. 2.44, in Anlagen zum KTB PzAOK 1, T313, R72, F7310527-30.
678 Bericht Major Kaestner, BA-MA MSg 2/3570, p. 25-27; Anlage 3 zum Gen.Kdo. XI. A.K. Ia Nr. 19/44 g.Kdos, "72. Inf.-Div. Gefechtsbericht," 23. 2.44, in Anlagen zum KTB PzAOK 1, T313, R72, F7310527-30.
679 Bericht Major Siegel, BA-MA RH 37/6609, Bl. 30-36; Anlage 3 zum Gen.Kdo. XI. A.K. Ia Nr. 19/44 g.Kdos, "72. Inf.-Div. Gefechtsbericht," 23. 2.44, in Anlagen zum KTB PzAOK 1, T313, R72, F7310527-30.
680 Bericht Major Siegel, BA-MA RH 37/6609, Bl. 30-36; Anlage 3 zum Gen.Kdo. XI. A.K. Ia Nr. 19/44 g.Kdos, "72. Inf.-Div. Gefechtsbericht," 23. 2.44, in Anlagen zum KTB PzAOK 1, T313, R72, F7310527-30.

681 Bericht Major Siegel, BA-MA RH 37/6609, Bl. 30-36; Anlage 3 zum Gen.Kdo. XI. A.K. Ia Nr. 19/44 g.Kdos, "72. Inf.-Div. Gefechtsbericht," 23. 2.44, in Anlagen zum KTB PzAOK 1, T313, R72, F7310527-30.

682 Bericht Major Siegel, BA-MA RH 37/6609, Bl. 30-36; Anlage 3 zum Gen.Kdo. XI. A.K. Ia Nr. 19/44 g.Kdos, "72. Inf.-Div. Gefechtsbericht," 23. 2.44, in Anlagen zum KTB PzAOK 1, T313, R72, F7310527-30.

683 Bericht Major Siegel, BA-MA RH 37/6609, Bl. 30-36; Anlage 3 zum Gen.Kdo. XI. A.K. Ia Nr. 19/44 g.Kdos, "72. Inf.-Div. Gefechtsbericht," 23. 2.44, in Anlagen zum KTB PzAOK 1, T313, R72, F7310527-30.

684 Bericht Major Siegel, BA-MA RH 37/6609, Bl. 30-36; Anlage 3 zum Gen.Kdo. XI. A.K. Ia Nr. 19/44 g.Kdos, "72. Inf.-Div. Gefechtsbericht," 23. 2.44, in Anlagen zum KTB PzAOK 1, T313, R72, F7310527-30.

685 Bericht Major Siegel, BA-MA RH 37/6609, Bl. 30-36; Anlage 3 zum Gen.Kdo. XI. A.K. Ia Nr. 19/44 g.Kdos, "72. Inf.-Div. Gefechtsbericht," 23. 2.44, in Anlagen zum KTB PzAOK 1, T313, R72, F7310527-30.

686 Bericht Major Siegel, BA-MA RH 37/6609, Bl. 30-36; Anlage 3 zum Gen.Kdo. XI. A.K. Ia Nr. 19/44 g.Kdos, "72. Inf.-Div. Gefechtsbericht," 23.2.44, in Anlagen zum KTB PzAOK 1, T313, R72, F7310527-30.

687 Bericht Major Siegel, BA-MA RH 37/6609, Bl. 30-36; Anlage 3 zum Gen.Kdo. XI. A.K. Ia Nr. 19/44 g.Kdos, "72. Inf.-Div. Gefechtsbericht," 23. 2.44, in Anlagen zum KTB PzAOK 1, T313, R72, F7310527-30.

688 Bericht Major Siegel, BA-MA RH 37/6609, Bl. 30-36.

689 Anlage 3 zum Gen.Kdo. XI. A.K. Ia Nr. 19/44 g.Kdos, "72. Inf.-Div. Gefechtsbericht," 23.2.44, in Anlagen zum KTB PzAOK 1, T313, R72, F7310527-30; for more on the strength of the 72nd Division before and after the breakout, see Abschlußmeldung Gruppe Mattenklott, 2.3.44, in PzAOK 1 Ia Anlagen, T313, R72, F7310414 and Gen.Kdo XXXXII. A.K., 24.2.44, in Anlagen zum KTB PzAOK 1 Ia, T313, R72, F7310513. Note that given the number of soldiers who succeeded in breaking out, it seems that the reported strength of 72nd Division before the breakout, 4,000 men, is too low, or else it only refers to those who assembled among the combat units.

690 Bericht Feldwebel Peter Reisch, BA-MA RH 37/6609.

691 Bericht Feldwebel Peter Reisch, BA-MA RH 37/6609.

692 Bericht Feldwebel Peter Reisch, BA-MA RH 37/6609.

693 Bericht Feldwebel Peter Reisch, BA-MA RH 37/6609.

694 Bericht Feldwebel Peter Reisch, BA-MA RH 37/6609.

695 Bericht Feldwebel Peter Reisch, BA-MA RH 37/6609.

696 Bericht Feldwebel Peter Reisch, BA-MA RH 37/6609.

697 Bericht Feldwebel Peter Reisch, BA-MA RH 37/6609; 389. Inf.Div. Kommandeur, Ia Nr. 200/44 geh, 22.2.44, in Anlagen zu, KTB PzAOK 1 Ia, T313, R72, F7310553-6.

698 Korps-Abteilung B Ia Nr. 200/44 geh., 24.2.44, in Anlagen zum KTB PzAOK 1 Ia, T313, R72, F7310523-4.

699 Korps-Abteilung B Ia Nr. 200/44 geh., 24.2.44, in Anlagen zum KTB PzAOK 1 Ia, T313, R72, F7310524-5.

700 Korps-Abteilung B Ia Nr. 200/44 geh., 24.2.44, in Anlagen zum KTB PzAOK 1 Ia, T313, R72, F7310524-5.

701 Proschek papers, BA-MA MSg 2/5650.

702 Proschek papers, BA-MA MSg 2/5650.

703 Proschek papers, BA-MA MSg 2/5650.

704 Proschek papers, BA-MA MSg 2/5650; G. Tessin, *Verbände und Truppen der deutschen Wehrmacht und Waffen-SS* (Mittler & Sohn, Frankfurt am Main and Biblio Verlag, Osnabrück 1966–1975) Namensverbände, entry "B."

705 Gen.Kdo XXXXII. A.K., 24.2.44, in Anlagen zum KTB PzAOK 1 Ia, T313, R72, F7310513.

706 5. SS-Pz.Div. Wiking Ia, Anlage 10 zu PzAOK 1 Ia Nr. 158/44, 28.2.44, in Anlagen zum KTB PzAOK 1 Ia, T313, R72, F7310541-2.

707 Fritz Hahl, *Mit "Westland" im Osten* (Woltersdorf, Munin 2001), pp. 132–3.

708 5. SS-Pz.Div. Wiking Ia, Anlage 10 zu PzAOK 1 Ia Nr. 158/44, 28.2.44, in Anlagen zum KTB PzAOK 1 Ia, T313, R72, F7310541-2.

709 5. SS-Pz.Div. Wiking Ia, Anlage 10 zu PzAOK 1 Ia Nr. 158/44, 28.2.44, in Anlagen zum KTB PzAOK 1 Ia, T313, R72, F7310541-2; Hahl p. 133–4.

710 5. SS-Pz.Div. Wiking Ia, Anlage 10 zu PzAOK 1 Ia Nr. 158/44, 28.2.44, in Anlagen zum KTB PzAOK 1 Ia, T313, R72, F7310542-3; Hahl p. 133–4.

711 5. SS-Pz.Div. Wiking Ia, Anlage 10 zu PzAOK 1 Ia Nr. 158/44, 28.2.44, in Anlagen zum KTB PzAOK 1 Ia, T313, R72, F7310542-3; Hahl, *Mit "Westland" im Osten*, p. 133-4.

712 Hahl, *Mit "Westland" im Osten*, p. 134.

713 Hahl, *Mit "Westland" im Osten*, p. 134.

714 Günter Bernau, *SS-Panzer-Artillerie – Regiment 5 in der Panzer –Division Wiking* (Eigenverlag Kameradschaft ehem.Pz.Art Rgt. 5, Wuppertal 1990), s. 112.

715 88. Inf. Div. Ia, Nr. 1/44 geh., 23.2.44, in Anlagen zum KTB PzAOK 1 Ia, T313, R72, F7310545-7.

716 88. Inf.Div. Ia, Nr. 1/44 geh., 23.2.44, in Anlagen zum KTB PzAOK 1 Ia, T313, R72, F7310546-7.

717 88. Inf.Div. Ia, Nr. 1/44 geh., 23.2.44, in Anlagen zum KTB PzAOK 1 Ia, T313, R72, F7310546-7.

718 88. Inf.Div. Ia, Nr. 1/44 geh., 23.2.44, in Anlagen zum KTB PzAOK 1 Ia, T313, R72, F7310547-8.

719 Abschlußmeldung Gruppe Mattenklott, 2.3.44, in PzAOK 1 Ia Anlagen, T313, R72, F7310414-23.

720 57. Inf.Div. Ia, Nr. 1/44 geh. 22.2.44, in Anlagen zum KTB PzAOK 1 Ia, T313, R72, F7310549-51.

721 57. Inf.Div. Ia, Nr. 1/44 geh. 22.2.44, in Anlagen zum KTB PzAOK 1 Ia, T313, R72, F7310549-51.

722 57. Inf.Div. Ia, Nr. 1/44 geh. 22.2.44, in Anlagen zum KTB PzAOK 1 Ia, T313, R72, F7310549-51.

723 57. Inf.Div. Ia, Nr. 1/44 geh. 22.2.44, in Anlagen zum KTB PzAOK 1 Ia, T313, R72, F7310549-51.

724 57. Inf.Div. Ia, Nr. 1/44 geh. 22.2.44, in Anlagen zum KTB PzAOK 1 Ia, T313, R72, F7310549-51.
725 389. Inf.Div. Kommandeur, Ia Nr. 200/44 geh, 22.2.44, in Anlagen zu, KTB PzAOK 1 Ia, T313, R72, F7310553-6.
726 Meiser, *Die Hölle von Tscherkassy*, pp. 267–8.
727 Meiser, *Die Hölle von Tscherkassy*, pp. 268–9.
728 Meiser, *Die Hölle von Tscherkassy*, pp. 269–70.
729 Meiser, *Die Hölle von Tscherkassy*, pp. 270–1.
730 Ibid.
731 Meiser, *Die Hölle von Tscherkassy*, pp. 271–2.
732 Meiser, *Die Hölle von Tscherkassy*, pp. 272–3.
733 Meiser, *Die Hölle von Tscherkassy*, pp. 273–4.
734 Meiser, *Die Hölle von Tscherkassy*, pp. 274–5.
735 Proschek papers, BA-MA MSg 2/5650.
736 Proschek papers, BA-MA MSg 2/5650.
737 Proschek papers, BA-MA MSg 2/5650.
738 Proschek papers, BA-MA MSg 2/5650.
739 Proschek papers, BA-MA MSg 2/5650.
740 Abschlußmeldung Gruppe Mattenklott, 2.3.44, in Anlagen zum KTB PzAOK 1 Ia, T313, R72, F7310414.
741 The Documents are not entirely in agreement. An entry in the 8th Army war diary on 11 February states that Gruppe Stemmermann consisted of 56,000 men of all ranks. However, another entry, on 14 February, gives the figure 54,000 men. At first glance it could be assumed that the difference is caused by wounded soldiers flown out of the pocket. This is however unlikely, as the air evacuation had ceased during the period 11–14 February. It seems also quite unlikely that losses in killed and missing would be more than a few hundred men. Either the figure 56,000 refer to a date much earlier than 11 February, or else the figure 54,000 is the result of a more careful investigation. Another report (AOK 8/O.Qu Nr. 277/44 geh. 11.2.44, T312, R63, F7581371) confirms the latter figure and also show that 3,904 wounded and sick had been evacuated by air since 29 January. Thus the total would have been 58,000 when the pincers closed. However to this must be added soldiers killed or taken prisoner since the pocket was formed. We estimate that number to approximately 1,000. Hence we arrive at the figure 59,000.
742 Tsamo RF, fond 4.gd.A.(320), opis 4522, delo 120, p. 52.
743 Gr. Matteklott Ia, Geschütz-Bestand der Gruppe Stemmermann, 17.2.44, in Anlagen zum KTB PzAOK 1 Ia, T313, R72, F7310472.
744 *The Korsun'-Shevchenkovskii Operation*, pp. 41 and 52; KTB PzAOK 1 Ia, 19.2.44, T313, R69, F7305908.
745 Konev, *Zapiski Komandujusjego Frontom*, p.105.
746 Jahnke & Lerch, *Der Kessel von Tscherkassy 1944*, p. 71.
747 Konev, *Zapiski Komandujusjego Frontom*, p.125.
748 *The Korsun'-Shevchenkovskii Operation*, pp. 31–32, 71, 141–143.
749 Tsamo RF, fond 4.gd.A.(320), opis 4522, delo 120, p. 60.
750 57. Inf.Div. Ia, Nr. 1/44 geh. 22.2.44, in Anlagen zum KTB PzAOK 1 Ia, T313, R72, F7310549; Anlage 3 zum Gen.Kdo. XI. A.K. Ia Nr. 19/44 g.Kdos, "72. Inf.-Div. Gefechtsbericht," 23.2.44, in Anlagen zum KTB PzAOK 1, T313, R72, F7310527-30; Anlage 4 zu PzAOK 1 Ia Nr 158/44 g.Kdos, v. 28.2.44, T313, R72, F7310650.
751 Karl-Heinz Schneider-Janessen, *Arzt im Krieg* (Lichentwys, Frankfurt am Main 1993), p. 222.
752 KTB PzAOK 1 Ia, 16.2.44, T313, R69, F7305896f.
753 KTB PzAOK 1 Ia, 16.2.44-19.2.44, T313, R69, F7305896-7305909.
754 *The Korsun'-Shevchenkovskii Operation* , pp. 41 and 52; Krivosheev, *Grif Sekretnosti Sniat*, p. 227.
755 Tsamo RF, fond 240, opis 2795, delo 173.
756 Krainjukov, *Ot Dnepra do Visly*, pp. 152-153.
757 See table 3.
758 For more on this see Zetterling & Frankson, *Kursk 1943*, pp. 136–7.
759 PzAOK 1, Stabsoffizier für Panzer-Bek., 3.3.1944, Fernschreiben PzAOK 1 Ia 423/44, Betr. Panzerausfälle, T313, R70, F7307174-6. It should be noted that the report does somewhat question the lack of recovery vehicles as a cause of the losses, but it only shows that the number of recovery vehicles on hand (for 1st, 16th, and 17th PzDiv plus the battalions II./23, 503 and 506) was 66 on 31 January, which was only marginally lower than the prescribed number of 71. However, only 37 were operational and some of these belonged to 503 Tank Battalion, whose recovery vehicles remained far away at the XXXXVI Panzer Korps. On 24 February there were actually 67 recovery vehicles on hand, but the report does not mention how many of these were operational. Given the poor weather conditions it seems likely that serviceability may have been low.

Another report (PzAOK 1 Abt. V, "Tätigkeitsbericht für die Zeit vom 1.2.–29.2.44," 5.3.44, T313, R75, F7313464) emphasizes that the available recovery vehicles for tanks were fully occupied but could still only partially cope with the needs. The lack of heavy recovery vehicles was specifically emphasized.
760 Gen.Insp. der Pz.Truppe, Panther Abteilungen 29.2.1944 nach Gen.Qu, BA-MA RH 10/70.
761 III. Pz.Korps Ia Nr. 367/44 geh, 24.2.44, T314, R209, F000664.
762 Anlagen zum KTB PzAOK 1 Ia, 24.2.44, 11.15 Uhr, T313, R70, F7307014. Note that the document also gives casualties for the period 1–20 February that are slightly lower than the casualties given in table 3. However, as the report which table 3 is based on was compiled slightly later, we have chosen to rely on it.
763 PzAOK 1, IIa, Verlustübersicht Monat Januar 1944, NARA T313, R74, F7312636. The low tank strength is evident from PzAOK 1 Kriegsgliederungen Stand 22.1.44 & 29.1.44 (T313, R69, Frames 75306351-2 & 75306485) plus the Tagesmeldungen VII. A.K. in Anlagen zum KTB PzAOK 1 Ia, 25.1.44 & 29.1.44, (T313, R69, F7306400 & F7306492).

764 XXXXVII. Pz.Korps Ia Nr 196/44, 15.3.44, Zustandberichte 376. I.D. & 13. Pz.Div., T314, R1132, F880-887; data for 8th Army losses in table 5.

765 AOK 8 Ia Nr. 272/44 geh.K., 27.2.44, T312, R64, F7582921; XXXXVII. Pz.Korps Ia Nr 196/44, 15.3.44, Zustandberichte 376. I.D. & 13. Pz.Div., T314, R1132, F880-887.

766 I./Pz.Rgt. 26 losses derived from KTB I./Pz.Rgt. 26 and Anlagen "Zusammenstellung der Pz.-Lagemeldungen, 14.7.44" and Anlage 25 zum KTB I./Pz.Rgt- 26, all found in BA-MA RH 39/599. Manpower losses for I./Pz.Rgt. 26 taken from XXXXVII. Pz.Korps Ia Nr 196/44, 15.3.44, Zustandberichte 376. I.D. & 13. Pz.Div., T314, R1132, F898.

767 KTB AOK 8 Ia Nr. 253/44, 23.2.44, T312, R64, F7582929.

768 Panther Abteilungen 20.1.1944 nach Gen. Qu., BA-MA RH 10/70; AOK 8 Ia Nr. 129/44 geh., 11.1.44, T312, R64, F7582998.

769 During the spring the Pz.Rgt. 31 received 79 Panthers, thus bringing it up to authorized strength before it went back to the Eastern Front in summer 1944 (see Lieferungen der Pz.-Fahrz., BA-MA RH 10/349). According to the latter file it seems that no tanks were sent to 11th Panzer Division from Germany in the period we study here.

770 KTB III./Pz.Rgt. 36, BA-MA RH 39/380.

771 See Appendix 2 for more information about these units.

772 *The Korsun'-Shevchenkovskii Operation*, pp. 41 & 52.

773 Anlage zum Gen.Kdo III. Pz.Korps Ia Tagesmeldung 18.2.44, T314, R209, F000325.

774 Krivosheev, *Grif Sekretnosti Sniat*, p. 371.

775 See for example, E. F. Ziemke, *Stalingrad to Berlin* (New York: Military Heritage Press, 1985), pp. 218–247; J. Erickson, *The Road to Berlin* (London: Grafton 1985), pp. 234–40; Zhukov, *The Memoirs of Marshal Zhukov*, pp. 494–513.

776 For example, the 18th and 20th Tank Corps were moved to the Dzhurzhintsy–Lisyanka area on 14 February; see *The Korsun'-Shevchenkovskii Operation*, p. 140.

777 Tsamo RF, fond 240, opis 2795, delo 173; *The Korsun'-Shevchenkovskii Operation*, p. 140.

778 Krivosheev, *Grif Sekretnosti Sniat,* pp. 146f.

Appendix I

ORDERS OF BATTLE

Commanders at the Korsun-Shevchenkovskii Operation January–February 1944

Soviet Forces

Unit	Commander	Chief of Staff
Fronts		
1st Ukrainian Front	General N.F.Vatutin	Gen.Lt A.N.Bogolyubov
2nd Ukrainian Front	General I.S.Konev	Gen.Col M.V.Zakharov
Guards Armies		
4.Guards Army	Gen.Maj A.I.Ryzhov Gen.Lt I.K.Smirnov (from 3 Feb 44)	Gen.Maj P.M.Verkholovich
5.Guards Army	Gen.Lt A.S.Zhadov	Gen.Maj N.I.Lyamin
5.Guards Tank Army	Gen.Col P.A.Rotmistrov	Gen.Maj V.N.Baskakov
7.Guards Army	Gen.Col M.S.Shumilov	Gen.Maj G.S.Lukin
Armies		
2.Tank Army	Gen.Lt S.I.Bogdanov	Gen.Maj A.M.Pavlov
6.Tank Army	Gen.Lt A.G.Kravchenko	Gen.Maj D.M.Zaev
27.Army	Gen.Lt S.G.Trofimenko	Gen.Maj G.S.Lukyanchenko
40.Army	Gen.Lt F.F.Zhmachenko Gen.Maj V.M.Sharapov (from 26 jan 44)	Gen.Maj L.B.Sosedov
52.Army	Gen.Lt K.A.Koroteev	Gen.Maj A.N.Kolominov
53.Army	Gen.Lt I.V.Galanin	Gen.Maj I.I.Vorobev
57.Army	Gen.Lt N.A.Gagen	Gen.Maj K.N.Derevyanko
Air Armies		
2.Air Army	Gen.Lt S.A.Krasovskii	Gen.Maj I.I.Terentev
5.Air Army	Gen.Lt S.K.Goryunov	Gen.Maj N.G.Seleznev
Guards Corps		
5.Guards Cavalry Corps	Gen.Maj S.V.Selivanov	Colonel N.I.Privalov
5.Guards Mech Corps	Gen.Maj B.M.Skvortsov	Colonel A.A.Shibaev
5.Guards Tank Corps	Gen.Lt A.G.Kravchenko Gen.Lt V.M.Alekseev (from 25 Jan 44)	Colonel A.M.Belov
20.Guards Rifle Corps	Gen.Maj N.I.Biryukov	Colonel V.F.Smirnov
21.Guards Rifle Corps	Gen.Maj P.I.Fomenko	Colonel I.F.Kurakin
24.Guards Rifle Corps		
25.Guards Rifle Corps	Gen.Maj G.B.Safiulin	Colonel A.P.Kolesnik
26.Guards Rifle Corps	Gen.Maj P.A.Firsov	Colonel Ya.I.Dubrovskii
32.Guards Rifle Corps	Gen.Maj A.I.Rodimtsev	Colonel P.I.Petrov
33.Guards Rifle Corps	Gen.Lt M.I.Kozlov	Colonel M.A.Khlyzov
35.Guards Rifle Corps	Gen.Lt S.G.Goryachev	Colonel V.A.Kleshchev
Corps		
3.Tank Corps	Gen.Maj A.A.Shamshin	Colonel B.I.Zakharov
5.Mech Corps	Gen.Lt M.V.Volkov	
7.Mech Corps	Gen.Maj F.G.Katkov	Colonel F.A.Lukin
8.Mech Corps	Gen.Maj A.M.Khasin Gen.Maj A.N.Firsovich (from 11 Jan 44)	Colonel M.N.Taradai
16.Tank Corps	Gen.Maj I.V.Dubovoi	Colonel A.A.Vitruk
18.Tank Corps	Gen.Maj K.G.Trufanov	
20.Tank Corps	Gen.Lt I.G.Lazarev	Colonel A.K.Pogosov
29.Tank Corps	Gen.Maj I.F.Kirichenko	Colonel P.A.Solovev
33.Rifle Corps	Gen.Maj A.I.Semenov	Colonel S.P.Duchenko

Unit	Commander	Chief of Staff
47.Rifle Corps	Gen.Maj S.P.Merkulov Gen.Maj I.S.Shmygo (from 18 Jan 44)	Colonel F.F.Tulikov
48.Rifle Corps	Gen.Maj Z.Z.Pogoznyi	Colonel G.A.Komarov
49.Rifle Corps	Gen.Maj G.N.Terentev	Colonel D.S.Chernykh
50.Rifle Corps	Gen.Maj S.S.Martirosyan	Colonel F.A.Dubovskii
51.Rifle Corps	Gen.Maj P.P.Avdeenko	Colonel A.P.Ryabov
64.Rifle Corps	Gen.Maj M.B.Anashkin	Colonel I.S.Chelyadinov
73.Rifle Corps	Gen.Maj P.F.Batitskii	Colonel M.A.Tkachenko
75.Rifle Corps	Gen.Maj S.A.Kozak Gen.Maj A.Z.Akimenko (from 19 Jan 44) Colonel M.I.Manokhin (from 7 Feb 44)	Colonel M.N.Belov
78.Rifle Corps	Gen.Maj G.A.Latyshev	Colonel D.P.Ivanyushin
104.Rifle Corps	Gen.Lt A.V.Petrushevskii	Colonel A.I.Shishlyannikov

Cavalry Divisions

11th Guards Cavalry Division	Colonel L.A.Slanov
12th Guards Cavalry Division	Generalmajor V.I.Grigorovich
63rd Cavalry Division	Generalmajor K.R.Beloshnichenko

German Forces

Unit	Commander	Chief of Staff
Army Group South	Field Marshal von Manstein	Gen.Lt Busse
1st Panzer Army	Gen. d. Pz.Tr. Hube	Gen.Maj. Wenck
8th Army	Gen. d. Inf. Wöhler	Gen.Maj. Speidel
III. Pz.Korps	Gen. d. Pz.Tr. Breith	Col. Merck
VII. Korps	Gen. d. Art. Hell	Col.Schwatlo-Gesterding
XI. Korps	Gen. d. Art. Stemmermann	Col. Gaedke
XXXXII. Korps	Gen.Lt. Lieb1	Col. Franz
XXXXVII. Pz.Korps	Gen.Lt. von Vormann	Col. Reinhard
1st Panzer Division	Gen.Maj. Koll	Lt.Col.von Zitzewitz
SS-Leibstandarte	Gen.Maj. Wisch	Maj. Lehmann
3rd Panzer Division	Col. Lang2	Lt.Col. Voss
SS-Wiking	Gen.Lt. Gille	Lt.Col. Schörfelder
11th Panzer Division	Gen.Maj. von Wietersheim	Major Drews
13th Panzer Division	Gen. Maj Mikosch	Lt.Col. Möller-Althaus
14th Panzer Division	Gen.Maj. Unrein	Major Butlar
16th Panzer Division	Col. Back	Lt.Col. von Baer
17th Panzer Division	Gen.Maj. von der Meden	Lt.Col. Neckelmann
34th Infantry Division	Gen.Lt. Hochbaum	Lt.Col. Schulz
57th Infantry Division	Gen.Maj. Trowitz	Lt.Col. Heidenreich
72nd Infantry Division	Col. Hohn	Lt.Col. Müller
88th Infantry Division	Gen.Maj. von Rittberg	Lt.Col. Hoheisel
106th Infantry Division	Gen.Maj. Forst	Lt.Col. Doepner
198th Infantry Division	Gen.Lt. Horn	Lt.Col. Schäfer
282nd Infantry Division	Gen.Lt. Frenking	Lt.Col. Löffelholz von Colberg
320th Infantry Division	Gen. Lt. Postel	Lt.Col. von Ohlen und Adlerscron
389th Infantry Division	Gen.Maj. Kruse	Lt.Col. Meyer-Welker
Korps-Gruppe B	Col. Foquet4	

Notes

1 Normally commander of Korps-Gruppe B, but acting as commander XXXXII. Korps, since Gen.Lt. Mattenklott was on leave.
2 Replaced Fritz Bayerlein as commander after the Kirovograd battle.
3 Promoted to Gen.Maj. on 1 February 1944.
4 Acting as commander since Gen.Lt Lieb temporarily commanded XXXXII. Korps.

Soviet Order of Battle for 2nd Ukrainian Front, 1st January 1944

Commander: Ivan Konev

4th Guards Army Commander I. Galanin, (from 6th January A.Ryzjov)	20th Guards Rifle Corps, 5th Guards Airborne Rifle Div, 66th Guards, 375th Rifle Division 21th Guards Rifle Corps, 69th Guards, 138th Rifle Division
Army units:	27th Anti-Aircraft Division, 33rd Anti-Tank Brigade, 452nd Anti-Tank Regiment, 466th Mortar Regiment, 48th Engineer Battalion
5th Guards Army Commander A. Zhadov	32nd Guards Rifle Corps, 6th Guards Airborne, 95th Guards, 97th Guards, 110th, Guards, 214th Rifle Division, 33rd Guards Rifle Corps, 9th Guards Airborne, 13th Guards, 111th Rifle Division, 35th Guards Rifle Corps, 93rd Guards, 94th Guards, 78th Rifle Division, 84th Rifle Division
Army units:	57th Guards Tank Regiment, 46th Light Artillery Brigade (16th Artillery Division), 91st heavy howitzer Artillery Brigade (13th Artillery Division), 29th Anti-Aircraft Division, 11th Anti-Tank Brigade, 34th Anti-Tank Brigade, 8th Guards Mortar Brigade, 27th Guards Rocket Artillery Brigade, 265th Guards Cannnon Artillery Regiment, 1327th Cannon Artillery Regiment, 301st Anti-Tank Regiment, 444th Anti-Tank Regiment, 469th Mortar Regiment, 308th Guards Rocket Artillery Regiment, 225.Guards Anti-Aircraft Regiment, 256th Engineer Battalion, 328th Engineer Battalion, 431st Engineer Battalion
7th Guards Army Commander M. Shumilov	24th Guards Rifle Corps, 8th Guards Airborne, 36th Guards, 41st Guards Rifle Division, 25th Guards Rifle Corps, 72nd Guards, 81st Guards, 409th Rifle Division 303rd Rifle Division
Army units:	27th Guards Tank Brigade, 34th Armoured Train Battalion, 38th Armoured Train Battalion, 11th Artillery Division (45th Can Art Brig, 40th How Art Brig), 5th Anti-Aircraft Division, 30th Anti-Tank Brigade, 161st Guards Cannon Artillery Regiment, 1110th Cannon Artillery Regiment, 114th Guards Anti-Tank Regiment, 115th Guards Anti-Tank Regiment, 1661st Anti-Tank Regiment, 1669th Anti-Tank Regiment, 263rd Mortar Reg, 290.Mtr Reg, 97.Guards Rocket Art Reg, 302.Guards Rocket Art Reg, 309.Guards Rocket Art Regiment, 162ndGuards Anti-Aircraft Regiment, 175th Engineer Battalion, 329th Engineer Battalion
37th Army Commander M. Sharokhin	27th Guards Rifle Corps, 48th Guards, 58th Guards Rifle Division, 57th Rifle Corps, 15th Guards, 29th Guards, 228th Rifle Division, 82nd Rifle Corps, 10th Guards Airborne, 28th Guards, 188th Rifle Division, 1st Guards Airborne Rifle Division
Army units:	61st Armoured Train Battalion, 42nd light Artillery Brigade (13th Artillery Division), 35th Anti-Aircraft Division, 10th Anti-Tank Brigade, 381st Cannon Artillery Regiment, 324th Anti-Tank Regiment, 1008th Anti-Tank Regiment, 562nd Mortar Regiment,315th Guards Rocket Artillery Regiment,8th Engineer Brigade,112th Engineer Battalion, 116th Engineer Battalion
52nd Army Commander K. Korotejev	73rd Rifle Corps, 7th Guards Airborne, 62nd Guards Rifle Division, 78th Rifle Corps 254th, 373rd Rifle Division, 294th Rifle Division
Army units:	173rdTank Brigade, 378th Tank Battalion, 379th Tank Battalion, 38th Anti-Aircraft Division, 568.Can Art Reg, 438th Anti-Tank Regiment, 1322nd Anti-Tank Regiment, 490th Mortar Regiment, 17th Guards Mortar Regiment, 366th Engineer Battalion, 32nd Ponton Battalion, 40th Ponton Battalion

53rd Army

Commander G. Tarassov, (from 5 January I. Galanin)

48th Rifle Corps, 14th Guards, 252nd, 299th Rifle Division, 75th Rifle Corps, 116th, 213th, 233rd Rifle Division

Army units.

34th Tank Regiment, 16th Artillery Division (61st Can Art Brig, 52nd How Art Brig, 90th Hvy How Art Brig, 14th Mtr Brig), 31st light Artillery Brigade (11th Artillery Division), 30th Anti-Aircraft Division, 6th Anti-Tank Brigade, 1328th Cannon Artillery Regiment, 232nd Anti-Tank Regiment, 1316th Anti-Tank Regiment, 461st Mortar Regiment, 89th Guards Rocket Artillery Regiment, 96th Guards Rocket Artillery Regiment, 11th Engineer Battalion, 17th Engineer Battalion

57th Army

Commander N. Gagen

49th Rifle Corps, 19th, 223rd Rifle Division, 64th Rifle Corps, 73rd Guards, 78th Guards, 52nd Rifle Division, 53rd Rifle Division

Support units:

96thTank Brigade, 374th Anti-Tank Regiment, 595th Anti-Tank Regiment, 523rd Mortar Regiment, 80th Guards Rocket Artillery Regiment, 258th Guards Anti-Aircraft Regiment, 71st Anti-Aircraft Regiment, 227th Anti-Aircraft Battalion, 251st Engineer Battalion, 252nd Engineer Battalion

5th Guards Tank Army

Commander P. Rotmistrov

18th Tank Corps (110th, 170th, 181stTank Brig, 32nd Mot Rifle Brig, 1438th, 1543rd SU Reg, 1000th AT-Reg, 292nd Mtr Reg, 1694th AA-Reg, 78th M/C Bn, 736th AT-Bn, 106th Guards Rocket Art Bn), 29th Tank Corps (25th, 31st, 32nd Tank Brig, 53rd Mot Rifle Brig, 1446th, 1549th SU Reg, 108th AT-Reg, 271st Mtr Reg, 75th M/C Bn, 11th Guards Rocket Art Bn), 8th Mech Corps (66th , 67th, 68th Mech Brig, 116th Tank Brig, 69th Tank Reg, 69th, 1822nd SU-Reg, 114th AT-Reg, 615th Mtr Reg, 1716th AA-Reg, 97th M/C Bn, 395th AT-Bn, 205th Guards Rocket Art Bn)

Army units:

53rd Guards Tank Regiment, 1st Guards M/C Regiment, 6th Anti-Aircraft Division, 678th Cannon Artillery Regiment, 689th Anti-Tank Regiment, 76th Guards Rocket Artillery Regiment, 377th Engineer Battalion

Front units:

26th Guards Rifle Corps, 25th Guards, 6th, 31st Rifle Division, 33rd Rifle Corps 50th, 297th Rifle Division, 5th Guards Mech Corps (24th Guards Tank Brig, 10th, 11th, 12th Guards Mech Brig, 104th Guards SU Reg, 1447th, 1529thSU Reg, 285th Mtr Reg, 2nd Guards M/C Bn, 737th AT-Bn, 409th Guards Rocket Art Bn)
1st Mech Corps (19th 35th , 37th Mech Brig, 219th Tank Brig, 75th AT-Reg, 294th Mtr Reg, 1382nd AA-Reg, 57th M/C Bn, 751st AT-Bn, 41st Guards Rocket Art Bn)
7th Mech Corps (16th, 34th, 64th Mech Brig, 41st Guards Tank Brig, 1440th, 1821st SU-Reg, 109th AT-Reg, 614th Mtr Reg, 1713th AA-Reg, 94th M/C Bn, 392nd AT-Bn, 40th Guards Rocket Art Bn), 20th Tank Corps (8th Guards, 80th, 155th Tank Brig, 7th Guards Mot Rifle Brig, 1834th, 1895th SU-Reg, 1505th AT-Reg, 291st Mtr Reg, 1711th AA-Reg, 69th M/C Bn, 735th AT-Bn, 406th Guards Rocket Art Bn)
5thGuards Cavalry Corps (11th Guards, 12th Guards, 63rdCavalry Division)

Support units:

167.Tank Reg, 10.Arm Train Bn, 109.Super Hvy How Art Brig (16.Art Div), 11th Anti-Aircraft Division, 26th Anti-Aircraft Division, 27.Can Art Brig, 1073rd Anti-Tank Regiment, 303rd Guards Rocket Artillery Regiment, 5th Engineer Brigade, 60th Engineer Brigade, 14.Assault Engineer Brigade, 27th Special Purpose Engineer Brigade, 1st Ponton Brigade, 1st Ponton Regiment, 8th Ponton Regiment, 6th Ponton Battalion, 7.Ponton Battalion, 19th Ponton Battalion, 125th Ponton Battalion, 69th Engineer Battalion, 246th Engineer Battalion, 247th Engineer Battalion, 248th Engineer Battalion, 250th Engineer Battalion

German Order of Battle for 8th Army, 5th January 1944

Commander: Otto Wöhler

LII. Korps

Commander E. Buschenhagen

Divisions:	13th Panzer Division, 2nd Fallschirmsjaeger Division, 76th, 384th Infantry Division
Corps troops:	Artillery Commander 137, 612th Artillery Regimental Staff for special purpose (mot), II./Artillery Regiment 52. (with 2 btys 10cm K, 1 bty 15 cm sFH) (mot), III./Artillery Regiment 40. (with 2 btys 15 cm sFH, 1 bty 10cm K) (mot), I./Artillery Regiment 735. (without.2nd bty) (mot), II./Artillery Regiment 54. (IFH) (mot), I./Artillery Regiment 77. (IFH) (mot), 934th Artillery Battalion (IFH) (mot), 935th Artillery Battalion (IFH) (mot), 1st bty/731st Artillery Battalion (15cm K) (mot), III./Rocket Artillery Regiment 55, 21st Panzer Rocket Artillery battery, 203rd & 286th Assault Gun Battalion, 52nd light Artillery Observation Battalion, 66th Position Artillery Observation Battalion, 107th Construction Regiment, 620th Mountain Engineer Regiment (mot), 255th & 651st Engineer Battalion (mot), 246th Construction Battalion, II./43rd Anti-Aircraft Battalion, 669th hvy Anti-Tank Battalion, 662nd hvy Anti-Tank Battalion (without 2nd Coy)

XXXXVII. Panzer Korps

Commander N. von Vormann

Divisions:	11th Panzer Division, 14th Panzer Division (with Alarmgroup167.ID), 10th Panzergrenadier Division, 3rd Panzer Division, 376th Infantry Division, 106th Infantry Division, 320th Infantry Division (with rest of SS-Cav Reg 15.), 167.ID (only staff and supply troops)
Corps troops:	Artillery Commander 130., 781st Artillery Regimental Staff for special purpose (mot), I./ Artillery Regiment 108. (IFH) (mot), II./ Artillery Regiment 818. (IFH) (mot), III./ Artillery Regiment 818. (IFH) (mot), I./ Artillery Regiment SS-Cav Div, 3rd battery/857th heavy Artillery Battalion (21cm Mörs), 7th battery /52nd Rocket Artillery Regiment, 228th Assault Gun Battalion, 911th Assault Gun Battalion, 8thTank Destroyer Battalion (Stug), 13th light Artillery Observation Battalion, I./31.Panzer Battalion (Panther), 678th Engineer Regiment (mot), 217th Construction Battalion, 127th Engineer Battalion (mot), 18th Penal Battalion

XI. Korps

Commander W. Stemmermann

Divisions:	SS-Wiking, 389th Infantry Division, 57th Infantry Division, 72nd Infantry Division (with Inf Rgt 331., II./A.R. 238), 282nd Infantry Division (with Inf Rgt 315., 339., Füs Bn167., I./AR 40)
Corps troops:	Artillery Commander 411, 842nd Artillery Battalion (10cm K) (mot), 8th battery / Artillery Regiment 139. (sFH) (mot), 2nd battery /800th heavy Artillery Battalion (15cm K) (mot), II./52nd Rocket Artillery Regiment, 261st Assault Gun Battalion, 905th Assault Gun Battalion, 44th light Artillery Observation Battalion, 67th Position Artillery Observation Battalion, 601st Engineer Regiment (mot), 666th Engineer Battalion (mot), 155. (K) & 410.Construction Battalion
Army troops:	444th Security Division, Higher Art Commander 310., 52nd Rocket Art Regiment (only staff), 31st light Artillery Observation Battalion, 68th Position Artillery Observation Battalion, 857th hvy Art Battalion (without 3rd battery), III./Art Reg 139. (without 8.battery), 472nd Tank Hunter Battalion (Panzerschreck), 616th Anti-Aircraft Battalion, 300th Anti-Aircraft Battalion, 545th Construction Regiment for special purpose, 52nd Engineer Battalion (mot), 923rd Bridge Column, 41st & 531st Bridge Construction Battalion, 112nd Construction Battalion, 676th Road Construction Battalion, 10th Penal Battalion, 17th Anti-Aircraft Division (12.AA Regiment with 541., 251., I./38., le 775. AA Battalion.)

Soviet Order of Battle for the Korsun-Shevchnkovskii Operation

Order of Battle for the Forces from the 1st Ukrainian Front, 25th January, 1944

27th Army	180th, 206th and 337th Rifle Division, 54th and 159th Fortified Region
Support units:	298th Guards SU Regiment, 713th and 1892nd SU Regiment, 881st Anti-Tank Regiment, 480th and 492nd Mortar Regiment, 329th Guards Rocket Artillery Regiment, 25nd and 38th Engineer battalion, 21st Ponton battalion.
40th Army ((50th and 51st Rifle Corps covering Army`s right flank)	
47th Rifle Corps	167th and 359th Rifle Division, 104th Rifle Corps, 58th and 133rd Rifle Division
50th Rifle Corps	4th Guards Airborne, 38th, 240th and 340th Rifle Division
51st Rifle Corps	42nd Guards, 163rd and 232nd Rifle Division, 74th and 136th Rifle Division
Support units:	1898th SU Regiment, 33rd Cannon Artillery Brigade, 111th Guards and 1528th Howitzer Artillery Regiment, 28th Anti-tank Brigade, 4th Guards, 317th Guards and 690th Anti-Tank Regiment, 9th and 10th Mountain Mortar Regiment, 493rd Mortar Regiment, 9th Anti-Aircraft Division (with 800th, 974th, 981st and 993rd Anti-Aircraft Regiment)
6th Tank Army 5th Mechanized Corps	(with 2nd, 9th and 45th Mech brigade, 233rd Tank brigade, 745th and 1228th SU reg, 1827th Hvy SU reg, 64th M/C bn, 458th Mtr reg, 35th Gds Rocket Art bn, 1700th AA reg.)
5th Guards Tank Corps	(with 20th Gds, 21st Gds and 22nd Gds Tank brigade, 6th Gds Mot Rifle brigade, 1416th, 1458th and 1462nd SU reg, 80th M/C bn, 1667th AT reg, 754th AT bn, 454th Mtr reg, 1696th AA reg)
Support units:	156th Tank regiment, 57th Guards Rocket Artillery Regiment, 181st Engineer battalion.

Order of Battle for Forces from the 2nd Ukrainian Front, 25th January, 1944.

52nd Army 73rd Rifle Corps 78th Rifle Corps	 254th and 294th Rifle Division 373rd Rifle Division
Support units:	1322nd Anti-Tank regiment, 38th Anti-Aircraft Division (with 1401st, 1405th, 1409th and 1712nd AA reg), 366th Engineer Battalion.
53rd Army 26th Guards Rifle Corps 48th Rifle Corps 75th Rifle Corps	 1st Guards Airborne, 25th Guards and 6th Rifle Division 14th Guards, 66th Guards and 89th Guards Rifle Division 138th, 213th, 233rd Rifle Division, 214th Rifle Division
Support units:	189th Tank regiment, 63rd and 122nd Anti-Tank Rifle battalion, 16th Breakthrough Artillery Division (with 61st Cannon Artillery Brigade, 52nd Howitzer Artillery

Brigade, 90th Hvy Howitzer Artillery Brigade, 109th Super-hvy Howitzer Artillery Brigade, 14th Mortar Brigade), 31st Light Artillery Brigade (from 11th Artillery Division), 1327th Cannon Artillery Regiment, 33rd Anti-Tank Brigade, 1316th Anti-Tank Regiment, 461st Mortar Regiment, 30th Anti-Aircraft Division (with 1361st, 1367th, 1373rd and 1375th AA reg), 11th and 13th Engineer Battalion.

4th Guards Army

20th Guards Rifle Corps	5th and 7th Guards Airborne, 62nd Guards, 31st Rifle Division
21st Guards Rifle Corps	69th Guards, 252nd and 375th Rifle Division
Support units:	175th Tank Brigade, 57th and 60th Tank Regiment, 42nd Light Artillery brigade (from 13th Br.Art Div), 97th and 98th Heavy Howitzer Artillery Brigade, 568th and 1328th Cannon Artillery Regiment, 438th and 452nd Anti-Tank Regiment, 466th Mortar Regiment, 27th Anti-Aircraft Division (with 1354th, 1358th, 1364th and 1370th AA reg). 27th Assault Engineer Battalion (from 6.Ass Eng brig), 48th and 69th Engineer Battalion.

5th Guards Tank Army

18th Tank Corps	(with 110th, 170th and 181st Tank brigade, 32nd Mot Rifle brig, 1438th SU reg, 1543rd Hvy SU reg, 78th M/C bn, 1000th AT reg, 736th AT bn, 292nd Mtr reg, 106th Gds Rocket Art bn, 1694th AA reg)
20th Tank Corps	(with 8th Gds, 80th and 155th Tank brigade, 7th Gds Mot Rifle brig, 1834th Hvy SU reg, 1895th SU reg, 96th M/C bn, 1505th AT reg, 735th AT bn, 291st Mtr reg, 406th Gds Rocket Art bn, 1711th AA reg)
29th Tank Corps	(with 25th, 31st and 32nd Tank brigade, 53rd Mot Rifle brig, 1446th SU reg, 1549th Hvy SU reg, 75th M/C bn, 108th AT reg, 271th Mtr reg, 11th Gds Rocket Art bn)
Support units:	53rd Guards Tank Regiment, 1st Guards M/C Regiment, 678th Howitzer Artillery Regiment, 689th Anti-Tank Regiment, 6th Anti-Aircraft Division (with 146th, 366th, 516th and 1062nd AA -Regiment), 377th Engineer Battalion.
Front Reserves	5th Guards Cavalry Corps (with 11th Guards, 12th Guards, 63rd Cavalry Division, 1896th SU reg, 150th Gds AT reg, 5th Gds AT bn, 72nd Gds Mtr bn, 9th Gds Rocket Art reg, 585th AA reg), 2nd Anti-Tank brigade, 804th Anti-Aircraft regiment

Order of Battle for 2nd Tank Army 1st February 1944

2nd Tank Army

3rd Tank Corps	(with 50th, 51st and 103rd Tank brigade, 57th Mot Rifle brigade, SU reg (w/o number), 1540th and1818th SU reg, 74th M/C bn, 728th AT bn, 234th Mtr reg, 126th Gds Rocket Art bn, 121st AA reg)
16th Tank Corps	(with 107th, 109th and 164th Tank brigade, 15th Mot Rifle brigade, 1441st and 1542nd SU reg, 51st M/C bn, 298th Gds AT reg, 729th AT bn, 226th Mtr reg, 89th Gds Rocket Art bn, 1721st AA reg.)
Support units:	11th Guards Tank Brigade, 87th M/C Regiment, 86th Gds Rocket Artillery Regiment, 357th Engineer Battalion

German Order of Battle, 25th January, 1944

Left Flank of 8th Army

Commander: Otto Wöhler

XI. Korps

SS-Wiking (includes SS-Wallonien), 57th , 72nd and 389th Infantry Division (includes part of 167th Infantry Division)

Support units: Artillery Commander 411., 842nd Artillery Battalion, I./108th Artillery Regiment, 2nd battery /800th Artillery Battalion, 228th Assault Gun Battalion, 601st Engineer Regimental Staff (mot), 666th Engineer Battalion (mot), 155th (K) and 410th Construction Battalion

XXXXVII. Pz.Korps

3rd, 11th and 14th Panzer Division, 106th and 320th Infantry Division, 167th Infantry Division (only HQ and supply troops)

Support units: Artillery Commander 130., II./818th Artillery Regiment, III./140th Artillery Regiment (without 7th bty), 3rd battery/ 735th Artillery Battalion, 8th battery /139th Artillery Regiment, 3rd battery /857th Artillery Battalion, 203rd, 905th and 911th Assault Gun Battalion, 8th Tank Battalion (Stug III), 678th Engineer Regimental Staff, 217th Construction Battalion, 18th Penal Battalion

Right Flank of 1st Panzer Army

Commander: Hans Hube

XXXXII. Korps

Corps-Detachment B, 88th Infantry Division

Support units: Artillery Commander 107., I./248th Artillery Regiment (from 168th Infantry Division), 417th Infantry Battalion (from 168th Infantry Division), 318th Security Regiment, 4th Engineer Regimental Staff (mot)

VII. Korps

34th, 75th, 82nd, 198th Infantry Division

Support units: Artillery Commander 124., 617th Artillery Regiment for special purpose, I./84th Artillery Regiment, 625th Artillery Battery, II./62nd Artillery Regiment, 202nd and 239th Assault Gun Battalion, 685th Engineer Regimental Staff (mot), 215th Engineer Battalion, 135th Construction Battalion, 677th Infantry Battalion (from Corps Det. B)

Order of Battle of the Encircled German Forces, 3rd February, 1944

XXXXII. Korps	SS-Wiking (with SS-Wallonien), Corps-Detachment B, 88th Infantry Division (with 2 bns from 213th Security Division, 1 bn from 168th Infantry Division)
Support units:	Artillery Commander 107., 239th Assault Gun Battalion, 26th Engineer Regimental Staff (mot), 213th Engineer Battalion (mot)
XI. Korps	57th, 72nd and 389th Infantry Division
Support units:	Artillery Commander 411., 842nd Artillery Battalion (10cm Cannon), I./108th Artillery Regiment (10,5cm How), 2nd battery /800th heavy Artillery Battalion (15cm Cannon), 228th Assault Gun Battalion, 601st Engineer Regimental Staff (mot), 666th Engineer Battalion (mot), 155th (K) & 410th Construction Battalion

III Panzer Korps Order of Battle, 2nd February, 1944

Divisions.	16. Pz.Div. plus attached s.Pz.Abt. 506, Brüko (J) 848 and 34. Inf.Div. (minus I./Art.Rgt. 34) 17. Pz.Div. plus attached 198.Inf.Div.,Stu.Gesch.Abt. 249, Brüko (J) 843 and two b Batteries from Korps-Abt. B (8. and 11./Art.Rgt. 86)
Directly subordinated to III. Pz.Korps	Art.Rgt.Stab z.b.V. 617, II./Art.Rgt. 62 (10 cm Kan), II./Art.Rgt. 67 (s.F.H.), s.Art.Abt. 628 (21 cm Mrs.), I./Art.Rgt. 34, II./Art.Rgt. 182, 2./Art.Rgt. 84 (17 cm Kan), Werfer-Brig. 1 (with s.Werf.Rgt. 1, Werf.Rgt. 54 & 57), Pi.Rgt.Stab (mot) 674, Pi.Btl. 127 (mot), Pi.Btl. 627 (mot), Eisb.Pz.Zug. 62
Corps troops.	Arko 3, Pz.Korps-Nachr.Abt. 43, Feldg.Trupp 403, Korps-Kos.Kp.
Comments:	*The 34. and 198. Inf.Div. were subordinated to the panzer divisions for the breakthrough phase.*
Source:	*III. Pz.Korps Ia Nr. 191/44, "Gliederung des III. Pz.Korps am 2.2.1944", NARA T314, R208, F000417.*

III Panzer Corps Order of Battle, 5th February 1944.

Divisions.	16. Pz.Div. plus attached s.Pz.Abt. 506, Brüko (J) 848 and II./Art.Rgt. 67 (s.F.H.) 17. Pz.Div plus attached s.Pz.Rgt.Bäke (with s.Pz.Abt. 503 and II./Pz.Rgt. 23) Stu.Gesch.Abt. 249, Brüko (J) 843 and II./Art.Rgt. 62 (10 cm Kan) 1. SS-Pz.Div.198. Inf.Div. plus attached 8./Art.Rgt. 86 (from Korps-Abt. B), 11./Art.Rgt. 86 (from Korps-Abt. B), F.E.B. 34 and F.E.B. 75, 34. Inf.Div. plus attached I./Gren.Rgt. 168, II./Art.Rgt. 182 Kampfgruppe Huppert from 1. Pz.Div. consisting of: II./Pz.Rgt. 1, II./Pz.Gren.Rgt. 1, Pz.A.A. 1 (except 3. Kp.) and I./Pz.Art.Rgt. 73
Directly subordinated to III. Pz.Korps	Art.Rgt.Stab z.b.V. 617, s.Art.Abt. 628 (21 cm Mrs.), 2./Art.Rgt. 84 (17 cm Kan), Werfer-Brig. 1 (with s.Werf.Rgt. 1, Werf.Rgt. 54 & 57), Pi.Rgt.Stab (mot) 674, Pi.Btl. 127 (mot), Pi.Btl. 627 (mot), Eisb.Pz.Zug. 62
Corps troops.	Arko 3, Pz.Korps-Nachr.Abt. 43, Feldg.Trupp 403, Korps-Kos.Kp.
Source:	*III. Pz.Korps Ia Nr. 216/44, "Gliederung des III. Pz.Korps am 5.2.1944", NARA T314, R208, F000518.*

Appendix II

GERMAN COMBAT UNITS IN THE BATTLE

This appendix presents all the information available on the condition and organization of the German units that took part in the battle.

We have opted to retain the German terminology as far as possible in this appendix, since often there is no direct translation available in English. Some terms that often appear in German strength returns and might need clarification are:[1]

Verpflegungsstärke	Ration strength, i. e. the number of men the unit was ordered to provide with necessary substance. Thus it could include sick, wounded, prisoners of war, non-military manpower and manpower from other military organisations.
Kopfstärke	This is a rather unusual term but it seems to be used to depict the same kind of strength as Verpflegungsstärke.
Iststärke	Actual strength, includes all men that are part of the units composition. Men on leave or temporarily detached to other units are included. Also men sick or wounded are included if they are assumed to return to service within eight weeks. Thus, despite its name, this strength category does not give the actual number of men available for service with the unit at the given time.
Tagesstärke	Daily strength, this includes all men momentarily available for service with the unit. Temporarily attached personnel is included too.
Gefechtstärke	Combat strength, i.e. the number of fit men in units of combat type, e. g. armour, infantry, combat engineer, reckon etc.
Kampfstärke	Front strength, i. e. those men in units of combat type who were up front, e. g. tank crews, rifle men, anti-tank gun crews, etc.

For the condition of battalions, another set of terms is used. The strength of battalions are often given by using the following terms[2]:

Starkes Battailon	Kampfstärke more than 400 men
Mittelstarkes Battailon	Kampfstärke 300–400 men
Durchschnittliches Battailon	Kampfstärke 200–300 men
Schwaches Battailon	Kampfstärke 100–200 men
Abgekäpftes Battailon	Kampfstärke less than 100 men

In the following pages we show the units in alphabetical order, with numbered units after those that only had a name or letter for identification. This appendix does not claim to give a complete coverage of the units involved, even though we have included all units shown in the organization charts of the armies and corps involved in the battle. However, the amount of information available on each unit varies considerably.

Divisions and Brigades

Korps-Abt. B

Korps-Abteilung B had been formed around the staff of 112th Infantry Division. To this was added elements from the 112th, 255th and 332nd Infantry Divisions.[3] These three formed "Divisions-Gruppen" within the Korps-Abteilung: Div.Gr. 112 with Rgts.Gr. 110 and 258, Div.Gr. 255 with Rgts.Gr. 465 and 475, Div.Gr. 332 with Rgts.Gr. 677 and 678. It is worth noting that the Regiments-gruppen were also referred to as the battalion that had provided most of its composition:[4]

Rgts.Gr. 110: III./Inf.Rgt. 110

Rgts.Gr. 258: II./Inf.Rgt. 258

Rgts.Gr. 465: I./Inf.Rgt. 465

Rgts.Gr. 475: III./Inf.Rgt. 465

Rgts.Gr. 677: I./Inf.Rgt. 475

Rgts.Gr. 678: II./Inf.Rgt. 475

When the battle began, the Rgts.Gr. 677 had been attached to 34. Inf.Div. The other five were with the Korps-Abteilung and four of them were rated as *mittelstark* and one as *durchschnittlich*.[5]

The Korps-Abt. also had a Füsilier battalion (from 112. Inf.Div.) which was rated strong.[6]

The engineer battalion was rated *schwach* and the field replacement battalion *mittelstark*.[7]

In addition to Rgts.Gr. 677, the Korps-Abt. B had sent away part of its artillery and its anti-tank guns. What remained was five batteries with 10.5 cm howitzers, three with captured Russian 7.62 cm guns and two batteries with 15 cm howitzers. It retained eleven medium anti-tank guns and five heavy (motor drawn).[8]

At the beginning of the battle, Korps-Abt. B was subordinated to XXXXII. Korps, but was soon forced to send some of its units to the ad hoc formation "Sperrverband Fouquet." It seems that 4,831 officers and men from the Korps-Abteilung B, plus 382 HiWi, managed to break out from the pocket.[9] Also 1,597 soliders who had returned from leave had assembled in Novo Ukrainka, Novo Archangelsk and Uman.[10] Probably there were further men who had been outside the pocket when the Soviet pincers closed.

Pz.Gren.Div. "Grossdeutschland"

Some books claim that elements of the Grossdeutschland Division took part in the Korsun battle. However, this seems to be a mistake, caused by the fact that some officers—e.g. Büsing and Wallroth from the Grossdeutschland—were involved. No combat units from the division seems to have reached the battlefield.

SS-Sturm Brigade "Wallonien"

Commander: Lt-Colonel Lucien Lippert (KIA)
Major Léon Degrelle

Formed from "Freiwillige Legion Wallonien" (verstärkt III. (Jäger) Battalion / 373.Infantry Regiment / 97.Jaeger Division) summer 1943. The brigade arrived on the Eastern Front and Army Group South in November 1943. It consisted of one infantry battalion, with a number of supporting companies. The infantry battalion had three infantry companies—each with 18 light MG, 2 heavy MG and 2 mortars—and a heavy company with 8 heavy MG and 6 mortars. The supporting companies included a Infanteriegeschütz company with four 7.5 cm infantry howitzers and two 15 cm infantry howitzers, the AT gun company had nine 7.5 cm Pzk 40, the light Flak company had 12 light Flak guns and the heavy Flak company had four 8.8 cm Flak guns and finally there was an assault gun company with 10 StuG III. The brigade had an authorized strength of 1,967 and on 1 January 1944 it was short of 199.[11]

Probably most of the brigade was encircled in the pocket. It seems that about 650 men from the brigade escaped during the breakout.

1. Pz.Div.

Commander: Generalmajor Richard Koll

The division was formed in 1935. It returned to Eastern Front in November 1943 from deployment in Greece. It had been fighting with Army Group South since then. The division was subordinated to 4th Panzer Army when the Red Army initiated the Korsun operation. Soon it was decided to transfer the 1. Pz.Div. to III. Pz.Korps for the relief of

Gruppe Stemmermann. However, it took time to relieve the 1. Pz.Div. and it arrived piecemeal. This is also reflected in the tank strength returns given below, as they only refer to operational tanks with the division employed for this operation. On 5 February the division had 33 Pz IV and 51 Panther operational.[12]

First to arrive was Kampfgruppe Huppert, which consisted of one Pz IV battalion (II./Pz.Rgt. 1), one panzer grenadier battalion (II./ Pz.Gren.Rgt. 1), the reconnaissance battalion, minus one company (Pz. Aufkl.Abt. 1 ohne 3. Kp.) and the SP artillery battalion (I./Pz.Art.Rgt. 73).[13] On 6 February elements of the division made contact with the enemy.[14]

The division was quite strong. According to its monthly report to the Inspector-general of Panzer troops, it had 39 Pz IV and 29 Panthers operational on 1 February and also 1 Pz IV and 7 Panthers in short term repair.[15]

Operational Tanks During the Operation:

6 February (early)	16: 30 Pz IV
7 February 17:	18 Pz IV, 2 Pz III (Bef)
9 February (early) 18:	18 Pz IV, 2 Pz III (Bef), 48 Panther, 1 Panther (Bef)
9 February (late) 19:	18 Pz IV, 48 Panther
10 February 20:	18 Pz IV, 48 Panther
13 February (early) 21:	12 Pz IV, 18 Panther
15 February (early) 22:	11 Pz IV, 9 Panther fully operational, 3 Panthers conditionally combat ready and four with only machine guns operational (probably caused by ammunition shortages due to supply difficulties).

The division did not suffer unduly during the relief attempt of Gruppe Stemmerman. Its casualties 1–20 February 1944 amounted to 35 killed in action, 212 wounded and 3 missing.[23]

Tank losses seem to have been more extensive. On 24 February it was reported that the division had lost 27 Panthers and 9 Pz IV. Of these, 9 Panthers and four Pz IV's had been knocked out by enemy fire. Also one Pz IV hit a mine and caught fire, causing a complete loss, while three further Panthers were also damaged by mines and subsequently blown up since they could not be towed away. Twelve Panthers and four Pz IV's suffered mechanical breakdowns and were subsequently blown up due to recovery difficulties in the mud. Finally two Panthers and one

Pz III got bogged down in the Lisyanka ford and could not be towed away. They were also blown up.[24]

However, as the III Panzer Corps retreated from the positions it had taken during its offensive, more damaged tanks had to be blown up as they could not be towed away in time. Eventually 51 tanks were irrevocably lost, as they were blown up before the advancing Soviet forces.[25]

1. SS-Pz.Div. "Leibstandarte SS Adolf Hitler"

LSSAH ("Leibstandarte SS Adolf Hitler") was formed as division in the summer of 1942. After *Operation Zitadelle* in the summer 1943 the division went to Italy for a short period before it returned the Eastern Front and Army Group South in October 1943. The division had been almost continuously engaged in action since its return. The 1. SS-Pz.Div. did not arrive in time to participate in the initial assault launched by III. Pz.Korps on 4 February, but elements of the division were employed, as soon as they arrived, to cover the left flank of the attacking 16. and 17. Pz.Div. The armor of the division included a Panther battalion, a Pz IV battalion, an assault gun battalion and a company with Tiger tanks.

Operational Tanks During the Operation:

2 February:[26]	16 Pz IV, 29 Panther, 3 Tiger, 22 StuG
3 February:[27]	In assembly area: 13 Pz IV, 11 Panther, 3 Tiger, 18 StuG III, 1 StuH III; En route: 9 Pz IV, 18 Panther, 3 Tiger
6 February (early):[28]	22 Pz IV, 29 Panther, 6 Tiger, 27 StuG III, 3 StuH III
6 February (late):[29]	7 Pz IV, 8 Panther, 4 Tiger, 12 StuG III, 1 StuH III
7 February:[30]	? Pz IV, 8 Panther, 4 Tiger, 10 StuG III, 1 StuH III
9 February:[31]	3 Pz IV, 3 Panther, 1 Tiger, 6 assault guns
10 February:[32]	3 Pz IV, 3 Panther, 1 Tiger, 6 assault guns
13 February (early):[33]	4 Pz IV, 3 Panther, 1 Tiger, 5 StuG III
15 February (early):[34]	4 Pz IV, 4 Panther, 1 Tiger, 5 StuG III

The division suffered only moderately during the relief attempt of Gruppe Stemmerman. Its casualties 1–20 February 1944 amounted to 82 killed in action, 219 wounded and 17 missing.[35]

Like many other units, mud took a heavy toll on the Leibstandarte's vehicles. On 7 February it reported that SS-Pz.Aufkl.Abt. 1 and III./

(gep.) SS-Pz.Gren.Rgt. 1 had to be employed as infantry as all the vehicles of these two battalions were inoperable.[36] The situation hardly improved. On 25 February the division reported that it had 1,392 trucks, 457 cars, 376 motorcycles and 115 prime movers in workshops, requiring major repairs.[37]

During the operation the division lost six Panthers, one Pz IV, ten StuG III and two Marder. It also lost one Wespe, one medium AT gun and one armored car.[38] Of the Panthers, none had been destroyed by enemy gun fire. Two had been damaged by enemy gun fire (at Tinovka and Lisyanka) and one had run on a mine at Oktyabr, but had to be blown up when the Germans retreated, as they could not be towed away.[39] Two had developed fires in the engine room, at Lisyanka and Rubannyi Most, respectively, and subsequently blown up.[40] Finally one had suffered from clutch problems at Lisyanka and had to be blown up.[41] On 22 January the Leibstandarte had three Panthers, four assault guns and one Pz IV operational,[42] but it also had 8 Tigers, 42 Panthers, 32 Pz IV and 13 StuG III in workshops.[43]

3. Pz.Div.

Commander: Lieutenant-General Fritz Bayerlein (—January 1944)
Oberst Lang

The division was formed in 1935. When *Operation Barbarossa* was launched on 22 June 1941 the 3rd Panzer Division participated and it had remained on the Eastern Front since that time.

Due to shortages of riflemen, the 3. Pz.Div. only had three combat ready infantry battalions on 22 January, two of them rated as *durchschnittlich* and one as *schwach*.[44] But the manpower problems were not new to the division. Its casualties were relatively modest during January, with 183 killed in action 539 wounded and 31 missing.[45] Hence shortages must have been a problem in late 1943 as well. The division only received 360 replacements and 173 returning convalescents during January.[46]

The division could only be described as partially motorized. The Germans rated the mobility in percent of the establishment transport capacity. On 22 January, the division was rated at only 36%, but the combat elements were somewhat better off.[47] There were two reasons for this: first there was a shortage of vehicles, but also shortages of spare parts caused many of the vehicles on hand to be inoperable.[48]

The division was also weak in tanks and only had one panzer battalion. It had 4 Pz IV and 4 Pz III operational on 1 January,[49] but otherwise its strength before 25 January is not known. By 1 February it had 18 Pz IV and 2 Pz III operational, plus 10 Pz IV and 3 Pz III in workshops expected to be repaired within three weeks.[50] This can be compared to the fact that it had 10 Pz IV and 2 Pz III operational on 1 January, with another 22 Pz IV and 4 Pz III in workshops expected to be repaired within three weeks.[51] Twenty new Pz IV were sent to the division on 21 December 1943,[52] but probably these arrived before 1 January 1944.

The Following Heavy Weapons were Available to the Division:

On 22 January:	6 Wespe, 3 Hummel, 10 10.5 cm howitzers, 3 15 cm howitzers, 5 8.8 cm Flak guns, 5 Marders, 4 7.5 cm AT guns and 1 5 cm AT gun.[53]
On 4 February:	12 Pz IV and 2 BW operational.[54]
On 13 February:	1 Pz III (7,5), 14 Pz IV, 1 BW were operational.[55]

Its equipment losses during the battle included 26 tanks, 8 tank destroyers, 4 8.8 cm Flak, 4 Wespe, 3 Hummel, 12 10.5 cm howitzers, 8 15 cm howitzers. To a significant degree, this was due to the lack of towing vehicles, which meant that equipment with slight damage or that had just bogged down in mud had to be abandoned.[56]

5. SS-Pz.Div. "Wiking"

Commander: SS-Brigadeführer Gille

This division had been formed late 1940 as a motorized infantry division. Wiking had been fighting on the Eastern Front since 22 June 1941 during which time the division lost one of it's infantry regiments (Nordland) and had acquired a panzer battalion. By October 1943 its official designation was 5.SS-Panzer Division.

The division had been in action for much of summer 1943 and most of the fall, and was seriously depleted by the beginning of 1944. On 1 January it reported that it had 15 Pz III, 11 Pz IV and 4 StuG III operational. Also, it had 4 Pz III and 2 Pz IV in workshops.[57] Since it did not recieve any new tanks during January 1944,[58] this sets the upper limit on the number of tanks it possessed on 25 January 1944.

By 16 February the division was still comparitively strong. It had five Pz III, two Pz IV and three StuG operational. Its artillery remained strong, with 25 le.FH 18, 6 s.FH 18, 4 10 cm K 18, 9 Wespe, 3 Hummel, all in all 47 artillery tubes.[59]

Hardly anything of their heavy equipment made it out of the pocket, but 8,253 officers and men, plus 25 HiWi, managed to break out.[60] Also about 1,500 soldiers were with the SS-Totenkopf Division further east.[61] Probably there were further men who had been outside the pocket when the Soviet pincers closed.

11. Pz.Div.

Commander: Gen.Maj. von Wietersheim

The division was formed after the fall of France in 1940. The panzer regiment in the new division came from 5th Panzer Division. The division had been on the Eastern Front since 22 June 1941.

On 20 January, the I./Pz.Rgt. 15 had 8 operational Panthers and 39 in workshops.[62] At the same time the I./Pz.Rgt. 31 had 11 operational Panthers and 28 in workshops.[63] The latter was ordered to hand over its Panthers to 11. Pz.Div.[64] This gave the division a total of 86 Panthers, but of these most were in workshops. It is doubtful that a significant number of them were repaired before the Soviet offensive began, since the division was seriously short of spare parts and recovery vehicles.[65]

The II. Abt. of the Panzer regiment seems to have been weak. On 1 January the division reported that it had five Pz III and two Pz IV operational, plus ten Pz IV in short term repair (repairable within three weeks).[66] This had changed little until 1 February, when it reported no operational Pz III, two operational Pz IV and seven and eight Pz III and Pz IV respectively in short term repair (repairable within three weeks).[67] During January no Pz III or Pz IV were shipped to the division,[68] thus it seems unlikely that the division had more than a handful combat ready Pz III and Pz IV on 25 January, especially since the division was involved in the Kirovograd battle in mid-January.

The division was fairly strong in manpower. On 22 January it had a ration strength of 12,305, but that included some non-divisional units.[69] Its infantry regiments had a ration strength of 1,100–1,200 men and a combat strength (*Gefechtsstärke*) of 605 and 412 respectively.[70]

The manpower situation remained much the same on 1 February, when the division had an authorized strength of 16,250, but a shortage of 3,786.[71] Casualties during January amounted to 220 killed in action, 704 wounded and 77 missing. Also 11 officers and 419 other ranks had been evacuated due to disease and another 490 had left the division for other reasons. The 276 replacements and 34 convalescents the division received during the month was insufficient to remedy the situation.[72]

The division reported five Panthers operational on 1 February.[73]

On 22 January the division had 14 10.5 cm howitzers, 6 15 cm howitzers and 6 10 cm guns. Also it had 4 8.8 cm Flak guns.[74]

Tank Strength (Operational Vehicles) During the Operation:

27 January:[75]	12 Panther, 3 Pz IV
4 February:[76]	21 Panther, 8 StuG (includes I./Pz.Rgt. 26 and probably 911. StuG.Abt. too)
13 February:[77]	8 Panther, 1 Pz IV, 1 StuG (includes I./Pz.Rgt. 26, Pz.Abt 8, StuG.Abt 911)
14 February:[78]	3 operational tanks
15 February (morning):[79]	6 operational tanks
1 March:[80]	10 Panther, 4 Pz III and 3 command tanks (also 54 Panthers, 7 Pz IV, 2 Pz III and 1 command tank in workshops)

13. Pz.Div.

Commander: Generalmajor Hans Mikosch

Hitler wanted more panzer divisions after the campaign in France so the 13th Motorized Infantry Division from Magdeburg was given a panzer regiment from 2nd Panzer Division and become 13th Panzer Division. The division had been fighting on the Eastern Front since *Operation Barbarossa* was launched.

On 28 January it was decided to send the 13. Pz.Div. to XXXXVII. Pz.Korps and on 1 February the 13.Pz.Div. went into action.[81]

The 13. Pz.Div. was very weak in tanks. On 1 February it only had seven Pz III and eleven Pz IV operational. Also it possessed three Pz III and one Pz IV that were in workshops and expected to be repaired within three weeks. In fact it had almost as many self-propelled AT guns, seventeen Marders operational and two in repair.[82]

In terms of manpower, the division was little better off. Its authorized strength was 15,373, including 1,214 HiWi, but it was short of 4,152 officers and men (including 191 HiWi).[83]

Artillery was in better supply. The division had six Hummel (15 cm SP Arty) operational plus two in repair. Also it had nine Wespe (10.5 cm SP Arty) operational and one in repair. Altogether, the division had 27 artillery pieces operational and 8 in repair.[84]

Tank Strength (Operational Vehicles) During the Operation:

4 February:[85]	5 Pz IV, 1 Pz III, 1 BW
13 February:[86]	3 Pz IV, 2 BW
1 March:[87]	5 Pz IV, 1 Pz III, 1 BW (also 7 Pz IV, 3 Pz III and 2 BW in workshops)

14. Pz.Div.

Commander: Generalmajor Martin Unrein

By reinforcing and reorganizing the 4th Infantry Division, the 14th Panzer Division was formed. The division was destroyed at Stalingrad but from the remnants (wounded outside the Stalingrad pocket, soldiers on leave, etc.) of the "old division" a new 14th Panzer Division was formed. The division arrived at the Eastern Front (Army Group South) in October 1943.

The 14. Pz.Div. was in reserve on the morning of 25 January, in the Slatopol–Novo Mirgorod area, but became subordinated to XI. Korps at noon.[88] Like many other panzer divisions participating in the operation it had few tanks. Its panzer regiment only had one battalion, the III./Pz.Rgt. 36.[89] On 21 January, this battalion reported seven Pz IV and five StuG III operational.[90] It also had a number of Pz III, but it has been impossible to establish how many.[91]

According to the divisional history it had seven Pz IV, four flamethower tanks and four StuG operational on 25 January, figures that are well in line with what we have found in the records.[92]

On 1 February the division had an authorized strength of 11,890 (including 707 HiWi) but it was short 2,948, thus it had an overall strength of less than 9,000. Its casualties during January included 354 killed in action, 692 wounded and 130 missing, while it received 240 replacements and 64 returning convalescents.[93] The tank strength amounted to four Pz IV and four StuG III operational.[94]

The manpower shortage was reflected in the condition of its two panzer grenadier regiments. They had a ration strength of 1,097 and 1,042 respectively on 22 January and all their battalions were rated *durschschnittlich*. The ration strength of the reckon and engineer battalions was 557 and 504 respectively. The panzer regiment had a ration strength of 838. The entire division had a ration strength of 8,831.[95]

The artillery comprised 5 Wespe, 3 Hummel, 10 towed 10.5 cm howitzers and 6 towed 15 cm howitzers operational on 22 January. The division also could call upon three 8.8 cm Flak guns and it also had a Flak-Kampftrupp with an additional 8.8 cm gun. The division possessed 3 medium and 12 heavy AT guns.[96]

Tank Strength (Operational Vehicles) During the Operation:

27 January:[97]	3 Pz IV, 2 StuG III
1 February:[98]	4 Pz IV, 4 StuG III
4 February:[99]	5 Pz IV, 4 StuG III
13 February:[100]	4 Pz IV, 2 StuG III
1 March:[101]	6 Pz IV, 2 Flamm-Pz., 4 StuG, 6 command tanks (also 4 Pz IV, 1 Pz III, 2 Flamm-Pz, 3 StuG and 2 command tanks in workshops).

From Kampfgruppe von Brese, which was caught inside the pocket, 467 men managed to break out.[102]

16. Pz.Div.

Commander: Col. Back (Promoted to Gen.Maj. on 1 February)

The 16th Infantry Division was used to form 16th Panzer Division during the second half of 1940. The panzer division suffered badly at Stalingrad and was re-constituted around surviving veterans. The new division went to Italy in May 1943 and returned to the Eastern Front in late 1943. The division fought briefly with Army Group Center before being deployed with Army Group South.

The 16. Pz.Div. assembled for *Operation Wanda* during the first days of February 1944. It was, together with 1. Pz.Div., the strongest of the German divisions that took part in the Korsun battle. Unlike most

Panzer divisions, its Panther regiment had three battalions, one with Panther tanks, one with Pz IV's and one with StuG III assault guns. Its authorized manpower strength was 15,790 and it reported a shortage of 2,144 on 1 February. It had been engaged in heavy combat during January, but casualties of 305 killed in action, 751 wounded and 58 missing can not be regarded as remarkably high for a month.[103]

On 1 February, the division had 38 Panthers, 24 Pz IV, 2 Pz III and 18 StuG III combat ready, while 15 Panthers, 30 Pz IV, 10 Pz III and 12 StuG III were in workshops and expected to be repaired within three weeks.[104]

On 2 February, the division reported that it had the following number of tanks operational: 40 Panthers (including two command Panthers), 26 Pz IV, 18 StuG III, 2 Pz III (both were command tanks). In addition the s.Pz.Abt. 506 was attached with 8 operational Tiger I's.[105]

The division had 267 SPW combat ready, which was quite good for a panzer division at the time. It had 30 artillery pieces, seven 15 cm infantry howitzers, eight 8.8 cm Flak guns and 9 heavy antitank guns operational on 1 February.[106]

On 3 February, the divisional artillery regiment had 8 10.5 cm howitzers, 4 15 cm howitzers, 4 10 cm guns, 4 Wespe and 4 Hummel available.[107] Also, the attached III./Art.Rgt. 34 had 8 10.5 cm howitzers.[108]

The division did not suffer unduly during the relief attempt of Gruppe Stemmerman. Its casualties 1–20 February 1944 amounted to 90 killed in action, 380 wounded and 50 missing.[109]

Tank Strength (Operational Vehicles) During the Operation:

2 February:[110]	40 Panther, 26 Pz IV, 18 StuG III, 2 Bef.Pz. III
5 February (early):[111]	16 Panther, 21 Pz IV, ? StuG III, 2 Bef.Pz. III
5 February (late):[112]	16 Panther, 27 Pz IV, ? StuG III, 2 Bef.Pz. III
6 February:[113]	18 Panther, 17 Pz IV, 14 StuG, 2 Bef.Pz. III
7 February:[114]	12 Panther, 17 Pz IV, 8 StuG III, 2 Bef.Pz. III
8 February:[115]	11 Panther, 6 Pz IV, 8 StuG III, 2 Bef.Pz. III
9 February (early):[116]	11 Panther, 6 Pz IV, 8 StuG III, 2 Bef.Pz. III
9 February:[117]	16 Panther, 16 Pz IV, 10 StuG III, 2 Bef.Pz. III
10 February:[118]	16 Panther, 15 Pz IV, 10 StuG III, ? Bef.Pz. III
15 February:[119]	4 Pz IV
17 February:[120]	2 Panther, 7 Pz IV, 1 StuG III

After the operation the division initially reported that it had lost four Panthers (one of them command version), three Pz IV, two StuG III and one command tank. It also lost four SPW and one Grille (SP 15 cm s.I.G.).[121] On 22 February it had five Panthers and two Pz IV operational,[122] but it also had 49 Panthers, 52 Pz IV and 22 StuG III in workshops.[123] Of the tanks lost three were blown up by the Germans, while four were destroyed by Soviet fire, as were the two assault guns.[124]

However, as the Germans retreated, it became clear that many more tanks, often without any major damage, had to be blown up as they could not be towed away in time. Thus the overall tank losses increased to 32.[125]

The 16th Panzer Division had scored an impressive claim of destroyed enemy tanks during its actions at Korsun and the Balabanova pocket. It reported 559 enemy tanks and assault guns destroyed or captured in the period. Of these over 250 had been destroyed by the Panther battalion. As always claims should be regarded with caution, but at least it can be concluded that the 16th Panzer Division had been engaged in major tank battles.[126]

After the Korsun battle the combat strength of the division was quite low, although it still retained a high manpower strength. This is shown by the manpower situation of some of its components:[127]

Unit	Combat strength	Ration strength
Pz.Rgt. 2	31	1950
Pz.Gren.Rgt. 64	141	1740
Pz.Gren.Rgt. 79	332	1500
Pz.Aukl.Abt. 16	210	900
Pz.Pi.Btl. 16	140	1000
Pz.Art.Rgt. 16	511	1350
Flak.Abt. 16	43	560

It seems reasonable to assume that the very great difference between combat strength (which did not include men who were sick, suffered from trench foot, were so exhausted that they could not fight, etc.) and ration strength (which included all men not evacuated) was caused by the hardships endured during the battle.[128]

17. Pz.Div.

Commander: Gen.Maj von der Meden

The 17th Panzer Division was formed from the Bavarian 27th Infantry Division during the autumn 1940. The division had been fighting on Eastern Front since the summer of 1941.

On 29 January the 17. Pz.Div. began assembling in the VII. A.K. area.129 The 17. Pz.Div. was rather weak. It had only one tank battalion. On 29 January it reported 11 Pz IV lg. and 1 Pz III lg.[130] operational. Two days later it had 13 Pz IV lg and no Pz III operational, while it had eleven Pz IV lg and five Pz III lg in workshops expected to be repaired within three weeks.[131] On 2 February, it had 15 Pz IV tanks operational.[132]

Nominally, its two infantry regiments consisted of two battalions each. One infantry battalion was considered *abgekämpft*, two *schwach* and one *mittelstark*. However, for the fighting during *Operation Wanda*, the infantry was amalgamated into two battalions, I./Pz. gren.Rgt. 40 and II./Pz.Gren.Rgt. 63, that were combined into Kampfgruppe Fink. The recon battalion was rated *durchschnittlich* and the engineer battalion *schwach*.[133]

On 1 February the division had 28 artillery pieces combat ready and 8 in repair. It had 5 15 cm infantry howitzers combat ready and six in repair, while its number of 8.8 cm Flak guns were two combat ready and two in repair.[134]

On 3 February, the divisional artillery regiment had 10 10.5 cm howitzers, 6 15 cm howitzers, 3 10 cm guns, 6 Wespe and 4 Hummel available.[135] Also, the attached Art.Rgt. 34 (minus III. Abt.) had 15 10.5 cm howitzers, 3 15 cm howitzers and 1 7.62 cm gun.[136]

The authorized manpower strength of the division was 14,474, but it was short of 4,376 officers and men. Casualties during January amounted to 188 killed in action, 559 wounded and 304 missing.[137] Thus, the division had had to operate with a considerable shortage for a long time.

Tank Strength (Operational Vehicles) During the Operation:

2 February:[138]	15 Pz IV, 1 Pz III
5 February:[139]	5 Pz IV, 1 Pz III
6 February (early):[140]	5 Pz IV, 1 Pz III

7 February (early):[141]	5 Pz IV, 1 Pz III
8 February:[142]	3 Pz IV, 1 Pz III
9 February (early):[143]	3 Pz IV, 1 Pz III
10 February:[144]	1 Pz III, 4 Pz IV
12 February:[145]	1 Pz IV
13 February (early):[146]	1 Pz IV
15 February (early):[147]	1 Pz IV

The division did not suffer unduly during the relief attempt of Gruppe Stemmerman. Its casualties 1–20 February 1944 amounted to 77 killed in action, 225 wounded and 25 missing.[148]

Initial reports showed that during the operation the division lost one Pz IV and one StuG III. It also lost two Hummel and one SP AT gun.[149] Both were blown up by the Germans.[150] On 22 January it had one Pz IV operational,[151] but it also had 23 Pz IV in workshops.[152]

However, the subsequent retreat forced the division to blow up a number of tanks, which could not be towed away in time, thus raising the total number of tanks lost to 16.[153]

34. Inf.Div.

Since this division was expected to take the brunt of the Soviet offensive, it was reinforced by Rgts.Gr. 677 from Korps-Abt. B.[154] Unfortunately the available reports do not give any information on the condition of the Rgts.Gr. 677. The Korps-Abt. B had also dispatched one 10.5 cm howitzer battery, one 15 cm howitzer battery and four heavy antitank guns to the VIIth Corps, probably these were deployed in the area of 34th Infantry Division.[155]

The division possessed three organic infantry regiments with two battalions each. Three were rated as *durchschnittlich* and three as *schwach*. Also one battalion (*schwach*) was subordinated from 75th Infantry Division.[156]

The 34th Division had an artillery regiment with ten 10.5 cm howitzer batteries and one battery with 15 cm howitzers.[157] The antitank defences relied on fourteen heavy AT guns, five heavy self-propelled, five towed by motor vehicles and four horse-drawn. The division had a Füsilier battalion (*schwach*) and an engineer battalion (*durchschnittlich*).[158]

57. Inf.Div.

Commander: Generalmajor Adolf Trowitz

The division had three infantry regiments, numbered 199, 217 and 676.[159] Of these, the 676. Gren.Rgt. was on its way to reinforce the 389. Inf.Div. on the morning of 25 January.[160] The rest of the division was deployed between Smela and Buda Orlovetskaja.[161] The division lacked a Panzerjäger battalion, but had a Panzerjäger company instead, with towed guns.[162] The other components, artillery regiment, Füsilier battalion and engineer battalion, seems to have been organized according to the normal lines.[163] The condition of the units is however unclear. It is known that on 1 February, the division possessed 29 10.5 howitzers, 3 15 cm howitzers, 15 captured Russian 7.62 cm guns, 6 7.5 cm AT guns and 2 captured Russian 7.62 cm AT guns.[164]

It seems that 2,697 officers and men from the 57th Infantry Division, plus 253 HiWi, managed to break out from the pocket.[165] Also 1,851 soliders who had returned from leave had assembled in Novo Ukrainka and Novo Archangelsk.[166] Furthermore, considerable parts of the rear services of the division were outside the pocket when the pincers of 1st and 2nd Ukrainian Front met on 28 January. Mainly these rear services were located in the Novo Archangelsk area.[167]

72. Inf.Div.

The division seems to have had a normal organization, with three infantry regiments (numbered 105, 124 and 266), a Füsilier battalion, a Panzerjäger battalion, an engineer battalion and an artillery regiment. The Artillery regiment had number 172, the non-regimental battalions had all number 72.[168] On 1 February, the division possessed 29 10.5 howitzers, 4 15 cm howitzers, 12 7.5 cm AT guns and 2 captured French 7.5 cm AT guns.[169]

It seems that 3,615 officers and men from the 72nd Infantry Division, plus 200 HiWi, managed to break out from the pocket.[170] Also 984 soliders who had returned from leave had assembled in Novo Ukrainka.[171] Furthermore, considerable parts of the rear services of the division were outside the pocket when the pincers of 1st and 2nd Ukrainian Front met on 28 January. Mainly these rear services were located in the Lipnyashka area.[172]

75. Inf.Div.

Since the Red Army was comparatively inactive on the sector defended by this division, it did not see much action during the battle. Rather it mainly guarded the flank of the German forces. Indeed, it can be called in question if the division actually participated in the Korsun battle. It is a matter of how the battle is defined. As it only suffered 93 casualties in the period 1–20 February,[173] it clearly saw very little action during the German offensive, and when Vatutin's forces conducted their offensive in January, they advanced north of the 75th Infantry Division. Nevertheless, it is included here in order to provide some information on the unit. On 22 January it had only three infantry battalions available, all rated *durchschnittlich*. As mentioned above, it also had one battalion detached to 34th division. In addition, it had a battalion detached to XIIIth corps (part of 4th Panzer Army).[174]

The Füsilier battalion was rated *abgekämpft*, while the engineer battalion was *durchschnittlich*. The division possessed 9 light field howitzer batteries and two heavy batteries. It only had seven antitank guns, all heavy, towed by motor vehicles.[175]

88. Inf.Div.

Commander: Georg Graf von Rittberg

In autumn 1943 the division was reorganized and absorbed elements of the 323. Inf.Div.[176] At the time of the Korsun battle, it also had elements of 213. Sich.Div. and 168. Inf.Div.[177] Its original infantry regiments had been restructured and its organization was somewhat confused. The 245. Gren.Rgt was the only infantry unit the division possessed that had a regular organization,[178] but it had been sent away to 68. Inf.Div. and did not take part in the operation.[179] The 246. Inf.Rgt. had been dissolved and its remains formed one of the battalions in 248. Inf.Rgt., whose II. Btl. was made the divisional Füs.Btl.[180] The absorbed 323. Inf.Div. was available as the Divisions-gruppe 323, with two infantry battalions (Rgts.Gr. 591 and Rgts.Gr. 593). Thus, at the beginning of the Soviet offensive the division had only four infantry battalions, plus the Füsilier battalion. Of the infantry battalions, one was rated as *mittelstark* and the rest as *durchschnittlich*. Attached to the division was the Rgt.Gr. 417, a battalion sized unit from 168. Inf.Div, which was rated as *durchschnittlich*.181 Also attached were two battalions from 318. Sich.Rgt, one rated as *durchschnittlich* and one as *abgekämpft* (these battalions also included remnants of the I./Sich.Rgt. 177).[182]

The artillery regiment comprised three of the divisions original battalions, plus one battalion from the 323. Inf.Div. Altogether, the division had seven batteries with 10.5 cm howitzers and one battery with 15 cm howitzers.[183]

The antitank weapons included eleven horse-drawn medium AT guns (probably 5 cm) and eight (six towed by motor vehicles and two by horse) heavy AT guns.[184]

It seems that 3,163 officers and men from the 88th Division, plus 200 HiWi, managed to break out from the pocket.[185] In addition 442 men from the attached elements of 318th and 177th Security regiments broke out.[186] Also 984 soldiers who had returned from leave had assembled in Novo Ukrainka.[187] Furthermore, considerable parts of the rear services of the division were outside the pocket when the pincers of 1st and 2nd Ukrainian Front met on 28 January. Mainly these rear services were located in the Lipnyashka area.[188]

There were also 632 men from 168th Division that broke out from the pocket. These belonged to the Div.Gr. 168, which was attached to 88th Division when the battle began, and the I./Art.Rgt. 248 which was subordinated to XXXXII. Korps at the beginning of the battle.[189]

106. Inf.Div.

Commander: Gen.Lt. Forst

This was one of the weakest divisions in the area, having a ration strength of only 6,028 on 22 January. The lack of manpower was especially apparent in its infantry regiments; the 239th had a ration strength of only 534 and the 240. Rgt. was even weaker at 457.[190] As the division's third infantry regiment the Divisions-Gruppe 39 served, which had a ration strength of 520.[191] The situation was not much better for the rest of the division. The Füsilier battalion had a ration strength of 199 and the engineer battalion 295.[192]

The problems were reflected in the rating of the units. Out of its scattered infantry, it formed four battalions, but two of them were still rated *abgekämpft* and the remaining two *schwach*.[193]

It was better provided with artillery, since it had 27 10.5 cm howitzers and four 15 cm howitzers operational on 22 January.[194] The picture was less bright for the anti tank weapons, since the division only had one 5 cm and five 7.5 cm AT guns, plus one captured Russian 4.5 cm AT gun.[195]

The division was subjected to Soviet attacks on 25 January, but the main effort fell further to the north.

According to the 1 February situation report the division remained weak. It had an authorized strength of 13,300, but reported a shortage of 5,243, which would thus mean the division had an actual strength of 8,057. However, this includes men on leave as weel as hospitalized, two categories that were far from insignifiacnt. During January the division had issued 1,250 tickets to soldiers scheduled for leave.[196]

The weakness of the division was caused by months of continous action. Casualties in January were 254 killed, 1,081 wounded and 193 missing. Also 8 officers and 353 men were evacuated due to desease. To counter this loss the division received 199 replacements during January. Also 733 convalescents returned to the division.[197]

As could be expected the infantry suffered from the worst shortage of manpower. The division had 2,699 infantry, including men on leave and soldiers wounded or sick, but remaining with the division.[198] Other shortages affected the division. Various specialists were missing, for example radio operators. Also it only had twelve antitank guns combat ready. The situation was better in the artillery regiment, as the division had 37 howitzers ready for action on 1 February.[199]

For most of the battle the 106. ID. was employed on the east flank.

198. Inf.Div.

The division did follow the regular prescribed organization relatively well. It had three infantry regiments with two battalions each.[200] Three of the battalions were rated as *durchschnittlich* and three were rated as *schwach*.[201] The division had a Füsilier battalion rated as *schwach* and the engineer battalion was rated as *durchschnittlich*.[202]

The panzer jäger battalion only had one company, with towed AT guns, as the other two companies had not yet been formed.[203]

The artillery comprised two batteries with 15 cm howitzers and ten batteries with 10.5 cm howitzers. The division had four medium AT guns and ten heavy, all of them towed by motor vehicles.[204]

Its casualties in January amounted to 211 killed in action, 887 wounded and 211 missing.[205] In the period 1–20 February it lost 105 killed in action, 509 wounded and 147 missing.[206] These figures do not include non-combat losses.

320. Inf.Div.

When the battle began on 25 January, the 320th Division was outside the actual battle area, but after a few days it was shifted to relieve some of the panzer divisions in XXXXVII. Pz.Korps.

On 1 February the division had an authorized strength of 12791, including 2,154 HiWi, but it reported a shortage of 3,580. Almost the entire shortage was found in the three infantry regiments and the Füsilier battalion, all of them being at approximately 50% strength. Also the division lacked its antitank battalion.[207]

Casualties during January numbered 163 killed in action, 594 wounded and 272 missing. In addition 303 soldiers were evacuated due to disease. Replecements were wholly inadequate. Only 12 officers arrived at the division and not a single NCO or other ranks. However, 315 convalescents returned to the division, but still the casualties remained significantly higher.[208]

The artillery was often the backbone of the German infantry divisions, especially when casualties accumulated in the infantry regiments. However, the artillery regiment of the 320. Inf.Div. was not particularly strong, as it only had 24 howitzers.[209]

Further shortages plagued the division. The lack of vehicles was serious. None of the regimental commanders had a vehicle, which made it difficult for them to effectively command their units. Serious vehicle shortages were also affecting the division staff and all signals units.[210]

376. Inf.Div.

The 376. Inf.Div. had been destroyed at Stalingrad one year earlier. It was reformed and sent to the Eastern Front in the autumn of 1943, where it found itself engaged in continous combat. After having been seriously depleted, the 376th Division received considerable replacements in January 1944, when it received 63 officers plus 3,460 other ranks, in addition to 115 returning convalescents.[211] This meant that on 1 February the division was still short of 2,728 officers and other ranks, compared to the authorized strength of 12,295, which included 2,154

HiWi.[212] Furthermore, a significant part of the replacements were actually soldiers from the 167. Inf.Div., which was in the process of being disbanded. With many soldiers from another division to mix into the existing formations, the 376th Division would actually have needed some time behind the front, a situation exacerbated by the fact that the division had been continously in action for almost four months. However the pressure of events denied it its much needed rest.[213]

The process to absorb the elements of 167. Inf.Div. proceeded for weeks. Not until 22 February was it reported that the process was completed.[214]

389. Inf.Div.

The 389. Inf.Div. was also among the divisions destroyed at Stalingrad. It was rebuilt in the summer 1943 and subsequently sent to the Eastern Front. It had three infantry regiments (544, 545 and 546), all of which originally had three battalions (numbered I., II. and III. in each regiment). However, both the II./544 and III./546 were sent to other formations before the division went into action. Also, the II./545 was made into the divisional Füsilier battalion. Hence, in the end the division had three two-battalion regiments. The original numbering of the battalions and companies was retained though. The 544. Inf.Rgt. consisted of I. Btl. with companies 1–4 and the III. Btl. with companies 9–12, with the 545. Rgt. being similarly numbered. The division also had an artillery regiment, a Panzerjäger battalion and an engineer battalion.[215]

On 1 February the division had 6 10.5 howitzers, 5 15 cm howitzers, 15 captured Russian 7.62 cm guns and 12 7.5 cm AT guns.[216]

The division was weak in infantry before the Soviet main attack began. On the afternoon of 24 January, it was reported that the division only had an infantry combat strength (*Gefechtsstärke*) of 1,500. This was supposed to cover 21 km.[217] On 8 February the combat elements of the division were distributed to other formations and the staff of the division employed for traffic control.

It seems that 1,899 officers and men from the 389th Division, plus 33 HiWi, managed to break out from the pocket.[218] Also 352 soliders who had returned from leave had assembled in Novo Ukrainka.[219] Furthermore, considerable parts of the rear services of the division were outside the pocket when the pincers of 1st and 2nd Ukrainian Front met on 28 January.[220]

Non-Divisional Combat Units:

s.Pz.Rgt. Bäke

This was an ad hoc formation. On 21 January it was ordered to form using the staff of 11. Pz.Rgt. (from 6. Pz.Div.) and two tank battalions: s.Pz.Abt. 503 (Tiger I) and II./Pz.Rgt. 23 (Panther).[221]

The regiment was first committed in the offensive operations conducted by XXXXVI. Pz.Korps during the last week of January. The regiment performed very well and was credited with the destruction of 268 enemy tanks in one week.[222]

On 31 January the regiment had 15 Panthers and 18 Tigers operational.[223] Thereafter, in mud and slush, it moved to the assembly area for *Operation Wanda* and it seems that it had 11 Tigers and 14 Panthers combat ready when the operation began.[224]

Of these only 8 Tigers and 8 Panthers had yet reached the front when the offensive began.[225]

Tank Strength (Operational Vehicles) During the Operation:

5 February:[226]	12 Tiger, 4 Panther
6 February (early):[227]	12 Tiger, 4 Panther
6 February (late):[228]	11 Tiger, 3 Panther
7 February (early):[229]	11 Tiger, 3 Panther
9 February (early):[230]	11 Tiger, 15 Panther
10 February:[231]	10 Tiger, 16 Panther
15 February (early):[232]	6 Tiger, 8 Panther

During the operation the regiment lost seven Tigers and 23 Panthers.[233]

It is notable that all the Tigers lost had been blown up by the Germans, as had seventeen of the Panthers. Also two Panthers were complete losses due to spontaneous engine room fires during the march.[234] Thus, of the 30 tanks lost by the regiment, only four were lost due to Soviet fire.

It seems that all of them fell vicitm in one single engagement, near Dashchukovka on the morning of 12 February.[235]

On 22 February the regiment had 34 Tigers in workshops.[236]

Kampfgruppe Haack

Orders to form Kampfgruppe Haack were issued by 8th Army on 5 February. Major-General Haack actually commanded the "Artillerie-Division zur besondere Verwendung," which in fact was only a staff. He was given the following units:[237]

Elements from Nachr.Abt. 389 (389. Inf.Div.)	
Feldgend.Trupp 72. Inf.Div.	
Urlauber-Rgt. Baake	(which consisted of soldiers from 57., 72., 88., 389. Inf.Div., that had been on leave when the Korsun battle began).
Urlauber-Btl. Korps-Abt. B	(consisted of soldiers from Korps-Abt. B that had been on leave when the battle began).
Pz.Zerst.Btl. 472	
II./Art.Rgt. 818	
III./Art.Rgt. 818	
III./Art.Rgt. 140	
StuG.Abt. 228	(5 Stug on 5 February, see also the entry for this unit for further information)
Werfer-Rgt. 55	
1 company from Pz.Jäg.Abt. 389	(from 389. Inf.Div., with three heavy AT guns)
Pi.Btl. 666	
s.Str.Bau-Btl. 676	(except one company)
Various rear services from 389th Infantry Division	
Alarm units formed from rear security units (approx. 450 men)	

On 13 February the Kampfgruppe had 4 operational StuG III.[238] The Kampfgruppe was dissolved after the battle.

Kampfgruppe Renz

Kampfgruppe Renz consisted of one infantry battalion, the I./Gren.Rgt. 168 and one artillery battalion, II./Art.Rgt. 182 from 82. Inf.Div.

This force was fighting against the Soviet units encircled near Tikhonovka.[239] On 3 February the artillery battalion had nine 10.5 cm howitzers and was subordinated temporarily to 17. Pz.Div.[240]

s.Werfer-Rgt. 1

The regiment arrived in February to support the III Pz.Korps relief attempt. The I. Abt had eight 15 cm rocket launchers, while the II. and III. Abt. each had twelve 30 cm rocket launchers each on 3 February, when the regiment was subordinated to III. Pz.Korps.[241]

Pz.Abt. 8 (R1132, F427)

This battalion was actually an organic part of 20. Pz.Gren.Div. and was equipped with assault guns.[242] During the Korsun operation it fought separated from its parent division. It had received 42 StuG III in September and October 1943 (and probably 3 command veheicles). Otherwise it did not receive any assault guns before March 1944.[243] On 23 January the battalion was with the 11. Pz.Div and had a ration strength of 516.[244]

Tank Strength (Operational Vehicles) During the Operation:

27 January:[245]	1 StuG III
1 February:	8 operational StuG III and 10 in short term repair (up to three weeks).[246]

II./Pz.Rgt. 23

See s.Pz.Rgt. Bäke

I./Pz.Rgt. 26

The battalion had recently arrived on the Eastern Front and had no previous combat experience. It seems to have been poorly trained and led. The commander, major Glässgen, was killed on the day the battalion made its combat debut and replaced by captain Wallroth from the Großdeutschland division, who arrived on 30 January.[247] The latter did not last long as battalion commander either, as he fell to a rifle bullet on 3 February. Lieutenant Wartman assumed command, but on 12 February he too was wounded in his right wrist by shrapnel. Lieutenant Weidinger took over temporarily until major von Wagner arrived on 14 February to take command.[248]

At first the battalion was attached to the Großdeutschland division, but it saw little action. On 26 January it reported 67 operational Panthers.[249] It moved to XXXXVII. Pz.Korps on 27 January and went into action near Pisarovka and Tishkovka on 28 January.[250] For most of the battle it was attached to 11. Pz.Div. In many of the reports for 11. Pz.Div., Panthers from I./26 are included.

Tank Strength (Operational Vehicles) During the Operation:

21 January:[251]	67 (including 2 command Panthers)
26 January:[252]	67 (including 2 command Panthers)
28 January (06.00):[253]	61 (including 2 command Panthers)
28 January (15.25):[254]	35 (approximately)
29 January (morning):[255]	17
31 January (probably evening):[256]	30
1 February (morning):[257]	32 (include 2 command Panthers), also 10 in short repair and 20 in long repair.
1 February (18.00):[258]	21
3 February (17.00):[259]	16 (include 2 command Panthers)
6 February (20.00):[260]	13
7 February:[261]	14
8 February:[262]	14
9 February:[263]	15
10 February (13.00):[264]	17
10 February:[265]	15 (include 0 command Panthers), also 13 in short repair and 33 in long repair.
11 February (12.00):[266]	15
12 February (12.15):[267]	10
13 February (evening):[268]	6
14 February (evening):[269]	6
15 February:[270]	6
16 February:[271]	5
17 February:[272]	8
20 February:[273]	2 (include 0 command Panthers), also 11 in short repair and 46 in long repair.
1 March:[274]	6 (include 0 command Panthers), also 23 in short repair and 29 in long repair.

Losses (complete write offs) during January and February 1944 were:[275]

1 Panther lost on 6 January, which caught fire during train loading.

1 Panther lost on 27 January, due to fire in engine room during march.

10 Panther (one of them from the battalion staff) lost on 28 January. Of these, four were destroyed by enemy fire, five were

damaged by enemy fire but could not be recovered, the fate of the last one is unclear.

2 Panther lost on 29 February, one destroyed by enemy fire (but recovered and sent to Germany by train, but the vehicle was nevertheless classified as written off), one slid down a sharp slope during darkness and could not be recovered.

1 Panther lost on 1 February, due to fire in engine room while on march.

1 Panther lost on 5 February, destroyed by enemy fire.

1 Panther lost on 12 February, destroyed by enemy fire.

1 damaged Panther cannibalized and written off on 23 February.

A great many more tanks were damaged, either by fire or due to mechanical breakdown. This is illustrated by the work of the repair services of the battalion. Between 27 and 31 January eight tanks were repaired. This work was intensified between 1 and 11 February, when no less than 57 Panthers were repaired. From 12 to 20 January another 40 were repaired. Obviously tanks went in and out of the workshops quite frequently.[276]

The ration strength of the battalion amounted to 907 officers and men on 21 January. This changed somewhat during the battle. On 1, 11 and 21 February the ration strength was 1,051, 1,028 and 964 respectively.[277]

On 1 March the battalion had 58 Panthers, of which 52 were in workshops. Its casualties during February 1944 amounted to six killed in action and four wounded.[278]

Werfer-Rgt. 54

The regiment arrived in February to support the III Pz.Korps relief attempt. The II. Abt had ten 15 cm rocket launchers, while the I. and III. Abt. each had twelve 15 cm rocket launchers each on 3 February, when the regiment was subordinated to III. Pz.Korps.[279] Also the regiment had a battery with Maultier Panzer-Werfer.[280]

Werfer-Rgt. 55

The regiment arrived at XXXXVII. Pz.Korps on 1 February and was directed to cooperate with the 11. Pz.Div.[281] It seems that its I. Abt. was missing, but the 21. Bttr. (Pz.Werfer) was present.[282] On 5 February it was decided to send the regiment to Kampfgruppe Haack. By this time the I. Abt. was included in the regiment.[283]

Werfer-Rgt. 57

The regiment arrived in February to support III Pz.Korps relief attempt. The I. and II. Abt. each had eighteen 15 cm rocket launchers each on 3 February, when the regiment was subordinated to III. Pz.Korps. The regiment had only two battalions present.[284]

II./Art.Rgt. 62

The II./Art.Rgt. 62 battalion was subordinated to VII. Korps at the beginning of the battle. It was equipped with 10 cm guns. On 3 February the II./Art.Rgt. 62 had six 10 cm guns available. By then, the battalion was subordinated to III. Pz.Korps.[285]

II./Art.Rgt. 67

The battalion fought with III. Pz.Korps in late January and followed the corps to its new assignment when the relief operation was to be launched. On 3 February it had two batteries with a total of six 15 cm howitzers available.[286]

On 7 February it was detailed to support 34. Inf.Div.[287]

I./Art.Rgt. 84

The battalion was only present with its staff and one of its batteries (the 2. Bttr.).[288] It was equipped with 17 cm guns.[289] At the beginning of the battle it was subordinated to VII. Korps, but on 3 February it was subordinated to III. Pz.Korps and had two 17 cm guns available.[290]

I./Art.Rgt. 108

On 24 January the I./Art.Rgt. 108 was ordered to immediately transfer to XI. Korps[291] and it got there in time to be encircled.[292] It seems to have had nine 10.5 cm howitzers.[293] It is unclear how many of its men managed to break out from the pocket.

Pi.Btl. 127 (mot)

On 22 January the battalion was on its way to 1st Panzer Army.[294] One week later it seems to have been with the XXXXVI Panzer Corps.[295] Before *Operation Wanda* began, it was transferred to III. Pz.Korps.[296] On 8 February the battalion was subordinated to 1. Pz.Div.[297]

III./Art.Rgt. 140

Late on 24 January, this battalion was ordered to leave the Großdeutschland division, which it was temporarily subordinated to, and assemble at Kapitanovka to be subordinated to XI Korps.[298] It seems this was not done immediately, since on 26 January 1944, it was ordered to transfer from LII. A.K. to XXXXVII. Pz.Korps.[299] It arrived at XXXXVII. Pz.Korps late on 27 January.[300] The battalion had two 15 cm howitzer batteries and one 10 cm gun battery. One battery, the 7./Art.Rgt 140, did not follow the battalion to the Korsun battle. Instead another battery, 3./s.Art.Abt. 735 with 21 cm howitzers, was subordinated to the battalion.[301]

On 6 February the battalion, including the attached battery, was ordered to join Kampfgruppe Haack.[302]

I./Gren.Rgt. 168

See Kampfgruppe Renz.

II./Art.Rgt. 182

See Kampfgruppe Renz.

Stug.Abt. 202

On 25 January the VII. Korps, to which the 202. assault gun battalion was subordinated, reported that it had 15 combat ready assault guns.[303] On 8 February, the battalion was with the 34. Inf.Div.[304]

Stug.Abt. 203

On 25 January the battalion was with Gruppe Schmidt, further to the south. In the evening it was ordered to move to XXXXVII. Pz.Korps at Pantshevo.[305] On 31 January the battalion had 6 operational StuG and 12 in workshops.[306]

On 1 February the battalion had 8 operational StuG III and evidently was subordinated to 106. Inf.Div.[307] On 13 February the battalion only had 1 operational StuG III.[308] On 1 March it had 4 operational StuG III and seven in workshops.[309]

Pi.Btl. 213 (besp.)

On 9 February the battalion was in Uman, on its way to III. Pz.Korps.[310]

Pi.Btl. 215

The battalion was subordinated to VII. Korps when the battle began.[311] It seems to have remained with VII. Korps for the remainder of the battle.[312]

Stug.Abt. 228

228. StuG.Abt. was attached to 389. Inf.Div. on the morning of 25 January.[313] How many assault guns it had on 25 January is unknown. It reported 19 operational assault guns on 1 January.[314] On 31 January the battalion had 6 operational StuG and 11 in workshops.[315] Probably the vehicles in workshops were located outside the pocket that had been formed. This is also supported by the fact that elements of 228. StuG.Abt. (with 5 operational StuG) were subordinated to Kampfgruppe Haack, outside the pocket on 6 February.[316]

Stug.Abt. 239

On 20 January the battalion had 17 StuG III,[317] but this is apparently including assault guns in workshops.[318] On 25 January the VII. Korps, to which the 239. assault gun battalion was subordinated, reported that it had 8 combat ready assault guns.[319]

The battalion was subordinated to VII. Korps when the Soviet offensive began, but on 26 January was soon ordered to transfer to XXXXII Korps, via Morentsy.[320] It seems just to have reach Lieb's korps when the Soviet pincers closed.[321] Thus it seems likely that the vehicles in workshops remained outside the pocket.

On 28 January it was reported that the battalion had six operational assault guns.[322] On 29 January it reported seven operational assault guns.[323]

It was reported that 150 men from the battalion broke out from the pocket.[324] Most likely there were many men from the battalion that were outside the pocket when the Soviet pincers closed at Zvenigorodka on 28 January.

I./Art.Rgt. 248

The battalion was originally a part of 168. Inf.Div., but it was subordinated to the XXXXII. Korps and had 3 batteries with 10.5 cm howitzers when the battle began.[325]

There were two units from 168th Division engaged in the battle, the I./Art.Rgt. 248 and the Rgts.Gr. 417 (see 88th Division). Both were surrounded in the pocket and altogether 632 men from them broke out.[326]

StuG.Abt. 249

On 31 January, the battalion had 6 operational StuG III and 21 in workshops.[327] However, on the following day it was reported that the battalion had only three StuG III operational.[328] It again had 6 assault guns operational on 6 February.[329]

For the first phase of III. Pz.Korps relief operation (4–9 February) the battalion seems to have been subordinated to 17. Pz.Div.[330]

Tank Strength (Operational Vehicles) During the Operation:

5 February:[331]	6 StuG
6 February (early):[332]	6 StuG III
7 February (early):[333]	6 StuG III
8 February:[334]	6 StuG III
9 February:[335]	6 StuG III
10 February:[336]	4 StuG III
12 February:[337]	2 StuG III
13 February:[338]	5 StuG III
15 February (early):[339]	3 StuG III

On 22 February it had only one operational assault gun,[340] but 22 in workshops.[341]

Pz.Zerst.Btl. 471

A few days before the Soviet attack was launched the VII. Korps was reinforced by the Panzer-Zerstörer-Btl. 471 and it was sent to the 34. Inf.Div., where the main Soviet attack was expected.[342] On 5 February the battalion was deployed mainly at 34th and 198th Divisions.[343]

s.Pz.Abt. 503

See s.Pz.Rgt. Bäke

Schwere Panzer Abteilung 506 (506. Heavy Tank Battalion)

Commander: Captain Eberhard Lange

The battalion was formed from III.Battalion/33.Panzerregiment (9. Pz.Div.) in July 1943. In September 1943 the battalion arrived to Army Group South with it's new Tiger tanks (Tiger I E).

The battalion was sent to participate in III. Pz.Korps attack *Operation Wanda* on 4 February. On 1 February it had 10 operational Tigers and 13 expected to be repaired within three weeks.[344]

One day later it reported 8 operational Tigers[345] and on 5 February it had 12 operational.[346] It was subordinated to the 16. Pz.Div. when *Operation Wanda* began.

Tank Strength (Operational Vehicles) During the Operation:

5 February:[347]	12 Tiger
6 February (early):[348]	12 Tiger
6 February (late):[349]	12 Tiger
7 February:[350]	4 Tiger
8 February:[351]	4 Tiger
9 February:[352]	2 Tiger
10 February:[353]	2 Tiger
12 February:[354]	6 Tiger
13 February:[355]	4 Tiger
15 February (early):[356]	4 Tiger

During the battle the battalion lost seven Tigers, all of which were mechanical failures blown up by the Germans when they retreated from the sailient created by III. Pz.Korps.[357] On 22 February the battalion had one operational Tiger.[358] It also had 19 in workshops.[359]

Art.Bttr. 625

The battery was equipped with 17 cm guns and subordinated to VII. Korps at the beginning of the battle.[360]

Pi.Btl. 627 (mot)

On 29 January the battalion was with the III. Pz.Korps and it seems to have followed the corps when it moved to the staging area for *Operation Wanda.*[361]

I./Art.Abt. 628

The battery had fought with III. Pz.Korps in late January and followed the corps to its new assignment when the relief operation was to be launched. On 3 February it had three 21 cm howitzers available.[362]

3./s.Art.Abt. 735

See III./Art.Rgt. 140.

II./Art.Abt. 818

The motorized battalion was equipped with towed 10.5 cm howitzers and seems to have been with the XXXXVII. Pz.Korps from the beginning of the Korsun battle.[363] On 6 February the battalion, including the attached battery, was ordered to join Kampfgruppe Haack.[364]

III./Art.Abt. 818

On 6 February the battalion, including the attached battery, was ordered to join Kampfgruppe Haack. It had until then been with the Grossdeutschland Division.[365]

Art.Abt. 842

The battalion, equipped with 10 cm guns, was subordinated to XI. Korps when the battle began.[366]

StuG.Abt. 905

The assault gun battalion was in the 3. Pz.Div. area on the morning of 25 January.[367] At 16.10 on 26 January, the battalion was transferred to 11. Pz.Div.[368] On 31 January, it had 14 combat ready StuG III and 8 in workshops.[369] On 1 February the battalion had 8 operational StuG III and was evidently subordinated to 320. Inf.Div.[370]

On 13 February the battalion had 13 operational StuG III, of which 4 were subordinated to 106. ID.371 On 1 March it had 11 operational StuG and eight in workshops.[372]

StuG.Abt. 911

Commander: Capt. Hoffmann

During the Korsun battle the 911. StuG.Abt. was subordinated to 11. Pz.Div. It was quite weak, having few assault guns and also experiencing shortages of other vehicles. It was almost up to strength in personell, having an authorized strength of 464 officers, NCO's, men and HiWi and short of only nine HiWi.[373]

Tank Strength (Operational Vehicles) During the Operation:

27 January:	4 StuG III.[374]
1 February:	6 operational StuG III and seven in workshops.[375]
1 March:	8 operational StuG III and ten in workshops.[376]

Notes on the Appendices

1 See OKH GenStdH/org.Abt. Nr. I/2000/44 geh., 25.4.44, Festlegung der Stärkebegriffe, BA-MA RH 2/60.

2 OKH GenStdH/Org Abt Nr. IZ/45 100/44 geh., 15 Juni 1944, T78, R421, R6390282.

3 G. Tessin, Verbände und Truppen der deutschen Wehrmacht und Waffen-SS (Mittler & Sohn, Frankfurt am Main and Biblio Verlag, Osnabrück 1966-1975), entry for units beginning with letter "B".

4 Ibid.

5 PzAOK 1 Ia Nr. 69/44, 24 January 1944, Wochenmeldung: Kampfwert der Divisionen, Stand 22.1.1944, T313, R69, F7306382. See also XXXXII. .A.K. Ia Fernschreiben an PzAOK 1, 26.1.44, 11.25 Uhr, T312, R69, F7306413 and PzAOK 1 Kriegsgliederung, Stand 22.1.11944, T313, R69, F7306485.

6 PzAOK 1 Ia Nr. 69/44, 24 Januar 1944, Wochenmeldung: Kampfwert der Divisionen, Stand 22.1.1944, T313, R69, F7306383.

7 PzAOK 1 Ia Nr. 69/44, 24 Januar 1944, Wochenmeldung: Kampfwert der Divisionen, Stand 22.1.1944, T313, R69, F7306383.

8 Ibid.

9 Meldung Gruppe Mattenklott, 29.2.44, 17.40 Uhr, in Anlagen zum KTB PzAOK 1 Ia, T313, R72, F7310423.

10 Gruppe Mattenklott, "Nicht im Kampfraum XI. und XXXXII. A.K. befindliche Teile", 18.2.44, in Anlagen zum KTB PzAOK 1 Ia, T313, R72, F7310470.

11 See 5. SS-Pz.Div. Zustandmeldung an Gen.Insp. der Panzer-Waffe, Stand 1.12.1943, BA-MA RH 10/316 and SS-Wallonien Zustandmeldung an Gen.Insp. der Panzer-Waffe, Stand 1.1.1944, BA-MA RH 10/332.

12 Anlagen zum KTB III. Pz.Korps Ia, Tagesmeldungen der Div. am 6.2.44, T314, R208, F000541.

13 PzAOK 1 Ia Nr 221/44 geh., 3.2.44, 14.30 Uhr, T313, R71, F7308399.

14 Anlagen zum KTB III. Pz.Korps Ia, Tagesmeldungen der Div. am 6.2.44, T314, R208, F000541.

15 BA-MA RH 10/140.

16 Anlagen zum KTB PzAOK 1 Ia, "Anruf III. Pz.Korps–Panzer- und Sturmgeschützlage," 6.2. 44, 12.05 Uhr, T313, R71, F7308419.

17 Anlagen zum KTB PzAOK 1 Ia, Panzerlage vom 7.2 – Meldung III. Pz.Korps, 8.2.44, 10.00 Uhr, T313, R70, F7306587.

18 Anlagen zum KTB PzAOK 1 Ia, Panzerlage III. Pz.Korps, 9.2.44, 10.00 Uhr, T313, R70, F7306601 and Nachmeldung zur Panzerlage III. Pz.Korps, 9.2.44, 11.00 Uhr, T313, R70, F7306602.

19 PzAOK 1 Ia, Tagesmeldung 9.2.44, T313, R70, F7306626.

20 PzAOK 1 Ia, Tagesmeldung 10.2.44, T313, R70, F7306649.

21 Anlagen zum KTB PzAOK 1 Ia, Panzerlage III. Pz.Korps 13.2, 10.15 Uhr, T313, R70, F7306713.

22 Anlagen zum KTB PzAOK 1 Ia, Panzerlage III. Pz.Korps 15.2, 11.10 Uhr, T313, R70, F7306803.

23 PzAOK 1 IIa Verlustübersicht vom 1. bis einschl. 20. Februar 1944, T313, R74, F7312637.

24 Anlagen zum KTB PzAOK 1 Ia, Meldung III. Pz.Korps, 24.2.44, 14.30 Uhr, T313, R70, F7307019.

25 PzAOK 1, Stabsoffizier für Panzer-Bek., 3.3.1944, Fernschreiben PzAOK 1 Ia 423/44, Betr. Panzerausfälle, T313, R70, F7307174-6.

26 Anlagen zum KTB III. Pz.Korps Ia, Morgenmeldungen der Div. am 3.2.44, T314, R208, F000418.

27 Anlagen zum KTB III. Pz.Korps Ia, Tagesmeldung 3.2.44, T314, R208, F000425.

28 Anlagen zum KTB PzAOK 1 Ia, "Anruf III. Pz.Korps–Panzer- und Sturmgeschützlage," 6.2. 44, 12.05 Uhr, T313, R71, F7308419.

29 Anlagen zun KTB III. Pz.Korps Ia, Tagesmeldungen der Div. am 6.2.44, T314, R208, F000543.

30 Anlagen zum KTB III. Pz.Korps, Tagesmeldungen der Div. am 7.2.44, T314, R208, F000603.

31 Anlagen zum KTB III. Pz.Korps Ia, Funkspruch von LSSAH, 9.2.44, 18.17 Uhr, T314, R208, F000713.

32 PzAOK 1 Ia Tagesmeldung 10.2.44, T313, R70, F7306649.

33 Anlagen zum KTB PzAOK 1 Ia, Panzerlage III. Pz.Korps 13.2, 10.15 Uhr, T313, R70, F7306713.

34 Anlagen zum KTB PzAOK 1 Ia, Panzerlage III. Pz.Korps 15.2, 11.10 Uhr, T313, R70, F7306803.

35 PzAOK 1 IIa Verlustübersicht vom 1. bis einschl. 20. Februar 1944, T313, R74, F7312637.

36 LSSAH Tagesmeldung an III. Pz.Korps am 7.2.44, T314, R3208, F603.

37 Fernspruch LSSAH an III. Pz.Korps, 25.2.44, in Anlagen zum KTB III. Pz.Korps Ia, T314, R209, F000821.

38 Anlagen zum KTB PzAOK 1 Ia, T313, R70, F7307094.

39 LSSAH Ia Fernschreiben an III. Pz.Korps Ia, 22.2.44, 21.00 Uhr, in Anlagen zum KTB III. Pz.Korps Ia, T314, R209, F000595-7.

40 Ibid.

41 Ibid.

42 Anlagen zum KTB PzAOK 1 Ia, Panzerlage III. Pz.Korps, 22.2.44, T313, R70, F7306966.

43 Anlagen zum KTB PzAOK 1 Ia, T313, R70, F7307094.

44 According to a report for 22 January, the division had three infantry battalions, two rated durchschnittlich and one schwach (See XXXXVII. Pz.Korps Ia Nr. 290/44 geh., Kurzzustandbericht, Stand 22.1.44, T314, R1132, F000574). According to the 1 February report (3. Pz.Div. Zustandmeldung, Stand 1.2.44, in Anlagen zum KTB XXXXVII. Pz.Korps Ia, T314, R1132, F000651-4), the I./Pz.Gren.Rgt. 394 had only its rear services, sicne its combat elements had been transferred to II./Pz.Gren.Rgt. 394.

45 3. Pz.Div. Zustandmeldung, Stand 1.2.44, in Anlagen zum KTB XXXXVII. Pz.Korps Ia, T314, R1132, F000651-4.

46 Ibid.

47 XXXXVII. Pz.Korps Ia Nr. 290/44 geh., "Kurzzustandbericht, Stand 22.1.44, T314, R1132, F000574.

48 3. Pz.Div. Zustandmeldung, Stand 1.2.44, in Anlagen zum KTB XXXXVII. Pz.Korps Ia, T314, R1132, F000651-4.

49 Anlagen zum KTB III. Pz.Korps Ia, Tagesmeldungen der Div. am 1.1.44, T314, R207, F000861.

50 3. Pz.Div. Zustandmeldung, Stand 1.2.44, in Anlagen zum KTB XXXXVII. Pz.Korps Ia, T314, R1132, F000651-4.

51 3. Pz.Div. Zustandmeldung an Gen.Insp. der Pz.Truppe, Stand 1.1.44, BA-MA RH 10/142.

52 Lieferungen der Pz.Fahrzeuge, Bd. ab Mai 1943, BA-MA RH 10/349.

53 3. Pz.Div. Zustandmeldung, Stand 1.2.44, in Anlagen zum KTB XXXXVII. Pz.Korps Ia, T314, R1132, F000651-4.

54 AOK 8 Ia Nr. 845/44 geh., Fernschreiben an HGr Süd, 4.2.44, 12.20 Uhr, T312, R64, F7582968.

55 XXXXVII. Pz.Korps Ia Tagesmeldung 13.2.44, T314, R1132, F000684.

56 KTB AOK 8 Ia Nr. 253/44, 23.2.44, T312, R64, F7582929.

57 BA-MA RH 10/316.

58 BA-MA RH 10/349.

59 Gen.Kdo XXXXII. A.K., 24.2.44, in Anlagen zum KTB PzAOK 1 Ia, T313, R72, F7310513.

60 Meldung Gruppe Mattenklott, 29.2.44, 17.40 Uhr, in Anlagen zum KTB PzAOK 1 Ia, T313, R72, F7310423.

61 Gruppe Mattenklott, "Nicht im Kampfraum XI. und XXXXII. A.K. befindliche Teile", 18.2.44, in Anlagen zum KTB PzAOK 1 Ia, T313, R72,

F7310470.

62 Panther Abteilungen 20.1.1944 nach Gen. Qu., BA-MA RH 10/70.

63 Ibid.

64 This was ordered on 11 January, see AOK 8 Ia Nr. 129/44, 11.1.44, T312, R64, F7582998. The I./Pz.Rgt. 31 was to return to Germany for refit. It is not clear exactly when the tanks were handed over, even though it clearly had taken place before 1 February. (See 11. Pz.Div. Zustandmeldung, Stand 1.2.44, in Anlagen zum KTB XXXXVII. Pz.Korps Ia, T314, R1132, F000655.)

65 11. Pz.Div. Zustandmeldung, Stand 1.2.44, in Anlagen zum KTB XXXXVII. Pz.Korps Ia, T314, R1132, F000656.

66 Monatszustandmeldung 11. Pz.Div, Stand 1.1.44, BA-MA RH 10/149.

67 11. Pz.Div. Zustandmeldung, Stand 1.2.44, in Anlagen zum KTB XXXXVII. Pz.Korps Ia, T314, R1132, F000655.

68 Lieferungen der Pz.Fahrz., BA-MA RH 10/349.

69 XXXXVII. Pz.Korps Ia Nr. 289/44 geh., 23.1.44, Verpflegungs und Gefechtsstärken, T314, R1132, F000575.

70 Ibid.

71 Monatszustandmeldung 11. Pz.Div, Stand 1.2.44, in Anlagen zum KTB XXXXVII. Pz.Korps Ia, T314, R1132, F000655.

72 Ibid.

73 XXXXVII. Pz.Korps Ia Tagesmeldung 1.2.44, T314, R1132, F000594.

74 XXXXVII. Pz.Korps Ia Nr. 290/44 geh., 23.1.44, Kurzzustandberich, Stand 22.1.44, T314, R1132, F000574.

75 11. Pz.Div. Ia, Fernschreiben an AOK 8, 27.1.44, found in Anlagen zum KTB AOK 8 Ia, T312, R66, F7584303.

76 AOK 8 Ia Nr. 845/44 geh., Fernschreiben an HGr Süd, 4.2.44, 12.20 Uhr, T312, R64, F7582968.

77 XXXXVII. Pz.Korps Ia Tagesmeldung 13.2.44, T314, R1132, F000684.

78 KTB AOK 8 Ia, 14.2.44, 19.15 Uhr, T312, R64, F7581886.

79 KTB AOK 8 Ia, 15.2.44, 08.10 Uhr, T312, R64, F7581886.

80 XXXXVII. Pz.Korps Ia, "Panzer- und Sturmgeschütz-Lage Stand 1.3.44", T314, R1132, F000724.

81 See KTB AOK 8 Ia, 28.1.44, T312, R64, F7581765 and 1.2.44, T312, R64, F7581798.

82 Monatszustandmeldung 13. Pz.Div, Stand 1.2.44, in Anlagen zum KTB XXXXVII. Pz.Korps Ia, T314, R1132, F000667.

83 Ibid.

84 Ibid.

85 AOK 8 Ia Nr. 845/44 geh., Fernschreiben an HGr Süd, 4.2.44, 12.20 Uhr, T312, R64, F7582968.

86 XXXXVII. Pz.Korps Ia Tagesmeldung 13.2.44, T314, R1132, F000684.

87 XXXXVII. Pz.Korps Ia, "Panzer- und Sturmgeschütz-Lage Stand 1.3.44", T314, R1132, F000724.

88 KTB AOK 8 Ia, 25.1.44, 11.40 Uhr, T312, R64, F7581727.

89 14. Pz.Div. Zustandmeldung, Stand 1.2.44, in Anlagen zum KTB XXXXVII. Pz.Korps Ia, T314, R1132, F000674.

90 Anlagen zum KTB III./Pz.Rgt. 36, Gefechts- und Verpflegungsstärken, BA-MA RH 39/380.

91 The annexes to the war diary of the battalion only indicates 2 Pz III (command vehicles) on 21 January. However, the divisional report for 1 February (14. Pz.Div. Zustandmeldung, Stand 1.2.44, in Anlagen zum KTB XXXXVII. Pz.Korps Ia, T314, R1132, F000674) shows 14 operatinal Pz III and none in short term repair. For the same day, the battalions papers still show 2 Pz III. Part of the explanation may be that some of the Pz III (command vehicles) were actually with the panzer regiment staff (thus not part of III./Pz.Rgt. 36).

92 R. Grams, Die 14. Pz.Div. 1940-1945 (Podzun, Bad Nauheim 1957) p. 164–166.

93 Zustandmeldung ZZ.

94 XXXXVII. Pz.Korps Ia Tagesmeldung 1.2.44, T314, R1132, F000594.

95 XXXXVII. Pz.Korps Ia Nr. 290/44 geh., 23.1.44, Kurzzustandberich, Stand 22.1.44, T314, R1132, F000574 and XXXXVII. Pz.Korps Ia Nr. 289/44 geh., 23.1.44, Verpflegungs und Gefechtsstärken, T314, R1132, F000575.

96 XXXXVII. Pz.Korps Ia Nr. 290/44 geh., 23.1.44, Kurzzustandberich, Stand 22.1.44, T314, R1132, F000574.

97 14. Pz.Div. Ia, Fernschreiben an AOK 8, 27.1.44, 23.40 Uhr, in Anlagen zum KTB AOK 8 Ia, T312, R66, F7584304.

98 XXXXVII. Pz.Korps Ia, Tagesmeldung 1.2.44, T314, R1132, F000594.

99 AOK 8 Ia Nr. 845/44 geh., Fernschreiben an HGr Süd, 4.2.44, 12.20 Uhr, T312, R64, F7582968.

100 XXXXVII. Pz.Korps Ia Tagesmeldung 13.2.44, T314, R1132, F000684.

101 XXXXVII. Pz.Korps Ia, "Panzer- und Sturmgeschütz-Lage Stand 1.3.44", T314, R1132, F000724.

102 Meldung Gruppe Mattenklott, 29.2.44, 17.40 Uhr, in Anlagen zum KTB PzAOK 1 Ia, T313, R72, F7310423.

103 16. Pz.Div., Monatszustandmeldung an Gen. Insp. der Pz.Tr., Stand 1.2.44, BA-MA RH 10/153.

104 Ibid.

105 See 16. Pz.Div. Ia, Tagesmeldung an III. Pz.Korps 2.2.44, T314, R208, F000402 and III Pz.Korps Ia Nr. 193/44, 2.2.44, "Korpsbefehl für den Angriff", T314, R208, F000411.

106 16. Pz.Div., Monatszustandmeldung an Gen. Insp. der Pz.Tr., Stand 1.2.44, BA-MA RH

10/153.

107 Gliederung der Div. u. Heeresartillerie im Bereich des III. Pz.Korps, Stand 3.2.44, Arko 3, T314, R208, F000441.

108 Ibid.

109 PzAOK 1 IIa Verlustübersicht vom 1. bis einschl. 20. Februar 1944, T313, R74, F7312637.

110 16. Pz.Div. Ia, Tagesmeldung an III. Pz.Korps 2.2.44, T314, R208, F000402 and III Pz.Korps Ia Nr. 193/44, 2.2.44, "Korpsbefehl für den Angriff", T314, R208, F000411.

111 Anlagen zum KTB III. Pz.Korps Ia, Morgenmeldungen der Div. am 5.2.44, T314, R208, F000479.

112 Anlagen zum KTB III. Pz.Korps Ia, Tagesmeldung 16. Pz.Div. Ia am 5.2.44, T314, R208, F000506.

113 Anlagen zum KTB III. Pz.Korps, 16. Pz.Div. Ia Morgenmeldung 7.2.44, T314, R208, F000570.

114 Anlagen zum KTB PzAOK 1 Ia, Panzerlage meldung vom 7.2, III. Pz.Korps, T313, R70, F7306587.

115 Anlagen zum KTB III. Pz.Korps Ia, Tagesmeldung der 16. Pz.Div. 8.2.44, T314, R208, F000606.

116 Anlagen zum KTB PzAOK 1 Ia, Panzerlage III. Pz.Korps 9.2, 10.00 Uhr, T313, R70, F7306601.

117 Anlagen zum KTB III. Pz.Korps Ia, Tagesmeldungen der Div. am 9.2.44, T314, R208, F000716.

118 PzAOK 1 Ia, Tagesmeldung 10.2.44, T313, R70, F7306649.

119 Anlagen zum KTB PzAOK 1 Ia, Panzerlage III. Pz.Korps 15.2, 11.10 Uhr, T313, R70, F7306803.

120 PzAOK 1 Ia, Tagesmeldung 17.2.44, T313, R70, F7306862.

121 Anlagen zum KTB PzAOK 1 Ia, T313, R70, F7307094.

122 Anlagen zum KTB PzAOK 1 Ia, "Panzerlage III. Pz.Korps," 22.2.44, T313, R70, F7306966.

123 Anlagen zum KTB PzAOK 1 Ia, T313, R70, F7307094.

124 Anlagen zum KTB PzAOK 1 Ia, 22.2.44, "Verluste und Bergung von Panzern und Großwaffen," T313, R70, F7306959.

125 PzAOK 1, Stabsoffizier für Panzer-Bek., 3.3.1944, Fernschreiben PzAOK 1 Ia 423/44, Betr. Panzerausfälle, T313, R70, F7307174-6.

126 Anlagen zum KTB III. Pz.Korps Ia, Nachmeldung zur Ziff. 8.) der Tagesmeldung, 25.2.44, T314, R209, F000735.

127 III. Pz.Korps Ia Nr. 357/44 geh. 22.2.44, 23.30 Uhr, Fernschreiben an PzAOK 1, Anlagen zum KTB PzAOK 1 Ia, T313, R70, F7306982.

128 III. Pz.Korps Ia Nr. 367/44 geh, 24.2.44, T314, R209, F000664.

129 VII. A.K. Ia Nr 337/44 geh. 29.1.44 in Anlagen zum KTB PzAOK 1 Ia, T313, R69, F7306496.

130 Ibid.

131 17. Pz.Div., Monatszustandmeldung an Gen.Insp. der Pz.Tr., Stand 1.2.44, BA-MA RH 10/154.

132 Anlagen zum KTB Ia III. Pz.Korps, Tagesmeldungen der Div. am 2.2.44, T314, R208, F000400.

133 PzAOK 1 Ia Nr. 91/44, 31.1.44, "Kampfwert der Divisionen, Stand 29.1.44," T313, R69, F7306526, KTB III. Pz.Korps Ia, 5.2.44, T314, R206, F001254, Anlagen zum KTB III. Pz.Korps Ia, 15.2.44, T314, R209, F000114.

134 17. Pz.Div., Monatszustandmeldung an Gen. Insp. der Pz.Tr., Stand 1.2.44, BA-MA RH 10/154.

135 Gliederung der Div. u. Heeresartillerie im Bereich des III. Pz.Korps, Stand 3.2.44, Arko 3, T314, R208, F000441.

136 Ibid.

137 17. Pz.Div., Monatszustandmeldung an Gen. Insp. der Pz.Tr., Stand 1.2.44, BA-MA RH 10/154.

138 Anlagen zum KTB III. Pz.Korps Ia, Tagesmeldungen der Div. am 2.2.44, T314, R208, F000400.

139 Anlagen zum KTB III. Pz.Korps Ia, Tagesmeldungen der Div. 5.2.44, T314, R208, F000504.

140 Anlagen zum KTB PzAOK 1 Ia, "Anruf III. Pz.Korps–Panzer- und Sturmgeschützlage," 6.2. 44, 12.05 Uhr, T313, R71, F7308419.

141 Anlagen zum KTB PzAOK 1 Ia, Panzer und Sturmgeschützlage III. Pz.Korps, 7.2.44, 11.15 Uhr, T313, R70, F7306569.

142 Anlagen zum KTB III. Pz.Korps Ia, Tagesmeldungen der Div. 8.2.44, T314, R208, F000648.

143 Anlagen zum KTB PzAOK 1 Ia, Panzerlage III. Pz.Korps, 9.2.44, 10.00 Uhr, T313, R208, F784.

144 Anlagen zum KTB III. Pz.Korps Ia, Tagesmeldung der 17. Pz.Div. am 10.2.44, T314, R70, F7306649.

145 Anlagen zum KTB PzAOK 1 Ia, Panzer und Sturmgeschützlage III. Pz.Korps, 12.2.44, 15.30 Uhr, T313, R70, F7306688.

146 Anlagen zum KTB PzAOK 1 Ia, Panzerlage III. Pz.Korps 13.2, 10.15 Uhr, T313, R70, F7306713.

147 Anlagen zum KTB PzAOK 1 Ia, Panzerlage III. Pz.Korps 15.2, 11.10 Uhr, T313, R70, F7306803.

148 PzAOK 1 IIa Verlustübersicht vom 1. bis einschl. 20. Februar 1944, T313, R74, F7312637.

149 Anlagen zum KTB PzAOK 1 Ia, T313, R70, F7307094.

150 Anlagen zum KTB PzAOK 1 Ia, 22.2.44, "Verluste und Bergung von Panzern und Großwaffen," T313, R70, F7306959.

151 Anlagen zum KTB PzAOK 1 Ia, Panzerlage III. Pz.Korps, 22.2.44, T313, R70, F7306966.

152 Anlagen zum KTB PzAOK 1 Ia, T313, R70,

F7307094.

153 PzAOK 1, Stabsoffizier für Panzer-Bek., 1.3.1944, Fernschreiben PzAOK 1 Ia 423/44, Betr. Panzerausfälle, T313, R70, F7307174-6.

154 PzAOK 1 Ia Nr. 69/44, 24 Januar 1944, Wochenmeldung: Kampfwert der Divisionen, Stand 22.1.1944, T313, R69, F7306382. See also XXXXII. .A.K. Ia Fernschreiben an PzAOK 1, 26.1.44, 11.25 Uhr, T312, R69, F7306413 and PzAOK 1 Kriegsgliederung, Stand 22.1.11944, T313, R69, F7306485.

155 PzAOK 1 Ia Nr. 69/44, 24 Januar 1944, Wochenmeldung: Kampfwert der Divisionen, Stand 22.1.1944, T313, R69, F7306383.

156 PzAOK 1 Ia Nr. 69/44, 24 Januar 1944, Wochenmeldung: Kampfwert der Divisionen, Stand 22.1.1944, T313, R69, F7306382.

157 Ibid.

158 Ibid.

159 Kriegsgliederung der 8. Armee (nur Divisionen) Stand 8.2.44, T312, R64, F7582623.

160 AOK 8 Ia Morgenmeldungen der Korps 25.1.44, T312, R66, F7584360.

161 Lagekarten XI. A.K., BA-MA RH 24-11/98.

162 Kriegsgliederung der 8. Armee (nur Divisionen) Stand 8.2.44, T312, R64, F7582623.

163 Ibid.

164 Gruppe Mattenklott Ia, Geschützbestand der Gruppe Stemmermann, 17.2.44, fouund in Anlagen zum KTB Ia PzAOK 1 Ia, T313, R72, F7310472.

165 Meldung Gruppe Mattenklott, 29.2.44, 17.40 Uhr, in Anlagen zum KTB PzAOK 1 Ia, T313, R72, F7310423.

166 Gruppe Mattenklott, "Nicht im Kampfraum XI. und XXXXII. A.K. befindliche Teile", 18.2.44, in Anlagen zum KTB PzAOK 1 Ia, T313, R72, F7310468.

167 Ibid.

168 Kriegsgliederung der 8. Armee (nur Divisionen) Stand 8.2.44, T312, R64, F7582623.

169 Gruppe Mattenklott Ia, Geschützbestand der Gruppe Stemmermann, 17.2.44, fouund in Anlagen zum KTB Ia PzAOK 1 Ia, T313, R72, F7310472.

170 Meldung Gruppe Mattenklott, 29.2.44, 17.40 Uhr, in Anlagen zum KTB PzAOK 1 Ia, T313, R72, F7310423.

171 Gruppe Mattenklott, "Nicht im Kampfraum XI.und XXXXII. A.K. befindliche Teile", 18.2.44, in Anlagen zum KTB PzAOK 1 Ia, T313, R72, F7310468.

172 Ibid.

173 PzAOK 1, IIa, Verlustübersicht vom 1. bis einschl. 20. Februar 1944, NARA T313, R74, F7312637.

174 PzAOK 1 Ia Nr. 69/44, 24 Januar 1944, Wochenmeldung: Kampfwert der Divisionen, Stand 22.1.1944, T313, R69, F7306382.

175 Ibid.

176 G. Tessin, Verbände und Truppen der deutschen Wehrmacht und Waffen-SS (Mittler & Sohn, Frankfurt am Main and Biblio Verlag, Osnabrück 1966–1975), entry for units with number 88.

177 PzAOK 1 Ia Nr. 69/44, 24 Januar 1944, Wochenmeldung: Kampfwert der Divisionen, Stand 22.1.1944, T313, R69, F7306382.

178 G. Tessin, Verbände und Truppen der deutschen Wehrmacht und Waffen-SS (Mittler & Sohn, Frankfurt am Main and Biblio Verlag, Osnabrück 1966–1975), entry for units with number 88 and 245.

179 PzAOK 1 Kriegsgliederung, Stand 22.1.11944, T313, R69, F7306352, also on subsequent Kriegsgliederungen the regiment is missing.

180 G. Tessin, Verbände und Truppen der deutschen Wehrmacht und Waffen-SS (Mittler & Sohn, Frankfurt am Main and Biblio Verlag, Osnabrück 1966–1975), entry for units with number 88.

181 PzAOK 1 Kriegsgliederung, Stand 22.1.11944, T313, R69, F7306352 and PzAOK 1 Ia Nr. 69/44, 24 Januar 1944, Wochenmeldung: Kampfwert der Divisionen, Stand 22.1.1944, T313, R69, F7306382.

182 PzAOK 1 Kriegsgliederung, Stand 22.1.11944, T313, R69, F7306352; PzAOK 1 Ia Nr. 69/44, 24 Januar 1944, Wochenmeldung: Kampfwert der Divisionen, Stand 22.1.1944, T313, R69, F7306382; XXXXII. .A.K. Ia Fernschreiben an PzAOK 1, 26.1.44, 11.25 Uhr, T312, R69, F7306413.

183 PzAOK 1 Kriegsgliederung, Stand 22.1.11944, T313, R69, F7306352 and PzAOK 1 Ia Nr. 69/44, 24 Januar 1944, Wochenmeldung: Kampfwert der Divisionen, Stand 22.1.1944, T313, R69, F7306382.

184 PzAOK 1 Ia Nr. 69/44, 24 Januar 1944, Wochenmeldung: Kampfwert der Divisionen, Stand 22.1.1944, T313, R69, F7306382.

185 Meldung Gruppe Mattenklott, 29.2.44, 17.40 Uhr, in Anlagen zum KTB PzAOK 1 Ia, T313, R72, F7310423.

186 Ibid.

187 Gruppe Mattenklott, "Nicht im Kampfraum XI. und XXXXII. A.K. befindliche Teile", 18.2.44, in Anlagen zum KTB PzAOK 1 Ia, T313, R72, F7310468.

188 Ibid.

189 Meldung Gruppe Mattenklott, 29.2.44, 17.40 Uhr, in Anlagen zum KTB PzAOK 1 Ia, T313, R72, F7310423.

190 XXXXVII. Pz.Korps Ia Nr. 289/44 geh., 23.1.44, Verpflegungs und Gefechtsstärken, T314, R1132, F000575.

191 Ibid.

192 Ibid.

193 According to the XXXXVII. Pz.Korps Ia Nr. 290/44 geh., Kurzzustandbericht, Stand 22.1.44, T314, R1132, F000573. See also XXXXVII. Pz.Korps Ia Nr. 414/44 geh., Kurzzustandbericht, Stand 29.1.44, T314, R1132, F000591 and 106. Inf.Div. Zustandmeldung, Stand 1.2.44, in Anlagen zum KTB XXXXVII. Pz.Korps Ia, T314, R1132, F000640.

194 XXXXVII. Pz.Korps Ia Nr. 290/44 geh., Kurzzustandbericht, Stand 22.1.44, T314, R1132, F000573.

195 Ibid.

196 106. ID. Monatszustandmeldung, Stand 1.2.44, in Anlagen zum KTB XXXXVII. Pz.Korps Ia, T314, R1132, F000638.

197 Ibid.

198 Ibid.

199 Ibid.

200 PzAOK 1 Kriegsgliederung, Stand 22.1.1944, T313, R69, F7306352.

201 PzAOK 1 Ia Nr. 69/44, 24 Januar 1944, Wochenmeldung: Kampfwert der Divisionen, Stand 22.1.1944, T313, R69, F7306383.

202 Ibid.

203 Gliederung 198. Inf.Div., Stand vom 1.1.1944, in Anlagen zum KTB III. Pz.Korps Ia, 3.2.44, T314, R208, F000439.

204 Ibid.

205 PzAOK 1, IIa, Verlustübersicht Monat Januar 1944, NARA T313, R74, F7312636.

206 PzAOK 1, IIa, Verlustübersicht vom 1. bis einschl. 20. Februar 1944, NARA T313, R74, F7312637.

207 320. ID. Monatszustandmeldung, Stand 1.2.44, in Anlagen zum KTB XXXXVII. Pz.Korps Ia, T314, R1132, F000642-5.

208 320. ID. Monatszustandmeldung, Stand 1.2.44, in Anlagen zum KTB XXXXVII. Pz.Korps Ia, T314, R1132, F000642-5.

209 320. ID. Monatszustandmeldung, Stand 1.2.44, in Anlagen zum KTB XXXXVII. Pz.Korps Ia, T314, R1132, F000642-5.

210 320. ID. Monatszustandmeldung, Stand 1.2.44, in Anlagen zum KTB XXXXVII. Pz.Korps Ia, T314, R1132, F000642-5.

211 376. ID. Monatszustandmeldung, Stand 1.2.44, in Anlagen zum KTB XXXXVII. Pz.Korps Ia, T314, R1132, F000647-8.

212 Ibid.

213 Ibid.

214 Gen.Kdo. XXXXVII. Pz.Korps Ia Nr. 66/44, 22.2.44, T314, R1132, F000699-703.

215 See G. Tessin, Truppen und Verbände der deutschen Wehrmacht und Waffen-SS (Mittler & Sohn, Frankfurt am Main and Biblio Verlag, Osnabrück 1966–1975) and Kriegsgliederung der 8. Armee (nur Divisionen) Stand 8.2.44, T312, R64, F7582623.

216 Gruppe Mattenklott Ia, Geschützbestand der Gruppe Stemmermann, 17.2.44, fouund in Anlagen zum KTB Ia PzAOK 1 Ia, T313, R72, F7310472.

217 See KTB AOK 8 Ia, 24.1.44, 18.20 Uhr and also 19.25 Uhr.

218 Meldung Gruppe Mattenklott, 29.2.44, 17.40 Uhr, in Anlagen zum KTB PzAOK 1 Ia, T313, R72, F7310423.

219 Gruppe Mattenklott, "Nicht im Kampfraum XI. und XXXXII. A.K. befindliche Teile," 18.2.44, in Anlagen zum KTB PzAOK 1 Ia, T313, R72, F7310468.

220 Ibid.

221 Michael Schadewitz, Einsätze des "schweren Panzerregiments Bäke" vom 24. Januar bis 17. Februar 1944, p. 2, BA-MA MSg 2/4396.

222 Ibid, p. 7. Note that this is "kills" as recorded by the Germans. Such figures are usually exaggerated.

223 PzAOK Ia, Tagesmeldung an HGr Süd, 31.1.44. Note that five of the Panthers were with 101. Jg.Div.

224 Michael Schadewitz, Einsätze des "schweren Panzerregiments Bäke" vom 24. Januar bis 17. Februar 1944, p. 8, BA-MA MSg 2/4396.

225 Anlagen zum KTB III. Pz.Korps. Ia, Morgenmeldungen der Div., 4.2.44, NARA T314, R208, F000448.

226 Anlagen zum KTB III. Pz.Korps Ia, Tagesmeldungen der Div. 5.2.44, T314, R208, F000504.

227 Anlagen zum KTB PzAOK 1 Ia, "Anruf III. Pz.Korps – Panzer- und Sturmgeschützlage," 6.2. 44, 12.05 Uhr, T313, R71, F7308419.

228 Anlagen zum KTB III. Pz.Korps Ia, Tagesmeldungen der Div. am 6.2.44, T314, R208, F000543.

229 Anlagen zun KTB PzAOK 1 Ia, Panzer und Sturmgeschützlage III. Pz.Korps, 7.2.44, 11.15 Uhr, T313, R70, F7306569.

230 Anlagen zun KTB PzAOK 1 Ia, Panzerlage III. Pz.Korps, 9.2.44, 10.00 Uhr, T313, R70, F7306601.

231 PzAOK 1 Ia Tagesmeldung 10.2.44, T313, R70, F7306649.

232 Anlagen zum KTB PzAOK 1 Ia, Panzerlage III. Pz.Korps 15.2, 11.10 Uhr, T313, R70, F7306803.

233 Anlagen zum KTB PzAOK 1 Ia, T313, R70, F7307094.

234 Anlagen zum KTB PzAOK 1 Ia, 22.2.44, "Verluste und Bergung von Panzern und Groß-

waffen," T313, R70, F7306959.

235 Michael Schadewitz, Einsätze des "schweren Panzerregiments Bäke" vom 24. Januar bis 17. Februar 1944, p. 8, BA-MA MSg 2/4396 p. 10.

236 Anlagen zum KTB PzAOK 1 Ia, T313, R70, F7307094.

237 AOK 8 Ia, Nr 918/44, 6.2.44, T312, R64, F7582954.

238 XXXXVII. Pz.Korps Ia Tagesmeldung 13.2.44, T314, R1132, F000684.

239 See VII. A.K. Ia Nr. 160/44, 24.1.44; Anlagen zum KTB PzAOK 1 Ia, T313, R69, F7306391 and III. Pz.Korps. Tagesmeldung 25.1.44 in Anlagen zum KTB PzAOK 1 Ia, T313, R69, F7306401.

240 Gliederung der Div. u. Heeresartillerie im Bereich des III. Pz.Korps, Stand 3.2.44, Arko 3, T314, R208, F000441.

241 Gliederung der Div. u. Heeresartillerie im Bereich des III. Pz.Korps, Stand 3.2.44, Arko 3, T314, R208, F000441.

242 Tessin ZZ.

243 Lieferungen der Pz.Fahrzeuge, BA-MA RH 10/349.

244 XXXXVII. Pz.Korps Ia Nr. 290/44 geh., Kurzzustandbericht, Stand 22.1.44, T314, R1132, F000575.

245 11. Pz.Div. Ia, Fernschreiben an AOK 8, 27.1.44, found in Anlagen zum KTB AOK 8 Ia, T312, R66, F7584303.

246 Monatszustandmeldung 8. Pz.Abt., Stand 1.2.44, in Anlagen zum KTB XXXXVII. Pz.Korps Ia, T314, R1132, F000658.

247 KTB I./Pz.Rgt. 26, BA-MA RH 39/599; KTB AOK 8 Ia, 30.1.44, 09.30 Uhr, T312, R64, F7581777.

248 KTB I./Pz.Rgt. 26, BA-MA RH 39/599.

249 KTB I./Pz.Rgt. 26, BA-MA RH 39/599.

250 KTB AOK 8 Ia, 27-28 January 44, T312, R64, F7581753-63 and KTB XXXXVII. Pz.Korps Ia, 28.1.44, T314, R1132, F000430.

251 KTB I./Pz.Rgt. 26, BA-MA RH 39/599.

252 KTB I./Pz.Rgt. 26, BA-MA RH 39/599.

253 KTB I./Pz.Rgt. 26, BA-MA RH 39/599.

254 KTB I./Pz.Rgt. 26, BA-MA RH 39/599.

255 KTB I./Pz.Rgt. 26, BA-MA RH 39/599.

256 Anlage 25 zum KTB I./Pz.Rgt- 26, BA-MA RH 39/599.

257 KTB I./Pz.Rgt. 26, Anlage "Zusammenstellung der Pz.-Lagemeldungen, 14.7.44", BA-MA RH 39/599.

258 KTB I./Pz.Rgt. 26, BA-MA RH 39/599.

259 KTB I./Pz.Rgt. 26, BA-MA RH 39/599.

260 KTB I./Pz.Rgt. 26, BA-MA RH 39/599.

261 KTB I./Pz.Rgt. 26, BA-MA RH 39/599.

262 KTB I./Pz.Rgt. 26, BA-MA RH 39/599.

263 KTB I./Pz.Rgt. 26, BA-MA RH 39/599.

264 KTB I./Pz.Rgt. 26, BA-MA RH 39/599.

265 KTB I./Pz.Rgt. 26, Anlage "Zusammenstellung der Pz.-Lagemeldungen, 14.7.44", BA-MA RH 39/599.

266 KTB I./Pz.Rgt. 26, BA-MA RH 39/599.

267 KTB I./Pz.Rgt. 26, BA-MA RH 39/599.

268 KTB I./Pz.Rgt. 26, BA-MA RH 39/599.

269 KTB I./Pz.Rgt. 26, BA-MA RH 39/599.

270 KTB I./Pz.Rgt. 26, BA-MA RH 39/599.

271 KTB I./Pz.Rgt. 26, BA-MA RH 39/599.

272 KTB I./Pz.Rgt. 26, BA-MA RH 39/599.

273 KTB I./Pz.Rgt. 26, Anlage "Zusammenstellung der Pz.-Lagemeldungen, 14.7.44", BA-MA RH 39/599.

274 KTB I./Pz.Rgt. 26, Anlage "Zusammenstellung der Pz.-Lagemeldungen, 14.7.44", BA-MA RH 39/599.

275 Derived from KTB I./Pz.Rgt. 26 and Anlagen "Zusammenstellung der Pz.-Lagemeldungen, 14.7.44" and Anlage 25 zum KTB I./Pz.Rgt- 26, all found in BA-MA RH 39/599.

276 Anlage 25 zum KTB I./Pz.Rgt. 26, BA-MA RH 39/599.

277 Gefechts- und Verpflegungsstärken der I./Panzer-Regiment 26, BA-MA RH 39/599.

278 Ibid.

279 Gliederung der Div. u. Heeresartillerie im Bereich des III. Pz.Korps, Stand 3.2.44, Arko 3, T314, R208, F000441.

280 Kriegsliederung PzAOK 1 Ia, Stand 29.1.44 & 10.2.44; T313, R69, F7306485 and T313, R70, F7306639.

281 KTB XXXXVII. Pz.Korps Ia, 1.2.44, T314, R1132, F000438.

282 AOK 8 Ia/Art, Nr. 266/44 geh, 31.1.44, T312, R64, F7582972; Kriegsgliederung der 8. Armee, Stand 3.2.44, T312, R64, F7582624.

283 AOK 8 Ia, Nr 918/44, 6.2.44, T312, R64, F7582954.

284 Gliederung der Div. u. Heeresartillerie im Bereich des III. Pz.Korps, Stand 3.2.44, Arko 3, T314, R208, F000441.

285 PzAOK 1 Kriegsgliederung, Stand 22.1.11944, T313, R69, F7306352 and Gliederung der Div. u. Heeresartillerie im Bereich des III. Pz.Korps, Stand 3.2.44, Arko 3, T314, R208, F000441.

286 Gliederung der Div. u. Heeresartillerie im Bereich des III. Pz.Korps, Stand 3.2.44, Arko 3, T314, R208, F000441.

287 III. Pz.Korps Ia Nr. 221/44 geh., "Korpsbefehl für den 7.2.44", T314, R208, F553.

288 PzAOK 1 Kriegsgliederung, Stand 22.1.11944, T313, R69, F7306352 and Gliederung der Div. u. Heeresartillerie im Bereich des III. Pz.Korps, Stand 3.2.44, Arko 3, T314, R208, F000441.

289 PzAOK 1 Kriegsgliederung, Stand 22.1.11944, T313, R69, F7306352.

290 Gliederung der Div. u. Heeresartillerie im Bereich des III. Pz.Korps, Stand 3.2.44, Arko 3, T314, R208, F000441.

291 AOK 8 Ia/Art, Nr. 212/44 geh., 24.1.44, T312, R64, F7582982.

292 Kriegsgliederung der 8. Armee, Stand 28.1.44, T312, R64, F7582625.

293 Gruppe Mattenklott Ia, Geschützbestand der Gruppe Stemmermann, 17.2.44, fouund in Anlagen zum KTB Ia PzAOK 1 Ia, T313, R72, F7310472.

294 PzAOK 1 Kriegsgliederung 22.1.44, T313, R69, F7306351.

295 PzAOK 1 Kriegsgliederung 22.1.44, T313, R69, F7306485.

296 III. Pz.Korps Ia Nr. 191/44, "Gliederung des III. Pz.Korps am 2.2.1944", NARA T314, R208, F000417.

297 III. Pz.Korps, "Korpsbefehl für den 8.2.44", T314, R208, F612.

298 KTB AOK 8 Ia, 24.1.44, T312, R64, F7581744.

299 AOK 8 Ia/Art Nr. 225/44 geh. 26.1.44, T312, R64, 7582977.

300 KTB XXXXVII. Pz.Korps Ia, 27.1.44, T314, R1132, F000430.

301 AOK 8 Ia/Art Nr. 237/44 geh, 28.1.44, 12.20 Uhr, T312, R64, F7582976.

302 AOK 8 Ia Nr. 918/44 geh., 6.2.44, T312, R64, F7582954.

303 Tagesmeldung VII. A.K. 25.1.44. - 19.30, Anlagen zum KTB PzAOK 1 Ia, T313, R69, F7306400.

304 34. Inf.Div. Tagesmeldung an III. Pz.Korps am 8.2.44, T314, R208, F649.

305 KTB XXXXVII. Pz.Korps Ia, 25.1.44, T314, R1132, F000426.

306 StuG-Lage Stand 31.1.44, BA-MA RH 10/20.

307 XXXXVII. Pz.Korps Ia Tagesmeldung 1.2.44, T314, R1132, F000594.

308 XXXXVII. Pz.Korps Ia Tagesmeldung 13.2.44, T314, R1132, F000684.

309 XXXXVII. Pz.Korps Ia, "Panzer- und Sturmgeschütz-Lage Stand 1.3.44," T314, R1132, F000724.

310 PzAOK 1 Ia Nr. 286/44 geh., 9.2.44, 16.20 Uhr, T314, R208, F706.

311 Ibid.

312 See PzAOK 1 Kriegsgliederungen charts, 29 Jan, 10 Feb and III Panzer Corps Kriegsgliederungen charts 2 and 5 February, T313, R69, F7306485; T313, R70, F7306639; T314, R208, F000417, T314, R208, F000508.

313 KTB AOK 8 Ia, 24.1.44, 14.30 Uhr, T312, R64, F7581741.

314 Anlagen zum KTB III. Pz.Korps Ia, Tagesmeldungen der Div. am 1.1.44, T314, R207, F000859.

315 StuG-Lage Stand 31.1.44, BA-MA RH 10/20.

316 AOK 8 Ia Nr. 918/44 geh. 6.2.44, T312, R64, F7582954.

317 Gruppe Mattenklott, 17. Febr. 1944, Geschütz-Bestand der Gruppe Stemmermann, in Anlagen zum KTB PzAOK 1 Ia, T313, R72, F7310472.

318 On both 19 and 21 January the battalion reported three operational assault guns, see Tagesmeldung VII A.K. Ia, 19.1.44 and 21.1.41, both found in Anlagen zum KTB PzAOK 1 Ia, T313, R69, F7306305 & 7306341.

319 Tagesmeldung VII. A.K. 25.1.44. – 19.30, Anlagen zum KTB PzAOK 1 Ia, T313, R69, F7306400.

320 KTB PzOAK 1 Ia, 26.1.44, T313, R69, 7305828.

321 Tagesmeldung XXXXII. A.K., 28.1.44, in Anlagen zum KTB PzAOK 1 Ia, T313, R69, F7306470.

322 Tagesmeldung XXXXII. Korps Ia 28.1.44, in Anlagen zum KTB AOK 8 Ia, T312, R66, F7584271.

323 Tagesmeldung XXXXII. Korps Ia 29.1.44, in Anlagen zum KTB AOK 8 Ia, T312, R66, F7584256.

324 Meldung Gruppe Mattenklott, 29.2.44, 17.40 Uhr, in Anlagen zum KTB PzAOK 1 Ia, T313, R72, F7310423.

325 PzAOK 1 Kriegsgliederung, Stand 22.1.11944, T313, R69, F7306352.

326 Meldung Gruppe Mattenklott, 29.2.44, 17.40 Uhr, in Anlagen zum KTB PzAOK 1 Ia, T313, R72, F7310423.

327 StuG-Lage Stand 31.1.44, BA-MA RH 10/20.

328 Anlagen zum KTB Ia III. Pz.Korps, Tagesmeldungen an PzAOK 1, 1.2.44, T314, R208, F000382.

329 PzAOK 1 Ia Anlagen zum KTB, Anruf an III. Pz.Korps, Panzer- und Sturmgeschützlage, 6.2. 44, 12.05 Uhr, T313, R71, F7308419.

330 See III. Pz.Korps Ia Nr. 191/44, "Gliederung des III. Pz.Korps am 2.2.1944", NARA T314, R208, F000417 and III. Pz.Korps Ia Nr. 216/44, "Gliederung des III. Pz.Korps am 5.2.1944", NARA T314, R208, F000518. According to the 17. Pz.Div. Tagesmeldung an III. Pz.Korps am 8.2.44, T314, R208, F648, the battalion was at 17. Pz.Div.

331 Anlagen zum KTB III. Pz.Korps Ia, Tagesmeldungen der Div. 5.2.44, T314, R208, F000504.

332 Anlagen zum KTB PzAOK 1 Ia, "Anruf III. Pz.Korps – Panzer- und Sturmgeschützlage," 6.2. 44, 12.05 Uhr, T313, R71, F7308419.

333 Anlagen zun KTB PzAOK 1 Ia, Panzer- und Sturmgeschützlage III. Pz.Korps, 7.2.44, 11.15 Uhr, T313, R70, F7306569.

334 Anlagen zum KTB III. Pz.Korps Ia, Tagesmeldungen der Div. 8.2.44, T314, R208, F000648.

335 PzAOK 1 Ia, Tagesmeldung 9.2.44, T313, R70, F7306626.

336 PzAOK 1 Ia Tagesmeldung 10.2.44, T313, R70, F7306649.

337 Anlagen zum KTB PzAOK 1 Ia, "Panzer und Sturmgeschützlage III. Pz.Korps," 12.2.44, 15.30 Uhr, T313, R70, F7306688.

338 Anlagen zum KTB PzAOK 1 Ia, "Panzer und Sturmgeschützlage III. Pz.Korps," 13.2.44, 10.15 Uhr, T313, R70, F7306713.

339 Anlagen zum KTB PzAOK 1 Ia, "Panzerlage III. Pz.Korps," 15.2, 11.10 Uhr, T313, R70, F7306803.

340 Anlagen zum KTB PzAOK 1 Ia, "Panzerlage III. Pz.Korps," 22.2.44, T313, R70, F7306966.

341 Anlagen zum KTB PzAOK 1 Ia, T313, R70, F7307094.

342 Anlagen zum KTB PzAOK 1 Ia, Fernschreiben VII. A.K. Ia an PzAOK 1 Ia 23.1.44, T313, R69, F7306370.

343 See PzAOK 1 Ia Nr. 105/44 geh. 5.2.44 in Anlagen zum KTB III. Pz.Korps Ia, T314, R208, F000513. See also III. Pz.Korps Fernschreiben an 34. I.D. and 198. I.D., 5.2.44, 23.00 Uhr, T314, R208, F515f.

344 BA-MA RH 10/220.

345 16. Pz.Div. Ia, Tagesmeldung an III. Pz.Korps 2.2.44, NARA T314, R208, F000402.

346 Anlagen zum KTB III. Pz.Korps Ia, T314, R208, F000504.

347 Anlagen zum KTB III. Pz.Korps Ia, Tagesmeldungen der Div. 5.2.44, T314, R208, F000504.

348 Anlagen zum KTB PzAOK 1 Ia, "Anruf III. Pz.Korps – Panzer- und Sturmgeschützlage," 6.2. 44, 12.05 Uhr, T313, R71, F7308419.

349 Anlagen zum KTB III. Pz.Korps, 16. Pz.Div. Ia Morgenmeldung 7.2.44, T314, R208, F000570.

350 Anlagen zum KTB III. Pz.Korps Ia, Tagesmeldung der 16. Pz.Div. 7.2.44, T314, R208, F000606.

351 Anlagen zun KTB PzAOK 1 Ia, Panzerlage III. Pz.Korps, 8.2.44, T313, R70, F7306586.

352 PzAOK 1 Ia, Tagesmeldung 9.2.44, T313, R70, F7306626.

353 PzAOK 1 Ia Tagesmeldung 10.2.44, T313, R70, F7306649.

354 Anlagen zum KTB PzAOK 1 Ia, "Panzer und Sturmgeschützlage III. Pz.Korps," 12.2.44, 15.30 Uhr, T313, R70, F7306688.

355 Anlagen zum KTB PzAOK 1 Ia, "Panzer und Sturmgeschützlage III. Pz.Korps," 13.2.44, 10.15 Uhr, T313, R70, F7306713.

356 Anlagen zum KTB PzAOK 1 Ia, "Panzerlage III. Pz.Korps," 15.2, 11.10 Uhr, T313, R70, F7306803.

357 PzAOK 1, Stabsoffizier für Panzer-Bek., 3.3.1944, Fernschreiben PzAOK 1 Ia 423/44, Betr. Panzerausfälle, T313, R70, F7307174-6.

358 Anlagen zum KTB PzAOK 1 Ia, Panzerlage III. Pz.Korps, 22.2.44, T313, R70, F7306966.

359 Anlagen zum KTB PzAOK 1 Ia, T313, R70, F7307094.

360 PzAOK 1 Kriegsgliederung, Stand 22.1.11944, T313, R69, F7306352.

361 PzAOK 1, Kriegsgliederung 29.1.44, T313, R69, F7306351; III. Pz.Korps Ia Nr. 191/44, "Gliederung des III. Pz.Korps am 2.2.1944", NARA T314, R208, F000417; III. Pz.Korps Ia Nr. 216/44, "Gliederung des III. Pz.Korps am 5.2.1944", NARA T314, R208, F000518.

362 Gliederung der Div. u. Heeresartillerie im Bereich des III. Pz.Korps, Stand 3.2.44, Arko 3, T314, R208, F000441.

363 Kriegsgliederungen der 8. Armee, Stand 16.2.44, 28.2.44 and 3.2.44, T312, R64, F7582624-6.

364 AOK 8 Ia Nr. 918/44 geh., 6.2.44, T312, R64, F7582954.

365 AOK 8 Ia Nr. 918/44 geh., 6.2.44, T312, R64, F7582954.

366 It was part of the XI. Korps according to Kriegsgliederuungen AOK 8 for 16 and 28 January 1944, T312, R64, Frames 7582626 & 7582630.

367 KTB AOK 8 Ia, 25.1.44, 08.12 Uhr, T312, R64, F7581745.

368 KTB XXXXVII. Pz.Korps Ia, 26.1.44, T314, R1132, F000427.

369 StuG-Lage Stand 31.1.44, BA-MA RH 10/20.

370 XXXXVII. Pz.Korps Ia Tagesmeldung 1.2.44, T314, R1132, F000594.

371 XXXXVII. Pz.Korps Ia Tagesmeldung 13.2.44, T314, R1132, F000684.

372 XXXXVII. Pz.Korps Ia, "Panzer- und Sturmgeschütz-Lage Stand 1.3.44," T314, R1132, F000724.

373 Monatszustandmeldung 911. StuG.Abt., Stand 1.2.44, in Anlagen zum KTB XXXXVII. Pz. Korps Ia, T314, R1132, F000662.

374 11. Pz.Div. Ia, Fernschreiben an AOK 8, 27.1.44, found in Anlagen zum KTB AOK 8 Ia, T312, R66, F7584303.

375 Monatszustandmeldung 911. StuG.Abt., Stand 1.2.44, in Anlagen zum KTB XXXXVII. Pz.Korps Ia, T314, R1132, F000662.

376 XXXXVII. Pz.Korps Ia, "Panzer- und Sturmgeschütz-Lage Stand 1.3.44," T314, R1132, F000724.

Index

Bäke, Franz, 155, 199, 212, 221, 223, 230, 296
Back, Major-General Hans-Ulrich, 154, 157, 240
Bessonov, Evgeni, 12-13
Bittl, Maj. Norbert, 122-123, 171-172, 174, 178
Breith, Gen. Hermann, 147-148, 150, 153, 159, 169, 171, 194, 196, 201, 204, 211, 213, 215-216, 221, 231, 235, 240, 251, 296
Büsing, Colonel, 85, 88-89, 91-93, 95
Busse, Theodor, 66-67, 82, 129-130, 169-170, 175, 181, 187, 238
der Meden, Major-General Karl-Friedrich von, 154, 158-159, 201
Ehlers, Olaf, 48, 173, 246-250
Gaedke, Col., 63, 65-66, 174
Geneva Convention, 182

GERMAN MILITARY UNITS:
1st Panzer Army, 22, 25-28, 30-31, 66, 100, 108, 111, 122, 133, 145, 147-149, 158-159, 161, 164, 175, 177-178, 226, 233, 281, 284, 287-289, 295
1st Panzer Division, 148, 150, 153, 158, 163, 165, 168, 177, 195-196, 198-199, 201, 214, 223-225, 232-233, 240, 251, 284-287
1st SS-Panzer Division, 111, 114, 150, 153, 158-159, 177, 198, 204, 253, 284- 285, 287
I Fliegerkorps, 228
2d Parachute Division, 170, 181, 209, 238
II SS-Panzer Corps, 9
3d Panzer Division, 45, 53, 55, 57, 59, 61-62, 68, 75, 77, 120, 133, 137, 139, 141, 153, 172-173, 175-176, 181, 190, 237-238, 288, 290
III Panzer Corps, 26, 28-30, 42, 100, 145, 147-149, 153, 157-159, 161-165, 171, 174-175, 177, 180-181, 184, 189, 193, 195-197, 199, 210, 213-216, 218- 220, 223-227, 229-231, 233, 235-239, 242-243, 244-245, 253-254, 259-260, 262, 269, 275, 277, 279, 281, 283-285, 287-288, 290, 293-294
4th Army, 296
4th Mountain Division, 226, 233
4th Panzer Army, 148
4th SS-Panzer Grenadier Division, 106
6th Army, 1, 6-7, 9, 96, 108, 114, 170, 179
6th Panzer Division, 226, 233
8th Army, 22, 31-32, 36, 39, 62-63, 73, 94-96, 108, 111, 122-123, 129-130, 133, 138-139, 148, 164, 169-170, 174-175, 177-178, 183, 187, 189, 191, 218, 226, 231, 288-289
8th Assault Gun Battalion, 66
10th Panzer Grenadier Division, 123, 185
11th Panzer Division, 32, 36, 45, 53, 62, 65-70, 74-75, 77-78, 80, 83, 89, 94, 104, 120-121, 123, 127, 133, 135, 137, 139, 144, 169, 172-173, 181, 185, 190, 193, 205-207, 216-217, 226-227, 237, 239, 246, 288-292
13th Panzer Division, 45, 48, 96, 123, 132-133, 135, 172-174, 181, 190, 193, 205-207, 216-217, 227, 239, 246, 288-289, 291
14th Panzer Division, 32, 36, 46, 53, 57-59, 61, 63, 66-68, 70, 74, 77-78, 80, 104, 120, 123, 127, 130, 132, 141,

173, 175, 177, 181, 185, 190, 216, 246, 278, 288, 291-292
15th Panzer Regiment, 216
16th Panzer Division, 147-150, 154-155, 157-158, 160, 163-165, 167-168, 195-196, 198-199, 201-202, 213, 215, 221, 223, 225, 232, 284-287
17th Panzer Division, 100, 118, 147-150, 154-155, 157-161, 163, 165, 167-168, 195-196, 198, 201, 213, 223, 225, 232, 284-286
17th Reconnaissance Battalion, 241, 251
20th Panzer Grenadier Division, 20
24th Panzer Division, 96, 123, 140, 145, 150, 169-172, 220
26th Panzer Division, 81
28th SS-Division, 297
32d Antitank Brigade, 162
34th Infantry Division, 29, 53, 99, 100-101, 148, 157, 163-164, 204, 226, 284-285, 288
57th Infantry Division, 36, 53, 55, 61-63, 65, 80, 109, 177, 242, 254, 269, 271-272, 278, 296-297
63d Cavalry Division, 227
72d Division, 53, 60-61, 63, 65-67, 69, 75, 80, 109, 122-123, 177, 180, 186, 189, 191, 205, 209-210, 238, 242, 254, 257-260, 262, 265-266, 278, 296
75th Infantry Division, 285
76th Infantry Division, 15, 27-30
88th Infantry Division, 28-29, 53, 99, 103-104, 109, 111, 131, 177, 242, 254, 266, 269-270, 278, 296-297
103d Infantry Regiment, 78
105th Infantry Regiment, 205
106th Infantry Division, 53, 57, 181, 185, 209
107th Infantry Regiment, 157, 245
108th Infantry Regiment, 257
108th Panzer Grenadier Regiment, 120
109th Infantry Regiment, 259
110th Infantry Regiment, 206
111th Panzer Grenadier Regiment, 68, 206
112th Infantry Division, 44
113th Panzer Grenadier Regiment, 224
124th Infantry Regiment, 260-261
198th Infantry Division, 53, 98, 101, 148, 157-158, 160, 163, 165, 167-168, 199, 201, 213, 225, 278, 284-285, 288
255th Infantry Division, 44
258th Infantry Division, 1
266th Infantry Regiment, 205, 259, 262
282d Division, 53
305th Infantry Regiment, 201
308th Grenadier Regiment, 98, 167
320th Infantry Division, 53, 96, 123, 127, 141, 181, 185
326th Infantry Regiment, 213
332d Infantry Division, 44, 278
376th Infantry Division, 96, 123, 133, 137, 139, 141, 181, 288-289
389th Infantry Division, 15, 31-32, 36, 38, 53, 55, 57-58, 60-63, 65-66, 69, 74-75, 106, 109, 122, 177, 186, 188-189, 272, 278, 296-297
676th Infantry Regiment, 55, 62, 271
Army Group South, 5, 17, 20, 25, 36, 66, 80, 111-112, 123, 129, 164, 169-170, 175, 181, 237
Das Reich SS-Panzer Division, 10
Divisionsgruppe 255, 104
Grossdeutchland Division, 10, 36, 74, 81, 83, 89, 127
Gruppe Stemmermann, 96, 132, 134, 138-139, 141, 143, 163-164, 171, 174-175, 177-178, 180, 183, 187, 189, 193, 196, 199, 209-211, 215-216, 223-225, 228- 229, 230-233, 235-240, 243, 251, 254, 257, 264, 266, 277, 279, 281, 283-285, 288, 292
Kampfgrappe von Sievers, 206
Kampfgruppe Blo..meke, 199, 213
Kampfgruppe Fink, 160, 201
Kampfgruppe Frank, 199-203, 214-215, 218, 233, 241, 251-253
Kampfgruppe Gehrig, 207
Kampfgruppe Haack, 190, 193, 205-208, 217, 238-239, 246
Kampfgruppe Heimann, 159
Kampfgruppe Huppert, 158, 161, 163, 165, 167
Kampfgruppe Pietsch, 201, 232-233, 240-241

Kampfgruppe Stelzner, 143
Kampfgruppe von Brese, 58-59, 68, 74, 83, 85, 120-121, 127, 131, 173
Kampfgruppe von Sievers, 205-207
Korps-Abteilung B, 28-29, 44, 53, 103-104, 109, 122, 138, 177, 190, 242, 256- 257, 264-266, 291, 297
LII Corps, 39, 181
Panzer Regiment Bäke, 13, 147-149, 155, 158, 160, 163, 165, 167-168, 195-196, 201-202, 212, 215, 221, 223, 225, 230, 232-233, 240-241, 252-254
SS-Panzer Division Leibstandarte Adolf Hitler, 147-148, 168, 195-196, 213, 225-226, 241, 287
SS-Panzer Grenadier Regiment 1, 159
SS-Wallonien Brigade, 53, 106, 108, 188-189, 191, 210, 228, 238, 245, 265, 274, 278, 292, 297
SS-Westland Regiment, 17, 109, 191, 267
SS-Wiking Division, 17, 32, 53, 55, 59, 61-63, 65, 69, 104-106, 108-109, 122-123, 131, 137-138, 180, 189, 204, 210, 238-239, 242, 245, 256, 258, 261, 265-268, 271, 276, 278, 292, 297
Totenkopf Division, 10
VII Corps, 25-28, 30, 53, 66, 98-101, 126, 133, 147-149, 213, 284, 288
VIII Fliegerkorps, 175, 181, 193
XI Corps, 31-32, 36, 53, 55, 57-58, 61-63, 66-67, 69-70, 75, 80, 82, 96, 102, 104, 122, 123-127, 131, 133, 138-139, 171, 174, 178-180, 184, 223, 238, 245, 257, 271, 295
XXXXII Corps, 1-2, 25, 27-31, 53, 66, 75, 82, 96, 99-104, 108, 122-123, 127, 130-131, 137, 171, 174, 178, 180, 184-185, 191, 223, 238, 277, 295
XXXXVI Panzer Corps, 28-30, 40, 42, 52-53, 57-58, 66, 70, 100
XXXXVII Panzer Corps, 79-81, 83, 94-96, 121, 123, 126, 128, 132, 135, 137, 140-141, 148, 150, 154, 162-164, 169, 171, 174-175, 181, 184-185, 193-194, 207, 218, 226-227, 229, 231, 233, 235, 239, 246, 283, 288, 290, 292
Glässgen, Maj., 79, 83, 85-86, 88-89, 94-95
Grossjohan, Capt. Georg, 98
Haack, Major-General Werner, 177-178
Hitler, Adolf, 5-6, 15-16, 27, 65-66, 131, 148, 169-170, 174, 190,-191, 297
Hube, Gen. Hans-Valentin, 22, 25-27, 30-31, 42, 100, 108, 159, 161-162, 196, 199, 226, 233, 295
Kaestner, Major, 209-210
Kirchhoff, Lt., 85-89, 91-94
Konev, Marshal Ivan, 1, 3, 18-20, 22-25, 37, 39, 60-62, 67, 81-82, 95-96, 118-119, 132, 138, 172, 177, 180, 184, 189, 191, 193-194, 204, 211-212, 216, 228-229, 237, 239, 244, 278-279, 283, 296
Krainyukov, Konstantin V., 20, 284
Kravchenko, Andrei, 117-119, 160, 179, 223, 296
Kruse, Major-General, 32-33, 35-36, 264, 272
Lampe, Heinz, 218-220
Langkeit, Col., 58, 67-68
Lazarev, Gen., 59, 244
Lemmer, Capt., 85-89
Lesselidse, Colonel-General (-), 20-21
Lieb, Gen. Theobald, 2-3, 29, 103-104, 123, 128-130, 137-138, 142-143, 171, 174, 184-185, 189, 191, 204, 215-216, 229, 237, 242, 244-246, 254, 256
Manstein, Field Marshal Erich von, 7, 17, 19-20, 22, 24-26, 111, 129, 149, 161-162, 170-171, 175, 184, 223, 233, 237, 246, 296
Mattenklott, Lieutenant-General, 277, 278
Mayer, Capt., 85, 87-89, 91-95
Meiser, Anton, viii, 15, 32-33, 35, 48-49, 69, 75-77, 106-108, 123-127, 130, 138, 142-143, 182-183, 186-189, 217-218, 243, 257, 273-275, 297
Mikosch, Major-General Hans, 132, 136, 140, 246
Operation Barbarossa, 5, 40
Operation Citadel, 7, 9-10, 40, 51
Operation Typhoon, 5

Operation Wanda, 148, 150, 158, 161, 197, 287
Operation Watutin, 22, 24, 27, 29, 42, 100-101, 118, 148
Paulus, Field Marshal Friedrich von, 24
Rotmistrov, Gen., 23-24, 37, 40, 55, 59, 61, 71, 73-75, 78, 81, 117, 120, 137, 139, 144, 171, 175, 179, 194, 208, 231, 235, 239, 244, 296
Rybalko, Gen., 18-19
Sapauschke, Johannes, 1-3
Savalev, Major General M.I., 99
Saveliev, Gen. M.I., 2
Scherf, Walter, 221-223, 240, 252-253
Schlieffen Plan, 112
Selivanov, Major-General, 121, 126, 180, 184, 189, 194, 204, 220, 227, 244
Shumilov, Gen., 39
Siedemann, Lieutenant-General, 180
Sievers, Major von, 83, 85, 89
Sorajewski, Lt., 69, 76, 125, 138, 143, 182-183

SOVIET MILITARY UNITS:
1st Belorussian Front, 22
1st Tank Army, 30, 101
1st Ukrainian Front, 1, 18, 20, 22, 24-25, 30-31, 37, 66, 75, 96-99, 101, 103-104, 120, 126, 155, 157, 162, 191, 197, 204, 211, 283-284, 294-295
2d Air Army, 184
2d Guards Airborne Division, 118,
2d Tank Army, 157-159, 161-162, 184, 204, 221
2d Ukrainian Front, 1, 18, 25, 37-39, 41, 54, 61, 66, 70, 73, 75, 78, 81, 96-97, 101, 117, 120-121, 126, 131, 138, 172, 194, 211-212, 216, 228, 235, 246, 254, 283-284, 294-295
3d Guards Airborne Division, 213
3d Guards Tank Army, 18-19, 21
4th Guards Army, 37-38, 55, 59-60, 63, 74-75, 119, 131, 180, 212, 231, 244, 277, 279
4th Tank Army, 12
5th Guards Airborne Division, 204
5th Guards Army, 39, 172
5th Guards Cavalry Corps, 70, 74-75, 78, 120-121, 126, 180, 191, 236, 244, 279
5th Guards Tank Army, 23, 37-38, 41, 55, 58-59, 61, 63, 66-69, 73, 86, 101, 111, 117, 119, 121, 139, 162, 171, 175, 194, 239, 244, 294
5th Guards Tank Corps, 29, 38, 97-98
5th Mechanized Corps, 29, 38, 97-98, 101-102, 117-118, 154
6th Tank Army, 37, 82, 97, 111, 117-119, 126, 154-155, 157, 159-160, 162, 184, 196, 294
7th Guards Airborne Division, 61
7th Guards Army, 24, 39, 172
8th Guards Tank Brigade, 63, 73
8th Mechanized Corps, 24
8th Tank Brigade, 82
11th Guards Cavalry Division, 126
12th Guards Cavalry Division, 126
12th Guards Cavalry Division, 227
13th Army, 211, 296
14th Guards Infantry Division, 57
18th Tank Corps, 39, 59, 71, 74-75, 78, 86, 96, 120-121, 194, 231
20th Guards Corps, 61
20th Tank Corps, 39, 59, 63, 67, 69, 73-75, 78, 82, 104, 120, 194, 208, 231, 238, 244
27th Army, 38, 104, 119-120, 132, 137, 141, 143, 191, 204, 211-212, 244, 279, 294
29th Tank Corps, 39, 59, 69, 74-75, 78, 120, 137, 144, 208, 231, 236, 244
31st Guards Rifle Division, 61
32d Guards Rifle Corps, 23
38th Army, 19
40th Army, 38, 100, 118-119, 126, 159-160, 185, 226, 294
41st Guards Rifle Division, 177
47th Rifle Corps, 118
49th Rifle Corps, 117, 144
52d Army, 119, 189, 244
53d Army, 37-38, 55, 57, 75, 77, 117, 119
54th Fortified Region, 212
58th Rifle Division, 98, 154, 213
60th Army, 211, 296
62d Rifle Division, 204, 236

63d Cavalry Division, 126, 131, 189
69th Guards Rifle Division, 61
104th Rifle Corps, 97, 98, 154
133d Rifle Division, 154
138th Infantry Division, 57
155th Tank Brigade, 66, 73, 82
180th Rifle Division, 212
189th Division, 103
198th Division, 98-99
202d Fortified Region, 212
202d Rifle Division, 162, 212, 236
206th Rifle Division, 204
213th Infantry Division, 57
233d Infantry Division, 57
233d Tank Brigade, 99, 118
254th Rifle Division, 236
337th Rifle Division, 212
340th Rifle Division, 162
359th Rifle Division, 30

Speidel, Major-General Hans, 63, 65-67, 80, 82, 123, 130, 132, 138-139, 164, 169-170, 177, 181, 185, 187, 220, 231, 238, 246
Stalin, Josef, 5, 7, 19, 36, 211
Stalingrad, Battle of, 1-3, 6, 14-15, 21, 24, 31, 107, 111, 114, 119, 142, 179
Stelzner, Maj., 143, 182-183, 186-187
Stemmermann, Gen. Wilhelm, 2-3, 31, 69, 103-104, 131, 134, 138, 141, 171, 180, 189-191, 199, 204, 215, 237-238, 242-246, 250-251, 254, 256, 265, 269-270
Strecker, Gen. der Infanterie Karl, 31
ten Brink, Lt., 86-88, 92
Vatutin, Gen. Nikolai, 1, 3, 18-22, 24-25, 38, 82, 96-97, 99, 101-102, 118- 120, 138, 157, 159, 161-162, 180, 184, 191, 193, 197, 204, 211-212, 225, 283-284, 294-296
Viebig, Col. Hans, 1-2
Vormann, Nikolaus von, viii, 120, 132-133, 136, 138-141, 144-145, 150, 154, 162, 168-171, 173-175, 184, 190, 193-194, 196, 205, 208-209, 216, 226, 231, 235, 238-239, 246, 296
Wartmann, Lt., 85, 88, 90-91
Wenck, Major-General Walther, 66, 133, 161, 164-165, 167, 177, 220, 231, 280
Wietersheim, Major-General Wend von, 77, 94, 127, 132, 135-136, 139-140, 173, 185, 205-206, 216, 227, 246, 290
Wöhler, Gen. Otto, 22, 36, 57, 61-62, 67, 75, 80, 120, 123, 127-129, 133, 135, 140-141, 169-173, 175, 181, 184, 193, 208, 217, 237-239, 246, 296
Zhadov, Gen., 23-24, 39
Zhmachenko, Gen. Filipp, 118, 226
Zhukov, Marshal G.K., 3, 18, 23, 211, 231, 244, 296